Eleventh Edition

Organizational Behavior in Education

Leadership and School Reform

Robert G. Owens

Distinguished Research Professor Emeritus

Hofstra University

Thomas C. Valesky

Florida Gulf Coast University

PEARSON

Boston   Columbus   Indianapolis   New York   San Francisco   Upper Saddle River
Amsterdam   Cape Town   Dubai   London   Madrid   Milan   Munich   Paris   Montreal   Toronto
Delhi   Mexico City   São Paulo   Sydney   Hong Kong   Seoul   Singapore   Taipei   Tokyo

Vice President and Editorial Director: Jeffery W. Johnston
Senior Acquisitions Editor: Meredith Fossel
Editorial Assistant: Janelle Criner
Executive Field Marketing Manager: Krista Clark
Senior Product Marketing Manager: Christopher Barry
Production Project Manager: Laura Messerly
Senior Operations Supervisor: Pat Tonneman
Senior Art Director: Jayne Conte
Cover Designer: Karen Salzbach
Cover Photo: Fotolia, © roblan
Media Project Manager: Noelle Chun
Full-Service Project Management: Peggy Kellar, Aptara®, Inc.
Composition: Aptara®, Inc.
Printer/Binder: Courier Westford
Cover Printer: Courier Westford
Text Font: Minion

> This book is lovingly dedicated to the memory of Barbara Owens

Credits and acknowledgments for material borrowed from other sources and reproduced, with permission, in this textbook appear on the appropriate page within the text.

Every effort has been made to provide accurate and current Internet information in this book. However, the Internet and information posted on it are constantly changing, so it is inevitable that some of the Internet addresses listed in this textbook will change.

Library of Congress Cataloging-in-Publication Data

Owens, Robert G.
  Organizational behavior in education : leadership and school reform/Robert G. Owens, Distinguished Research Professor Emeritus Hofstra
University, Thomas C. Valesky, Florida Gulf Coast University.—
Eleventh edition.
     pages cm
  Includes bibliographical references and index.
    ISBN 978-0-13-348903-3—ISBN 0-13-348903-5   1. School management and organization—United States.
2. Organizational behavior.   I. Title.
  LB2806.O9 2015
  371.2—dc23
                                                                              2014000895

10 9 8 7 6 5 4 3 2 1

ISBN 10:   0-13-348903-5
ISBN 13: 978-0-13-348903-3

9/23/16

CONTENTS

PREFACE

NEW TO THIS EDITION

Four major goals of this new edition are the following:

1. We provide the reader with additional practical applications by adding "Voices From the Field" in appropriate chapters.
2. We update the treatment of the subject of organizational behavior in schools so that it includes new research and current trends.
3. We incorporate a better connection between organizational behavior, critical theory, and critical race theory.
4. We integrate theory and practice throughout the text by discussion and expansion on initial concepts in succeeding chapters to provide additional depth of analysis and synthesis.

The following are the specific major changes to this 11th edition of *Organizational Behavior in Education*:

- We have added "Voices From the Field" in appropriate chapters. We solicited examples from practicing administrators to show how concepts are being applied in the schools today. These "Voices" provide the reader with a connection between theory and practice as well as help the reader critically apply "book knowledge" to organizational behavior.
- Although we briefly defined critical theory in the 10th edition in the chapter on leadership, we have expanded the concept. We believe critical theory and critical race theory in education have been elevated to major theories since their initial introduction in the mid-1990s. We also believe it is important to focus on eliminating racism in schools and schooling through a focus on CRT at all levels in the organization.
- The Critical Incidents introduced in the previous edition are being updated and moved to the end of each chapter. Our reviewers felt that readers were not prepared to critically analyze the Critical Incident until after they read the chapter, and we agree with our reviewers. After reading each chapter, a Critical Incident presents the reader with practical issues based on the chapter content. The Critical Incident requires the reader to respond to decision-making questions based on the facts presented and the reader's own theory of practice. This approach is important to the reader because (a) it develops understanding of the practical application of the knowledge of organizational behavior to the practice of leadership, and (b) it helps the reader to develop and internalize a personal commitment to a practical and effective theory of practice.
- New charts and figures to support new and previously presented material have been added in several chapters. This material helps the visual learner by presenting research findings in easy-to-view displays. Several charts and figures were also removed as we and our reviewers did not believe these were helpful.
- The book has been updated to make it more current in today's fast-paced era of No Child Left Behind (NCLB), Race to the Top (RTTT), accountability, and high-stakes testing. New updated research and recent developments in the field have been added in most of the book's 12 chapters to replace older material. For example, we introduce the Common Core State Standards along with a discussion of the two new assessment consortia: Smarter Balanced Assessment Consortium and Partnership for Assessment of Readiness for College

and Careers (PARCC). In addition, we maintained the classical research and theories that have been the foundation of progress in educational leadership.
- Our reviewers provided us with many excellent ideas for additions and changes to this edition. Here are a few of the major changes in addition to some of those listed above:
  - We moved the chapter on motivation from the end of the book to its new location as Chapter 5. We made this change because the theory and practice of motivation underlies the implementation of good leadership.
  - We added back to this edition in Chapter 3 a discussion of Mary Parker Follett's contribution to management theory.
  - We have added to Chapter 8 some of the many contributions Michael Fullan has provided on organizational change.
  - The Marzano, Waters, and McNulty research on leadership has been included in the discussion on leadership in Chapter 9.
  - We added a discussion on data-based decision making to Chapter 10.
  - Also, new to Chapter 10 is the presentation of Total Quality Management concepts to assist in organizational decision making.
  - The name and content of the chapter related to conflict in organizations (Chapter 11) has been changed to reflect a better focus on the topic of communications: *Conflict and Communications in Organizations.* In addition, we added a discussion on how principals should deal with difficult teachers, using ideas from Todd Whitaker's work.
- Many of the Reflective Activities at the end of each chapter have been revised and updated. These activities further challenge each student to develop and internalize personal commitment to a defensible theory of practice in educational leadership. By studying this book and completing the activities, the learner will develop a thoughtful and well-grounded approach to the practice of leadership in any school setting.

The 11th edition also offers updated support to instructors via two supplements, a Test Bank and PowerPoint® presentations. Both of these supplements can be downloaded at www .pearsonhighered.com/educators. The supplements can be located within the Instructor's Resource Center, which you can access after a one-time registration.

ACKNOWLEDGMENTS

We are grateful to those individuals who assisted us with information and reviews of the 11th edition: Heather Duncan, University of Wyoming; Maria Hinojosa, Texas A&M University–Commerce; Ricardo D. Rosa, University of Massachusetts–Dartmouth; and Rosemarye Taylor, University of Central Florida. This group of reviewers was particularly thorough and provided excellent guidance for revising this edition and future editions.

In addition, we want to acknowledge the following practicing administrators who add great meaning to many of the chapters through their "Voices From the Field," connecting the research, theory, and concepts in this book to the "real world" of schooling:

- Peggy Aune, Principal, Manatee Middle School, Naples, Florida
- Scot Croner, K-12 Instructional Coordinator, Marion Community Schools, Marion, Indiana
- James Gasparino, Principal, Pelican Marsh Elementary School, Naples, Florida

- Kevin Gordon, former Principal, Gibbs High School, St. Petersburg, Florida; currently Provost St. Petersburg College, St. Petersburg, Florida
- Kendall Hendricks, Director of Finance, Brownsburg Community Schools Corporation, Brownsburg, Indiana
- Rocky Killion, Superintendent, West Lafayette Community School Corporation, West Lafayette, Indiana
- Brain Mangan, former Principal, Mariner High School, Cape Coral, Florida; currently Principal East Lee County High School
- Jorge Nelson, former Head of School in Vienna, Austria; currently administrator for Myanmar International School, Burma
- LaSonya Moore, Assistant Principal, Pinellas County Schools, Florida
- Steve Ritter, Principal, Lakeland High School, Deepwater, Missouri

Finally, and most importantly, we wish to thank Christopher Parfitt, a doctoral graduate student and graduate assistant at Florida Gulf Coast University, for his research assistance, his help in assuring our references were accurate, his help in editing and proofreading, and for his assistance in revising the PowerPoint® slides.

R.G.O.
T.C.V.

EDUCATIONAL LEADERSHIP POLICY STANDARDS FOR 2008
(Formerly Known as the ISLLC Standards)

The Interstate School Leaders Licensure Consortium (ISLLC) Standards have been at the center of Educational Leadership program reform for over a decade. In 2008, with support from the Wallace Foundation, the standards were revised and are now called the Educational Leadership Policy Standards. Originally, each of the six ISLLC standards included a list of knowledge, skills, and dispositions (KSDs), totaling nearly 200 KSD indicators. About these indicators, Joseph Murphy (2003), who was one of the primary authors of the ISLLC standards, wrote the following:

> [T]hese indicators are examples of important knowledge, practices, and beliefs, not a full map. No effort was made to include everything or to deal with performances in the myriad of leadership contexts. Leadership is a complex and context-dependent activity. To attempt to envelope the concept with a definitive list of indicators is a fool's errand.

The authors of the ISLLC standards assumed that an entire university preparation program, not any single course, should engender all knowledge, dispositions, and performances of the ISLLC standards, but even then, programs were not to be evaluated based on these indicators alone. In practice, however, the KSD indicators were used as standards themselves, which was not the intent of the original ISLLC developers. In the revised standards document, the authors state that "the very nature of listing examples of leadership indicators was unintentionally limiting and negated other areas that could have been included in an exhaustive listing" (Council of Chief State School Officers, 2008, p. 5). Therefore, the KSD indicators were abandoned in the revised standards, and "functions" were added to define each standard and to assist administrators in understanding the behaviors expected for each. The revised standards are purposely called "policy standards" to help guide policy-level discussions related to educational leadership, rather than direct practical applications.

The ISLLC standards provide the basis for evaluating university programs by the National Council for Accreditation of Teacher Education (NCATE) and the National Policy Board for Educational Administration (NPBEA). A brief history of the development of the ISLLC standards might help the reader understand the importance of these standards.

The NPBEA was formed in 1988 with membership from the following 10 national associations:

- American Association of Colleges for Teacher Education (AACTE)
- American Association of School Administrators (AASA)
- Association of School Business Officials (ASBO)
- Association for Supervision and Curriculum Development (ASCD)
- Council of Chief State School Officers (CCSSO)
- National Association of Elementary School Principals (NAESP)
- National Association of Secondary School Principals (NASSP)
- National Council of Professors of Educational Administration (NCPEA)

- National School Boards Association (NSBA)
- University Council for Educational Administration (UCEA)

Later, ASBO dropped its membership in NPBEA and the National Council for Accreditation of Teacher Education (NCATE) joined.

In 1994, the NPBEA formed the Interstate School Leaders Licensure Consortium (ISLLC) to develop standards for our profession. ISLLC was funded by a grant from the Pew Charitable Trusts, and the process of developing the standards was managed by the Council of Chief State School Officers (CCSSO) under the direction of Joseph Murphy and Neil Shipman. The NPBEA adopted the ISLLC standards in 1996. The NPBEA then formed a working group from among its membership to form the Educational Leadership Constituent Council (ELCC), which worked to develop a set of standards for evaluating programs in educational leadership to be used by NPBEA and NCATE.

There was considerable controversy surrounding the original ISLLC standards, which included the following issues: (1) the standards did not provide a supporting research base; (2) no weighting was given to the standards in terms of which standards (and the knowledge, dispositions, and performances) were more likely to lead to higher student achievement; and (3) the standards did not include or emphasize the importance of some critical areas, such as technology. The NPBEA acknowledged some of these criticisms and in the summer of 2005 formed a working group to begin a revision of the ISLLC standards. A 10-member steering committee was formed from nine of the member organizations (all except the National School Boards Association). The NPBEA agreed that the standards would be revised under important assumptions, including the following:

- Revamping the ISLLC and the ELCC standards would be done at the same time.
- The ISLLC *Standards for School Leaders* need to be updated, not rewritten from scratch.
- The context in which both sets of standards are being revised has changed dramatically in the past decade.
- NPBEA will own the copyright to the revised two sets of standards.

The plan was to present the final revision of the standards to the NPBEA for approval in the spring of 2008, a goal that was achieved early because the new Educational Leadership Policy Standards were approved in December 2007 by the NPBEA. The first of the criticisms listed above was resolved in this revision. A research base was developed and each of the new functions is directly connected to supporting research publications (National Policy Board for Educational Administration, 2009). The resulting document was titled *Educational Leadership Policy Standards: ISLLC 2008.*

Although we recognize that the ISLLC standards are not comprehensive of all aspects of school leadership and that there has been significant critical discourse in the profession about the standards, we also recognize that, as of 2008, 43 states adopted or adapted the ISLLC standards as the basis for state certification in educational leadership and as the basis for evaluating and approving university preparation programs (Council of Chief State School Officers, 2008). Those states not adopting or modifying the ISLLC standards as their own have standards with marked similarities to the ISLLC standards (Sanders & Simpson, 2005). In view of their importance, therefore, we want to identify for you the ISLLC standards and their accompanying functions that are significant aspects of this book. The tables on pages xx–xxii are matrices of each ISLLC standard and indicate the functions that are contained in each chapter. By looking at each standard table, you can see which chapters in our book contain related content. It is clear that some standards are covered more thoroughly than others. For example, you can see from the table that Standard 4 has less related content than Standards 3 and 5. By scanning across the rows for the functions, you can determine which chapter contains related material. We hope that this information is of value to students and professors alike, and we welcome any feedback that might guide us in making this information more useful in future editions.

ISLLC Functions by Chapter

STANDARD 1: An education leader promotes the success of every student by facilitating the development, articulation, implementation, and stewardship of a vision of learning that is shared and supported by all stakeholders.

Functions	Chapters											
	1	2	3	4	5	6	7	8	9	10	11	12
A. Collaboratively develop and implement a shared vision and mission	•							•	•		•	
B. Collect and use data to identify goals, assess organizational effectiveness, and promote organizational learning	•							•	•	•	•	•
C. Create and implement plans to achieve goals	•			•		•		•	•	•		
D. Promote continuous and sustainable improvement	•	•				•		•	•	•		•
E. Monitor and evaluate progress and revise plans								•	•	•		•

STANDARD 2: An education leader promotes the success of every student by advocating, nurturing, and sustaining a school culture and instructional program conducive to student learning and staff professional growth.

Functions	Chapters											
	1	2	3	4	5	6	7	8	9	10	11	12
A. Nurture and sustain a culture of collaboration, trust, learning, and high expectations	•				•	•	•	•	•	•	•	•
B. Create a comprehensive, rigorous, and coherent curricular program		•			•	•			•		•	•
C. Create a personalized and motivating learning environment for students	•	•			•	•	•	•			•	•
D. Supervise instruction						•			•			•
E. Develop assessment and accountability systems to monitor student progress	•				•		•	•	•	•		•
F. Develop the instructional and leadership capacity of staff	•				•	•	•		•		•	
G. Maximize time spent on quality instruction		•			•	•					•	•
H. Promote the use of the most effective and appropriate technologies to support teaching and learning	•	•		•	•			•	•	•	•	•
I. Monitor and evaluate the impact of the instructional program					•		•		•	•		•

STANDARD 3:   An education leader promotes the success of every student by ensuring management of the organization, operation, and resources for a safe, efficient, and effective learning environment.

Functions	Chapters												
	1	2	3	4	5	6	7	8	9	10	11	12
A. Monitor and evaluate the management and operational systems			•	•					•	•		
B. Obtain, allocate, align, and efficiently utilize human, fiscal, and technological resources		•	•	•					•	•		
C. Promote and protect the welfare and safety of students and staff						•					•	
D. Develop the capacity for distributed leadership	•			•	•	•	•	•	•	•	•	
E. Ensure teacher and organizational time is focused to support quality instruction and student learning						•			•			•

STANDARD 4:   An education leader promotes the success of every student by collaborating with faculty and community members, responding to diverse community interests and needs, and mobilizing community resources.

Functions	Chapters												
	1	2	3	4	5	6	7	8	9	10	11	12
A. Collect and analyze data and information pertinent to the educational environment	•					•		•	•	•		•
B. Promote understanding, appreciation, and use of the community's diverse cultural, social, and intellectual resources	•				•	•		•	•	•		
C. Build and sustain positive relationships with families and caregivers	•			•	•	•	•	•	•	•		
D. Build and sustain productive relationships with community partners	•			•				•	•	•		

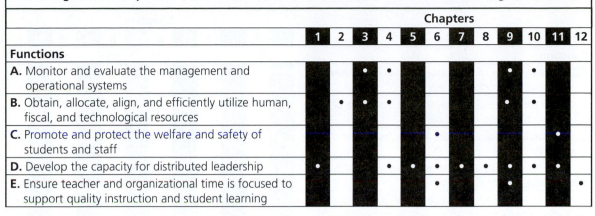

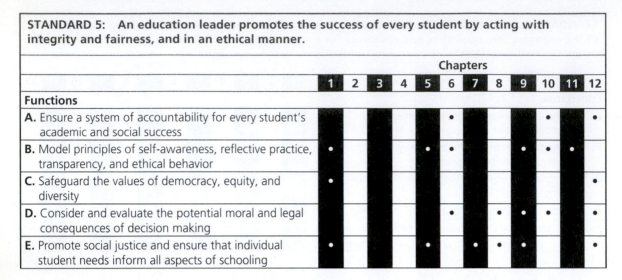

STANDARD 5: An education leader promotes the success of every student by acting with integrity and fairness, and in an ethical manner.

Functions	\- Chapters - 1	2	3	4	5	6	7	8	9	10	11	12
A. Ensure a system of accountability for every student's academic and social success							•			•		•
B. Model principles of self-awareness, reflective practice, transparency, and ethical behavior	•				•	•			•	•	•	
C. Safeguard the values of democracy, equity, and diversity	•											•
D. Consider and evaluate the potential moral and legal consequences of decision making							•	•	•	•		•
E. Promote social justice and ensure that individual student needs inform all aspects of schooling	•				•		•	•	•			•

STANDARD 6: An education leader promotes the success of every student by understanding, responding to, and influencing the political, social, economic, legal, and cultural context.

Functions	\- Chapters - 1	2	3	4	5	6	7	8	9	10	11	12
A. Advocate for children, families, and caregivers									•			•
B. Act to influence local, district, state, and national decisions affecting student learning	•	•		•				•	•	•		•
C. Assess, analyze, and anticipate emerging trends and initiatives in order to adapt leadership strategies	•						•	•	•	•		•

NPBEA DISTRICT-LEVEL STANDARDS

New to national standards in 2011 were district level standards developed by the National Policy Board for Educational Administration (NPBEA). The document is entitled *Educational Leadership Program Recognition Standards: District Level* (National Policy Board for Educational Administration, 2011). These standards, based on the ISLLC standards, were designed primarily for university preparation programs to receive national accreditation by the Educational Leadership Constituent Council (ELCC). The major difference with the ISLLC standards is the addition of Standard 7 related to internship programs. Due to their importance to preparation programs, we list these standards below. Matrices (or crosswalks) mapping these district-level standards to the ISLLC standards and comprehensive research support for each standard are provided in the NPBEA document listed above. In addition, Canole and Young (2013) provided an in-depth analysis of the ISLLC and ELCC standards in their report published by the Council of Chief State School Officers (CCSSO). In their report, Canole and Young provided the history of the standards; the research base for the standards; and crosswalks of the ELCC standards to not only the ISLLC standards but also to other national standards, such as InTASC teacher standards, NASSP, and NAESP standards. They also report their analysis of the Wallace Foundation Principal Pipeline Initiative in which six districts adapted the ELCC standards to develop strong principal preparation and succession programs (Charlotte-Mecklenburg in North Carolina; Denver, Colorado; Gwinnett County in Georgia; Hillsborough County in Florida (Tampa area); New York City; and Prince George's County in Maryland).

To receive national recognition by the Educational Leadership Constituent Council (ELCC), university preparation programs are evaluated on the *Educational Leadership Program Recognition Standards: District Level* (National Policy Board for Educational Administration, 2011).

ELCC STANDARD 1.0:

A district level education leader applies knowledge that promotes the success of every student by facilitating the development, articulation, implementation, and stewardship of a shared district vision of learning through the collection and use of data to identify district goals, assess organizational effectiveness, and implement district plans to achieve district goals; promotion of continual and sustainable district improvement; and evaluation of district progress and revision of district plans supported by district stakeholders.

ELCC Standard Elements:

ELCC 1.1: Candidates understand and can collaboratively develop, articulate, implement, and steward a shared district vision of learning for a school district.

ELCC 1.2: Candidates understand and can collect and use data to identify district goals, assess organizational effectiveness, and implement district plans to achieve district goals.

ELCC 1.3: Candidates understand and can promote continual and sustainable district improvement.

ELCC 1.4: Candidates understand and can evaluate district progress and revise district plans supported by district stakeholders.

ELCC STANDARD 2.0:

A district-level education leader applies knowledge that promotes the success of every student by sustaining a district culture conducive to collaboration, trust, and a personalized learning environment with high expectations for students; creating and evaluating a comprehensive, rigorous, and coherent curricular and instructional district program; developing and supervising the instructional and leadership capacity across the district; and promoting the most effective and appropriate technologies to support teaching and learning within the district.

ELCC Standard Elements:

ELCC 2.1: Candidates understand and can advocate, nurture, and sustain a district culture and instructional program conducive to student learning through collaboration, trust, and a personalized learning environment with high expectations for students.

ELCC 2.2: Candidates understand and can create and evaluate a comprehensive, rigorous, and coherent curricular and instructional district program.

ELCC 2.3: Candidates understand and can develop and supervise the instructional and leadership capacity across the district.

ELCC 2.4: Candidates understand and can promote the most effective and appropriate district technologies to support teaching and learning within the district.

ELCC STANDARD 3.0:

A district-level education leader applies knowledge that promotes the success of every student by ensuring the management of the district's organization, operation, and resources through monitoring and evaluating district management and operational systems; efficiently using human, fiscal, and technological resources within the district; promoting district-level policies and procedures that protect the welfare and safety of students and staff across the district; developing district capacity for distributed leadership; and ensuring that district time focuses on high-quality instruction and student learning.

ELCC Standard Elements:

ELCC 3.1: Candidates understand and can monitor and evaluate district management and operational systems.

ELCC 3.2: Candidates understand and can efficiently use human, fiscal, and technological resources within the district.

ELCC 3.3: Candidates understand and can promote district-level policies and procedures that protect the welfare and safety of students and staff across the district.

ELCC 3.4: Candidates understand and can develop district capacity for distributed leadership.

ELCC 3.5: Candidates understand and can ensure that district time focuses on supporting high-quality school instruction and student learning.

ELCC STANDARD 4.0:

A district-level education leader applies knowledge that promotes the success of every student by collaborating with faculty and community members, responding to diverse community interests and needs, and mobilizing community resources for the district by collecting and analyzing information pertinent to improvement of the district's educational environment; promoting an understanding, appreciation, and use of the community's diverse cultural, social, and intellectual resources throughout the district; building and sustaining positive district relationships with families and caregivers; and cultivating productive district relationships with community partners.

ELCC Standard Elements:

ELCC 4.1: Candidates understand and can collaborate with faculty and community members by collecting and analyzing information pertinent to the improvement of the district's educational environment.

ELCC 4.2: Candidates understand and can mobilize community resources by promoting understanding, appreciation, and use of the community's diverse cultural, social, and intellectual resources throughout the district.

ELCC 4.3: Candidates understand and can respond to community interests and needs by building and sustaining positive district relationships with families and caregivers.

ELCC 4.4: Candidates understand and can respond to community interests and needs by building and sustaining productive district relationships with community partners.

ELCC STANDARD 5.0:

A district-level education leader applies knowledge that promotes the success of every student by acting with integrity, fairness, and in an ethical manner to ensure a district system of accountability for every student's academic and social success by modeling district principles of self-awareness, reflective practice, transparency, and ethical behavior as related to their roles within the district; safeguarding the values of democracy, equity, and diversity within the district; evaluating the potential moral and legal consequences of decision-making in the district; and promoting social justice within the district to ensure individual student needs inform all aspects of schooling.

ELCC Standard Elements:

ELCC 5.1: Candidates understand and can act with integrity and fairness to ensure a district system of accountability for every student's academic and social success.

ELCC 5.2: Candidates understand and can model principles of self-awareness, reflective practice, transparency, and ethical behavior as related to their roles within the district.

ELCC 5.3: Candidates understand and can safeguard the values of democracy, equity, and diversity within the district.

ELCC 5.4: Candidates understand and can evaluate the potential moral and legal consequences of decision making in the district.

ELCC 5.5: Candidates understand and can promote social justice within the district to ensure individual student needs inform all aspects of schooling.

ELCC STANDARD 6.0:

A district-level education leader applies knowledge that promotes the success of every student by understanding, responding to, and influencing the larger political, social, economic, legal, and cultural context within the district through advocating for district students, families, and caregivers; acting to influence local, district, state, and national decisions affecting student learning; and anticipating and assessing emerging trends and initiatives in order to adapt district-level leadership strategies.

ELCC Standard Elements:

ELCC 6.1: Candidates understand and can advocate for district students, families, and caregivers.

ELCC 6.2: Candidates understand and can act to influence local, district, state, and national decisions affecting student learning in a district environment.

ELCC 6.3: Candidates understand and can anticipate and assess emerging trends and initiatives in order to adapt district-level leadership strategies.

ELCC STANDARD 7.0:

A district-level education leader applies knowledge that promotes the success of every student in a substantial and sustained educational leadership internship experience that has district-based field experiences and clinical practice within a district setting and is monitored by a qualified, on-site mentor.

ELCC Standard Elements:

ELCC 7.1: Substantial Experience: The program provides significant field experiences and clinical internship practice for candidates within a district environment to synthesize and apply the content knowledge and develop professional skills identified in the other Educational Leadership District-Level Program Standards through authentic, district-based leadership experiences.

ELCC 7.2: Sustained Experience: Candidates are provided a six-month concentrated (9–12 hours per week) internship that includes field experiences within a district environment.

ELCC 7.3: Qualified On-site Mentor: An on-site district mentor who has demonstrated successful experience as an educational leader at the district level and is selected collaboratively by the intern and program faculty with training by the supervising institution.

REFERENCES

Canole, M., & Young, M. (2013). *Standards for educational leaders: An analysis.* Washington, DC: CCSSO.

Council of Chief State School Officers. (2008, June). *Educational leadership policy standards: ISLLC 2008. As Adopted by the National Policy Board for Educational Administration,* Washington, DC: Council of Chief State School Officers. Retrieved from http://www.ccsso.org/Documents/2008/Educational_Leadership_Policy_Standards_2008.pdf

Murphy, J. (2003, September). *Reculturing educational leadership: The ISLLC standards ten years out.* Paper prepared for the National Policy Board for Educational Administration. Retrieved from www.npbea.org/Resources/catalog.html

National Policy Board for Educational Administration. (2011). *Educational leadership program recognition standards: District level.* Alexandria, VA: NPBEA.

National Policy Board for Educational Administration. (2009, June). *Major projects.* Retrieved from http://www.npbea.org/projects.php

Sanders, N. M., & Simpson, J. (2005). *State policy framework to develop highly qualified administrators.* Washington, DC: CCSSO.

CHAPTER 1

Organizational and Critical Theory

A school is a world in which people live and work. Like any other social organization, the world of the school has power, structure, logic, and values, which combine to exert strong influence on the ways in which individuals perceive the world, interpret it, and respond to it. In short, the behavior of people at work in an educational organization—individually as well as in a group—is not merely a reflection of their individual unique personalities but is powerfully shaped and molded by the social norms and expectations of the culture that prevail in the organization. This interplay between individuals and the social environment of their world at work is a powerful agent in the creation of organizational behavior, the behavior of people in the school organization. Those who want to be effective educational leaders must have a clear grasp of the essentials of organizational behavior in deciding how to engage in the practice of leadership. As you read this text, you should think about what you read, question it, challenge it, and ask yourself—and discuss with other people—how it all fits into the practical realities of your work, your experience, and your personal view of the world. By being a reflective practitioner, this text will be much more useful to you both now and in the future.

SCHOOLS AS EDUCATIVE ORGANIZATIONS

Although U.S. schools have tended throughout their history to reflect the values and views of industry, commerce, and the military, it is becoming increasingly clear that schools are in fact distinct, if not unique, kinds of organizations that differ in important ways from industrial, commercial, governmental, or military organizations. Because schools are unique among organizations, they require ways of thinking, styles of leadership, and approaches to administrative practice that are especially suited to them.

The uniqueness of educational organizations resides in their educative mission. Many organizations are created for the basic purpose of making money by manufacturing products, selling them, or providing for-profit ancillary services that support those activities. Governments create a vast array of organizations that, collectively, are intended to provide public order and security. The distinctive mission of the schools to educate requires organizations that, by their very nature, enhance the continuing growth and development of people to become more fully functioning individuals. Such organizations must foster the learning, personal growth, and development of *all participants, including student as well as adults at work in the school.*

Educative organizations seek to increase the personal and interpersonal competencies of their participants, to develop the skills of the group in collaborating, to make hidden assumptions explicit and to examine them for what they mean in terms of individual and group behavior, to enact cooperative group behavior that is caring and supportive of others, to manage conflict productively and without fear, and to share information and ideas fully. They place high value on and support openness, trust, caring, and sharing; they always strive for consensus but support and value those who think differently; and they prize human growth and development above all. Effective educational leaders, then, strive for a vision of the school as one that seeks to be engaged in a never-ending process of change and development, a "race without a finish line" (or *kaizen*, as the Japanese call constant growth achieved through small incremental steps), rather than one that seeks the big dramatic breakthrough, the mythical silver bullet, that will, supposedly, finally make everything right.

The processes of becoming (McGregor, 1960)—of people growing and developing as individuals and as group members, and of the organization doing so, too—combine to create the essence of enduring vitality in organizational life, while academic outcomes are transient, ephemeral evidence that the processes are working. The conundrum of power is a major concern in the environment of the educational organization: Hierarchy prevails. We have never found a substitute for hierarchy in organizational life, but there is much that we can ethically and honestly do to share power and distribute it more equitably in efforts to minimize its deleterious effects on the behavior of people in the organization. In the process, we can make the school a more growth-enhancing environment, which is a very different concept of organization from what one generally finds in industrial and business organizations, and it should be because the essential, unique mission of schools is educative.

ORGANIZATIONAL THEORY

Discussion of different perspectives that may be used in thinking about organizations, bureaucratic and nonbureaucratic, is really discussion of organizational theory. Practicing educational administrators are commonly skeptical of theory, often thinking of it as some ideal state or idle notion—commonly associated with the pejorative term *ivory tower*. This attitude is often rationalized by those who work in schools by stating they must deal with the tough practicalities of daily life in the "real world." Far from being removed from daily life, however, theory is crucial in shaping our everyday perception and understanding of commonplace events. School leaders need to know about organizational theory so that they can think more clearly about making better-informed choices in a world where things are characteristically ambiguous, uncertain, unclear, or unknown.

Theory Defined and Described

Theory is not a guess or a hunch. Theory is systematically organized knowledge thought to explain observed phenomena. Good theory is based on good research (we discuss research practices later in this chapter). Just as we have theories about the causes of disease, the forces that make it possible for airplanes to fly, and the nature of the solar system, we also have theories about organizations and how they work. Just as there are theoretical reasons that underlie the fact that we know we should wash our hands frequently, exercise regularly, and maintain a nutritionally sound diet, there should be theoretical underpinnings to our understanding of schools as organizations and how to make them more effective.

Theory is useful insofar as it provides a basis for thinking systematically about complex problems, such as understanding the nature of educational organizations. It is useful because it enables us to *describe* what is going on, *explain* it, *predict* future events under given circumstances, and—essential to the professional practitioner—think about ways to exercise *control* over events.

Two Major Perspectives on Educational Organizations

Since the dawn of organizational studies in the twentieth century, people have generally elected to conceptualize organizations in one of two ways. One way is traditional theory, usually called bureaucratic, though it is often sardonically referred to by staunch critics of public schooling as the factory model of organization. Whatever name is used, bureaucratic organization conjures in one's mind some well-worn stereotypes:

- The eighteenth-century army of Frederick the Great, with its characteristically robot like regimentation, top-down authority, all controlled by extensive written detailed rules and directives—the "book" by which the organization is run
- Franz Kafka's famously vivid, indelible images that depict bureaucracy as a nightmarish, maddeningly indecipherable, obtuse organization that creates bizarre unpredictable outcomes in the name of sweet reason

Nevertheless, bureaucratic organization remains by far the most common theory of organization worldwide. Indeed, to many people in the world, bureaucracy is the defining concept, the very essence, of what an organization is. However, as time passed and the world changed, a second way of understanding organizations arose.

The second way is the contemporary nonbureaucratic theory that developed in large part from the constant growth and accelerating tempo of change in today's world. The present-day acceleration in the development of technology and changes in politics, economics, and society have generally left rigid bureaucracies floundering and unresponsive. To thrive in today's rapidly changing world, schools must be nimble, adaptive to change, and constantly evolving. These are the kinds of organizations that Peter Senge (1990) called learning organizations. They are not only adaptable to new challenges emerging in the world but are also adaptable to the worldwide rise in expectations for increased democracy, personal freedom, individual respect and dignity, and opportunities for self-fulfillment.

BUREAUCRATIC THEORY   The bureaucratic approach tends to emphasize the following five mechanisms in dealing with issues of controlling and coordinating the behavior of people in the organization:

1. *Maintain firm hierarchical control of authority and close supervision of those in the lower ranks.*   The role of the administrator as inspector and evaluator is stressed in this concept.
2. *Establish and maintain adequate vertical communication.*   This practice helps to ensure that good information will be transmitted up the hierarchy to the decision makers, and orders will be clearly and quickly transmitted down-the-line for implementation. Because the decision makers must have accurate information concerning the operating level in order to make high-quality decisions, the processing and communicating of information up-the-line is particularly important but often not especially effective. The use

of computers to facilitate this communication is highly attractive to adherents of bureaucratic concepts.

3. ***Develop clear written rules and procedures to set standards and guide actions.***   These include curriculum guides, policy handbooks, instructions, standard forms, duty rosters, rules and regulations, and standard operating procedures.

4. ***Promulgate clear plans and schedules for participants to follow.***   These include teachers' lesson plans, bell schedules, pull-out schedules, meeting schedules, budgets, lunch schedules, special teacher schedules, bus schedules, and many others.

5. ***Add supervisory and administrative positions to the hierarchy of the organization as necessary to meet problems that arise from changing conditions confronted by the organization.***   For example, as school districts and schools grew in size, positions such as assistant principal, chairperson, director, and coordinator appeared. As programs became more complex, positions for specialists (director of special education, coordinator of substance abuse programs, school psychologist, compliance officer, and school social worker, to name a few) appeared.

The widespread acceptance of these bureaucratic mechanisms as the preferred way for exercising control and coordination in schools is illustrated by the reform movement that emerged in 1983, when *A Nation at Risk* was published during the Reagan presidency. The effectiveness of schools became a major theme in the political agenda on education and joined the linked duo that had been inherited from the 1970s—equality and access. Although there had been a steadily growing body of research literature on effective schools and what they were like, a nearly unrelated reform movement suddenly erupted in 1983 that—in the popular press and electronic media, at least—seized the center stage and strongly influenced numerous efforts to improve the functioning of schools. This point is of interest to us here because it illustrates the very strong conviction of many political leaders that bureaucratic methods are appropriate in thinking about schools and how to improve them.

Clearly, there is a strong tendency for some educational reformers to keep in mind bureaucratic methods or some other set of assumptions about the nature of schools on which the logic of their efforts pivots. Often those assumptions are the same as those underlying the traditional factory, in which management decides what is to be done, directs the workers to do it, then supervises them closely to be sure that the directives are followed in full. But as Doyle and Hartle (1985) observed:

> It simply doesn't work that way. The impulse to reform the schools from the top down is understandable: it is consistent with the history of management science. The explicit model for such reform was the factory; Frederick Taylor's scientific management revolution did for the schools the same thing that it did for business and industry—created an environment whose principal characteristics were pyramidal organization. . . . The teacher was the worker on the assembly line of education; the student, the product; the superintendent, the chief executive officer; the school trustees, the board of directors; and the taxpayer, the shareholder. (p. 24)

These beliefs seem to undergird the current reform strategy, as the No Child Left Behind (NCLB) Act of 2001 demonstrates. At the time of this writing, a year into President Barack Obama's second term, it seemed clear that this trend would continue. It also seemed clear, based on Race to the Top (RTTT) foci, that the scope and power of the federal role in education policy would be expanded on an unprecedented scale. Both NCLB and RTTT made extraordinary amounts of funding available to the states from Washington, DC. But the money awarded by RTTT to some states came with strict requirements, such as states must use common standards assessed by common assessments, and they must develop teacher and administrator accountability evaluation systems, in part based on student test scores.

Also, at the time of this writing, we were still awaiting the revision of the Elementary and Secondary Education Act (ESEA), delayed by the eruption of the overwhelming worldwide economic downturn in 2008 and 2009. We expect the ESEA to be reauthorized sometime in 2014. While it was recognized that the 2001 version of ESEA, which had been named the No Child Left Behind Act of 2001, had been a major breakthrough in the history of U.S. public education, it had also given rise to significant problems. The outcome of the entire enterprise would unquestionably hinge on the extent to which the conviction of those with political power in Washington and the state capitals would remain unshakable about the following:

1. That they have the best ideas about how to bring about improvement in school outcomes in the classrooms of the 95,000 or so schools in the United States
2. That they have sufficient knowledge about the circumstances in the classrooms in those school districts to make the judgments necessary to draw up action plans and legal mandates to implement the top-down organizational strategy in the belief that it is incontestably the most promising option available to bring about the desired changes that are sought in the schools

The NCLB Act was—in the history of the Republic until that time—the boldest venture on the part of the federal government to redirect the schooling of children throughout the land. By 2013, federal participation continued to escalate on an unprecedented scale. It will take more time to see how well founded the beliefs so confidently held by politicians in Washington and in the state capitals actually were. We will discuss NCLB later in this chapter and refer to it throughout this book as it touches on many topics in the study of organizational behavior.

HUMAN RESOURCES DEVELOPMENT THEORY   As we have suggested, there is a very different set of assumptions about the organizational characteristics of schools and the behavior of teachers in their classrooms. It is a view that places the teacher foremost in creating instructional change and therefore questions the wisdom of any change strategy that seeks to force change upon the teacher arbitrarily and without his or her participation in the processes of deciding what should be done. As we have seen, this is far from a new view of organization. But recent failures of bureaucratic methods to rectify severe organizational difficulties—especially in the corporate world—coupled with the emergence of newer organizational perspectives (such as the power of organizational cultures to influence behavior) has brought newer, nonbureaucratic concepts to the fore as a major way to think about organizational issues.

Bureaucratic organizations strive to create organizational cultures that place strong emphasis on the primacy of the organization's officially prescribed rules, and their enforcement, as the central means of influencing individual participants to perform dependably in predictable ways. Nonbureaucratic approaches, in contrast, emphasize developing a culture in the organization that harnesses the conscious thinking of individual persons about what they are doing as a means of involving their commitment, abilities, and energies in achieving the goals of the organization. The central mechanism through which the nonbureaucratic organization exercises coordination and control is the socialization of participants about the values and goals of the organization, rather than through written rules and close supervision. Through this intense socialization, participants identify personally with the values and purposes of the organization and are motivated to see the organization's goals and needs as being closely congruent with their own. Thus, the culture of the organization epitomizes not only what the organization stands for and expects but also the core beliefs and aspirations of the individual participants themselves. The culture of an organization makes clear what the organization stands for—its values, its beliefs, its true (often as distinguished from its publicly stated) goals—and provides tangible ways by which individuals in the organization may personally identify with that culture. The culture of an organization is communicated through symbols: typically in the form of stories, myths, legends, and rituals that establish, nourish, and keep alive the enduring values and beliefs that give meaning to the organization and make clear how individuals become and continue to be part of the saga of the organization as it develops through time.

In this view, close inspection and supervision are far from the only means of ensuring the predictable performance of participants. Personal identification with and commitment to the values of the organization's culture can provide powerful motivation for dependable performance even under conditions of great uncertainty and stress. Consider, for example, what causes an individual to join an organization, stay in it, and work toward that organization's goals. For principles of human resources development theory to work, leaders need to believe in a particular philosophy of human behavior in the organization. Douglas McGregor helps us understand leader philosophy about people and the organization. His depiction of leader philosophy is called Theory X and Theory Y (McGregor, 1960).

THEORY X AND THEORY Y   Theory X rests on four assumptions that the administrator may hold:

1. The average person inherently dislikes work and will avoid it whenever possible.
2. Because people dislike work, they must be supervised closely; they must be directed, coerced, or threatened with punishment in order for them to put forth adequate effort toward the achievement of organizational objectives.
3. The average worker will shirk responsibility and seek formal direction from those in charge.
4. Most workers value job security above other job-related factors and have little ambition.

Administrators who—tacitly or explicitly—think that these are basic facts of organizational life will, of course, use them as a guide when dealing with employees in the organization.

Theory Y embraces very different assumptions about the nature of people at work:

1. If it is satisfying to them, employees will view work as natural and as acceptable as play.
2. People at work will exercise initiative, self-direction, and self-control on the job if they are committed to the objectives of the organization.
3. The average person, under proper conditions, learns not only to accept responsibility on the job but also to seek it.
4. The average employee values creativity—that is, the ability to make good decisions—and seeks opportunities to be creative at work.

Administrators who—tacitly or explicitly—accept this explanation of the nature of human beings at work could reasonably be expected to deal with subordinates in ways that are quite different from those who hold Theory X views.

These theories are not something for you to accept or reject; they are merely a simple illustration of how theoretical views of the organization are actually used by practitioners of educational administration in their work—a guide to rational decisions and actions on the firing line. Those of us with administrative, management, or leadership responsibilities tend to believe that one of these theoretic statements more accurately represents the nature of reality in the organization than the other does. Leaders will generally act in ways that are harmonious with the theoretic statement that they think is true. Those who tend to hold a Theory X view of people, for example, tend to believe that motivation is basically a matter of the carrot and the stick; they tend to readily accept the necessity for close, detailed supervision of subordinates, and they tend to accept the inevitability of the need to exercise down-the-line decision making. Collegial approaches to organizational life tend to be viewed as perhaps a nice ideal in the abstract but not very practical in the real world of schools.

As Chris Argyris (1971) put it, Theory X views give rise to Behavior Pattern *A* on the part of leaders. This pattern of behavior may take one of two principal forms:

1. Behavior Pattern *A, hard,* is characterized by no-nonsense, strongly directive leadership, tight controls, and close supervision.
2. Behavior Pattern *A, soft,* involves a good deal of persuading, "buying" compliance from subordinates, benevolent paternalism, or so-called "good" (that is, manipulative) human relations.

In either case, Behavior Pattern *A,* whether acted out in its hard or its soft form, has the clear intention of motivating, controlling, and managing in the classical sense. It is based on Theory X assumptions about the nature of human beings at work.

Theory Y assumptions that leaders hold about people at work are very different. Theory Y assumptions give rise to Behavior Pattern *B* on the part of the leader. This style is characterized by commitment to mutually shared objectives, high levels of trust, mutual respect, and helping people in the organization to get satisfaction from the work itself. Pattern *B* leadership may well be demanding, explicit, and thoroughly realistic, but it is essentially collaborative. It is a pattern of leader behavior that is intended to be more effective and productive than Pattern *A* because it is thought to reflect a more accurate understanding of what people at work are really like.

In this discussion of the relationship between theory and understanding organizational behavior in schools, it should be emphasized—as Argyris cautioned—that Behavior Pattern *A, soft,* is often superficially mistaken for Behavior Pattern *B.* This ambiguity has caused considerable confusion among those trying to apply these theoretic ideas to schools:

> Behavior associated with Theory Y assumptions is basically developmental. Here supervisors focus on building identification of and commitment to worthwhile objectives in the work context and upon building mutual trust and respect in the interpersonal context. Success in the work and the interpersonal contexts are assumed interdependent, with important satisfactions for individuals being achieved within the context of accomplishing important work. (Siepert & Likert, 1973, p. 3)

But the Behavior Pattern *A, soft,* approach often used by supervisors to manipulate teachers into compliance with what is basically highly directive management—in the guise of "good human relations"—has done much in U.S. education to discredit the plausibility of Theory Y as applicable to the real world of schools and school systems. Siepert and Likert concluded that "by treating teachers in a kindly way it is assumed that they will become sufficiently satisfied and sufficiently passive so that supervisors and administrators can run the school with little resistance" (p. 4).

LIKERT'S FOUR SYSTEMS   The practical usefulness of thinking in this way is illustrated by the work of Rensis Likert. In more than 30 years of research in schools as well as in industrial organizations, Likert identified a range of management styles, called Systems 1, 2, 3, and 4. The definitions of each system are explained in terms of leader behavior and how others in the organization are involved in decision-making processes: These systems range on a continuum from authoritarian leader behavior and no involvement by others in decision-making process in System 1, to collaborative leadership and broad involvement by others in decision making in System 4. Figure 1.1 defines each system and juxtaposes Likert's four systems with McGregor's Theory X and Theory Y. Likert's studies supported the hypothesis that the crucial variable that differentiates more effective from less effective organizations is human behavior in the organization. Blake and Mouton (1969) found that effective organizations involve individuals in important organizational decisions. They submitted that System 4 management is most effective and System 1 least effective. In examining extensive research on school organizations specifically, Gordon Lippitt (1969) agreed with Blake and Mouton's conclusions.

Both McGregor and Likert were basically concerned, not with being nice to people or making work pleasant, but with understanding how to make organizations more effective, which is as pressing a need in business and industry as it is in education. This general point of view is widely

THEORY X	*System 1*	*Management is seen as having no trust in subordinates.*
		a. Decision imposed—made at the top.
		b. Subordinates motivated by fear, threats, punishment.
		c. Control centered on top management.
		d. Little superior—subordinate interaction.
		e. People informally opposed to goal by management.
	System 2	*Management has condescending confidence and trust in subordinates.*
		a. Subordinates seldom involved in decision making.
		b. Rewards and punishment used to motivate.
		c. Interaction used with condescension.
		d. Fear and caution displayed by subordinates.
		e. Control centered on top management but some delegation.
	System 3	*Management is seen as having substantial but not complete trust in subordinates.*
		a. Subordinates make specific decisions at lower levels.
		b. Communication flows up and down the hierarchy.
		c. Rewards, occasional punishment, and some involvement are used to motivate.
		d. Moderate interaction and fair trust exist.
		e. Control is delegated downward.
THEORY Y	*System 4*	*Management is seen as having complete trust and confidence in subordinates.*
		a. Decision making is widely dispersed.
		b. Communication flows up and down and laterally.
		c. Motivation is by participation and rewards.
		d. Extensive, friendly, superior—subordinate interaction exists.
		e. High degree of confidence and trust exists.
		f. Widespread responsibility for the control process exists.

FIGURE 1.1   Likert's Management Systems Theory Related to McGregor's Theory X and Theory Y

and strongly supported by a vast amount of organizational research. Robert R. Blake's and Jane Srygley Mouton's (1969) organizational research, Gordon Lippitt's (1969) studies of organizational renewal, and Paul Berman's and Milbrey McLaughlin's (1978) extensive studies of change in U.S. schools are only a few of the many early studies that supported the general theoretic position that pioneers such as McGregor and Likert held.

Traditional classical organizational views (bureaucratic theory) would indicate the opposite practices: tighten up rules and procedures, exercise stronger discipline and tougher management, and demand more work from subordinates. In the parlance of neoclassical theory exemplified in NCLB, the focus is on teacher accountability, specified performance objectives, and market-based approaches to reform. Yet much of the best research in organizational behavior strongly suggests that this latter approach would be, at best, self-defeating. Throughout this book, we present evidence to support this claim.

A word of caution is in order here. Bureaucratic and human resources perspectives have been compared and contrasted as ideal cases for the purpose of clarifying and delineating the very real, basic differences between them. In the real world of schools, of course, one rarely encounters ideal cases, which is not to suggest that organizations cannot properly be classified as being bureaucratic or nonbureaucratic. Indeed, they can be and often are. Nor does it mean that, to be described as nonbureaucratic, an organization must be totally devoid of policies, regulations, and standard operating procedures, or that to be described as bureaucratic, an organization must be totally devoid of sensitivity to or respect for people. This fact is particularly true of schools, which are bureaucratic in some ways and nonbureaucratic in some very important ways. What it does suggest is that organizations may be properly described as *relatively* bureaucratic or *relatively* nonbureaucratic. It also suggests that schools are undoubtedly far more organizationally complex than is generally understood.

CRITICAL THEORY

A group of educational academicians who subscribe to a type of social criticism known as critical theory (CT) have had a major impact on how we view organizations and leadership. These theorists have been especially sensitive to and vociferous about shortcomings in the school hierarchy, particularly traditional bureaucratic institutions with top-down authority and limited allowances for typically marginalized groups to add their voices to organizational governance.

Critical theory holds that institutionalized oppression of groups of people in a society—cultural, ethnic, racial, and gender groups—is often supported by the oppressed peoples themselves, who believe the system to be in their own best interests. This coercion, critical theorists contend, is achieved by the manipulation of meaning by those in power to legitimate the values and beliefs of the power elite: "In essence, the oppressed groups work to support the interest of the dominant groups. By doing so, they consent to their own oppression" (Palmer & Maramba, 2011, p. 439). In that view, some critical theorists in the Marxian tradition would say—indeed have said—that workers in capitalist societies are oppressed by the powerful capitalist class but do not perceive it because, through control of the press, education, organized religion, and other social institutions, those in power systematically induce workers to believe that the values and beliefs of the capitalist class are legitimate and in the workers' best interests.

Paulo Freire (1970) is often credited with bringing CT to education in his famous work *Pedagogy of the Oppressed,* in which he analyzed educational practices and their impact on the poor and other marginalized groups. He contended that education should not treat children as empty, passive vessels into which teachers implant knowledge, which he called *banking*; education in his view should be *problem-posing* in which teachers and students engage in dialogue and students are proactive learners in their own knowledge acquisition. These concepts gave rise to the term *critical pedagogy*. In this way, he believed that education could mobilize social transformation. Freire was from Brazil, and although his work had an impact in the United States, CT was firmly planted in the United States by the works of Michael Apple (1971, 1986) and Henry Giroux (1983). Other notables in their field are Derek Bell (1992), Richard Delgado (1995), and Peter McLauren (1998), among others. Often Jonathan Kozol (1991, 1995, 2005) is considered a critical theorist for exposing the problems of poverty on children in U.S. schools, beginning with *Savage Inequalities* in 1991; his research brought to light the effects of poverty on schools and children to many in mainstream education circles. Kozol showed how students living in poverty were typically in schools with insufficient funding and fewer highly qualified teachers; this condition, Kozol showed, hindered students' ability to meet educational standards set by states and school districts.

Critical Race Theory

When CT is applied to race, and specifically in education to the achievement gap, it is also termed Critical Race Theory (CRT), which is defined by Solórzano (1997) as scholarship and discourse on race and racism in an attempt to eliminate racism and racial stereotypes from society, including laws, social policy, and organizational cultures. Box 1.1 presents the tenets of CRT as defined by DeCuir and Dixson (2004).

A major contributor in bringing CRT to education is Gloria Ladson-Billings who credited others with its origins: "Our work owes an intellectual debt to both Carter G. Woodson and W. E. B. DuBois, who, although marginalized by the mainstream academic community, used race as a theoretical lens for assessing social inequality" (Ladson-Billings & Tate, 1995, p. 50). Ladson-

BOX 1.1

Tenets of CRT (DeCuir & Dixson, 2004)

1. *Counter-storytelling*—gives a voice to people of color as "a means of exposing and critiquing normalized dialogues that perpetuate racial stereotypes" (p. 27).
2. *The permanence of racism*—racism exists and this fact suggests "that racist hierarchical structures govern all political, economic, and social domains" (p. 27).
3. *Whiteness as property*—this stems from the historical view of Whites having exclusive privileges, such that Whiteness is much like having a property right. For example, "tracking, honors, and/or gifted programs and advanced placement courses are but the myriad ways that schools have essentially been re-segregated" (p. 28).
4. *Interest convergence*—decisions by the majority power structure will favor people of color only when it is also in the interest of the majority.
5. *The critique of liberalism*—"arguing that society should be colorblind ignores the fact that inequity, inopportunity, and oppression are historical artifacts that will not easily be remedied by ignoring race in the contemporary society. Moreover, adopting a colorblind ideology does not eliminate the possibility that racism and racist acts will persist" (p. 29). In addition, liberal ideology supports incremental change and "those most satisfied with incremental change are those less likely to be directly affected by oppressive and marginalizing conditions" (p. 29).

Billings also credited the more recent work of Jonathan Kozol. She wrote: "Kozol's research did give voice to people of color. His analysis of funding inequities provides insight into the impact of racism and White self-interest on school funding policies" (1998, p. 20). Ladson-Billings, among others (e.g., Bell, 1992; Brookfield, 2013; Closson, 2010; Delgado, 1995; DeCuir & Dixson, 2004; Smith & Colin, 2001; Solórzano, 1997), proffered that if we are to use CRT in education successfully, it must begin with understanding that racism exists, and it is normal. We should not deny it exists or shy away from discussing it; we accept its existence and try to understand it and expose it in an attempt to eliminate it. To do this is to foster antiracist practices and perspectives among everyone in the organization, and it cannot be done without using the lived experiences of African Americans. Although Whites and other non-Black individuals cannot fully empathize with the Africentric view (the term Smith and Colin preferred) because they have not lived it, they need to be aware of it and understand how it impacts schools in terms of curriculum, students' views on themselves and other races, as well as school and district culture in terms of how minorities are viewed and treated. Smith and Colin (2001) wrote that we should use Africentric views to "make the invisible visible" (p. 65).

The authors of this text, Owens and Valesky, do not share an Africentric experience, but this fact does not mean we cannot reflect on, discourse about, and empathize with the Africentric experience and use it analytically to examine and improve practices in schools. Giving people of color a voice through counter-story-telling regarding their lived experiences with racism helps heal their wounds, allows the oppressor to understand, and "is required for a deep understanding of the education system" (Ladson-Billings, 1998, p. 14). Giving people of color a voice is a major tenant of CRT supported throughout the literature (e.g., DeCuir & Dixson, 2004; Ladson-Billings, 1998). There have been some rather successful large-scale events in our recent history that gave voice to people of color and some of these are listed in Box 1.2.

BOX 1.2

Large-Scale Events in the United States to Give Voice to People of Color

Some large-scale attempts nationally in the United States to uncover and stop racism, and to give a voice to people of color, began most importantly with the August 28, 1963, Great March on Washington, led by Dr. Martin Luther King Jr. where he gave his famous "I Have a Dream" speech. Second, an annual march across the Edmund Pettus Bridge in Selma, Alabama, attracts many prominent politicians and marks the anniversary of March 7, 1965—Bloody Sunday—when Alabama state troopers viciously beat the voting rights marchers attempting to go from Selma to the state capital of Montgomery. Third, the Million Man March of October 16, 1995, took place on the National Mall in Washington, DC, and was a major event to bring voice to people of color who continued to face racial problems in the United States. Fourth, one of the more important permanent structures giving a voice to the African-American population is the Martin Luther King Jr. memorial on the National Mall, which opened in 2011. Fifth, another important structure was placed in the U.S. Capitol Building in 2013—a statue of Rosa Parks, one of the female heroines of the civil rights movement, and now the first Black woman to have a statue in the Capitol's Statuary Hall. Finally, we would be remiss if we did not highlight the historical election in November 2008 and again in 2012 of the first U.S. president of African descent, Barack Obama, who became the 44th president of the United States.

What specifically can we do to implement CRT in schools? Solórzano (1997) provided four activities to combat racism:

1. Identify Examples—give specific examples of racism and racial stereotyping as well as the effects on both minorities and nonminorities.
2. Identify Media Stereotypes—"identify racial stereotypes in the popular media such as film, television, and print and show how they are used to justify attitudes and behavior toward Students of Color" (p. 14).
3. Identify Professional Stereotypes—we need to find ways to challenge the standard curricula and textbooks, which do not portray many professional people of color in quality professional roles.
4. Find Examples That Challenge—expose students to positive examples of people of color, challenging racial stereotypes: "There are rich sources of material in individual and family oral and pictorial histories, institutional and community studies, and artistic and cultural artifacts and ideologies that would change the racial stereotyping found in the popular and professional media" (p. 15).

These are the things school leaders and teachers must do if critical theory and critical race theory are to have any impact in schools.

What is the legacy of CT and CRT in education? Will it make an impact? Will educational researchers use CT and CRT to make improvements—not incremental improvements but radical improvements—for students of color? Will educators use CRT "to expose racism in education *and* propose radical solutions for addressing it" (Ladson-Billings, 1998, p. 22)? The practical impact on what we do in education based on CT and CRT, however, has not been as successful as most critical theorists would have hoped. In 1998, Ladson-Billings wrote the following:

What, then, might happen to CRT in the hands of educational researchers and school personnel? Well to be honest, . . . I doubt if it will go very far into the mainstream. Rather, CRT in education is likely to become the "darling" of the radical left, continue to generate scholarly papers and debate, and never penetrate the classrooms and daily experiences of students of color. (p. 22)

As of 2013, it seems that Ladson-Billing's prophecy was correct. We do not see much to challenge racism in our schools in the way CRT would imagine. Yet, liberalism has brought a focus on multicultural curriculum and the concept of diversity is clearly a topic of interest in classroom instruction, among faculty and administrators when discussing school and district mission and vision, and with school policy in hiring practices. Since mid-1990s, when Ladson-Billings and Kozol presented their work to educators, some progress has been made, such as improved equity in school funding across school districts in many states, yet funding equity among schools within school districts still remains a question. Maybe multicultural education, a focus on diversity, and some funding equity are steps in the right direction, but are they enough to meet the goals of CRT?

The Concept of Social Justice

Multiculturalism, according to Ladson-Billings and Tate, is insufficient and "a liberal ideology offering no radical change in the current order" (Ladson-Billings & Tate, 1995, p. 56). However, perhaps the focus on *social justice* takes us a step toward the goals of CRT. The concept of social justice, which seems to be taking root in U.S. schools and in colleges of education, is part of the CRT framework in its attempt to eliminate racism (Solórzano, 1997). Social justice takes on broad categories of issues as described by Dantley and Tillman (2010):

> Discussion about social justice in the field of education generally, and in educational leadership more specifically, have typically framed the concept of social justice around several issues (e.g., race, diversity, marginalization, gender, spirituality). Although these areas are vitally important to any discussion of social justice, we add the formidable issues of age, ability, and sexual orientation to this discourse. (pp. 19–20)

THE RELEVANCE TO SCHOOL LEADERSHIP TODAY

One may well question how relevant the ideas that have been discussed thus far are to the practice of educational leadership in schools. Are these ideas merely the playthings of academics and philosophers, or do they have real meaning to those who seek to make a difference as leaders in education?

The key to understanding how and why these ideas are important to educational leaders lies first in understanding that the processes of developing educational leadership are highly dynamic with constant, ongoing change and development. They have been changing and developing over the course of many years and will continue this dynamic process in the future. Knowing and accepting this evolution as an enduring characteristic of the education enterprise is basic to preparing oneself to be an educational leader. Of the many wellsprings from which the dynamic processes of change and development in education are shaped and molded, two are of foremost importance:

- *The emergence of new knowledge about how people function in organizations*   Research and study are constantly modifying our understanding of the human experience in educational organizations, which is why it is necessary for the educational leader to stay abreast of current relevant studies of organizational behavior.
- *The dynamic impact of changes in the larger society in which the schools exist*   The affairs of humankind possess an unremitting ebb and flow of overarching changes that challenge all social institutions to adapt to new conditions, and schools are no exception. War and peace, economic prosperity and recession, the evolution of social values and beliefs, and sweeping technological-industrial changes are obvious among them. Some are more subtle, such as the worldwide rise of conservative thought—economic, political, religious—that emerged in the waning years of the twentieth century and swept across the globe as the twenty-first century unfolded. This ideology may appear to have little to do with educational leadership, but in fact, as we shall describe, it may have at least as much impact as all the discoveries or inventions of new knowledge by scholars.

The relentless, ceaseless interplay between the search for a better understanding of human nature and human behavior, on the one hand, and the evolutionary development of social and political beliefs and values in our culture, on the other, creates a dynamic environment in which the basic concepts of education and educational leadership are endlessly incomplete, always works in progress. This can be an uncomfortable environment for those who seek certitude and finality in the ideas that guide their professional work. But this versatility is hardly unique to educational leadership: the need to be nimble, adaptable, and flexible is a central characteristic of all kinds of effective organizations in every profession today.

To react to changing environments, to be nimble, and to adapt, leaders need to work with others to examine the organizational vision and mission to ensure the organization is on track for success. We examine these ideas in the next section.

VISION AND EDUCATIONAL LEADERSHIP

The vision that leaders seek to share with followers is a protean thing, continually being revised and annotated by changing values, emerging developments, and events that vindicate or repudiate aspects of the worldview previously held by leaders, followers, or both. Indeed, one of the pivotal activities of leaders is to engage constantly in the dynamic process of stating a vision of things to come; then revising in light of emerging events, ideas, and beliefs; and restating the vision of "where we are and where we are going" that binds the members of the organization in mutual purpose and resolve. But in all its iterations, the vision of a leader is always uplifting, pointing to new directions, calling for progress from where followers are to where they want to be, and describing how they will get there. Dramatic examples abound in the realm of politics and social movements: one thinks of Churchill's magnificent rallying cry to the British facing almost certain defeat in World War II, "We shall fight on"; the stirring inspiration of Lincoln's low-key "Gettysburg Address"; and the immortal vision of King's speech, "I Have a Dream." Educational leaders rarely have opportunities to exercise such dramatic flair and personal charisma, yet they must always be prepared to articulate their personal vision for the organization as a rallying cry for the daily work to be done.

The purpose of the ongoing process of stating and discussing the vision is to buttress and develop the most critical factors in the development of organizational culture: the web of shared assumptions, beliefs, and values that unites the group in mutual solidarity. In the ordinary bureaucratic organization, these factors are rarely examined and discussed, rarely made explicit and public, rarely challenged. Indeed, in ordinary organizations, there is little even in the way of vocabulary for talking about such things, and the time-consuming minutiae of professional meetings usually drives such conversation out so that the norm in the organization's culture is to avoid such discussion altogether.

The goal of forging agreement on the vision or mission of the organization is, ideally, to seek consensus as nearly as it can be practically achieved, but always consensus on a new and better state in the future. We define a *vision* for an organization as the ideal toward which the organization is focused, whereas the *mission* is how the organization will achieve the vision, that is, a clear statement of the methods and strategies to be used, which contain the beliefs and values of the organizational culture. Throughout the process of developing or revising a vision and mission, the leader strives always to marshal consensus in support of something better: a higher plane of functioning, an elevated sense of motivation and commitment, an organization that is constantly metamorphosing into something better than it was. The point to remember is that the ongoing discussion of the organizational vision is a crucial dialogue through which the leader and the followers mutually engage in the process of forging the destiny that unites them in common cause. Therefore, it is a powerful engine for the empowerment of teachers. By participating in the never-ending process of creating, maintaining, and evolving a vision of the future of the school, teachers are themselves involved in a process of self-development and growth. Because the process is open, ongoing, and collaborative, the principal is also engaged in personal self-development and growth: The process engages the leader as much as anyone and in the end helps to forge and refine the leader's own vision.

Engaging in the give and take of the ongoing colloquy required to forge and maintain an evolving vision and mission of the organization requires one to rethink assumptions, beliefs, and values that previously guided behavior at work. One must either reaffirm them or modify them in the light of this reflection, as well as in the light of newly emerging realities. The process has a name—reflective practice—and many believe that it is essential if one is to continue to develop and improve one's professional practice over the years rather than stagnate and become increasingly irrelevant.

Whose Vision Is It Anyway?

At a time when school reform cries out for leadership rather than bureaucratic command, schools should be evolving from top-down hierarchical management toward a more collaborative, collegial, participative form of leadership. Because the new form of organization facilitates and encourages the active participation of people who are on the lower rungs of the organizational hierarchy, it is sometimes popularly referred to as bottom-up organization. In such an organization, the glue that binds the organization's participants together, that motivates them to unite in common purpose, is a vision of a different school, new and better, in the future. But whose vision is it anyway?

Bureaucrats assume that experts high in the hierarchy are especially qualified to set the goals of the organization and determine how to reach them. The experts may or may not consult those on the lower levels of the organization when they set goals. Leaders, on the other hand, assume that those on the lower levels of the organization have valuable knowledge about and insights into what the organization is about and that must be an integral part of the mix that we call a vision of the organization.

Leaders assume that the ability to lead is widely distributed throughout the organization and often manifests itself when participants express new ideas, challenge traditional practices, and synthesize and express the ideas of a collegial group. That is why it is important for leaders to empower others to participate fully in the unending processes of creating and refining a vision of the school's mission. But leadership is not a spectator sport: leaders do not stand passively on the sidelines hoping that others will lead the way and shape the future.

Leaders are not merely catalysts of the ideas of others, much as they encourage and facilitate participation; they have their own clearly thought-out vision of the future, their own sense of direction. Leaders have something important to say in the dialogue about where we are going, something that engages the aspirations of others and raises their hopes about what can and should be achieved in their work. Leaders move them forward to engage vigorously with others in building a new and better future in the organization. But leadership is not a solo performance. The leader's role in the process of developing a vision of the school, in addition to offering ideas and participating in discussion, emphasizes facilitating the involvement of others in an ongoing dialogue about the direction for the future.

Therefore, vision building is not always a placid process but also often requires engagement with different worldviews of people in the group, different temperaments, different personal agendas, different levels of understanding, different hopes and aspirations, and different pedagogical approaches to the future. Whereas the school principal, for example, must avoid imposing a prepared vision or mission statement on the teachers for ratification by them, he or she must have developed a clearly thought-out position from which to contribute, unhesitatingly and convincingly, to the discussion.

Perhaps the leader can do nothing more important in empowering teachers to create a process for forging and reworking the vision, or mission, of the school than to signal that this process is not only important but also acceptable. Traditionally, schools have not been places where adults can easily share the collegial relationships that are essential to leadership (as distinct from management) and teacher empowerment. The school leader, then, must demonstrate convincingly an interest in promoting collegiality and shared leadership, an interest in shifting the norms of the school's culture from the traditional to more collaborative ways of working together. Making this shift in the cultural norms of the school, translating the intent into daily practices that reduce the sense of isolation that is typical teaching, will more than likely be gradual because teachers have learned, through experience, to be cautious in talking about their work. In traditional schools, teachers rarely see one another practice their craft; rarely discuss pedagogy in a serious way; and almost never deal with such matters in staff meetings, which are ordinarily filled with minor routine matters.

The educational leader—like leaders in all fields of human endeavor—inevitably faces a career in which new, resilient responses are constantly required to meet the challenges that will inescapably and unremittingly arise in the future. These challenges are likely to occur in cycles, as they have for over a century. Rest assured: The problems that seem overwhelming to us now will in time recede into the background as new and apparently more demanding challenges emerge in the future. In view of this unyielding progression, educational leaders not only need to develop responses to the urgencies of the moment but also to develop a set of values, beliefs, and principles to guide them in developing effective strategies and actions in the uncertain future. Taken together, these values, beliefs, and principles mold and shape the educational leader's vision of what the school ought to be like, the direction in which it should be going, and the end state for which it should be striving. A core element in such a vision must be the ability to see the school as a nimble, adaptive organization that is able to proactively detect problems as they are emerging and create effective solutions to them before the problems develop into crises. It is generally agreed today that a school administrator who does not have a clear and well-developed vision will find it difficult, if not impossible, to be an effective educational leader in the days ahead.

This incessant social-political process of change has been commented upon many times as being characteristic of the American approach to educational problems: New solutions to problems are invented, rise in popularity, and are enthusiastically tried for a few years. Then, when they fail to solve the problems, Americans grow impatient and cast them aside in favor of applying a new fad to a fresh set of different problems. The chronicle of schooling in the United States since the mid-twentieth century clearly supports the view that this pattern has been an enduring characteristic of the American approach to educational problems. It seems certain to be repeated in the future, and the debate and contention that accompany each new proposed quick fix invariably involve clashes concerning assumptions about people, values, and beliefs about human nature. The current iteration of this peculiarly American approach was launched with the passage by Congress in 2001 and the signing by the president in 2002 of the NCLB Act.

THE NO CHILD LEFT BEHIND ACT

The power of the ideas that have been briefly discussed here to forge and give direction to practical matters in the tough world of educational leadership is clearly demonstrated in the federal Elementary and Secondary Education Act, an omnibus bill on education that became the law of the land in 1965. The law was then reauthorized with major revisions and given the new moniker of NCLB in January 2002. All the ideas that have been discussed here were contested in the rough-and-tumble world of national politics. Parties and players battled for dominance in shaping and molding new rules and new dynamics in educational policy and practice. Clearly, in the process, one set of values and beliefs won the day in that legislative process; competing values and beliefs did not prevail. And yet in the give and take of the democratic process, losers seek to become winners, and we would be naïve to assume that the pendulum might not, in due course, swing back. But that is not the situation at this moment, although it is a possibility in the future. By any measure, the passage of the historic NCLB Act demonstrates that the ideas discussed here are not merely academic fluff but are at the heart of the need to make practical decisions about education.

When signed by President George W. Bush on January 8, 2002, the act reauthorized the Elementary and Secondary Education Act of 1965 in ways intended to be the most far-reaching reform of the nation's public education system since the creation of the Department of Education in 1979 (Kiely & Henry, 2001). It can be seen as "perhaps the greatest achievement of the U.S. Department of Education in its then 29-year history [because] it signified a clear shift from the department's early role as data keeper and dispenser of student-aid funds to its emergent role as leading education policy maker and reformer" (Dodge, Putallaz, & Malone, 2002, p. 674). Conversely, it has also been described as a historic, even breathtaking, intrusion by the federal government into the rights of states to control the education enterprise within their borders. At any rate, either as an intrusion or as an achievement, it marked a tectonic shift in the roles and the relationships between the federal and the state governments in the arena of public schooling.

The NCLB Act promised to increase federal expenditures in education by 20% over the previous year, and it had three major goals:

- Improving the preparation of teachers and increasing their compensation so that every classroom in the United States would be staffed by a "highly qualified" teacher by the end of the 2005–2006 school year
- Closing the achievement gap for disadvantaged students by having all children at proficient levels or better in reading and math by 2014
- Instituting closely monitored systems of accountability for students, teachers, and schools

By 2013, the first of these goals had fallen well short of its target; the second goal seemed, at best, unlikely to be achieved; and the third eluded the best of intentions. It had been envisioned that these goals would be accomplished by a number of federally issued mandates. For example, a centerpiece of the effort to close the achievement gap was a provision in the act creating the Early Reading Initiative. It pledged $900 million per year over a 6-year period to bolster reading instruction primarily in schools in poverty-stricken areas and an additional $75 million per year for preschool instruction in reading. The funding was not to be doled out automatically to the states, but it had to be applied for by proposals from the then cash-starved states that described in detail the programs they would develop with the money from Washington to achieve the initiative's intention of raising the achievement of disadvantaged students in learning to read.

But the language of the act, some 1,184 pages long, bristles with 246 references to the word *research* and 116 references to the terms *scientific* and *scientifically* in describing the kinds of approaches to instruction that were desired by Congress in enacting the law. It was clear that what Congress wanted to accomplish was to support instruction based on evidence from scientific research, but this quickly gave rise to a controversy over what exactly "scientifically based" research or instruction means. Since the beginning of NCLB, the U.S. Department of Education (ED) has worked to define what this means, which has resulted in an ED website containing information to assist educators in researching "scientifically-based" programs. This is called the *What Works Clearinghouse* (ies.ed.gov/ncee/wwc/). We discuss this in more detail in Chapter 12. In the next section, we will discuss research in education to identify key elements in good research, and we provide some examples from both education and medicine.

RESEARCH IN EDUCATION

Some advocates for improving educational research seemed to insist that only controlled laboratory experimentation in the tradition of double-blind studies used in medical and pharmaceutical research could be the *gold standard* for judging the scientific adequacy of the research on instructional methods. Studies may properly be called controlled laboratory experiments if they use two basic techniques:

- They employ a control group, whose members would unknowingly receive a placebo, and an experimental group, whose members, also unknowingly, receive the medication under study. If neither the researcher nor the subjects know who is getting which treatment, it is usually called a double-blind study.
- They include systematic efforts to control or minimize other variables that might be confusing such as the age of the subjects, sex, race, financial status, and even variables that are unknowable.

Research in elementary and secondary education has, for over a century, been generally scorned in the academic community as being trivial, shallow, and largely lacking what is usually called scientific or academic rigor. Indeed, many academics contend that, because they perceive the field as lacking rigorous theoretical and scientific underpinnings, education cannot properly be called an academic discipline at all. It is also a major reason why educational research does not attract the financial support that is common in many other disciplines such as agriculture, medicine, physics, and business.

It cannot be denied that the quality of research in education has been and still is uneven. Research in education is hampered by the fact that education is not recognized as a bona fide scholarly discipline. By definition, a scholarly discipline includes the following:

- A well-defined body of knowledge that arises from recognized theory
- The use of research methods accepted as being appropriate to study the questions under investigation

This, of course, refers to what Thomas Kuhn called a scientific paradigm, which we will address in more detail later in this text. History is a typical example of a well-recognized academic discipline: it has well-defined body of knowledge that we call history, and that body of knowledge is constantly under development and expansion by researchers who investigate interesting questions by using systematic methods of study and recognized rules of evidence. Historians, for example, employ theory unique to their discipline and well-recognized methods of historical research such as historiography. Education, on the other hand, must draw its knowledge as well as its theory and research methods from a number of related disciplines, including psychology, sociology, anthropology, political science, and economics.

The quality of educational research has been rapidly improving since the middle of the twentieth century, as have the academic qualifications of those who are engaged in educational research. However, in academic circles, it takes time, sometimes a lot of time, to painstakingly bring an emerging discipline to maturity and recognition. Psychology went through this process as it began to develop from biology; sociology required a long time to become accepted as an academic discipline, and so on.

The Framingham Heart Study—A Medical Example

Studies in education lack the strong support of their institutions as well as commitment from external sources of funding. Not surprisingly, few rigorous, large-scale, breakthrough studies exist in education comparable to, say, the legendary Framingham Heart Study, which has been so powerful in shaping the modern practice of medicine and, indeed, the way most of us live today. The study began collecting data in 1948 from 5,209 men and women between the ages of 30 and 62 and continues today, having now enrolled 5,124 of the adult children of the original participants and their spouses. Consider a few of the major findings of that research—the year of the findings are in parentheses (Arruda, 2013):

- Cigarette smoking was found to increase the risk of heart disease (1960).
- Cholesterol level and hypertension were found to increase the risk of heart disease (1961).
- The level of physical activity was found to be correlated with the risk of heart disease (1967).
- High blood pressure was found to increase the risk of stroke (1970).
- Menopause was found to be related to the risk of heart disease (1976).
- Sociopsychological factors were found to be related to the risk of heart disease (1978).
- High levels of high density lipid (HDL) cholesterol were found to reduce the risk of death (1988).
- Obesity was found to be a risk factor for heart failure (2002).
- Fat around the abdomen has been associated with smaller, older brains in middle-aged adults (2010).

This extraordinary program of research has directly contributed to more than a thousand articles published in refereed medical journals and has transformed, in important ways, the curriculum in medical schools and the practice of medicine itself. This is indeed powerful research by any standard. But notice: There was no control group, no laboratory controls, none of the arcane mystery that is popularly thought to be inherent in good medical research. Conceptually, the design of the Framingham Heart Study was classically simple: Data were systematically collected from a large, stratified random sample of individuals over the course of many years and examined for statistical relationships. Carrying out the research, however, has been complex, expensive, and difficult. This was a large-scale longitudinal study whose execution included two basic steps:

- Gathering data from a selected population using repeated questionnaires, interviews, and tests over time
- Seeing how, over time, selected factors (e.g., diet, exercise, genetic inheritance, smoking habits) correlated with the incidence of the onset of heart disease

It is a truly elegant research design, simple and straightforward, and executed with remarkable precision and fidelity. Of course, being a large and long-lasting study, it has required careful and highly competent management. But the point to be noted in the present discussion is that it is a classic correlational study. The Framingham Heart Study has great power to inform us, on the one hand, of certain associations between cardiovascular health and selected lifestyle practices and, on the other hand, to suggest new and important questions for researchers to explore more fully using equally rigorous, though perhaps different, research designs.

The Tennessee STAR Study—An Education Example

Education research has few well-designed, large-scale studies similar to the Framingham study. One example that most educational researchers can agree meets the gold standard for research is the longitudinal study done in Tennessee entitled Student-Teacher Achievement Ratio, popularly known as the STAR study. We also present this study as it has been one of the most widely cited studies and has impacted a good deal of legislation and education policy across the United States. This was a legislated study that was conducted by the Tennessee State Department of Education and was carried out by representatives from four state universities. From 1985 to 1989, 79 elementary schools—stratified by inner city, urban, suburban, and rural settings with approximately 7,500 students in 300 kindergarten through third-grade classes—were involved in this research (Tennessee State Department of Education, 1990).

In the STAR study (Finn & Achilles, 1999), some students were randomly assigned to small classes ranging from 13 to 17 students, others to regular classes ranging from 22 to 26 students, and a third group to regular classes ranging from 22 to 26 students with a full-time aide. Findings from standardized test measures of math and reading indicated that students in small classes benefited significantly among all types of schools when compared to regular classes or regular classes with aides. Regular classes with aides showed some increased achievement results when compared to regular classes, but these results were not significant. The most striking findings were that gains made in small classes in kindergarten and first grade were maintained over the four years of the study, that low socioeconomic status (SES) student gains outpaced high SES student gains, and that small class sizes reduced grade retention. Because significant differences can be found statistically with small gains, the researchers were also interested in knowing how large the gains actually were. To do this, they calculated the effect size. Effect sizes were found to range from .15 to .34 for all students across the 4 years of the study, which means that students in small classes gained from 15% to 34% of one standard deviation compared to the larger classes.

What this study found to be not significant is also important. There were no differences found in levels of in-service training that teachers had had, teacher grouping practices, and parent volunteer interaction with classes. In other words, small class size made the difference in achievement, not these other variables. Due to its research design, the STAR study is perhaps the best known, large-scale longitudinal study in U.S. education, and befitting this stature, STAR has been influential in many education policy decisions.

Research and NCLB

In light of the role of research in school improvement, and the many competing claims being made for research "evidence" that advocates proffer in support of the use of particular, commercially produced instructional methods and materials, the educational leader should remember to examine the research designs and procedures on which the claims are based, as well as the statistical treatments given to the data reported, instead of taking the evidence reported by the press or, worse, book publishers at face value. The NCLB Act ushered in a new era for educational leaders, one in which school leadership was expected to be driven by data concerning educational outcomes to an unprecedented degree, an era in which one increasingly needed statistical evidence to support claims and beliefs about instructional practices, much as the Framingham Heart Study guides us today in dealing with choices about diet and exercise.

Indeed, these two emphases immediately raised a storm of questioning, debate, and argument because it was not clear what either of those provisions meant: Did they mean that phonics drill was now to be the order of the day to the exclusion of other methods of early reading instruction? And what did "scientifically based" instructional methods mean? To some, it appeared that quantitative laboratory research methods were being emphasized as a base for professional knowledge to the exclusion of knowledge obtained through other research methods. To some, it seemed evident that the emphasis on phonics in the provisions concerning reading instruction was an effort by a political majority to dictate the outcome of the long-running controversy over what constituted appropriate pedagogical strategies and techniques in the teaching of reading. Thus, it seemed manifest that the federal government was, for the first time in history, dictating how reading should be taught in the kindergartens and primary grades of schools throughout the land. Similarly, to others, it seemed equally manifest that the Washington bureaucracy had decided to back quantitative laboratory research in the study of teaching methods as the only acceptable form of research, despite the fact that research in the social and behavioral sciences had generally, over the years, stressed the importance of qualitative field studies, too.

Clearly, the writing of the NCLB Act, and the debate and disputation that led to its final passage by Congress, had involved a battle in which modernist (who believe in quantitative research), and postmodernist (who accept and value qualitative research in addition to quantitative) beliefs, values, and understandings had clashed and the modernist view of the world had won the political battle. This was hardly some unfathomable academic discussion by intellectuals that had little to do with the hard realities of leadership and day-to-day life in schools. It was a struggle between people with different understandings of human nature, human behavior, values, and beliefs about the human condition.

The political struggle to control unfolding events is not over. These issues will be revisited many times in the twenty-first century as the application of the law unfolds and the effects are experienced with all their ramifications. The contention over the NCLB Act is a political struggle for the heart and soul of schooling in the United States, a struggle to wrest control of the direction in which schools had been going from those who had been in control and to force a change of course in a strikingly new and hopefully more successful direction. But, more important, it was and continues to be, a political struggle. It involves educational issues and problems, but, nevertheless, it continues to be a political struggle.

States, education associations, and parent groups successfully flexed their own political muscles, and, in 2005, the Bush administration eased up on some accountability measures. For example, some, though not all, special education children were permitted to take alternative state achievement tests if individualized educational plan (IEP) teams decided that a student was making progress, but his or her disability was preventing him or her from reaching grade level in the same time frame as other students. By the spring of 2005, 21 states sought some changes to NCLB resulting in lawsuits, state legislation, resolutions, and other actions such as requests for waivers from NCLB requirements. Connecticut became the first state to sue the federal government for not providing sufficient funding to support the mandates of NCLB, and the National Education Association (NEA) sued (in *Pontiac School District v. Spellings*) on behalf of nine school districts in Vermont, Texas, and Michigan, asking for exemptions from all NCLB requirements that were not funded by the federal government. The NEA (2005) claimed that from the inception of NCLB in 2002 to early 2005, states had to pay a $28 billion shortfall between the required costs of NCLB and federal funding. They cited the law's own words in its reasoning (No Child Left Behind, 2002):

> Nothing in this Act shall be construed to authorize an officer or employee of the Federal Government to mandate, direct, or control a State, local education agency, or school's curriculum, program of instruction, or allocation of State or local resources, or mandate a State or any subdivision thereof to spend any funds or incur any costs not paid for under this Act. (Section 9527)

In November 2005, the U.S. District Court for the Eastern District of Michigan granted the federal government's motion to dismiss *Pontiac v. Spellings*. It ruled that the federal government has the authority to require states to spend their own money to comply with the law. Education associations such as the NEA, American Association of School Administrators (AASA), the National Association of Secondary School Principals (NASSP), the National Association of Elementary School Principals (NAESP), the Council for Exceptional Children (CEC), and the National Parent-Teacher Association (NPTA) became strong advocates for school districts in their lobbying efforts for changes to NCLB. It was an attempt to establish a new scientific paradigm in education by political action rather than by scientific revolution. It has everything to do with the day-to-day realities of being a leader in the schools. Anyone who would be an effective leader in U.S. schools of the future must have a clear understanding of the assumptions and beliefs that underlie the arguments on both sides of this confrontation.

VOICES FROM THE FIELD

Rise Above the Mark

Public Education Reforms That Work

Rocky Killion, Superintendent of Schools, West Lafayette Community School Corporation, West Lafayette, Indiana

West Lafayette Community School Corporation (WLCSC), located in West Lafayette, Indiana, is one of the highest achieving school districts in the nation. Despite its success, Indiana legislators, driven by "corporate education reforms" are diverting the school district's tax-supported revenues to charter and private schools. In essence, these "reforms" are leading to the dismantling of public schools under the guise of providing "school choice." This dismantling then paves the way for national privatization of public schools by state legislatures whose efforts are often supported and rewarded by large corporations and foundations. Note the absence of educators in this process. Superintendent of Schools Rocky Killion, supported by the Board of School Trustees, the West Lafayette Schools Education Foundation, administration, and staff, are working together to produce an education documentary that will give public school educators a voice about what this process is doing to public schools.

Purpose

The purpose of *Rise Above the Mark*, narrated by Peter Coyote, is to educate the general public about the "corporate takeover" of Indiana public schools and what parents, community members, and educators can do to protect their local public schools. Legislators are calling the shots and putting public schools in an ever-shrinking box. WLCSC Board of School Trustees and Superintendent of Schools, Rocky Killion, want to secure resources and legislative relief necessary to achieve the school district's mission of creating a world-class educational system for all children. The school district's strategic plan will introduce a model of education that puts decision making back into the hands of local communities and public school teachers, rather than leaving it in the hands of legislators and ultimately lining the pockets of corporations.

Documentary Themes

Major participants who have been interviewed for this documentary will address the following:

1. The corporate takeover of public schools and diversion of public funds to private entities
2. The dismantling of public schools disguised as "school choice" and "school vouchers"
3. The adverse impact standardized testing and using test scores to evaluate teachers is having on the teaching profession and public school students
4. The money grab of private companies that benefit from the so-called reform, which are not required to play by the same rules as public schools
5. The research on the best education systems in the world and what we can learn from them
6. A blueprint for parent, community member, and educator involvement in the "reform"
7. A request for support and resources to achieve our school district's mission which is *to engage our students in a world-class educational experience that prepares them to be well-rounded, innovative, creative, productive, and adaptive citizens who will shape our global society*

National Message

This scenario is not limited to Indiana. Nationally, legislators and policymakers are trying to privatize public schools by offering "school choice." With this mechanism, they are diverting public tax dollars from public schools and giving it to corporations. If public schools are dismantled, equal educational access for all children will disappear. The end result, if unchallenged, will cripple our society, destroy our economy, and create generations of impoverished children. WLCSC School Board members, staff, and administrators are ready to take on this fight so that all children can have equal access to an educational model in which educators, not legislators, are making the decisions. To view the current trailers for *Rise Above the Mark*, go to riseabovethemark.com.

The current educational reforms being used throughout the United States are based on competition, standardized test scores, and are being mandated by U.S. legislators and policy makers. As a nation, if we are interested in reforming public education, all Americans must first consider if the aforementioned mechanism really works. The National Center on Education and Economy indicates that the problem we face in public education is caused by the political system, not by the educators: "We have built a bureaucracy in our schools in which, apart from the superintendent of schools, the people who have the responsibility do not have the power, and the people who have the power do not have the responsibility" (National Center on Education and the Economy, 2008, p. xxvi). Legislators craft and pass educational legislation. Then, they direct school boards and administrators to implement their legislation. When their legislation doesn't work, school boards, educators, and administrators are generally blamed for the failure.

If the United States is to have the best education system in world, then the influence of political agendas must be removed from the equation, which does not mean that politics will never play a role in supporting the education system. What it does mean is politicians and policy makers must allow a public education system that empowers local school boards, administrators, and educators to make educational decisions for their respective communities and then hold them accountable for their decisions. When this type of governance is truly embedded within the U.S. public education system, then and only then will true education reform begin to work because those working closest with the students, educators, are making the educational decisions and not some political or special interest group hundreds of miles away from the classroom.

In order for U.S. public schools to become competitive with the world's best education systems, educational reforms that include early childhood education, equitable education opportunities for all students, raising requirements for entrance into the teaching profession, and paying beginning teachers' salaries comparable with other professions must be considered. The countries that have implemented these kinds of reforms have risen above the mark.

Major Participants

The Creative Team of the WLCSC has garnered the support of the following experts and supporters of public education to participate in this documentary:

Dr. Diane Ravitch—former U.S. Assistant Secretary of Education and Education Historian (dianeravitch.com)

Dr. Marc Tucker—President and CEO of the National Center on Education and the Economy (ncee.org)

Dr. Pasi Sahlberg—Director General of National Centre for International Mobility and Cooperation in the Ministry of Education in Helsinki, Finland (pasisahlberg.com/blog/)

Mr. Jamie Vollmer—Author, speaker, and supporter of public schools—former CEO of the Great Midwestern Ice Cream Company and former critic of public schools. (jamievollmer.com /about.html)

Dr. Linda Darling-Hammond—Charles Ducommun Professor of Education, Stanford University (ed.stanford.edu/faculty/ldh)

Mr. Peter Coyote—Award winning actor and narrator, appearing in more than 100 films and narrating over 165 documentaries (petercoyote.com)

Source: The National Center on Education and the Economy, 2008.

ASSUMPTIONS, BELIEFS, BEHAVIORS

Everyone in every culture accepts certain implicit, basic assumptions about people, their human nature, the nature of human relationships, the nature of human activity, and the nature of the relationships between people and their physical and social environments. These assumptions are called basic assumptions because they give rise to our beliefs and values and, ultimately, the way we behave toward others (Schein, 1985). Basic assumptions are learned beginning in infancy and develop as we mature and are educated. Over time, they become so thoroughly internalized that they are taken for granted and are shared with and supported by others around us. The assumptions become an invisible part of the warp and woof of organizational life, and they are rarely thought about enough to be considered or discussed. These basic assumptions become "the way we do things around here."

These basic assumptions—invisible and so taken for granted as to be rarely thought about, much less talked about—give rise to values and beliefs that we are more readily aware of. Because we may discuss those values and beliefs from time to time, they are more public than the basic assumptions from which they arise. For example, one of the marvels of the *Declaration of Independence* is that it publicly articulated the clear linkage between basic assumptions about the nature of humankind held by the founding fathers and the political beliefs and human values that, in their view, ultimately arose from those assumptions. In a similar vein, but in more commonplace examples, this concept explains why we unquestioningly adopt one set of behaviors when we go to church and a remarkably different set of behaviors when we are at a ball game.

Actions—that is, behaviors—flow from the values and beliefs that we embrace. In the case of the founding fathers, the compelling logic of their assumptions about human nature, that all men are created equal, led them to the treasonable acts of declaring independence from and ultimately taking up arms against arguably the mightiest kingdom of the time. Few of us have the intellectual or the moral integrity of the founding fathers, however, and sometimes a peculiar dissonance separates the beliefs and values we publicly espouse and the organizational behavior in which we engage. In the case of the founding fathers, an example of this dissonance is easily seen in the discrepancy between the soaring pronouncement in the *Declaration of Independence* that all men are created equal and the fact that slavery was an accepted institution in the new Republic. As we know, this contradiction was the fountainhead of seemingly endless political struggles and compromises that began at the Constitutional Convention in Philadelphia and has wracked the nation through generations until this very day, more than two centuries later. Indeed, the contradiction nearly destroyed the nation in the bloody Civil War. Yet some 87 years after the writing of the *Declaration of Independence*, in his celebrated "Gettysburg Address," Abraham Lincoln restated the proposition that all men are created equal and made clear to Americans that the purpose of the Civil War was to finally achieve that reality in practice. But while the basic assumption that all men are created equal endured and was thus powerfully reinforced, resistance also persisted, and the struggle to achieve equality in daily human behavior and political practice has endured as well. The low point of this saga was the Jim Crow period in the South. That period began in the 1870s and was finally broken by the enactment of the Civil Rights Act of 1964, after the great civil rights struggles that wracked the nation in the 1950s. This dissonance between underlying assumptions about the nature of humanity, on the one hand, and the things that we do—our behaviors—on the other hand, continues to exist in our own time.

Examples of dissonance abound in education, as they do everywhere in our culture. Much is said about the need for children to get an early start in schooling with a rich and diverse program to lay a strong foundation for success in later years, yet we persist in spending minimal amounts for preschool and early childhood education. Women's rights activists, people of color, the growing impoverished underclass, and oppressed racial and ethnic minorities in our culture discomfit many by pointing to similar discrepancies between espoused beliefs and values in the schooling enterprise, on the one hand, and actual schooling practices, on the other. If we want to make a difference in the organization we call school, it is first necessary to carefully make our basic assumptions manifest and consider how logical the connections are between those assumptions, our publicly espoused values and beliefs, and the organizational behavior that we use in professional practice.

Certainly, at least until the mid-twentieth century, the pervasive assumption in Western cultures was that the world we live in must be characterized by some underlying patterns of logic, system, and order. This assumption is called structuralism, which is

> a pervasive and often unacknowledged way of thinking [that] has influenced twentieth-century thinking in important ways. It promises order, organization, and certainty. Structuralism is consistent with teaching for objectives, standardized educational assessment, quantitative empirical research, systematic instruction, rationalized bureaucracies, and scientific management. As long as structural assumptions remain unacknowledged, they are immunized against criticism. (Cherryholmes, 1988, p. 30)

However that is not the way things work in the real world of schools. There is often an obvious disjunction between publicly espoused values and what we do in schools. We say, for example, that we believe in equity and equality, but many women, people of color, and poor people find inequality and inequity to be dominant characteristics of their lives in schools. But it is difficult for members of minority groups to raise questions about that issue because those who control the schools are usually able to suppress, sidetrack, redefine, or otherwise control the colloquy. There is an invisible web of power in the culture that controls our aspirations, how we think of ourselves, and how we deal with those issues in our lives (Foucault, 1980). Through that invisible web of power, those who control the culture decide what may be discussed, who is credible, and who is allowed to speak.

That is why most people today believe that it matters very much what kind of climate or culture prevails in a school. As teachers know well, many schools tend to evoke behavior that is conventional, conforming, submissive, and controlled—many would describe such schools as oppressive (students tend to say "jails")—by emphasizing powerful social norms and expectations that support and reward such behavior. Conversely, the norms of such schools discourage behavior that questions the established order and proposes changes that challenge the conventional ways of the past. It is essential for principals and others who want to be leaders in schools to explore ways of understanding the extraordinarily powerful relationship between the school as an organization and the behavior of people who work in it, and what implications for professional practice these understandings suggest about the behavior of leaders.

Knowledge of organizational behavior is very powerful and is arguably central to the most pressing issues in educational leadership today. This is a time of great intellectual turmoil in the field of education, a time of great epistemological skepticism in which all ideas rooted in the past are suspect. Indeed, some people seek to reject all theory and insist on a pragmatic approach to understanding organizational life in schools without seeming to understand that pragmatism is, in itself, a theory and an epistemological philosophy. Although we take a pragmatic approach to understanding behavior in education, it is based on understanding and accepting the fact that pragmatism is both an epistemological theory and a philosophy. Because of the epistemological skepticism that is rampant today and the antitheory bias that is sweeping through all the behavioral sciences, let us consider at least the essence of the growing intellectual heritage that underlies this book.

THE NATURE OF SCIENTIFIC PROGRESS

Dissatisfaction with public schooling has deepened over time, but the search for simple direct solutions has not borne fruit in the sense of an emerging broad national consensus that points the way to effective school reform. Rather, efforts to improve the performance of schools have produced not widespread agreement as to how to bring about improvement, but a frustratingly broad array of very different concepts, proposals, and programs, some of which are in conflict. By the time the NCLB Act came before Congress for consideration, many people who wished to bring order out of seeming chaos seized the notion that what was needed was a more scientific, or evidence-based, approach to deciding what to do. They wanted, in other words, to see the emergence of a consensus on what should be done to make schools more effective. Apparently, the hope was to legislate a simpler, more transparent understanding of what the problems were and therefore of what the solutions were. The prevailing view at the time of the debate and adoption of the act by Congress was that an infusion of more rigorous scientific thought and methods would be instrumental in improving the performance of schools. However, this view embodies some critically important assumptions about the nature of science and scientific progress. *It requires those who would be educational leaders to think more carefully about those assumptions and about the nature of science and scientific progress.*

People used to think, and many still do, that science brings about a steady cumulative acquisition of knowledge over the course of time. This view assumes that the nature of scientific inquiry is to use the discoveries of earlier investigations to explore further and thus extend our knowledge and understanding in an orderly and systematic way. This view envisions the growth and development of a science as a continuous, ever-expanding, increasingly certain understanding of the world.

This view of science and scientific methods was challenged by Thomas S. Kuhn (1962) with the publication of a 180-page essay entitled *The Structure of Scientific Revolutions*. Clearly "a profoundly influential landmark of twentieth-century intellectual history" (Van Gelder, 1996, p. B7), it has been translated into 16 languages and has sold well over one million copies—a remarkable number for such an intellectually rigorous book. Still in print today, Kuhn's work is studied not only by those in the so-called mature sciences (such as physics, chemistry, and astronomy) but also by those in the less-mature sciences (such as economics, history, education, and sociology) as well. As the demand for increased use of scientifically rigorous approaches to improving teaching and learning rises, it becomes important for educational leaders to understand the issues that Kuhn discussed.

Central to Kuhn's thesis was the recognition that science—contrary to conventional belief—does not produce a steady cumulative acquisition of knowledge. Rather, the history of science is characterized by a pattern consisting of tranquil periods during which "normal science" is practiced, punctuated occasionally by intellectually vigorous—or even, at times, intellectually violent—scientific revolutions. These scientific revolutions bring to the fore whole new conceptual understandings about the world.

During periods of normal science, the basic task of scientists is to apply established theory to explain and understand the mysteries that abound in our universe, to grapple with the confounding intricacies, and to discern patterns in the apparent muddle of the world. In the conduct of normal science, there is wide general agreement within the profession as to what theory is acceptable and what methods are appropriate to use in conducting studies and investigations. Thus, during periods of normal science, the work of scientists consists largely of using currently accepted theory to frame explorations of questions that the theory has not yet explained. Usually, this work results in strengthening and extending the currently accepted theories, ideas, and practices.

Kuhn described scientific work during periods of normal science as being rather routine, what he called puzzle solving: filling in the remaining pieces of the puzzle to further demonstrate and support the currently accepted theory. Such scientists are neither breaking new ground to extend scientific knowledge nor being objective, independent thinkers in the popular stereotype of scientific work. They are generally conservative individuals who accept what they have been taught and seek to apply it to solving the problems that prevailing theory dictates.

Kuhn used the term *paradigm* to describe this worldview shared by scientists, this intertwined set of theoretical and methodological beliefs and values that is accepted as being fundamental to a field of science. This scientific paradigm then establishes a set of agreed-upon understandings—the rules of the game, if you will—subscribed to by those in the profession as accepted and approved ways that problems are to be understood and explained. But a paradigm is more than merely a set of understandings and agreements arising from objective facts. A paradigm, even a scientific paradigm, is a system of beliefs that exists within a larger ideological context: it consists of interlocking scientific, social, as well as political views and commitments. Thus, it is not simply some esoteric scientific phenomenon isolated from the rest of the world; it is closely entwined with the realities of the social and political world. These realities of time and place are powerful players in shaping and molding a scientific paradigm.

A classic example of this—one that Kuhn used—is in the realm of astronomy, which had for centuries been dominated by the Ptolemaic paradigm that described the Earth as the center of the universe around which the sun and the planets revolve, which was of practical importance because the calendar was based on celestial activity. Yet as time passed, astronomers encountered ever-increasing difficulties in resolving the escalating number of awkward discrepancies between their observations and the dictates of the well-accepted Ptolemaic paradigm. During the sixteenth century, as the need for calendar reform made it vital to resolve these discrepancies, a great furor was stirred by the swelling debate over the revolutionary, new paradigm arising from the work of Copernicus. His was a heliocentric theory whose evidence showed that Ptolemy had been wrong, that in fact the sun was at the center of the solar system; around it, the Earth and other planets revolved. Thus arose what was indeed a paradigmatic crisis; it finally resulted in a scientific revolution that brought about the downfall of the time-honored Ptolemaic paradigm and gave rise to the then-new Copernican paradigm that still prevails today in astronomy.

Many other examples have been used to illustrate the concept of paradigms, scientific revolutions, and scientific progress. Four main points should be emphasized here:

- Scientific progress is characterized by periods of normal science, during which the established paradigm is refined and strengthened, followed by the emergence of a new paradigm to replace the old.
- In a scientific revolution, the new paradigm is very different from the old. It is not a modification of what went before, and it takes the science in a new direction. It renders the old paradigm incorrect and replaces it.
- The emergence of a revolutionary paradigm is strongly resisted and denied by the established "normal" science community. Thus, a scientific revolution is inevitably turbulent, volatile, and even intellectually violent. This is not a peaceful process, though, at its best, it may well be a civil process.
- Like a political revolution, a scientific revolution can succeed only when it wins the approval and acceptance not only of those in the scientific community but also of other relevant constituents.

The presence of a scientific paradigm is the most critical criterion that identifies a field as a mature science because it guides the research efforts of those who work in that scientific community. An immature science, on the other hand, lacks such an overarching paradigm to unify the efforts of the members of its community. In other words, the paradigm identifies and defines a field of science. As an immature science, education has no overarching paradigm. This is a fundamental reason that the effort to improve schools, teaching, and learning is currently characterized by many different theories, ideas, programs, and approaches—all of which are said by their adherents to work, but none of which has unified the relevant constituencies in acceptance and endorsement. The last paradigm in American schooling was progressive education, which is currently maligned by many critics.

Progressive education was not overthrown as incorrect by the breakthrough discovery of a new and different scientific paradigm; it was never demonstrated to be wrong or ineffectual through clinical trials or other scientific research. Rather, many of the basic pedagogical practices developed under progressive education continue to be widely in evidence and lauded as exemplary in American classrooms today, even as vigorous efforts to stamp them out persist. The drive to force a pedagogical shift away from progressive pedagogy is fueled not by any scientific breakthrough, but by a rising conservative social and political outlook that chooses to reject the essence of the ideas about human nature and human behavior on which progressive education was built. In this context, American educational leaders may correctly understand the bold changes in direction embodied in the NCLB Act as an attempt to legislate the establishment of a new paradigm in teaching and learning, rather than as a result of a scientific revolution. In fact, the legislation called for scientific work to be done to justify the new paradigm after the fact instead of establishing a new paradigm based upon new knowledge arising from a scientific revolution, which effectively turns Kuhn's analysis on its head.

But do not be misled: Paradigm shifts and scientific revolutions occur from time to time in all sciences, no matter how mature they may be. This is the very nature of scientific progress. It is also why we continually witness previously well-established ideas and practices being challenged and overthrown either by the discovery of new scientific insights or by mounting evidence that the established ways are not producing the results that were predicted. In our modern scientific age, these changes have become the stuff of daily newspaper headlines. For almost three decades, for example, menopausal women were routinely advised by their doctors to take hormones, which were thought to ease the problems normally associated with the onset of menopause. Medical practitioners thought their advice was based on a well-developed body of solid scientific, clinical evidence. Yet early in the twenty-first century, this practice was thrown into great doubt and confusion; accumulating evidence clearly contradicted earlier beliefs and expectations held by medical practitioners and underscored the potential dangers of hormone therapy that had been largely unknown. The earlier scientific studies had not been badly done; however, accumulating experience with the use of hormones produced unanticipated outcomes for many patients, which constituted new evidence that could not ethically be ignored.

IMPACT OF BEHAVIORAL SCIENCE

William Wundt established the first psychology laboratory at the University of Leipzig in 1879, which was the dawn of the science of psychology. Similar laboratories were quickly established in other European universities, many of them by Wundt's students. Among these were American students, who commonly pursued graduate studies in Europe at that time, seeking the cutting-edge teaching and scholarship that did not exist then in American universities. Upon returning, many of them quickly established psychology laboratories in their universities and began teaching experimental psychology as the new scientific paradigm. This school of thought became known as behaviorism, which took root in American higher education and flourished well into the twentieth century.

Behaviorism emphasizes the scientific study of behavior using apparatus under the controlled conditions of a laboratory that permitted the experimenter to reinforce desired behaviors by controlling rewards such as food or gentle unpleasant consequences such as mild electric shocks. The experiments always focused on behavior that could be observed and quantified, excluding the consideration of possible internal states of the subject such as motivation or other mental activity such as thinking. Ivan Pavlov conditioned the reflexes of dogs so that he could cause them to involuntarily salivate when he wished. Edward L. Thorndike conditioned cats so that they could escape from puzzle boxes only by selecting and pressing the correct lever. Similarly, a popular experimental approach was to condition rats so that they could improve their abilities to navigate out of the laboratory mazes in which they had been placed.

B. F. Skinner invented a simple yet sophisticated piece of equipment for the psychology laboratory when he was a graduate student in the 1930s. It is called an operant conditioning chamber and has been and still is widely used in laboratory research work. Skinner went on to produce a prodigious body of research, much of which used the operant conditioning chamber (or Skinner Box, as it was often sardonically called).

After William James established an early laboratory at Harvard, the discipline of psychology developed rapidly in American universities and, in the process, has produced a number of scientific paradigms that are very different from behaviorism. Five of these paradigms are briefly described here because they are particularly germane to the study of organizational behavior in education.

Behaviorism had clearly emerged by 1933 as the definitional approach to understanding human behavior in academic departments of psychology in U.S. universities. Skinner is undoubtedly the practitioner best known to U.S. teachers and educators for his widely practiced proposals for applying behaviorism to schooling, especially the pedagogical methods for teaching children with maladaptive behavior. Behaviorism was very popular among those in business and industrial management for many years because it supported the idea that management had the moral and ethical right to control and dominate people. Employees were, in this view, more or less passive objects that should be controlled and manipulated by management using behaviorist techniques. This procedure, it was reasoned, would be done in the best interests of the employees—whether or not they believed in or understood what they were doing.

By the 1970s, behaviorism, and particularly its Skinnerian form, had mushroomed into a large-scale movement in U.S. schooling and remained so well into the 1980s. Behaviorism still remains influential in curriculum and instruction circles. It has been embraced, knowingly or otherwise, by many advocates of school reform. Such pedagogical notions as programmed instruction, scripted teaching, diagnostic-prescriptive teaching, and behavior modification (e.g., the popular program called Positive Behavior Support [PBS]) draw upon behaviorist ideas familiar to many U.S. teachers. Much of the use of computers in the classroom is based on behaviorist understandings of pedagogy: "The technology of behaviorism that Skinner [advocated] for the schools is to decide on goals, to find the reinforcers to produce those responses, to implement a program of reinforcers that will produce the desired behaviors, and finally to measure very carefully the effects of the reinforcers and to change them accordingly" (Schmuck & Schmuck, 1974, p. 45). Thus, behaviorism, especially Skinner's brand, was far from some idle academic theory that had little relevance to the real world of schools; in fact, it has been a powerful force in defining how U.S. teachers, administrators, reformers, and others think about students, teaching methods, and the organization and leadership of schools. In the behaviorist view, "Evidence of learning consists of prescribed responses to stimuli presented in a program, on a standardized test, or by the teacher's question. In a good [behaviorist] program, the objectives are behaviorally defined, the information is presented in a logical and sequential manner" (Schmuck & Schmuck, 1974, p. 49), and there are systematic methods for evaluating behaviors to be used as evidence of reaching the program's objectives. Systematic methods for evaluating the outcomes of instruction should be, in the behaviorist view, *objective* and tend to emphasize standardized testing. Skinner made it very clear that, because the processes of learning are neither directly visible nor quantifiable, the pedagogical techniques of behaviorism "are not designed to 'develop the mind' or to further some vague 'understanding' . . . they are designed on the contrary to establish the very behaviors which are taken to be *evidence of learning* [italics added]" (Skinner, 1968, p. 26).

That was in 1968, but it is not some academic babble that has been rendered obsolete with the passage of time and the advancement of knowledge. Clearly, this view of teaching and learning is alive and well in our own time of school reform: many who advocate the standards movement and high-stakes testing in education reform today are comfortable with it. It is one of two recurring themes in the debate and discussion of schooling that have clashed repeatedly for well over a century.

Psychoanalytic Psychology

A 180-degree turn away from the behaviorist approach was the psychology of psychoanalysis. It was founded around the year 1900 by Sigmund Freud and a group of followers, notably Carl Jung. Whereas behaviorism was often spoken of as first-force psychology, psychoanalytic psychology emerged as the second force.

Psychoanalysis was the key method of choice to explore the unconscious drives and internal instincts that were thought to motivate people and thus were the causes of behavior. In fact, it was Freud who introduced the revolutionary notion of psychic energy: a previously overlooked source of energy, different from physical energy, from which human thoughts, feelings, and actions arose. Both Freudian and Jungian psychoanalytic approaches tended to focus on the need to diagnose and treat what was thought to be deviant or at least problematic behavior and tended to concentrate on issues such as social maladjustment and behavior disorders. The preferred method of treatment of perceived behavioral disorders was, and still is, psychotherapy.

Jungian psychology also gave us the terminology and concepts that are used in many organizations, including schools, to help us understand ourselves and others. Jung distinguished between two major psychological types, extravert and introvert, and he indicated that each person has four basic psychological functions: sensation, intuition, thinking, and feeling. These concepts were later used by Isabel Myers and Katherine Briggs to develop their famous personality instrument called the Myers-Briggs Type Indicator (MBTI), which will be discussed in more detail in Chapter 5. This instrument and other similar personality profile measures are used extensively in business organizations.

Sociological and Psychological Points of View

Psychoanalysts and psychotherapists of various types were important actors in some academic departments of psychology in U.S. universities in 1933, but they were far from dominant in the field because their research methods had little to do with ideas such as the design and execution of laboratory experiments, objective measurement, and mathematical analyses—all of which had become the hallmark of the scientific method and academic respectability among the status-conscious denizens of the upwardly mobile U.S. academy of the time. Nevertheless, the psychoanalytic/psychotherapeutic concepts of psychology were—as they still are—a widely known and influential force in the development of psychology.

Today, many U.S. teachers have studied the application of psychotherapeutic concepts to schooling through the work of practical psychoanalysts such as Bruno Bettelheim. Bettelheim's writing has been very popular among the general public as well, especially among parents and others interested in his chosen field of children with emotional disturbances.

Cognitive Psychology

Cognitive psychology is generally acknowledged as having begun in the 1960s as a major paradigm shift away from the then-dominant behaviorism. An important factor that triggered the paradigm shift was a devastating review by Noam Chomsky of some of Skinner's work on verbal behavior. Chomsky's work made it clear that the creative use of language cannot be explained by behaviorist theories.

Cognitive psychologists concentrate on what part the following phenomena play in generating human behavior:

- Attention
- Motivation

- Perception
- Memory
- Learning
- Information processing
- Reasoning
- Problem solving
- Judgment
- Decision making
- Language processing
- Sensation

They often apply their theories and paradigms to matters such as the following:

- *Critical thinking,* for example, how we apply these cognitive phenomena to evaluating arguments and analyzing complex discussions
- *Creative thinking,* for example, how we generate new insights, understandings, and alternatives that are different from the norm

Those who trigger scientific or artistic revolutions by inventing new paradigms (such as Einstein, Mozart, and Monet) are typically skilled in thinking critically and creatively. This area of cognitive psychology opens up consideration of the contrasts between convergent thinking and divergent thinking. It is also closely related to the currently popular concept of left-brain and right-brain orientation in thinking.

Cognitive psychology, having been widely accepted as a principal component of the scientific paradigm of education, has had considerable impact on the practice of teaching and learning in school classrooms. Thus, of course, excellent instruction is seen as emphasizing outcomes such as the perception of relationships between and among the elements of a problem, in contrast with emphasis on rote memorization. Contemporary teachers who are considered excellent tend to strive to develop the motivations of students as well as to incorporate a variety of ways of knowing and understanding in their teaching and thus the learning of their students. Therefore, considerable emphasis is given to the teaching of ideas such as study skills, social skills, problem solving, and organizational skills along with subject-matter mastery. This perspective clashes remarkably with the views of many who are active in the political realm of school reform, as is evident in much of the NCLB Act.

Social Psychology

Social psychology is particularly useful in informing the educational leader about organizational behavior. Behaviorism focused on the study of observations of manifest behavior and assumed nothing about possible inner factors that might influence it, and psychoanalytic psychology and cognitive psychology sought to study the cognitive and thought processes of individuals as causes of behavior. But social psychology interprets behavior as arising from an interaction between two factors: (a) the distinctive personality characteristics of the individual and (b) the distinctive social characteristics of the group or the organization in which the behavioral action occurs.

FIELD THEORY OF BEHAVIOR   This insight is largely credited to Kurt Lewin, who is widely regarded as the founder of social psychology. It may be expressed in equation form as $B = f(p \cdot e)$, meaning that behavior is a function of the person in the context of the social environment. This simple yet powerful concept was a major breakthrough, and it is called the *field theory* of human behavior. Social psychology encompasses a wide range of human behavior, including the following:

• Leadership
• Socialization
• Motivation
• Social interaction
• Interpersonal relations
• Group processes
• Group dynamics
• The formation and role of attitudes
• Public opinion
• Group behavior
• Intercultural behavior

It is part of the core of organization studies and has been very influential in the development of sociological and anthropological concepts of organizational life. Many social-psychological concepts underlie modern approaches to classroom management and teaching-learning practices as well. An understanding of the basics of social psychology is indispensable to the educational leader.

When working in schools, as in any organization, an extraordinarily powerful aspect of the environment in shaping and molding the behavior of participants is the culture and the climate provided by the organization. Although educational leaders have scant influence over the temperaments or personalities of the individuals whom they lead, they have a wide range of possibilities for influencing the characteristics of the culture and the climate of the organization. Because the organization has no independent physical reality but exists only as a socially constructed reality, and because our construction of reality is dependent on our perception of what is real, we can easily see how the organization emerges as a primary factor in evoking the behavior of people in it. This web of interactions between people and organization, and its implications for leadership, is not simple, but it is powerful in influencing and shaping the behavior of people at work in educational organizations.

In its early years, sociology developed with almost no reference to schools other than as institutions that were involved in issues such as social class, the effects of desegregation, and the role in society. By the late 1970s, however, a small number of sociologists began to take interest in applying sociological concepts and research methods to the study of organizations, including educational organizations. Their groundbreaking view was that every organization constitutes a distinctive culture. They began to pick up on some of the ideas that had been explored by the sociologists who conducted studies in industrial settings, notably in units of the Western Electric Company, and to extend that field of inquiry. As the school reform movement of the 1980s unfolded, educators became disenchanted with many of the proposals coming from psychologists—for example, proposals for more testing, increased emphasis on basic skills, and refinement of pedagogical techniques—and they began to listen more carefully to the thoughts of sociologists.

In thinking about schooling, psychologists and sociologists generally agree that the goals of schooling are as follows:

• Academic achievement
• Effective work habits

- Civic values
- Social behavior
- Self-esteem
- Self-reliance (Wells, 1989, p. 17)

But they disagree on what must be emphasized to achieve these outcomes effectively. Psychologists tend to focus on the ways in which individuals learn, including their learning styles, motivation, and relationships with both the teacher and classmates. "Sociologists," on the other hand, "look at the entire school and how its organization affects the individuals within it" (Wells, 1989, p. 17). Thus, to achieve the goals of schooling, social psychologists tend to focus on the following:

- The expectations that teachers have for the achievement of students
- The relationships between students and teachers
- The motivation of students
- Time spent on teaching and learning
- The relationships between individual students and their peers

To achieve the same goals, organizational and educational sociologists tend to emphasize the following:

- How schools are led and managed
- How students are grouped
- How parents and community people are involved
- How students and teachers are assigned to work together
- How important decisions are made in the school

We should be careful about emphasizing the apparent dichotomy of these two different points of view. It is not a new idea in psychology that behavior is heavily influenced by the characteristics of the organizational environment on which organizational sociologists tend to focus. Working independently, both Kurt Lewin (1935) and Henry A. Murray (1938), each a giant in the founding of modern psychology, accepted the premise as early as the 1930s that behavior is a function of the interaction between the person and the environment. This remains a basic concept in understanding organizational behavior. In this book, that idea is expressed as follows:

$$B = f(p \cdot e)$$

This formula represents a powerful understanding that has informed and inspired much of the study of organizational culture and the organizational climate in schools. The study of organizational behavior is, in fact, the study of the internal needs and personality characteristics of individuals and groups in dynamic interaction with the environment of the organization.

The emphasis increasingly given to the restructuring of schools to achieve school reform comes largely, but by no means exclusively, from the contemporary thought of organizational sociologists. Many currently popular buzzwords in school reform reflect the renewed understanding that the interface of people with the organization is the nexus of school reform efforts. Thus, the vernacular of school reform resounds with calls for empowerment and power sharing, "reinventing" the school, school site management, restructuring the school, participative decision making, humanizing the school, and organizational culture and organizational climate. All of these terms suggest the need for major changes in the organization of the schools to improve the growth-enhancing characteristics of their environments.

LEADERSHIP AS COACHING

Since the 1980s, as we have discussed, much has been said in the literature on school reform and school leadership about the importance of educational leaders having a vision of what schools should ideally be like and how they can be changed from their present imperfect state to more nearly achieve the ideal that the leader and, presumably, the people in the school community envision. This evolution is, of course, offered as an antidote to the popular received wisdom that school administrators have traditionally been mindless bureaucrats who blindly follow the dictates of the frequently demonized "educational bureaucracy" that some critics claim is the organizational bane of public schooling.

Coaching as a Method of Teaching

Coaching is a time-honored and respected method of teaching, and it is one that school leaders must master. Mortimer Adler (1982) pointed out that there are three principal methods of teaching well, and each method is distinctive.

- *Didactic instruction*   This method of teaching relies on clearly presenting information to students, often through lectures by teachers and activities such as having students read books, watch films, and do practice exercises. These instructional techniques are commonly supplemented by techniques such as discussions, demonstrations, the use of examples, and field trips—all intended to link new concepts to previously learned concepts to build and strengthen learning. Most readers of this book are skilled in didactic instruction, but as they assume the role of educational leaders, they will find that it is a way of working with teachers that is generally not productive. Many in-service programs intended to improve the instructional skills of teachers flounder because they emphasize didactic teaching methods, which are not always well received by adult learners.
- *Socratic teaching method*   This method is often useful when the students have already learned a great deal of information but the goal is to get them to connect relevant ideas, to think critically, to analyze, to hypothesize about and explore the pros and cons of ideas, to assess the quality of countervailing claims, and to internalize new learning so that they will be applied in daily life. In using the Socratic method, the teacher often poses a conceptual conundrum and encourages the students to explore and discuss the issues that the conundrum raises. This teaching method has limited but sometimes useful applications for the school leader when he or she is working with teachers.
- *Coaching*   Coaching assumes that the learners have a basic understanding of what they are doing, which has been previously imparted by both didactic and Socratic teaching. The coach "stands back to observe performance and then offers guidance, identifies weaknesses, points up principles, offers guiding and often inspiring imagery, and decides what kind of practice to emphasize" (Perkins, 1982, p. 55). As former teachers, school leaders learn that coaching is a familiar basic teaching method that they find very useful in working with teachers.

To many readers, the coaching metaphor immediately conjures up the imagery of sports. It is quite true that coaching is front and center in football, basketball, gymnastics, and other sports. However, coaching is also a basic approach to leadership and teaching that is widely used in many situations where one is dealing with advanced students or professional colleagues. High schools that are successful in teaching advanced students, such as those who are preparing to enter challenging competitions in fields as diverse as science, music, dance, and mathematics, usually find coaching to be the method of choice. University professors normally use coaching techniques in working with advanced graduate students, and it is commonly the method of choice in working with students at the doctoral level. Coaching is often sought by many accomplished professionals with proven track records—among them presidents, opera stars, world-class athletes, and international luminaries of the theater—many of whom routinely seek the help of coaches even as they are recognized as masters of their professions. In contemporary business management, which emphasizes leadership as does educational administration, coaching is also widely accepted as an effective way to motivate and enhance the competencies of others—that is, to lead.

Final Thoughts

We have described some of the different perspectives and paradigms that are commonly used in thinking about and trying to understand issues of human behavior in educational organizations. The fact that various people use different paradigms in trying to understand human behavior in organizations inevitably means that educational leaders will be confronted with conflict and controversy as a normal part of their work. We emphasize that there is no *single* paradigm that will unify and give direction to the diverse ways of thinking about schools, teaching, and learning.

Precisely because there is no overarching paradigm, it becomes especially important for educational leaders to think through the issues and develop a clear understanding of their own position on the different, often conflicting, points of view. It is vital for the educational leader to develop a clear vision for change in the school, and of teaching and learning, and how that vision can be implemented in the schools. It is equally crucial for the leader not only to share this vision for change with others—particularly teachers and parents—but to encourage their collegial participation in developing it and adopting it as their own vision for the future, which we call the school's game plan. The vision for change—which, in the corporate world, would be called the *strategic vision* for the school—is crucial to developing this game plan.

A contribution from athletic coaching to the language of American English is the concept of a game plan, and it is very useful in dealing with the problem of turning an educational vision into effective leader behavior that brings about improvement in the learning of all the students in the school. By developing a game plan and supervising its implementation in the midst of the uncertainties, confusion, and stress of the game, the coach transforms the vision of the game into a coherent plan of action that is intended not only to achieve results but to motivate and enhance the abilities of the players as well.

This is precisely what effective educational leaders do, too. While it is unarguable that a clear, articulate, well-grounded vision of learning in the school is absolutely necessary for effective instructional leadership, it is also clear that it is not sufficient. To be effective (to get results), the vision must be developed into a workable implementation plan. Let us repeat: The game plan must not only get results in terms of improved student learning but, at the same time, it must motivate and enhance the competencies of the teachers. It is the responsibility of the school leader, the coach, to develop and supervise the implementation of that plan.

This is a theme you will encounter in each chapter as we encourage you to think more deeply about your educational vision and the game plan you need to make it happen. In the next chapter, this theme is further discussed and its relationship to the concept of theory of practice, the well-accepted academic term for this concept, is explained. In succeeding chapters, you will find opportunities and, we hope, challenges for you to examine your own beliefs and values about leading people and coaching them to improve the instructional outcomes of the students in the school.

It is generally accepted today that school leaders are administrators whose professional practice is dedicated to promoting the success of all students, regardless of their race; family background; gender; or any other social, financial, or personal characteristics. As a basis for developing such a practice, it is essential for leaders to create, articulate, and implement a vision of learning in the school that they seek to make a reality. This vision of learning gives direction and shape to the leader's day-to-day activities and priorities. By sharing the vision with others—teachers, students, and parents—the leader engages them to unite in the effort to make it happen. Quite simply, the vision of learning in the school—having been thought through and embraced as the organizing core for exercising leadership—becomes the way in which the central issues of learning, teaching, and school improvement are constantly held in the foreground as the administrator confronts the never-ending necessity to make choices in a world where resources, such as time and money, are never enough, and expectations are always beyond our full grasp.

In this book, that vision for learning is called a game plan because it is not just wishful thinking or an idle dream: The vision becomes a plan that will guide you in choosing effective strategies and ways of implementing them in the real world of schools. The metaphor of the game plan is taken from sports, of course. The vision becomes a plan that organizes the work of the leader and establishes priorities for action. In other words, where do you want to go and how do you intend to get there? When communicated to others in a way they can embrace it as their own, the vision organizes their work and establishes the priorities of everyone on the school's team. No serious coach would take an athlete into an arena or send a team into a game without a strategy and a plan for implementing it, and no serious school leader should try to lead a faculty and staff in making the school more effective without a game plan either. You will find more about the concept of a game plan in Chapter 2.

However, to get started, focus now on the notion of a vision for the school that you would like to lead. The vision is the end state, the intentions of where you want to go with the school. Perhaps nothing is more important than educational leaders lifting their eyes from the mundane world of the present and envisioning the future possibilities—not a dream—of what a school really should be. The vision that you have of the school you would like to lead will express not merely the direction in which the school should be moving but what, in the end, such a school would be like. Free yourself now from the fetters of past practice, custom, or the way in which things are done in your school district. Think afresh: How do you envision what a school should be like? What really should be going on in such a school? How would you describe an effective school to others? What values and beliefs about learning in schools do you think are very important to address? What vision do you have for a really effective school?

Reflective Activities

1. Revisit the three main theories presented at the beginning of this chapter: (a) bureaucratic theory, (b) human resources development theory, and (c) critical theory. How do you see each of these being implemented in your organization—whether it be from the perspective of the school district level, the school level, a district department, a university, or some other organizational entity in which you work. State the organizational entity, and then how you would use, or not use, these concepts. These ideas will be the beginning of your game plan, which is discussed at the end of this chapter. Dream a little. Write freely. This is not the end; this is the beginning.

2. Kurt Lewin, in his *Field Theory of Behavior*, gave us the expression $B = f(p \cdot e)$. Define this expression in your own words and describe what this means to you in terms of organizational behavior.

CRITICAL INCIDENT   The Vision for South Shore High School

Ran Nordhoff, professor of educational leadership at a major state university, had been compiling a series of studies of the work life of U.S. school principals. His research method was, essentially, to follow and observe a school principal at work all day, every day, for a period of several months in order to develop a case study. Doing this required that he first develop a comfortable relationship with the principal, one that was characterized by mutual trust and ease with one another, which in turn required time before the observational study began, time that was spent both during and outside school hours, in developing that relationship. That phase of the current study was over now, and today was the day that Ran would begin the data-gathering phase: going into the school and actually "shadowing" Bill Johnson, the principal of South Shore High School. Bill and Ran had agreed to start by having breakfast together at a local diner, which had been Bill's longtime custom, then driving to the school to start the day.

The two men had finished breakfast and were leaving the diner to drive to the school in Bill's car to begin the day's work. Ran felt a surge of quiet anticipation: Weeks of carefully cultivating Bill's trust and confidence were about to be put to the test. Today he would accompany Bill to the school to begin the task that the two had agreed on: The professor would shadow the principal throughout every school day for a period of five months. He had invested a lot of time and effort to get this far, and now he must be very careful. He had come to learn that Bill Johnson, while always projecting the very image of confidence and self-assuredness, also felt vulnerable. Bill was keenly aware that, as school principal, he was an important actor with a number of audiences:

students, staff members, parents, and most important of all certain members of the ever-watchful school board.

Bill parked the car in his reserved space near the front doors of the school. Just as the two men were opening the car doors, Bill turned to Ran, saying, "Now, from this minute on, I expect you to 'shadow' me but we can't be friends while I am on the job. Don't talk to me during the day. Don't ask me questions while I am on the job. Because right now I am stepping on the stage and my role is that of principal of this school. And I am principal 100% of the time while I'm in that school. Okay?"

Ran said, "Sure, okay. But before we do that, tell me, what are your plans for the day? Can you give me an idea of what you are trying to accomplish today?"

Bill replied, "Oh, I don't make a lot of plans for each day. When I enter that building, there will be more than enough to keep me busy every minute of the day. The problems come to me. I don't have to go looking for them. Come on. You'll see."

With that Bill stepped out of the car, stood to his full six-foot height, and strode purposefully toward the school. He could see a small clutch of teachers, perhaps two or three, waiting behind the glass doors for him, the principal, to arrive.

1. What are the strengths of Bill Johnson's approach to the job? What are the drawbacks?
2. Do you think that you would approach the job differently? If so, in what ways?
3. You may have already observed the principals at work where you have been a teacher. In what ways would you say that Bill Johnson's approach was typical of (or different from) those principals?

Suggested Reading

Acker-Hocevar, M. A., Ballenger, J., Place, A. W., & Ivory, G. (Eds.). (2012). *Snapshots of school leadership in the 21st century: Perils and promises of leading for social justice, school improvement, and democratic community (The UCEA Voices from the Field Project)*. Charlotte, NC: Information Age Publishing.

This book is the third stage of a series of studies called *Voices From the Field* sponsored by the University Council on Educational Administration that began in the mid-1990s. Based on interviews of 81 superintendents and 85 principals from across the United States, researchers used the data to conduct a series of qualitative research studies on a number of topics in the field of organizational behavior. These topics include such areas as NCLB, leadership practices, assessment, decision making, and social justice. Some of these studies have been referenced in this textbook in subsequent chapters.

Educational Researcher. (2002). *31*(8).

The theme of this issue of *Educational Researcher* is "scientific research in education." It contains six articles, by nine distinguished authors, that discuss aspects of the report *Scientific Inquiry in Education* (which is listed in this section). This discussion was triggered by the emphasis in the No Child Left Behind Act on the importance of using scientific research methods in designing programs for improving instruction. The articles contained in this issue of *Educational Researcher,* together with the original report, *Scientific Inquiry in Education,* provide the educational leader with an invaluable guide to the issues and problems that comprise the current controversy about educational research. These readings are strongly recommended to anyone who hopes to be an educational leader.

Hamilton, L. S., Stecher, B. M., & Yuan, K. (2008). *Standards-based reform in the United States: History, research, and future directions.* Palo Alto, CA: The RAND Corporation.

This book is *must* reading for anyone studying school leadership in the United States today. It is a well-researched study of where we are and where we are likely to be going with standards-based school reform in the United States, from a highly reliable and well-respected research organization. It is a very accessible report: clearly written in straightforward English.

Kuhn, T. S. (1962). *The structure of scientific revolutions.* Chicago, IL: The University of Chicago Press.

This important book is must reading for educational leaders today. It not only helps us to understand how scientific progress is shaped and developed but also explains some of the difficulties that immature sciences— such as education—have in increasing their scientific credibility. Given the recent attempts to legislate a paradigm for teaching in the United States, instead of encouraging a scientific paradigm, the issues discussed by Kuhn take on new importance for educational leaders.

National Policy Board for Educational Administration. (2008). *Educational leadership policy standards: ISLLC 2008.* Washington, DC: Council of Chief State School Officers.

This publication is the source for the ISLLC Standards that are described elsewhere in this textbook. Having been adopted for use in some 40 states, they are highly influential in the training of school leaders. It gives some history of how the standards came to be, with particular emphasis on the recent research used as their base. A well-written presentation that we think should be on the shelf of every future school leader.

Shavelson, R. J., & Towne, L. (Eds.), National Research Council Committee on Scientific Principles for Education Research. (2002). *Scientific inquiry in education.* Washington, DC: National Research Council, National Academy Press.

One of the most powerful and controversial provisions of the No Child Left Behind Act requires those who receive federal funds under the act to use evidence-based strategies in their school reform efforts. This requirement put education research at center stage as questions arose about what the term *evidence-based strategies* means. In an effort to clarify this issue, the National Research Council convened a committee that produced this report, which defines and discusses issues in scientific inquiry in education and what standards are appropriate to use in judging its quality. The main thrust of the report is to encourage the development of a scientific culture in the education profession. It is a landmark document that promises to have a long-term impact on the much-delayed development of research in education. Some practitioners may think that such dull stuff is best left to those in the ivory tower, but that would be wrong: Of all the provisions in the No Child Left Behind Act, this one has the greatest promise, over time, of finally moving education into the ranks of a full-fledged profession.

References

Adler, M. (1982). *The Paedeia Proposal: An educational manifesto.* New York, NY: Macmillan.

Apple, M. (1971). The hidden curriculum and the nature of conflict. *Interchange, 2*(4), 27–40.

Apple, M. (1986). *Teachers and text: A political economy of class and gender relations in education.* New York, NY: Routledge.

Argyris, C. (1971). *Management and organizational development.* New York, NY: McGraw-Hill.

Arruda, H. (Ed.). (2013). Framingham Heart Study: A project of the National Heart, Lung and Blood Institute of Boston University. Retrieved from http://www .framinghamheartstudy.org/about/milestones.html.1713

Bell, D. (1992). *Faces at the bottom of the well.* New York, NY: Basic Books.

Berman, P., & McLaughlin, M. W. (1978). *Federal programs supporting educational change: Implementing and sustaining innovations* (Vol. VIII). Santa Monica, CA: RAND Corporation.

Blake, R. R., & Mouton, J. S. (1969). *Building a dynamic corporation through grid organization development.* Reading, MA: Addison-Wesley.

Brookfield, S. (2013). Racializing criticality in adult education. *Adult Education Quarterly, 53*(3), 154–169. doi:10.1177/0741713603251212

Cherryholmes, C. H. (1988). *Power and criticism: Poststructural investigations in education.* New York, NY: Teachers College Press.

Closson, R. B. (2010). Critical race theory and adult education. *Adult Education Quarterly, 60*(3), 261–283. doi:10.1177/0741713609358445

Dantley, M. E., & Tillman, L. C. (2010). Social justice and moral transformative leadership. In C. Marshall & M. Oliva (Eds.), *Leadership for social justice: Making revolutions in education* (pp. 19–34). Boston, MA: Allyn & Bacon.

DeCuir, J. T., & Dixson, A. D. (2004). "So when it comes out, they aren't that surprised that it is there": Using critical race theory as a tool of analysis of race and racism in education. *Educational Researcher, 33*(5), 26–31.

Delgado, R. (1995). *Critical race theory: The cutting edge.* Philadelphia, PA: Temple University Press.

Dodge, K. A., Putallaz, M., & Malone, D. (2002, May). Coming of age: The Department of Education. *Phi Delta Kappan, 83*(9), 674.

Doyle, D. P., & Hartle, T. W. (1985, September). Leadership in education: Governors, legislators, and teachers. *Phi Delta Kappan, 67*(1), 21–27.

Finn, J., & Achilles, C. M. (1999). Tennessee's class size study: Findings, implications, misconceptions. *Educational Evaluation and Policy Analysis, 21,* 97–109.

Foucault, M. (1980). *Power/knowledge.* New York, NY: Pantheon Books.

Freire, P. (1970). *Pedagogy of the oppressed.* New York, NY: The Continuum International Publishing Group.

Giroux, H. (1983). *Theory and resistance: A pedagogy for the opposition.* South Hadley, MA: J. F. Bergin.

Kiely, K., & Henry, T. (2001, December 17). Will no child be left behind? *USA Today,* p. D4.

Kozol, J. (1991). *Savage inequalities.* New York, NY: Crown.

Kozol, J. (1995). *Amazing grace.* New York, NY: Crown.

Kozol, J. (2005). *The shame of the nation.* New York, NY: Crown.

Kuhn, T. S. (1962). *The structure of scientific revolutions.* Chicago, IL: The University of Chicago Press.

Ladson-Billings, G. (1998). Just what is critical race theory and what's it doing in a nice field like education? *Qualitative Studies in Education, 11*(1), 7–24.

Ladson-Billings, G., & Tate, W. F., IV. (1995). Toward a critical race theory of education. *Teachers College Record, 97*(1), 47–68.

Lewin, K. (1935). *A dynamic theory of personality.* New York, NY: McGraw-Hill.

Lippitt, G. L. (1969). *Organizational renewal: Achieving viability in a changing world.* New York, NY: Appleton-Century-Crofts.

McGregor, D. M. (1960). *The human side of enterprise.* New York, NY: McGraw-Hill.

McLauren, P. (1998). *Life in schools.* Boston, MA: Pearson.

Murray, H. A., et al. (1938). *Explorations in personality.* New York, NY: Oxford University Press.

National Center on Education and the Economy. (2008). *Tough choices or tough times: The report of the New Commission on the Skills of the American Workforce.* San Francisco, CA: John Wiley & Sons.

National Education Association. (2005). NEA stands up for children and parents, files first-ever national lawsuit against administration for not paying for education regulations. Retrieved from http://www.nea.org/home/17497.htm

No Child Left Behind Act. 20 U.S.C. 7907 Section 9527(a) (2001).

Palmer, R. T., & Maramba, D. C. (2011). African American male achievement: Using a tenet of critical theory to explain the African American male achievement disparity. *Education and Urban Society, 43*(4), 431–450. doi:10.1177/0013124510380715

Perkins, D. (1982). *Smart schools: Better thinking and learning for every child.* New York, NY: Free Press.

Schein, E. H. (1985). *Organizational culture and leadership.* San Francisco, CA: Jossey-Bass.

Schmuck, R. A., & Schmuck, P. A. (1974). *A humanistic psychology of education: Making the school everybody's house.* Palo Alto, CA: National Press Books.

Senge, P. (1990). *The fifth discipline.* New York, NY: Doubleday.

Siepert, A. F., & Likert, R. (1973, February 27). *The Likert school profile measurements of the human organization.* Paper presented at the American Educational Research Association National Convention, New Orleans, LA.

Skinner, B. F. (1968). *The technology of teaching.* New York, NY: Appleton-Century-Crofts.

Smith, S. E., & Colin, S. A. J., III. (2001). An invisible presence, silenced voices: African Americans in the adult education professoriate. In V. Sheared & P. A. Sissel (Eds.), *Making space: Merging theory and practice in adult education* (pp. 57–69). Westport, CT: Bergin & Garvey.

Solórzano, D. G. (1997). Images and words that wound: Critical race theory, racial stereotypes, and teacher education. *Teacher Education Quarterly, 24*(3), 5–19.

Tennessee State Department of Education. (1990). *The State of Tennessee's Student/Teacher Achievement Ratio (STAR) project: Final summary report 1985–1990.*

Van Gelder, L. (1996, June 19). Thomas Kuhn, 73. Devised science paradigm [Obituary]. *The New York Times,* p. B7.

Wells, A. S. (1989, January 4). Backers of school change turn to sociologists. *The New York Times Education Supplement,* p. 17.

CHAPTER 2

Guiding Concepts for a Theory of Practice

As you move into the ranks of educational leadership, you may be certain of at least one thing from the outset: the world in which you will work as an educational leader is, and will continue to be, embedded in controversy, conflict, and contention. Perhaps some people in our culture may go through life as detached observers; leaders may not. Leaders engage in the business of not merely observing the human condition but also—however modestly—making a difference in the outcomes of the issues of their day. Educational leaders do not merely survive in their competitive, conflicted, fast-paced world of work. To paraphrase William Faulkner, they prevail: They succeed in the work and find it challenging, zestful, and rewarding.

If you choose the path of leadership for your professional future, even if you do not now aspire to a high position in the scheme of things, you must prepare yourself to prevail in that new role if you want to be successful. There is a great deal of scholarly evidence to support the commonplace observation that effective leaders are characteristically confident and self-assured even in the face of uncertainty. This need to deal confidently with ambiguity is a core factor in making the transition from teaching or counseling to school administration. Such a move is more than a step to extend or enrich one's career. It is a career change: a move from one career to another. Normally, one leaves teaching to take up administration. At the moment of appointment to a position as an administrator, one no longer holds the title of teacher but has a different title: assistant principal, principal, or whatever the case may be. Also at that moment—at least at the level of school principal and often at lower ranks in the organization—you not only leave the classroom but also leave the teachers' union bargaining unit and are classified as management. Training and experience in teaching are clearly important to success in educational administration. It is also indisputable that a career in leadership requires knowledge, skills, and attitudes that are not necessarily required to the same degree for effective teaching.

Preparation for leadership in education includes becoming increasingly familiar with and comfortable working in an environment characterized by uncertainty, paradox, and—not infrequently—confusion. Upon appointment to an administrative position, leaders acquire power and cachet, no matter how minor or trivial their new role may seem, and they are therefore inevitably pulled and hauled from many different directions by those who want to enlist that power and cachet in support of their causes. Preparation for prevailing in this environment is, in part, cognitive: learning basic principles of organization and the behavior of people who work in them, which this text is about. But acquiring the essential organizational knowledge is, in itself, inadequate. Preparation for leadership also requires an individual to internalize this knowledge. Only by internalizing organizational knowledge can one use it as a guide to developing the kinds of leader behavior that will be authentic, consistent, and effective, even under conditions that may seem to be contentious or bordering on the chaotic. That part of the preparation process is in your hands. Only you can develop a *theory of practice* that will guide *your* practice of educational leadership.

Later in this book, we will discuss more fully the idea that conflict is a normal part of organizational life and that how you deal with conflict as an educational leader must become part of your theory of practice. Differences of opinion, dispute, debate, and discussion are not to be avoided, nor should we seek to eliminate them entirely. Properly managed, conflict in an organization—as well as in one's own life—can and should be welcomed as a source of dynamism that strengthens and energizes both the individual and the organization and offers opportunities for leaders to lead. It is very difficult to be an effective leader in an organization in which the participants are complacent with things as they are, one in which raising questions or proposing new ideas is frowned upon, one in which no one feels a need to change the way things are done. Organizations with participants who seem to be smug and complacent may be unwittingly revealing symptoms of deep organizational malaise. In fact, one of the important things that leaders do is to raise the awareness of people that change is needed and convince them that it can be accomplished.

Dealing with divergent opinions and disputation is a given for anyone who exercises leadership in any organization because leadership is, by definition, exercised in an environment that demands choices be made from among competing points of view. After all, if everyone in the organization agreed from the beginning on what should be done, there would be little need for leadership.

TWO PRINCIPAL SOURCES OF CONFLICT

Leaders in education are likely to encounter conflict that arises from various sources, many of which may be idiosyncratic to their local community, or their particular school system, or the region in which they are located. However, all educational leaders, regardless of where or at what level they work, are certain to encounter two overarching sources of conflict:

- One source lies in the different ways in which different people can and do understand what educational organizations are and how they are best led and managed.
- The second source lies in the pervasive disagreement among people in our society about the nature of education itself and what the goals of schooling should be.

The educational leader encounters conflict as an ordinary part of practice. In a dynamic and open society such as ours, in which education is clearly in the public realm, the level and intensity of conflict are closely related to the extent to which there is broad agreement in society about the purposes and methods of schooling. We like to think, fantasize perhaps, that some time in the past there was little controversy over schools and schooling, that there was broad agreement about what schools should be accomplishing and how. Whatever the truth may be, that time (if it ever existed) is in the past and is not relevant to the situation we face today. All school districts and all states abound with groups and coalitions of single-issue critics: ethnic groups, gays, conservatives, women, tax cutters, liberals, the poor—one could go on and on.

The "Great Debate": Traditional Versus Progressive Education

One single, overarching, long-standing struggle has dominated educational thought in the United States for well over a century, beginning in the 1870s, with each side declaring victory from time to time. While progressive ideas have steadily increased in popularity and have occasionally been in ascendancy, early in the second millennium it is clear that traditional conservative concepts of schooling have seized the momentum of the school reform movement. Thus, many teachers and parents, believing in the tenets of progressive education, are dismayed to find their views at odds with the prevailing educational philosophy of the day.

Traditional concepts of schooling emphasize the primacy of subject matter, the importance of passing an inherited body of knowledge on to the young, drill, memorization of facts, the authority of the teacher, and formal instructional methods. Although those holding such traditional views have consistently presented tough-minded challenges to progressive educational thought, the signature ideas and practices of progressivism had already irrevocably transformed the practice of teaching in the United States by the 1940s and had become generally recognized as the standard of good educational practice (Ravitch, 1983). Progressive ideas and classroom instructional practices such as the primacy of practical experience in learning (learning by doing), individual instruction, informality in the classroom, group discussion, team learning, and laboratory instruction had become defining characteristics of good teaching and good schools, and they were important standards by which regional accrediting agencies and state evaluators judged the quality of schools. The belief that art, music, poetry, dance, athletics, and other cultural pursuits are important contributors to the history of the human race tends to be a central value in such schools. It remains so today, even as the clash between traditional and progressive approaches to schooling in the United States continues unabated. These ideas, beliefs, and practices are, and will remain, important standards for judging the quality of teaching and schooling even as the dispute continues in the twenty-first century.

The Beginnings of the Great Educational Debate

The conflict and dispute over public schooling that you have personally witnessed and experienced during your career is nothing new; it has been going on since the 1870s. Much of the present-day conflict over schooling in the United States is a continuation and extension of the clash of two very different and very opposing points of view about schooling that erupted in the late 1800s and that have been battling for dominance in the United States literally for generations.

> At its simplest level, one could say it is a debate between education broadly and narrowly conceived, between the primacy of the child and the primacy of subject matter, between spontaneous and formal approaches to schooling, and between education designed to transform the nation's cultural heritage and one designed to preserve it. (Olson, 1999, p. 25)

The clash has often been referred to as the progressive versus the traditional. It has waxed and waned "with bitter intensity throughout the 20th century. And it is no less heated or closer to resolution today than it was in the beginning" (Olson, 1999, p. 25).

During the era in which progressive education developed and flourished, spanning the years from 1873 through the depths of the Great Depression in the 1930s, immigration seemed to be flooding the United States and large-scale industrialization was rapidly transforming it from an agricultural society into an urban-industrial one. It was a time that was, in some remarkable ways, much like our own. It was the era that saw the emergence of new super-rich corporate giants such as the original shipping and railroad robber barons, Cornelius Vanderbilt and Jay Gould, financier John Pierpont Morgan, steel magnate Andrew Carnegie, oil tycoon John D. Rockefeller, and automaker Henry Ford. It was also a time of new technology that was, then as now, the province of young entrepreneurs. For example, Thomas Edison was 28 when he sold a license to use the wax-process stencil that he had invented to 19-year-old Albert Blake Dick, who created the mimeograph machine with it and became rich and famous. John D. Rockefeller founded his first oil venture in Titusville, Pennsylvania, when he was 20. Charles A. Lindbergh flew over the Atlantic when he was 25. Chauncy "Chance" Vought founded Chance Vought Aircraft to manufacture the airplanes that he was designing when he was 27 and then went on to be instrumental in creating the United Aircraft Corporation.

It was a time of transformation in the nation, fueled not only by the financiers, entrepreneurs, and technical wizards who were building the great new industries, transportation systems, and communications systems that would alter life in the United States forever, but also by the great masses of immigrants from abroad and migrants from the farms to cities. It was the latter group who would provide the muscle and energy in the factories and on the construction sites. For most of them, it would be a new life, very often one of squalor. Unlike their forebears, they would now be city dwellers, tenants in rented housing, employees dependent on their weekly pay envelopes, living away from the traditional support systems of their families and communities.

In this era of massive industrialization and urbanization, many became very concerned about the welfare of the large number of workers and their families who were, in a single generation, being relocated and socialized into a new way of life, a new culture that was just in the process of being invented. Corporate abuse of workers abounded, government agencies were often corrupt, social support for those in need was skimpy, and health care was often nonexistent. It was the time of the muckrakers, who documented the plight of the urban poor and exposed corruption in education and city government and the often deplorable working conditions that powerless workers had to endure. Lincoln Steffens, editor of *McClure's* magazine, may have invented investigative reporting by exposing corruption in city government. Ida Tarbell published a book that revealed the seamy side in the history of the Standard Oil Company. Jacob Riis, using flash photography for the first time to create incredibly powerful pictures of the human condition in inner cities, revealed to middle- and upper-class Americans how the other half lived. Nobel laureate Jane Addams, founder of Hull House in Chicago, was a feisty and powerful activist for better working conditions, improved city services, and expanded social and health services. Pulitzer Prize-winner Upton Sinclair wrote a series of books documenting widespread abysmal working conditions. *The Jungle,* perhaps his most notable work, focused on the Chicago stockyards. He then went on to write exposés of other kinds of organizations.

A political movement soon emerged that

> sought to curb the excesses of modern capitalism by regulating industry and commerce, emphasizing concern for human over corporate welfare, and placing the scientific expertise of the university at the service of the government. . . . It was in this heady, fractious period that reformers turned to the schools. (Olson, 1999, p. 26)

In 1873, Francis Wayland Parker—the superintendent of the Quincy, Massachusetts, public schools—became prominent by establishing perhaps the first schools using what were to become known as progressive methods. These methods used group instructional activities and informal instruction methods, stressed science and the real world in which the children lived, and eschewed harsh disciplinary methods. Parker was a true educational pioneer who took up academic life only after he had demonstrated the practicality of his ideas convincingly in the real world of public schools in less than idyllic communities.

> At a time when public schools were dominated by recitation, memorization, and drill, Parker advocated placing the child at the center of education and building schools around their students' motivation and interests. Under the Quincy System, as it came to be called, textbooks gave way to magazines, newspapers, and materials developed by teachers. Students learned geography by exploring the local countryside. And they studied an integrated curriculum that stressed learning by doing and expression through the arts. (Olson, 1999, p. 25)

These ideas appealed to many people and they took root and flourished: Progressive education was on the upswing and it spread rapidly. The most pressing problems were in the cities, and many cities across the nation were in the vanguard of the progressive movement: The public schools of Gary (Indiana), Denver, Houston, and St. Louis were prominent among them. While each community developed its own unique approach to implementing the new ideas, they tended to be "associated with more active learning, cooperative planning by teachers and students, a greater recognition of individual differences, attempts to relate learning to 'real life,' and efforts to broaden the school's mission to address health, vocational, social, and community issues" (Olson, 1999, p. 25).

In the early years of the twentieth century, this new approach to public schooling involved legendary figures such as John Dewey, a world-class philosopher and educator; psychologist Edward L. Thorndike, internationally acclaimed for his original work on the nature of intelligence; G. Stanley Hall, an eminent psychologist and president of Clark University, who did pioneering work in the study of adolescence; and educator William Heard Kilpatrick of Teachers College, Columbia University, who was Dewey's most noted acolyte.

The Backlash of the 1950s

The progressive education movement had been a powerful force in rescuing U.S. schooling from the formalistic rote-recitation constrictions of traditional teaching and moving it toward a more enlightened recognition of the central role of students as growing, developing individuals; over time, however, some of its adherents went too far. Some advocated rejecting traditional concepts of subject matter altogether and advocated schools that prepared students for—among other things—worthy home membership, the use of leisure time, and entry-level vocational preparation (National Education Association of the United States, 1918). In 1944, the National Education Association (NEA) spearheaded the concept of Education for All American Youth that envisioned high schools that would track some students into college preparation courses and would send 60% of the students into lower-level courses that would presumably prepare them for entry-level employment. In 1945, the life adjustment movement appeared. Backed by the U.S. Office of Education, it advocated simplified courses for the 60% of high school students who were not expected to go to college, courses that emphasized skills such as the ability to read a newspaper, fill out a job application form, or balance a checkbook. "The result was a proliferation of nonacademic and often pedestrian high school courses," (Olson, 1999, p. 28) which led directly to a powerful backlash from a broad spectrum of people who had become increasingly uneasy about the "modern" changes in U.S. schooling.

One of the first critics was Arthur E. Bestor, who had earned a reputation as a historian of the nineteenth-century New Harmony communal colony on the banks of the Wabash River in southern Indiana. His hit book in 1953 was *Educational Wastelands: The Retreat from Learning in Our Public Schools* (Bestor, 1953, 1985). It was a devastating, shocking, and hugely profitable critique in the era of the Brave New World, when many hoped and dreamed that, in contrast to their own lifetimes—which had been dominated by the Great Depression followed by the enormity of World War II—the old contests for international dominance would not be inherited by their children. In the cold war years, there was not much to cheer them, however.

Vice Admiral Hyman G. Rickover, the iconoclastic and strangely magnetic individual in charge of developing the U.S. atomic-powered attack submarine to confront the much-feared and mysterious Soviet opponent in the depths of the world oceans, foresaw the collapse of the American way of life being deliberately and carelessly engineered in the schools of the nation in competition with the schools of the Soviet Union (Rickover, 1959). A 1959 book buttressed with a foreword by the venerated Edward R. Murrow and a preface by Charles Van Doren, then still admired in his role as a youthful and popular intellectual on a television game show, was a runaway bestseller and raised primordial fears that, in the life-and-death contest with the fearsome Soviet Union, the future of the nation was being decided—most unfavorably—in the high school classrooms. Meanwhile, former school board member Albert Lynd (1969) had published a sensational exposé titled *Quackery in the Public Schools*. In a similar vein, another former school board member, Mortimer Smith, had found publishing gold in *The Diminished Mind: A Study of Planned Mediocrity in Our Public Schools*. In his criticism of the progressive movement in education, Smith wrote:

> I do not think anyone will challenge the statement that pragmatism has become the official philosophy of the public education; there may be an occasional maverick scattered here and there but the great majority of the professors of education are committed to this philosophy and they transmit it to the future teachers and administrators whom they train to run the American public school system. (Smith, 1954, pp. 78–79)

By *pragmatism,* Smith meant *progressive education* principles.

Amidst these sensational and highly popular exposés, the esteemed chancellor of the University of Chicago weighed in with the more sober but nonetheless devastating *Education for Freedom,* which, predictably, decried the public schools' straying from the heritage of the Great Books, which Robert Maynard Hutchins (1943) thought contained the essence of human civilization. These critics lambasted the schools for denigrating academic learning, lacking serious goals, and undermining the traditions of liberal education. Summing up these critics' conclusions on the direction of progressive education, Hutchins wrote, "The world is probably closer to disintegration now than at any time since the fall of the Roman Empire" (p. 23).

All of this became mere background, however. It was the warm-up for the main event, which came when the Soviet Union launched a 184-pound satellite on October 4, 1957, to orbit the earth every 90 minutes and followed it the next month with *Sputnik II,* which had a live dog aboard as a passenger. In the paroxysm of deep foreboding and fear that swept across the United States, schooling was quickly identified as a major culprit for the national embarrassment and became a primary target for immediate and massive change. Suddenly, school had to be made more demanding; the future of the nation required a tougher curriculum and greater effort from children in school. The schools of the Soviet Union were extolled as models because they emphasized demanding academic training; made heavy use of authoritarian, traditional teaching methods; made heavy use of examinations; and eschewed frills such as sports, driver training, and other extracurricular activities. The National Defense Education Act (NDEA) was swept through the Congress, and it provided substantial funding for strengthening instruction in mathematics, sciences, and foreign languages. Notions of progressive education were widely shouldered aside as U.S. schools and teachers were pressed to prepare their students for the grim and dangerous future of global competition that many thought surely lay ahead.

The Neoprogressives Emerge in the 1960s

The cyclical nature of the pulling and hauling that is the signature of the ongoing struggle between traditional, conservative views of schooling and more liberal, progressive views was powerfully manifest in the 1960s. Against a backdrop of the protracted tragedy of the Vietnam War, spectacular and disheartening assassinations of political and racial leaders, noisy rebelliousness among youth, and urban uprisings against institutional injustice, progressive views surged to the fore of education. During this time, a new group of critics cried out against the social inequities and the dull, mindless coursework they saw as the lot of those hapless children trapped in the public schools of inner cities. This group of largely youthful critics once again sounded progressive themes and practices as urgent and necessary to deal with the realities, often harsh, that they saw firsthand in urban schools. John Holt (1953), in simple yet withering prose, described vividly how the schools that children were required to attend doomed them to failure in coping with the realities of the world they lived in. Jonathan Kozol, in *Death at an Early Age*, wrote a searing indictment from the frontlines, the classrooms of the Boston public schools that vividly described discriminatory treatment of the Negro (his term which was acceptable vernacular of the time) children in the public schools (Kozol, 1967). In *36 Children*, Herbert Kohl described his experiences in his first year of teaching (Kohl, 1967). He told, for example, of his efforts to find ways (often subversive ways, in the eyes of the system) to breathe life and freshness into classroom routines and encourage children to explore, invent, create, and find excitement in their learning.

THE CONTEMPORARY DEBATE ON SCHOOLING

Former president of Yale University and commissioner of baseball A. Bartlett Giamatti described truth as being perhaps a dynamic compound of opposites, savage contraries for a moment conjoined. If this is so, then the polemic dispute one finds so readily in current literature on the state of U.S. education may represent the process of interfusing a new amalgam that may eventually be generally accepted as the basis for understanding the state of affairs in schooling. As the twentieth century drew to a close, however, the student of educational leadership found a literature characterized more by *Sturm und Drang* than by coolly reasoned analyses in search of truth.

   In retrospect, the confrontational, heated discussion of issues and problems in education is thought by many to have been touched off by an opening salvo in 1983, when the White House released an incendiary document highly critical of U.S. education. The document was called *A Nation at Risk* (1983), and its release by the Reagan White House amidst a well-orchestrated nationwide publicity blitz was an astonishing event in U.S. history, let alone U.S. schooling. The report had been prepared by a prestigious committee under the direction of the Secretary of Education. The president, Ronald Reagan, took the extraordinary step of endorsing the report in a speech, which was in itself a historic intervention in education by any president—especially one who had campaigned on the promise to eliminate the United States Office of Education, which had sponsored the report. Subsequently, as president, George H. W. Bush also endorsed the report.

The title of the work was alarming at a time when the cold war was still tense and fraught with danger, the Berlin Wall was intact, and nuclear-capable bombers flew in relays 24 hours a day ready to retaliate in the event of nuclear attack. It immediately catapulted issues in U.S. education into the realm of the highest possible concern: literally, the security of the nation itself. It was, to put it mildly, a new, if not novel, thesis: What went on in U.S. classrooms posed a threat to the security of the nation.

A Nation at Risk made many allegations of numerous "failures" of U.S. schools and went on to charge that the educational achievement of U.S. students was dismal in comparison with that of students in other lands. It described U.S. schools as being not very well organized and not well run, and it depicted educators in them as being a dispirited and not very able lot. Upon its release, scholars eagerly examined the report and quickly noticed that the "evidence" on which the claims of failures and shortcomings were based was not in the document, nor were the claims cited so that one could examine the basis for the charges. The document was therefore difficult to discuss meaningfully, let alone challenge, while it became the basis for any number of startling sound bites and breathless discussions in both print and electronic media.

Clearly, the school reform movement that was thus kicked off has been the greatest and most sustained concerted national effort to change the central core of assumptions and structures of the public schools in the history of the Republic. Since its inception "the country has been searching for some magical way to reform and restructure public schools. We have tried—and are still trying—all sorts of alchemical nostrums [that we hope] will turn educationally leaden schools into schools of educational gold" (Clinchy, 1993, p. 28). Over the years, the discourses on school reform have been well leavened with bold calls for sweeping changes such as restructuring education, reinventing schools, and re-creating the nation's educational goals. During the same years, instead of finding a new amalgam of truth, some *conjoining* of contraries that Giamatti hoped for, the discourses have grown increasingly polarized, tendentious, and partisan. As Clark Kerr, president emeritus of the University of California, observed, "Seldom in the course of policymaking in the U.S. have so many firm convictions held by so many been based on so little convincing proof" (Kerr, 1991, p. 30). We will cite only three critical examples from this large body of literature. The very titles of the first two of these books make manifest how far we have drifted from reasoned discourse in the public discussion of these issues.

Three Critical Books

Thomas Sowell (1993), a senior fellow at the Hoover Institution, chose to title his book *Inside American Education: The Decline, the Deception, the Dogmas.* Its title, a stark reminder of William L. Shirer's history-making exposé of the Nazi regime, is a tendentious polemic that, in 368 pages of relentless attack, found almost nothing of value in U.S. schools. To deliver his message, Sowell chose to load it with hot button words by speaking of "deception" (p. 12) and "dogmas about education" (p. 15), with such topics as "self-esteem, role models, diversity" (p. 15). He even contended that schools use "brainwashing techniques developed in totalitarian counties" (p. 36) to deliver these dogmas.

In summing up, Sowell asserts that the schools must be reorganized and that this process first requires that "[w]e need to face the harsh reality of the kind of people we are dealing with, the kind of bitter fight we can expect from them if we try to disturb their turf and perks—and the bleak future of our children if we don't" (p. 296). What kind of people are these educators in the schools, and what have they done? Sowell's answer began thus:

> They have taken our money, betrayed our trust, failed our children, and then lied about the failures with inflated grades and pretty words. They have used our children as guinea pigs for experiments, targets for propaganda, and warm bodies to be moved here and there to mix and match for racial balance, pad enrollments. . . . They have proclaimed their special concern for minority students, while placing those students into those colleges where they are the most likely to fail. (pp. 296–297)

David C. Berliner and Bruce J. Biddle (1995) presented a remarkably different view in their book, *The Manufactured Crisis: Myths, Fraud, and the Attack on America's Public Schools.* Using somewhat more restrained language than Sowell, their blunt analysis starts with the proposition that the current crisis in education is based on a series of specific myths that—though they have become widely believed—are simply and demonstrably not true. This deception did not happen by accident, nor was it the product of dynamic social forces: This deception, the authors contend, was planned and orchestrated "by identifiable persons to sell America the false idea that their public schools were failing and that because of this failure the nation was in peril" (p. 9). Thus, *A Nation at Risk* and its aftermath is seen by them as a campaign of misinformation by the Reagan administration to put the con into play and that this was later supported by the Bush presidency. Many of the myths, half-truths, and outright lies that make up the manufactured crisis—the massive and orchestrated con game—are described in this text, each of them being countered with carefully marshaled evidence and reason that destroys the myth. A few of the myths are as follows:

1. Student achievement in U.S. primary schools has recently declined.
2. The performance of U.S. college students has also fallen recently.
3. The United States spends a lot more money on its schools than other nations do.
4. Investing in the schools has not brought success. Indeed, money is unrelated to school performance.

Berliner and Biddle, both highly reputable scholars with acknowledged strong research credentials, leave little doubt that efforts to perpetuate these myths in attacking the public schools clearly arise from deliberate distortion for the purpose of furthering certain sociopolitical intentions. They do their best to help the reader understand why they think so by encouraging examination of the data on which the mythical claims are based. To their great credit, the last 135 pages of *The Manufactured Crisis* are devoted to a quiet and level-headed discussion of "real problems in American education," which many readers will find useful.

Berliner and Biddle are not alone in their skepticism. There is growing dismay in the ranks of education scholars at the widespread propagation of distortions and misinformation about the condition of public education that have become daily grist for the U.S. press and U.S. politicians as well. For example, Gerald Bracey (1997) published a series of reports in the journal *Phi Delta Kappan* as well as in books that have diligently examined and documented the sources of some of the most egregious and damaging myths and untruths that are routinely passed off as facts about schools and the achievement of students in them. Sadly, Bracey passed away in the fall of 2009.

In a book entitled *The Way We Were?: The Myths and Realities of America's Student Achievement*, Richard Rothstein (1998) pointed out that the popular indictment of the public schools— including the alarming *A Nation at Risk* report in 1983—rests not on clear and documented evidence but on generalizations that "everyone seems to know," beginning with the conviction that "our schools are in desperate need of reform" (p. 9). Thus, everyone seems to know that "[t]he quality of public education seems to have declined, and schools are not up to the task of readying young people for the challenges" (p. 9) that lie ahead. Everyone seems to know, Rothstein continues, that a watered-down curriculum ensures that all students, regardless of whether they have mastered necessary skills, can graduate. "Social promotion" without a requirement to master grade-appropriate skills is said to be commonplace now, so even elite colleges must run remedial courses for freshmen in basic math and literacy. Instead of teaching basic skills, everyone seems to know that schools concentrate on "self-esteem" and "values clarification" while discarding traditional values along with traditional skills so that students no longer absorb the moral values that schools once inculcated. And so the litany of things that "everyone seems to know" about the apparent decline of the public schools goes on and on.

Rothstein continues, "Most Americans agree with these indictments. . . . Most adults remember that when they were students, public schools were safer, more academically serious, and focused both on basic learning and on more advanced thinking skills. They believe schools now do worse, even though a modern economy demands that they do better" (p. 10). But Rothstein's research reveals that "this story, whatever partial truths it contains, is more a culturally embedded fable that has remained unchanged for a century rather than a factual account" (p. 10).

Rothstein began his study by asking this question: If schools are worse today than they used to be, then when, exactly, was the golden—or at least silver—age of education? Was the golden age in the 1960s and 1970s? Apparently not, because that was the time that bestselling author Vance Packard's thundering accusation was that we were becoming a nation of illiterates, asserting that there was "indisputable evidence that millions of presumably educated Americans can neither read nor write at satisfactory levels" (Packard, 1974, pp. 81–82). And it was in 1961 that the Council for Basic Education (Walcutt, 1961) issued its startling report, *Tomorrow's Illiterates*, charging that a third of ninth-graders could read at only the second- or third-grade level because phonics had been abandoned in the schools. And it was in 1967 that Jeanne Chall published a widely read textbook on reading instruction, entitled *Learning to Read* (Chall, 1967), that alleged that most problems in reading instruction were traceable to the abandonment of phonics in that decade. Clearly, the decades of the 1960s and 1970s were not the golden age of education. Perhaps it was in the 1950s? Rothstein looked there.

The 1950s were dominated by the cold war, the centerpiece of which was the intense competition between the Soviet Union and the United States, and that was serious business indeed. It was the time of McCarthyism, blacklisting of suspect intellectuals—such as writers, directors, and actors—and the fear that communism had insidiously infiltrated all aspects of U.S. life and culture, including education, to undermine U.S. institutions and sap values from within. Indeed, the nadir of the cold war was in 1957, when the Soviet Union launched *Sputnik I* and *Sputnik II* and when our national humiliation at believing that we had lost the space race was largely ascribed to the abysmal failure of public schools, which were described as having become weak, flabby, and ineffectual.

So in search of the golden age of U.S. schooling, Rothstein looked back to the 1940s, then the 1930s, back to World War I, the early 1900s, and even to the nineteenth century, and he never did discover a golden age. What he did find, however, was an endless recycling of complaints much the same as those we hear in our own day. In 1902, for example, the editors of the *New York Sun* asserted that when they went to school, children "had to do a little work . . . spelling, writing and arithmetic were not electives, and you had to learn." But now, in 1902, schooling seemed to them to be a vaudeville show in which the child must be kept amused and learns what he pleases (Butterworth, 1958). Thus, Rothstein concludes (paraphrasing a well-worn Will Rogers adage), "The schools ain't what they used to be and probably never were," despite the unending din of criticism with which we are all familiar today. It seems clear that "what everyone seems to know" is, as Rothstein has described, a culturally embedded fable.

This is a fast-paced world, one that is dominated by ceaseless global change. Our educational organizations must be nimble and adaptable, so we must always strive to do better, achieve more. While much has been accomplished in U.S. education, we may not rest on our laurels; much work lies ahead. We must never slacken our efforts to develop ever better schools, equalize educational opportunity, and administer greater social justice in schooling. On the other hand, there is no cause for despair by educational leaders: While there is much that can be fairly criticized and much room for improvement, there is also a great deal of evidence that we have done well and are continuing to do well. The evidence is not only in the great achievements in the social, political, economic, and cultural life of our society but also in the remarkable resilience demonstrated by the schools themselves in adapting to social changes of nearly incredible scope. These include rapidly changing demographics in the schools arising from ongoing massive immigration and migration, evolving social-political policies of inclusion and the education of children with special needs, and the continuing push for greater equality in dealing with issues such as gender, race, and ethnicity. While the agenda is incomplete—a work in progress— educational leaders can and should face the challenges of the future with justifiable confidence, optimism, and enthusiasm. If it is true that every challenge presents an opportunity, this time of challenge is also a moment of great opportunity for educational leaders. That opportunity may lie in a tectonic shift—or, more precisely, a scientific paradigm shift—that is now underway in U.S. education.

A PARADIGM SHIFT IN EDUCATION

We appear to be in the midst of a true scientific revolution in education, a major paradigm shift that makes it likely that the traditional concept of equality of educational opportunity is being fundamentally transformed. The paradigm shift pivots on understanding the nature of human intelligence on which rests the learning theory that we use to organize schools and programs of instruction in them. That paradigm—the consensus among scientists about what intelligence is—has direct and significant implications for educational leadership because it is the basic foundation upon which all else in education stands. The paradigm concerning the nature of human intelligence is the only foundation on which educational leaders may build the "visions" for educational excellence that are now so much demanded of them. The paradigm drives how we organize schools, what we teach in them, how we teach, how we group students for instruction, and everything else for which educational leaders are responsible. Thus, the scientific paradigm of human intelligence drives and shapes the educational vision of schools that school leaders hold and is therefore the key to developing a game plan for educational leadership.

A Passion for Equality

The American people are remarkably passionate idealists in many ways. A primary American ideal is that of equality, especially equality of opportunity. This ideal is embodied in the noble sentiments that Thomas Jefferson wrote in the introduction to the *Declaration of Independence*: "We hold these truths to be self-evident, that all men are created equal, that they are endowed by their Creator with certain unalienable Rights, that among these are Life, Liberty, and the pursuit of Happiness." Since that time, when those words were penned in one of the most revered American documents, virtually enshrined as American Scripture, the concept of equality has been embraced, observed, and embellished by successive generations that have struggled ceaselessly to make it a reality in daily life rather than merely regarding it as a lofty and distant goal (Maier, 1997). As a result, today, Americans seek literal equality. Differences in outcome—whether in voting rights, access to housing, job opportunities, fairness in lending, access to schooling, or whatever—are taken as legally sufficient evidence of unequal opportunity. Thus has evolved a remarkably egalitarian, if still flawed, society that is engaged in the apparently unending process of perfecting itself, and it is distinctively American.

The current brouhaha over the quality and effectiveness of U.S. schooling takes on a different perspective from the past when viewed through the prism that this egalitarian ideal provides. Though often obscured in the hardball vehemence of public controversy over school reform as well as controversy that involves many agendas only tangential to education, perhaps the central educational issue is that of equal educational opportunity. This is no longer understood to be merely equal opportunity must be present in the schoolhouse, which desegregation was largely about. Equal educational opportunity today implies that, once in the schoolhouse, each individual will have equal access to effective teaching that will achieve desired educational outcomes. To a remarkable extent, this issue revolves around one's understanding of the nature of intelligence.

The Traditional Paradigm of Intelligence

In 1994, a group of 52 internationally known scholars, who viewed themselves as working in the mainstream of science, described what Kuhn might call the existing or traditional paradigm of science on intelligence in this way:

1. Intelligence is a very general mental capability that, among other things, involves the ability to reason, plan, solve problems, think abstractly, comprehend complex ideas, learn quickly, and learn from experience. It is not merely book learning, a narrow academic skill, or test-taking smarts. Rather, it reflects a broader and deeper capability for comprehending our surroundings—"catching on," "making sense" of things, or "figuring out" what to do.
2. Intelligence, so defined, can be measured, and intelligence tests measure it well. They are among the most accurate (that is, reliable and valid) of all psychological tests and assessments. They do not measure creativity, character, personality, or other important differences among individuals, nor are they intended to.
3. While there are different kinds of intelligence tests, they all measure the same intelligence. Some use words or numbers and require specific cultural knowledge (such as vocabulary). Others do not, and instead they use shapes or designs and require knowledge of only simple universal concepts (many/few, open/closed, up/down). ("Mainstream Science," 1994, p. A19)

This paradigm of intelligence that has prevailed in the cognitive sciences for a century has two characteristics that are particularly important in this discussion:

- *Intelligence is a unitary whole: a single, though complex, phenomenon.*
- Like one's body build or skin color, IQ is a fixed and unchangeable personal characteristic.

But what is the source of intelligence? Is it a fixed inherited characteristic? That is, is it genetically determined? Or is intelligence amenable to development from environmental sources such as nutrition, social support, and opportunities to learn? These questions, of course, raise the nature-nurture controversy that educators know so well.

The existing traditional paradigm of intelligence began to unfold and develop just about a century ago—in 1904—when Alfred Binet was asked by the French minister of education to develop a way to identify those children in school who needed special help. Binet promptly set about devising a way to measure intelligence so that one could express the results in numerical terms, much as one weighs and measures the physical characteristics of the bodies of children. By comparing the intelligence test score of an individual child with the distribution of all of the scores of many children taking the same test, one could discern whether the score of an individual was above or below the average of scores of many other children of that age. This gave rise to the concept of *mental age*: If, for example, 10-year-old François's test score equaled that of most 12-year-olds, he would be considered bright—that is, 2 years ahead of his peers—having a mental age of 12. If, however, his 10-year-old classmate Hélène scored at the level of most eight-year-olds, she would be considered less intelligent, having a mental age of eight. Within a few years, a German psychologist came up with the idea of dividing the mental age by the chronological age of the child and multiplying the resulting quotient by 100 to yield the intelligence quotient (IQ). Thus, François would be said to have an IQ of 120, while Hélène's IQ would be 80.

If one obtained the IQs of a large sample of individuals, their frequency distribution would predictably fall into a bell-shaped pattern that is familiar to most readers of this text. This pattern is predictable because the distribution of data from any measure of individuals, such as height, shoe size, or weight, would also normally fall into this bell shape, which is why it is called the *normal curve of distribution* or the *normal curve*. Not surprisingly, it is also popularly called the *bell curve* (because it somewhat resembles a cross section of a bell such as the Liberty Bell). In a normal distribution, the bell curve shows, as would be expected from such measures of individuals, a small number of very low scores, a small number of very high scores, and a strong tendency for most of the scores to cluster toward the middle of the distribution. The dispersion of the data, from low scores to high, is shown along the horizontal axis; it can be spread out or compressed, depending on the shape and appearance desired for display purposes. The unit of the spread is called a *standard deviation*, and ordinarily a standard deviation of 15 is used to array scores from intelligence tests; a smaller standard deviation produces a narrow, sharply arched curve, while a larger standard deviation produces a lower, more elongated curve. In any case, the data—that is, the distribution of the scores from the intelligence test—remain the same; only the graphic depiction changes. A typical ideal bell curve that might display the distribution of IQ scores is shown in Figure 2.1.

The distribution of scores shown in Figure 2.1 shows that about 68% of those who took the test are within one standard deviation of the mean score. Many people, thinking of this group as within the "average" range, would say that the scores of about 16% of those who took the test are below the average range and those of another 16% are above it. One could readily use such a distribution to identify the "best and the brightest," on the one hand, and the "losers," on the other; as we all know, this evaluation has often been done in making decisions not only in schools but also in hiring practices and other highly important matters.

A New Paradigm of Intelligence—or the Lake Wobegon Syndrome?

The traditional paradigm of intelligence has long had a powerful impact on educational leadership at all levels of schooling and continues to be the scientific paradigm in cognitive psychology. School leaders have generally accepted this paradigm and the learning theory that it implies, and therefore they have recognized the need for some means for sorting students according to

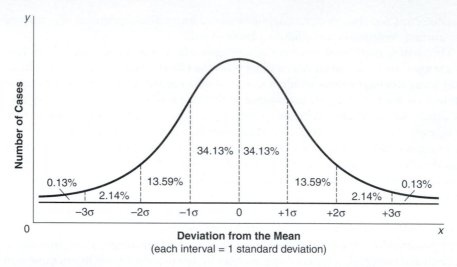

FIGURE 2.1   When displayed in graph form, the distribution of IQ scores from a large population typically takes the form of a bell-shaped curve.

ability as a basis for organizing curriculum and instruction. Recognizing that there is a spread of abilities in the student population, schools have commonly been organized using variations of the concept of ability grouping for instruction to conform to this perceived reality. For example, a time-honored standard of excellence in elementary school teaching is the skill that teachers demonstrate in using ability grouping to organize instruction within their classrooms. At the secondary level, it is common practice to offer courses at different levels of difficulty, when practical, and to sort students into them using scheduling techniques. College instructors have, not infrequently, tried to assign marks to students competitively according to the normal curve of distribution, so-called marking on the curve, even though the small numbers of students in such classes frequently make this statistically indefensible.

But in an era where schools are expected to "leave no child behind," there is an increasing conviction that all children—in the United States, at any rate—start out in life with equal intellectual abilities. There has been, as we have pointed out, a notably persistent gap between the learning outcomes of poor children and those of children from affluent families, and the gap has continued to exist despite efforts to close it. Because there are many minority people in the ranks of the poor, the educational achievement gap takes on racial overtones. In the emerging view, it is the task of the school to teach each child so that equality is not merely the opportunity for all individuals to be present in school and to receive instruction, but that the actual learning of all children is more nearly equal than historically has been the case. This is more than an important shift; it is a tectonic shift: from accepting equality of opportunity to learn as the standard of excellence in schooling to demanding equality of educational achievement, or outcomes, as the standard.

But one may protest, how can this be? We accept as a scientific verity that there is a normal distribution of intellectual abilities in the population. More than a century of scholarly work devoted to developing and refining intelligence tests around the world has demonstrated this time and again, and this distribution is predictably depicted by the curve of normal distribution. How, then, is it reasonable to expect that the intervention of schooling can yield achievement outcomes that are significantly different from the curve of normal distribution? Yet it seems clear that this is exactly the expectation with which many people approach the issue of school reform.

To skeptics, this sounds much like Lake Wobegon, the mythical Minnesota bastion of small-town values and rural innocence that humorist Garrison Keillor, on his weekly radio show *A Prairie Home Companion,* unfailingly describes as being a place where all the women are strong, all the men are good-looking, and all the children are above average. It's an idea so preposterous that it is an exemplar of humor, and it has drawn an appreciative chuckle from his large radio audience for years. To many educators, it so aptly describes the emerging new demands on schools—which seem similarly preposterous—that the term *Lake Wobegon syndrome* has become standard in the professional jargon of educators.

The point, of course, is that it seems to many teachers and other educators as though, when schools are properly run, all the pupils and students should score above average on their examinations. But the issue takes on a markedly different perspective if we consider the possibility that the current well-established paradigm theory of intelligence is fundamentally wrong. If this is the case, and if we become convinced that American public schools and their pedagogical practices are organized on the basis of a flawed understanding of the nature of intelligence and therefore a flawed learning theory, it may not be surprising that the educational achievement gap between the poor and the affluent has persisted for so long despite continued diligent efforts to close it. If a new and more correct understanding of the nature of intelligence exists, educational leaders need to learn what it is and perhaps reconsider the learning theory that they use, in the light of the new paradigm, to decide how schools should be reorganized and how pedagogical practices in them should be revised to be more effective. It seems that we may be at the beginning of a scientific revolution that, if it succeeds in supplanting the existing paradigm, could pave the way to the emergence of a new paradigm and great opportunities for educational leadership.

MULTIPLE INTELLIGENCES THEORY

First, let's review briefly a few of the core theories on which the traditional paradigm of intelligence is constructed:

- Intelligence is a single, unitary mental factor that is often referred to as the *g* factor (meaning general intelligence), which is what intelligence tests are designed to measure.
- Intelligence processes are neural processes, and the quality of these processes depends on the nervous system that is present in the individual at birth.
- The nervous system is inborn, dependent on inherited chromosomes, and the level of its functioning is little changed by external events in life such as schooling or poverty. Intelligence is therefore relatively stable over time.

This was summarized in a classic statement by Henry H. Goddard—the scholar whose opus magnum was the translation of Binet's work into English. Goddard (1919) observed:

> [O]ur thesis is that the chief determinant of human conduct is a unitary mental process which we call intelligence: that this process is conditioned by a nervous mechanism which is inborn: that the degree of efficiency to be attained by that nervous mechanism and the consequent grade of intellectual or mental level for each individual is determined by the kind of chromosomes that come together with the union of the germ cells: that it is but little affected by any later influences except such serious accidents as may destroy part of the mechanism. (Gould, 1981, pp. 159–160)

Goddard's work was followed by generations of research studies into the working of the brain and the mind, which produced a much better understanding of intelligence and learning theory and, at the same time, a steady erosion in the confidence that Goddard's beliefs are correct. Jean Piaget (1929) and later Jerome Bruner (1960), for example, fundamentally challenged the notion that external influences—such as schooling—had little effect on cognitive functioning.

Many readers of this text know something of the work of the Swiss scholar Jean Piaget, who regarded learning as part of child development. He described learning as a progressive growth process during which—over time and with proper stimulation and guidance—the individual builds on the simpler processes that were learned in earlier years by integrating higher-order logical processes and thus the growth in logical thought matures and develops. Piaget's work had great influence on the education and work of schoolteachers, especially American schoolteachers, in the 1970s and 1980s. Jerome Bruner, working in the constructivist theoretical framework, was much influenced by Lev Vygotsky's thinking (Vygotsky, 1934) and also had great influence on teachers and their methods in the later decades of the twentieth century. Bruner's view was that learning is an active process in which students construct new understandings based on their existing knowledge. The active process involves the learner in selecting and transforming information, constructing hypotheses, and—in short—developing logical cognitive processes and ways of discovering and learning new ideas and new information. But this, in Bruner's view, required carefully structured, skillful, Socratic-type teaching for it to happen.

Piaget, Vygotsky, and Bruner had clearly challenged the notion that intellectual functioning was fixed and unchangeable. They believed that, by aiding and abetting the inborn tendency of individuals to develop cognitively, teachers and schools could facilitate the growth and maturity of their students' cognitive skills. They also challenged the conviction of the behaviorists, which represented the clearly dominant approach to psychology at that time, that (a) one could not deal with the internal functioning of learners because it was unseen and not capable of being manipulated and that (b) the manipulation of rewards and punishments was key to designing successful teaching-learning strategies. But they had not directly challenged the belief that intelligence is a fixed, inborn, unitary characteristic of each individual. That would be done by a later generation of scholars whose work began to appear near the end of the twentieth century.

As the millennium approached, for example, Daniel Goleman began to study and describe that the important competencies in life included self-awareness, self-discipline, persistence, and empathy, and that these are more important for success in life than traditional IQ. He contended that this cluster of competencies, that he called social and emotional intelligences, can be taught to children. Furthermore, he explained that these competencies are more important for outstanding performance and leadership than either intellect or technical skill.

Gardner's Multiple Intelligences Theory (MIT)

In his landmark work on the nature of human intelligence or, more correctly, human intelligences, Howard Gardner (1983) has drawn attention to the shift during the twentieth century of psychologists away from focusing on the external objects of the physical world in explaining human behavior to focusing on the preoccupation with the mind, and especially cognitive thought, that depends so heavily on symbols such as language, mathematics, the visual arts, body language, and other symbols. Gardner's great contribution in explaining human thought and behavior has been to give us a new way to think about intelligence: not as a single characteristic or even as a group of characteristics that can be summed up with the single measure of IQ. Gardner explained that there are several kinds of intelligence that are independent of one another, yet each of them enables one to engage in intellectual activity in different ways. Many have found it persuasive that Gardner, who has taught neurology in medical school, has identified specific areas in the brain that are involved in each of the different kinds of intelligence.

Gardner (1993) observed:

> In the heyday of the psychometric and behavioristic eras, it was generally believed that intelligence was a single entity and that it was inherited; that human beings— initially a blank slate—could be trained to learn anything, provided that it was presented in an appropriate way. Nowadays an increasing number of researchers believe precisely the opposite; that there exists a multitude of intelligences, quite independent of each other; that each type of intelligence has its own strengths and constraints; that the mind is far from unencumbered at birth; and that it is unexpectedly difficult to teach things that go against early "naive" theories or that challenge the natural lines of force within an intelligence and its matching domains. (p. xxiii)

Howard Gardner described seven principal dimensions of intelligence:

- *Linguistic intelligence*   The ability to understand words and how they are combined to produce useful language. This is important for writers, poets, and journalists.
- *Logical-mathematical intelligence*   The ability to see patterns, order, and relationships in seemingly unrelated events in the world around us and to engage in logical chains of reasoning. One thinks of scientists, mathematicians, engineers, and architects.

Before we present the remainder of the list of intelligences, we should point out that Gardner believes that a major problem in schools as they are organized and operated today is that they tend to restrict much of their curriculum and teaching to the linguistic and the logical-mathematical dimensions of intelligence. Learning in these areas is especially esteemed, is considered by many to be of a higher order, and is usually emphasized in assessing the outcomes of schooling. There are, however, five other intelligences that are widely recognized in our culture and that, Gardner argues, are valid ways of learning and thinking:

- *Musical intelligence*   The ability to discern pitch, melody, tone, rhythm, and other qualities of musical symbolism and integrate them into intellectual activity such as reasoning. Musicians, composers, singers, and rap artists come to mind.
- *Spatial intelligence*   The ability to accurately perceive and think in terms of the visual qualities of the world and its dimensions, and to manipulate and transform them in creative ways. This is important for architects, artists, sculptors, photographers/cinematographers, and navigators.
- *Bodily-kinesthetic intelligence*   The ability to control one's bodily motions, the capacity to handle objects skillfully, and the skill to combine these into a language with which one may express oneself "with wit, style, and an esthetic flair," as Norman Mailer said with boxers in mind (as cited in Lowe, 1977, p. 255). Gardner's example of mimes, particularly Marcel Marceau, makes vivid the concept of bodily-kinesthetic intelligence, but one thinks also of dancers, figure skaters, and many athletes.
- *Intrapersonal intelligence*   The ability to access and understand the inner self: feelings, reactions, aspirations. This refers to the self-aware individual who understands and is comfortable with his or her personal emotions and is able to differentiate between

various feelings and use them in thinking about the world. One thinks of novelists and playwrights such as Alice Walker, Eugene O'Neill, Marcel Proust, and James Baldwin, all of whom used autobiographical themes to examine humanity. Cinema *auteurs* ranging from Marcel Pagnol to Woody Allen also readily come to mind, as do gurus whose wisdom transcends their own provincialism.

- *Interpersonal intelligence*   "The ability to notice and make distinctions among other individuals and, in particular, among their moods, temperaments, motivations, and intentions." This ability "permits a skilled adult to read the intentions and desires—even when these have been hidden—of many other individuals and, potentially, to act upon this knowledge—for example, by influencing a group of disparate individuals to behave along desired lines" (Gardner, 1983, p. 239). Outstanding examples include Martin Luther King Jr., Eleanor Roosevelt, Lyndon B. Johnson, and Mohandas Gandhi. Such intelligence might well be useful in exercising educational leadership, but it is a form of intelligence rarely sought by university programs in educational administration.

Gardner's description of intelligences illuminates some important ways in which people bring different inner resources to the behavioral equation in organizations—not only students but also adults such as teachers and administrators. It is important to remember that these different kinds of intelligence are present in each of us, but that the mix in each of us is so idiosyncratic that in any group one will find some range of individual differences, which suggests that an approach to developing an educational game plan that fails to take these differences into account is flawed at the outset.

It is important to remember that these intelligences are human characteristics, not options or preferences that individuals choose. As Gardner has shown, though one's intelligences develop over time as one matures physiologically, their development also depends to a great extent on learning from the environment. Thus, one does not learn to read, write, and calculate simply because one has matured (and is, therefore, presumably "ready" to learn), but also because, for example, one has seen others read, write, and calculate. This underscores the importance of interaction between the person and the environment in shaping human behavior.

Gardner's insights have had a profound impact on the learning theory that underlies the practice of American teachers and school leaders and is currently being used in many schools across the country as a basis for organizing curriculum and instruction. Many of these schools participated in a study called Project SUMIT (Schools Using Multiple Intelligence Theory) under the sponsorship of Harvard University's Project Zero. Project SUMIT published case studies, descriptions of teaching methods and practices, and other information that is useful to those who want to learn more about the application of MIT to the improvement of school outcomes.

Perkins's Learnable Intelligence Theory

Clearly, Gardner has raised credible objections to the paradigmatic theory that intelligence is a single unitary human characteristic and has convinced many that there are, in fact, at least seven kinds of intelligence. These provide the educator with the keys to a learning theory for organizing the school, creating the curriculum, and selecting pedagogical methods that will facilitate learning and achievement in a much broader spectrum of students than had previously been thought possible. Gardner's colleague in Project Zero at the Harvard University Graduate School of Education, David Perkins, took aim at the second fundamental concept of traditional IQ: the theory that intellectual capability is inherited and fixed. Perkins (1995a) wrote the following:

> [T]he old IQ lives! Many people firmly believe in intelligence as a fixed, genetically determined characteristic of themselves and others. Historically, many people have thought that some racial groups differ in their fundamental intellectual capacities. It is unpopular to express such a view today, but certainly the attitude persists. More broadly, a view of intelligence as fixed pervades our reasoning about human performance. . . . We attribute failure to fundamental lack of ability. Likewise, when people succeed conspicuously, we laud their talent and envy their genes. Curiously, this pattern of thinking figures much more in United States culture than, for instance, in Japan [where] parents lay much more emphasis on the role of effort in success: The way to deal with a difficult problem or a puzzling concept is to persevere systematically until you have mastered it. (p. 16)

But Perkins agreed with Gardner in emphasizing that intelligence is not a single characteristic. He is not so sure that there are seven dimensions, however. He believes that there are three dimensions of intelligence, which he calls "the new intelligence" (Perkins, 2008, pp. 102–103):

- "*The neural dimension of intelligence (neural intelligence for short)*: The contribution of the efficiency and precision of the neurological system to intelligent behavior," much as the theorists and psychometricians in the traditional paradigm have claimed.
- "*The experiential dimension of intelligence (experiential intelligence for short)*: The contribution of context-specific knowledge to intelligent behavior. This contribution is learned, the result of extensive experience thinking and acting in particular situations over long periods of time."
- "*The reflective dimension of intelligence (reflective intelligence or mindwave for short)*: The contribution to intelligent behavior of strategies for various intellectually challenging tasks, attitudes conducive to persistence, systematicity, and imagination in the use of one's mind, and habits of self-monitoring and management. Reflective intelligence is in effect a control system for the resources afforded by neurological and experiential intelligence, bent on deploying them wisely."

The latter two kinds of intelligence, Perkins argues, are not recognized by those who support traditional IQ theory—who claim that intelligence cannot be learned—yet they are the keys to learnable intelligence. You can, Perkins argues, know your way around in much the same sense that you can know your way around your neighborhood, the game of baseball, or the stock market. To acquire such knowledge, people can "learn their way around" important kinds of thinking, gaining concepts, beliefs, feelings, and patterns of action that allow them to handle problem solving, decision making, explanation, and other intellectually demanding activities better (Perkins, 2008, p. 15).

This analysis brings to mind the age-old dichotomy between the ability of one who has "street smarts" to thrive and succeed in an environment that one with "book smarts" cannot cope with. The point is that to be "smart" is to be intelligent, and Perkins emphasizes that this is not limited to either facility in understanding words and how they are combined or facility in understanding logical-mathematical patterns of order in the world around us, though these are the two aspects of intelligence and learning that have long been emphasized in schools. And to make the point, Perkins draws upon a report from the RAND Corporation entitled *Global Preparedness and Human Resources*:

> The report examined what people from the corporate and academic sectors felt was needed to meet the escalating challenges of the times. Their answer: General cognitive skills were rated more highly than knowledge in an academic [subject], social skills, [or] personal traits. Good thinking counts most. (Perkins, 1995a, p. 7)

Similarly, a study of the international role of schooling found that success in today's global market of competitiveness and economic productivity depends on workers who are skillful thinkers and learners, yet in U.S. schools they found the following (Marshall & Tucker, 1992):

> [F]ewer than four in ten young adults can summarize in writing the main argument from a lengthy news column—one in four whites, one in four blacks, and two in ten Hispanics. Only twenty-five out of 100 young adults can use a bus schedule to select the appropriate bus for a given departure or arrival—three in 100 blacks and seven in 100 Hispanics. Only 10 percent of the total group can select the least costly product from a list of grocery items on the basis of unit-pricing information—twelve in 100 whites, one in 100 blacks, and four in 100 Hispanics. . . . These findings make it clear that only a tiny fraction of our workers can function effectively in an environment requiring strong communications skills and the application of sophisticated understanding to complex real-world problems. (p. 67)

Of course, observations such as these are commonplace to readers of this text as we contemplate the educational outcomes that are essential today and increasingly so in the years ahead. Many seize upon observations such as these to mount insistent demands to go back to basics; for more readin', writin', and 'rithmetic; for tougher academic standards; more drill and practice; and more demanding examinations. Perkins (1995b) takes a very different tack, and it has proven to be very popular: Schools should be increasingly engaged in teaching more thinking skills because real learning is a consequence of thinking. We should, he argues, be developing "smart schools" that teach better thinking and therefore better learning to every child.

Smart Schools

Perkins asserts that "we need schools that put to work, day in and day out, what we know about how to educate well. We can call such schools 'smart schools'—schools wide awake to the opportunities of better teaching and learning." In Perkins's view, smart schools exhibit three characteristics:

1. *They are informed*   "Administrators, teachers, and indeed students in the smart school know a lot about human thinking and learning and how it works best. And they know a lot about school structure and collaboration and how that works best."
2. *They are energetic*   "The smart school requires spirit as much as information. In the smart school, measures are taken to cultivate positive energy in the structure of the school, the style of administration, and the treatment of teachers and students."
3. *They are thoughtful*   "Smart schools are thoughtful places, in the double sense of caring and being mindful. First of all, people are sensitive to one another's needs and treat each

other thoughtfully. Second, both the teaching/learning process and school decision-making processes are thinking centered . . . putting thinking at the center of all that happens is crucial." (Perkins, 1995b, p. 3; Perkins, 2008, p. 3)

These are important ideas for an educational leader who is engaged in the process of creating a vision for teaching and learning in the school, which we have called a game plan. We have added emphasis to the important linkage that Perkins makes between the values and behavior of the educational leader, on the one hand, and the quality of educational life in the school, on the other.

Perkins goes on to say that these characteristics of smart schools—being informed, energetic, and thoughtful—are not revolutionary and, indeed, they are not. Perkins readily admits that they go back at least as far as John Dewey and were central to the progressive education movement that provided the dominant theory of learning until the mid-1940s, when the pendulum of popularity began to swing away from the progressive movement and toward life adjustment education. The three characteristics of smart schools are largely common sense, Perkins points out, yet *they are not common practice in schools.* And that observation is a consistent theme in this text because it is a central theme for understanding organizational behavior in schools.

Emotional Intelligence

We briefly described the emerging understanding that emotional intelligence (EI) is today seen as being an important form of intelligence, one of the multiple intelligences that individuals possess. A common cliché in our culture is that of the individuals who were recognized as "brains" in traditional school coursework, people who seemed to do well effortlessly in examinations and could "send an IQ test sky-high, but who don't quite make good in either their personal or working lives. They rub others the wrong way; success just doesn't seem to pan out" (Stein & Book, 2000, p. 14). Of course, on the flip side of the cliché are the individuals who—though not outstanding in either coursework or examinations at school or in IQ tests—do well at other things such as socializing easily with others, immersing themselves in creative work such as music or new technologies, or being respected members of a team. Such individuals may go on in life and, to the surprise of many of their erstwhile classmates, become respected members of the community, successful in their personal lives, and in their business or professional lives as well.

This, you will recognize, is the old "book smarts" versus "common sense" dichotomy, which has attracted the attention of cognitive scientists since the early twentieth century. In 1920, for example, in the heyday of developing IQ tests, Edward Thorndike pondered the importance of what he called social intelligence, which he recognized as being quite different from general intelligence. Twenty years later, in 1940, David Wechsler, one of the founding fathers of IQ testing, urged that measures of emotional and social intelligence should be included along with intellective aspects of general intelligence to get a more complete assessment of general intelligence. In 1948, shortly after the end of World War II, R. W. Leeper explored the idea that "emotional thought" was intertwined in the development of "logical thought." But through all these years, the boom in IQ testing continued, largely undeterred by these ideas. Although this understanding of the emotional side of intelligence is hardly new, it has only recently entered the mainstream of the conversation.

When Howard Gardner began writing about multiple intelligences in 1983, as we have described, he drew on previous scholarship, of course, but he also spelled out afresh the meanings and the power of *intrapersonal intelligence* and *interpersonal intelligence.* Gardner had been talking about emotional intelligence and social intelligence, though he did not use those terms, and how the two are mutually interconnected. Gardner demonstrated how these intelligences—while markedly different from more traditionally respected *linguistic intelligence* and *logical-mathematical intelligence*—are crucially important for the achievements in life of many people. In 1990, Peter Salovey of the University of New Hampshire and John D. Mayer of Yale University coined the term *emotional intelligence* and described it as being "the ability to monitor one's own and others' feelings and emotions, to discriminate among them and to use this information to guide one's thinking and actions" (Salovey & Mayer, 1990, p. 189). Building on this definition, Nelson and Low (2003) conceptualized EI as a process of understanding and expressing emotions in healthy ways, and more important, they found that EI can be learned. Specifically, they indicated EI is:

1. knowing and valuing self;
2. building and maintaining a variety of strong, productive and healthy relationships;
3. getting along and working well with others in achieving positive results; and
4. effectively dealing with the pressures and demands of life and work.

In a book called *Emotional Intelligence,* Daniel Goleman (1995) suddenly transformed the subject from being an obscure academic field of interest for a handful of cognitive scientists to one that is today of wide interest. His book was on the bestseller lists for a long time. Goleman vividly delineates the relevant research of modern neuroscience as it describes our "two minds"—the rational and the emotional—that are rooted deep in the brain and how, often undetected by us, they interact to shape the way that we perceive and react to the world around us. He convincingly explains that emotional abilities are not fixed and inherent but that individuals can learn to harness both their rational and emotional minds so that they effectively work together. Goleman explains that if one does not learn to harness the two minds together, the emotional can cripple the rational. This fact, of course, readily helps to explain why it is common to see bright, even learned individuals who stumble as leaders. Goleman goes on to advocate that schools need to learn a new approach to curriculum that includes developing emotional intelligence as well as rational intelligence and thus make possible an entirely new concept of the meaning of excellence in educational achievement.

A good deal of research links emotional intelligence (EI) to effective leadership and organizational outcomes (Ozcelik, Langton, & Aldrich, 2008; Barbuto & Burbach, 2006; Riggio & Riechard, 2008), with some specific studies done with school principals showing similar results (DeLorenzo, 2012; Heiken, 2007; Williams, 2008). In other words, leaders who are determined through reliable and valid inventories to have higher EI were perceived more positively by followers and, in some cases, had better organizational outcomes than those leaders with lower EI.

The Debate Continues

It's a remarkable thing: "The more we try to change schools," the mantra goes, "the more they stay the same." Why is it so difficult to bring about change in schools that is both meaningful and long-lasting? After generations of effort, it seems obvious to many observers that schools remain remarkably similar to the schools that our parents attended. Is it because teachers and principals are united in a conspiracy to maintain the status quo? Many people think so, and not a few fault the unions for aiding and abetting the conspiracy. Or is it that the teachers and principals are simply incompetent and should be fired and replaced? Many people think that, too. In fact, replacing the principal is one of the first approved fixes prescribed by the No Child Left Behind (NCLB) Act to improve the performance of underperforming schools. Indeed, it is increasingly popular for urban school district superintendents to cite the numbers of school principals who have been dismissed as evidence of positive action being taken in the district to improve school performance. The University of Virginia, under prodding by Governor Mark Warner, devised a program to produce cadres of elite principals who are specially trained to become "turnaround specialists" for school districts across the country. It is envisioned that the turnaround specialists will go around from school to school "turning around" those that are deemed to be underperforming. Yet recent research casts serious doubt on the wisdom of this approach because it results in an accelerating carousel of principal succession, in which the principals spin around and around while the schools just go up and down (Hargreaves, Moore, Fink, Brayman, & White, 2003).

SUSTAINABILITY   A major finding from an in-depth longitudinal study of eight American and Canadian high schools through the period of the 1970s, 1980s, and 1990s was that the lack of sustainability was a primary characteristic of change in those schools during that heady period of dynamic change in North American life and culture. Principals rotated through the schools under study at an average rate of less than every five years, while the teachers tended to remain on a much more permanent basis. Teachers were typically insiders in the school while principals tended to arrive as outsiders and then leave before they could become insiders, and the teachers simply waited them out. This is an organizational fact of life that is often reported in the literature on change in schools: a principal arrives, change initiatives are launched, and then the principal leaves and the change efforts are abandoned before they are completed and begin to pay off (Hargreaves et al., 2003).

Hargreaves and Goodson (2006) reported the following:

> From the mid-to-late 1990s . . . teachers were seeing their leaders as being more like anonymous managers who had less visibility in the school, seemed to be more attached to the system [school district] or their own careers than the long-term interests of the school, and, . . . rarely remained long enough to ensure that their initiatives would last. (p. 21)

They concluded that pressures on the urban principalship of the NCLB legislation, in which one of the prescribed options for repeated annual failure to improve involves removal of the principal, does not bode well for building sustainable change into urban schools.

Many other well-informed observers simply do not find much mystery in the fact that schools tend to remain stable and are slow to change. This is characteristic of all organizations that have well-developed cultures; by definition, the culture of an organization not merely endures over time but develops strength and refinement with the passage of time. Many Americans, for example, have watched in astonishment over the years as major automobile manufacturing companies, such as General Motors, slipped slowly and irretrievably from the status of titans that once dominated the world's marketplaces into bankruptcy. Over the years, as the irresistible downward slide continued its implacable course at a glacial pace, General Motors frantically did everything it could think of: close factories, open others, create new brands of cars and new models, automate production, use every marketing tool in the book, and much more. All the while, a steady stream of organization consultants reiterated the same advice: the company's famously bureaucratic culture was deeply involved in the problem and needed to be changed if the company was to survive. There seemed to be little need, for example, to question *satisficing*: that is, a core belief in the company that it was not necessary to build the *best* cars on the market. They were convinced that they needed to make cars that were *good enough* for the market. In

2009, after major downsizing and filing for bankruptcy, many observers wondered if GM had then reached the point at which it could change the culture—including a new sense of mission and commitment—that was essential for the very survival of the company.

Every school has a strong and durable organizational culture, and *any* culture tends to be powerful in shaping the long-term beliefs and behavior of those who live and work in that culture. Therefore, those who seek *sustainability* as a characteristic of change in a school would be well advised to attend to the culture of the school and the need to develop a penchant for developing ongoing change processes in the culture. Whenever a school leader joins the school and then leaves after a tenure so brief that he or she is still an outsider, it is almost certain that he or she will have had little influence on the development of the organizational culture. This fact puts the spotlight on the need to develop change processes in the school that become an enduring, ongoing aspect of life in the organization.

THEORY OF ACTION

A *theory of action* is a theory that gives rise to some judgment, given the nature of truth that the theory describes, about how theoretical knowledge can be applied in dealing with practical problems. For example, in the nineteenth century, as the theory that germs can cause infection and disease gradually became credible to surgeons and physicians, it ceased to be merely an academic theory and became a theory of action. Doctors slowly began to recognize the value of antiseptic methods in surgery, and they sought to use them in their medical practice. A great breakthrough came in the work of Joseph Lister, who, in 1865, discovered that carbolic acid was an effective antiseptic that killed dangerous microorganisms. Soon, standard antiseptic methods in surgery included liberal use of carbolic acid: Instruments and even patients were scrubbed and sprayed with carbolic acid in efforts, which seem draconian by today's standards, to kill the germs that were thought to cause infection. In time, however—still using the germ theory of disease—doctors gradually changed the ways in which they applied it in practice. Aseptic methods became the more accepted way of applying the theory: The concept was one of keeping the surgical environment clean and sterile, free of germs, in the first place. Surgeons took to washing their hands, wore surgical gowns and masks, and found better ways to sterilize than using liberal scrubs of carbolic acid. As early as 1874, Robert Wood Johnson had developed the first ready-to-use sterile dressings, directly applying Lister's knowledge of germ theory to medical practice. By 1885, his company, the Johnson & Johnson Company, was manufacturing sterile self-adhesive dressings—the forerunner of the now-ubiquitous Band-Aid. Today, of course, the same germ theory guides the actions of doctors, but their actions in practice are different. Those who believe in the theory and practice of modern Western medicine take things such as disposable rubber gloves, autoclaving, the use of disposable instruments, maintaining sterile environments in the surgical unit, and the use of antibiotics as the actions that one in the modern world ordinarily expects of healthcare providers as they practice medicine.

To illustrate the basic interaction between theory of action and theory of practice, we have chosen to use simple examples from the realm of modern Western medicine. It is important to note, however, that in medicine—just as in the realms of education, organization, and leadership—a number of theories of practice compete in the marketplace of ideas to inform the practitioner. Modern Western medicine is far from being the only source for medical theory in action. Today, there are many alternative approaches to medical practice, each supported by its own unique body of theory and research. Many patients, for example, prefer to be attended by doctors of osteopathy rather than doctors of medicine. Holistic medicine and homeopathic medicine are surging in popularity in the West and around the world, as is an array of alternative medical practices that often have roots in ancient non-Western cultures. Acupuncture has a wide following and is slowly finding its way into the practice of some Western medical practitioners. Relaxation therapy, once thought to be exclusive to the ashrams of Indian yogis, has been embraced by many in the West, including an increasing number of highly respected practitioners of modern Western medicine. Various forms of faith healing (which draw their theories in action from many different concepts of religious faith and practice), homeopathy, and folk medicine continue to be the accepted basis for medical practice for large numbers of people worldwide. Those who practice medicine must decide which of these many competing theories—which explanations for events observed in nature—they will accept and act on to guide their actions in practice.

It can be reasonably argued that U.S. school administrators and supervisors are among the most skeptical professionals in the world when it comes to theory. As a group, they tend to reject what is often characterized as the ivory tower thinking of academic theorists, which many practicing school administrators see as fuzzy and reflecting little understanding of the hard realities that confront the practitioner on the job. To many, the word *theory* itself conjures images of impractical or esoteric thought or perhaps idle daydreaming. It often suggests the notion of some unattainable ideal state or speculation or even guesswork. In contrast, practicing educational administrators tend to view themselves as confronting a demanding and fast-moving environment in which action is required in order to solve problems and temporizing is not tolerated. Perhaps when the word *theory* is heard, many conjure an image of the intrepid TV defense attorney announcing that he has "a theory about this case," when all he means is that he has a hunch—shrewd or otherwise. Because the word *theory* means none of these things, let us begin by demystifying it.

As we explained in Chapter 1, the term *theory* is used for *systematically organized knowledge thought to explain observed phenomena*. The alternative to using theoretical knowledge is to scurry through the maze of professional leadership practice mindlessly hoping to take the right actions but guessing all the way. In that sense, there is perhaps nothing more practical than good theory because it provides the foundation for taking appropriate action in a busy, complex world where few problems are truly simple, where time is chronically short, and where any decision usually leads only to the need for additional decisions. Such is the nature of administrative work in which educational leaders are normally involved.

While it is true that some academic theorizing can be enormously complex, with arcane subtleties beyond the ken of nonexperts, this is not true of all theory, nor is it a necessary characteristic of elegant, powerful theory. Consider, for example, the story of Isaac Newton observing an apple falling from a tree in an orchard in 1666 and then—brilliant mathematician that he was—calculating what eventually were recognized as the laws of gravity. Gravity: what a simple, exquisite, powerful—and, one must add, theoretical—concept. Understanding how to calculate the relationships between the mass and speed of two bodies may be beyond many of us, but the central concept has become basic to our understanding about the world we live in.

But many common events that we observe in daily life are not so simple. For generations, for example, people generally believed that the center of the universe was the Earth. Evidence to support that idea had been developed in the second century by Claudius Ptolemy, a Greco-Egyptian astronomer, and had been elaborated into a geocentric theory of the universe that was not seriously challenged for well over 13 centuries. That theory held, of course, that the Earth stood still while the sun and the other planets orbited around it. To many who lived during those years, evidence that supported Ptolemaic theory included the common observation that, when dropped, things tend to fall downward—toward what was thought to be the center of the universe. When an earthling looked up, he or she could readily observe that the sun was moving about the Earth, causing day and night as it arced across the sky. Using this geocentric explanation of easy-to-observe everyday events, our forebears spoke confidently of the obvious: People were sure that they could easily see the sunrise in the morning, travel around the Earth during the day, and then set in the evening. Plainly, the evidence then available strongly supported the theory that the Earth was the center of the solar system.

In the early 1500s, however, the Polish astronomer Nicholas Copernicus recorded and published careful systematic observations of celestial events that eventually convinced some cognoscenti that, in fact, the sun is at the center of the solar system and the Earth rotates and is in orbit around the sun. This was confirmed in 1632 when Galileo published his *Dialogue Concerning the Two Chief World Systems,* which was based on the observations that Galileo made directly with the aid of his telescope. Even though Galileo was imprisoned and forced to renounce his findings in 1633, the genie was out of the bottle: The Copernican, or heliocentric, view of the solar system has not been seriously challenged since. Indeed, Galileo's work became a turning point in the development of Western science.

Today, because of this theorizing and testing of theory, when you look up at the heavens you may speak of the sunrise and the sunset, but we use those terms merely as figures of speech. Most of us are quite certain that the Earth rotates on its axis and is in orbit around the sun, which helps us to understand better what is going on, to explain it, and to comprehend predictions of future events. While it is helpful to us individually at that level, modern heliocentric theory is much more powerful than that. For example, it provides scientists and engineers with basic, indisputable ways of understanding and explaining the solar system, and it continues to be used in the designing and carrying out of our huge programs for exploring the solar system and of space beyond. Clearly, this theory is not some idle speculation; it is part of the theoretical bedrock on which our achievements in space have been built since the 1950s, and on which our plans for future space exploration have been constructed. This theory—like every good theory—is part of the practical stuff of living effectively in the real world. This theorizing continues to be explored and extended in our time and will continue to be tested into the foreseeable future. To paraphrase Kurt Lewin, the founder of social psychology: nothing is more practical than good theory (Marrow, 1977).

Just as we have theories of the causes of disease and theories about the solar system, life in our scientific-technological era relies on a rich base of theoretical understandings. Theories of aerodynamics describe and explain the forces that make it possible for heavier-than-air machines to fly. Reasonably able middle school children can explain why steel ships float because they understand the theory involved. Not surprisingly, we also have theories about organizations and the people who work in them. Just as there are theoretical reasons that underlie the beliefs that we should wash our hands frequently, exercise regularly, and maintain a nutritionally sound diet, there are theoretical underpinnings to our understanding of schools as organizations and how to make them more effective.

If you accidentally cut your finger, what would you do? Very likely you would wash the cut, then apply some antiseptic, and cover it with a sterile bandage. To most readers, this would be an ordinary, unremarkable response to having cut one's finger. But it is an ordinary, unremarkable response only to someone who knows about, and accepts, the germ theory of disease and the prophylactic practices that have been developed from that theory. To such people, the germ theory of disease is a theory of action. That is, it is a systematic explanation of phenomena that guides us to take actions that seem to be sensible, logical, and reasonable because they are compatible with the explanation of reality that the theory provides.

Theory is useful because it provides a basis for thinking systematically about complex problems, such as understanding the nature of educational organizations. Theory enables us to do four useful things: (a) *describe* what is going on, (b) *explain* it, (c) *predict* future events under given circumstances, and (d) (essential for the professional practitioner) think about ways to exercise *control* over events. This process lays the groundwork for the professional practice of school leadership. When we accept, internalize, and act on a theory of action, that theory becomes an important element in our theory of practice.

THEORY OF PRACTICE

A *theory of practice* is a composite of theories of action that underlies, and gives direction to, one's professional practice. A theory of practice is one's personal understanding of causal relationships: It arises from the processes of gathering, organizing, and integrating facts and experiences that one has encountered. It is the theory of practice that coheres, unifies, consolidates, makes consistent, and makes sense of hundreds of daily decisions and actions that the leader takes and that guide the leader inexorably to a seemingly unerring sense of what is right. Because the typical reader of this text is already a demonstrably successful teacher and has almost certainly been entrusted with other leadership roles, the focus of the text is on further developing the intellectual underpinnings of leadership in schools. The focus is on combining one's various theories of action into a coherent theory of practice. The foundation for a theory of practice in educational leadership rests on three intellectual pillars:

- *A systematic understanding of the behavior of adults at work in the school*   Thus, we focus on understanding aspects of human behavior such as motivation, decision making, and conflict. This realm of behavior theory seeks to explain the different ways in which we may attempt to understand the behavior of people, whether or not they are functioning in the context of organizational life. There are many, often competing, theories of human behavior that can be used to guide our understanding.
- *An understanding of the organizational context in which people work*   This realm of organizational theory seeks to explain the different ways in which we may approach the problem of organizing and coordinating the cooperative efforts of many people in order to achieve things that cannot be done individually. The central concern in the study of organizational behavior is the dynamic interaction between the organization and the people who populate it.
- *Leader behavior*   This aspect of organizational theory examines how leaders interact with people in the organization in ways that cause them to be understood and accepted as leaders—not only by followers but also by other participants in the organization.

But do not be misled: while it is important for potential school leaders to have a solid grasp of the knowledge that underlies leadership, knowledge alone is not sufficient. Each of us who would lead must develop and articulate a coherent theory of practice based on our idiosyncratic understanding of that knowledge and how it may be used in action. It is your theory of practice that informs your method of school leadership; guides you in deciding what to do and what not to do when choices are difficult and urgent; and renders your behavior as a leader understandable, believable, and therefore trustworthy to others.

Throughout this text, you will be challenged to reflect on ideas that you have read and to use them in thinking through the ways in which you hope to engage in the practice of being a school leader. By engaging in this reflective thinking, it is hoped that you can move beyond merely *knowing about* some of these ideas to a higher level of thinking in which you consider how you can *use these ideas* in your professional practice. How, for example, can you incorporate them into ways of thinking about problems and issues that confront you? How can you use them in developing the plans you make, the actions you take, and the ideas that you propose as a school leader? The concept of developing theories of action and combining them to form a theory of practice lends itself very well to the study of organizational behavior in education.

VOICES FROM THE FIELD

How One Principal Implements Her Theory of Practice

Peggy Aune, Principal, Manatee Middle School, Naples, Florida

As the leader of a middle school, my goal is to build positive momentum with the majority of stakeholders. When I assumed the principalship four years ago, our work centered on building a united school culture, specifically in the area of student behavioral expectations. Conversations abounded and meetings were held to determine what our end goals were for our students, how we wanted them to behave, ways to help the students internalize the common school expectations, and what we ultimately wanted our students to be able to accomplish as adults. A basic tenet of Positive Behavior Support (PBS) is that students should be extrinsically acknowledged for positive choices and that this will ultimately lead to a stronger internal locus of control. As with any initiative, there was some conflict among faculty at the outset. Shouldn't students behave for the sake of behaving? Why are we rewarding students for things they should be doing anyway? A starting point was to define our vision and logistically detail the steps we would need to achieve this vision. A committed group of teachers set the parameters and overall structure that would define our united school culture. After a time, faculty members who may have had some initial reservations saw that PBS was working to improve the culture at our school. With hard work and through a shared commitment, the school has been recognized as a PBS Gold School for the last three years. Our collective vision for the school in terms of positive behavior support has been realized.

A larger issue, however, that is critical to our students' success, is more adaptive and requires collaborative expertise over time. As a faculty, we needed our students to be actively involved in the learning process, understand and set their own goals, and pursue abstract outcomes. All stakeholders need to be emboldened to believe that our students are fully capable of achieving optimally in high school, college, and careers. As a school, we need students to understand their data and grades, teachers to actively monitor student progress and adjust instruction accordingly, and parents to partner with us in the entire process. We were ready, as a school, to enter into academic discussions within the faculty where there may be some strong opinions. We had moved beyond examination of behavioral expectations and were ready to really set the course for our students.

The district was supportive of our efforts, as we were motivated by district data dialogues in which each school set goals for student achievement. These data dialogues occurred routinely between district administrators and school leaders. School leaders identified areas of concern, strategies, and resources that may be needed at each particular school. These district data dialogues charged each school to periodically take stock, and this raised accountability at the school level. Ultimately, the change process for our school, motivated by the district data dialogues, has turned out to be challenging and exhilarating at the same time. We are currently in the midst of our change effort, and our methods and strategies continue to evolve.

Students at our school now engage in a daily intervention and enrichment time in which they monitor grades and quarterly progress results, have at least one data chat with a teacher every two weeks, and set short- and long-term goals. Teachers monitor their own benchmark data through data chats with school leaders and in department data teams and set goals individually and within departments. Parents actively participate in student-led conferences; in this past academic year, approximately 70% of parents engaged in student-led conferences. At one time, these types of outcomes may have seemed daunting for a middle school that has had numerous challenges as defined by state testing measures. At our school, it is indicative of a shared expectation that students are stewards of their own success, and we serve as facilitators.

Some of the positive byproducts of this student ownership have been a 100% increase in students taking algebra for high school credit, an exponential increase in students earning industry certifications, and a marked increase in students earning college scholarships.

The power of change at our school is that it is clear, collaborative, and has evolved over time. Teachers, instructional coaches, and department chairs among them, led the faculty in defining the specific steps we needed to take to empower our students and boost achievement. At times, we have had to recalibrate our expectations, adjust timelines, and justify ideas to one another. The work at our school is in progress and each year brings challenges, new ideas and most importantly the drive to accelerate student achievement. The entire faculty has the opportunity to offer insights, express needs, and reflect on goals for our students. Through collaborative leadership, our students' needs are prioritized and expertise in various areas is voluntarily extended for the greater good.

THE GAME PLAN: A COACHING METAPHOR

Another way of thinking about theories of action and combining them into a theory of practice is to apply the metaphor of the coach of a sports team. This is the preferred metaphor in many popular books intended for an audience of managers in business and industrial organizations. Coaches are unquestionably leaders and, arguably, theoreticians. Every successful coach is, above all, a student of the game, just as you are being urged to become a student of educational organization. We expect that the coach is able to analyze and think through the game as a basis for planning and developing strategies and tactics that will win in the future. As spectators of sports contests, we know that every team—in football, basketball, hockey, or any other sport—must operate from a game plan that is understood and shared by all who are involved.

The coach must also weave the dynamics of the human behavior of the team players with the strategic notions that underlie the plan. That is called team building. Those who are being coached must not merely know of the game plan; in addition, each individual in the group must be personally committed to the game plan and be confident that the plan is solid and will work. This process involves the use of playbooks, classroom sessions, tutoring, practice sessions, one-on-one encounters, and all of the teaching techniques that teachers and coaches know so well. More important, it involves developing the dynamics of human relationships on the team that build trust, collaboration, and high morale. The coach does not hope or assume that the team members will somehow understand that there is a plan that governs how the game is played; an important part of coaching is to make sure that everyone understands the game plan and what role each has in executing it. Ultimately, the coach uses the game plan in the heat and confusion of the action as a guide for making decisions as the situation develops and conditions change. One would hardly expect a coach to go into a game without a game plan.

Unpredictable developments and rapid, unforeseen changes constantly confront coaches, just as they confront all organizational leaders. Therefore, an essential characteristic of the game plan is that it be a guide to action—a plan that can be readily modified and adapted to new emerging conditions, not something that is fixed and rigid. This adaptability is, in fact, a crucial element in the game plan, just as it is in a theory of practice. It makes it possible for the team to respond nimbly and deftly to emerging circumstances that were unforeseen, rather than to continue hammering away using a game plan that is not working. In the context of this discussion, it is appropriate to think of your theory of practice as a game plan.

Final Thoughts

The central purpose of this text is to help you to begin the career-long process of developing, testing, and refining a theory of practice, or a game plan, in school leadership. While the focus is on understanding the interface between organization and human behavior as a basis for making a difference in schools, one must be very aware of one key factor that frames all actions in educative organizations—that is, the long-running fundamental disagreement between those who hold a traditional-conservative view of what education should be and how schools should be organized and run, on the one hand, and those who have a more progressive vision, on the other. Your challenge is to think through a clear and committed position on these contentious issues as an important step in developing a game plan, or theory of practice, for educational leadership.

Reflective Activities

1. Apply the three characteristics of Perkins's smart schools by describing several organizational structures, or common routines, that once established might lead to the type of school Perkins identifies as smart.

2. The long-term nationwide political drive to close the educational achievement gap between minority students and majority students has resulted in a set of national goals for education, the establishment of educational standards in each state, and a push for tough accountability measures using high-stakes testing. NCLB made these tests a reality. Students of educational leadership should be knowledgeable about the key issues involved in all of this and take a stand that guides their actions as education professionals. Where do you stand on these issues at this point in time? Write a paragraph or two describing your beliefs. Use one or more references from the research literature to support your beliefs.

3. Identify and describe a specific *theory* that guides your actions in your answer to Reflective Activity 2.

4. *Working on the Game Plan.* A game plan normally takes into consideration two principal factors: first, the strategies and tactics that are most likely to gain your objectives based on your analysis of the game and, second, the dynamic relationship between these strategies and tactics with the people on your team. Reflecting on the contemporary debate on education and school reform, which is an important part of the context of educational leadership today, discuss each of the following:

   A. How will you use the concept of multiple intelligences, including emotional intelligence, in your theory of practice?

   B. Describe at least one additional key idea from Chapter 2 that will guide your behavior as an educational leader. Explain the rationale for your choice. Why is it a key idea? What are the behavior implications of the idea for educational leadership? Show how your behavior based on this idea should improve the performance of those whom you lead.

CRITICAL INCIDENT   Controversy at the Principals' Meeting

Superintendent Dr. Geraldine Claxton was just about to call an end to the monthly principals' meeting when Olson Collins, principal of Roosevelt High School, rose and asked to make some comments.

"Dr. Claxton," Olson started, "It's time we quit pussy-footing around and tinkering with everything in hopes we will improve test scores. A group of us high school principals have been talking about some changes that we think are necessary. A lot of you have been complaining about No Child Left Behind, but we think No Child Left Behind has been a godsend for us. It has shown us that we are not meeting the needs of the kids in the lowest quartile. Look at our scores. They are low and going lower. We need to go back to the basics. We believe that we need to put these kids into classes with others who are on the same level so that we can work with them intensely and meet their needs. This should be started in kindergarten, so by the time they get to high school they are on grade level and know what career track they will pursue. Some kids will go to college, but college is not for everybody. For those kids who are not going to college, we need to go back to the type of vocational education we used to have that prepared these kids for a job when they graduate, and one other thing—"

Olson Collins was interrupted by Joan Sizemore, principal of James Adams Middle School. "Olson, excuse me for interrupting, but not everyone agrees with your philosophy. You are right about one thing though, we are not meeting the needs of the kids in the Title I schools, but not for the reasons you state. It's because we treat them like they are robots. We drill and kill them on preparation for the state achievement test, and we don't work on critical thinking skills. We try to make them memorize everything, and we are just killing their enthusiasm for learning. We need to treat all kids like they are in gifted classes. They should have hands-on projects, work in cooperative teams, and learn from a curriculum that integrates the content areas with real-world work assignments. Have you never heard of multiple intelligences, and how they should impact instructional practices and assessment?"

With a practiced eye, the superintendent saw people examining their cell phones, glancing at their watches, and closing their notebooks and knew it was too late in the day to let this go on. Yet there were other principals sitting up and really paying attention to their colleagues. "I hate to cut off this discussion so quickly," Dr. Claxton interjected, "but it *is* late and I need to get to tonight's board meeting. This is a very interesting discussion, but it's not something we can deal with quickly. I will put it on the agenda for the next meeting. In the meantime, perhaps Olson and Joan would agree to form a steering committee to meet before our next principals' meeting and bring us some recommendations about how to tackle our discussion of this issue."

1. If you had to choose at this time, would you side with Olson or Joan? Why?
2. Is there another point of view that you would like to put forward?
3. Have you experienced similar debates in your school or school district? If so, share the experience with your class. If not, share with the class why you think this debate has not occurred.

Suggested Reading

Calkins, A., Guenther, W., & Belifore, G. (2007). *The turnaround challenge. Executive summary.* Boston, MA: Mass Insight.

This book summarizes the argument for "America's best opportunity to dramatically improve student achievement," from a corporation that is in the business of providing consultant support for turnaround efforts, with the support of the Bill & Melinda Gates Foundation. Very clearly and forcefully stated. Recommended reading for all school leaders.

Gardner, H. (1999). *The disciplined mind: What all students should understand.* New York, NY: Simon and Schuster.

This text is a rarity in the literature on schooling: a thoughtful, superbly informed, and well-disciplined analysis of the problems that lie at the heart of the education profession. Gardner articulately stakes out a position that defines present-day progressive-liberal views on education and clarifies the issues that differentiate those views from the traditional-conservative approach. Educational leaders who do not know Gardner are at a great disadvantage in the current incarnation of the great debate on schooling.

Goleman, D., Boyatzis, R., & McKee, A. (2004). *Primal leadership: Learning to lead with emotional intelligence.* New York, NY: Perseus.

This book draws on decades of research in world-class organizations and demonstrates with many cases and critical incidents the power of emotional intelligence in leading organizations. Chapter 10, "Reality and the Ideal Vision," is powerful in helping the leader understand how to give life to the organization's future.

Hamilton, L. S., Stecher, B. M., & Yuan, K. (2008). *Standards-based reforms in the United States: History, research, and future directions.* Santa Monica, CA: RAND Corporation.

A report of research conducted for the National Science Foundation's project on Rethinking the Federal Role in Education as the time for reconsideration of the NCLB legislation drew near. This is a reliable, comprehensive overview from a reputable source of where we were and where we seemed to be going at that time.

Hargreaves, A., & Goodson, I. (2006). Educational change over time? The sustainability and nonsustainability of three decades of secondary school change and continuity. *Educational Administration Quarterly, 42*(1), 3–41.

This article is not poolside reading. It is a professional-level research report that describes most mainstream change theory as neglecting the political, historical, and longitudinal aspects of change to its detriment. Perhaps its singular contribution is its emphasis on sustainability as a key characteristic to successful change in secondary schools and, by logical extension, to all schools.

Kohn, A. (1999). *The schools our children deserve: Moving beyond traditional classrooms and "Tougher Standards."* Boston, MA: Houghton Mifflin.

This important book is a cautionary discourse on the future of U.S. schooling and must reading for anyone who would be an educational leader. Former teacher Kohn questions whether today's schools are really floundering or whether some romanticized notions about "the good old days," which he calls "aggressive nostalgia," are coloring our perceptions. Drawing on a wealth of research, Kohn argues that the demand for tougher standards reflects a lack of understanding of how children actually learn and why.

Rothstein, R. (1998). *The way we were? The myths and realities of America's student achievement.* Washington, DC: The Brookings Institution.

While this book carefully dispels the fantasy that there was at one time a golden age in which schooling in the United States was far better and more effective than it is today, it has much more to offer than a trip down memory lane. In particular, Rothstein's informative discussions of the ins and outs of tests such as the much-talked-about School Achievement Tests and the Iowa Tests of Basic Skills, how they came to be what they are, and how they are affected by factors such as the socioeconomic status of students and dropout rates in schools make this must reading for anyone preparing for leadership in American schooling.

Rothstein, R. (2004). *Class and schools.* New York, NY: Economic Policy Institute, Columbia University Press.

Rothstein exposes the myth that public school educators are the primary causes of the achievement gap that exists between the majority and minority communities. He uses solid research evidence to make his point that, to rectify these problems, we must develop public policy that addresses social and economic conditions, not just call for schools alone to change.

References

Barbuto, J. E., & Burbach, M.E. (2006). The emotional intelligence of transformational leaders: A field study of elected officials. *Journal of Social Psychology, 146*(1), 51–64.

Berliner, D. C., & Biddle, B. J. (1995). *The manufactured crisis: Myths, fraud, and the attack on America's public schools.* Reading, MA: Addison-Wesley.

Bestor, A. E. (1953). *Educational wastelands: The retreat from learning in our public schools.* Urbana, IL: University of Illinois Press.

Bestor, A. E. (1985). *Educational wastelands: The retreat from learning in our public schools* (2nd ed.). Urbana, IL: University of Illinois Press.

Bracey, G. R. (1997). *The truth about America's schools: The Bracey reports, 1991–1997.* Bloomington, IN: Phi Delta Kappa.

Bruner, J. (1960). *The process of education.* Cambridge, MA: Harvard University Press.

Butterworth, E. L. (1958, December). You have to fight for good schools. *Education Digest,* 83.

Chall, J. (1967) *Learning to read: The great debate.* New York, NY: McGraw-Hill.

Clinchy, E. (1993, December 8). Magnet schools matter. *Education Week,* 28, p. 28.

DeLorenzo, D. (2012). Emotional intelligence and school climate: A study to compare middle school teacher descriptions of principal emotional intelligence and school climate in low and high need schools that have demonstrated low and high growth in student achievement. (Doctoral Dissertation, University of Florida). Proquest, UMI Dissertations Publishing. (UMI No. AA13472672)

Gardner, H. (1983). *Frames of mind: The theory of multiple intelligences.* New York, NY: Basic Books.

Gardner, H. (1993). *Multiple intelligences: The theory in practice.* New York, NY: Basic Books.

Goddard, H. H. (1919). *Psychology of the normal and subnormal.* New York, NY: Dodd, Mead.

Goleman, D. (1995). *Emotional intelligence.* New York, NY: Bantam Dell.

Gould, S. J. (1981) *The mismeasure of man.* New York, NY: W. W. Norton.

Hargreaves, A., & Goodson, I. (2006). Educational change over time? *Educational Administration Quarterly, 42*(1), 3–41.

Hargreaves, A., Moore, S., Fink, D., Brayman, C., & White, R. (2003). *Succeeding leaders? A study of secondary school principal rotation and succession.* Toronto, Canada: Ontario Principals' Council.

Heiken, S. E. (2007). The perceived relationship between emotional intelligence and leadership effectiveness in school leaders: A comparison of self ratings with those of superiors and reports (Doctoral Dissertation, Wilmington College). *Proquest, UMI Dissertations Publishing.* (UMI No. 3246674)

Holt, J. (1953). *How children fail.* Boston, MA: Little, Brown.

Hutchins, R. M. (1943). *Education for freedom.* Baton Rouge, LA: Louisiana State University Press.

Kerr, C. (1991, February 27). Is education really all that guilty? *Education Week, 30,* p. 1.

Kohl, H. (1967). *36 children.* New York, NY: New American Library.

Kozol, J. (1967). *Death at an early age: The destruction of the hearts and minds of Negro children in the Boston public schools.* Boston, MA: Houghton Mifflin.

Lowe, B. (1977). *The beauty of sport: A cross-disciplinary inquiry.* Englewood Cliffs, NJ: Prentice-Hall.

Lynd, A. (1969). *Quackery in the public schools.* New York, NY: Greenwood Press.

Maier, P. (1997). *American scripture: Making the Declaration of Independence.* New York, NY: Alfred A. Knopf.

Mainstream science on intelligence. (1994, December 13). *The Wall Street Journal,* p. A19.

Marrow, A. J. (1977). *The practical theorist: The life and work of Kurt Lewin.* New York, NY: Teachers College Press.

Marshall, R., & Tucker, M. (1992). *Thinking for a living: Education and the wealth of nations.* New York, NY: Basic Books.

National Commission on Excellence in Education. (1983). *A nation at risk.* Washington, DC: Government Printing Office.

National Education Association of the United States, Commission on the Reorganization of Secondary Education. (1918). *Cardinal principles of secondary education.* Washington, DC: Government Printing Office.

Nelson, D. B., & Low, G. R. (2003). *Emotional intelligence: Achieving academic and career excellence.* Upper Saddle River, NJ: Prentice-Hall.

Olson, L. (1999, April 21). Tugging at tradition. *Education Week, 25,* p. 25.

Ozcelik, H., Langton, N., & Aldrich, H. (2008). Doing well and doing good: The relationship between leadership practices that facilitate a positive emotional climate and organizational performance. *Journal of Managerial Psychology, 23*(2), 186–203.

Packard, V. (1974, April). Are we becoming a nation of illiterates? *Reader's Digest,* 81–85.

Perkins, D. (1995a). *Outsmarting IQ: The emerging science of learnable intelligence.* New York, NY: Free Press.

Perkins, D. (1995b). *Smart schools: Better thinking and better learning for every child.* New York, NY: Free Press.

Perkins, D. (2008). *Smart schools: Training memories to educating minds.* New York, NY: Simon and Schuster.

Piaget, J. (1929). *The child's conception of the world.* London, England: Routledge and Kegan Paul.

Ravitch, D. (1983). *Troubled crusade: American education, 1945–1980.* New York, NY: Basic Books.

Rickover, H. G. (1959). *Education and freedom.* New York, NY: Charles E. Dutton.

Riggio, R. E., & Riechard, E. J. (2008). The emotional and social intelligences of effective leadership: An emotional and social skill approach. *Journal of Managerial Psychology, 23*(2), 169–185.

Rothstein, R. (1998). *The way we were? The myths and realities of America's student achievement.* New York, NY: Century Foundation.

Salovey, P., & Mayer, J. D. (1990). Emotional intelligence. *Imagination, Cognition, and Personality, 9,* 185–211.

Smith, M. (1954). *The diminished mind: A study of planned mediocrity in our public schools.* Chicago, IL: Henry Regnery.

Sowell, T. (1993). *Inside American education: The decline, the deception, the dogmas.* New York, NY: Free Press.

Stein, S. J., & Book, H. E. (2000). *The EQ edge: Emotional intelligence and your success.* Toronto, Canada: Stoddart.

Vygotsky, L. (1934/1986). *Thought and language.* Cambridge, MA: Massachusetts Institute of Technology Press.

Walcutt, C. C. (1961). *Tomorrow's illiterates: The state of reading instruction today.* Boston, MA: Atlantic Monthly Press.

Williams, H. W. (2008). Characteristics that distinguish outstanding urban principals: Emotional intelligence, social intelligence and environmental adaptation. *Journal of Management Development, 27*(1), 36–54.

CHAPTER 3

Mainstreams of Organizational Thought

Over the course of the past century, we have learned that essentially there are two ways of thinking about educational organizations. One is the traditional way: to think of organizations as hierarchical systems in which power and intelligence are concentrated at the top; hence, initiative and good ideas originate at the top and are passed down through command and control as programs and procedures that people in the lower levels put into practice. The other, newer way—discovered in chrysalides fashion over the course of the twentieth century—is to think of organizations as cooperative, collegial, even collaborative systems in which good ideas exist everywhere in the organization and can be made manifest and put into action only when those in the hierarchy of command and control act in ways that release the capabilities and motivations of subordinates. There is a lot more to it than that, of course, and this chapter gives you some background on the history of the development of these ideas in education. Without that background, one cannot intelligently engage in the current debate on school reform because the debate—though often openly political rather than educational—nearly always arises from the different concepts that the debaters have about issues such as how to make an organization more effective and what leadership is.

ORGANIZATIONAL BEHAVIOR

Because educational leaders work with and through other people to achieve organizational goals, understanding the behavior of people at work is fundamental to the success of their efforts. All human behavior is mediated and modulated by the context in which it occurs. The context can be overarching and distant, such as the long-term impact of the historical culture of our social and ethnic traditions, or it can be highly proximate. Normally our behavior can and does appropriately shift—usually very swiftly as we move from one context to another—depending, for example, upon whether we are at home for a quiet time with our family, engaged in a job interview, participating in a religious service, or attending a casual gathering of a few friends.

Organizational behavior is both a field of scientific inquiry and a field of applied practice. As a field of scientific inquiry, organizational behavior seeks to illuminate the behavior of individuals and groups of people in the social and cultural context of organizations. Like education, organizational behavior is a cross-disciplinary field: no single academic discipline claims it as its exclusive realm. Students of organizational behavior from a number of recognized disciplines can, and do, legitimately conduct inquiry in this field. Collectively, these disciplines are known as the social and behavioral sciences.

The social sciences are the disciplines from which organizational behavior derives (a) its intellectual base of knowledge and theory and (b) the research methods that give credence to claims of scientific legitimacy. Thus, scholars in organizational behavior tend to have academic grounding in one or more of five principal social science disciplines: cultural anthropology, sociology, social psychology, political science, and economics. Although all these disciplines seek to shed light on understanding the behavior of people in organizational environments, people from each of these disciplines tend to frame problems and choose research methods in ways that fit the particular traditions of the discipline with which they are associated. Not surprisingly, political scientists often focus on the ways in which people in organizations tend to form coalitions and use power. Cultural anthropologists tend to look at the values and belief systems of people in the organization and how these are revealed through the artifacts that are used, the customs of the place, the history of the organization, and the myths and stories that are told. Social psychologists are inclined to study the behaviors of people as they are influenced by the social milieu in the organization. Yet the boundaries separating these disciplines are not as impermeable as one may think. When designing, executing, and interpreting inquiry into issues of organizational behavior in real-world organizations, a great deal of overlapping of ideas and methods occurs between and among these various disciplines.

Indeed, collaborative interdisciplinary inquiry has been a hallmark of organizational behavior inquiry since the field first began to emerge in the 1930s. One of the celebrated collaborations in the history of organizational behavior inquiry was that of Kurt Lewin, who is generally credited with founding the discipline of social psychology, and cultural anthropologist Margaret Mead in the 1940s. Lewin, a renowned field researcher in social psychology, and Mead, equally renowned as a field researcher in cultural anthropology, demonstrated and modeled interdisciplinary collegiality in studying human social behavior. Their pioneering discoveries about the ways in which groups make decisions has long since become a central concept in organizational behavior.

Organizational behavior is also a field of applied science—that is, it is a field of professional practice that seeks to apply knowledge from the social sciences to solve practical problems in improving the performance of organizations. For example, organizational behavior is a standard subject for study at both the undergraduate and graduate levels of schools of business administration in U.S. universities. The intent, of course, is to improve the leadership and management, and thus the performance, of business organizations in today's global, fast-changing, competitive environment. Organizational behavior is studied in military institutions of higher education as well as for application in that field. This text examines some of the knowledge and theory that social scientists have been building for over half a century, with a view to their application to improving leadership and administration in education.

We define organizational behavior as *a field of social-scientific study and application to administrative practice that seeks to use knowledge of human behavior in social and cultural settings for the improvement of organizational performance.* Thus, organizational behavior is an arena in which social scientists and school administrators can seek to collaborate, however imperfectly, to bridge the gulf between arcane academic inquiry and the everyday challenges of improving the performance of schools.

Two Concepts of Organization and Behavior

Two concepts gradually began to be linked as the second half of the twentieth century unfolded. In the beginning, ideas about organization tended to come from people with engineering backgrounds. Military tradition has, for centuries, provided much of the logic that underlies organizational concepts, which continue to be taken for granted even today. These organizational concepts tend to emphasize the linear, logical, hierarchical, authoritarian, and disciplinary structure that one would expect of the military tradition. Generally, these concepts were adopted uncritically by the large-scale industrial and business organizations that developed so rapidly in the late nineteenth and early twentieth centuries. The people who took the lead in designing and managing these organizations were usually engineers whose interest in human factors was largely focused on fitting people into the machine system to create more efficient and manageable human-machine systems.

As the twentieth century unfolded, social scientists came to realize that the ubiquity of organizational life mandated that they seriously consider the nature of organizations as human environments. Beginning as early as the 1930s, serious scientific studies of the human side of organization began to be undertaken. This was a period that ushered in the Great Depression and an era of unprecedented labor-management strife in industry, and the topic had become too significant to ignore. By the end of the 1940s, the engineers had largely been displaced as organizational theorists. From that time on, the major thinkers in the field of organization would come almost exclusively from the ranks of the social and behavioral scientists.

Why Study Organizational Behavior?

The short answer to this question is because organizational behavior provides the indispensable foundation of knowledge that is absolutely essential if one hopes to achieve success in educational leadership. After all, leadership, and administration as well, means working with and through other people to achieve organizational goals. Although those who are appointed as school principals are usually selected from the ranks of teachers who are thought to be especially effective, after their appointments they engage very little in the technical aspects of teaching that earned them their reputations. Indeed, the shift from classroom teaching to a school leadership position, such as the principalship, is really a career change. So different are the skills needed to do the work, and the outcomes by which one's success is judged, that one literally leaves teaching and enters a new and very different occupation. Often, newly appointed school leaders find that knowledge of traditional subjects in the curriculum of educational administration—such as school law, curriculum theory, or educational finance—does little to ensure success in leadership.

After appointment as principal, one's work consists primarily of working with and through other adults: Principals confer with people, individually and in small groups; they plan and run meetings, sometimes small and sometimes large; they have innumerable encounters with people, some planned but many impromptu and necessarily hurried. It is often assumed that intelligent adults, such as successful teachers, are smart enough to work with and through other people effectively. Yet if you are a teacher, you may have already witnessed school principals at work who are simply not as capable as they should be in motivating teachers and parents, leading them, and developing the dynamic teamwork in the school and its community that is demanded in this era of school reform. A major cause of such failure is often the fact that the principal simply does not have a strategic plan—that is, a theory of practice—for dealing with the all-critical human dimension of the school enterprise.

Many newly appointed principals have good intentions about improving the performance of the school by improving morale, enriching the quality of life in the school, and building teamwork. Many wish to introduce new technical changes as well: adding new curricula, perhaps, or reorganizing the structure of the school. But very often they are ill prepared by either their experience in the classroom or traditional coursework in graduate school to think through and plan their approach to school leadership, and they have given little thought to the relationship between their day-to-day and hour-by-hour behavior on the job and the outcomes that they so earnestly desire as leaders.

Study of organizational behavior in education can help, first, by focusing your attention on the issues listed in the paragraph above and, second, by encouraging you to make some personal decisions about how you would plan to practice being a leader on the job. Aside from a general knowledge of pedagogy and schooling, perhaps the single most useful professional tool that the teacher can bring to the role of educational leader is skill in planning for both long- and short-range activities on the job. One of the outstanding characteristics of successful teachers is their skill in planning their work, both in the formal sense of written plans as well as in the sense of coherent mental maps of what work to do and how to do it. Astonishingly, this is the very skill that many people seem to abandon first when appointed to the principalship and, instead, go in to work every day more or less waiting to see what crises will unfold. Every principal quickly finds that there are always many, many crises and emergencies that seem to fill every hour of the day, compete urgently for attention, and keep one "putting out fires" from early in the morning until the evening. Such a demanding job, with its never-ending time pressures, requires a principal who not only understands organizational behavior and its importance to school leadership, but who has also internalized a personal commitment to keep leadership and human concerns high on the list of priorities.

IMPACT OF THE INDUSTRIAL REVOLUTION

At about the close of the nineteenth century—the time of Woodrow Wilson's scholarly contributions—businesspeople in Western Europe and the United States were stepping up their efforts to increase profits from industry. In that burgeoning era of industry, as now, it was generally believed that greater profitability required lowering the unit cost of producing goods. One way to do this, of course, was to step up mass production through the use of innovations such as the assembly line. The leadership of pioneering industrial giants such as Henry Ford is widely recognized in connection with such technological breakthroughs. In this era of industrial expansion, the key people were the engineers and technically oriented scientists—as they are in our own day of technological revolution. These were the people who could build the machines and then combine them into assembly line units. This was the era of the engineering consultant and the drive for efficiency.

Frederick W. Taylor and Scientific Management

Frederick W. Taylor is a name well known to many students of administration. He was an engineer at the Midvale and Bethlehem steel companies at the close of the 1800s and, in the early 1900s, became one of the top engineering consultants in U.S. industry. We know that Taylor read Woodrow Wilson's essay, "The Study of Administration," and was influenced by it. From about 1900 to 1915, as he worked to solve practical production problems in factories all over the United States, Taylor developed what later became known as his four principles of scientific management:

1. Eliminate the guesswork of rule-of-thumb approaches to deciding how each worker is to do a job by adopting scientific measurements to break the job down into a series of small, related tasks.
2. Use more scientific, systematic methods for selecting workers and training them for specific jobs.

3. Establish a clear division of responsibility between management and workers, with management doing the goal setting, planning, and supervising while workers execute the required tasks.
4. Establish the discipline whereby management sets the objectives and the workers cooperate in achieving them.

Notice, especially, the last two of Taylor's principles: They formally differentiate between the roles and responsibilities of managers, on the one hand, and those of workers, on the other. They mandate a top-down, hierarchical relationship between managers and workers. This traditional concept of labor–management relationships was hardly original with Taylor, but its formalization as a basic principle of organization and management has proven to be extremely powerful in shaping the assumptions and beliefs of managers and thus their thinking about concepts such as collaboration and teamwork, which were to emerge in the years ahead. These two of Taylor's principles still provide the justification for many school administrators and school board members to resist—openly or covertly—ideas such as collegial, collaborative approaches to goal setting, planning, and problem solving and other bottom-up approaches to school reform in favor of more traditional authoritarian approaches. Indeed, over the course of the next 75 years—certainly until the present time—these two of Taylor's principles of scientific management would be the arena in which new and very different ideas about management behavior would evolve.

Frederick Taylor's principles of scientific management became enormously popular, not only in industry but also in the management of all kinds of organizations, including the family. A bestseller of the 1950s, *Cheaper by the Dozen*, vividly recounts how efficiency invaded every corner of the family life of Frank B. Gilbreth, one of Taylor's closest colleagues and an expert on *time-and-motion study*—the study of efficient body movement in individual job skills. Taylor's principles of scientific management were aimed primarily at lowering the unit cost of factory production, although he and his followers claimed that these principles could be applied universally (Taylor, 1911). These principles became almost an obsession in the press and throughout our society. In practice, Taylor's ideas led to time-and-motion studies; rigid discipline on the job; concentration on the tasks to be performed, with minimal interpersonal contacts between and among workers; and strict application of incentive pay systems (Etzioni, 1964).

The Beginning of Modern Organizational Theory

At the same time that Taylor's ideas and their application were having an enormous impact on life in the United States, a French industrialist was working out some powerful ideas of his own. Henri Fayol had a background quite different from Taylor's, which helps account for some of the differences in perception of the two men. Whereas Taylor was essentially a technician whose first concern was the middle-management level of industry, Fayol had the background of a top-management executive. It would be useful to mention briefly some of the ideas Fayol advanced to give us a better perspective on what he contributed to the growth of thought in administration.

1. Unlike Taylor, who tended to view workers as extensions of factory machinery, Fayol focused his attention on the manager rather than on the workers.
2. Fayol clearly separated the processes of administration from other operations in the organization, such as production.

3. Fayol emphasized the common elements of the process of administration in different organizations.

Fayol believed that a trained administrative group was essential to improving the operations of organizations, which were becoming increasingly complex. As early as 1916, Fayol wrote that administrative ability "can and should be acquired in the same way as technical ability, first at school, later in the workshop" (Fayol, 1949, p. 14). He added that we find good and bad administrative methods existing side by side "with a persistence only to be explained by lack of theory" (p. 15).

In his most notable work, *General and Industrial Management,* Fayol established himself as the first modern organizational theorist. He defined administration in terms of five functions: (a) planning, (b) organizing, (c) commanding, (d) coordinating, and (e) controlling. It should be noted that, in the sense in which he used these terms, *commanding* and *controlling* mean what are now called "leading" and "evaluating results." More than 60 years after its initial publication, many still find Fayol's insightful approach to administration practical and useful.

Fayol went further by identifying a list of fourteen principles, among which were (a) unity of command, (b) authority, (c) initiative, and (d) morale. Avoiding a rigid and dogmatic application of his ideas to the administration of organizations, Fayol emphasized that flexibility and a sense of proportion were essential to managers who adapted principles and definitions to particular situations—quite a different interpretation from that of Taylor, who held firmly to the uniform, emphatic application of principles.

Emergence of Bureaucratic Organizational Theory

By the time of Fayol and Taylor, it was clear that the Western world was becoming an organizational society. As giant industrial organizations grew in the early 1900s, so did government and other organizational aspects of life. The relatively simple social and political structures of the preindustrial era seemed inadequate in an urban industrial society. Life was not always completely happy in this new social setting, and a great deal of friction—social, political, and economic—resulted. The increasing sense of conflict between people and organizations became a major factor in the struggle of learning to live successfully in this new kind of world, this industrial world in which the individual was, at every turn, part of some organization. The years before World War I were punctuated by frequent outbursts of this conflict, such as labor unrest, revolution, and the rise of communism. In this setting, a German sociologist, Max Weber, produced some of the most useful, durable, and brilliant work on an administrative system; it seemed promising at that time and has since proved indispensable: *bureaucracy.*

At a period when people and organizations were dominated by the whims of authoritarian industrialists and entrenched political systems, Weber saw hope in bureaucracy. Essentially, the hope was that well-run bureaucracies would become more fair, impartial, and predictable—that is, more rational—than organizations subject to the caprices of powerful individuals. Weber felt that well-run bureaucracies would be efficient; in fact, they would be the most efficient form of organization yet invented. Such a viewpoint may not reflect modern experiences with bureaucracies, but Weber was convinced that a *well-run* bureaucracy would be very efficient for a number of reasons, one of which was that bureaucrats are highly trained technical specialists, each skilled in a specific, limited portion of an administrative task.

According to Weber, the bureaucratic apparatus would be very impersonal, minimizing irrational personal and emotional factors and leaving bureaucratic personnel free to work with a minimum of friction or confusion. This environment, he concluded, would result in expert, impartial, and unbiased service to the organization's clients. In the ideal bureaucracy, Weber envisioned certain characteristics that are, in a sense, principles of administration:

1. A division of labor based on functional specialization.
2. A well-defined hierarchy of authority.
3. A system of rules covering the rights and duties of employees.
4. A system of procedures for dealing with work situations.
5. Impersonality of interpersonal relations.
6. Selection and promotion based only on technical competence. (Hall, 1963, p. 33)

Part of Weber's genius lay in his sensitivity to the dangers of bureaucracy, while at the same time he recognized the merits of bureaucracy in *ideal* circumstances. He emphasized very strongly the dangers of bureaucracy, even warning that massive, uncontrollable bureaucracy could very well be the greatest threat to both communism and free-enterprise capitalism (Mayer, 1943). It is helpful, in trying to understand the flow of ideas that guided the development of administration, to be aware that, although Weber produced his work at about the same time that Taylor and Fayol did (that is, from about 1910 to 1920), Weber was almost unknown in the English-speaking world until translations of his work began to appear in the 1940s, which helps to explain why his systematic work on bureaucracy did not receive widespread attention in educational administration until after World War II.

Thus far, we have considered the ideas of three people who represent many others and a prodigious amount of effort in their time. Each pointed to the need for the principles and the theories that, by 1900, were generally regarded as essential if the administration of our growing organizations was to become more rational and more effective. The American, Taylor, emphasized the principles that viewed administration as management—the coordination of many small tasks to accomplish the overall job as efficiently as possible. Efficiency was interpreted to mean the lowest net-dollar cost to produce the finished article. Taylor assumed that labor was a commodity to be bought and sold, as one buys oil or electricity, and that by using scientific management, the manager could reduce to a minimum the amount of labor that must be purchased.

The Frenchman, Fayol, emphasized broader preparation of administrators so that they would perform their unique functions in the organization more effectively. He felt that the tasks that administrators perform are, presumably, different from those that engineers perform but equally important.

Germany's Max Weber held that bureaucracy is a theory of organization especially suited to the needs of large and complex enterprises that perform services for large numbers of clients. For Weber, the bureaucratic concept was an attempt to minimize the frustrations and irrationality of large organizations in which the relationships between management and workers were based on traditions of class privilege.

THE RISE OF CLASSICAL ORGANIZATIONAL THEORY

These three individuals—Taylor, Fayol, and Weber—were giants in the early years and led the way in the efforts to master the problems of managing modern organizations. There is no precise and universally agreed-upon beginning or end of this era; however, the period from 1910 to 1935 generally can be thought of as the era of scientific management, which had a profound and long-lasting impact on the ways in which schools were organized and administered.

Raymond E. Callahan (1962), in *Education and the Cult of Efficiency,* vividly described how school superintendents in the United States quickly adopted the values and practices of business and industrial managers of that time. Emphasis was on efficiency (that is, low per-unit cost); rigid application of detailed, uniform work procedures (often calling for minute-by-minute standard operating procedures for teachers to use each day throughout a school system); and detailed accounting procedures. Though some educational administrators harbored doubts about all of this, there was a rush among school superintendents to get on the bandwagon of the day by adopting the jargon and practices of those with high status in the society—business executives. Typifying this, Ellwood Cubberley—long one of the leading scholars in U.S. education—took the clear position in 1916 in a landmark textbook that schools were "factories in which the raw materials [meaning students] are to be shaped and fashioned into products to meet the various demands of life" (Cubberley, 1916, pp. 337–338).

This view was widely held over the period roughly from before World War I until very close to the outbreak of World War II. Because the concept of scientific management called for the scientific study of jobs to be performed, professors of educational administration undertook to describe and analyze what school superintendents did on the job. Fred Ayer at the University of Texas, for example, surveyed superintendents to find out what kind of work they did in 1926–1927. Nearly all reported "attending board meetings, making reports, and supervising teachers, 80 percent . . . reported that they went to the post office daily; and each week half of them operated the mimeograph machine, . . . 93 percent inspected toilets, and 93 percent inspected the janitor's work" (Tyack & Cummings, 1977, p. 61). To prepare individuals to become school superintendents, therefore, programs of study often featured courses in budgeting, heating and ventilating, methods for performing janitorial services and sanitation tasks, writing publicity releases, and record keeping. Professors of educational administration, in turn, commonly conducted studies to determine, for example, the cheapest methods of maintaining floors—such as the most efficient techniques for mopping or sweeping, oiling, and/or waxing—so that they could provide prospective school superintendents with the skills necessary to train janitorial workers.

As the study of the problems of organization, management, and administration became established more and more firmly in the universities (just as Wilson and Fayol had predicted), the principles of scientific management received increased attention and also challenge from scholars and practitioners. In particular, as the hierarchical-authoritarian notions of organizational life formalized by Taylor and his followers gained ascendancy, mounting conflict arose from the clash between the demands of the organization for submissiveness and discipline on the part of workers and the need of individuals to experience a reasonable sense of reward and satisfaction from their work. This tension was publicly manifested in the 1920s and 1930s by increasing labor unrest. Nevertheless, management specialists continued to focus on developing and refining top-down hierarchical ideas about the management of organizations.

Luther Gulick and Lyndall Urwick stand out among the many scholars who attempted to synthesize what is now known as the "classical" formulation of principles, which would be useful in developing good, functional organizations. Central to the work of these two men was the idea that elements of the organization could be grouped and related according to function, geographic location, or similar criteria. They emphasized drawing formal charts of organizations that showed the precise ways in which various offices and divisions were related. Gulick and Urwick (1937) published a widely acclaimed book in 1937 and were still highly influential after World War II (Gulick, 1948).

Scientific Management Versus Classical Organizational Theory

Frederick Taylor was an engineer who spent many years designing and perfecting the machines and machine systems of mass-production factories that were mushrooming in his day. He got into management through his concern about the unique ability of human beings to interfere with the reliability, orderly predictability, and linear logic of his beloved machine systems. Scientific management therefore focused on ways to make individuals at work more reliable, more predictable, and less prone to human failings such as fatigue. Its focus, we would say today, was on the human-machine interface.

Scientific management taught that it was important to hire the right people, train them well to work with the machine, and keep the job requirements within the physical limits of the individual. Taylor urged consideration of worker motivation and that meant, to him, only money. The motivation to work, as he saw it, was a simple economic transaction between the individual worker and the employer. Pay should be closely pegged to the difficulty of the job and the productivity achieved.

Much of what Taylor taught now seems both commonsensical and old-fashioned, almost banal. In the first quarter of the twentieth century, it was not so; these were new and powerful ideas at that time. In fact, they were widely seen as a serious threat to the American worker because they demanded the surrender of individuality and the human spirit in return for dollars.

It is testimony to Taylor's greatness that we still accept many of his ideas and have moved beyond those that have not stood the test of time. Many people are surprised to learn that Taylor was a true pioneer in connecting motivation to performance on the job. Few today think that money is the only motivator, but before Frederick Taylor few had thought of motivation as being important at all.

Classical organizational theory, in contrast to Taylorism, came to view the total organization, rather than the individual worker, as the focus of attention. Classical organizational theorists tend to view motivation as being more important than Taylor did and also as being a more nuanced concept: Money is not the only motivator for people at work. Classical theorists understand that an organization is much more than the interface of human and machine; it is a complex web of social relationships and interdependencies, and motivation often involves more than money. It includes ideals, values, beliefs, and the need for personal satisfaction. Also, classical theorists—such as Max Weber and Elton Mayo, among many others—were concerned with organizational issues such as division of labor, organizational hierarchy and power, and defined lines of authority. One can learn a great deal about classical ideas about organizational theory, leadership, and motivation from viewing films such as *Twelve O'Clock High* and *The Godfather*.

Organizational Concepts of Classical Theory

Classical organizational theorists have sought to identify and describe some set of fixed principles (in the sense of rules) that would establish the basis for management. The best known of these dealt with organizational structure. For example, central to the classical view of organization is the concept of hierarchy, which, in the jargon of classical theorists, is the *scalar principle*. (In practice it is usually referred to as line and staff.) The contention is that authority and responsibility should flow in as direct and unbroken a path as possible from the top policy level down through the organization to the lowest member. This general principle is rather widely accepted by organizational theorists today, being most often attacked because of the rigid insistence with which many classical thinkers tend to apply the concept in practice, limiting lateral relationships between parts of the organization. Thus, it is no accident that organizational charts of U.S.

school districts today frequently show vertical lines of authority and responsibility with little or no interconnection between operating divisions of the organization. The organizational chart of a typical school district shows the elementary schools reporting up the line through the director of elementary education to the superintendent, with no interconnections to the middle schools or the secondary schools. In fact, in such a district, there is ordinarily no functional connection among the three levels or divisions of the district.

Another central classical principle of organization is *unity of command*—essentially, that no one in an organization should receive orders from more than one superordinate. Fayol, a strict interpreter of this point, was sharply critical of Taylor because the latter favored something called functional foremanship, which permitted a worker to receive orders from as many as eight bosses (each being a specialist). As organizations and work became more complex over time, this principle has been greatly weakened by the need to modify it so often to meet changing conditions. The organizational charts of school districts frequently reflect this principle, although in actual operation, it is routinely ignored.

For example, a teacher of music in the elementary schools may be assigned to several schools and spend time as an itinerant going from one school to another to offer classes and organize groups in music. Although the organizational chart of the school district may show the music teacher as reporting to the director of music, and although the teacher may be formally evaluated by the director, when working in a given school this teacher actually comes under the direction of the principal. In these situations, teachers receive instructions from at least two superordinates and are held responsible by both of them—although the principal and the director may neither coordinate their interests and intentions nor be in agreement on them.

The *exception principle* holds that when the need for a decision recurs frequently, the decision should be established as a routine that can be delegated to subordinates (in the form of rules, standard operating procedures, or administrative manuals). This process frees those in higher positions from routine detail to deal with the exceptions to the rules. This principle, too, has received wide acceptance: It underlies the delegation of authority and the concept that all decisions should be made at the lowest possible level in the organization, which has proven to be the most generally applicable principle of classical theory.

Span of control is the most widely discussed of the major ideas from classical organizational theory. The essence of the concept is to prescribe (and thereby limit) the number of people reporting to a supervisor or administrator. Much of the thinking about this principle arose from military organizations, which—under highly stressful, unstable, emergency conditions—need a dependable system of control and coordination. The problems in applying the concept to other kinds of organizations have led to more controversy than understanding. Whereas many theorists suggest having a small number of people (usually between three and six) reporting to an administrator, many firms deliberately put executives in charge of larger numbers of people to force them to delegate more decision making to their subordinates.

Classical and Neoclassical Administrative Concepts

Though classical concepts of organization and administration—that is, the concepts associated with bureaucracy and scientific management—were developed early in the twentieth century and were unchallenged by competing concepts for a time, it would be incorrect to view the classical approach as something that once flourished and is now gone. Bureaucracies flourish today; government bureaucracies, such as the Internal Revenue Service and state departments of motor vehicles, are among the obvious examples encountered every day. Even in the case of nonbureaucratic organizations, however, many scholars as well as administrators essentially believe that the classical views are the best foundation for administrative practice. Many contemporary advocates of accountability programs, competency-based programs, management by objectives, and value-added evaluation models, operate from classical organizational concepts. These newer manifestations of the older classical concepts are often referred to as *neoclassical* or in some cases *neoscientific*.

The Ideas of Mary Parker Follett

The work of Mary Parker Follett (1918, 1924) was unique in the development of management thought. Her ideas were rooted in the classical traditions of organizational theory but matured in such a way that she, in effect, spanned the gap between scientific management and the early industrial psychologists. Follett's first organizational study, done for her master's thesis at Radcliffe, was a major analysis of the speakership of the House of Representatives of the United States Congress, a significant administrative and leadership position that had received little systematic study until that time. It was published as a book that was a standard in the field for years.

Then, for many years, Follett managed an innovative volunteer program in Boston that offered a large-scale program of educational and recreational opportunities in public school facilities during the afternoon and evening hours. The program was designed specifically to meet the needs of the large number of homeless boys, street kids, who lived in Boston and other major U.S. cities at the turn of the century and who badly needed safe places where they could study in the evening, receive supportive guidance, and engage in wholesome recreational activities. Much of the financial support for this volunteer social program came from business executives, and through working with them, Follett came to learn a great deal about U.S. corporate leaders and what they thought about organizations and workers. She increasingly became concerned that corporations, through their management practices, were doing much to create the problems that her programs were attempting to ameliorate. The stock market crash of 1929, followed by the Great Depression, was a galvanizing event for her and for many others that starkly illuminated the realization that large business corporations had become social institutions whose concentration of power called into question the U.S. tradition of unrestrained corporate action.

Follett, first, viewed management as a social process and, second, saw it inextricably enmeshed in the particular situation. She did not see authority as flowing from the top of the organization's hierarchy to be parceled out among those in lower ranks. It was better practice, in her view, that orders should not be given by one person; rather, all should seek to take orders from the situation itself. She saw that the administrator has three choices of ways to handle conflict: (a) by the exercise of power, (b) by compromise, or (c) by "integration" (that is, bringing the conflict into the open and seeking a mutually acceptable, win-win resolution).

In 1932, Follett sought to summarize her views by developing four principles of sound administration. The first two were *coordination by direct contact of the responsible people concerned* and *coordination in the early stages.* These clashed with the typical classical preoccupation with hierarchical communication and control: Follett advocated placing control in the hands of those in the lower levels of the organization, which requires opening up communication horizontally across the organization as well as down the hierarchy. The third principle was *coordination as the reciprocal relating of all the factors in the situation* (which laid the basis for the "law of the situation"). This point emphasized the importance of linking departments in ways that enabled them to self-adjust to the organization's needs at lower levels of the organization. Finally, *coordination as a continuing process* recognized that management is an ever-changing, dynamic process in response to emerging situations—a sharp contrast to traditional, static, classical views that sought to codify universal principles of action.

Her ideas were instrumental in modifying the trend toward rigidly structuralist views in classical management theory, provided a rationale that was helpful in ushering in the human relations movement, and pioneered conceptualizing about what today is called contingency theory.

THE HUMAN RELATIONS MOVEMENT

In time, as the principles of scientific management were applied to industry with greater care, people felt a need to be more precise about the effect of human factors on production efficiency. The Western Electric Company was one of the more enlightened industrial employers of the time and, in routine fashion, cooperated with the National Research Council in a relatively simple experiment designed to determine the optimum level of illumination in a shop for maximum production efficiency. Western Electric's Hawthorne plant near Chicago was selected for the experiment. Before the research was over, an impressive team of researchers was involved; of its members, Elton Mayo is probably the best known to educators.

The original experiment was very well designed and executed, and it revealed that there was no direct, simple relationship between the illumination level and the production output of the workers. Because one of Taylor's principles suggested strongly that there would be such a relationship, this study raised more questions than it answered.

The Western Electric Studies

The original experiment in what became known as the Western Electric Studies (often called the Hawthorne Studies) was really quite simple, but analyses of the results were complex. The question to be studied could be put this way: In a room where women sit at benches assembling devices from parts, what is the optimum level of illumination that is required for the workers to be most productive in their jobs? An experiment was designed and conducted to find out.

In 1927, the investigators divided the workers into two groups. One group was the *control group*: Throughout the experiment, their work went on as it had before, with no changes made. For the other group, the *experimental group,* there would be some experimental interventions. In this case, the interventions consisted of nothing more than installing electric lightbulbs of different sizes. They started with the rather low-wattage lamps that the workers were accustomed to and that were ordinarily used in such workshop situations, and the experimenters noted the productivity of the workers. Then they installed lightbulbs with higher illumination and recorded the productivity of the workers. Productivity rose.

Because productivity went up, and because the only change that was known to have occurred was the amount of illumination, it seemed evident that there was some causal relationship between the level of illumination and the productivity of workers. It appeared that the level of illumination might be a *cause* of variations in productivity. A reasonable hypothesis might be that productivity increases as the level of illumination increases. Or would there be some limit, some level of illumination beyond which productivity would no longer increase? Is it possible that there is an optimum level of illumination that, if exceeded, would result in declining productivity? Because the researchers had started these studies with the intention of finding the optimum illumination required for optimum output, these kinds of questions hinted at interesting hypotheses that could be confirmed or rejected only through further experimental study. The experimenters again increased the light output of the bulbs in order to see what would happen. Productivity rose.

Taylor's principles of scientific management had clearly suggested that there would be an optimum amount of illumination to trigger optimum output by the workers. But the Western Electric Studies could not find any optimal amount of illumination that was associated with maximum productivity. When the wattage of the bulbs in the work areas was increased, the productivity of the workers increased. But when the wattage of the bulbs was held steady, productivity continued to rise. The confused experimenters undertook studies in which the amount of illumination was actually *reduced,* and productivity did not decline. Meanwhile, the people in the control group continued working at the same rate of productivity that they had experienced before the studies. The experiments did not confirm any of the hypotheses that were being tested. Something was afoot here, and those who were in control of the studies did not know what it was.

Quietly, one of the breakthrough moments of modern organizational behavior had arisen. After pondering the surprising results from the initial series of studies, the investigators drew up a list of six questions that clearly revealed a broadening of their concept of the working environment and its impact on human behavior. The questions also revealed deepening awareness of possible connections between productivity and the attitudes and beliefs of workers as well as their physical selves. The questions that sparked the continuation of the Hawthorne Studies were these:

1. Do employees actually become tired?
2. Are pauses for rest desirable?
3. Is a shorter working day desirable?
4. What is the attitude of employees toward their work and toward the company?
5. What is the effect of changing the type of working equipment?
6. Why does production decrease in the afternoon?

These were rather simple, straightforward questions, but it was obvious that the answers to a number of them would be psychological rather than physical in nature. These questions triggered one of the most far-reaching series of experiments in the history of administration; they became known as the Western Electric Studies and led to discoveries that are not yet fully understood. However unexpected it may have been, one major finding of these studies was the realization that human variability is an important determinant of productivity. Thus, in the 1920s, the basis for the human relations movement was established (Roethlisberger & Dickson, 1939).

New concepts were now available to the administrator to use in practice. Among them were (a) morale, (b) group dynamics, (c) democratic supervision, (d) personnel relations, and (e) behavioral concepts of motivation. The human relations movement emphasized human and interpersonal factors in administering the affairs of organizations. Supervisors, in particular, drew heavily on human relations concepts, stressing notions such as democratic procedures, involvement, motivational techniques, and the sociometry of leadership.

Sociometry

The human relations movement attracted social and behavioral scientists, particularly group dynamicists who had already been studying the human behavior of individuals interacting with one another in dyads and in groups. Numerous studies carried out in group and organizational settings laid the groundwork for better understanding of the nature of human groups and how they

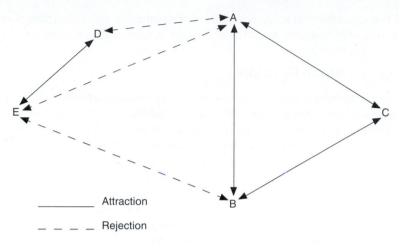

_____ Attraction

_ _ _ _ Rejection

FIGURE 3.1 Simple Sociogram of Five-Person Group

function. Illustrative of the better early work of group dynamicists is that of Jacob Moreno, who developed and refined the techniques of sociometric analysis. Moreno sensed that within groups are informal subgroups—identifiable clusters of people that form essentially on the basis of how much they like or dislike one another (Moreno, 1947). Moreno developed techniques of gathering information from members of organizations about the attraction they had for one another; the data were often gathered by interview, but other techniques (such as simple questionnaires) also were used. From such information, *sociograms* were developed that portrayed the dynamics of the *informal social structure* of human groups. A typical sociogram of a group of five people might look like Figure 3.1. By asking the members of the group simple questions (such as: with whom are you most willing to work?), it is possible to ascertain a great deal about the informal social structure of the group.

Behavior Patterns in Groups

Another fruitful line of investigation emanating from the human relations approach was the work of Robert Bales. He developed a systematic technique for analyzing the patterns of interaction among the members of a group. Essentially, Bales's interaction analysis technique consisted of recording key facts about the discussions that occurred between individuals: how many took place between specific individuals, who initiated them, which of these were between two individuals and which were addressed to the group as a whole, and so on (Bales, 1950). Bales's work not only provided a workable technique that others could use to study the interaction patterns of groups; it also permitted him to draw some generalizations about groups that have proved to be useful.

For example, Bales was the first to document that successful groups tend to include people who play two key roles:

1. It is necessary for someone (or perhaps several individuals in a group) to keep the group focused on *accomplishing its task*;
2. It is necessary for someone to see that the group pays attention to *maintaining productive human relations* within the group.

These two dimensions of group behavior—task orientation and maintenance orientation—have proved to be of lasting value in understanding the dynamics of group functioning.

Leadership as a Group Function

Leadership has long been a subject of great interest to those concerned with organizations, and social scientists were not long in realizing that—unlike the classical view—leadership is not something that "great people" or individuals with formal legal authority provide for their subordinates; rather, it is a process involving dynamic interaction with subordinates. Benjamin Wolman (1956), for example, found that members of groups tend to elect to leadership positions those individuals who are perceived to have the ability (or "power") to satisfy the needs of the group and who are, at the same time, perceived as ready to accept the responsibility. Bales (1953) noted that groups tend to confer leadership on individuals not so much on the basis of how well they are liked as on the basis of the ideas that the individuals contribute to the groups and the help that they give the groups in carrying out the ideas. Helen Jennings (1950) found that dominant, aggressive people are not likely to be perceived by group members as leaders but, in fact, are likely to be rejected and isolated by the group.

These few examples may serve in this discussion to illustrate some of the kinds of sociological, psychological, and social-psychological investigations that were undertaken in large numbers during the human relations era. This was a time when, in fact, social psychology began to mature as a scientific and academic discipline. Kurt Lewin (1939, 1947) contributed richly to studies of organizational behavior during this period, especially in the area of group decision making. More important, Lewin developed crucial insights and theoretical views that were of great help to those who came after him. His work and that of his students, for example, inspired the laboratory method of personal growth training (that is, T-groups or sensitivity training), which in turn laid the basis for the contemporary practice of organization development (discussed later in this book).

Muzafer Sherif (1948), whose studies of street gangs as human social systems became landmarks of insight and research methodology, went on to produce one of the early textbooks in social psychology. George Homans (*The Human Group*, 1950), Felix Roethlisberger (*Management and Morale*, 1950), William Foote Whyte (*Human Relations in the Restaurant Industry*, 1948), Fritz Redl (*Group Emotion and Leadership*, 1942), Philip Selznick (*The Leader as the Agent of the Led*, 1951), and Alvin W. Gouldner (*Studies in Leadership*, 1950) are only a few of the more famous contributors to the outpouring of theory and research during this period that was to establish an irreversible trend in thought and understanding about behavior in human organizations.

In U.S. education, the human relations movement had relatively little impact on school district administrators (for example, superintendents of schools), as compared with a substantial impact on supervisory and school site levels (for example, supervisors, school principals). In general, superintendents continued to emphasize classical concepts such as hierarchical control, authority, and formal organization, whereas supervisors emphasized, to a much greater extent, human relations concepts such as morale, group cohesiveness, collaboration, and the dynamics of informal organization. A review of the proceedings and publications of representative organizations, such as the American Association of School Administrators (AASA) and the Association for Supervision and Curriculum Development (ASCD) readily reveals that, for the most part, those who saw their roles as educational administrators tended to emphasize attention to budgets, politics, control, and the asymmetrical exercise of power from the top down, whereas those who were primarily concerned with instruction and curriculum placed much more emphasis on participation and communication and deemphasized status-power relationships. This difference in emphasis persisted at least into the 1980s, although gradually most administrators moved somewhat to embrace human relations ideas.

The Paradox of Organizational Structure

So much has been said and written about organizational structure that many people have come to think of organizations as real, tangible, and concrete: almost like buildings, with their foundations deep in the earth and their structures soaring aloft. But organizations are not real. They exist merely as concepts in our minds and in the minds of other people. As much as anything, organizations are social conventions. Palpable though they may seem, they cannot be touched or grasped; you cannot seize an organization in your hand or weigh it, kick it, or measure it. Organizations are human inventions and only concepts at that. If you learn nothing else about organizations, this is one basic bedrock idea that you must learn. *Organizations are what we think they are and what others think they are.*

THE ORGANIZATIONAL THEORY MOVEMENT

Classical and bureaucratic approaches to organizations tend not only to emphasize organizational structure and the highly rational logic of hierarchical control over people but also to reify these concepts, treating the organization as tangible, concrete, touchable, and nearly living. In the early literature on organization, this was called the *formal* organization. Today, it is generally known as *structuralism.* Structuralists tend to think that a properly structured organization will improve organizational performance. When we combine small school districts into larger ones, adopt school-based management, or modify the interface between elementary schools and high schools by creating middle schools, structuralist thought is guiding our administrative practice.

But the organization, with all its formal structure and the rules and regulations to interpret and reinforce that structure, is populated by human beings, with their very human and personal beliefs, attitudes, assumptions, hopes, and fears. The inner states of these people, collectively, go a long way to make the organization what it actually is. Thus, psychological thinking enters the study of organization and administration. Those who emphasize this concept of organization are convinced that changes in the relations between and among human beings in the organization have enormous power to affect the performance of the organization. This is variously called the *informal* organization or, as it was indelibly labeled in 1960, the *human side* of the organization (McGregor, 1960). Today, it is often referred to simply as *people approaches* to organization. When we seek to involve people more fully in making decisions that affect them, attend to their motivational needs more adequately, or increase collegiality and collaboration through teamwork, we are using people approaches to organizational problems.

In the 5-year period between 1937 and 1942, however, three significant books laid the groundwork for what was to develop during the post-World War II era into a new major influence on thought and practice in administration. The first of these landmark books was Chester Barnard's *The Functions of the Executive,* which appeared in 1938. Barnard, a vice president of the New Jersey Bell Telephone Company, selected and integrated concepts from the many schools of thought that had appeared since the publication of Woodrow Wilson's essay, *The Study of Administration,* and he introduced a number of new insights of his own. Barnard was in close communication with the scientists who conducted the Western Electric Studies. One of his most important contributions, and one that is germane to this discussion, was to illuminate the crucial importance of better understanding the relationship between the formal organization and the informal organization. In this pioneer work, Barnard (1938) made it clear that (a) it was illusory to focus exclusively on the formal, official, structural facets of administering organizations and (b) the effective executive must attend to the interaction between the needs and aspirations of the workers, on the one hand, and the needs and purposes of the organization, on the other.

The next year, the second of these three significant books appeared: *Management and the Worker,* by Felix J. Roethlisberger and William J. Dickson (1939). These two scholars presented a new view of the dynamic mutual interaction between the formal organization and the informal organization. Based on evidence gathered from the Western Electric Company research, the authors described and documented, for example, the surprising sophistication of the informal organization and its power to exercise control over not only the behavior of workers but also (without their realizing it) over the behavior of supervisors and managers (who thought that they were exercising the control). Their emphasis on "individual needs, informal groups, and social relationships was quickly endorsed by other social scientists and led to a 'philosophy of management' concerned primarily with human relationships in formal organizations" (Cartwright, 1965, p. 2).

The third of these early books was Herbert A. Simon's *Administrative Behavior: A Study of Decision-Making Processes in Administrative Organizations,* which was published in 1947. Even the title, with its emphasis on behavior, foreshadowed a fresh approach to understanding administrative practice. Simon—a professor with a strong background in political science, psychology, and business administration—sought to illuminate the importance of human behavior in critical administrative processes such as making decisions. This book (Simon, 1947), more than any other, established a fresh new concept of administration and set the pace for social and behavioral scientists who sensed in the post-World War II era that there was great promise in this new approach.

Although the adherents of classical and human relations approaches did not vanish in the years that followed, the most vigorous administrative research was in the areas of extending and developing the newer behavioral concepts. Scientists from a number of disciplines, or traditions, were to publish a steady stream of research and theory during the ensuing years. A list of a few of the better-known books published in the 1950s and 1960s, roughly classified by the academic tradition of their authors and listed chronologically within these classifications, presents a rather clear overview of the way the field developed:

Psychology and Social Psychology

ALVIN W. GOULDNER, ED., *Studies in Leadership* (1950)

CHRIS ARGYRIS, *Personality and Organization* (1958)

BERNARD M. BASS, *Leadership, Psychology, and Organizational Behavior* (1960)

MUZAFIR SHERIF, ED., *Intergroup Relations and Leadership* (1962)

RENSIS LIKERT, *The Human Organization: Its Management and Value* (1967)

Sociology

AMITAI ETZIONI, *A Comparative Analysis of Complex Organizations* (1961)

PETER M. BLAU and W. RICHARD SCOTT, *Formal Organizations* (1962)

CHARLES PERROW, *Organizational Analysis: A Sociological View* (1970)

Anthropology

William Foote Whyte, *Men at Work* (1961)

Eliot Dismore Chapple and Leonard R. Sayles, *The Measure of Management* (1961)

Harry F. Wolcott, *The Man in the Principal's Office* (1973)

Political Science

Victor A. Thompson, *Modern Organization* (1961)

Robert V. Presthus, *The Organizational Society* (1962)

Marilyn Gittel, *Participants and Participation: A Study of School Policy in New York City* (1967)

Management

Douglas McGregor, *The Human Side of Enterprise* (1960)

Rensis Likert, *New Patterns of Management* (1961)

Alfred J. Marrow, David G. Bowers, and Stanley E. Seashore, *Management by Participation* (1967)

Human Relations and Organizational Behavior

The term *human relations* is a broad one that refers to the interactions between people in all kinds of situations in which they seek, through mutual action, to achieve some purpose. Thus, it can be properly applied to two people seeking to develop a happy and productive life together, a social club, a business firm, a school, an entire government, or even a whole society. The social structure that regulates the human interactions that are the subject of human relations may be formal, clear, and readily apparent (for example, a government, a firm), or it may be informal, even diffuse, and therefore difficult to describe accurately (for example, the power structure of a group of prison inmates, the social system of a school faculty, a neighborhood).

   Organizational behavior is a narrower, more precise term that falls under the broader, more general meaning of human relations. *Organizational behavior is a discipline that seeks to describe, understand, and predict human behavior in the environment of formal organizations.* A distinctive contribution and characteristic of organizational behavior as a discipline is the explicit recognition that (a) organizations create contextual settings, or environments, that have great influence on the behavior of people in them and that (b), to some extent, the internal environment of an organization is influenced by the larger context in which the organization itself exists (for example, the social, political, economic, and technological systems that support the organization). The internal environment or context of the organization (which is so influential in eliciting and shaping human behavior) is not merely physical and tangible but also includes the social and psychological characteristics of the living human system.

   Management and administration necessarily must bear responsibility for establishing internal arrangements of the organization to achieve maximum effectiveness. In the early years of the study of human relations, it was common for managers and administrators to speak of the human relations of employees or human relations of the firm as though the organization and the wellsprings of its employees' behavior were separate though related. Contemporary administrative science, on the other hand, views goal-directed organizational behavior as essential to results-oriented, cooperative endeavors that cannot be teased out from the management policies and administrative practices of the system.

Educational administration was little affected by the evolution of administration as a field of study until the middle of the twentieth century, largely because the teaching of educational administration was sequestered from the mainstreams of scholarly thought and research. Schools of education in even the most prestigious universities tended to have almost no contact with the business schools and the behavioral science departments on their own campuses. Traditionally, educational administration had been taught by former school superintendents whose knowledge of their subject came largely from years of hard-earned experience in the frontlines. Courses in educational administration tended to focus on practical, how-to-do-it problems, drawing on the past experience of practicing administrators. Emphasis was typically given to sharing the techniques of these administrators for solving problems—techniques that had been tried in school districts such as the ones with which the students were familiar.

Research in educational administration during the first half of the twentieth century consisted principally of status studies of current problems or the gathering of opinion. With rare exceptions, little research in educational administration dealt with the testing of theoretical propositions, and almost none of it involved the insights and research methods that had been developed by behavioral scientists. As Van Miller (1965) observed:

> A lot of the study of administration has been a matter of looking backward or sideways at what was done or what is being done. It is striking to contemplate how much administrative experience has been exchanged and how little it has been studied scientifically. The current excitement arises from the fact that within recent years educational administration has become a field of study and of development as well as a vocation. (pp. 544–545)

By the mid-1950s, a new concept of organization was gaining wide acceptance among students of educational administration. This new concept recognized the dynamic interrelationships between (a) the structural characteristics of the organization and (b) the personal characteristics of the individual. It sought to understand the behavior of people at work in terms of the dynamic interrelationships between the organizational structure and the people who populated it.

Using this insight, students of organization began to conceptualize organizations—such as school systems and schools—as *social systems*. Although it is true that nearly any human group constitutes a human social system (including groups as diverse as street gangs, hobby clubs, and church congregations), the concept that began to emerge in this post–World War II era was that *organizations* constitute a *particular kind* of social system: Essentially, they are characterized by a clear and relatively strong *formal* structure. For example, unlike informal human social systems such as the office bowling team or the secretaries who eat lunch together, school systems and schools (and, indeed, all formal organizations) may be characterized as follows (Abbott, 1966):

1. They are specifically goal-oriented.
2. The work to be done to achieve goals is divided into subtasks and assigned as official duties to established positions in the organization.
3. These positions are arranged hierarchically in the formal organization, and authority relationships are clearly established.

4. General and impersonal organizational rules govern, to a large extent, what people do in their official capacity and also, to a large extent, shape and delimit the interpersonal interactions of people in the organization.

Beginning in the mid-1950s, increasing effort was expended to better understand the relationships among (a) these characteristics of organizational structure, (b) the personality (and consequent "needs") of individuals in the organization, and (c) behavior on the job. For example, numerous studies of leader behavior conducted in the 1950s and 1960s revealed remarkable agreement on the point that leadership can best be understood in terms of two specific kinds of behavior: (a) behavior that gives structure to the work of the group (for example, how the work is to be done, when, by whom, and so forth) and (b) behavior that is perceived by subordinates as showing consideration for the subordinates as human beings. These empirically derived insights were widely applied to business, industry, the military, and many other kinds of organizations, as well as to school systems and schools (Hemphill & Coons, 1950; Halpin & Winer, 1952; Halpin, 1956).

The generalization that seemed to arise from empirical tests of this view was that one leadership style promised to be more effective than any other, namely, a style characterized by behavior that emphasized *both* initiating structure *and* consideration for people. In this way, of course, both the demands of the organization and the needs of individuals in dealing with the organization would be met. One study typical of this period by Daniel Griffiths (1969), using the popular social systems model, found that school principals who displayed a style that emphasized concern for people tended to view teachers as professionals to a greater extent than did principals who stressed the role of initiating structure in the work group.

In the years from roughly 1955 to 1970, there was a great outpouring of theorizing and research in educational administration that explored the basic concepts of social system (either explicitly or implicitly) as applied to public school systems and schools. Neal Gross (1958), using sociological methods of inquiry, sought to illuminate the reasons school board members and school superintendents in New England made the decisions that they did. Daniel Griffiths (1959) initiated landmark work on decision making in educational administration that added considerably to our understanding of the importance of the decision-making behavior of administrators. One of many studies based on Griffiths's work, for example, suggests that if the administrator confines him- or herself to establishing clear processes and procedures for making decisions (rather than actually making the final decisions), the administrator's behavior will be more acceptable to subordinates.

A team of researchers who were especially interested in understanding the processes of curriculum change in schools conducted a study to explore the following question: To what extent do administrators and teachers in a given school system tend to agree or disagree in their perceptions of decision-making roles and responsibilities? Among the many findings arising from this complex and comprehensive study, one of the most outstanding—according to Griffiths—was that consideration for subordinates is more valuable behavior for the superintendent to exhibit than behavior intended to initiate structure in the group.

University graduate programs of study for educational administrators soon reflected the influence of social and behavioral science views of organizational behavior. In many cases, courses featuring some of the newer behavioral views—such as leadership, motivation, decision making, organizational climate, conflict management, and organizational change—took their place alongside courses on budgeting; financing; law; and school plant, site, and facilities. It soon became standard practice for writers of textbooks on the school principalship, general administration, and personnel administration to attempt to establish the relevance of organizational behavior research and concepts to the specific areas that the book addressed. Many professors, in their research and consulting activities, used these new ideas in their analysis of practical problems in actual schools, as well as in the design of in-service training activities.

Final Thoughts

Much of the current debate about school reform and educational leadership—whether in academic literature, in the popular press, or in discussions between practitioners—manifests different, frequently incompatible ideas about the nature of schools as organizations and the behavior of people who work in them. This debate has its roots in the larger debate about whether organizations are best understood as hierarchical, bureaucratic systems or as collegial, collaborative systems. That debate emerged in the first half of the twentieth century with the publication of the Western Electric Studies and has been continually stimulated by the growth and spread of research in group dynamics and human resources development. Though the human resources view has steadily grown in influence in the realms of business and the military as well as in education, many individuals in executive and leadership positions still cling to classical notions of hierarchical power relationships. It is important for the student of education to be aware of this fact, and it is especially important to examine the issues and make a clear personal commitment on where to stand on those issues as a guide to professional practice in educational leadership.

The struggle to develop understanding of human resources approaches to organizational behavior has led to the development of a number of theoretical views that can be helpful in clarifying issues confronting the educational leader. Chapter 4 examines a number of the newer views.

Reflective Activities

1. Examine the concepts from this chapter related to scientific management, bureaucratic organizational theory, and classical organizational theory. Which concepts, if any, do you believe are viable for today's schools? Describe why you believe these can still be effective.

2. Organizations have elements of scientific management, bureaucratic organizational theory, classical organizational theory, and/or human relations concepts that predominate. Using the concepts presented in this chapter, describe the management model of the organization (for example, school) where you are employed. In your opinion, is the existing model of management in your school or work environment the most effective for the organization? If so, explain why. What specific outcomes do you believe are attributable to this model of management? If it is not a desirable organizational model, what would you suggest as an alternative?

3. Complete a sociogram of the teachers and administrators in your grade level, department, and/or school, whichever is most helpful to you in analyzing informal relationship structures. Analyze the results in terms of how many informal groups exist and the size of these groups. Are they influential? Are they loners? Are they connected to the formal decision-making structure of the school?

4. *Working on Your Game Plan.* This text described two different approaches to understanding organizations and behavior. One is from the classical perspective (organizations are characteristically hierarchical and bureaucratic), and the other is from the human relations perspective (organizations are characteristically collegial and collaborative). In our present era of school reform, both of these perspectives are alive and well and competing for your attention and your allegiance as a leader. Write a paragraph for your game plan about exercising leadership in schools. Express your thoughts and present commitment on two issues:

   • What ideas from these two perspectives on organization and human behavior do you find most useful in analyzing the problems of being a leader in schools? How would you translate those ideas into things that you do (or how you would do them) as a leader on the job?

   • What connection do you perceive between the ideas that you discussed and present-day human problems in the schools (such as motivation, student achievement, or morale)?

CRITICAL INCIDENT   A Philosophical Disagreement on Administration

Jason is a new student at the local state university working on his master's degree in educational leadership. He intends to be a principal and eventually a superintendent like his father. Throughout his youth, he heard many stories from his father about dealing with teachers and other school professionals. He idolized his father and now holds his father's teachings as important life lessons in leadership.

In Jason's first class in organizational development, the professor introduced concepts about the importance of developing leadership among all stakeholders in the organization, involving stakeholders in the change process, and using collaborative decision making in all important decisions. Never one to shy away from an argument, Jason raised his hand and when called on stated, "I respectfully disagree. My father was a successful school superintendent in the 1980s and a principal for 20 years before that. He taught me how to run a school, and frankly, he would disagree with everything you said. He told me about the problems of allowing teachers to be involved in decisions, particularly those in the union. They were always trying to run the schools, and that if you gave an inch, they would just continue to grab as much power as they can. He said that administrators must maintain control of decisions and not let anyone take that power away. My father would say that administrators set the goals, establish the procedures, and tell the workers how to get the job done. Getting others involved in the decision just slows down change and winds up with bad decisions. The principals I had as a kid worked for my father and they were in total control. Our schools were good. We all learned, and there weren't terrible behavior problems like you have today."

Muriel chimed in, saying, "Yes, that's the way things are done in the real world. I've been teaching for nine years now, and what I do is I sit through the grade-level meetings and not get too involved. I'm friendly and sociable with everyone but I've learned that, frankly what goes on there is window-dressing. And every time the principal 'consults with his colleagues,' the teachers, he always knows what he wants and, while he's a nice guy and I like him, we always wind up agreeing with whatever he wants to do. So what I do is, when the meetings are over, I go to my classroom, shut the door, and teach in the quiet and privacy of my own room. And except for those occasional interruptions blasting out from the intercom boombox, that's where teaching is meaningful and almost fun for me. Working with kids is what it's all about for me."

1. Do you agree or disagree with Jason and Muriel?
2. If you agree, defend your position.
3. If you disagree, tell why. Does the professor make any valid points?
4. Would you agree with Jason that schools were administered somewhat differently in the past than they are today?

Suggested Reading

Callahan, R. E. (1962). *Education and the cult of efficiency*. Chicago, IL: University of Chicago Press.

This book recounts the events of an early period in the twentieth century when U.S. business and industrial leaders sought to improve public schooling by forcing school boards across the country to adopt their organizational values and goals. If you think that what goes around comes around, you will find a powerful message for today in this fascinating account.

Etzioni, A. (1964). *Modern organizations*. Englewood Cliffs, NJ: Prentice-Hall.

A remarkably lucid, easy-to-read explanation of the fundamentals of modern organizational thought. Truly a classic in the literature of organization and behavior.

Morgan, G. (1986). *Images of organization*. Beverly Hills, CA: Sage Publications.

This well-written book describes seven different ways of thinking about organizations, using metaphors for organizations such as machines, political systems, cultures, and so on. The author describes the advantages and disadvantages of using each metaphor.

Rothewell, W. J., & Sullivan, R. L. (2005). *Practicing organizational development: A guide for consultants* (2nd ed.). Hoboken, NJ: Pfeiffer: A Wiley Imprint.

This book, first published in 1995, includes chapters from many of the authors we highlight, such as Margaret Wheatley, Edgar Schein, and Robert Tannenbaum. It includes both theory, hands-on activities, and cases that can be used to help schools undergoing organizational development processes.

References

Abbott, M. G. (1966). Intervening variables in organizational behavior. *Educational Administration Quarterly 1*(1), 1–14.

Bales, R. F. (1950). *Interaction-process analysis: A method for the study of small groups.* Reading, MA: Addison-Wesley.

Bales, R. F. (1953). The equilibrium problem in small groups. In T. Parsons, R. Bales, & E. Shils (Eds.), *Working papers in the theory of action* (pp. 111–161). Glencoe, IL: Free Press.

Barnard, C. I. (1938). *The functions of the executive.* Cambridge, MA: Harvard University Press.

Callahan, R. E. (1962). *Education and the cult of efficiency.* Chicago, IL: University of Chicago Press.

Cartwright, D. (1965). Influence, leadership, control. In J. March (Ed.), *Handbook of organizations* (pp. 1–47). Chicago, IL: Rand McNally.

Cubberley, E. P. (1916). *Public school administration: A statement of the fundamental principles underlying the organization and administration of public education.* Boston, MA: Houghton Mifflin.

Etzioni, A. (1964). *Modern organizations.* Englewood Cliffs, NJ: Prentice-Hall.

Fayol, H. (1949). *General and industrial management* (C. Storrs, Trans.). London: Sir Isaac Pitman & Sons.

Follett, M. P. (1918). *The new state: Group organization, the solution of popular government.* New York, NY: Longmans, Green.

Follett, M. P. (1924). *Creative experience.* New York, NY: Longmans, Green.

Griffiths, D. (1969). Administrative theory. In R. L. Ebel (Ed.), *Encyclopedia of educational research* (pp. 17–22). Toronto, Canada: Macmillan.

Griffiths, D. E. (1959). *Administrative theory.* New York, NY: Appleton-Century-Crofts.

Gross, N. (1958). *Who runs our schools?* New York, NY: John Wiley & Sons.

Gulick, L. (1948). *Administrative reflection on World War II.* Tuscaloosa, AL: University of Alabama Press.

Gulick, L., & Urwick, L. (Eds.). (1937). *Papers on the science of administration.* New York, NY: Institute of Public Administration, Columbia University.

Hall, R. H. (1963). The concept of bureaucracy: An empirical assessment. *American Journal of Sociology, 69*(1), 33.

Halpin, A. W. (1956). The behavior of leaders. *Educational Leadership, 14,* 172–176.

Halpin, A. W., & Winer, B. J. (1952). *The leadership behavior of the airplane commander.* Columbus, OH: Ohio State University Press.

Hemphill, J. K., & Coons, A. E. (1950). *Leader behavior description.* Columbus, OH: Ohio State University Press.

Jennings, H. H. (1950). *Leadership and Isolation* (2nd ed.). New York: Longman.

Lewin, K. (1939). Field theory and experiment in social psychology: Concepts and methods. *American Journal of Sociology, 44,* 868–896.

Lewin, K. (1947) Group decision and social change. In T. M. Newcomb & E. L. Hartley (Eds.), *Readings in social psychology* (pp. 330–344). New York, NY: Holt, Rinehart & Winston.

Mayer, J. P. (1943). *Max Weber and German politics.* London, England: Faber & Faber.

McGregor, D. (1960). *The human side of enterprise.* New York, NY: McGraw-Hill.

Miller, V. (1965). *The public administration of American school systems.* New York, NY: Macmillan.

Moreno, J. L. (1947). Contributions of sociometry to research methodology in sociology. *American Sociological Review, 12,* 287–292.

Roethlisberger, F. J., & Dickson, W. J. (1939). *Management and the worker.* Cambridge, MA: Harvard University Press.

Sherif, M. (1948). *An outline of social psychology.* New York, NY: Harper & Row.

Simon, H. A. (1947). *Administrative behavior: A study of decision-making processes in administrative organizations.* New York, NY: Free Press.

Taylor, F. (1911). *The principles of scientific management.* New York, NY: Harper & Row.

Tyack, D. B., & Cummings, R. (1977). Leadership in American public schools before 1954: Historical configurations and conjectures. In L. Cunningham, W. Hack, & R. Nystrand (Eds.), *Educational administration: The developing decades* (pp. 46-66). Berkeley, CA: McCutchan.

Wolman, B. (1956). Leadership and group dynamics. *Journal of Social Psychology 43,* 11–25.

CHAPTER 4

A Systems Approach to Organization

In Chapter 1, we emphasized two major overarching theoretical ways that leaders think about schools as organizations: One is traditional bureaucratic theory and the other is more recent human resources theory. We also described McGregor's Theory X and Theory Y, which clarifies the very different assumptions that leaders hold about people at work in organizations that cause them to choose to follow one or the other of these two very different approaches. In this text, we briefly describe and discuss six widely used theoretical frameworks *that build on and extend the three fundamental organizational theories outlined in Chapter 1.*

Describing theoretical models of organizational life is a great deal like the electronic version of chalk-talk diagrams that a television commentator uses during a football game. They can lay out and describe the concepts that underlie the game, but they must be understood in the context of the uncertainty and unpredictability that are always present in human endeavor. Models are useful for giving you a mental road map of how organizations work, something that you can use in the practical business of sorting out organizational issues, and how to be an effective leader in dealing with them. Thus, theories and models are helpful in clarifying important issues involving organizational behavior. But they are not *literal* depictions of an organizational mechanism, as they are sometimes mistakenly taken to be.

For example, some people have rhapsodized about systems theories of organizations using the metaphor of old-fashioned clockworks, in which pendulums swing with unerring predictability, gears whir, springs unwind, and other parts all move synchronously in near-perfect predictable relationships to produce the desired result, namely, to tell the correct time. Organizations, especially educational organizations, are human endeavors, and—to the despair of those seeking simplicity, precision, system, order, and certainty—cannot be reduced to mechanistic systems. Understanding that we are dealing with *human social systems* is basic to knowing how to deal effectively with them.

ORGANIZATIONAL STRUCTURE AND PEOPLE

A major theme, perhaps the dominant one, in organizational theory for well over a half-century has been the interaction between organizational structure and people. It can be argued, for example, that the structure of an organization is the prime determinant of the behavior of people in the organization. For example, one study stated:

[O]ne of the persistent complaints in the field of penology, or juvenile correctional institutions, or mental hospitals, or any of the "people-changing" institutions is the need for better workers. Their problems, we hear, stem from the lack of high-quality personnel. More specifically, the types of individuals they can recruit as guards, or cottage parents, or orderlies typically have too little education, hold over-simplified views about people, tend to be punitive, and believe that order and discipline can solve all problems. (Perrow, 1970, pp. 3–4)

However, in this study, Perrow described previous research in which applicants for positions in a juvenile correction institution were tested and found to be quite enlightened and permissive, but after they had worked in the institution for a while, they became less permissive and showed a punitive, unenlightened view regarding the causes of delinquency and the care and handling of delinquents. Such is the power of organizations to shape the views and attitudes—and thus behavior—of participants.

Nevertheless much of the literature of organizational theory is devoted to the belief that the people in the organization tend to shape the structure of the organization. This ideology focuses attention on the impact of the behavior of people—in the processes of making decisions, leading, and dealing with conflict—on the structure, values, and customs of organizations. Attention has been devoted increasingly to strategies for improving the performance of organizations not by changing their structures as a way of inducing more effective organizational behavior, but by dealing with participants in ways that bring about desirable changes in the structure of the organization and—more important—in the character and quality of the social environment in which people work. *We are talking about changing the organizational culture and the organizational climate of the school.*

General Systems Theory

Attempts to describe, explain, and predict organizational behavior generally depend—as does all modern scientific thought—on systems theory. A biologist, Ludwig von Bertalanffy (1950), is generally credited with having first described what is now known as general systems theory. Here is one way to describe the basic concepts of general systems theory (Lwoff, 1966, p. 1216):

> An organism is an integrated system of interdependent structures and functions. An organism is constituted of cells and a cell consists of molecules which must work in harmony. . . . Each molecule must know what the others are doing. Each one must be capable of receiving messages and must be sufficiently disciplined to obey. You are familiar with the laws that control regulation. You know how our ideas have developed and how the most harmonious and sound of them have been fused into a conceptual whole which is the very foundation of biology and confers on it its unity.

This passage captures the basic way of thinking about complex situations that is now generally used in both the physical and the social sciences. If we substitute *organization* for organism, *group* for cell, and *person* for molecule in the above statement about biology, it has relevance for thinking about organizations (Berrien, 1976, p. 43):

> An *organization* is an integrated system of interdependent structures and functions. An *organization* is constituted of *groups* and a *group* consists of *persons* who must work in harmony. Each *person* must know what the others are doing. Each one must be capable of receiving messages and must be sufficiently disciplined to obey.

Take a simple example. A young child might think of a nearby pond as a wonderful playground, away from the ever-watchful eyes of grown-ups. A fisherman might see it as a great place in which to fill his creel. A farmer might think of it as a good source of water for irrigating crops. A biologist, however, would tend to view the pond as a system of living things, all of which are interdependent in many ways and all of which are dependent in some ways on the larger environment in which the pond exists (for example, the air and sunlight). In terms of understanding the pond and being able to describe it, it is obvious that we are dealing with different levels of insight. However, in terms of being able to predict more accurately the consequences of things that might be done to the pond—such as pumping a large volume of water from it or removing large numbers of its fish—the biologist clearly has the advantage when he or she thinks of the pond as a system.

It is this advantage in dealing with cause and effect that has made systems theory so powerful in the study of organizational behavior. There is a strong tendency in our culture to ascribe single causes to events; in fact, the causes of even relatively simple organizational events are often complex. We may be unwilling to accept this fact and, as a way of rejecting it, choose to apply simplistic cause-and-effect logic to our problems.

This point was illustrated by congressional interest in reducing automobile accidents in this country, which started out by concentrating on the automobile as a primary cause of accidents. From this flowed a logical line of thought: If we require automobile manufacturers to improve the design of their cars and install certain mechanical safety features, the result would be a reduction in the carnage on our highways.

In fact, however, more careful study seemed to show that automobile accidents are caused by an enormously complex, interrelated set of variables. Automobile design is one, but others include road conditions and intangible factors such as social mores and the psychological state of the driver. As we dig behind each of these conditions (for example: Why was the road built that way? Why was the driver talking on a cell phone? Why didn't the driver yield the right of way?), we find that each is part of a complex set of interrelated factors of its own. Clearly, significant

BOX 4.1

Peter Senge and the Fifth Discipline

New ways of thinking are required in a world that is dominated by change; ambiguity; and the need for nimble, sure-footed organizational performance. Under those conditions, schools must become quick learners. In some very popular publications over the years, Peter Senge has sought to clarify how systems thinking is essential in helping an educational organization become a learning organization. Senge calls systems thinking the fifth discipline because he sees it as essential to integrate with four other disciplines: personal mastery, mental models, team learning, and shared vision. "Within every school district, community, or classroom," Senge (2000) wrote, "there might be dozens of different systems worthy of notice: the governance process of the district, the impact of particular policies, the labor-management relationship, curriculum development, the approaches to disciplining students, and the prevailing modes of staff behavior. Every child's life is a system. Every educational practice is a system" (p.78). In this complex environment, Senge believes, people who have experience with systems thinking can act with more leverage than a short-attention-span culture generally permits.

reduction in automobile accidents must eventually require analysis of the interrelated factors of these complex subsystems of causative factors.

Systems theory should put us on guard against the strong tendency to ascribe phenomena to a single causative factor. Similarly, if our car is not running well, we often take what is, in effect, a systems approach to the problem: We get a tune-up from someone who understands the functions and interrelatedness of the subsystems (for example, the ignition system, the fuel system, the exhaust system) that comprise the engine.

These two concepts—the concept of subsystems and the concept of multiple causation—are central to systems theory.

Social Systems Theory

Systems can be divided into two main classes: open systems, which interact with their environments, and closed systems, which do not interact with their environments. Social systems theory generally deals with open systems because it is almost impossible to envisage a social system, such as a school, that is not interactive with its environment. When observers describe certain schools or school systems as closed systems, they generally mean that those organizations tend to try to limit the influence of the community and tend to proceed as though unrelated to the larger real world in which they exist. Thus, we often describe unresponsive school systems that resist constructive change as closed systems. Though this criticism has a certain ring of credibility, it is technically impossible. The input-output relationship of the school to its larger environment is an endless cyclical interaction between the school and its larger environment.

Figure 4.1 shows this interactive process as involving (a) *inputs* from the larger societal environment (for example, knowledge that exists in that society, social and community values, goals that are desired, and money available), (b) the *process* that occurs within the social system we call a school (involving subsystems of organizational structure, people, technology, and work tasks), and resulting from that process (c) *outputs* to society (in the form of learning by individuals and groups). In this sense, it is impossible for a school to be, in fact, a closed system. Indeed, in recent years educators have become increasingly aware of the extent and importance of the interaction between the school and its environment—which is, conceptually, the basis for much of what goes on under the rubrics of accountability and community involvement.

A CONTEXTUAL APPROACH   This input-output concept is often called a linear model; it is, in effect, a theory that attempts to explain how things can be described in the real world. It is a seductive concept—seemingly logical, rational, and orderly. It lends itself well to concepts of efficiency, such as cost effectiveness; one can relate the value of inputs to the value of outputs and arrive at relative cost efficiency. For a long time, it was a popular concept in analyzing the apparent relative effectiveness of competing programs and technologies. It is now generally recognized that this theoretical model contributed little to our understanding of the ways in which educative organizations function. For example, it presupposes that when students and teachers go to school each day, their dominant concerns are to achieve the formal, official goals of the school. Even a casual observer soon learns, however, that students and teachers actually bring to school a host of their own beliefs, goals, hopes, concerns—and their smart phones and iPods—that are more significant to them. Clearly, the many subtle ways in which teachers, administrators, and students accommodate to the rules, regulations, and discipline of the school have more to do with the need to survive in a frustrating, crowded environment than with commitment to the achievement of some remote and often ambiguous educational goals.

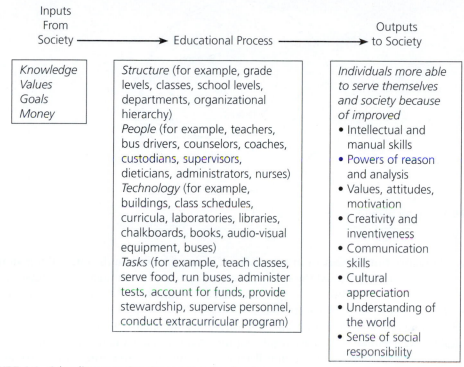

Inputs From Society ⟶ Educational Process ⟶ Outputs to Society

| *Knowledge*
Values
Goals
Money | *Structure* (for example, grade levels, classes, school levels, departments, organizational hierarchy)
People (for example, teachers, bus drivers, counselors, coaches, custodians, supervisors, dieticians, administrators, nurses)
Technology (for example, buildings, class schedules, curricula, laboratories, libraries, chalkboards, books, audio-visual equipment, buses)
Tasks (for example, teach classes, serve food, run buses, administer tests, account for funds, provide stewardship, supervise personnel, conduct extracurricular program) | *Individuals more able to serve themselves and society because of improved*
• Intellectual and manual skills
• Powers of reason and analysis
• Values, attitudes, motivation
• Creativity and inventiveness
• Communication skills
• Cultural appreciation
• Understanding of the world
• Sense of social responsibility |

FIGURE 4.1 Schooling as an input-process-output system.

A more useful approach to understanding educative organizations and the behavior of people in them is to focus our attention on what actually goes on in them. Thus, our attention is centered on examining the inner workings of that system we call an organization. This focus requires us to see the organization as a whole system that creates the setting, or the context, in which the whole pattern of human behavior that characterizes the organization occurs. With this approach, we seek to study organizations as systems that create and maintain environments in which complex sets of human interactions (both group and individual) occur with some regularity and predictability. In this view, our understanding of educative organizations requires us to examine the relationships between human behavior and the context (environment, ecology) that are characteristic of the organization. Thus, as we shall describe in detail in Chapter 7, the organizational culture (climate, ecology, ethos) of the system we call an organization is critical to our understanding.

The realm of organizational behavior tends to focus primarily on the school district or on the school as a human social system. Some scientists, in studying organizational behavior, have unwittingly encouraged the illusion that a school can, in fact, be a closed social system. Andrew Halpin and Don Croft (1962), for example, in their highly influential study of the organizational climate of schools *concentrated on internal organizational characteristics as though they function independently from external influences* and used the terms *open* and *closed* to describe the profiles of schools that represented selected characteristics of what they chose to call *organizational climate*. This was, to some extent, a convenience for the researchers: It is, indeed, difficult to study and discuss the behavior of people in a system without assuming (implicitly or otherwise) that the organization is separate from its environment. Many early

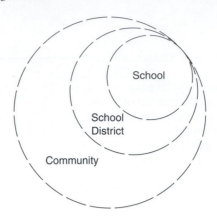

FIGURE 4.2   A social systems view of the school.

studies of organizational behavior in schools have, in fact, focused on the internal functioning of schools—that is, have treated the schools as closed systems—as though they function independently of influences from their larger outside environments (Anderson, 1968; Berman & McLaughlin, 1977; Gross & Herriott, 1965).

A burning candle has become a classic illustration of an open system: It affects its environment and is affected by it, yet it is self-regulating and retains its own identity. If a door is opened, the candle may flicker in the draft, but it will adjust to it and return to normal at the first opportunity—provided, of course, that the environmental change (the draft) is not so overwhelming that it destroys the system (that is, extinguishes the flame).

But, it is not so simple to describe *social* systems on even this superficial level. We can think of the organization (the system) as existing in an environment (the suprasystem) and having within it a subsystem (such as the administrative system). We must bear in mind that these boundaries are permeable, permitting interaction between the systems and their environments. One application of this viewpoint can be illustrated by labeling the figure, as in Figure 4.2. It then becomes obvious that factors that interfere with the interactive and adaptive relationships among the components of the interrelated parts of the system could pose a threat to the functioning of the whole. One form of interference would be a loss of permeability of one or more of the boundaries, thus tending to make the system closed and less sensitive to environmental change.

Where does the individual fit into all of this? Here, again, relabeling the diagram can specify—a little more clearly at least—one way in which the view would apply to people working in schools. The individual is functioning in the organization not only as an individual but also as one who occupies a certain *role* within the social system in the organization. In the hypothetical case illustrated in Figure 4.3, the person occupies the role of teacher in the chemistry department of John F. Kennedy Senior High School, a situation possessing a number of useful implications for anyone interested in analyzing, predicting, and perhaps controlling organizational behavior.

When we consider the individual person carrying out a unique role in an organization, we become concerned with the complex web of human involvement and its attendant behavior in organizational life. As the individual, with all the needs, drives, and talents that human beings have, assumes an official role, he or she shapes that role to some extent and is also shaped by it.

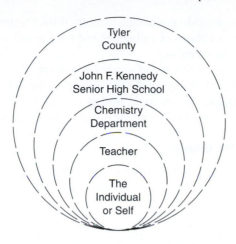

FIGURE 4.3 A social systems view of the individual in a hypothetical school organization.

Role Conflict

The dynamic interaction of people, with their idiosyncratic personalities, in the organizational setting is the domain of role theory. Everyone in the organization has a role to play based on the job description and expectations about how a person should perform the job. Katz and Kahn (1978) stated that the concepts one has about the role he or she plays in an organization are "the major means for linking the individual and organizational levels of research and theory; it is once the building block of social systems and the summation of the requirements with which such systems confront their members as individuals" (p. 219). But when different stakeholders have differing expectations, *role conflict* occurs. Role conflict comes from many sources, all of which inhibit optimum performance of the person in the role. A common source of tension from role conflict is the expectation that the person in the role, perhaps an administrator, will be empathetic and understanding in dealing with his or her subordinates and will still enforce the rules of the organization and strongly support the school board in dealing with teachers as members of a collective bargaining unit. Many administrators feel this sort of conflict when they zealously attempt to build trust, confidence, and high morale in the teaching staff and then are required to conduct a formal evaluation or to participate in a grievance procedure that seems to be in conflict with those goals.

Role Ambiguity

Role ambiguity arises when the role prescription contains contradictory elements or is vague. Katz and Kahn (1978) define role ambiguity as "uncertainty about what the occupant of a particular office is supposed to do" (p. 206). For example, role ambiguity is rather commonly observed in the attempt to preserve the distinction between administration and supervision: The first is generally seen as a line authority, whereas the other is thought to be a staff responsibility. Yet supervisors are often perceived as being in hierarchical authority over teachers; not infrequently, supervisors feel that they are being maneuvered, against the spirit of their role, into the exercise of authority over teachers, which threatens their more appropriate collegial relationship with them.

Role conflict and role ambiguity such as those described above produce tensions and uncertainties that are commonly associated with inconsistent organizational behavior. In turn, this inconsistent behavior, being unpredictable and unanticipated, often evokes further tension and interpersonal conflict between holders of complementary roles. Frequently, those who must perform their roles under the conditions of ambiguity and tension outlined here develop dysfunctional ways of coping with the situation.

To possess knowledge of role theory and some of its concepts is, in itself, of little use. However, the construct can be useful in analyzing some of the interpersonal behavior that we encounter in the work groups of organizations. For example, leaders are concerned with facilitating the acceptance, development, and allocation of roles that are necessary for the group to function well.

Functional Roles in the Group

Group task roles help the group to achieve its tasks (Katz & Kahn, 1978). The leader must either assume these essential roles or see that they are allocated to other members of the group. They include the roles of

1. initiating action and contributing ideas,
2. seeking information,
3. seeking opinions from the group,
4. giving information,
5. giving one's opinion,
6. coordinating the work of group members,
7. helping to keep the group focused on goals,
8. acting as the evaluator-critic,
9. prodding the group to action,
10. attending to routine housekeeping tasks of the group, and
11. recording.

An important responsibility of the group leader is to provide for the creation of an environment in the group in which these roles can be developed and carried out.

In the same way, the leader must see to it that other specific roles are fulfilled to ensure that the group will not only maintain itself over time but that it will develop increasing effectiveness over time. Group building and maintenance roles help the group develop a climate and processes that enable the members to work harmoniously and with a minimum of lost time. These roles include (a) encouraging members to keep at the task, (b) harmonizing differences between ideas and between individuals, (c) facilitating communication (for example, by helping silent individuals to speak up and encouraging equal use of "air time"), (d) setting high standards of performance for the group, and (e) providing the group with feedback about its own processes and actions. These roles are obviously quite different in nature and function from the group task roles. Of course, it is possible that an individual group member will take on more than one role or that two or more members will share a given role.

ROLE RELATED TO SOCIAL SYSTEMS THEORY

The foregoing discussion enables us to return to social systems with somewhat more insight. The basic notion is that the organization may be understood as a social system as described by Getzels and Guba (1957) in this way:

> We conceive of the social system as involving two major classes of phenomena, which are at once conceptually independent and phenomenally interactive. There

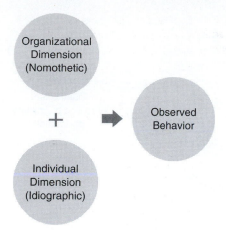

FIGURE 4.4 Social System model.

are, first, the *institutions* with certain *roles* and *expectations* that will fulfill the goals of the system. Second, inhabiting the system are the *individuals* with certain *personalities* and *need-dispositions,* whose interactions comprise what we generally call "social behavior." (p. 423)

Figure 4.4 graphically depicts the interaction of the two dimensions that result in the observed behavior. The nomothetic (organizational) dimension is comprised of the institutional role and role expectations; the idiographic (individual or personal) dimension is comprised of each individual and his or her needs.

Each behavioral act stems simultaneously from the nomothetic and the idiographic dimensions. But how do these dimensions interact? What proportion of each dimension is present in organizational behavior? That depends, of course, on both the individual and on the institutional role and is best expressed as a function of the interplay between the two dimensions. Getzels and Guba (1957) gave us the following general equation to express it:

$$B = f(R \cdot P)$$

where   B = observed behavior
         R = institutional role
         P = personality of the role incumbent.

Thus, the school, as an organization, creates certain offices and positions that are occupied by individuals. The offices and positions represent the nomothetic dimension of the organization, and role expectations held by the organization for incumbents are specified in a number of ways. These may range from elaborate written job descriptions to the more subtle (and usually more powerful) group norms established by custom and tradition. By this we mean, the organization not only establishes some formal, minimal level of job performance that would be acceptable but also communicates rather elaborate specifications of behavior in roles that may well extend to the kinds of clothes worn on the job, the manner of speech used, and so on.

But the individuals in these offices and positions have their own personality structures and needs, which represent the idiographic dimensions of the organization. To some extent, even in

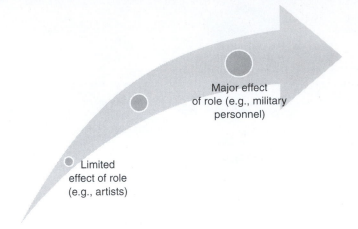

Major effect
of role (e.g., military
personnel)

Limited
effect of role
(e.g., artists)

FIGURE 4.5   The effect of role on different career types such as artists versus military personnel.

highly formal organizations, the people in these roles mold and shape the offices in some ways in order to better fulfill some of their own expectations of their roles.

The mechanism by which the needs of the institution and the needs of the individual are modified and come together is the work group. There is a dynamic interrelationship in the work group, then, not only of an interpersonal nature but also between institutional requirements and the idiosyncratic needs of individual participants. The shaping of the institutional role, the development of a climate within the social system, and the personalities of the participants all interact dynamically with one another. Organizational behavior can be viewed as the product of this interaction.

How much organizational behavior can be ascribed to role expectation and role prescription, and how much is traceable to the personality needs of the role incumbent? In other words, if $B = f(R \cdot P)$, what values can be assigned to R and P, respectively? For some people, a role can have far greater influence in prescribing behavior than it does for other people. Figure 4.5 displays this relationship.

Different kinds of roles in different kinds of organizations do suggest that some role players are more affected by the nomothetic dimension. One generally supposes that the role of an army private is very largely prescribed and clearly limits the extent to which the private can meet his or her individual personality needs. Closer to the other extreme would be an artist who exhibits highly creative behavior, with a minimum of organizational constraint, and who expresses personal idiosyncratic needs to a great degree.

Equilibrium

People participate in organizations to satisfy certain needs. Presumably, the organization has needs of its own, which are fulfilled by the participants who function in its various roles. This is illustrated by the Getzels-Guba social systems model with its stress on the interplay between the nomothetic (organizational) needs and the idiographic (personal) needs of the "actors" who fill the various roles. There is obviously a quid pro quo relationship between the role player and the organization, the maintenance of which can be thought of as a state of equilibrium between the needs of the organization and those of the individual. As long as this state of equilibrium exists, the relationship presumably will be satisfactory, enduring, and relatively productive.

BOX 4.2

Idiographic–Nomothetic

In the study of human social behavior, as in the organization sciences, two modes of analysis are generally used. One mode seeks to discover scientific principles or laws that are generally true, applicable in all situations, and are endlessly repeatable. It is called the *nomothetic* approach (from the ancient Greek *nomos,* or "law," and *thetos,* "prescribed"). Another approach, sometimes thought to be antithetical, is called "idiographic" (from the Greek *idios,* "personal" or "private," and *graphos,* "to display or write"). The idiographic mode focuses on the human beings who populate the organization and their uniqueness from one organization to another and from time to time, even in the same roles. Nomothetic analyses focus on the formal structure of the organization (typically described in organization charts, operations manuals, and other rules and "laws") that is generally thought to be replicable from organization to organization and from time to time. More commonly, we speak of the *structure* of the organization (nomothetic) and the *human* side of the organization (idiographic). These terms and concepts are widely used in the study of history, psychology, geography, and other human sciences.

On a very rudimentary level, the notion of equilibrium between the needs of the organization and its participants is illustrated by the well-known case of Schmidt at Bethlehem Steel. Schmidt, as he was called in Frederick W. Taylor's description (Taylor, 1911), was a pig-iron handler who picked up, carried, and loaded pig iron—12.5 tons in a 10-hour day for $1.15 per day. Obviously, the company needed men to do the pig-iron handling, and this need was satisfied by the men whose role was that of handler. Presumably, as long as the needs and satisfactions exchange was in a state of balance or equilibrium, the organization functioned adequately. In his account, Taylor described how he applied his scientific principles to the task of rigorously training Schmidt to increase Schmidt's daily workload to 47.5 tons. The needs-inducements balance was maintained by boosting the pay to $1.85 per day. Schmidt and the company apparently found the needs-inducements arrangements mutually satisfactory because Schmidt was described as staying on the job for "some years."

Chester Barnard (1938) discussed equilibrium as "the balancing of burdens by satisfactions which results in continuance" of participation of both the individual and the organization in a mutual relationship. In his lexicon, the term *effectiveness* was the "accomplishment of the recognized objectives of cooperative action" (p. 55). *Efficiency* referred to the ability of the organization to sustain the continued participation of individuals by offering adequate satisfactions to them.

Barnard described the organization as inducing cooperation by distributing its "*productive results*" to individuals. "These productive results," he wrote, "are either material or social, or both. As to some individuals, material is required for satisfaction; as to others, social benefits are required. As to most individuals, both material and social benefits are required in different proportions" (p. 58). Barnard pointed out—and this is familiar to us all—that the definition of what constitutes "adequate satisfactions" to individuals in the organization varies, depending in great measure on the makeup and circumstances of the individual involved. Some people certainly find great satisfaction in material reward, especially money, and to get it will accept an organizational role that may be insecure, unpleasant, or strenuous. Regardless of the many possible negative aspects of such a role, as long as there is enough material reward, such people may well find the inducement satisfying. Others, for whatever reasons, might find a higher income not worth the price that must be paid.

In the recent history of educational administration, this point can be seen in connection with the role of the superintendent of schools and, to a lesser degree, with that of the high school principal. Although the salaries being offered to superintendents are reaching very high levels, many qualified people are not attracted to this role, and many incumbents have shifted to university teaching or to other fields altogether. Long working hours, arduous demands, and enormous pressures are some of the drawbacks of the job of superintendent; in many cases, there is little reward in terms of achievement or self-fulfillment. To attract and hold capable people as superintendents, school districts must proffer a combination of material and psychological rewards incumbents will find attractive.

Not many years ago, an important problem in the United States was attracting good teachers to rural areas and keeping them there despite the low pay, inadequate school facilities, and limited cultural opportunities, which made teaching in such areas relatively unrewarding to many. Today, the situation is somewhat reversed; schools in nonurban areas offer considerable reward to many teachers, whereas the bleak, hostile, frustrating environment of the teacher in the poor urban school is barely adequate—both in terms of money and a sense of fulfillment—for many capable teachers.

In discussing organizational equilibrium from the systems theory point of view, we must remember that there is not only a needs-inducements relationship between the individual participant and the organization; the organization itself is part of a larger system. If the system is open—as in the case of schools and school systems—the organization will interact actively with the external systems that comprise its environment. An expanded version of the Getzels-Guba social system model depicts this interaction of the school with its larger environment. Presumably, changes in the environment will stimulate a reaction by the organization, either *static* or *dynamic*. If the reaction is static, the system responds to keep relationships in their original state, that is, the status quo is maintained. Dynamic equilibrium, however, is characterized by a rearrangement of the internal subsystems of the organization or by a change in its goals in order to adjust to changing circumstances in its external environment. Dynamic equilibrium, in other words, helps to keep the system in a steady state by being adaptable.

Homeostasis

Homeostasis, a biological term, has been applied to organizations and refers to the tendency of an open system to regulate itself to stay constantly in balance. The biological organism tends to retain its own characteristics, to maintain itself, and to preserve its identity, but at the same time, it has compensatory mechanisms that enable it to adapt to and survive environmental changes within certain limits. Homeostatic processes in human beings include the body's tendency to maintain a constant temperature and to maintain blood pressure by repairing a break in the circulatory system through coagulation. Homeostatic mechanisms in school systems and schools, such as well-developed communication systems and decision-making processes, enable them to adapt to and deal effectively with changes in their environment.

Feedback

Systems that do not have sensitive antennas picking up accurate feedback information or—perhaps worse—that do not provide for the accurate transmission of feedback information to decision makers, find it difficult to react appropriately to environmental changes. Such systems tend to be in a static, rather than in a dynamic, equilibrium with their environments. They tend to lack the self-correcting, homeostatic processes essential to maintaining themselves in environments characterized by change.

We have, in the social systems view, an organization that is, by definition, an open system, which means that the organization has internal subsystems (e.g., schools) *and* that it is part of a suprasystem (e.g., community). The organization is in an interactive relationship with this suprasystem: The organization exchanges inputs and outputs with it. To some extent, the organization affects its environment (the suprasystem) and is also affected by changes that occur in the suprasystem.

The organization can resist and deny changes in the suprasystem or environment by ignoring or fighting them or by attempting to insulate itself from them (that is, by becoming more closed). It can attempt to accommodate to environmental change by homeostatic adaptation (that is, by adopting a policy of "business as usual"). Or the organization can adapt to environmental changes by developing a new balance, a new equilibrium. In a world such as ours, dominated by rapid and extensive change, the organization with poor feedback mechanisms or weak homeostatic characteristics would show declining performance and increasing evidence of disorganization.

It is important to remember that essential to systems theory is the concept that *systems are composed of subsystems that are highly interactive and mutually interdependent.* The Getzels-Guba model of the school as an open social system (which has already been described) assumed at least two subsystems can be identified and their interaction suggested: (a) the organizational or institutional system and (b) the human system. Useful as this model was in the early attempts to understand the dynamics of organizational behavior, it is incomplete. By the mid-1980s, students of organizational behavior understood that organizations possess more than these two subsystems and that the analysis of organizational behavior requires us to use more complex concepts. One of the more currently useful approaches is to conceptualize organizations—for example, the school system and the school—as *sociotechnical systems.*

SOCIOTECHNICAL SYSTEMS THEORY

By definition, an organization exists for the purpose of achieving something: reaching some goal or set of goals. It seeks to do this by accomplishing certain tasks. Logically, of course, the organization is structured, equipped, and staffed appropriately to accomplish its mission. The main goal of a school district, for example, requires it to operate schools, a transportation system, and food services. The district must employ people, provide legally mandated services, and perhaps engage in collective bargaining. The school district must organize numerous tasks internally in order to achieve its goals (Owens & Steinhoff, 1976).

To achieve an assigned task—which may include a large number of subtasks and operationally necessary tasks—we build an organization: That is, we give it *structure,* which gives an organization order, a system, and many of its distinctive characteristics. The structure establishes a pattern of authority and collegiality, thus defining roles: There are top-management executives and middle-management supervisors, bosses and workers, each of whom attempts to know the extent of his or her own legitimate authority as well as that of others. Structure dictates, in large measure, the patterns of communication networks that are basic to information flow and therefore to decision making. Structure also determines the system of workflow that is presumably focused on achieving the organization's tasks.

The organization must have *technological resources* or, in other words, the tools of its trade. The word *technology*, used in this sense, does not include typical hardware items only, such as computers, milling machines, textbooks, chalk, and electron microscopes. Technology may also include program inventions: systematic procedures, the sequencing of activities, or other procedural inventions designed to solve problems that stand in the way of organizational task achievement. Thus, the teacher's daily lesson plan, the high school class schedule, and the district's curriculum guides are illustrative of technology in educational organizations.

Finally, of course, the organization must have *people*. Their contribution to the task achievement of the organization is ultimately visible in their acts—that is, their organizational behavior. This behavior selects, directs, communicates, and decides.

These four internal organization factors—*task, structure, technology,* and *people* (Leavitt, 1964)—are variables that differ from time to time and from one organization to the next. Within a given organization, these four factors are highly interactive, each tending to shape and mold the others. As in any system, the interdependence of the variable factors means that a significant change in one will result in some adaptation on the part of the other factors. Important in determining the nature and interrelationship of these internal organizational arrangements in a school district or school is the response of the organization to changes occurring in the larger system in which it exists.

Suppose, for example, that an academically oriented high school admits limited numbers of talented students by competitive examination for the express purpose of preparing them for college. If the board of education rules that the school must be converted into a more comprehensive high school to meet the needs of the total youth population (which, of course, would be a change in the organization's goal), a number of internal adjustments would be necessary for the school to achieve its new goal reasonably well. Many of these changes would be compensatory in nature. For example, to accommodate those students interested in a business career, it would be necessary to teach courses in business (task). To do this, business education equipment would have to be installed (technology), business education teachers would have to be employed (people), and a department of business education might be created (structure). However, some of the changes flowing from the board's directive might be retaliatory rather than compensatory. For example, if some people in the school sought to resist these changes, their former cooperative and productive behavior would be replaced by alienation and conflict. This resistance could disrupt the normal communications patterns in the school, thereby producing a structural change.

A technological change, such as the introduction of a comprehensive, computer-related instructional system in a high school, could bring about important side effects: It could change the goals of the school by making it possible to achieve new things and, simultaneously, by rendering certain traditional tasks obsolete. A change in people would include the employment of new personnel with technical skills, affecting the work activities of others in the school by making some activities unnecessary and requiring certain new activities to be introduced. Finally, the introduction of new departments and changes in those involved in the decision-making processes would be structural changes flowing out of the technical change originally initiated.

Thus, in coordinating the internal processes of the school district or school, it is necessary to attend to the dynamic interaction of the four subsystems: people, structure, technology, and task. However, if it is proposed to introduce a significant change primarily through one of the target variables, it is clear that the other variables soon will be affected. Change efforts that are basically technological in nature result in some compensatory or retaliatory behavior on the part of people and in some structural adjustments within the organization. Those who seek to bring about significant structural rearrangements in the school, such as differentiated staffing plans, must reckon with the people involved and the way they will react to the change.

Although it is easy to speak of different administrative strategies and to categorize various tactics and procedures as "belonging" to one strategy or another, we must recognize the symbiotic interrelationship that exists among the internal organizational subsystems with which we are concerned: task, technological, structural, and behavioral.

The schematic diagram in Figure 4.6 illustrates the key internal and external relationships of a school system or school. The figure provides only a few illustrative examples of the many things that are normally included in the task, technology, and structure subsystems. In conceptualizing the human subsystem, the reader is cautioned to note that it is insufficient to name or label the occupational roles of participants (such as teachers, nurses, and custodians). In terms of the dynamics of internal organizational functioning, the values, beliefs, and knowledge possessed

VOICES FROM THE FIELD

A Systems Approach to District Budget Development

Kendall Hendricks, Director of Finance, Brownsburg Community School Corporation, Brownsburg, Indiana

A school corporation budget is a pretty complex beast I have discovered in my first year as Director of Finance. I have held a variety of positions in a couple of different school corporations in central Indiana. My roles have ranged from fourth grade high ability classroom teacher to summer school computer teacher, from middle school science teacher to elementary administrator, and from track coach to my current position as a central office administrator in charge of a $65 million plus budget. Needless to say, I've seen a whole host of leadership styles, both good and bad, and have a pretty good sense for the "hot buttons" within a building. One of the hottest topics at any staff lounge table would undoubtedly include dollars spent for the students. The budgeting process for the following year begins in earnest during March of the previous year. In my school corporation, each building has some degree of control over the direction of repairs and improvements, the purchase of equipment, and the specific technological desires that would best assist the staff and students with curricular needs.

A particular goal of mine in my first year on the job as Director of Finance was to gather specific input from the building level while going out in the field on "their turf." I gathered three additional key figures from within the corporation to help with this endeavor; they included the Chief Operations Officer, the Coordinator of Technology, and the Maintenance Supervisor. The Chief Operations Officer's administrative assistant organized some scheduling for us, and we were off to uncharted waters. On our Traveling Tour that consisted of multiple visits over a 2-week timeframe, the four of us visited six elementary schools, two middle schools, the high school, our alternative school, and the athletic director.

This face-to-face approach allowed us to get into the field and gather specific input from the individual components of the system. I have come to realize over my career the most vital people within any organization are those who make the day-to-day decisions at the building level. By obtaining their vibrant proposals, I could then turn my focus to developing a workable budget within the framework of our overall school system. Building administrators were very appreciative of this approach, and the methodology allowed for great conversations. This systematic approach also allowed for some specific building tours in some instances to get a first-hand look at their individual desires. My ultimate goal will be to put these distinct desires into motion for the overall good of our system within the framework of our budget.

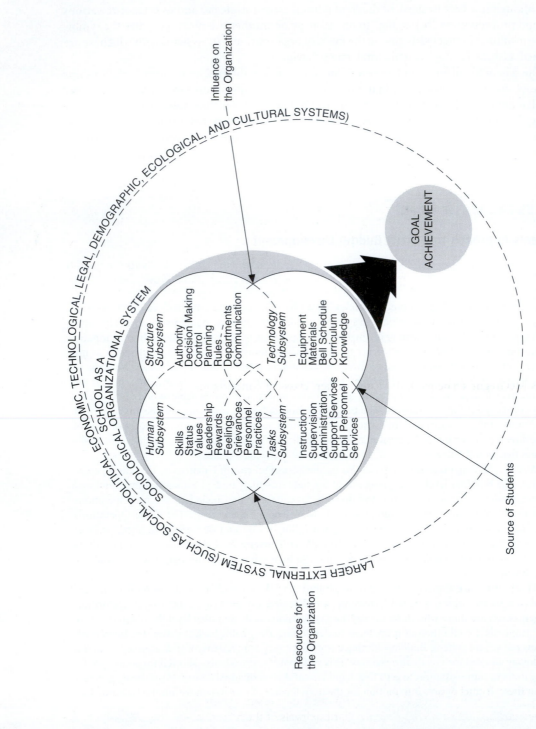

FIGURE 4.6 Four primary organizational subsystems characterize the internal arrangements of school systems and schools. Adapted from Robert G. Owens and Carl R. Steinhoff, *Administering Change in Schools* (Englewood Cliffs, NJ: Prentice Hall, 1976), p. 143.

by individuals in the human system are just as important as the facts that the individuals are present and that the organization has formalized ways of dealing with them (such as rules, grievance procedures, and personnel policies). It should be obvious that the human subsystem is the only one that has nonrational (that is, affective, not irrational) capability.

CONTINGENCY THEORY

Theorizing, thinking, research, and experience with organizations have been accompanied by an observable tendency for individuals (whether theorists or practitioners) to adopt advocacy positions. Those who favor classical approaches to organization, for example, have consistently supported the notion that a hierarchy of authority based on rank in the organization is essential to the very concept of organization. Human relations adherents may differ on many points but are almost unanimous in espousing supportive, collaborative, people-centered leadership and highly participative management styles as superior to other approaches. Behavioral adherents have, with a fair degree of consistency, sought to find the best, most productive way to integrate the key elements of the classical and human relations approaches. The result, for many years, was the development of competing advocacy positions, which showed mixed results when attempts were made to apply any one of the positions to organizations: None of the three approaches is demonstrably superior in *all* situations.

Traditional (classical or neoclassical) approaches to the administration of school systems and schools have tended not only to use a hierarchical model of organization (drawn from the tradition of the military and large corporations) but also to emphasize the importance of rational, logical, and potentially powerful control systems, whereby decisions are made at the top of the hierarchy and implemented at the bottom. As a conceptually ideal state, at least, the whole is characterized by hierarchically maintained order, system, and discipline. Remember, like Douglas McGregor's Theory X discussed earlier, classical concepts may be used in either hard (coercive) or soft (manipulative) form.

Rational Planning Models

Rational planning models, such as planning, programming, and budgeting systems (PPBS), program evaluation and review technique (PERT), management by objectives (MBO), and zero-based budgeting (ZBB), are adapted from massive, military-industrial enterprises that were created for purposes such as building and maintaining huge fleets of enormous, technologically complex systems of weapons. The approach, characterized by the use of modern rational systems concepts and technology (as differentiated from *social* systems concepts), is traditional, classical in viewpoint, and *mechanical* in operation. Organizations are said to be mechanical when the primary basis for managing the system features the following:

1. Highly differentiated and specialized tasks with precise specification of rights, responsibilities, and methods
2. Coordination and control through hierarchical supervision
3. Communication with the external environment controlled by the top offices of the hierarchy
4. Strong, top-down chain of command
5. Leadership style emphasizing authority-obedience relationships
6. Decision-making authority reserved for top levels of the hierarchy

The concepts of *mechanical* and *organic* systems are widely discussed in the literature of organizational theory. These concepts help us to discuss and analyze specific organizational situations without resorting to potentially pejorative dichotomies such as the bureaucratic-humanistic or democratic-authoritarian ones, which are obviously value laden. Organic organizational systems, which in today's parlance might be called *learning organizations*, are recognizable by the fact that they emphasize a different approach to managing the system:

1. Continuous reassessment of tasks and responsibilities through interaction of those involved, with functional change being easy to arrange at the working level
2. Coordination and control through interaction of those involved, requiring considerable shared responsibility and interdependence
3. Communication with the external environment that is relatively extensive and open at all levels of the organization
4. Emphasis on mutual confidence, consultation, and information sharing—up and down, laterally, and diagonally across the organization—as the basis of organizational authority
5. Team leadership style, featuring high levels of trust and group problem solving
6. Wide sharing of responsibility for decision making at all levels in the organization

These two views of organization in public education have long been described as two irreconcilable modes of thought that have struggled for dominance.

The ebb and flow of the tides of rhetoric and viewpoint—alternately bringing a mechanical-bureaucratic-hierarchical emphasis to the fore, then a soft human relations-humanistic sweep, followed perhaps by a more manipulative, soft mechanical emphasis—historically has been painfully evident in the administration of U.S. public schooling. Many school superintendents, principals, and others, having witnessed this reality, have decided to eschew any theoretical or analytical approach and have elected what is generally described by practitioners as an eclectic or pragmatic approach: to go out into the real world of school districts and do whatever seems to work. After all, the argument goes, theory doesn't make any difference. This is not only a gross misreading of what organizational studies have to teach us but also it offers no hope whatsoever of setting educational administration on a solid foundation of knowledge from which systematic administrative practice may be developed.

A contingency approach to organization takes a different view: Although there is no one best way to organize and manage people in all circumstances, there are certain designs of organizational structure and certain management methods that can be identified as being most effective under specific situational contingencies. The key to understanding and dealing effectively with organizational behavior, from a contingency point of view, lies in being able to *analyze* the critical variables in a given situation. Effective administrator behavior (that is, behavior likely to increase achievement of the organization in attaining its goals, to improve the culture for working and learning, and to deal as productively as possible with conflict) is not seen as characterized by a universal fixed style (for example, nomothetic or idiographic) but reveals a repertoire of behavioral styles tailored to the contingencies of the situation. In sum, three basic propositions underlie the contingency approach to organizational behavior in schools:

1. There is no one best universal way to organize and administer school districts or schools.
2. Not all ways of organizing and administering are equally effective in a given situation: Effectiveness is contingent upon appropriateness of the design or style to the situation.

3. The selection of organizational design and administrative style should be based on careful analysis of significant contingencies in the situation.

Open System Related to Contingency Theory

Contingency theory represents "a middle ground between (a) the view that there are universal principles of organization and management and (b) the view that each organization is unique and that each situation must be analyzed separately" (Kast & Rosenzweig, 1973, p. ix). Contingency approaches represent a rather sensible theoretical development that seems to have value in dealing with the theory-practice gap (Moberg & Koch, 1975). The basic contribution of contingency thinking lies not in providing ready-made, pat answers to complex problems or easy recipes; it lies, rather, in providing us with new ways of analyzing the interrelationships within and among the interacting parts of the organizational system. One critical set of relationships arises from the interaction of the organization (which, remember, is an open system) with its environment.

Organizations are open systems that are capable of differentiating their internal subsystems in response to a variety of environmental contingencies. Organizations that deal successfully with uncertain environments (that is, environments that are apt to call for relatively sudden change in the organization) tend to differentiate internally more than less successful organizations do, yet they are able to maintain high levels of integration between the various subunits. Such organizations are characterized by joint decision making, clear interdepartmental linkages, and well-developed means of dealing with conflict between units of the organization. Organizations that function in environments characterized by change and instability must organize differently to be effective, to meet the need for planning, decision making, and conflict management—more so than those organizations that deal with relatively stable environments.

As environmental conditions change, the organization needs to adapt by responding with an appropriate structure and administrative system. Stable technologies and stable environmental conditions call for mechanistic organizations, characterized by rigidity and by explicitly defined tasks, methods, and job descriptions. In contrast, organizations facing unstable or changing technologies and environments require relatively flexible structures, with emphasis on lateral rather than vertical communications, expert power (rather than hierarchical power) as the predominant base of influence, loosely defined responsibilities, and emphasis on exchanges of information rather than on giving direction (Robbins, 1976).

Technological Change in the Suprasystem

Critics who fault U.S. schools for failing to make full use of modern technology often have hardware technologies in mind (such as computers, interactive whiteboards, and other machines) and have a limited grasp of the extensive software technology that is widely used in U.S. education. The term *technology* properly includes "software" such as procedures for sequencing instruction; scheduling the interface of time, people, and material resources; specialized programs and curriculum guides; and techniques for generating and managing information. Thus, the term—when applied to school organizations—must include diverse forms such as curriculum guides; the high school schedule; biology laboratories and band rooms; the testing program; and methods for classifying, grouping, and promoting students. The array of technology utilized in schooling has considerable power to affect behavior in the entire sociotechnical system, as was suggested earlier.

But, again, technology is usually developed outside the school system or school; its impact is a result of the interaction of the open sociotechnical system with its environment. New technological developments of every description tend to alter the contingencies that affect the internal arrangements of the school. They are, in effect, one aspect of the large environment in which school systems or schools as organizations exist.

Interaction with the External Environment

The school system or school, as a sociotechnical system, is in constant dynamic interaction with the larger external environment in which it exists. As used here, *environment* refers to the suprasystem in which the school district or school exists: the social, political, and economic systems of our culture. Thus, demographic shifts resulting in changing enrollments and increasing percentages of older people in the population, changing attitudes toward individual freedom, emphasis on women's right to equality, shifting patterns of social mobility, dissatisfaction with the performance of schools, massive changes in legal-judicial philosophy, increased taxpayer resistance, organization of teachers into labor unions, and even mounting distrust of authority and institutions in our society in general are among the many environmental contingencies to which public school organizations have had to adapt.

Internal arrangements of the organization are largely contingent upon circumstances in that environment. Changes in the environment cause the organizational system to respond with changes in its internal arrangements. Those internal arrangements are best understood as containing four dynamically interactive subsystems: *tasks* to be performed, *structure* of the organization, *technology* utilized to perform the tasks, and the *human* social system.

One way that the social, political, and cultural environment of the school district or school has an impact is in setting goals to be achieved. Although educators play a part in establishing the goals of schooling, the process is ultimately in the political realm: State legislatures representing the body politic, for example, are normally instrumental in formalizing important aspects of the goals of schooling. Legislation of minimum competency standards for graduation and/or promotion can have a powerful impact on what schools seek to achieve. Federal initiatives have had a widespread, direct effect on school goals—not only for youngsters with special educational needs but for almost all other students, too. Of course, the presence and involvement of the federal government has been increasing rapidly in recent years and promises to continue expanding in the years ahead.

Other political processes, such as approving budgets and levying taxes or electing school board members, also serve as a means for influencing the goals of schools. Frequently, a display of potential political power is sufficient to effect reassessment and revision of organizational goals. Not infrequently, of course, judicial intervention is a means of implementing goal changes in schooling. This is readily observable in situations in which federal district courts not only have ordered the desegregation of school districts but also have specified the means by which this process is to be achieved (for example, intradistrict transportation and interdistrict transportation). Courts also have required changes in curricula, testing procedures, and methods of selecting and assigning staff. All of these represent some of the ways in which the environment of the school organization affects the internal functioning of the organization. The organization will either adapt smoothly and easily, or it may resist.

Thus, a groundswell of popular support for a move back to basics might appear in a local school district that motivates the board of education and the administrative staff to initiate a goal-setting and educational planning project with community involvement. As a result, the schools would likely revise their curricula, shift their teaching style, perhaps reorganize their grade structure, and adopt new textbooks—that is, make internal rearrangements in response to changes in the organization's environment.

Frequently, however, schools will resist external changes and maintain the status quo, almost regardless of the degree or power of the new environmental contingencies. Our history with regard to desegregation, equal rights, and nondiscriminatory practices—even in the face of concentrated, massive, statutory, judicial, and political action—makes it clear that schools often attempt to close off the organizational system in order to deflect the impact of changes in the larger environment, rather than seek ways of making appropriate internal rearrangements to adapt to them. From a contingency point of view, this action tends to put the school or school system out of touch with the real-world contingencies in which these organizations exist. In terms of organizational behavior, a negative result in such a case is likely to be leadership and administrative styles that—in the long run—are not the most effective and may even be counterproductive.

Contingency Theory and Organizational Behavior in Schools

Operationally, using the contingency approach in the practice of school administration does not necessarily have to be terribly exotic or require highly sophisticated methods. It does, however, require the administrator to use some analysis of relevant contingencies in the situation at hand as a basis for selecting a way of dealing with them. Because administration is working with and through individuals and groups to achieve organizational goals, a fundamental question to consider is the following: What will likely yield the most productive behavior (in terms of achieving organizational goals) from my subordinates in this situation? An important assumption underlying this question is, of course, that different administrative styles are likely to evoke predictably different responses from people.

For example, an issue that often confronts the administrator concerns leadership style. Is a good leader one who sets goals, directs subordinates, and checks closely to see that they do things as directed? Or is a good leader one who involves subordinates in setting goals, collaborates with them in deciding what to do and how to do it, and provides coordination of the group in evaluating progress and results? In the parlance of public school administrators, which is better: "directive" leadership or "collaborative" leadership?

A contingency approach to this issue starts with clarifying what is meant by the word *good*. Because the administrator's intent is to maximize the achievement of organizational goals, *good* is probably best redefined as "effective." The question then becomes as follows: Which leadership style is most effective—that is, which will likely contribute most to the goal performance of the school system or school?

Contemporary understanding of the dynamics of leader behavior makes it clear that there is apparently no one most effective style: Effectiveness of leadership style clearly depends on its appropriateness in terms of the critical contingencies in a given situation. The power of the leader, the quality of relationships with subordinates, the clarity of the structure of the task to be done, the degree of cooperation required to implement decisions, and the levels of skill and motivation of subordinates are a few of the many contingencies that can be assessed by the administrator and related to predictable outcomes of various specific alternative ways to lead. In the contingency view, the effective leader is able to match leadership style to the contingencies of the situation in order to achieve the behavior on the part of subordinates that will contribute most to achieving the goals of the school district or school.

A contingency orientation is helpful in dealing with issues of motivation, decision making, organizational change, organizational culture, and conflict management. The remaining chapters of this book explore these aspects of organizational behavior in schools.

Final Thoughts

Open social systems theory is the basis for contemporary analysis of organizational behavior. Social systems theory, such as the Getzels-Guba model, has provided a useful way of conceptualizing organizational behavior as a function of the interaction between the demands of organizational requirements and the needs-dispositions of individuals in the organization. Although the Getzels-Guba model has often been used to stress this internal dynamic relationship of the organization, the expanded version of the model clearly illustrates the dynamic relationship between the organizational system itself and its external larger environment, the suprasystem.

Role theory not only helps us to understand the idiographic-nomothetic relationship in greater detail but also illuminates many of the broader interpersonal relationships that exist in schools and school systems. Although role theory lacks the power to explain the organization in its entirety, it is useful as a framework for examining relationships between person and organization, as well as interpersonal behavior.

Sociotechnical concepts help us to understand the dynamic interrelationship among the structure, tasks, technology, and human aspects of educational organizations as a force in evoking and molding the behavior of people. In the typical high school, for example, people's daily lives are deeply affected by the schedule, which governs all and often defines the possible. Architects design buildings that evoke psychological responses and shape behavior. The choice to equip a classroom with movable desks or screwed-down desks has an impact on behavior. A curriculum that mandates individually prescribed instruction also mandates behavior. The need to transport students to and from school on buses has an impressive impact on the school as an organization and on the behavior of people in it.

But the fact that educational organizations are *open* systems has additional behavioral consequences. A school, for example, is subject to two major external forces that define the very nature of its internal arrangements. One of these forces is the fact that the school *is* a school: It is probably more like other schools from coast to coast than it is different from them. Professional standards and expectations expressed through teacher training institutions, accrediting associations, the entrance requirements of colleges, the wares of the educational-industrial complex, and the speakers at annual conventions—all of these are but a representative few of the many professional influences that reach in from the outside and define what a school *is* in behavioral terms.

The *second* cluster of these forces represents the broader social-cultural influences that reach in from the outside and establish norms for behavior in the school. These include diverse sources such as community standards, tradition, judicial decisions, statutory law, and—not least, by any means—the broad generalizations embodied in concepts such as Western culture. More specifically, perhaps, is the impact of the youth subculture that has become so influential in Western nations. Because the school is an open system, this facet of the school's environment has a powerful impact on its internal functioning. The fact that children watch television and Internet videos; are exposed to a drug culture; and are developing new concepts of sex, marriage, and the family does shape the nature of life in schools. All of these combine to create an *organizational* culture that is powerful in determining how people perceive things, value them, and react to them.

Thus, the concept of the educative organization as an open sociotechnical system enables us to see the internal arrangements of a particular organization as at once unique and part of an interaction with its larger suprasystem. This is the view of schools that people like John Goodlad (1978) take when they speak of the culture of the school. In contemporary organizational theory, this concept is coupled with contingency theory: the view that there is no one universal best way of dealing with organizational issues. Contingency approaches to organizational behavior require developing a systematic understanding of the dynamics of organizational behavior in order to be able to diagnose or analyze the existing specific situation.

Organizational theory provides a systematic body of knowledge on which we base assumptions about the nature of organizations and the behavior of people in them. Far from being the impractical plaything of scholars, theory is used constantly by administrators—albeit often in an intuitive and unexamined way—as a basis for the professional work they do every day.

Bureaucratic theory has long been the most widely used perspective, by an overwhelming margin, in developing assumptions about educational organizations. Human resources theory has been steadily developing and gaining greater acceptance, however, as research following the tradition of the Western Electric Studies has been pushed forward and as bureaucratic responses to the problems of schools have failed to work as well as had been expected. Since the 1960s, human resources development theory has been considerably strengthened by the emergence of newer perspectives such as concepts of loose coupling and an understanding of motivation that will be more fully described in the next chapter.

Reflective Activities

1. Using role theory and the Getzels-Guba model as described in this chapter, analyze your organization as a social system. Briefly define the group roles, individual roles, and organizational expectations that seem to define or direct the goal behaviors of your organization. Can you identify any changes in roles or expectations that might help improve organizational effectiveness?

2. *Working on Your Game Plan.* How will you use the concepts of role theory and sociotechnical systems theory as a school leader? When combined, these two theories have the potential for innovative organizational structures among various roles and systems within the organization. How might you implement them?

CRITICAL INCIDENT   A Tale of Two Principals

Mavis

Mavis is thought of by the staff as a very capable and intelligent leader. Mavis has worked with the staff to set up an organization in which a variety of committees that focus on schoolwide goals has significant decision-making authority. There are committees for technology, social, curriculum, discipline, staff development, organization/scheduling, reform, and several other ad hoc committees as needed. Staff members are asked to indicate which three committees they would like to serve on, and then the leadership committee chooses members to ensure that there are individuals who always seem to be task-oriented and others who are always very collaborative and supportive of others. Mavis and the leadership team select the chairs for committees who they believe are the most knowledgeable about the committee charges and who are well organized. The chairs also serve on a school steering committee to ensure that all committees work in tandem toward schoolwide goals. Team leaders and the principal's leadership committee also serve on the steering committee.

Charley

Charley is thought of by the staff as highly organized and decisive. He has been at this school for 15 years as principal. The school organization is composed of grade-level teams. Charley believes that too many committees waste staff time that can best be spent in planning for instruction. Each grade-level team meets with Charley once a month. He sets the agenda for these meetings and after getting ideas from the group, he makes the final decisions. Charley believes that by being in charge of the teams, he can ensure that the entire school is on track to meet schoolwide goals.

1. Analyze each of the organizational structures set up by these two principals. Which one is most likely to lead to effective decisions that will meet schoolwide goals? Why?
2. For which principal would you rather work? Why?

Suggested Reading

Two items below should be read in tandem: *first,* Weick's now-classic article that has had wide influence on thought in American education, *then* Elmore's piece, written 24 years later, which attempts to reinterpret the original ideas of Weick in the context of the twenty-first century.

Elmore, R. F. (2000). *Building a new structure for school leadership.* Washington, DC: The Albert Shanker Institute.

This book is a serious analysis of present-day organizational problems of schools based on the conviction that Weick got it all wrong.

Firestone, W. A., & Wilson, B. L. (1985). Using bureaucratic and cultural linkages to improve instruction: The principal's contribution. *Educational Administration Quarterly, 21*(2), 7–30.

This article discusses the two kinds of linkages available for principals to use in influencing the instructional behavior of teachers: first, traditional bureaucratic linkages and, second, cultural linkages. This piece has an excellent list of references to the literature for those who wish to probe this topic more fully.

Flood, R. L. (1999). *Rethinking the fifth discipline: Learning within the unknowable.* New York, NY: Routledge.

This book contains an excellent introduction to systems thinking, which underlies all modern approaches to scientific thought, and presents a readily accessible discussion that uses nontechnical language. Flood compares systems thinking to other kinds of thinking—such as scientific reductionism and spiritualism/theism—and shows the historical connection to its emergence during the Enlightenment. We recommended it for the educational leader who seeks to better understand the emerging emphasis on scientific methods in educational research.

Meyer, J. W., & Rowan, B. (1983). The structure of educational organizations. In J. W. Meyer & W. R. Scott (Eds.). *Organizational environments: Ritual and rationality* (pp. 71–98). Beverly Hills, CA: Sage Publications.

This chapter provides a provocative analysis of schools from a sociological perspective that challenges the conventional tradition of bureaucratic logic and order. The entire book, of which this chapter is part, will be of great interest to the serious student.

Meyer, M. W. (1977). *Theory of organizational structure.* Indianapolis, IN: Bobbs-Merrill Educational Publishing.

In this 78-page book, sociologist Meyer first discusses the various functions of organizational theory. He then goes on to describe a theory of organizational structure that departs from traditional bureaucratic concepts.

Weick, K. E. (1976). Educational organizations as loosely coupled systems. *Administrative Science Quarterly, 21*(1), 1–19.

While Weick did not invent the concept of loosely coupled systems, in this article he did lay the foundation for a major shift in the theory of schools as organizations. This piece is a classic that should be read in the original.

References

Anderson, J. G. (1968). *Bureaucracy in education.* Baltimore, MD: Johns Hopkins University Press.

Barnard, C. I. (1938). *The functions of the executive.* Cambridge, MA: Harvard University Press.

Berman, P., & McLaughlin, M. W. (1977). *Federal programs supporting educational change: Factors affecting implementation and continuation* (Vol. VII). Santa Monica, CA: RAND Corporation.

Berrien, F. K. (1976). A general systems approach to organizations. In M. D. Dunnette (Ed.), *Handbook of industrial and organizational psychology* (pp. 43–61). Chicago, IL: Rand McNally.

Getzels, J. W., & Guba, E. G. (1957). Social behavior and the administrative process. *School Review, 65,* 423–441.

Goodlad, J. I. (1978). Educational leadership: Toward the third era. *Educational Leadership, 35*(4), 330.

Gross, N., & Herriott, R. E. (1965). *Staff leadership in public schools: A sociological inquiry.* New York, NY: John Wiley & Sons.

Halpin, A. W., & Croft, D. B. (1962). *The organizational climate of schools.* Washington, DC: Cooperative Research Report, U.S. Office of Education.

Kast, F. E., & Rosenzweig, J. E. (1973). *Contingency views of organization and management.* Chicago, IL: Science Research Associates.

Katz, D., & Kahn, R. L. (1978). *The social psychology of organizations* (2nd ed.). New York, NY: John Wiley & Sons.

Leavitt, H. J. (1964). *Managerial psychology* (2nd ed.). Chicago, IL: University of Chicago Press.

Lwoff, A. (1966). Interaction among virus, cell and organization. *Science, 152,* 12–16.

Moberg, D., & Koch, J. L. (1975). A critical appraisal of integrated treatments of contingency findings. *Academy of Management Journal, 18*(1), 109–124.

Owens, R. G., & Steinhoff, C. R. (1976). *Administering change in schools.* Englewood Cliffs, NJ: Prentice Hall.

Perrow, C. B. (1970). *Organizational analysis: A sociological view.* Monterey, CA: Brooks/Cole.

Robbins, S. P. (1976). *The administrative process: Integrating theory and practice.* Englewood Cliffs, NJ: Prentice Hall.

Senge, P. (2000). *Schools that learn: A fifth discipline fieldbook for educators, parents, and everyone who cares about education.* New York, NY: Doubleday.

Taylor, F. W. (1911). *The principles of scientific management.* New York, NY: Harper & Row.

von Bertalanffy, L. (1950). An outline of general systems theory. *British Journal of Philosophical Science, 1,* 134–165.

CHAPTER 5

Motivation: Understanding Self and Others

Organizational behavior has been described as arising from interactions between the person in the organization and characteristics of the organizational environment, or B = f (p • e), this chapter focuses on the person—the individual—in that equation. The previous chapters of the book focused on characteristics of the organizational environment in the equation.

THE MEANING AND PATTERNS OF MOTIVATION

Motivation deals with explanations of why people do the things they do. Why, for example, do some teachers regularly come to work and do as little as necessary, whereas others are full of energy and ideas and throw themselves zealously into the job? Why do some principals seem to focus only on the day-to-day operations in the school, with no apparent vision of where the school should be headed, whereas others seem to embrace a clear, coherent vision of the school as it ought to be and pursue it consistently over the course of years? Why are some professors boring, monotonous lecturers whose classes students avoid, whereas other professors are so enthusiastic, vibrant, and creative that their classes are interesting, always fresh, and so popular with students that they are closed out early during registration?

For millennia, the mysteries of why people behave as they do have fascinated dramatists, artists, writers, composers, philosophers, theologians, and other observers of the human condition, as the libraries and museums of the world attest. For a century now, scholars have added their efforts to probing the enigma of human motivation and have produced a body of literature that is staggering in scope and size and illuminating, too. From all this, we have learned a great deal about the links between motivation and human behavior, and we still have more to learn. In this chapter, we discuss some of what is known about motivation and the pragmatic implications of that knowledge for the practice of leadership in educational organizations.

Although many theories of motivation exist, there is much disagreement about them among scholars, but there is substantial agreement on what we are talking about when we are discussing motivation. Scholars generally agree, for example, that when we observe the variation in human behavior in organizations, at least three motivational patterns are evident.

First Pattern: Direction in Making Choices

One of the first indicators of motivation is the apparent pattern of choices that individuals make when confronted with an array of possible alternatives. When a person attends to one thing rather than others, the observer may make some motivational inference from the behavior of choosing but, of course, cannot know what actually caused the choice to be made. For example, one teacher might habitually arrive at school early in the morning, pick up the mail promptly, and proceed briskly to the classroom to prepare for the day's work and be ready and relaxed before the students arrive. Another teacher might wander in much later, chat and socialize in the office until the last moment, then dash to the classroom to begin work by fumbling with papers as the students sit at their desks waiting. A similar example is the professor who, seeing the academic job as demanding only three days a week on campus, regularly spends two days on the golf course or at the tennis club, whereas a colleague spends every spare moment studying and preparing articles for publication in academic journals that do not pay for them but also reject three times more manuscripts than they publish.

Second Pattern: Persistence

A second critical indicator of motivation is the persistence with which one pursues the chosen course of action. One dimension of persistence is the amount of time a person devotes to the chosen activity. Whether it is refinishing antiques or creating plans for a new teaching project, some people will work intensely for long hours seeking to produce meticulous, high-quality results, whereas others may give the task a "lick and a promise," consider the result good enough to get by, and let it go at that. Indeed, an individual may show great persistence in pursuing one activity meticulously and show remarkably little persistence in pursuing others. Another dimension of persistence is observed when an individual returns to a task time and again to achieve the desired results. Some teachers, for example, never seem to have the job done and frequently take work home to spend more hours on it, whereas others usually close up shop as soon as the buses have left and won't think about their work again until tomorrow. Some professors pull old yellowed lecture notes from the file year after year, whereas others spend many hours every year not merely editing, revising, and polishing their lectures but creating new methods of instruction in the hope of making classes more informative and more interesting.

Third Pattern: Intensity

The intensity with which a person attends to doing something is a third behavioral indicator that seems to be linked to motivation. One person can work with apparent high energy, seemingly concentrating intensely, engrossed in the work, whereas another might be much less intensely involved when attending to a task. Observations of intensity have to be interpreted more carefully than observations of either direction or persistence because factors beyond the control of the individual may be involved, such as the environment and the skill of the individual. For example, observing work behavior in environments with many uncontrolled interruptions, as is common in some schools, makes it difficult to determine whether the level of intensity is a matter of individual choice or the result of environmental disturbance. Similarly, an individual may be observed as being little involved as a participant in meetings, apparently merely waiting quietly for the meeting to close. The problem here could easily be environmental, such as a social climate in the meeting not being conducive to participation, or maybe the individual has never developed the behavioral attitudes and skills that one needs to participate confidently in the give and take of effective meetings, or maybe the topic under consideration is neither interesting nor relevant to the individual.

THE EXTRINSIC-INTRINSIC DEBATE

Two major approaches dominated thinking about motivation in organizational behavior during the twentieth century. One has been described by Levinson (1973) as *The Great Jackass Fallacy*. That is the age-old metaphor of the carrot and the stick, which prescribes that a combination of proffering some mix of rewards and punishments is a way to motivate people in organizational life. It is associated with behaviorist psychology in which external control of the individual is emphasized. The other approach, associated with both cognitive psychology and humanist psychology, emphasizes the psychic energy of internal thoughts and feelings as the primary source of motivation.

Extrinsic, or Behaviorist, Views

Managers have traditionally sought to motivate people with a carrot and a stick. They long ago found that people who are hurt tend to move in order to avoid pain and that people who are rewarded tend to repeat the behavior that brought the reward. This is a behaviorist concept of motivation, and it has long been highly influential in management thought. Managers using such techniques would say, "We're motivating the employees!"

The behaviorist view of motivation, that people can be motivated through manipulation of positive reinforcers (the carrot) and negative reinforcers (the stick), has been widely embraced and used in educational organizations. Merit pay plans, demands for accountability, emphasis on formal supervision, annual performance reviews tied to reappointment to position, and teacher recognition days are but a few of the many ways that this motivational concept is routinely used in public school praxis. Universities often practice an up-or-out policy to motivate newly appointed junior faculty members. They are commonly given a stipulated number of years to demonstrate growing research production through publication of their works; at the end of the time period, they know that they may be either rewarded for their behavior by being promoted and granted tenure or punished by dismissal.

Intrinsic Views of Motivation

Some contend that the behaviorist approach has nothing to do with motivation. As Frederick Herzberg said of the carrot-and-the-stick approach, "Hell, you're not motivating them. You're moving them" (as cited in Dowling, 1978, p. 44). Herzberg's observation points to a major criticism of the behaviorist approach to motivation: It in fact does not deal with motivation at all.

The view is that, although people can be *controlled* by external forces such as rewards and punishments, a crucial factor in the *motivation* of people lies within the individuals themselves. The cognitive and humanistic views of motivation spring from an understanding of people as unfolding and developing both physiologically and psychologically from biological givens. The internal capacities of individuals, primarily emotional and cognitive, give rise to feelings, aspirations, perceptions, attitudes, and thoughts, and these are what can be motivating or nonmotivating. In this view, motivation is thought of as creating conditions in the organization that facilitate and enhance the likelihood that the internal capacities of members will mature both intellectually and emotionally, thus increasing their motivation. In sum, the behaviorist tends to view motivation as something that one does *to* people, whereas the cognitive or humanist tends to view motivation as tapping the inner drives of people by creating growth-enhancing environments.

INDIVIDUAL AND GROUP MOTIVATION

Let's now focus on the motivation of people in organizations, as distinguished from the more general, broader concept of motivation of individuals qua individuals. A crucial point to remember in understanding organizational behavior is that, as a member of an organization, the person does not act alone and independently: The organization member always acts as a member of a group. That concept is probably central to understanding organizational behavior. Groups are dynamic social systems that establish interdependent relationships between and among people.

Thus, if you find yourself hurrying along a crowded city street, you would hardly think of the throng as a group of which you are a member. On the other hand, if you step to the curb and take your place in a queue to wait for a bus, you have joined a group, albeit a primitive one. The members of that group, the bus queue, share certain purposes, values, and expectations for behavior that bond them in common purpose and modify not only each individual's behavior but each person's attitudes and beliefs, too. Thus, if someone had the temerity to cut in line near the front of the queue, you would probably become concerned and join with fellow group members in remonstrating with the individual in an effort to get him or her to abide by the behavioral norms tacitly shared by the group.

The character and quality of the group's internal dynamics are often described in terms of group cohesion and morale. These dynamics of the group give rise, in turn, to basic assumptions and values that are shared between and among the members of the group as "truth" and "reality." The latter point, which is the essence of group climate and culture, will be discussed in greater depth in Chapter 7.

The power of group norms in motivating people at work, having been first clearly identified in the Western Electric Studies almost 80 years ago, is well established in the literature of organizational behavior and is widely understood and accepted. Let's take a moment to consider once again and more exactly what was learned in those studies.

The Western Electric Studies Revisited

Most students of education have heard something about the Hawthorne Studies or the Western Electric Studies, if in no other way than to have learned about the so-called Hawthorne effect, about which we shall say more in a moment. This classic research has had such a profound impact on the understanding of motivation at work, and has been so widely misunderstood in educational circles, that we should take a moment to review it here. This discussion draws on only two of the many studies that composed this very sizable research project.

THE ILLUMINATION STUDIES   The Hawthorne Works of the Western Electric Company, located in Cicero, near Chicago, was chosen as the site for an experimental study that was started in 1924 and ended 10 years later. This particular site was selected for the experiment largely because the management of Western Electric was considered enlightened and likely to be cooperative with the investigators. The purpose of the study was to find out how much illumination was required to achieve the maximum output from workers. The researchers varied the levels of illumination of an experimental group, while maintaining the same illumination of a control group. Initial results revealed no significant differences in worker productivity between the two groups.

In fact, there was some increase in output by the workers regardless of the level of illumination provided. Clearly, the workers in the experimental group were responding to *their perceptions* of the expectations of the experimenters and not to the changes in the physical environment. Thus, the workers were responding to *psychological* factors that motivated their behavior at work and, at the time of the experiments, the nature of these psychological factors was unknown to the investigators (Homans, 1951).

The significance of this study was not lost on the researchers. Whereas traditional management theory would have posited that changes in the physical environment would have an impact on worker productivity, this experiment showed a direct relationship between productivity and *psychological* phenomena, such as the expectations of others and being the focus of attention. This is sometimes called the *Hawthorne effect*, which has often been misinterpreted by many educators as suggesting that merely paying attention to people, changing some things in their environment, and expecting higher achievement from them will increase their motivation. As we shall see, there is much more to it than that.

THE RELAY INSPECTION GROUP STUDIES   After the study on the relationship between illumination and productivity was concluded, leaving more questions than answers, a new experimental study was organized in the Hawthorne Works involving workers who assembled telephone relays. The researchers, led by George Elton Mayo, used a control group, which worked in the regular shop, and an experimental group, which was given a separate work area.

Working methodically for over a year, the researchers kept careful production records while trying different experimental interventions: rest pauses, special lunch periods, a shorter working day, and a shorter working week. Throughout the period of the experimental work, output rose slowly and steadily. In each period of the experiment, output was higher than in the preceding period. Finally, the work conditions of the group were, with the consent of the workers, returned to the same as they had been prior to the start of the research (no rest periods, no special lunch periods, a regular-length workday and workweek). The result: Productivity *continued to rise*. In sum, the group had (a) become more productive and (b) had maintained that high productivity even after the experimental interventions were taken away (Homans, 1951). If rest periods and shorter working hours, plus the "special attention" of being in an experimental group, could not account for the change, what could?

CENTRAL FINDINGS OF THE STUDIES   It took a number of people some years to analyze all the data and gradually put together a picture of what had happened. The salient facts are these:

1. The workers liked the experimental situation and considered it fun.
2. The new form of supervision (encouraging them to work at a normal pace and not to try to hurry) made it possible for them to work freely and without anxiety.
3. The workers knew that what they did was important and that results were expected.
4. The workers were consulted about planned changes, often by the superintendent himself or herself, and during that process were encouraged to express their views and were, in fact, permitted to veto some ideas before they were ever implemented.
5. As a result, the group itself had changed and developed during the course of the experiment. Though the last step of the experiment was an attempt to return the group to the original conditions of work by taking away the experimental rest periods, new hours, and the like, it was in fact impossible to return the group to its original state because the group itself had been transformed. It had become more cohesive, it had developed a distinctive esprit, and it was functioning at a significantly more mature level than it had been in the beginning.

In sum,

> the women were made to feel that they were an important part of the company . . . .
> They had become participating members of a congenial, cohesive work group . . .
> that elicited feelings of affiliation, competence, and achievement. These needs,
> which had long gone unsatisfied at work, were now being fulfilled. The women
> worked harder and more effectively than they had previously. (Hersey & Blanchard,
> 1977, p. 46)

Or in the vernacular of today's educational reform, the women had been empowered, had
participated in making decisions that were important to them and their work, had been treated
in ways that fostered personal feelings of dignity and respect, and had gained "ownership" of
their work and how it was performed. However it is expressed, clearly this experience had transformed the group into a much more effective team than it had been before, as the sustained
increase in productivity over time showed.

IMPACT OF THE STUDIES   One very interesting aspect of this research is that at the time (it
was not unknown for companies in the 1920s to send goons to beat up dissident workers), it
was so unusual for a company to relate to workers in these ways that many years passed before
it dawned on anyone (except a very few advanced scholars) what had happened in the Hawthorne
plant during those experiments. For decades, many students of organization and management
chose to believe that the Hawthorne Studies showed that if you pay a little attention to people
by changing some of their working conditions, their motivation will take an upward tick and
productivity will increase. As mentioned above, this misreading of the research is often called the
Hawthorne effect.

It is now clear, however, that the Western Electric Studies set the stage for the evolution of widespread research seeking to better understand the nature and needs of human beings at work and to apply this knowledge to the development of more effective organizations.
Drawing on that large and still growing body of research, plus extensive practical experience in
applying the emerging new knowledge to a variety of organizations, we now understand that
the higher productivity achieved during the Western Electric research resulted from the fact
that, under participative leadership, the groups of workers themselves developed greater cohesiveness, higher morale, and values that were highly motivating. Once collaborative group
processes had been established, the individual participants were no longer merely working
side by side but became interrelated in ways that were unique to that specific group. Today,
of course, that is commonly called *teamwork,* and it is at the heart of motivational concepts
in work groups. As the Western Electric Studies showed, once established, teamwork can become a powerful motivator that tends to endure. School boards, school administrators, and
managers who like to view themselves as being tough failed for decades to understand the
power and significance of this simple, crucial discovery even as it was being reconfirmed in
study after study over the years. Eventually, however, it emerged in the 1980s as the central
idea in the transformation of organizational life and leadership in U.S. business, industry, and
finally in education.

CONTEMPORARY VIEWS OF THE WESTERN ELECTRIC STUDIES   The Western Electric Studies
are arguably the seminal research of the twentieth century on organizational behavior in the

workplace. They introduced a whole new approach to understanding the subject and paved the way for modern notions such as participative management, democracy in the workplace, empowerment, and more. The foundations of organization and management as we know it today, including the field of organizational behavior, were built on the Western Electric Studies, and they have stood the test of time and trial for seven decades. Contemporary scholarship developed on those foundations has added a great deal to our knowledge, but little of it has dimmed the luster of that early seminal research.

INDIVIDUAL DIFFERENCES

Thus far, the discussion has focused on some notable *environmental* factors in the basic organizational behavior equation, $B = f(p \cdot e)$. We turn now to a discussion of useful ways of thinking about the differences in the intrinsic characteristics of the *person* in that dynamic concept. One question about motivation that commonly arises is: What gets people "turned on" or "turned off"? Why is it, for example, that one person will select a particular thing to do, stick with it, and work intensively on it, whereas another person might show no interest whatever? Psychologists call this "turning on" to something, this energizing of human behavior, "arousal": It is clearly an internal aspect of self, seemingly involving emotional processes as well as cognitive processes, a characteristic that lies close to the personality of the individual. Clearly, then, the individual brings unique personal characteristics to the dynamic social interaction processes of the group. The characteristics of these internal capacities literally determine how one perceives the environment and makes judgments about it.

In Praise of Diversity

In today's world, when all people of goodwill seek to avoid the bigotry of stereotyping and labeling of others, any effort to type or categorize people tends to be met with suspicion. Yet

> people are different from each other, and no amount of getting after them is going to change them. Nor is there any reason to change them, because the differences are probably good, not bad. People are different in fundamental ways. They *want* different things; they have different motives, purposes, aims, values, needs, drives, impulses, urges. Nothing is more fundamental than that. They *believe* differently: they think, cognize, conceptualize, perceive, understand, comprehend, and cogitate differently. (Keirsey & Bates, 1984, p. 2)

Because such inner attributes—cognitions, urges, values, perceptions, and so on—are crucial in prompting us to say what we say and do what we do, the individual differences between and among us can and do evoke a vast range of behaviors. From those behaviors, we can deduce a great deal about the motivations of individuals and create useful descriptive categories. But one must be extremely cautious not to slip into the error of labeling one behavioral style good and another bad.

Because we are describing here the inner characteristics of the person, his or her temperament or personality, we are unsure of the extent to which these characteristics are either learned or innate. Therefore, we cannot be sure about the extent to which they can be intentionally modified. Some take a fairly absolutist view of this, comparing psychological type to other fixed characteristics. For example, just as short persons cannot make themselves tall and one cannot change the pattern of fingerprints or the color of one's eyes, one cannot change inner drives and attributes. Others believe that some modification of inner characteristics may be possible but always at the risk of distorting, destroying, or scarring the original instead of transforming it into something new.

However, a problem in this debate is the all-too-common tendency to confuse various ways of perceiving, thinking, feeling, and behaving as shortcomings or flaws that need to be corrected. Keirsey and Bates reminded us of the Pygmalion story from Greek mythology and cautioned that efforts to sculpt others so that they conform to our own standard of perfection are doomed to failure at the outset. Educators deal with this all the time; for example, we may understand, and perhaps accept, the idea of multiple intelligences, yet in our schools there is powerful social and cultural pressure to put a premium on certain kinds of intelligences, especially the linguistic and logical-mathematical, and value the others less in varying degrees. Thus, the logic of cultural traditions prods schools to emphasize and extol in the official curriculum languages, math, and sciences for all students and to marginalize music, the arts, and bodily kinesthetic opportunities for development. In the minds of many, for example, a "good" kindergarten curriculum stresses formal instruction in reading, language, and arithmetic and "wastes" little time on activities in which children move about, engage others in play, and participate in physical activities.

So we proceed from the assumption that people are fundamentally different in many ways, that we can understand important patterns of those differences, and that we can learn to make that understanding work productively for us. The converse assumption would be that people are, or should be, fundamentally all alike and our goal is to get them to behave alike. That, however, appears to be a twentieth-century confusion that arises from the growth of democracy in the Western world: the idea that if we are equals, then we must be alike. Today, in the twenty-first century, we celebrate a different idea: Even as we are equals, we may be different from one another.

Understanding and accepting diversity between and among people in a nonjudgmental way is important to understanding and working with organizational behavior in education. This acknowledgment does not mean, however, that we don't challenge prejudices and have an open dialog dealing with individual and collective differences. In fact, leaders should strive to create a culture that supports an *Ethic of Critique*—a by-product of critical theory (Starratt, 2004). In Starratt's *Multidimensional Ethic*, including, as well, the *Ethic of Caring* (for children and one another) and the *Ethic of Justice* (promotion of a just social order for students and staff), the *Ethic of Critique* promotes dialog about questions of power, decision making, relationship-building; essentially asking questions about why we do what we do and how we do it in the administration of the organization. Critical theory suggests that as part of this critique in developing a socially-just environment of caring and acceptance is examining our understanding and application of adult education and learning (Sheared & Sissel, 2001). In praxis, this means that educational administration and leadership emphasizes creating environments in organizations that do both of the following at the same time:

- Foster and enhance the growth and development of participants in terms of their own perceptions, needs, aspirations, and self-fulfillment.
- Accept the fact that individuals differ from one another and that this diversity can be a source of great strength to the organization.

Critical Race Theory:

Being Prepared to Pay the Price

LaSonya Moore, Vice Principal,
an urban school district in Florida

I began my first administrative experience as a young, focused visionary committed and loyal to my district, school, principal, students, teachers, families, and community. As an African American female in a "White dominated culture," I soon came to realize with every commitment comes a cost. Whether I'm criticized in public, private, marginalized in front of faculty and staff members, and ignored, there is a cost. As an instructional leader, I had to stop and ask myself, "Can I afford to pay the cost of my commitment? Could I afford the backlash of being ignored, ostracized, and, in a worst case scenario, transferred or replaced?" The response was always a resounding "no."

As an educated, African American female in a leadership role, it can be difficult to share my honest thoughts without fear of retribution. As a vice principal, my current role allows me the opportunity to listen to controversial conversations about organizational change as it relates to students, parents, faculty, and staff. Many of those conversations are filled with inconsistencies and stereotypical viewpoints, not by choice, but by lack of background. As one African American female in a large, urban school district, my race seems to somehow make a big splash. I have been a vice principal for six years, and in those six years I have become accustomed to conversations that are in dire need of cultural sensitivity. Whether intentionally or unintentionally, the fact remains the same, race continues to play a major role in the decision-making process.

I recently attended a team meeting at an educational institution. The meeting members consisted of a school dean, three vice principals, three counselors, and one intern. My heart tells me that these individuals are dedicated, educated, student-first individuals. The meeting agenda focused on processes, policies, and programs for the following school year. The organizational structure of specific programs was the focal point of the meeting discussion (specifically the behavior academy). The behavior academy housed approximately six to 10 male minority students.

The dean posed the following question during the meeting, "Should we have another Behavior Academy next year?" The room became silent, numb, and almost lifeless. After a difficult silence, the dean repeated the question; this time his tone became more forceful as if the silence made him angry. The team's unresponsiveness was not due to disrespect, but due to fear of future repercussions. Will it affect our evaluation, job, or future professional opportunities? Finally, a counselor stated, "I don't think the program is beneficial unless the instructional methods are changed." The environment of the room became unpleasant, smiles became straight-faced. Feeling a bit worried (as I have in the past) about my position, I began to have internal conversations. Asking myself, "Will I sit idly by (without speaking up) allowing students to be underserved in a public educational environment?" The fear of backlash traveled through my bones like fire. Although, previously the principal has labeled the administrative meeting room as "Vegas" or "cone of silence" meaning what's stated in here remains in here, sadly, it has been proven on several occasions that this was not the case. Statements were repeated to faculty and staff members in an effort to assist with a process or program, but inadvertently caused poor morale amongst the organization as a whole.

Stepping out on the edge, I took a deep breath and made the following statement: "First off, thank you for asking my opinion. With all due respect, I cannot continue to support a program that is exclusive and not in the best interest of *all* students—the current program targets male minority students." This remark allowed some to feel a sense of relief while others gasped. The dean immediately became defensive and stated the following, "Well, I guess this means we won't have a Behavior Academy next year since all the black kids are being targeted." I then responded, "That was not the statement I made." Before I could continue, the guidance counselor immediately began speaking. He stated, "I don't think Mrs. Moore said anything about black students, but a concern that ALL students having the opportunity to be placed in the program as it relates to their individual educational needs." The dean then looked over at the vice principal of curriculum (VPC) and said "Remove the Behavior Academy from the master schedule." The VPC replied with "I didn't expect to have the adequate numbers to support the program next year, anyways." The room again became quiet and unresponsive. Shortly after this moment, the meeting was adjourned. I later asked the dean what his thoughts were on the Behavior Academy. I suggested that we should get teacher and parent input as well, in addition to looking at the student data. The response I received was, "Do you think these teachers care? The teachers don't care—they just want *them* out of their classroom."

As the vice principal in charge of the School Based Leadership Committee, I knew the answer to both questions and was sure she was aware based on our previous conversations. He simply responded with "It doesn't matter; I won't lock your black kids away in the Behavior Academy." And with those final remarks, she simply walked away down the hall, which ironically featured a variety of flags from different countries around the world which represented our diverse population at the school. Upon my arrival to this school, there was a limited amount of minority faculty and staff members. Since the new dean's arrival, he has hired several minority faculty (including myself) and staff to meet the needs of the changing culture. By no means was the dean a racist, but did he lack a certain level of cultural proficiency, certainly.

I look forward to a time in my life in which all educational leaders are able to sit down and have frank conversations about students, families, achievement, politics, policies, and organizational procedures without the fear of being punished or ostracized at a future point in time. As a leader, I'm obligated to speak up for those who cannot speak for themselves. Social justice is a major issue in our country as a whole. It is my sincere hope that on this day I created some thought-provoking ripples that will be dealt with in the long run—ripples that will positively affect the lives of students, parents, teachers, and ultimately the community as a whole. I do realize, however, there will always be public and private racism at all levels. There will always be inappropriate and unprofessional backlash. The critical race theory is alive and well. My race is not theory, it is a reality that I have dealt with and will continue to deal with forever.

Archetypes

We commonly make the great diversity between and among people manageable by thinking of individuals as archetypes: "Oh," we say, "he's that kind of guy!" or "Did you hear what she asked? That's vintage Harriet Smith!" Psychologists do the same thing.

- Howard Gardner described the differences between and among people in terms of seven kinds of intelligence.
- Based on the work of Carl Jung, many psychologists describe individuals in terms of their temperaments or personality types.

HUMAN INTELLIGENCE

Earlier in this book, we discussed intelligence as a critical variable in the ways in which people differ. In his landmark book on human intelligences (which we discussed in Chapter 2 of this book), Howard Gardner (1983) drew attention to the shift during the twentieth century of philosophers and psychologists from focusing on the external objects of the physical world in explaining human behavior to focusing on the mind, and especially cognitive thought, which depends so heavily on symbols such as those from language, mathematics, the visual arts, body language, and other human symbols. Gardner explained that there are several kinds of intelligence and that they are independent of one another; each kind enables a person to engage in intellectual activity in different ways.

In describing the historical underpinnings of his theory of multiple intelligences, Gardner recounted the noted meeting between William James, the first world-renowned psychology scholar from the United States, and Sigmund Freud, which took place in Worcester in 1909. The occasion was Freud's only trip to the United States, which was at the invitation of G. Stanley Hall, the psychologist who was then president of Clark University. The meeting between Freud, who had already achieved celebrity in Europe, and the aging James is acclaimed in the history of the development of psychology because it set the stage for the eventual emergence of modern psychology that was to transcend the radical behaviorism that was so dominant in the United States at that time.

Gardner (1983) explained:

> What united Freud and James and what set them apart from the mainstream of psychology both on the Continent and in the United States, was a belief in the importance, the centrality, of the individual self—a conviction that psychology must be built around the concept of the person, his personality, his growth, his fate. Moreover, both scholars deemed the capacity for self-growth to be an important one, upon which depended the possibility of coping with one's surroundings. (p. 25)

Curiously, Gardner did not mention the presence of another person on that historic occasion, one who was to play a pivotal role in explaining human personality and its capacity for self-growth and adaptation to the environment. Carl Jung, then 34 years old and a close collaborator of Freud's, would soon thereafter break away from his older colleague and create new ways of understanding the differences between and among individuals that have proven to be invaluable in understanding organizational behavior.

TEMPERAMENT AND ORGANIZATIONAL BEHAVIOR

Early psychology was dominated by the notion that people are motivated from within by a single instinct. The scholar's challenge was to identify that instinct. To Freud, it was Eros, which manifested itself in different guises at different times. Adler thought that the motivating instinct was to acquire power. Others thought that the desire for social belonging was the central motivational instinct. To the existentialists, it was the search for self that informed and drove our behavior. Keirsey and Bates (1984) noted, "Each appealed to instinct as purpose, and each made one instinct primary for everybody" (pp. 2–3).

Carl Jung's masterwork on motivation revealed that this was not so, that individuals are motivated by different inner forces, and there is wide variation in these motivational forces from person to person. But Jung identified a pattern in these individual differences. Understanding the pattern of individual differences enables one to better understand the behavior of others and to predict their likely behaviors under different circumstances. This development was the basis for understanding the concept of personality types.

Like Freud, his senior and sometime mentor, Carl Jung was a clinical psychologist. Having observed many people in his clinical practice, he began to think that the personalities of various individuals could be sorted into categories according to types. He compared his observations with studies of literature, mythology, and religions and found that the idea was often used by writers and other observers of human behavior. He published a treatise on the subject in 1920 (Jung, 1971), and a student of his translated it into English in 1923; both publications were largely ignored. Why? Because as Benfari and Knox (1991) informed us:

> [I]n 1923, other approaches to psychology were dominant in Europe and North America. Freudian psychology was in vogue in Europe and on both American coasts, while grass-roots America was under the overwhelming influence of behaviorism. Scientific circles of the time regarded Jung as mystical and his approach antithetical to their own penchant for logic and facts. (pp. 4–5)

The Four Psychological Types

Cutting through the confusion that abounds in trying to understand the essential personality differences between and among people, Jung's observations led him to a simple analysis: human personality has three basic dimensions. The mix of these dimensions varies from person to person, although they cluster into patterns that are called psychological types. In the 1950s, as we shall describe, Isabel Myers and her mother, Katheryn Briggs, added a fourth dimension to the analysis, laying the basis for identifying four *psychological types*—or four temperaments—of people, an analysis that is widely accepted today.

When we speak of four psychological types, we are speaking of the ways in which people perceive the world around them, how they interpret what they perceive, and how they form judgments about their perceptions—that is, the extent to which people are (a) introverted or extraverted,[1] (b) sensing or intuitive, (c) thinking or feeling, and (d) perceiving or judging. From the perspective of psychological types, therefore, there is no objective independent reality that we call the environment: The "real" environment, for any individual, depends largely on how one perceives and interprets it. This is an important point in understanding organizational behavior and a central tenet of postmodern thought: The reality of organizational life lies largely in the eye of the beholder. An understanding of one's own temperament not only puts one in a better position to understand how one sees and deals with the organizational world, it also gives one greater ability to understand the behavior of others in the organization.

The Myers-Briggs Type Indicator (MBTI)

After World War II, when the field of psychology underwent extraordinary ferment and many alternatives to traditional academic behaviorism emerged, Jung's idea that psychological types existed and could be identified was revisited. Myers and Briggs triggered widespread interest in the possibilities and uses of this idea when they created a simple questionnaire that was said to be reliable and valid in determining the psychological type of individuals. The MBTI makes it easy to use the four behavioral dimensions that have just been described to sort people according to the preferences that they tend to use in dealing with the world around them. The MBTI and its offshoots have also been widely advocated in popular literature for individuals to use as a

---

[1]The atypical spelling of the word *extraversion* became the accepted spelling in the subject index of *Psychological Abstracts* in 1974 and has been the accepted spelling in the literature on individual differences since that time.

way of assessing their own personality type. On the Myers-Briggs website (myersbriggs.org) one can take the original MBTI (for a fee) that is scored by a trained professional, which includes a 1-hour phone consultation. This website also provides a referral network of professionals around the world. In addition, several websites offer free inventories that measure the same dimensions as the MBTI (see examples in Reflective Activities section at the end of this chapter).

Despite criticisms that the MBTI has limited validity and reliability studies to support it, it has received worldwide popularity. Many find the information very useful in understanding themselves and those around them. To anyone who wants to be an educational leader, having a clear understanding of how one functions in the world—how one "reads" the environment, the kinds of information one attends to, how one interprets what is perceived—is, of course, a great advantage in dealing effectively with many kinds of people.

FOUR BASIC DIMENSIONS OF HUMAN PERSONALITY   The MBTI is an instrument that identifies 16 different patterns of action that people are likely to follow in responding to certain situations. The 16 patterns of action are combinations of four dimensions that describe the preferences that one might have in dealing with the situations. Three of the dimensions were described by Jung in the 1920s:

- Introversion-extraversion (I-E)
- Sensation-intuition (S-N)
- Thinking-feeling (T-F)

Myers and Briggs used these three dimensions as scales to create the MBTI. They devised questions to represent these scales and to which people taking the test would respond. During their work, Myers and Briggs created a fourth dimension that they believed was needed:

- Perceiving-judging (P-J)

The MBTI inventory is scored on each dimension and results in 16 possible personality types. The results of taking the inventory are reported for a test taker using a letter from each of the dimensions that was the test taker's strongest indicator, such as ISTJ, INFP, ENTP, ESFJ, and so forth.

The MBTI became popular in U.S. corporate organizations as a self-assessment instrument for those who wanted to learn more about themselves as managers as well as about their colleagues. It has also been used in corporate training programs to help work groups gain a better understanding of ways to become more effective in dealing with various types of colleagues in the organization. Aside from its uses as a self-assessment instrument, the dimensions on which the MBTI is built provide an interesting way to analyze and understand organizational behavior.

INTROVERSION-EXTRAVERSION (ATTITUDE)   Jung "used the term *attitude* to refer to the ways that individuals direct their psychic energy. He described two attitudes: the extraverted and the introverted" (Keirsey & Bates, 1984, p. 6). Some people characteristically receive great psychic energy from external sources: people, events, and things in the environment. Typically these are very sociable individuals who like to talk to people, play, and work with them. They find that meeting and interacting with others is fun; it invigorates them and recharges their psychic batteries. They are the extraverts, and whether at work, at play, or on vacation, they gravitate to other people and want to be involved where the action is. Working alone in quiet places is wearisome to the extravert, who tends to find activities such as research in the library or puzzling alone over a complex problem tiring and draining.

Introverts usually like people and often enjoy being around them, but they tend to find socializing taxing, tiring, and draining of their energies rather than energizing. The introvert prefers quiet, even being alone at times, and in this environment is recharged and invigorated.

These dimensions—introversion and extraversion—are useful in thinking about motivation because they reveal deep-seated orientations about how one literally perceives the world, where one gets information about the world, and how one makes judgments about what is real in the world. Two individuals, one an extravert and the other an introvert, tend to experience identical events differently, understand them differently, and respond to them differently. It is important to remind ourselves, however, that one is not *either* an introvert *or* an extravert. This is a dimension that describes the intensity of a personality characteristic. Each of us may tend to emphasize either extravert attitudes or introvert attitudes, but most of us find that both attitudes coexist in each of us.

A Dimension Rather Than Either-Or.   In thinking about introversion-extraversion attitudes, however, it must be underscored that we are dealing with a dimension with two poles: introversion at one end and extraversion at the other. One's attitude leans toward one pole or the other, but it would be rare indeed to find a "pure" type. Thus, an introvert is not totally without the ability to enjoy other people, to socialize, or to share with them, nor is an extravert unable to enjoy concentrating on tasks alone or a break away from the "pressure cooker" of the organization. It is the balance, chiefly between sociability and territory, that identifies types in this dimension.

SENSATION-INTUITION (PROCESSES OF PERCEPTION) AND THINKING-FEELING (PROCESSES OF JUDGMENT)   In describing the ways in which different types of people relate to their environments, Jung saw that there were two rational functions, thinking and feeling, and two nonrational functions, sensing and intuition. These allude to how one experiences, judges, and reacts to events in the environment. Normally one or perhaps two tend to dominate in an individual.

PERCEIVING-JUDGING (DEALING WITH THE OUTSIDE WORLD)   As Myers and Briggs developed an instrument for identifying personality types, they added a fourth dimension of behavior that people use in dealing with the world around them: perceiving and judging. A *perceiving* person is one who tends to use either sensing or intuition to make sense of the environment. On the other hand, one who tends to use either thinking or feeling in interactions with the environment is described as a *judging* type of individual. For example, a person who is a sensing-judging personality is thought to be more logical in his or her lifestyle, while a feeling-judging personality is more empathetic.

An Educational Application—True Colors®

A popular application of temperament types in education has been the True Colors concept. True Colors was developed by Don Lowry in 1978 and is based on the Myers-Briggs Type Indicator. True Colors presents real-life applications of the use of psychological typing in schools and organizations. In fact, in the 1980s the State Department of Education in Tennessee endorsed this concept and provided training around the state. The goal was to help promote understanding of others and to embrace diversity. True Colors uses four colors to represent different psychological types. They are blue, gold, green, and orange. Some characteristics or adjectives describing individuals of various colors would be as follows:

- Blue: sensitive, friendly, helpful
- Gold: responsible, organized, dependable, efficient

- Green: analytic, calm, logical
- Orange: outgoing, playful, energetic

In school, both teachers and children take the personality quiz to determine their primary and secondary color types. True Colors then provides workshops and training in teambuilding, communication strategies, working with parents, coaching, and learning styles. We have not found any independent research on the success of True Colors, but the True Colors website provides a research article by Whichard (2006) describing the reliability and validity of the personality inventory. Whichard concluded True Colors had content validity when measured against the MBTI, and "the True Colors program, assessments and products were judged as highly accurate by study participants in predicting and assessing behavioral characteristics and preferences" (Executive Summary section, para. 4). One of the authors of this text was trained in True Colors, and I can attest to the interest by both teachers and students in True Colors concepts and the usefulness in bringing issues related to diversity to the table for discussion.

Final Thoughts on Temperament and Organizational Behavior

Keirsey and Bates (1984) thought that about 75% of the population in the U.S. was extroverted and about 25% introverted, but according to a study by Myers, McCaulley, Quenk, and Hammer (1998), reported in the MBTI manual, 49.3% of the population are extroverts, and 50.7% are introverts. Surprisingly, more females were found to be extroverts (52.5%) versus introverts (47.5%) compared to males (45.9% extroverts; 54.1% introverts). Table 5.1 displays the percentages for each dimension as reported in the MBTI manual.

With the exception of the Sensation-Intuition dimension, there is a remarkable difference between males and females, with the most notable difference in the Thinking-Feeling dimension.

In Western cultures, it is common to think that there is something wrong with those individuals who prefer a little peace and quiet, perhaps some solitude, and a little territorial breathing room. "Indeed," noted Keirsey and Bates (1984), "Western culture seems to sanction the outgoing, sociable and gregarious temperament. The notion of anyone wanting or needing much solitude is viewed rather often as reflecting an unfriendly attitude" (p. 17). When one considers that the attitudes of people in non-Western cultures often tend to be more supportive and approving of those who prefer to direct their psychological energy inward than those whose energy

TABLE 5.1 Percentage of Population in Each Dimension of the MBTI.

Dimension	Males	Females	Total Population
Extroversion	45.9	52.5	49.3
Introversion	54.1	47.5	50.7
Sensation	71.7	74.9	73.3
Intuition	28.3	25.1	26.7
Thinking	56.5	24.5	40.2
Feeling	43.5	75.5	59.8
Judging	52.0	56.2	54.1
Perceiving	48.0	43.8	45.9

Source: Adapted from data in MBTI manual (Myers, McCaulley, Quenk, & Hammer, 1998).

is primarily directed outward, it becomes clearer that Jung was close to being right in believing that introversion-extraversion reveals some combination of innate, inherited attitudes and skills that reflect learning to conform to cultural norms. For example, the introverted individual may very well learn the social skills and attitudes to deal effectively with the expectation that one occasionally attends large, noisy cocktail parties as part of professional life. The extravert, on the other hand, may learn to "work the room" expertly. The difference is that the introvert will find the experience demanding, perhaps tiring, while the extravert will find it exhilarating and just plain fun.

As we have seen, using the examples of intelligences and personality types, many psychologists focus on the role that various personal characteristics play in motivation. These personal characteristics are thought to be basic to motivation: In large measure, they literally construct the environment of the individual by defining and describing what is perceived and understood; they cause a person to attend to one thing rather than another; they explain why the individual is persistent in some tasks and desultory in others. Sense making, viewed through the lenses of individual differences, is informed by the way one thinks, feels, and experiences as one interacts with the organizational environment. To what extent are these personal characteristics innate or learned? In pragmatic terms, we don't know: for scholars, the debate continues. However, many theories of motivation have been constructed on the assumption that humans universally respond to certain innate needs.

INTRINSIC MOTIVATION

Other than behaviorist theories of motivation, which emphasize motivational factors external to the individual (e.g., the carrot and the stick), there are two main perspectives on motivational thought: the cognitive perspective and the humanistic perspective. Both view motivation as intrinsic, or arising from within the individual.

Cognitive Views of Motivation

One cognitive perspective on motivation is based on the belief that human beings have an innate drive to understand the world, make sense of it, gain control over their lives, and become increasingly self-directed, which is thought to give rise to certain innate characteristics that arouse and energize individuals to work toward these ends. Following Piaget (1977), the cognitive perspective assumes that people are motivated by a need for order, predictability, sensibleness, and logic in dealing with the world. This is equilibrium, an idea central to Piaget's theory. Piaget used the term *equilibration* to describe the processes of seeking equilibrium. In applying the notion of equilibrium to organizational life, one would tend to emphasize organizational routines to develop regularity, predictability, and dependability as desirable motivating processes.

ACHIEVEMENT MOTIVATION   John Atkinson (1960) thought that every individual was driven by two learned characteristics: the desire or need to achieve success (n Achievement or n-Ach) and/or the desire to avoid failure. Some people are high in their n-Ach and low in the need to avoid failure (low avoidance), whereas others are low in their n-Ach and high in avoidance of failure (high avoidance). The behaviors of people with these two different motivational traits obviously tend to be different. Atkinson's work, which was carried on and extended by his close colleague and longtime collaborator, David McClelland (1961, 1976, 1988), has had an enormous impact on thinking about the behavior of managers in corporate America and in conceptualizing entrepreneurship in free-market capitalism. In addition to n-Ach, McClelland's theory also focused on two additional needs: the need for power (n-Pow) and the need for affiliation (n-Affil). N-Pow emphasizes an individual's need to lead others and to make an impact, and n-Affil is the need for human interaction and friendly relations—to feel liked and be accepted. Our motivation and behaviors, then, are influenced by how high or low our needs are in relation to n-Ach, n-Pow, and n-Affil.

Woven into achievement motivation theory is a very strong element of competition. It would appear that high n-Ach people thrive on competition and find it zestful and energizing, whereas high avoidance people tend to shun competition and find it stressful. But it should be made clear that the approach-avoidance concept is about *potential in human characteristics*. One may exhibit high avoidance behavior in some situations, yet in other circumstances one's n-Ach motives may be aroused and one may engage in highly competitive behavior. A shy, self-effacing young woman, for example, may shun public appearances and large, glittering celebrity parties, yet step onstage before a world-class orchestra and an audience of thousands and deliver a brilliant violin solo knowing that the critics as well as her older colleagues are listening perceptively, looking for the slightest flaw.

In the literature on achievement, success-oriented people (high approach to success—low avoidance of failure) are extolled as achieving above and beyond the standards, beating the competition, being winners. High-approach people were mythologized during the Reagan/Bush presidencies as hard driving, risk taking, tough, relentless, narrowly focused on achieving a limited goal, driven by the clock, often with little consideration for others. Failure avoiders (low approach—high avoidance), on the other hand, act more defensively, are more careful to avoid losses, and often restructure the situation so that failure may be redefined as success.

Although people high in n-Ach anticipate and savor success and victory in competition, their counterparts seek to avoid humiliation and failure. Just as achievers work hard and relentlessly to ensure success, failure avoiders may tend toward inaction or may lower their aspirations to more closely match their perception of the likelihood of success. One has to be very careful, however, not to overgeneralize. Failure avoiders can, and often do, strive very hard and are often highly successful in the process. Covington (1992) described it as

> a frontal assault on failure—avoiding failure by succeeding! …These fear-driven successes can be extraordinary. Many failure-threatened students are merit scholar finalists, class valedictorians, and National Science Fair winners. Despite such outward signs of success, however, being driven to succeed out of fear may be the ultimate academic ordeal. The individual's sense of worth comes to depend to an increasingly perilous degree on always succeeding, relentlessly, and against lengthening odds. (p. 89)

The central point is that those who seek to avoid failure can be, and often are, highly motivated people.

Ferdinand Hoppe did landmark research on the roles of self-confidence, expectations, and aspirations in the motivation of people when he was Kurt Lewin's laboratory assistant in 1930 and 1931. Hoppe's research involved the game of ring toss. He found that individuals perceived themselves to be successful depending on their *expectancy* to achieve at a certain level. Their levels of aspiration would shift based on prior experience—aspirations would shift upward after success and downward after failure. Hoppe's experiments gave meaning to the term *self-confidence* (Covington, 1992).

> There is no accounting for self-confidence in objective terms. Some individuals may discern a gleam of hope in a situation that seems hopeless to everyone but themselves. At the same time, others may express a vote of no confidence despite the fact that they have everything going for them. Basically, self-confidence reflects the extent to which the individual believes himself or herself able to win the prize, to turn back the foe, or in Hoppe's experiment to toss enough rings correctly. (Covington, 1992. p. 26)

MCCLELLAND AND THE "SPIRIT OF CAPITALISM"   Having identified the need to achieve and the avoidance of failure as personality traits that are relatively stable and have some value in predicting behavior in various circumstances, McClelland proceeded to extend his thinking to the larger society and to the economic growth of nations around the world. His hypothesis was that, first, highly motivated people can change society itself, and, second, a society experiences economic growth when it promotes the advancement and use of achievement motivation by its people. This could be done, McClelland believed—and many still believe strongly—by placing high value on the orientation to achievement and teaching this value in the home and in the schools, as well as teaching the attitudes, skills, and habits that might develop high n-Ach.

Thus, McClelland elevated discourse on motivation to the realms of social, political, and economic policy. For example, to transform a society into a highly motivated one with a "spirit of capitalism," which he called *The Achieving Society,* McClelland (1961) advocated child-rearing practices and schooling as primary points of intervention.

The belief that there is a link between high achievement motivation as a sociocultural norm and the economic productivity of a people is remarkably similar to Max Weber's observations during the Belle Époque that led to his work *The Protestant Ethic and the Spirit of Capitalism* (Weber, 1930). Weber lived at a time when both Roman Catholicism and Protestantism were vigorous social forces omnipresent in the daily lives of European people. Both had a powerful impact on their ethical beliefs as well as child-rearing practices and schooling. Thus, it was significant when Weber observed that the productivity and economic development of European Protestant countries and European Roman Catholic countries differed from one another. Weber believed that the "Protestant ethic"—with its emphasis on individual faith and independence, rejection of personal pleasure, and the belief that hard work is inherently good—accounted for much of the observed difference. As one can imagine, this view aroused a good deal of controversy over the years; however, it also has had a powerful impact on Western thought about the inner versus outer issues in motivation. The extensive research carried out by McClelland and his followers lends strong support to the notion that the society that emphasizes the need for personal achievement, hard work, and personal responsibility may be inculcating the characteristics that will ultimately lead to the society's high productivity and economic development. Indeed, in our time, with the demise of communism, we have witnessed an unfolding of this line of thought as the Eastern European countries of the old Soviet empire struggle to transform their societies and their economies by trying to cast off Soviet-style bureaucracy and adopt the outlook, values, and work behavior of free-market, capitalist cultures.

SOCIAL COGNITIVE THEORY AND SELF-EFFICACY   The work of Albert Bandura has had a significant impact on psychology in general and on educational psychology in particular. He

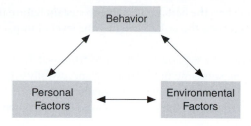

FIGURE 5.1 Graphic representation of triadic reciprocality.

saw limitations in behaviorist principles that focused on external forces that affect individual behavior and limitations in human functioning theories that focused on biological traits. He believed human functions are the result of dynamic connections among personal factors, such as cognition, environmental factors, and behavior. This fact takes our equation for individual and organizational behavior, $B = f(p \cdot e)$, one step further, by stating that "behavior, cognition and other personal factors, and the environmental influences all operate interactively as determinants of each other" (Bandura, 1986, p. 23). Bandura called this *triadic reciprocality*. People are viewed as self-motivating, self-reflective, and proactive rather than as reactive organisms that are controlled by their environment or motivated by innate traits. Triadic reciprocality can be portrayed visually, as shown in Figure 5.1.

Initially called *social learning theory*, Bandura changed the name to *social cognitive theory* because he found that cognitive processes mediated social learning. The hallmark of this theory is that individuals can proactively control their development and make things happen by taking action. However, what people do is affected by what they believe they are capable of performing, which is termed *self-efficacy*. People tend to avoid those situations in which they don't believe they are capable of performing well, and they will enthusiastically perform those behaviors when they feel capable of performing them well. This fact is combined with an individual's perception of the value or importance of the particular activity, and thus both have an effect on motivation. Some theorists have called this *expectancy theory* of motivation—a person is motivated if he or she believes in his or her capacity to successfully perform a task and whether or not it is of importance to them; the latter is called the *valence*, or value, of performing the task. The valence is established by the internal and external rewards of completing the task. Victor Vroom (1964) is credited with the first description of expectancy theory, which led to the expression that motivation is a function of the valence and the expectation the task can be accomplished successfully or $M = (V^*E)$.

Self-efficacy influences the choices we make, how much effort we put into those choices, and how long we persist in our choices if we encounter difficulties. If individuals overestimate their capability, then they may become involved in activities they are not able to complete well and perhaps get themselves and others into difficulties. On the other hand, if individuals underestimate their ability to complete a task, they will shy away from activities that may be potentially rewarding to them, which could improve their self-efficacy for a particular task. All of this has enormous implications for leaders in the areas of instruction and staff development.

Self-efficacy comes from four sources:

1. ***Enactive Attainment***—one's experience in performing a particular task, either successfully or not: "Enactive attainments provide the most influential source of efficacy information because it is based on authentic mastery experiences" (Bandura, 1986, p. 399). The more

mastery successes one has, the better one is able to sustain failure in the same task. Also, the more difficult one perceives the task, the higher the level of impact on one's self-efficacy to perform that task.

2. *Vicarious Experience*—the experience one gains from watching or visualizing others perform a task. Observing someone perform a task successfully affects one's belief that he or she can also perform that task. Conversely, watching someone fail has a negative impact on self-efficacy. This result, of course, is influenced by one's own experience with the task (enactive attainment).

3. *Verbal Persuasion*—information one receives from others, positive or negative, about one's ability to perform a task and the perceived importance or value of a task. Although more limited in influencing self-efficacy than the previous two sources, it is most useful in helping an individual create greater effort and persistence in performing a task, particularly if the person has some belief in his or her ability to perform. Verbal persuasion is more effective when the person giving feedback is viewed as skilled in performing the same task, and when the feedback is presented positively: "In the case of teaching, the expertise and knowledge of the supervisor, mentor or consultant must be respected for performance feedback to be effective in enhancing personal efficacy beliefs" (Labone, 2004, p. 348).

4. *Physiological State*—one's reaction to internal physiological reactions to performing a task. High stress or anxiety decreases one's ability to perform a task successfully, and this internal feedback only increases the stress and fear reaction.

We need to distinguish self-efficacy from self-concept or self-esteem. Although related to self-concept, self-efficacy is context-specific about one's ability to perform a specific task, or type of task; self-concept is a more global assessment about one's general capabilities and judgment of self-worth (self-esteem). Self-concept and self-esteem are based on a lifetime of experiences and feedback from significant others. Self-efficacy, however, can certainly affect one's self-concept when supported by many positive enactive experiences, vicarious experiences, and verbal persuasion of one's ability to perform certain tasks. One may feel highly efficacious about performing a specific task, for example, mathematics, yet have a low self-concept about one's overall academic skills and hence not take pride in one's accomplishments in math. Conversely, one may have a positive self-concept yet feel unable to perform a variety of specific tasks. To avoid the feelings associated with low self-concept, individuals may be drawn to more limited activities in which they have high self-efficacy.

Organizations, like individuals, can have a sense of collective efficacy. Bandura (1986) put it this way:

> The strength of groups, organizations, and even nations lies partly in people's sense of collective efficacy that they can solve their problems and improve their lives through concerted effort. Perceived collective efficacy will influence what people choose to do as a group, how much effort they put into it, and their staying power when group efforts fail to produce results. (p. 449)

If groups have a strong sense of efficacy that they can sustain a change, for example, then they will be able to resist or cope with outside efforts to undermine the change. In this particular example, self-efficacy and collective efficacy contributes to the resiliency of the group, that is, their ability to bounce back from adversity. The reverse, however, is also true. If a group faces obstacles and it does not believe it is capable of surmounting them, it will cease trying. This shutdown can have a monumental impact on an organization trying to implement change.

All of these factors become important to organizational leaders who need to be aware of the status of employee self-efficacy and collective efficacy. Employees who perceive themselves as highly efficacious will be more likely to put forth effort that is sustainable to produce successful outcomes, and of course, the reverse is true. Employees who see themselves as unable to complete a task either will not vigorously pursue the task or they will cease their efforts prematurely. This fact has been shown to be true through research. In a meta-analysis by Stajkovic and Luthans (1998) of self-efficacy in the workplace, a strong, positive correlation was found between self-efficacy and work-related task performance, which translated to an impressive 28% gain in task performance. The strength of the relationship, however, is moderated by the complexity of the task and the locus of control, that is, how much control participants felt they had over the implementation of a task. This has huge implications for organizations in terms of ensuring that individuals have the skills and belief that they can perform a task, and that they have control over its implementation.

Using self-efficacy theory and research, leaders can ensure that staff members have the best chance at successfully implementing change by following some simple guidelines:

1. First and foremost, staff must be trained, so they have a clear understanding of the tasks to be performed, and they have the skills necessary to perform the tasks.
2. Training should provide active practice at implementing the tasks so that individuals and groups experience success (enactive attainment).
3. Part of the training process should involve observing others model successful implementation (vicarious experience).
4. Leaders should take every advantage during training and during implementation to provide positive feedback and encourage others to provide feedback in individual and group implementation (verbal persuasion).
5. Leaders need to protect the organization from outside negative influences that seek to impose obstacles. The staff must see itself as having complete control of implementation and feel they are supported from the outside (locus of control).
6. Standards of performance against which individuals and the group can judge their accomplishments must be provided.

The Humanistic Perspective

The cognitive perspective on motivation is that we are motivated from within to make sense of the world as we perceive it, to exercise control of our lives, and to be inner-directed. The humanistic perspective maintains that personal needs to constantly grow and develop, to cultivate personal self-esteem, and to have satisfying human relationships are highly motivating drives. This perspective, as described by Hamachek (1987), is a "searching to understand what goes on inside us—our needs, wants, desires, feelings, values, and unique ways of perceiving and understanding what causes us to behave the way we do…it is what teachers practice as they help students to see the personal relevancy of what they are learning" (p. 160).

Accordingly, motivation is internal—not something that is done *to* us—and emphasizes nurturing an inherent ongoing human proclivity to continue growing, developing and maturing, and being enriched by new experiences. Hence, one is always in the process of becoming. In this view, there is no such thing as an unmotivated person. The experienced teacher who shows little enthusiasm for the latest twist in curriculum and instruction being advocated by the superintendent is not unmotivated—that teacher may not be motivated to do what the superintendent would prefer, but she or he probably sees little connection between what is being demanded and her or his internal sense of fulfillment.

ABRAHAM MASLOW: MOTIVATION AS A HIERARCHY OF NEEDS One of the most powerful and enduring ways of understanding human motivation was developed by Abraham Maslow, who, unlike the experimental psychologists of his day, decided to study the motivation patterns shown by people as they lived. He believed that people are driven from within to realize their full growth potential. This ultimate goal is sometimes called *self-fulfillment,* sometimes *self-realization,* but Maslow called it *self-actualization.* Some people—such as Eleanor Roosevelt, Thomas Jefferson, and Albert Einstein, all of whose lives Maslow studied—achieve self-actualization in the course of their lives, and many people do not, but they all strive in that direction.

The genius of Maslow's work lies in his hierarchy of needs, which is shown in Figure 5.2. Human needs start with survival, then unfold in an orderly, sequential, hierarchical pattern that

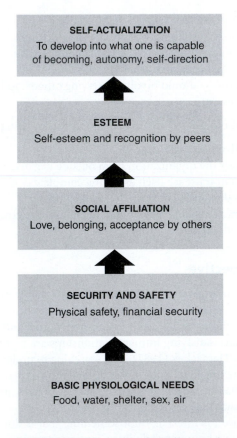

FIGURE 5.2 Hierarchy of needs as used in Maslow's theory of motivation.

takes us toward continued growth and development (Maslow, 1970). *Prepotency* is the term that Maslow used to describe the fact that one cannot be motivated by a higher need until the lower needs are met first. For example, we all start out with the need to survive, and the basics for that are food, water, clothing, and shelter. The next higher need is safety: to be without fear of physical or psychological harm. The need for survival is prepotent, however: One cannot attend to the need for safety unless the needs for survival are met first. After the need for safety is met, one seeks affiliation: belonging, acceptance by others, love. Once one's prepotent needs for affiliation are adequately met, one is motivated by the next higher need in the hierarchy: the need for self-esteem. Self-esteem comes from recognition and respect from others.

Deficiency Needs and Growth Needs.   The lower four needs in Maslow's hierarchy are called *deficiency needs* because (a) their deficiency motivates people to meet them, and (b) until the deficiencies are met, people find it difficult to respond to a higher order need. Thus, the teacher who feels unsafe at school is unlikely to be highly motivated to seek acceptance by other members of the faculty or by the need for recognition or approval. In Maslow's view, trying to create a more supportive, accepting climate in the school or to use participative methods of decision making are likely to be problematic if the prepotent need—the need for safety—is not met first.

The higher order needs are called *growth needs,* and they are different. The growth needs are never fully met. For example, as one learns more and develops aesthetic appreciation, the need for growth is not met; rather, it expands. The music aficionado never wearies of fine music but studies more, collects recordings, and continues attending concerts, always striving to achieve greater depth and scope of understanding and new levels of appreciation. Civil war buffs may not satisfy their curiosity by reading a book and visiting a battlefield or two; they may soon be involved to the extent of using their weekends and vacation time to attend seminars, travel to historic sites, and otherwise pursue their quest for knowing and understanding with increasing energy.

People motivated by growth needs seem insatiable in their search for knowledge and understanding as the need for growth and self-development expands. Many develop an enormous scope of interests, and others probe ever more deeply into their understanding of fewer interests. Thus, responding to growth needs leads to increased growth; the cycle of personal growth is seemingly endless.

This is a very different perspective on motivation than behaviorist views, which primarily emphasize carefully regulated rewards and punishments: the prospect of modest annual increases in compensation and ultimately retirement income as the reward for being a "good" teacher; the threat of being demoted or sacked for being a "poor" teacher. The hierarchy-of-needs view of motivation envisions the realistic possibility of generating enormous psychic energy within and among teachers and principals, and seeing that energy expand and increase over time, first, by meeting their deficiency needs and, second, by encouraging their growth and development needs. This is the essence of creating growth-enhancing environments in schools as an organizational approach to motivating participants.

Application to Work Motivation.   Lyman Porter (1961) adapted Maslow's concept of the hierarchy of needs to create growth-enhancing environments in work organizations. An interpretation of his work is shown in Figure 5.3. In Porter's view, Maslow's hierarchy fits the organizational environment better by adding a new level in the hierarchy: *autonomy.* Autonomy refers to the individual's need to participate in making decisions that affect him or her, to exert

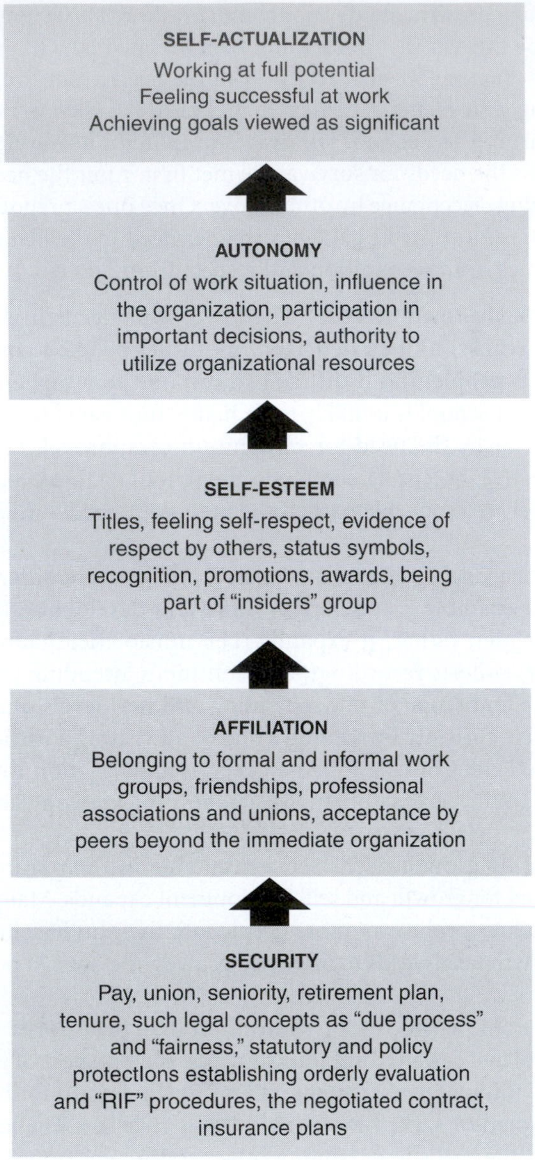

SELF-ACTUALIZATION
Working at full potential
Feeling successful at work
Achieving goals viewed as significant

AUTONOMY
Control of work situation, influence in
the organization, participation in
important decisions, authority to
utilize organizational resources

SELF-ESTEEM
Titles, feeling self-respect, evidence of
respect by others, status symbols,
recognition, promotions, awards, being
part of "insiders" group

AFFILIATION
Belonging to formal and informal work
groups, friendships, professional
associations and unions, acceptance by
peers beyond the immediate organization

SECURITY
Pay, union, seniority, retirement plan,
tenure, such legal concepts as "due process"
and "fairness," statutory and policy
protections establishing orderly evaluation
and "RIF" procedures, the negotiated contract,
insurance plans

FIGURE 5.3   A hierarchy of work motivation based
on Porter's model.

influence in controlling the work situation, to have a voice in setting job-related goals, and to
have authority to make decisions and latitude to work independently. Using Porter's concept
of the needs hierarchy, it is relatively easy to see the ways in which work organizations, such as
school districts, schools, and institutions of higher education, can be sources for fulfilling these
motivating needs.

Porter went on to conduct research that is representative of a whole line of inquiry that followed. Among the characteristics he attempted to measure concerning the managers he studied were the following:

1. To what extent the need characteristic (of any level of the hierarchy) was being met by the manager's job
2. To what extent the manager thought the job should meet the need characteristic

The differences between the first question (to what extent need was being met) and the second question (to what extent the job should meet the need) provide a measure of either (a) the amount of *need satisfaction* the person is experiencing or (b) the perceived *need deficiency* that the person is experiencing. Research such as this has been conducted widely in an effort to understand the relationship between need satisfaction and/or need deficiency and the performance of people on the job (Kuhn, Slocum, & Chase, 1971; Lawler & Porter, 1967).

Because such studies

contend that human behavior is goal-directed toward fulfilling unsatisfied needs, an individual's need satisfaction should be related to his job performance. And, as Maslow's theory would predict, higher order needs should be more closely linked to job performance than lower order needs that can be readily satisfied. (Hellriegel & Slocum, 1974, p. 308)

One generalization that seems to arise from the substantial body of research of this kind is that it is situation-bound. That is, when or where times are good and jobs are plentiful, such research tends to pick up little concern for the lower order needs (for example, security and physiological needs) because they are not a significant part of reality. But when or where there is employment instability, there appears to be a closer connection between the lower order needs and job satisfaction. This admittedly general observation may be disconcerting to those who seek a broad, generally applicable explanation of human motivation.

It is probably unrealistic to assume that teachers are, as a group, motivated by any particular needs inducement that is applicable only to that group; the variables among teachers are too great. There are personal variables, such as life and career goals, and differing family and financial obligations. There also are differing situational contingencies; teachers who work in schools where they may have their coats stolen, be robbed, or be in danger of being raped may very well reveal needs dispositions that are different from those of teachers in a more secure environment. Again, the point here is the critical importance of the function of situational contingencies in attempting to describe, explain, and predict the needs inducements that lie behind the behavior of people in educational organizations.

We should consider the studies reported by Sergiovanni and Carver (1973) which sought to find out "at what level teachers are with respect to the hierarchy [of prepotent needs]. We need to know their level of prepotency" (pp. 58–59) for the simple reason that we cannot (according to the hierarchy-of-needs theory) motivate insecure teachers by offering them greater autonomy or, on the other hand, motivate teachers seeking autonomy by offering them security. Perhaps worse is the likelihood that "freshly trained school executives who overestimate the operating need level of teachers and scare them off with ultra-participatory self-actualizing administration are as ineffective as others who deny teachers meaningful satisfaction by underestimating operating need levels" (p. 59). To shed light on what he calls the "operating need levels" of teachers, Sergiovanni and his colleagues conducted two studies: one of the teachers and administrators of an upstate New York suburban school district and the other of the teachers in 36 Illinois high schools.

These studies are of interest on two levels:

1. The data-gathering instruments and techniques for analyzing the data that were used to demonstrate one way to study systematically important situational contingencies in the motivation of people in education organizations, and
2. The results drawn from the populations they studied provide some useful insights.

In general, "esteem seems to be the level of need operation showing greatest need deficiency for these professionals. Large deficiencies are also reported for autonomy and self-actualization, and these gaps will continue to rise as teachers make gains in the esteem area" (Sergiovanni & Carver, 1973, p. 59). In other words, these studies suggest that (in the populations studied and at the time of the study) the teachers—as an overall group—(a) had satisfied the lower order needs and (b) were generally ready to respond to higher order needs. They felt reasonably secure and reasonably affiliated with their colleagues, and therefore more of these kinds of inducements were unlikely to be very motivating. But if these teachers were given opportunities to feel better about themselves and opportunities to have greater influence in the processes of making decisions, they would likely be highly motivated. The groups of people studied were not monolithic; the researchers report (not surprisingly, to be sure) some differences related to age. In this case, age probably was an indicator of where individuals were in the development of their careers. They found, for example, that the younger teachers (that is, those ages 20 to 24) seemed to be the most concerned with esteem. Slightly older teachers (ages 25 to 34), on the other hand, showed the most unmet motivational needs across the board. One could speculate that this is the period in a teacher's career when he or she hits a dead end; for most, there will be little opportunity for professional growth, advancement, and significant achievement in the years ahead. Perhaps even more disturbing, however, are some insights concerning older teachers (45 years or older). At first glance, the data seemed to indicate that older teachers had the smallest need deficiencies of all; this point tends to suggest that, in the later years of their careers, teachers were finding their work rather highly motivating at all levels. When the researchers examined this phenomenon, however, there appeared to be quite a different explanation: older teachers "are not getting more in terms of need fulfillment as the years go by but, rather, are expecting less. Levels of aspiration seem to drop considerably with age. Teachers become more 'realistic' or resigned to things as they are" (Sergiovanni & Carver, 1973, p. 61).

The significance of findings such as these looms very large, indeed, for those who are concerned with improving the effectiveness of public schools. There is strong support for believing that job security, salaries, and benefits have little likelihood of motivating teachers, though they are far from being irrelevant to them. A greater motivational need, it seems clear, is for teachers to achieve feelings of professional self-worth, competence, and respect—to be seen increasingly as people of achievement, professionals who are influential in their workplaces, growing persons with opportunities ahead to develop even greater competence and a sense of accomplishment. But in an era in which public schools (and institutions of higher education) have more and more adversarial relationships between teachers and management, there appears to be little support from the organizational hierarchy of many schools to meet these needs. Indeed, the negotiating posture of most school districts has been highly defensive on this point, viewing every gain by teachers in opportunities to develop their autonomy and participation and to increase their scope of influence as a loss of jealously guarded management authority and prerogatives.

Similarly, the widespread loss of confidence in the effectiveness of schools has led to a rash of actions that have had a direct impact on the motivating environment of education organizations. Reductions in force (RIF), slashed budgets, mandated competency programs, legislated school reforms, and massive federal interventions at the local school level all, of course, have laudable intent in terms of overall social policy. But in terms of Maslow's needs hierarchy theory of motivation, as applied to the organizational behavior of people working in schools, they tend to produce disastrous results in combination.

HERZBERG'S TWO-FACTOR THEORY OF MOTIVATION   The two-factor theory of motivation posits that motivation is not a single dimension that can be described as a hierarchy of needs but rather is composed of two separate, independent factors:

1. *Motivational factors,* which can lead to job satisfaction.
2. *Maintenance factors,* which must be present in sufficient amounts in order for motivational factors to come into play. When they are not present in sufficient amounts, they can block motivation and lead to job dissatisfaction.

The work of Frederick Herzberg began to appear about 12 years after Maslow's and has become widely influential in management thought around the world, particularly in profit-making organizations. Herzberg started with systematic studies of people at work, thereby producing an empirically grounded theory rather than using an "armchair" approach. In his research, Herzberg (1966) asked people to recall the circumstances in which (a) they had, at specific times in the past, felt satisfaction with their jobs and in which (b) they had been dissatisfied with their jobs. Analysis of the responses indicates that there is one specific, describable cluster or group of factors that is associated with motivation and satisfaction at work and another, equally specific, group of factors that is associated with dissatisfaction and apathy. Perhaps no other theory of motivation in the workplace has been more extensively researched and argued about than this one, and in all likelihood none has been as widely applied to complex organizations.

Traditionally, it had been believed that the opposite of job satisfaction is job dissatisfaction; thus, by eliminating the sources of dissatisfaction from work, the job would become motivating and satisfying. But Herzberg suggested that this is not so, that the opposite of satisfaction is no satisfaction (see Figure 5.4).

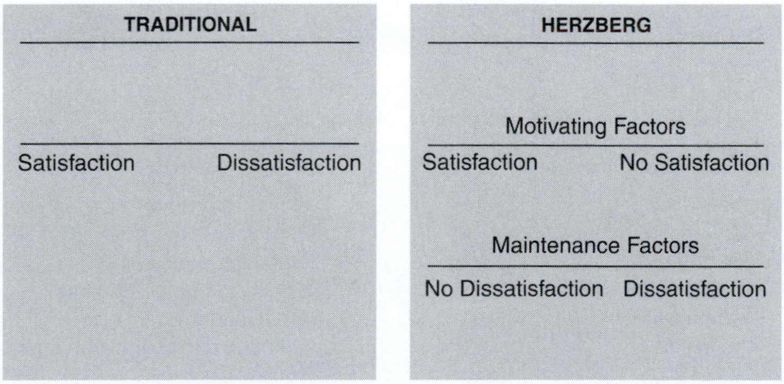

FIGURE 5.4 Traditional concept of job satisfaction-dissatisfaction contrasted with Herzberg's concept.

Thus, by eliminating sources of dissatisfaction, one may placate, pacify, or reduce the dissatisfaction of a worker, but this elimination does not mean that such reduction either motivates the worker or leads to job satisfaction. For example, salary, fringe benefits, type of supervision, working conditions, climate of the work group, and attitudes and policies of the administration can be sources of dissatisfaction. However, if one improves the salary-benefits package and working conditions and develops a more humane, concerned administration, one can expect to reduce dissatisfaction, but one cannot expect to motivate the workers by such means. Conditions such as these, taken together, originally were called *hygiene factors*. That term was chosen because—to Herzberg, at least—they have a preventive quality. Today, they are called *maintenance factors*, and that is the appellation that is used in this book.

Motivation appears to arise from a separate cluster of conditions, different from and distinct from those related to the sources of dissatisfaction. For example, achievement, recognition, the challenge of the work itself, responsibility, advancement and promotion, and personal or professional growth appear to motivate people and are therefore associated with job satisfaction. They are called *motivating factors* or *motivators*.

The theory, which is shown schematically in Figure 5.5, suggests that it is not possible to motivate people at work through maintenance factors. Reducing class size, developing a more amiable atmosphere, and improving fringe benefits may well accomplish two goals: (a) reduce or eliminate the dissatisfaction of teachers and (b) create conditions wherein they may be motivated. But these kinds of efforts in themselves are not motivating. It does not follow, however, that the maintenance factors are unimportant: Minimum levels must be maintained if we are to avoid so much dissatisfaction that motivators will not have their expected effect. For example, failure to keep the salary schedule at a level that teachers think is reasonable, or threats to job security

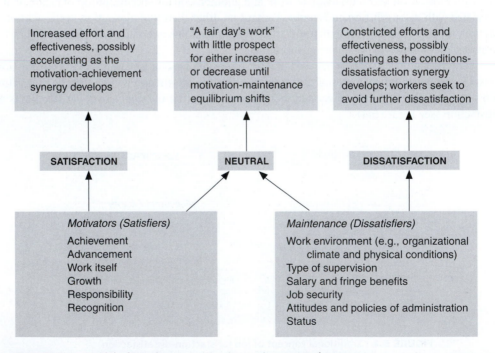

FIGURE 5.5   Model of Herzberg's motivation-maintenance theory.

can generate such dissatisfaction that teachers cannot respond to opportunities for professional growth, achievement, or recognition. Although maintenance factors are not in themselves motivating (or do not lead to job satisfaction), they are prerequisite to motivation.

An important concept in the two-factor theory is that people tend to see job satisfaction as being related to intrinsic factors such as success, the challenge of the work, achievement, and recognition, whereas they tend to see dissatisfaction as being related to extrinsic factors such as salary, supervision, and working conditions. In other words, they attribute motivational characteristics to themselves and attribute dissatisfaction to characteristics of the organization. In this context, Herzberg has suggested three main ideas for those who wish to practice his theory:

1. *Enrich the job,* which involves redesigning the work that people do in ways that will tap the motivation potential in each individual. This process would include making the job more interesting, more challenging, and more rewarding.
2. *Increase autonomy* on the job. Note that it was *not* suggested that complete autonomy be somehow granted to workers but that autonomy be increased. This point suggests more participation in making decisions about how the work should be done.
3. *Expand personnel administration* beyond its traditional emphasis on maintenance factors. The focus of personnel administration should be on increasing the motivational factors present in the work. In this view, school districts in which personnel administration focuses almost exclusively on details such as contract administration, the routines of selection-assignment-evaluation-dismissal, and teacher certification and pension plans are attending to important details but not to motivating details. Because 80% or more of the current operating budget of many school districts is allocated directly to salaries, wages, and related items, it would seem that the personnel function should be deeply involved in creating or redesigning jobs that motivate the incumbents and thus increase the effectiveness or productivity of the district's employees. This is the view that, for many, underlies the concept of human resources administration in contrast to more traditional views of personnel administration.

Herzberg's motivation-maintenance theory has been widely accepted and applied to the management of organizations, especially to U.S. business and industrial corporations. At the same time, it has provided the basis for considerable academic debate. The four principal criticisms that crop up in that debate are often expressed as follows:

1. Herzberg's basic research methods tended to foreshadow the responses he got. When things went well and people felt satisfied, they tended to take the credit for it; when things went badly on the job and the respondents were not satisfied, they tended to project the fault onto other people or onto management.
2. The reliability of his research methods is also open to question. The research design required a number of trained individuals to score and interpret the responses from the respondents. Obviously, there may be some differences in the way individuals do the rating, with one rater scoring a response in one way and another rater scoring a similar response in another way (so-called interrater reliability).
3. No provision in the research covers the likely possibility that a person may get satisfaction from one part of his or her job and not from another part.
4. The theory assumes that there is a direct relationship between effectiveness and job satisfaction, yet the research studies only satisfaction and dissatisfaction and does not relate either of them to the effectiveness (or productivity) of the respondents.

The first three of these criticisms are easily dealt with as merely representing typical problems of designing research that requires us to infer causes of behavior from observations of the behavior itself. They make the basis for nice arguments, but in fact, Herzberg's research—after exhaustive review in the literature over a period of two decades—must be accepted as representing the state of the art. The fourth criticism, however, is not so simple.

There is the chicken-or-the-egg aspect to the research literature on job satisfaction and its presumed link to effectiveness on the job. Roughly, investigators with a human relations orientation tend to think that satisfied workers are likely to be productive. Herzberg, however, is among those scholars who tend to think that satisfaction at work arises from the work itself or, more precisely, that job satisfaction comes from achievement. There is a massive body of research literature in this area; because of methodological problems as well as ideological conflicts, the overall results are inconclusive. Conversely, scant support exists for the notion that dissatisfied workers are likely to be more effective than those who report a higher level of satisfaction; the question, then, revolves around the sources of satisfaction (that is, maintenance factors or motivating factors). The Herzberg theory has been tested numerous times in school situations and—in this organizational setting, at least—appears to be well supported.

Savage (1967), using interviews to obtain data from Georgia teachers, reported that Herzberg's theory was generally supported, as did Wickstrom (1971) in reporting a study of teachers in the province of Saskatchewan, Canada. Gene Schmidt (1976) studied 132 high school principals in districts in the Chicago suburbs and found that, again, the two-factor theory appeared to be strongly supported by these school administrators, indicating that "recognition, achievement, and advancement are major forces in motivating them to lift their performance to approach their maximum potential" (p. 81). In operational terms, Schmidt concluded that "encouragement and support for administrators who desire to be creative, to experiment with new educational programs, and to delve into different educational endeavors are needed to allow more opportunities for achievement" (p. 81).

Sergiovanni and Carver (1973), after replicating Herzberg's work among teachers, reported that the theory appeared to be supported. Their findings were that achievement and recognition were very important motivators for teachers, along with the work itself, responsibility, and the possibility of growth. Among the dissatisfiers were (not surprisingly) routine housekeeping, taking attendance, paperwork, lunch duty, insensitive or inappropriate supervision, irritating administrative policies, and poor relationships with colleagues and/or parents. They made the point that advancement, frequently an important motivator in studies conducted in private-sector corporations, was missing in the study of teachers. On this significant point, they observed that "advancement was simply not mentioned by teachers because teaching as an occupation offers so little opportunity for advancement. If one wishes to advance in teaching, he [*sic*] must leave teaching for a related education profession such as administration, supervision, and counseling" (p. 77).

Comments on Herzberg's Two-Factor Theory. Herzberg's two-factor theory of motivation was developed through research in which people were asked to describe critical incidents in their work lives that involved motivation and job satisfaction. Subsequently, it has been strongly supported by additional research carried out by a number of investigators using similar techniques. These provide strong support for the concept. However, some investigators find it troubling that studies that use other research techniques generally fail to support the theory. Herzberg's theory has been widely influential, however, and commonly appears in the literature of business and industry as well as that of education. Although some advocate abandoning it in favor of the newer and more complex expectancy theory, the two-factor theory remains a powerful explanation of motivation in the workplace.

INTEGRATION OF HERZBERG'S AND MASLOW'S THEORIES Some of the essential differences between Maslow's hierarchy-of-needs theory and Herzberg's motivation-maintenance theory have already been pointed out. The central difference is that Maslow thought of every need as a potential motivator, with the range of human needs in a prepotent hierarchical order, whereas Herzberg argued that only the higher order needs are truly motivating (the lower order needs being conceptualized as maintenance factors). Another difference—not quickly apparent, perhaps—is that Maslow's was a general theory of human motivation, whereas Herzberg tried to illuminate motivational issues specifically in the workplace.

Nevertheless, a comparison of the two theories, as shown in Figure 5.6, reveals that they are basically highly compatible and, in fact, support one another. We feel (as Figure 5.6 shows) that the Porter version of the hierarchy-of-needs model lends itself to such a comparison, for the

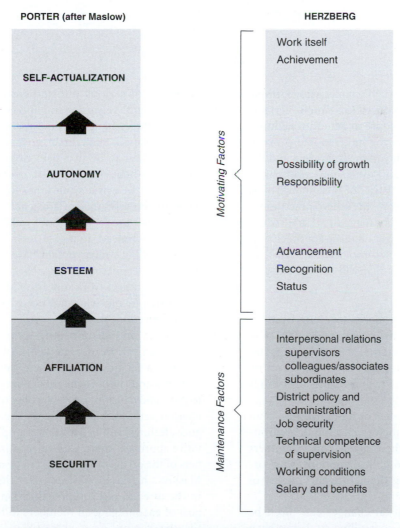

FIGURE 5.6 Need-priority model compared with motivation-maintenance model.

simple reason that basic physiological drives such as the need for food, water, and air have little relevance for motivating behavior at work in U.S. educational organizations. Even so, we agree with Robbins (1976):

> The lower-order needs on Maslow's hierarchy tend to closely approximate the maintenance factors as outlined by Herzberg. Salary, working conditions, job security, [school district] policy and administration, and supervision are generally physiological and safety-oriented needs. In contrast, the intrinsic motivational factors of recognition, advancement, responsibility, growth, achievement, and the work itself tend to be closely related to the desire for esteem and self-actualization. The integrated model would also suggest that organizations have traditionally emphasized lower-order needs. If workers are to become motivated on their jobs, it will be necessary for administrators to make the alterations necessary to stimulate the motivational factors in the [jobs themselves]. (p. 312)

Final Thoughts

Motivating people who work in schools is not a simple matter, and it cannot be reduced to a simple, certainly not a mechanical, procedure or set of procedures. Each of the two factors in the motivational process, the idiosyncratic personality of the individual and the idiosyncrasies of the organization's environment, is complex, and the precise nature of their interactions is not fully known. Therefore, the school practitioner must proceed, not with aphorisms or simple reductionism, but with an intelligent holistic approach that takes these complex variables into account. Here are some pragmatic principles that will help to support such an approach:

1. Individuals are not motivated only by their internal perceptions, needs, and characteristics or only by external demands, expectations, and environmental conditions, but by an interaction of the two: the generalization is $B = f(p \cdot e)$.
2. The educational leader or administrator is an important part of the organizational environment with which the organization's members interact and therefore, by definition, is important in determining the nature and quality of their motivation.
3. Short-term behavioral changes can often be achieved by highly controlling strategies such as threats of serious punishments, promises of meaningful rewards, and forced competition, but these changes should not be confused with motivation. Such direct, coercive attempts to motivate may be useful in bringing about changes in behavior when immediate action is required in crisis situations, for example, when the performance of a teacher is so unacceptable that the school cannot wait for corrective action. Indeed, in a case such as this one, the controlling strategy might have a beneficial effect by permitting the teacher to achieve enough success at work that he or she becomes responsive to motivational needs of a higher order than survival.
4. To induce and sustain long-term evolution of the motivation of organizational members requires a facilitative approach, one that encourages and supports members in their efforts to grow and develop their ways of perceiving the environment in which they work, their personal goals, feelings, and beliefs. For example, a facilitative approach might seek to encourage members of the organization always to be moving up Maslow's hierarchy of needs over time, always in the direction of self-actualization, with the goal of encouraging all members to become all that they can be.

5. One strategy for developing a facilitative approach to motivation in educational organizations is to change the environment factor in $B = f(p \cdot e)$, that is, to create growth-enhancing environments, which involves working with the organizational culture and organizational climate. In this realm, the educational leader emerges as a key actor in the environment of the organization.

Reflective Activities

1. Using the information about the four psychological types and the Myers-Briggs Type Indicator, write a self-assessment concerning these concepts. Describe the predominant types that you believe you possess. Give examples of behaviors that illustrate your self-assessment. You can also find some free MBTI-type survey instruments online that will give you an assessment of your profile. Here is a website from HumanMetrics: humanmetrics.com/cgi-win/JTypes2.asp

2. Using McClelland's motivation theory based on n-Ach, n-Pow, and n-Affil, complete a self-assessment and give specific examples as to why you think you meet your self-assessed criteria.

3. Assuming that all lower order needs have been met (in Maslow's theory), and using Herzberg's motivating factors, complete the following: Develop a plan to meet the higher order needs of school personnel or individuals in your organization. You may choose to focus on a specific school level (for example, elementary) or develop a generic plan that would be good for any school level. Within your plan, be sure to briefly outline at least two major programs, projects, or activities that will help meet higher order needs in the faculty or staff.

4. Describe how you can use Bandura's theory of motivation in your organization to establish a meaningful plan to involve staff in changes suggested by upper administration. Use a specific example from your experience.

5. *Working on Your Game Plan.* Over time you have observed leaders and other people working in organizations. Think about those observations and relate them to what you have read in this chapter. Then create two lists. First, list five things leaders do that are highly motivating to staff. Then list five things leaders do that kill motivation in staff. After creating the two lists, describe what generalizations for leadership you draw from your observations.

CRITICAL INCIDENT   Changes at Washington High School

Kinsey Jenks had accepted the position as principal of Washington High School a year ago knowing that it was going to be a difficult job. Historically, the school's student population had drawn from mostly white middle-income to upper-middle-income parents, and the school generally performed very well on state achievement tests. School climate was positive and student and staff morale was high. Within the district, the school was often spoken of as "the country club."

The principal whom Kinsey had succeeded had been at Washington High for 13 years. Though he did have something of a patrician manner, the teachers, who were a stable teaching force in the school, loved him. He had been removed by the superintendent last year, however, because of growing problems both with declining test achievement scores and increasing discipline problems. The teachers

opposed both the principal's removal as well as the appointment of Kinsey Jenks, whom they distrusted and viewed as an unwelcome outsider.

All the trouble seemed to begin about 5 years ago, when the district had to rezone the high schools due to increasing enrollments brought on mostly by two new manufacturing plants that had been built in the area. Since then, Washington High School had been drawing increasing numbers of students from the migrant farm-labor families who lived in the rural areas as well as factory workers' families who were moving into the new development houses that were going up "out there." These students, mostly from low socioeconomic families, did not perform as well on the state achievement tests and Washington's reputation as a "good school" suffered. In addition, friction quickly developed between the "new" students and the "old" students. In sports, for example, a more intense conflict developed in the usual competition for spots on the teams. The coaches agreed that it was largely a reflection of tension between the Hispanic students and the non-Hispanic white students. Fighting incidents, as well as other behavioral problems in both the cafeteria and the classrooms, increased dramatically. For the most part, teachers no longer felt as safe as they once did on campus, and over time, more teachers were asking for transfers to other schools than had been the experience at Washington High.

Kinsey viewed the issue of mistrust as the main problem at Washington High, so she introduced a new idea to teachers and students at the beginning of her first year as principal. Most of the teachers and students decided to give Kinsey's idea a try because they knew that something had to change. A consultant was hired to train teachers and students in a personality identification program called True Colors, which uses four different colors to represent different personality traits. The idea is that if everyone becomes more knowledgeable about individual personality and motivation and has a common language to discuss indi-vidual and group differences, everyone will become more trusting of one another.

At the end of Kinsey's first year, and the time for her annual evaluation approached, the superintendent could assure the school board that progress had been made in reduced behavioral problems. Although the test scores improved a little, student achievement was far from the levels that he knew the board wanted to see.

Kinsey knew that, of course, and she knew that she had to be ready at her evaluation to make a convincing case for reappointment.

1. If Kinsey asked your advice, what kind of three-point plan would you suggest that Kinsey have ready to discuss with the superintendent at her annual evaluation?
2. What rationale underlies your suggestions to Kinsey?
3. Should the True Colors program be continued? Why or why not? If yes, suggest ways that it could be used to continue improvements in behavior and learning.

Suggested Reading

Bandura, A. (1986). *Social foundations of thought and action: A social cognitive theory.* Englewood Cliffs, NJ: Prentice Hall.

This is a landmark book in the field of psychology that has had a remarkable influence on the field since its publication. It presents the research and theory of human motivation called social cognitive theory, which is based in part on the concept of self-efficacy.

Benfari, R., & Knox, J. (1991). *Understanding your management style: Beyond the Myers-Briggs Type Indicators.* Lexington, MA: D.C. Heath and Company.

This book applies four theoretical orientations to the understanding of one's own personality structure: (1) the Myers-Briggs Type Indicators, which are drawn directly from Jung's theory of personality; (2) the needs that motivate you; (3) the conflict management style that you use; and (4) the kinds of power that you use. It stresses the importance of assessing your own personality characteristics so that you can work from your own strengths. It's a do-it-yourself book, in a way, complete with a self-assessment test that you can take. It is also scholarly, sound, and readable.

Covington, M. V. (1992). *Making the grade: A self-worth perspective on motivation and school reform.* New York, NY: Cambridge University Press.

While this book is focused on the motivation of students in the classroom rather than on the motivation of adults who work in the educational organization, it is an informative and provocative discussion that has much to say to those who are interested in organizational behavior in education. Drawing heavily on the work of Atkinson and McClelland, Covington starts with the thesis that "every achievement situation implies the promise of success as well as the threat of failure. This means that all achievement situations involve approach-avoidance conflict to one degree or another" (p. 32). Entwined with this approach-avoidance, in which many students wind up struggling to avoid failure in school, is the sense of self-worth of the individual. A scholarly yet highly practical resource for educational leaders.

Keirsey, D., & Bates, M. (1984). *Please understand me: Character and temperament types.* Del Mar, CA: Prometheus Nemesis Book Company.

This book explains the psychological types of Carl Jung and provides a useful vocabulary and phraseology for applying the Jung-Myers concepts of different types to one's work in organizations. As the title suggests, it focuses on the communication distortions and blockages that commonly arise between and among different kinds of people who perceive and respond to the world in different ways. Readers can get feedback on their own psychological type by taking The Keirsey Temperament Sorter found on pages 5–13. The instrument can also be taken online at keirsey.com/sorter/register.aspx

Sheared, V., & Sissel, P. A. (2001). *Making space: Merging theory and practice in adult education.* Westport, CT: Bergin & Garvey.

This book gives voice to the traditionally unheard voices in adult education. Taking a staunch postmodern focus, this collection of articles has contributions of individuals and of topics in adult education and learning that have historically been marginalized.

References

Atkinson, J. W., & Litwin, G. H. (1960). Achievement motivation and test anxiety conceived as motive to approach success and motive to avoid failure. *Journal of Abnormal and Social Psychology, 60,* 52–63.

Bandura, A. (1986). *Social foundations of thought and action: A social cognitive theory.* Englewood Cliffs, NJ: Prentice Hall.

Benfari, R., & Knox, J. (1991). *Understanding your management style: Beyond the Myers-Briggs Type Indicators.* Lexington, MA: Lexington Books, D. C. Heath.

Covington, M. V. (1992). *Making the grade: A self-worth perspective on motivation and school reform.* New York, NY: Cambridge University Press.

Dowling, W. (Ed.). (1978). *Effective management and the behavioral sciences.* New York, NY: AMACOM.

Gardner, H. (1983). *Frames of mind: The theory of multiple intelligences.* New York, NY: Basic Books.

Hamachek, D. E. (1987). Humanistic psychology: Theory, postulates and implications for educational processes. In J. A. Glover & R. R. Ronning (Eds.), *Historical foundations of educational psychology* (pp. 160–175). New York, NY: Plenum Press.

Hellriegel. D., & Slocum, J. W., Jr. (1974). *Management: A contingency approach.* Reading, MA: Addison-Wesley.

Hersey, P., & Blanchard, K. H. (1977). *Management of organizational behavior: Utilizing human resources* (3rd ed.). Englewood Cliffs, NJ: Prentice-Hall.

Herzberg, F. (1966). *Work and the nature of man.* Cleveland, OH: World.

Homans, G. C. (1951). The Western Electric researches. In S. D. Hoslett (Ed.), *Human factors in management* (pp. 210–241). New York, NY: Harper and Brothers.

Jung, C. (1971). *Psychological types.* Princeton, NJ: Bollingen Series.

Keirsey, D., & Bates, M. (1984). *Please understand me: Character and temperament types.* Del Mar, CA: Prometheus Nemesis.

Kuhn, D. G., Slocum, J. W., & Chase, R. B. (1971). Does job performance affect employee satisfaction? *Personnel Journal, 50,* 455–460.

Labone, E. (2004). Teacher efficacy: Maturing the construct through research in alternative paradigms. *Teaching and Teacher Education, 20*(4), 341–359.

Lawler, E. E., III, & Porter, L. W. (1967). The effect of job performance and job satisfaction. *Industrial Relations, 6,* 20–28.

Levinson, H. (1973). *The great jackass fallacy.* Boston, MA: Harvard University Press.

Maslow, A. (1970). *Motivation and personality* (2nd ed.). New York, NY: Harper & Row.

McClelland, D. C. (1961). *The achieving society.* New York, NY: Free Press.

McClelland, D. C. (1976). *Power: The inner experience.* New York, NY: John Wiley & Sons.

McClelland, D. C. (1988). *Human motivation.* Cambridge, England: Cambridge University Press.

Myers, I. B., McCaulley, M. H., Quenk, N. L., & Hammer, A. L. (1998). *MBTI manual: A guide to the development and use of the Myers-Briggs Type Indicator* (3rd ed.). Palo Alto, CA: Consulting Psychologists Press.

Piaget, J. (1977). Problems in equilibration. In M. H. Appel & L. S. Goldberg (Eds.), *Topics in cognitive development: Equilibration: theory, research and application* (Vol. 1, pp. 3–13). New York, NY: Plenum Press.

Porter, L. W. (1961). A study of perceived need satisfaction in bottom and middle-management jobs. *Journal of Applied Psychology, 45,* 1–10.

Robbins, S. P. (1976). *The administrative process: Integrating theory and practice.* Englewood Cliffs, NJ: Prentice Hall.

Savage, R. M. (1967). *A study of teacher satisfaction and attitudes: Causes and effects.* Unpublished doctoral dissertation, Auburn University, Auburn, Alabama.

Schmidt, G. L. (1976). Job satisfaction among secondary school administrators. *Educational Administration Quarterly, 12*(2), 68–86.

Sergiovanni, T. J., & Carver, F. D. (1973). *The new school executive: A theory of administration.* New York, NY: Dodd, Mead.

Sheared, V., & Sissel, P. A. (2001). *Making space: Merging theory and practice in adult education.* Westport, CT: Bergin & Garvey.

Stajkovic, A. D., & Luthans, F. (1998). Self-efficacy and work-related task performance: A meta-analysis. *Psychological Bulletin, 124,* 240–261.

Starratt, R. J. (2004). *Ethical leadership.* San Francisco, CA: Jossey-Bass.

Vroom, V. H. (1964). *Work and motivation.* New York, NY: John Wiley & Sons.

Weber, M. (1930). *The protestant ethic and the spirit of capitalism* (T. Parsons, Trans.). New York, NY: Charles Scribner's Sons. (Original work published 1904.)

Whichard, J. A. (2006, June). *Reliability and validity of True Colors.* Retrieved from http://www.true-colors.com/userfiles/file/Research%20Whichard%20Presentation%207-09%5B1%5D.pdf

Wickstrom, R. A. (1971). *An investigation into job satisfaction among teachers.* Unpublished doctoral dissertation, University of Oregon, Eugene.

CHAPTER 6

The Human Dimension of Organization

In previous chapters, we introduced some systematic ways of thinking about organizations and the people who work in them, which is the field of systems theory of organization. Many of these ways of thinking, or theories, such as the Getzels-Guba model, have proven almost indispensable to students in educational administration. In this chapter, however, we shall see that these ways of thinking have some distinct limitations. Perhaps the most serious one is that, although they depict relationships between the organizational structure and the people who populate the organization in graphic ways, they tend to subscribe to a theory of action that emphasizes bureaucratic control over the human realities in organizations.

In this text, we describe some aspects of the very important shift in the organizational paradigm from traditional modernism, with its emphasis on perfecting and refining bureaucratic management strategies and techniques, to an approach that emphasizes the potential for improving organizational performance from within, from the bottom up, by fostering the growth and development of the people who inhabit the organization. The overarching concept of this paradigm is that of building human capital. Organizations become more effective as the people in them grow and develop personally and professionally over time. In this way, they become increasingly effective not only in their individual work but as participants in a work group that is also becoming increasingly adept and effective in cooperative endeavors. We also discuss ways in which leaders engage, treat, and develop individuals and groups to improve potential for organizational success.

RECONCEPTUALIZING THE NATURE OF ORGANIZATIONS TO FOCUS ON PEOPLE

This text addresses the problem of understanding the behavior of people at work in educational organizations. This is the central problem confronting educational administrators because administration is defined as "working with and through other people, individually and in groups, to achieve organizational goals." In terms of administrative practice, then, we need to address an essential question: Which are the best and most effective ways of working with and through other people?

This is not an arcane academic question. How you answer it goes to the heart of how you conduct the work of school administration, whether as a department chairperson, a school principal, a superintendent of schools, or a person in any other leadership position. Nor is it a simple question. Teachers know, from working with children and their parents, that people are complex, idiosyncratic, and full of contradictions, and that their behavior often seems baffling and difficult to grasp.

We understand now much better than we did 20 years ago that schools, like all organizations, are complex and confusing places. At their best, they are filled with contradiction, ambivalence, ambiguity, and uncertainty. These understandings help us realize that many of the most important problems confronting school administrators are neither clear-cut nor amenable to technical solutions.

This is not a problem peculiar to school administration, nor is it limited to schools as organizations. It is a problem that is generally shared by all professions and all organizations. Consider how Donald Schön described what he called a "crisis of confidence in professional knowledge" (Schön, 1987, p. 3). Schön described two types of problems faced by all organizations: the high ground problems and the lowland, swampy problems. In the high ground, problems are easy to recognize and solutions rather simple to implement by using known theory-based applications. In the lowlands of the swamps, problems are not easily understood and solutions difficult to uncover.

For many years now, educational administrators have been urged to concentrate on technical solutions to the high-ground problems of education. Essentially, those who back the standards movement believe that establishing new detailed curriculum standards at the state level that are directly linked to required statewide, high-stakes, objective achievement tests that must be taken by children at the local level will force local administrators and teachers to revamp practices in their schools to achieve the demanded results. Adherents of this strategy usually refer to this as "setting educational standards." Other popular technical approaches include not only the use of electronic technology, such as computers and the Internet, but also structural technology, such as the creation of magnet schools, charter schools, and other forms of school choice, as well as instructional technology, such as the invention of new pedagogical techniques in the classroom.

The perspective of schools and school reform that has been adopted by many people who advocate these various technologies has been tightly bound to the image of schools as production organizations in which teaching is viewed as routinized labor. Such labor, if properly systematized and subjected to bureaucratic controls, should lead logically to the desired outcomes. Adherents of these views of schools have tended to believe that teachers can learn only through formal training that normally consists of lectures, directed workshops, and formal conferences, all of which are controlled and directed by external experts who know what the problems are and what the teachers need to deal effectively with them. Thus, we have witnessed the development of training programs to meet every conceivable problem confronting the schools as well as a proliferation of "expert" consultants ready to fly in to dispense their wisdom and quickly depart with their high fees safely in their pockets.

But important educational problems, those that are in the swampland that Donald Schön (1987) described, are typically messy: poorly defined, poorly understood, and complicated. Messy problems tend to be understood, or framed, in terms of the things about them that we are apt to notice. What you may notice, though, comes mainly from your own background, values, and perspectives.

As administrators seek to deal with the problems of education, their approach depends primarily on how they conceptualize their options, how they frame the problems. As in the case of malnutrition of children, there are many ways of framing a response. But people are limited in their ability to make sense of problems, in their ability to frame them, and by the number and variety of frames with which they are familiar and on which they can draw to give them insight and perspective on the messy, ill-defined problems that every professional encounters in the swampy lowlands. As we have described, for much of the last century, one single perspective dominated thinking about educational organizations: the structural perspective. This is the familiar notion of hierarchical control, bureaucratic offices, the organization chart, and rules and regulations such as standard operating procedures.

After 1975, organizational thought took a major turn away from such formal theorizing, which emphasized the machinelike characteristics that many scholars believed underlay the ways in which organizations worked, toward a markedly increased emphasis on the human dimensions of organization. This shift was caused by a combination of several forces that came together simultaneously. One of these forces was intellectual: the development of a new analysis of the fundamental concept of what an organization actually is.

A New Paradigm of Organizational Theory

As we have described, the period from the early 1950s to the mid-1970s produced an outpouring of theory and research in educational administration, so much so that in retrospect, the period—the modern period—is often called the era of the theory movement in educational administration. By the 1970s, however, many began expressing concern that the theories and the research that had been spawned did not fully describe schools as they were experienced by people in them. Research, and indeed the academic establishment in leading universities at that time, was dominated by those who accepted logical-positivist assumptions about schools as organizations and about ways of understanding them. In other words, they assumed that there was some rational, logical, systematic order underlying the organizational realities of schools that must be discovered. They thought that the means of discovery must be the approach to inquiry that emphasizes measurement, sampling, quasi-experimental methods, and quantification. It was believed that these assumptions and these methods of discovery were the only way to improve the training of educational practitioners. Wayne Hoy and Cecil Miskel (1982) claimed, for example, that "[t]he road to generalized knowledge can lie only in tough-minded scientific research, not in introspection and subjective experience" (p. 82).

T. Barr Greenfield (1975), however, articulated serious concerns about then-existing organizational theory that had been developing among both practitioners and a growing number of scholars. The crux of the concerns was that academicians, in their search to understand educational organizations and the behavior of people in them—to make sense of the "swamp" that Donald Schön spoke of—had become transfixed with the wish to be objective and to emphasize mathematical descriptions and, worst of all, they had come to think of organizations as tangible, concrete entities that exist independently and that are governed by systematic laws and principles. "In common parlance," Greenfield said, "we speak of organizations as if they were real" (p. 71). But they are not real, he went on to explain: "[T]hey are invented social realities" (p. 81) that exist only in the minds of people, rather than as tangible, independent realities. Thus, the argument runs, we anthropomorphize when we speak of organizations as imposing themselves on people or of organizational systems "behaving" in certain ways. The essence of an organization is the human beings who populate the organization; they choose, act, and behave, even if in their own minds they reify the organization as they do so.

Nevertheless, we are continually confronted by evidence that academic assumptions often contrast remarkably with the experiences of individuals engaged in the work of school administration. For example, Barth and Deal (1982) described striking differences that existed between academic literature on the principalship and principals' written reflections on their own practices:

- Principals describe concrete everyday experiences, whereas academics emphasize theory and abstract relationships.
- Principals communicate through metaphors, examples, and stories, whereas academics use models and the language of science.
- Principals are aware of limits on rationality, whereas academics stress rationality and the definition of problems in formal terms.
- Principals describe schools in human and emotional terms, as places wherein school personnel agonize over and celebrate their daily ups and downs; academics describe them in terms of detached abstraction.
- Principals see schools as ambiguous and even chaotic places, whereas academics describe an image of rationality and orderliness.

A Focus on People: The Rise of Qualitative Research Methods

As early as 1964, James Bryant Conant—Nobel laureate, former president of Harvard University, and chairman of the National Defense Research Committee during World War II—had reported that when he undertook studies of U.S. schools in the 1950s, it became necessary for him to eschew the hypothetico-deductive way of thinking that he had used for so many years in chemistry; instead, he had to learn to use inductive reasoning because the nature of educational problems was so different from that of scientific problems. In a readable little book called *Two Modes of Thought: My Encounters with Science and Education* (Conant, 1964), he discussed the differences between kinds of thinking appropriate to the sciences and education. He suggested that understanding the behavior of individuals in schools and post-secondary institutions is practical art.

Carl Rogers (1963) agreed and discussed "three ways of knowing" about human behavior and the contexts in which it occurs:

1. Subjective knowing is integral to every experience and human interaction since individuals interpret their surroundings based on their own subjective analysis.
2. Objective knowing is not really objective but actually more of a consensus between and among trusted colleagues who were thought to be qualified to make judgments about the "truth" of observed events.
3. Interpersonal, or phenomenological, knowing involves the frame of mind of an individual by checking hypotheses with the individual or, alternatively, by validating hypotheses by checking independently with several other observers. Rogers gave a simple example in describing the situation in which you may feel that a colleague is sad or depressed. How can you confirm that hypothesis? One way would be to simply ask the person in an empathetic way. Another would be to wait and see if others comment to you on their own independent observations and feelings about the colleague's state of mind. Rogers believed that in a mature behavioral science, all three ways of knowing would be acknowledged and used in combination, rather than using one way and ignoring the others.

Twenty-five years later, Arthur Blumberg (1988) enriched this line of thinking about educational organizations when he suggested that it is useful to think of school administration as a craft rather than as a science, so to think about knowledge and understanding as craft workers do. A craft, he contended, is unlike science in important ways. A craft (he used pottery as one example) is learned in day-to-day practice with tools and materials in which the practitioner develops "a nose for things," an intimate feel for the nature of the materials being worked with, a sense of what constitutes acceptable results, an almost intuitive sense of process, an understanding of what to do and when to do it, and a feel for the need for action. Blumberg argued convincingly that by shifting from the concept of science to the concept of craft, one discovers new and useful ways of knowing about organizational behavior in education. However, like many people who advocate the use of pragmatic approaches such as this one in our search for understanding of behavior in schools, Blumberg failed to recognize that the use of the craft metaphor is but another theoretical approach to understanding, as had been the work of Rogers, Conant, and so many others who sought to break out of the straitjacket of logical positivism.

By the 1980s, many students of education, who were well aware of these discrepancies, began to eschew traditional formal theorizing and the limitations of traditional quasi-experimental research methods and to find better ways of studying human behavior in schools. They began to go into the schools, instead of sending questionnaires and compiling statistics, to see what was going on and to talk to individuals at schools in order to understand how they were experiencing their lives. The results of such inquiries produced lively, rich narrative descriptions of life in present-day schools that illuminated the confusions, inconsistencies, ambiguities, and general messiness so characteristic of schools' organizational life.

Indeed, studies using these research methods, called *qualitative* or *ethnographic methods,* became the intellectual backbone of the educational reform movement of the 1980s. There were fewer of the spare statistical studies, so often elegant in style but yielding "no significant difference"; they were enhanced by lively, richly documented accounts of human beings at work that yielded insight and understanding of what was happening to people and how they were responding to their experiences.

This was a major shift in ways of thinking about and studying organizational behavior, and it arose directly from abandoning the old certainties of logical positivism in favor of significant new directions in understanding organizational behavior in schools. To get some flavor of the newer thinking, we now present a brief explanation of some of the ideas about organization that began to emerge as traditional organizational theory collapsed.

Educational Organizations as Loosely Coupled Systems

We are often apt to think of and describe a school system or a school in classical structural terms: for example, as a hierarchically linked pyramid of units subject to strong central control and command (as bureaucracies and military organizations are usually described). Students of organization have recognized for quite some time, however, that school systems and schools are in fact characterized by structural looseness: Schools in a district have considerable autonomy and latitude, and teachers in their classrooms are under only very general control and direction of the principal. As Bidwell (1965) noted, this is a functionally necessary arrangement, given the nature of the school's task, clients, and technology. It has been described vividly in this way:

> Imagine that you're either the referee, coach, player or spectator in an unconventional soccer match: the field for the game is round; there are several goals scattered

haphazardly around the circular field; people can enter or leave the game whenever they want to; they can throw balls in whenever they want; they can say "that's my goal" whenever they want to, as many times as they want to, and for as many goals as they want to; the entire game takes place on a sloped field; and the game is played as if it makes sense. And if you now substitute in that example principals for referees, teachers for coaches, students for players, parents for spectators, and schooling for soccer, you have an equally unconventional depiction of school organizations. The beauty of this depiction is that it captures a different set of realities within educational organizations than are caught when these same organizations are viewed through the tenets of bureaucratic theory. (Weick, 1976, p. 1)

We can contrast this image of reality with the conventional explanation of how schools go about doing things: namely, by planning, goal setting, and applying rational processes such as cost-benefit analyses, division of labor, job descriptions, authority vested in official office, and consistent evaluation and reward systems. The only problem with this latter conventional view is that it is rare to find schools that actually work that way; more often than not, people in educational organizations find that rational concepts such as these simply do not explain the way the system functions.

Because so much of educational organization defies explanation by existing rational concepts, the suggestion is that we give serious thought to more unconventional ideas that may lead us to more accurate understanding, such as the notion of "loose coupling." In general, the term *loose coupling* means that, although subsystems of the organization (and the activities that they carry out) are related to one another, each preserves its own identity and individuality. In a high school, for example, the guidance office is usually shown on an organization chart as reporting to the principal's office, yet the linkage is usually loose, with relatively infrequent interaction and typically a slow response of one to the other. The linkage is, in short, relatively weak and unimportant. The coupling—the very glue that holds the organization together—may be described as "loose."

Educational Organizations as Dual Systems

The concept of loose coupling as a distinctive characteristic of schools and other educational organizations has been powerful in explaining aspects of their organization that were previously ill understood. It does not explain them fully, however; an observer can easily find much in schools that smacks of bureaucratic or classical organization as well as much that is loosely coupled.

There has long been general agreement among students of organizations that educational organizations are loosely coupled in some significant ways and are highly bureaucratic in other ways and that this structure is important in understanding them and the behavior of people in them. For example, in an important study done by Meyer and Rowan (1983), the results of from 188 elementary schools in 34 school districts in the San Francisco area showed that

the inspection of instructional activity is delegated to the local school and takes place infrequently. For example, only one of the thirty-four superintendents interviewed reported that the district office evaluates teachers directly. Nor does it appear that principals and peers have the opportunity to inspect and discuss teachers' work: Of the principals surveyed, 85 percent reported that they and their teachers do not work

together on a daily basis. Further, there is little evidence of interaction among teachers: A majority of the principals report that there are no day-to-day working relations among teachers within the same grade level, and 83 percent report no daily
work relations among teachers of different grades. Teachers reaffirm this view of segmented teaching. Two-thirds report that their teaching is observed by other teachers
infrequently (once a month or less), and half report a similar infrequency of observation by their principals. (p. 74)

Considerable other research evidence corroborated the observation that supervision by
school administrators is rather infrequent; that teachers work in isolation, with little adult interaction throughout the day; and that when supervisors do visit classrooms, it is infrequent and
mainly for summative evaluation purposes (Morris, Crowson, Hurwitz, & Porter-Gehrie, 1981;
Newberg & Glatthorn, 1983). In the 30 years since these studies, little has changed, though the
accountability movement led by No Child Left Behind (NCLB) has resulted in some increased
presence in classrooms by administrators. For example, the concept of *classroom walkthroughs*
has received considerable attention. And although there are many variations of classroom walkthroughs, they generally involve administrators' presence in a classroom for a short period of
time during which they collect specific information about their observations. They may use a
hand-held electronic device or paper and pencil to record their observations. Whether or not,
and in what format, feedback from this data collection is provided to the teachers to assist them
in improving their instruction depends on the school and district vision for using walkthroughs.
Of course, teachers benefit from immediate individual feedback, and grade-level or department
teams can learn from collated data soon after it has been collected, but this type of quick feedback rarely occurs (David, 2008). David points out that too often when trust is at low levels between teachers and administrators, walkthroughs are viewed by teachers as compliance strategies,
and they only serve to create poor climates. In these cases, walkthroughs do nothing to improve
human capital.

Of course, control may be exerted by means other than direct supervision. For example,
evaluating student learning, maintaining close and detailed specification of the curriculum, and
ensuring that students have mastered the work of a previous grade before being promoted to the
next are among the many ways that schools may exercise strong control over teaching. These
views are, of course, at the core of the NCLB Act.

Thus, the central core activities of the school—instruction and learning—are viewed
as being loosely coupled to the extent that they are not directly controlled by administrators.
Although administrators bear general responsibility for the instructional programs of schools,
their ability to monitor the instructional behavior of teachers and the learning of students is
rather limited due to time and manpower constraints. For example, the San Francisco research
reported that only 12% of the principals studied indicated they had real decision power over the
methods that teachers use, and a mere 4% said that they are extremely influential in determining the instructional methods used by teachers. These data have been sustained over the years by
other studies, and they are one reason that NCLB began focusing on "research-based strategies."
In other words, to participate in NCLB, for the state to receive NCLB money, the state has to
show that its schools are implementing programs that have a research base, preferably quantitative studies that show improvement in student achievement.

On the other hand, administrators have access to bureaucratic means by which to structure
the work of teachers and thereby have indirect means of influencing the instructional behavior in

the school. *The control of time* is one means: Time schedules, the frequency with which students are pulled out for special classes and other activities, the frequency of interruptions of classroom instruction, and the burden of paperwork required of teachers all mold the teaching behavior of teachers, and all are influenced by the administrator as a key actor. *The assignment of students to classes* (how many and what kind) is also considerably influenced by administrators and constrains the teachers' work behavior. *Grouping* is another way in which administrators can influence instruction—for example, students may be grouped heterogeneously or homogeneously; teachers may work alone in self-contained classrooms, on teaching teams, or in departments. Principals also influence instructional behavior of teachers through their *control of resources*: teaching space, the availability of equipment, access to the copying machine, and even the availability of mundane basic supplies such as paper and pencils. Figure 6.1 displays visually these bureaucratic methods of controlling instruction.

Although these bureaucratic means are powerful in some ways in influencing the instructional behavior of teachers, they are relatively indirect in terms of how much students are learning. Thus, the core technical activity of the school is loosely coupled (as contrasted with what one would expect from a classic bureaucratic organization), but noninstructional activities are often tightly coupled. The issuing of paychecks in timely fashion, the deployment of buses, the management of money, and student accounting (attendance, for example) are among the numerous noninstructional activities that are closely controlled by administrators and therefore may be described as tightly coupled. In contrast to the nebulous authority that administrators reported

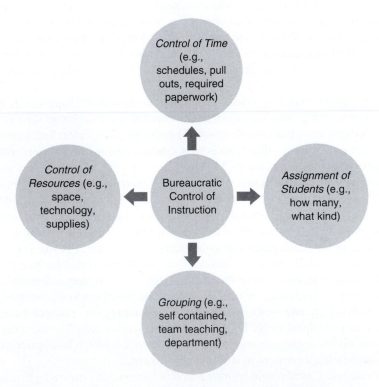

FIGURE 6.1 Examples of how administrators control instruction bureaucratically.

over the instructional activities of teachers, the San Francisco research reported that 82% of the principals surveyed claim to make decisions about scheduling, 75% made decisions about the assignment of students to classes, and 88% (either alone or in consultation with other school administrators in the district) made decisions about hiring new personnel. These activities may be said to be tightly coupled inasmuch as they are carefully controlled by direct administrative oversight.

One may conclude that looseness in controlling the instructional behavior of teachers is somehow wrong and insist—in the tradition of classic bureaucratic thought—that it be tightened up. Indeed, many contemporary observers take such a view, which explains many political initiatives undertaken in recent years by governors, legislatures, and a few state departments of education to tighten standards and educational requirements by imposing new requirements and limitations on schools. These often include adding required instruction to the curriculum, increased testing of both students and teachers, and more detailed specification of teaching methods. However, the issue being raised here is not whether schools ought to be loosely coupled or tightly coupled. Our interest is in better understanding the organizational characteristics of educational organizations *as they exist* (rather than as someone may wish they were) so that we may better understand the leadership of people in them *and their vision for the future of the school.*

We may think of organizations as exercising control exclusively through formal mechanisms such as supervisory authority, but a more useful perspective is that powerful control can be exercised through the use of far more subtle and indirect means: the development of positive organizational culture by building human capital. Understanding this point can be a powerful insight in understanding schools and universities and how to lead them effectively.

BUILDING HUMAN CAPITAL

Capital is ordinarily thought of in terms of tangible assets such as cash; raw materials; real estate; machinery and equipment; and even intellectual property such as ideas, inventions, and creations. But economists have understood for a long time the concept of *human* capital: that is, that people's knowledge, technical skills, attitudes, and social skills are also assets to any human enterprise. The human resources available to an organization are therefore a form of human capital. In fact, it turns out that they are potentially highly valuable assets that can increase in value over time—which, by definition, assets should do—or decrease in value, depending largely on how they are managed.

Applied to societies, nations, or regions, this concept helps to explain why some societies, though rich in tangible assets such as minerals or water power, may be less productive than others. Those societies and nations in which people have high levels of education and well-developed work skills, are favorably disposed toward the discipline of the workplace, and have a social tradition that places high value on hard work and productivity tend to become wealthier than those that do not.[1] As far back as the birth of our nation in 1776, Adam Smith, in the *Wealth of Nations*, noted the value of improving human capital by providing workers with additional skills. But it was not until the Nobel Prize-winning economist Theodore Schultz published his work in 1963 that the concept was shown to be mathematically true. Schultz's work found that roughly

---

[1]Economists have long recognized the value of human resources. See Schultz, T. W. (1960). Capital formation by education. *The Journal of Political Economy, 68*, 3–72.

one-third of economic growth in the United States was attributable to increases in labor and physical capital. The remaining "residual" he found was attributable to investment in educating the workers (Schultz, 1963). This concept was demonstrated spectacularly in Western Europe shortly after World War II with the Marshall Plan.

Most of Europe lay in ruins after World War II: many factories were gone, equipment was ruined or worn out, currency systems were in shambles, distribution and transportation systems were nearly wrecked, and many cities and towns were reduced to rubble. As a result, unemployment was rampant, poverty was commonplace, and despair was everywhere. George C. Marshall and Harry S. Truman persuaded a reluctant Congress to fund a large-scale plan, the Marshall Plan, to rebuild the currency and banking systems, the cities, the factories, and the transportation and communications systems to get people back to work and productive once again. A key to the plan was that the human capital needed to bring about recovery was already in place in Western European nations: Western Europeans were a well-educated populace, possessing high levels of work skills and managerial skills; they wanted to work; and they had a long tradition of pride in high-quality work and achievement. Because these human resources were in place, the infusion of a substantial amount of startup money enabled Western Europe to rebuild quickly, and citizens rapidly achieved levels of productivity higher than those that had existed prior to the war. In the United States after World War II, some important legislation led to great advances in the U.S. economy during the 1950s and 1960s, including the Servicemen's Readjustment Act of 1944 (commonly known as the GI Bill) that provided postsecondary education tuition (as well as other benefits) for returning war veterans. The GI Bill is credited with doubling college enrollment by 1950. We continue to see reports about the value of increasing human capital to individuals, in terms of both lower unemployment rates and higher earnings potential, and to society for increased economic expansion (Greenstone & Looney, 2013).

The concept of building human capital underlies much of the historic effort to improve the lot of societies through the spread of education and the development of social infrastructures, including the physical and economic infrastructures of Third World nations through international aid. Today, many developing nations that are emerging as prosperous societies with rising standards of living, especially countries in the Pacific Rim area such as Japan, South Korea, Taiwan, Hong Kong, Thailand, Singapore, and China, manifest the power of the concept of human capital. Not a few business leaders in the United States view the need to reform U.S. schooling through the lens of human capital, often referring to the reform of education as an investment in human capital. The concept is apt for application to thinking about organizations as well and lies at the heart of the notion of human resources management. But unfortunately, during difficult economic times, professional development budgets in schools are often cut, thereby decreasing chances of accomplishing instructional goals.

Administrators are customarily held accountable for the financial and physical assets of the school district, such as buildings, equipment, and money. The processes of preparing and approving the annual budget, then the administration of the budget over the course of the fiscal year, and finally a formal accounting of stewardship are familiar and important activities in every school district. Permitting tax-levy funds to be used unwisely or allowing assets to deteriorate through misuse or neglect are justifiably considered to be evidence of mismanagement. Only in the 1970s, however, did accountants as well as organizational theorists begin to realize the extent to which mismanagement of an organization's human resources can be detrimental to the organization's effectiveness.

One form of mismanagement is to spend too much on human resources, which has led to downsizing, outsourcing, contracting for services, using temporary and part-time employees, and other efforts to reduce payroll costs. Another way of mismanaging human resources, perhaps more important because it is less obvious and often unseen immediately, is failing to place adequate value on the skills, abilities, motivations, and commitment of the people in the organization.

In a typical U.S. school district, over 80% of the annual operating budget is allocated to personnel services and related costs. Obviously, the human resources of the school enterprise require a substantial outlay of tax-levy funds. Not only are the administrators responsible for maintaining the quality and effectiveness of these resources, but they also must manage them—as one would manage any assets—so that their value to the school district increases over time. Therefore, people should be managed so that their skills, motivations, attitudes, and knowledge develop, improve, and increase over time rather than level off at a steady pace or, worse yet, decline. This way of managing, to develop and increase the value of the organization's human resources, is the process of building human capital.

Human Resources as Assets

In building human capital, it is insufficient to assume that if employees do not actually quit, the state of the organization's human resources is acceptable. We have known for a long time, for example, that the processes of building and administering the budget are often handled in ways that create considerable pressure on individuals and groups, which leads to strife, apathy, tension, strain, aggression, and a pervasive feeling of failure. These responses tend to give rise, of course, to counterproductive behaviors that are directly related, not to the fact that budget decisions had to be made, but to the leadership processes that leaders and administrators choose to employ in dealing with the budget (Argyris, 1953).

As Rensis Likert (1967) observed, "if bickering, distrust, and irreconcilable conflict become greater, the human enterprise is worth less; if the capacity to use differences constructively and engage in cooperative teamwork improves, the human organization is a more valuable asset" (p. 148). Many problems stem from a negative climate in the organization—such as low morale, inadequate effort, lack of cooperation, complaints, and employee turnover (Killian, 1976). Thus, there is impressive evidence that the internal characteristics of the organization that tend to evoke destructive organizational behavior arise largely from the choices that administrators make in deciding how to carry out their work. Indeed, it is often largely the behavior of administrators that causes the needless dysfunctional feelings and behaviors commonly observed in struggling or failing organizations. When leaders behave in ways to alienate employees, they weaken the capacity of the organization to improve. So, not only do leaders need to improve human capacity, they need to ensure they don't purposely or inadvertently decrease human capacity through mismanagement of human resources.

The Dark Side of Leadership

Such administrator mismanagement of human resources was described by Joseph and Jo Blase (2002) in a research article entitled "The Dark Side of Leadership." In a qualitative study of 50 teachers from the United States and Canada who had experienced long-term abuse of six months or more, the authors showed the aftermath of mistreatment by school principals, which is consistent with boss abuse and bullying literature outside education (Glomb, 2002; Harlos &

BOX 6.1

Examples of Mistreatment by Principals

Level 1 (indirect, moderately aggressive)

- Discounting teachers' thoughts, needs, and feelings
- Favoring a select group of teachers
- Isolating and nonsupport of teachers
- Withholding resources and denying approval, opportunities, and credit

Level 2 (direct, escalating aggression)

- Public (in front of students, parents, or colleagues) and private criticism (the most pervasive Level 2 mistreatment)
- Spying (e.g., listening on intercom)
- Sabotaging (e.g., preventing others from helping in a grant)
- Stealing (e.g., teacher's journal)
- Destroying teacher instructional aids (e.g., dismantling a teacher's learning centers)
- Making unreasonable demands

Level 3 (direct, severe aggression)

- Explosive behavior (in public meetings and in private)
- Threats (e.g., threatening adverse effects on an evaluation)
- Unwarranted reprimands
- Unfair evaluations
- Mistreating students (occurred mostly when students had "misbehaved")
- Forcing teachers out of their jobs (e.g., reassignment, termination)
- Preventing teachers from advancing (e.g., negative letters of reference after lying to them that they would write a positive letter)
- Sexual harassment
- Racism (from both black and white teachers, indicating that this resulted in poor school climate)

Axelrod, 2005) Five of the teachers were male and 45 were female, with a good distribution from urban, suburban, and rural schools, as well as grade levels. These teachers described abuse from 28 male and 22 female principals. Blase and Blase (2006) found that mistreatment runs along a continuum from what they term Level 1 mistreatment, such as discounting teachers' ideas, to Level 3 mistreatment, which is highly abusive. See Box 6.1 for examples of the different levels of mistreatment behavior by principals. Such behaviors have devastating adverse effects to individuals and the school. Box 6.2 displays examples of the resulting negative effects of mistreatment.

Blase and Blase (2006) found

that the effects of such mistreatment are extremely harmful to teachers' professional and personal lives.... Beyond the teachers' responses of shock and disorientation,

BOX 6.2

Examples of the Effects of Principal Mistreatment

- Psychological and emotional responses, including shock and disorientation, humiliation, loneliness, lower self-esteem, and guilt
- Long-term, chronic psychological and emotional problems, including anxiety, fear, anger, and depression
- Physical and physiological problems
- Damaged schools, such as impaired school-level decision making
- Resigning from teaching at the school

humiliation, loneliness, and injured self-esteem, principal mistreatment seriously damaged in-school relationships, damaged classrooms, and frequently impaired all-school decision making. In addition, principals' abuse resulted in severe psychological/emotional problems including chronic fear, anxiety, anger, and depression. (pp. 714–715)

The effects of mistreatment by abusive principals don't stop with the individual. In a later article, Blase and Blase reported abusive principals "undermined the development of innovative and collaborative structures among faculty as well as teachers' overall level of involvement in their schools" (p. 123). This behavior led to teachers withdrawing from voluntary participation in school activities and, although showing up for required meetings, not actively participating. This research supports other studies (Murphy & Seashore-Louis, 1994; Reitzug & Cross, 1994) that principal or boss misuse of power through coercive or manipulative tactics has negative effects on implementation of reform initiatives.

In a more recent study, Blase and Blase (2008) completed a quantitative study that surveyed 172 teachers (51 males; 121 females). In responding to the questions about the level of harm to themselves, to the workplace, and to their families, 79% of the participants reported at least moderate harm to themselves and 49% reported serious or extensive harm, with similar percentages reporting moderate to serious harm to the workplace, 75% and 49%, respectively. Moderate harm to their families was reported by 58% and serious harm was reported by 31%. To cope with the stress of mistreatment, the top three coping strategies reported by more than 50% of the participants were (a) avoid the principal (80%), (b) talk with others for support and ideas (77%), and (c) endure the principal's mistreatment (61%). Although the main coping strategies seemed to be avoidance and submissive types, another coping strategy was to assert oneself with the principal (45%). Those more likely to assert themselves were male, senior teachers, and union members. The most surprising finding was that a large majority (77%) indicated that they would likely leave their position because of the mistreatment. The types of mistreatment reported by more than 50% of the respondents were as follows:

1. Failed to recognize or praise me for work-related achievements (70%)
2. Favored "select" teachers (63%)

3. Tried to intimidate me (59%)
4. Failed to support me in difficult interactions with students and/or parents (57%)
5. Ignored or snubbed me (55%)
6. Nitpicked about time or micromanaged me (54%)
7. Was insensitive to my personal matters (53%)
8. Made unreasonable demands (52%)
9. Stonewalled or failed to respond to me (52%)

It seems clear that students of educational leadership need to be aware of the potential for mismanagement of human resources by principals that lead to harmful effects on teachers and schools. Because of the difficulty of doing the type of research that Blase and Blase have pursued (e.g., finding teachers to admit abuse and protecting their identities), the percentage of principals who exhibit mistreatment behaviors is not known. Nonetheless, we report this research because we do not believe there should be any leaders who mistreat staff, students, or parents. There should be no need for an association such as the National Association of Prevention of Teacher Abuse (endteacherabuse.org), which began in 2002 and grew to over 1000 teachers and parent members as of 2013.

Human Resources Development

A continuing difficulty is finding ways to make administrators aware of the dense relationship between their behaviors, policies, and practices, on the one hand, and their impact on the human side of the enterprise, on the other. In dealing with tangible assets, such as money or real estate, accountants can demonstrate with numbers the bottom-line results of choices that managers make, thus showing the effect on the value of tangible assets entrusted to managers' care. One can show that deferring maintenance on buildings is an expensive practice, that purchasing wisely can save money, or that turning down thermostats reduces fuel costs. It is much more difficult to make such cause-and-effect linkages between administrative practices and their impact on the value of human resources. A local taxpayer association may cheer on a heavy-handed administrator who ruthlessly cuts teaching positions to slash the budget, but what is the cost if student achievement nosedives and dropout rates soar? Antiunion residents may be elated to see the superintendent of schools get tough at contract bargaining time, but what is the cost if resentment undermines the motivation of teachers and the teamwork between administrators and classroom teachers falters? The American Accounting Association has supported a great deal of work to develop ways of dealing with such human resources issues in industrial and commercial organizations, which is called human resources accounting. The central continuing problem with human resources accounting lies in the difficulty of measuring and quantifying the impact of management behavior on human attitudes, motivation, and work behavior. However, this work has given rise to a set of concepts that are helpful in understanding organizational behavior.

Human resources are valuable. In fact, in the case of educational organizations, they are often the most valuable resources available to create and maintain a high-performing organization. If thought of and treated as assets, the people in the organization—the human resources from which human capital is formed—are expected to have greater value in the future than at the present time. This is the essential nature of assets. Therefore, one can properly think of the costs of recruiting and hiring new people, training and supporting them, encouraging their professional growth and development, and managing them sensitively and skillfully as investment in people and—one would hope—their eventual higher productivity as return on that investment.

Instead of increasing in value over time, however, it is commonplace to assume that the human resources in schools decline in value over the years. For example, many observers of schooling complain that school faculties contain a lot of older teachers, who are often described as "burned out." This situation is often thought to be a consequence of tenure, which allegedly causes teachers to become complacent and uncaring. If this is true, it is not only costly but—worse—hinders the school's effective performance. But if it is true, one must ask: What is the cause? Is it that teachers tend to be a basically selfish and uncaring lot who, once they have some job security, shed any sense of professional responsibility? Is it that teaching is somehow a young person's game and at some point, teachers should be dismissed because of age? Little of what we know about organizational behavior supports either of these propositions. Rather, research in organizational behavior suggests that it is more likely that in a supportive organizational environment, one that facilitates continuous personal growth and professional fulfillment, teachers turn out to be increasingly effective over time. This fortuitous state of affairs is ordinarily found to exist in schools described as highly effective. Creating such a growth-enhancing organizational environment is the responsibility of those in charge of the schools, namely, school administrators. It is the process through which one builds human capital in schools.

DEVELOPING HUMAN CAPITAL THROUGH POSITIVE ORGANIZATIONAL CULTURE

Like all workplaces, an educational organization—each school and each university—is characterized by a distinctive organizational culture. In this sense, the term *organizational culture* refers to the *norms* that inform people about what is acceptable and what is not, the dominant *values* that the organization cherishes above others, the *basic assumptions and beliefs* that are shared by members of the organization, the *rules* of the game that must be observed if one is to get along and be accepted as a member, and the *philosophy* that guides the organization in dealing with its employees and its clients. These elements of organizational culture are developed over time by the people in the organization working together. They evolve during the history of the organization and are shared and subscribed to by those who are part of that history.

The culture of the educational organization shapes and molds assumptions and perceptions that are basic to understanding what it means to be a teacher. The culture informs the teachers about what it means to teach, what teaching methods are available and approved for use, what the students are like—what is possible, and what is not. The culture also plays a large role in defining for teachers their commitment to the task: It evokes the energy of the teachers to perform the task, loyalty and commitment to the organization and what it stands for, and emotional bonds of attachment to the organization and its ideals. These give rise to teachers' willingness not only to follow the rules and norms governing their behavior in the organization but, more than that, to accept the ideals of the organization as their own personal values and to work energetically to achieve the espoused goals of the organization (Firestone & Wilson, 1985).

Do certain kinds of organizational cultures promote greater effectiveness in educational organizations? The consensus is a resounding *yes*, as we describe more fully in Chapter 7. It is widely accepted today that the single most critical factor in improving the performance of individuals in an organization is to change its culture. For example, Bolman and Deal (1984) have contended that it is strong organizational culture that distinguishes high-performing companies from less-successful companies in competitive markets. In a highly popular and bestselling book, Thomas J. Peters and Robert H. Waterman, Jr. (1982) argued that successful U.S. corporations are characterized by the presence of specific, describable cultures that clearly differentiate them from others that seek to compete with them. Similarly, Rosabeth Moss Kanter (1983) argued persuasively that companies having what she called an "open culture" are more innovative and more successful than those that do not. Edgar Schein (1985) has described the relationship between organizational culture and the ability of administrators to exercise leadership. A growing body of literature concerning the role of organizational culture in educational organizations (discussed in later chapters of this book) strongly suggests that organizational culture is as powerful in creating effective human capital in educational organizations as it is in creating profit-making corporations.

FIVE BASIC ASSUMPTIONS OF EFFECTIVE SCHOOLS

We discuss the concept of effective schools in this chapter because without high-quality human capital working together in specific ways schools cannot be successful. For well over two decades, researchers have studied the characteristics of effective schools, seeking to find out what they tend to be like in contrast with less-effective schools. The result is an accumulated body of research that suggests that effective, or high-achieving, schools tend to be organized and operated on five basic assumptions (Purkey & Smith, 1985):

1. Whatever else a school can and should do, its central purpose is to teach: Success is measured by students' progress in knowledge, skills, and attitudes.
2. The school is responsible for providing the overall environment in which teaching and learning occur.
3. Schools must be treated holistically: Partial efforts to make improvements that deal with the needs of only some of the students and break up the unity of the instructional program are likely to fail.
4. The most crucial characteristics of a school are the attitudes and behaviors of the teachers and other staff, not material things such as the size of its library or the age of the physical plant.
5. Perhaps most important, the school accepts responsibility for the success or failure of the academic performance of the students. Students are firmly regarded as capable of learning regardless of their ethnicity, sex, home or cultural background, or family income. "Pupils from poor families do not need a different curriculum, nor does their poverty excuse failure to learn basic skills," Stewart Purkey and Marshall Smith have asserted, adding, "Differences among schools do have an impact on student achievement, and those differences are controllable by the school staff" (p. 355).

Thus, the effective schools concept turns 180 degrees from traditional educational thought that tends to blame the victim, namely, the student, for low academic achievement. Though one of the outstanding characteristics of effective schools is that collectively staff take responsibility for meeting the educational needs of students to a greater degree than their less-successful counterparts, this is still a concept that many educational practitioners find difficult to accept. Nevertheless, this is the essential lesson from the effective schools research.

The question remains: what is it, specifically, that some schools do in order to meet the educational needs of students? Read a quote from Purkey and Smith (1985), who developed a penetrating analysis of the effective schools research literature in the mid-1980s:

> The most persuasive research suggests that student academic performance is strongly affected by school culture. This culture is composed of values, norms, and roles existing

within institutionally distinct structures of governance, communication, educational practices and policies and so on. Successful schools are found to have cultures that produce a climate or "ethos" conducive to teaching and learning . . . efforts to change schools have been most productive and most enduring when directed toward influencing the entire school culture via a strategy involving collaborative planning, shared decision making, and collegial work in an atmosphere friendly to experimentation and evaluation. (p. 357)

Purkey and Smith's survey of the research literature identified a cluster of 13 organizational and operational characteristics that effective schools tend to exhibit. They fall into two groups. The first group contains nine characteristics that can be implemented quickly at minimal cost by administrative action. These involve such characteristics as collaborative decision making, improving human capital through professional development, strong leadership distributed throughout the school, a coordinated curriculum, parental involvement, recognition for and a focus on academic success, and an emphasis on teaching and learning. A more detailed description of what we call *tactical* characteristics of effective schools is displayed in Box 6.3:

BOX 6.3

Nine *Tactical* Characteristics of Effective Schools That Can Be Implemented Quickly at Minimal Cost by Administrative Action

---

1. School-site management and democratic decision making, in which individual schools are encouraged to take greater responsibility for, and are given greater latitude in, educational problem solving.
2. Support from the district for increasing the capacity of schools to identify and solve significant educational problems, which includes reducing the inspection and management roles of central office people while increasing support and encouragement of school-level leadership and collaborative problem solving
3. Strong leadership, which may be provided by administrators but also may be provided by integrated teams of administrators, teachers, and perhaps others
4. Staff stability to facilitate the development of a strong cohesive school culture
5. A planned, coordinated curriculum that treats the students' educational needs holistically and increases time spent on academic learning
6. Schoolwide staff development that links the school's organizational and instructional needs with the needs that teachers themselves perceive should be addressed
7. Parental involvement, particularly in support of homework, attendance, and discipline
8. Schoolwide recognition of academic success, both in terms of improving academic performance and achieving standards of excellence
9. An emphasis on the time required for teaching and learning, for example, reducing interruptions and disruptions, stressing the primacy of focused efforts to learn, and restructuring teaching activities

BOX 6.4

**Four *Strategic* Characteristics Necessary
in Achieving Effective Schools**

1. Collaborative planning and collegial relationships that promote feelings of unity, encourage sharing of knowledge and ideas, and foster consensus among those in the school
2. Sense of community, in which alienation—of both teachers and students—is reduced and a sense of mutual sharing is strengthened
3. Shared clear goals and high achievable expectations, which arise from collaboration, collegiality, and a sense of community and which serve to unify those in the organization through their common purposes
4. Order and discipline that bespeak the seriousness and purposefulness of the school as a community of people—students, teachers and staff, and other adults—that is focused by mutual agreement on shared goals, collaboration, and consensus

The characteristics of effective schools listed in Box 6.3 are necessary, but in and of themselves will not lead to effective schools. They set the stage for the development of a second group of four characteristics that have great power to renew and increase the school's capacity to continue to solve problems and increase effectiveness over time. This second group is characterized by long-term commitment to developing a staff who work collaboratively to develop a sense of community with shared goals that have high, but achievable, expectations. These long-term characteristics, that we call *strategic,* are displayed in Box 6.4.

Clearly, the critical school characteristics listed in the second, *strategic,* group are more complex than those in the first group, more difficult to achieve and sustain over time, yet they combine to produce great power to establish the improvement of educational effectiveness as a central focus of life within the school. The power, of course, lies in developing within the school a culture—norms, values, and beliefs—that unites those in the school in their unending quest for increased educational effectiveness. Many if not most school-improvement plans can be faulted precisely for seeking to "install" the relatively simpler, *tactical,* characteristics and falling short of seriously engaging in the culture rebuilding suggested by the more complex, strategic, characteristics.

These characteristics are found in the research that Carl Glickman, Stephen Gordon, and Jovita Ross-Gordon (2007) call *school-improvement research.* They suggest that school-improvement research indicates how we can, over time, sustain effective school characteristics resulting in improved student and school outcomes. Their review of the school-improvement literature resulted in a list of the most important factors that are responsible for developing effective schools. These factors are listed in Box 6.5. Schools that model the second-order effective school characteristics of improving schools are schools that value human resources, treat human resources as professionals, and continue to improve those human resources through professional development.

BOX 6.5

Characteristics of Improving Schools (Glickman, Gordon & Ross-Gordon, 2007, p. 42)

- Varied sources of leadership, including teacher leadership
- Consideration of individual school context and culture
- Parental involvement
- Shared vision and continuous revisioning
- External and internal support, including time, moral, and technical support
- Focus on teaching and learning
- Ongoing professional development, including continuous analysis, reflection, and growth
- Instructional dialogue
- Teacher collaboration
- Democratic, collective inquiry, including action research
- Integration of improvement efforts into a coherent program
- Data-based feedback on improvement efforts using multiple measures

VOICES FROM THE FIELD

Curriculum and Professional Development

Scot D. Croner, K-12 Instructional Coordinator,
Marion Community Schools, Marion, Indiana

Much discussion has taken place amongst educators in recent years regarding "intended curriculum" and "taught curriculum." From the district level, it is critical that systems be in place to ensure that all intended curriculum is taught (and more importantly learned). Many times, the quality of the professional development will play the key factor in determining whether this goal is accomplished.

Over the past years, our district has struggled with the concept of ensuring a consistently taught curriculum. Many times, without guidance and an opportunity to collaborate upon curriculum, teachers will become isolated and teach what is comfortable. This factor alone can adversely affect student learning. An inconsistent curriculum, however, becomes exponentially more detrimental when working with a transient student population, which is the case within our district.

To assist us with this challenge, this past year our district implemented a common formative assessment program across all grade levels and all buildings. On a monthly basis, grade level teachers from each building were provided half-day professional development to meet as a grade level team with a district-level administrator. During these meetings, instructors reviewed data from previous assessments, discussed instructional strategies that provided success, and collaboratively wrote the next common assessment based upon student data and their curriculum maps. This process required us not only to reflect upon our curriculum but also to give our teachers a deeper understanding of the standards. In addition, this process held us accountable to ensure that our curriculum was rigorous and (most importantly) helped us determine whether it was learned.

Anecdotally, we have observed improvements in our student learning throughout the course of the year. In addition to a consistently taught and assessed curriculum, our team has also developed a consistent schedule for each of our four elementary schools with specific Tier 2 (RtI) time to provide additional reading instruction for our struggling students. Tier 2 instruction is designed to meet the needs of our students based upon the results of our formative assessments. These two improvements have helped raise the results of our reading comprehension scores as measured by Indiana Reading Evaluation and Determination for third grade (IREAD 3) from 72% proficiency (2011–2012 school year) to 78% proficiency (2012–2013 school year). Results from our formative assessments also indicate a significant improvement in our State Accountability assessments although this data is not available at this time.

The expertise within a building is one of the most underutilized professional development resources available to educators. Through our purposeful approach of guiding our teachers through their curriculum with the use of formative assessments, we were able to see significant gains in our teacher pedagogy and student learning. After each monthly meeting, our teachers returned to their classroom with a laser-like focus on their curriculum, new instructional tools to help improve student learning, and the knowledge that expertise and support was available through their neighbor across the hallway.

Professional Development

To achieve the effective school characteristics described in the preceding section, leaders must value human resources in the organization and understand that improving the knowledge base of the workers is paramount. While professional development budgets are often the first to be downsized in times of retrenchment, skillful leaders will do all they can to ensure that professional development continues for the staff because they realize that unless they can focus on continually improving human resources, the organization will backslide, or at least remain stagnant. Research studies support these statements; the work by Linda Darling-Hammond (2000), for example, has shown that teacher preparation and certification are the strongest correlates of student performance in reading and math. This fact holds true regardless of student socioeconomic status or language background. Darling-Hammond concludes:

> Reforms underway to create more thoughtful licensing systems, more productive teacher education programs, and more effective professional development strategies are producing evidence of the stronger effects on teaching and learning of approaches that strengthen teachers' abilities to teach diverse learners with a keen diagnostic eye and a wide repertoire of strategies supporting mastery of challenging content. (p. 33)

Understanding the importance of teacher preparation, certification, and professional development, Congress requires that districts prove they have "highly qualified teachers." Highly qualified teachers must have a bachelor's degree, have full state licensure, and prove that they know each subject area in which they teach. To assist local education agencies (LEAs) in having highly qualified teachers for all students, Title II of NCLB includes grants for the improvement of human resources in schools. These include areas such as funding for professional development; alternative routes to teacher certification that are likely to attract second-career individuals from noneducation backgrounds; and recruiting and retaining highly qualified teachers, principals, and other personnel. Other, more controversial sections of Title II involve funding to reform teacher tenure systems to make it easier to terminate marginal teachers, funding to implement teacher testing for subject-matter knowledge in order to obtain teacher certification, and funding to support LEAs in developing merit-based performance systems in the belief that merit pay will improve the performance of teachers.

Whether or not school leaders are able to tap the Title II funding, the improvement of human resources through professional development is paramount. All educators, however, have horror stories of poor inservice training workshops they have had to endure; thus, it is quite common for teachers to criticize professional development plans in their district or their school.

BOX 6.6

Characteristics of Effective Professional Development Programs

- Involvement of participants in planning, implementing, and evaluating programs
- Schoolwide goals form the basis for improvement, but individual and group goals are integrated with school goals
- Long-range planning and development
- Incorporate research and best practice on school improvement and instructional improvement
- Administrative support, including provision of time and other resources as well as involvement in program planning and delivery
- Adherence to the principles of adult learning
- Attention to the research on change, including the need to address individual concerns throughout the change process
- Follow-up and support for transfer of learning to the school or classroom
- Ongoing assessment and feedback
- Continuous professional development that becomes part of the school culture

But professional development can be highly effective if it is planned properly by including those to be trained in the process; by insuring that the training is focused on the district and school improvement objectives; and by having continuous training, not one-shot workshops. Box 6.6 lists these and other characteristics of successful staff development programs (Glickman et al., 2007, pp. 353–354).

Improving human resources through staff development is the leader's responsibility. Regardless of whether the professional development budget has been cut, the principal must find ways to offer learning opportunities to the staff. Even with a tight budget, one can provide a very effective method of staff development through use of scheduling and class coverage. Having teachers observe each other and then having discussions about what was observed and how one can improve is a highly effective method of learning. This method and others that cost little but are excellent learning opportunities should be developed by the staff. The goal, even in times of retrenchment, is to improve human resources.

Final Thoughts

The essay "The Study of Administration," which Princeton's assistant professor Woodrow Wilson (and future President of the United States) published in *Political Science Quarterly* in the summer of 1887, marked the beginning of the serious study of administration. During the century that followed, students of organization struggled to do what had never been done before: to increase through systematic inquiry our understanding of organizations and the behavior of people who work in them. Two very clear long-term trends developed that, together, set the stage for where we are now and where we are going.

THE EFFORT TO CREATE AN ADMINISTRATIVE SCIENCE

The search for deep and stable principles believed to be the foundations of administrative thought and practice led first to the quest for a science of administration. The effort was fueled by the conviction that some fundamental rational logic, system, and order must underlie organization. These were to be discovered through objective, value-free scientific research using measurement and expressing descriptions in mathematical terms.

Once these factors were discovered, it was thought, systematic principles for engaging in the practice of administration could be scientifically derived from them. By the middle of the twentieth century, though, many observers were having doubts, not merely about the assumptions of system and rationality in organizations that guided the processes of scientific discovery but also whether the assumed order and logical system even existed at all. These doubts arose from two main observations. First, practicing administrators saw little relationship between the realities of organizational life as they experienced it and the theories of organizational life that academics espoused. Second, scant convincing evidence was generated to support the "scientific" assumptions as being more valid than other insightful, thoughtful views.

Formal challenges to this logical-positivist paradigm began to be published in 1974, the so-called theory movement collapsed, and today students of educational administration have coalesced around a new paradigm that is still in the process of being developed. The new paradigm rejects anthropomorphism, which can lead us to reify organizations and think of them as existing in some sort of freestanding way, independent of human beings. Organizations actually are social inventions that exist only in the minds of people. We now think not so much of analyzing organizations in mathematical terms but of making sense of them in human terms. We accept that organizations do not act or think; people do.

Thus, at the dawn of the second century of organizational study, few seriously believe that the time is ripe to develop a science of administration if, indeed, such a science ever will be developed. This fact does not mean, however, that we have failed either to discover some basic principles of organizational behavior or to develop increased understanding of organizational life. Far from it. The patient theorizing and research carried out over the course of a century has produced a rich legacy of knowledge that administrators can use in practice. But it is not marked by the logical precision and mathematical certitude that the pioneer scholars had expected it to have.

CENTRALITY OF THE HUMAN DIMENSION OF ORGANIZATION

Perhaps the most powerful learning to have arisen during the first century of organizational studies concerns what is now obvious: that the key to understanding organization lies in understanding the human and social dimensions. Early scholars emphasized organizational structure chiefly as a hierarchy of power. Those in the lower ranks were to submit to the power and authority, perceived as legitimate, of those in the higher ranks of the hierarchy. Toward the middle of the twentieth century, after the completion of the Western Electric research, students of organization began to grasp what Douglas McGregor was later to describe as "the human side of enterprise," which was the realization that human motivation, aspiration, beliefs, and values have wondrous power in determining the effectiveness of efforts to lead and develop organizations.

At first, the conviction of the legitimacy of hierarchical authority was still widely held, and the human side of organizations was interpreted as "human relations," meaning taking steps to ameliorate and reduce the resistance of workers to their powerlessness. Human relations, as it was interpreted by administrators, typically became ameliorative inducements for people to submit to organizational authority. The inducements ranged from health insurance plans to simple civility in daily encounters, from providing pleasant working environments to legitimizing the feelings of employees about their work. But throughout the human relations era, administrators clung to the notion that while they might act civilly, even kindly, toward subordinates, power in the organization is hierarchical and by right ought to be exercised asymmetrically from the top down.

But the "battle of the century," both in organizational studies and in the larger world, has been the struggle between centralized authority and individual freedom, between entrenched power elites and ordinary people. Organizations of all kinds, often once revered, are now suspect, viewed with hostility, and often described as oppressive. The ability to establish and maintain organizational discipline through traditional top-down hierarchical exercise of power has been rapidly eroding in all kinds of organizations, from nation-states to school districts. The larger canvas, the backdrop, is revealed in the collapse of traditional political hegemonies that began to unfold in the late 1980s in Eastern Europe, the former Soviet Union, and South Africa as people around the world demanded greater power and freedom from centralized organizational constraints as well as greater control over their own lives and destinies.

In the world of U.S. education, this theme is insistently echoed, if in muted tones, in oft-repeated themes that call for efforts to improve the performance of schools by restructuring them to increase the power of teachers to make critical educational decisions, facilitate collaborative decision making, and create collegial growth-enhancing school cultures. This is a marked departure from traditional thinking and is based on the conviction that overemphasis on bureaucratic structures, top-down exercise of power, and centralized control have demonstrably failed to produce the organizational results that advocates of traditional organizational theory had claimed it would.

WHERE WE ARE AND WHERE WE ARE GOING

Today, traditional bureaucratic approaches to organization and the newer approaches that emphasize the human dimensions of organization exist side by side and often compete for the attention and loyalty of educational administrators. Bureaucratic approaches are far from dead in educational organizations, and many people are confident that imposing change from the top down is the most effective way to reform schools. Unfortunately, NCLB and Race to the Top (RTTT) support bureaucratic methods of human resources development. These approaches include programs based on tough accountability systems for schools and districts that link student achievement to standards (e.g., Common Core State Standards—to be discussed in later chapters) for teacher and principal evaluation systems that impact placement, teacher tenure, promotion, dismissal, and salary increases. These systems, often called the Value-Added Model (VAM), are unproven, yet purport to motivate and improve staff by determining how much value an individual adds to student and school improvement and using the results in the evaluation system (Ravitch, 2013).

On the other hand, nonbureaucratic approaches to organizing and administering have been rapidly gaining support in recent years among many educators and education organizations. These two approaches will continue to compete in the marketplace of ideas for years to come, with the concept of building human capital continuing to gain ground because it so well meets contemporary conditions.

Reflective Activities

1. In this chapter, we pointed out the discrepancies between the academic view of the world and that of the practitioner. As an aspiring leader, what is your opinion of these discrepancies? How does your opinion affect the way you will lead an organization?
2. Locate a primarily quantitative research article and a primarily qualitative research article about organizational behavior, focusing on the human dimension or improving human capital. Compare and contrast the different research design and data-collection methods.

Describe the findings in these articles. How are the research methods in each type of article useful in understanding organizations? In your view, which type of research paradigm is best?
3. Reflect on the results from the Meyer and Rowan study. Analyze how the leadership in your organization uses bureaucratic means to influence the instructional behavior of teachers. Are these ideas effective? Suggest others ideas that might be effective in influencing instruction.

4. Using the research on effective school characteristics and on characteristics of improving schools, identify the characteristics currently used and those that are not used in your school. Are those characteristics used in your school effective? If they are effective, why is this so? If they are not, what do you suggest to improve their effectiveness?

5. Reflect on the characteristics of effective professional development. Describe professional development planning at your school in terms of these characteristics.

6. *Working on Your Game Plan.* Consider the following advertisement, which appeared (except for changes in the names and dates) in a national newspaper.

Assume that you are interested in applying for the principalship that is advertised. After reviewing the work that you have done thus far on your game plan, and after reviewing this chapter, prepare a draft of the letter of interest that the ad requests. Focus your letter on your beliefs about building human capacity to help create or maintain an effective school.

Because you are limited to a one-page letter (including the heading block, inside address, and signature block), you cannot address every point raised in the ad. In preparing your draft, you must choose, at most, a few points that you consider important and with which you can present yourself to advantage.

It would be interesting, and probably a learning opportunity, to discuss with others how they handled this problem and why they chose to say what they did.

CRITICAL INCIDENT   Turning Madison High Around

Dr. Frances Weinstein liked the ring of her new title, Doctor of Education, recently acquired at the state university's main campus. And now she was thrilled to have the honor —and the challenge—of being principal of Madison High School. After all, Madison was still a respected school, even though its former prestige was now threadbare. Her new job, Superintendent Renaldo Carreras had told her plainly, was to return Madison High to the prestige of its glory days. Dr. Weinstein had no doubt that she could do that: After all, her graduate studies had focused on the effective schools research, and she had done an outstanding job as assistant principal for administration at Wallingford High School. That job hadn't been a walk in the park either!

Mr. Wentworth, the founding principal at Madison, had retired graciously and everyone on the faculty had known that it was time for him to go. Superintendent Carreras clarified with Dr. Weinstein the issues that were troubling him the most about Madison High: (1) Attendance was poor and getting worse, (2) achievement test scores were on a persistent downward slide, (3) Scholastic Aptitude Test (SAT) scores were going the same way, and (4) the dropout rate was steadily climbing.

The first year at Madison went well, Dr. Weinstein thought. She had followed a carefully thought-out strategic plan. She would spend the first semester accomplishing the following four tasks:

1. Get to know the school and the way things were done there, and confirm that the indicators of poor performance that Superintendent Carreras had given her were correct.
2. Get to know, and develop collegial relationships with, the faculty of 119 teachers and counselors.
3. Take every opportunity to present herself and represent the school to the parents and to important community members.
4. Make a diagnosis of the issues that underlie the indicators of poor performance in the school and develop and initiate an action plan for her second year.

She learned that Carreras's four performance indicators were of concern to people on the faculty, too. Teachers and counselors expressed concern that cutting classes was a growing problem, as was lateness in coming to school. And discipline problems were, they thought, verging on disorder in the hallways during passing time, in the cafeteria, and in some classes. It also seemed that the following pattern was emerging for a growing group of students: come to school on time, check in as "present," perhaps go to a class or two that the students liked (such as gym or shop), have lunch, and then drift off and not be seen for the rest of the day.

In the March faculty meeting, Dr. Weinstein launched her action plan by announcing that the school would develop a freshman academy. Faculty meetings were held in the school's large-group lecture room that had an in-the-round design, with seats stepped up and the lectern in the center. Dr. Weinstein proudly took the occasion to show her PowerPoint presentation that introduced the idea of freshman academy, explained what it was about, and encouraged discussion following it. The discussion was unusually lively and included a number of expressions of doubt and reservations about whether it was appropriate for Madison High. Many of the faculty's reservations centered on concern about how such a thing could be worked into the school's class schedule. Others thought the idea was off target altogether: that Madison High's problems came from demographic change. They were, of course, alluding to the fact that more and more low-income families were moving into Madison High's attendance zone. The rising trend in the numbers qualifying for subsidized lunch testified to that.

Dr. Weinstein drew the meeting to a close, and she assured faculty members that they would have plenty of opportunity to discuss the freshman academy in the months ahead. She, the counselors, and the assistant principal for administration would get to work on next year's schedule immediately and had no doubt that it could be worked out. She summarized the main points of the freshman academy idea: "It will help new high school kids adjust to the change of moving from middle school to a high school, provide a cadre of caring teachers and a school counselor whom they know and can confide in, and provide students with a culture of caring that supports them academically, making it less likely that they will drop out."

Dr. Weinstein concluded by enthusiastically saying: "We are going to make Madison High a place where the students want to be because they know we care about them. We need to treat these kids holistically, not just send them to different classes and hope for the best. You are going to take individual responsibility for the children in your academy. This is a change you can do now. It doesn't take a lot of money, time, and training. You are all professional teachers and you know how to help these kids."

Dr. Weinstein energetically launched the new freshman academy at the opening of the next school year, her second year at Madison High. She invested considerable time, energy, and personal attention to support and encourage its implementation and development. But she was discouraged as the months went by to see little, if any, change in the way freshmen were treated. Teachers as well as counselors told her frankly that the academy idea wasn't having much impact and, sadly, the trend data bore that judgment out. The teachers and counselors were convinced that they had always cared for and supported their students, and they did not embrace this idea of a freshman academy. They felt that this change was simply dumped on them and that they had little training and no extra time to implement the changes that they believed were needed to make such a program work effectively.

1. Analyze the change process at Madison High School. What went wrong with the changes the principal implemented?
2. Can you suggest a different approach that might be more effective?
3. In your response, include concepts from this chapter that focus on developing human capacity and relationships.

Suggested Reading

Blase, J., & Blase, J. (2003). *Breaking the silence: Overcoming the problem of principal mistreatment of teachers.* Thousand Oaks, CA: Corwin Press.

This book describes the research literature on boss abuse or bullying behaviors of supervisors, and it details the research findings reported in this chapter that the authors completed on principal mistreatment of teachers. They call this "The Dark Side of Educational Leadership."

Meyer, M. W. (1978). *Environments and organizations.* San Francisco, CA: Jossey-Bass.

In the classical bureaucratic tradition, structuralism has long dominated thinking about organizations in sociology. This important book marks a sharp departure from that tradition and introduces the newer organizational theorizing that is emerging in the discipline of sociology. Excellent chapter on "The Structure of Educational Organizations." Highly recommended.

Mink, O. G., Mink, B. P., & Owens, K. Q. (2000). *Developing high performance people: The art of coaching.* Reading, MA: Addison-Wesley Longman.

The authors describe coaching as the art of encouraging others to experience their own power, and they try to show how leaders can use coaching to create high-performance environments, as present-day school reform efforts demand. Starting from understanding how people learn and grow on the job, they deal with issues involved in helping workers to deal with barriers to their performance, participate with others in self-managed teams, and work toward improving the performance of the organization.

Mintzberg, H. (1979). *The structuring of organizations.* Englewood Cliffs, NJ: Prentice Hall.

A well-organized, comprehensive, and lucid discussion of contemporary problems of designing and building organizations. Describes the characteristics of five specific kinds of organizations and their implications for administration.

Parker, G. M. (1994). *Cross-functional teams: Working with allies, enemies, and other strangers.* San Francisco, CA: Jossey-Bass.

Though primarily concerned with corporate management, this book about managing and leading collaborative teams does include among its examples some noteworthy team efforts in public school education in the United States. It is a how-to manual that gives advice and practical guidance on issues such as overcoming communication barriers, building bridges between groups, and working together to produce fluid and productive collaboration.

Peters, T. J., & Waterman, R. H., Jr. (1982). *In search of excellence: Lessons from America's best-run companies.* New York, NY: Harper & Row.

Long on the bestseller lists, this book is a must read for those who want to find out how modern organizational theory is being used in the competitive corporate world. Though it focuses on business and industry, it contains a great deal of food for thought for educators.

References

Argyris, C. (1953). Human problems with budgets. *Harvard Business Review, 31,* 97–110.

Barth, R. S., & Deal, T. E. (1982). *The effective principal: A research summary.* Reston, VA: Association of Secondary School Principals.

Bidwell, C. E. (1965). The school as a formal organization. In J. G. March (Ed.), *Handbook of organizations* (pp. 972–1022). Chicago, IL: Rand McNally.

Blase, J., & Blase, J. (2002). The dark side of leadership: Teacher perspectives of principal mistreatment. *Educational Administration Quarterly, 38*(5), 671–727.

Blase, J., & Blase, J. (2006). Teachers' perspectives on principal mistreatment. *Teacher Education Quarterly, 33*(4), 123–142.

Blase, J., & Blase, J. (2008). The mistreated teacher: A national study. *Journal of Educational Administration, 46*(3), 263–301.

Blumberg, A. (1988). *School administration as a craft: Foundations of practice.* Boston, MA: Allyn and Bacon.

Bolman, L. G., & Deal, T. E. (1984). *Modern approaches to understanding and managing organizations.* San Francisco, CA: Jossey-Bass.

Conant, J. B. (1964). *Two modes of thought: My encounters with science and education.* New York, NY: Trident Press.

Darling-Hammond, L. (2000, January). Teacher quality and student achievement: A review of state policy evidence. *Education Policy Analysis Archives, 8*(1). Retrieved from http://epaa.asu.edu/epaa/v8n1/

David, J. L. (2008). What research says about classroom walk-throughs. *Educational Leadership, 65*(4), 81–82.

Firestone, W. A., & Wilson, B. (1985). Using bureaucratic and cultural linkages to improve instruction: The high school principal's contribution. *Education Administration Quarterly, 21*(2), 7–30.

Glickman, C., Gordon, S., & Ross-Gordon, J. (2007). *Supervision and instructional leadership: A developmental approach.* Boston, MA: Allyn and Bacon.

Glomb, T. M. (2002). Workplace anger and aggression: Informing conceptual models with data from specific encounters. *Journal of Occupational Health Psychology, 7*(1), 20–36.

Greenfield, T. B. (1975). Theory about organization: A new perspective and its implication for schools. In M. G. Hughes (Ed.), *Administering education: International challenge* (pp. 71–99). London, England: Athlone.

Greenstone, M., & Looney, A. (2013). Is starting college and not finishing really that bad? *The Hamilton Project at The Brookings Institution.* Retrieved from http://www.hamiltonproject.org/files/downloads_and_links/May_Jobs_Blog_20130607_FINAL_2.pdf

Harlos, K. P., & Axelrod, L. J. (2005). Investigating hospital administrators' experience of workplace mistreatment. *Canadian Journal of Behavioural Sciences, 37*(4), 262–272.

Hoy, W. K., & Miskel, C. G. (1982). *Educational administration* (2nd ed.). New York, NY: Random House.

Kanter, R. M. (1983). *The change masters: Innovation and entrepreneurship in the American corporation.* New York, NY: Simon & Schuster.

Killian, R. A. (1976). *Human resource management.* New York, NY: AMACOM.

Likert, R. (1967). *The human organization: Its management and value.* New York, NY: McGraw-Hill.

Meyer, J. W., & Rowan, B. (1983). The structure of educational organizations. In J. W. Meyer & W. R. Scott (Eds.), *Organizational environments: Ritual and rationality* (pp. 71–98). Beverly Hills, CA: Sage.

Morris, V. C., Crowson, R. L., Hurwitz, E., Jr., & Porter-Gehrie, C. (1981). *The urban principal: Discretionary decision making in a large educational organization.* Chicago, IL: University of Illinois Press.

Murphy, J., & Seashore-Louis, K. (1994). *Reshaping the principalship: Insights from transformational reform efforts.* Thousand Oaks, CA: Corwin Press.

Newberg, N. A., & Glatthom, A. G. (1983). *Instructional leadership: Four ethnographic studies of junior high school principals.* Washington, DC: National Institute of Education.

Peters, T. J., & Waterman, R. H., Jr. (1982). *In search of excellence: Lessons from America's best-run companies.* New York, NY: Harper & Row.

Purkey, S. C., & Smith, M. S. (1985). School reform: The district policy implications of the effective schools literature. *Elementary School Journal, 85,* 353–389.

Ravitch, D. (2013). *Reign of error: The hoax of the privatization movement and the danger to America's public schools.* New York, NY: Alfred A. Knopf.

Reitzug, U. C., & Cross, B. E. (1994, April 5). *A multisite case study of site-based management in urban schools.* Paper presented at the annual meeting of the American Educational Research Association, New Orleans, LA.

Rogers, C. R. (1963). Toward a science of the person. *Journal of Humanistic Psychology, 3*(2), 17–31.

Schein, E. H. (1985). *Organizational culture and leadership.* San Francisco, CA: Jossey-Bass.

Schön, D. A. (1987). *Educating the reflective practitioner.* San Francisco, CA: Jossey-Bass.

Schultz, T. W. (1960). Capital formation by education. *The Journal of Political Economy, 68,* 3–72.

Schultz, T. W. (1963) *The economic value of education.* New York, NY: Columbia University Press.

Weick, K. E. (1976). Educational organizations as loosely coupled systems. *Administrative Science Quarterly, 21,* 1–19.

CHAPTER 7

Organizational Culture and Organizational Climate

Because the behavior of people in organizational life arises from the interaction between their motivational needs and characteristics (temperaments, intelligences, beliefs, perceptions) and characteristics of the environment, or because B = f (p • e), it follows that the organizational environment is a key to influencing organizational behavior. Although educational leaders have little ability to alter the inner drives and motivational forces of individuals in the organization, they have considerable latitude in altering the organizational environment.

But remember that the organization, and therefore its environment, is a socially constructed reality: It is not tangible. Of course, the building is tangible enough, as are the furniture, equipment, files, and other artifacts that make up the physical entity that we often call school. But these are not the organization. The organization exists largely in the eye and the mind of the beholder: It is, in reality, pretty much what people think it is.

Coordinating and influencing the behavior of people to achieve the goals of the organization is the central concern of administrators and leaders. Earlier in this book, we pointed out two different, contrasting ways of thinking about and acting on this issue. That is, there are two different theoretical approaches to it: One is the traditional bureaucratic approach; the other uses the concept of building human capital through human resources development. These two theoretical approaches were compared and contrasted in some detail earlier in this book.

If educational administrators have little ability to directly alter or influence the inner state of organizational participants—in other words, their motivation—they have considerable ability to do so through indirect means. By fostering the creation of organizational environments that enhance the personal growth of organization members—environments that are supportive of creativity, team building, and participation in solving problems—school leaders can tap into the powerful energy of inner motivational forces that traditional organizational environments routinely repress and discourage. What we are discussing here is, of course, largely the social-psychological environment of the organization rather than only the physical environment. It is the realm of organizational climate and organizational culture.

DEFINING AND DESCRIBING ORGANIZATIONAL CULTURE AND CLIMATE

The inner state of organizational participants is an important key to understanding their behavior. Thus, although immediate antecedent conditions may well evoke behavioral responses, so do the perceptions, values, beliefs, and motivations of the participants. In other words, participants commonly respond to organizational events very much in terms of learnings that have developed through their experience over time and not merely to events immediately preceding their behavior. Therefore, the educational leader is much concerned with the forces and processes through which organizational participants are socialized into the organization: how they develop perceptions, values, and beliefs concerning the organization and what influence these inner states have on behavior. In contemporary organizational behavior literature, these are the realms of organizational climate and organizational culture.

Organizational climate and organizational culture are not new concepts. They have a long tradition in the literature of organization studies, going back at least as far as the Western Electric research of the 1930s, which noted that some management styles elicited feelings of affiliation, competence, and achievement from workers, leading to more productive work than had been done previously, as well as eliciting greater satisfaction from workers than under other and different styles of management (see Chapters 3 and 5). Beginning in the 1940s, Kurt Lewin, his colleagues, and students conducted numerous studies to explore the proposition that organizations could be made more effective by using planned interventions designed to shift the social norms of managers and workers alike.

Many different names have been used over the years to allude to the subtle, elusive, intangible, largely unconscious forces that comprise the symbolic side of organizations and shape human thought and behavior in them. Very early in the study of organizations, Chester Barnard (1938) described culture as a social fiction created by people to give meaning to work and life. In the 1940s, Philip Selznick (1949) used the term *institution* to describe what creates solidarity, meaning, commitment, and productivity in organizations; in the 1960s, the term *organizational climate* became very popular with students of organization, in no small measure due to the research on elementary schools by Andrew Halpin and Don Croft (1963). In the 1970s, Rutter, Maughan, Mortimore, and Ouston (1979) noted the importance of "ethos" in determining the effectiveness of the high schools that they studied. In the 1990s, we learned from Heifetz (1994) that cultural norms we learn from the voices of authority figures can then somewhat fulfill the social functions of authority, though not entirely. In 2001, Fullan (2001) told us about our responsibility to establish a culture to fulfill our *moral purpose* of making a difference in the lives of children. Marzano, Waters and McNulty (2005) informed us that successful principals fostered shared beliefs and a sense of community in building a positive culture. And critical theorists, according to McLaren (2007), define schooling as *cultural politics* (to be discussed in more detail in this chapter). These studies are illustrative of a substantial body of research that seeks to describe and explain the learned pattern of thinking, reflected and reinforced in behavior, that is so seldom seen yet is so powerful in shaping people's behavior. This pattern of thinking and the behavior associated with it provide stability, foster certainty, solidify order and predictability, and create meaning in the organization.

An observer who moves from school to school ineluctably develops a sense that each school is distinctive, unique in some almost indefinable yet powerful way. This sense, seemingly palpable when we are in a school, more than describes that school: It *is* that school. As we have said, many different terms have been used to identify that sense of the unique characteristics that organizations have. People sometimes use terms such as *atmosphere, personality, tone,* or *ethos* when speaking of this unique characteristic of a school. But the term *organizational climate* has come into rather general use as a metaphor for this distinctive characteristic of organizations. But just what is organizational climate? And how is it created?

Climate is generally defined as the characteristics of the total environment in a school building (Anderson, 1982; Miskel & Ogawa, 1988). But we need to understand what those

ECOLOGY
PHYSICAL AND MATERIAL FACTORS

BUILDING AND FACILITIES	TECHNOLOGY
Facilities	***Scheduling/sequencing inventions***
Age of building	*(e.g., bell schedule, scope and sequence*
Size of building	*of curriculum)*
Design of building	***Information/communication***
Accessibility for individuals with disabilities	***inventions***
Equipment and furniture	*Books*
Condition of building	*Computers*
	Video
	Film
	Chalkboard
	Pedagogical inventions
	Student grouping
	Instructional techniques
	Testing

FIGURE 7.1 Some illustrative examples of the characteristics that give rise to the ecology of a school.

characteristics are, and to lay the groundwork for that understanding, we turn to the work of Renato Tagiuri (1968), who described the total environment in an organization, that is, the organizational climate, as composed of four dimensions:

1. *Ecology* refers to physical and material factors in the organization: for example, the size, age, design, facilities, and condition of the building or buildings. It also refers to the technology used by people in the organization: desks and chairs, chalkboards, elevators, everything used to carry out organizational activities. See Figure 7.1.
2. *Milieu* is the social dimension in the organization, which includes almost everything relating to the people in the organization—for example, how many people and what they are like. Milieu would also include race and ethnicity, salary level of teachers, socioeconomic level of students, education levels attained by the teachers, the morale and motivation of adults and students who inhabit the school, level of job satisfaction, and a host of other characteristics of the people in the organization. See Figure 7.2.
3. *Social system* (organization) refers to the organizational and administrative structure of the organization. It includes how the school is organized, the ways in which decisions are made

MILIEU OF THE SCHOOL
HUMAN SOCIAL SYSTEM FACTORS

Skills	*Morale*
Motivation	*Size of the group*
Job satisfaction/rewards	*Race, ethnicity, and gender issues*
Status	*Socioeconomic level of students*
Feelings	*Education levels attained by teachers*
Values	*Leadership*

FIGURE 7.2 Some illustrative examples of the characteristics that give rise to the milieu of a school.

ORGANIZATION OF THE SCHOOL
ORGANIZATIONAL STRUCTURE FACTORS

Organization of:

Instruction	*Communication patterns*
Supervision	*Control mechanisms*
Administration	*Patterns of hierarchy/collegiality*
Support services	*Planning practices*
Pupil personnel services	*Formal structure*
Decision-making practices	*(e.g., departments, emphasis on rules)*

FIGURE 7.3   Some illustrative examples of the characteristics that give rise to the organization of a school.

and who is involved in making them, the communication patterns among people (who talks to whom about what), what work groups there are, and so on. See Figure 7.3.

4. *Culture* refers to the values, belief systems, norms, and ways of thinking that are characteristic of the people in the organization. It is "the way we do things around here." See Figure 7.4. This aspect of the organization's total environment is described more fully a little later.

As you can see in Figure 7.5, these four dimensions or subsystems are dynamically interrelated. In creating Figure 7.5, we have substituted the term *organization* for Tagiuri's original term *social system* because it seems more descriptive of what this dimension actually encompasses. Many of the organizational dimensions of climate arise from factors that administrators control directly or strongly influence. It is important that administrators understand the close connections between the choices they make about the way they organize and the climate manifested in the organization. To some, *social system* conveys a sense of a somewhat uncontrollable natural order of things, whereas *organization* makes the influence of the administrator's responsibility for establishing that order a little clearer.

However, contemporary thought does not view each of the four dimensions as being equally potent in producing the character and quality of the climate in a given organization. Recent research has concentrated attention on the primacy of the *culture* of the organization in defining the character and quality of the climate of an organization.

CULTURE OF THE SCHOOL
PSYCHOSOCIAL CHARACTERISTICS

Assumptions	*History*
Values	*Heroes/heroines*
Norms	*Myths*
Ways of thinking	*Rituals*
Belief systems	*Artifacts*
	Art
	Visible and audible behavior patterns

FIGURE 7.4   Some illustrative examples of the characteristics that give rise to the organizational culture of a school.

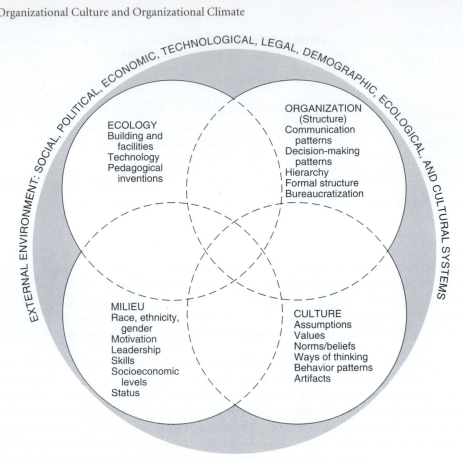

FIGURE 7.5 The four internal dimensions or subsystems of the organization—ecology, milieu, organization, and culture—are dynamically interactive within the organization, whereas the organization itself is dynamically interactive with its external environment.

THE IMPORTANCE OF ORGANIZATIONAL CULTURE

Research on organizational culture, which had stood for some time in the wings of organization studies, shifted to center stage in 1981–1982. It was a dramatic shift and was due to the publication of two books. The first of these, William Ouchi's *Theory Z*, appeared in 1981 and became the first book by a researcher of organizational behavior to enjoy a lengthy stay on the nonfiction bestseller lists (Ouchi, 1981). Published at a moment when U.S. corporate managers were groping for some solution to their difficulties in meeting Japanese competition, Ouchi—a Japanese American—compared and contrasted the management styles used in the two nations. He found that Japanese management practices tended to be quite different from those applied in the United States and that some of these Japanese practices (not all, due to societal differences) could profitably be adopted by U.S. corporations. Taking his cue from McGregor's Theory X and Theory Y, he named his approach Theory Z to suggest a new alternative. Theory Z accepts the main assumptions of human resources development (HRD):

> Of all its values, commitment of a Z culture to its people—its workers—is the most important…. Theory Z assumes that any worker's life is a whole, not a Jekyll-Hyde

personality, half machine from nine to five and half human in the hours preceding and following. Theory Z suggests that humanized working conditions not only increase productivity and profits to the company but also the self-esteem for employees…. Up to now American managers have assumed that technology makes for increased productivity. What Theory Z calls for instead is a redirection of attention to human relations in the corporate world. (Ouchi, 1981, p. 165)

In 1982, another research report appeared on the bestseller lists. Called *In Search of Excellence,* it described eight management characteristics that 62 successful U.S. corporations had in common (Peters & Waterman, 1982). Cutting across the eight characteristics was a consistent theme: The power of values and culture in these corporations, rather than procedures and control systems, provides the glue that holds them together, stimulates commitment to a common mission, and galvanizes the creativity and energy of their participants. These values are not usually transmitted formally or in writing. Instead, they permeate the organization in the form of stories, myths, legends, and metaphors—and these companies have people who attend to this awareness of organizational culture: "The excellent companies are unashamed collectors and tellers of stories, of legends and myths in support of their basic beliefs. Frito-Lay tells service stories. Johnson and Johnson tells quality stories. 3M tells innovation stories" (Peters & Waterman, 1982, p. 282).

Why did organizational culture stay in the wings in the United States so long? And why is it today a central concern in U.S. management? One answer to the first question is that the human underpinning of organization has long been considered to be soft. Technology is hard. Money is hard. Organizational structure, rules and regulations, policy decisions—these are hard, in the lexicon of many administrators and managers. The things that one can measure, quantify, and control are hard. In this view, the human side of organization is soft. Values, beliefs, culture, and behavioral norms have widely been believed to be less powerful in getting things done.

But it helps to clarify what culture is: a system of shared values and beliefs that interact with an organization's people, organizational structures, and control systems to produce behavioral norms. In practical terms, *shared values* means "what is important;" *beliefs* means "what we think is true;" and *behavioral norms* means "how we do things around here." With the obvious success of companies using these ideas, and with the ideas themselves clarified, the concept of organizational culture suddenly became of practical importance to managers and administrators. As Peters and Waterman (1982) put it, "Now, culture is the 'softest' stuff around. Who trusts its leading analysts—anthropologists and sociologists—after all? Businessmen surely don't. Yet culture is the hardest stuff around, as well" (p. 319).

It became clear to U.S. businesspeople that an organizational culture that stifles innovation and hard work may be the biggest stumbling block to adapting to uncertain times. The lesson was not lost on educational administrators: Confronted by shrinking finances, faltering public support, divided constituencies with conflicting interests, and rampant charges of organizational ineffectiveness, they became riveted by the implications of organizational culture for educational organizations.

ORGANIZATIONAL CULTURE AND ORGANIZATIONAL CLIMATE COMPARED AND CONTRASTED

The terms *culture* and *climate* are both abstractions that deal with the fact that the behavior of persons in organizations is not elicited by interaction with proximate events alone but is also influenced by interaction with intangible forces in the organization's environment. As we shall explain more fully, *culture* refers to the behavioral norms, assumptions, and beliefs of an organization, whereas *climate* refers to perceptions of persons in the organization that reflect those norms, assumptions, and beliefs.

Organizational Culture

Though many definitions of organizational culture are found in the literature, the high degree of agreement between and among them makes it relatively easy to understand what culture is and how it relates to and differs from organizational climate. *Organizational culture* is the body of solutions to external and internal problems that has worked consistently for a group and that is therefore taught to new members as the correct way to perceive, think about, and feel in relation to those problems (Schein, 1985).

Culture develops over a period of time and, in the process of developing, acquires significantly deeper meaning. Thus, "such solutions eventually come to be assumptions about the nature of reality, truth, time, space, human nature, human activity, and human relationships—then they come to be taken for granted and, finally, drop out of awareness" (Schein, 1985, p. 20). Therefore, "culture can be defined as the shared philosophies, ideologies, values, assumptions, beliefs, expectations, attitudes, and norms that knit a community together" (Kilmann, Saxton, & Serpa, 1985, p. 5). In this case, the community is an organization—a school, for example—and all of these interrelated qualities reveal agreement, implicit or explicit, among teachers, administrators, and other participants on how to approach decisions and problems: "the way things are done around here" (Kilmann et al., p. 5).

According to Terrence Deal (1985), "At the heart of most…definitions of culture is the concept of a learned pattern of unconscious (or semiconscious) thought, reflected and reinforced by behavior, that silently and powerfully shapes the experience of a people" (p. 301). This pattern of thought, which is organizational culture, "provides stability, fosters certainty, solidifies order and predictability, and creates meaning" (Deal, p. 301). It also gives rise to simpler, though highly compatible, commonsense definitions, such as the following: "[Organizational culture] is the rules of the game; the unseen meaning between the lines in the rulebook that insures unity" (Kilmann, 1985, p. 352). Or, as Wilkins and Patterson (1985) have phrased it, "Culture consists of the conclusions a group of people draws from its experience. An organization's culture consists largely of what people believe about what works and what does not" (p. 267).

Critical theorists agree with much of the above discussion of culture but expand on the definition to include a focus on power issues within the organization. For example, McLaren (2007) defined culture as

> the particular ways in which a social group lives out and makes sense of its "given" circumstances and conditions of life. In addition to defining culture as *a set of practices, ideologies, and values from which different groups draw to make sense of the world*, we need to recognize how cultural questions help us understand who has power and how it is reproduced and manifested in the social relations that link schooling to the wider social order. The ability of individuals to express their culture is related to the power which certain groups are able to wield in the social order. (p. 201)

In McLaren's definition, in society there is a *dominant culture* ("social practices and representations that *affirm the central values, interests, and concerns of the social class in control of the material and symbolic wealth of society*" [p. 201]), a *subordinate culture* ("groups who live out social relations in subordination to the dominant culture of the ruling class" [p. 201]), and *subcultures* within each of these that are "frequently organized around relations of class, gender, style, and race" (p. 202). Critical theorists believe that giving *voice* to the lived experiences of subcultures is key to promoting a culture of social justice and establishing *revolutionary multiculturalism* identified by discourse on racial, gender, and social equality, and that the results of this discourse lead to *critical pedagogy* to prepare students for life in society. In McLaren's view, "schooling is a form of *cultural politics*; schooling always represents an introduction to, preparation for, and legitimation of particular forms of social life" (p. 188). It is, therefore, a leader's responsibility to develop a school culture that promotes *revolutionary multiculturalism,* that is, giving voice to the subordinate culture and subcultures to empower them.

MULTIPLE CULTURES   Although a given organization will have an overall organizational culture, as McLaren noted, many organizations also have additional workplace cultures. In other words, in describing organizational culture, we must be aware that subunits of the organization have cultures of their own that possess distinctive attributes. As an example, consider the school district that has central administrative offices, a senior high school, a junior high school, and several elementary schools.

Whereas the school board and top-level administrators in such a district may understand that the district as an organization has a shared set of understandings, assumptions, and beliefs reflected in and reinforced by the behaviors of people—in short, an organizational culture—they should also understand that each school is characterized by its own culture. The culture of a given school is likely to reflect certain aspects of the principal characteristics of the school district's organizational culture and yet is different in some ways. The cultures of the various schools are also likely to differ. It is probable that the central office will exhibit an organizational culture of its own that is distinctive from that of any of the schools.

To carry the illustration further, consider the organizational culture of the senior high school in that district. The school itself has an organizational culture, as we have described, and it also has workplace cultures within it. For example, the counselors in the guidance and counseling department of the school may interpret their roles—and that of the department—as being supportive and helping in their relationship to students, encouraging students to grow and mature in the ability to make informed decisions regarding their lives and to take charge of their lives. In their work, such counselors tend to value developing high trust relationships with students in order to engender openness in dealing with problems. Across the hall, however, one might find the unit responsible for managing attendance and discipline. Quite possibly, the faculty in this unit could adopt—for whatever reasons—a shared understanding that toughness counts along with fairness, that it is the responsibility of the school to be sure that students obey, to mete out punishment when they fail to do so, and to leave no mistake as to who is in charge. One could go on, demonstrating that other departments in the school are likely to exhibit cultures of their own—in some ways distinctive and in other ways mirroring the culture of the school as a whole.

The fact that multiple cultures are likely to be found in school districts and schools is not surprising inasmuch as the subunits of the organization do many of the same culture-building things that the larger organization itself does. The subunits—such as schools and departments—regularly bring together people who share some constellation of interests, purposes, and values; they are the settings in which people seek social affiliation in face-to-face groups; they facilitate the sharing and cooperative effort required to get the work done. These functions of the subunits provide the impetus for developing multiple cultures in the organization, rather than a single organizational culture from top to bottom.

Indeed, it appears likely that Theory X administrators tend to think of organizational culture as being conceptualized at top levels in the organization and managed so that they are implemented down the line of authority. This approach to the development of organizational culture, which is in harmony with classical concepts of organization, is problematic because it is difficult to change the assumptions of people and compel their sharing of assumptions with others by issuing directives. On the other hand, Theory Y administrators are likely to more readily accept the concept of multiple cultures existing within the organization. The development of multiple cultures within the organization is facilitated by the use of participative methods associated with human resources development—similar to Ouchi's Theory Z approach.

No concept in the realm of organizational behavior relies more heavily on social systems concepts than does organizational culture. Clearly, however, the culture of an organization is seen as important to eliciting and shaping the behavior of participants, which gives rise to the notion of *person-environment interaction*, which will be discussed later.

TWO MAJOR THEMES IN A DEFINITION OF ORGANIZATIONAL CULTURE   Two themes consistently pervade the literature describing and defining organizational culture: One theme is *norms* and the other is *assumptions*. Norms and assumptions are widely regarded as key components of organizational culture.

Norms.   An important way in which organizational culture influences behavior is through the norms or standards that the social system institutionalizes and enforces. They are, of course, unwritten rules that nonetheless express the shared beliefs of most group members about what behavior is appropriate in order to be a member in good standing (Cohen, Fink, & Gadon, 1984).

Assumptions.   Underneath these behavioral norms lie the assumptions that comprise the bedrock on which norms and all other aspects of culture are built. These assumptions deal with what the people in the organization accept as true in the world and what is false, what is sensible and what is absurd, what is possible and what is impossible. We agree with Edgar Schein (1985): These are not values, which can be debated and discussed. Assumptions are tacit, unconsciously taken for granted, rarely considered or talked about, and accepted as true and nonnegotiable. The cultural norms in the organization—informal, unwritten, but highly explicit and powerful in influencing behavior—arise directly from the underlying assumptions. It is these underlying assumptions that critical theorists argue we must bring to the forefront and discuss. By having this discourse, we potentially expose assumptions that are not based on *voices* from all subcultures in the organization, and by exposing these voices we begin to include all subcultures into the underlying assumptions (McLaren, 2007).

Levels of Culture

Edgar Schein (1985) described organizational culture as being composed of three different but closely linked concepts. Thus, organizational culture may be described as follows:

1. It is a body of solutions to external and internal problems that has worked consistently for a group and that is therefore taught to new members as the correct way to perceive, think about, and feel in relation to those problems.
2. These eventually come to be assumptions about the nature of reality, truth, time, space, human nature, human activity, and human relationships.
3. Over time, these assumptions come to be taken for granted and finally drop out of awareness. Indeed, the power of culture lies in the fact that it operates as a set of unconscious, unexamined assumptions that is taken for granted.

Thus, culture develops over a period of time and, in the process of developing, acquires significantly deep meaning.

In Schein's model, the most obvious manifestations of organizational culture are visible and audible: the first level of culture includes artifacts such as tools, buildings, art, and technology, as well as patterns of human behavior, including speech. They are readily observable and have been frequently studied, usually using naturalistic field research methods such as observations, interviews, and document analysis—that is, qualitative research methods. Though these manifestations are readily observable, they are merely symbolic of the culture itself, which is not observable and which is not even in the awareness of the people we observe. Therefore, to make sense of the artifacts and the behaviors that we observe, we must decipher their meaning, and this decoding is difficult to do.

Below the publicly visible level of the manifestations of culture lies the second level of culture, the values of the organization, sometimes encoded in written language such as in a mission statement, a statement of philosophy, or a credo. Documents such as these move us closer to understanding the basic assumptions of the organization, but they, too, merely reflect the basic assumptions that are the essence of the culture.

At the third and lowest level, we find the essence of the culture: those assumptions that are taken for granted, invisible, and outside consciousness. They are such concepts as the relationships of individuals to the environment; the nature of reality, time, and space; human nature; the nature of human activity; and the nature of human relationships. These assumptions, of which the organization's members are unaware, form patterns, but they remain implicit, unconscious, and taken for granted unless they are called to the surface by some process of inquiry, such as that recommended by critical theorists.

How Organizational Culture Is Created

The organizational culture of the school arises over time and is shaped and defined by intersecting and overlapping symbolic elements. See Figure 7.6.

The traditions of the school and its rituals, developing as time passes, are told, retold, and embellished to newcomers and old-timers alike in the stories and myths that convey the history of this particular school. These embody the values and beliefs of the people in the school and exert great power in establishing and maintaining the behavior norms that characterize the place—often more powerfully than rules and regulations can. The heroes and heroines of the school are very important in conveying organizational culture because they embody these symbolic elements and are important in enacting them.

An important aspect of organizational culture, as it is for culture in general, is that it endures through the generations. Each school is different because its history is unique, and that history is constantly in development as the school moves toward its future. Anyone hoping to alter the culture of a school must seek to alter the course of the school's history, and the leverage points for that are in the symbolic elements that define and shape the organizational culture of the school.

SYMBOLISM AND CULTURE   Though organizational culture is usually studied through inferences derived from the observation of organizational behavior, the focus is not limited to the impact of the environment on the behavior of individual persons. It extends to understanding what the elements of such environments are, how they develop, and how these elements relate to one another to form (in effect) the lexicon, grammar, and syntax of organization. The study of symbolism is central to the study of organizational culture: the rituals, myths, traditions, rites,

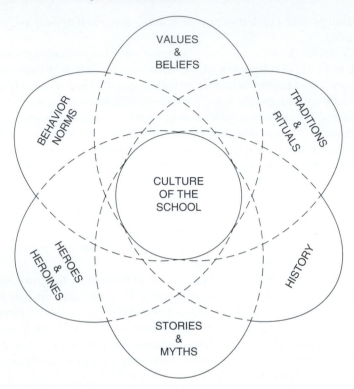

FIGURE 7.6   Overlapping symbolic elements describe the culture of a school.

and language through which human meanings and values are transmitted from one generation of the organization to the next.

A school climate may be characterized by certain perceptions held by participants about the nature of the organization ("what things are really like here"), but how are those perceptions developed, communicated, and transmitted? A school may be viewed by members as holding certain values, extolling particular virtues, standing for describable standards and practices that have a deep effect on the behaviors of the members. But how are these made explicit and communicated to the members? What are the mechanisms used by the organization to influence and control behavior in predictable, desired ways? In schools, as well as in societies, the answer is through institutionalized rituals and symbols. Understanding these is essential to understanding culture.

In many societies, for example, marriage rites constitute powerful symbols that evoke a great deal of behavior considered right and proper, if not inevitable, which might include deciding where the married couple lives, how the members of the family take on new roles (such as mother-in-law), and the division of labor between the sexes. Thus, the institution of marriage, symbolized by ceremonies and rituals handed down through the generations, communicates values to people that the society deems important. Much more than that, the communication results in behaviors that may seem ordinary and even mundane to the participants but that are powerful in developing their perceptions about what is right or wrong or even possible.

Similarly, to join the faculty of a typical U.S. high school brings with it many obligations and expectations. Some of these are inexorably demanded by the daily schedule of classes (the bell schedule), which signals powerfully to participants who should be where—and doing what—almost every minute of the day. To many educators, the schedule is such an inherent part of the culture of the school as to be taken for granted, accepted without question, an overriding symbol of what defines the school itself. The bell is a powerful cultural feature of the high school, and it has great impact on what participants do, see as possible, and value as important in the life of the school. The bell schedule is one of many powerful cultural symbols that help to create the organizational climate found in a high school in the United States.

AFFECTIVE ASPECTS   The culture of an organization exerts a powerful influence on the development of climate. Inasmuch as the culture of the organization (even though it is intangible) influences the way participants perceive events and make sense of those events, it is clear that culture has influence on the attitudes and feelings of participants. Rosabeth Moss Kanter (1983) captured much of the impact of organizational culture and climate in reporting her studies comparing highly successful and less-successful U.S. corporations. She described high-performing companies as having a *culture of pride* and a climate of success.

A "culture of pride" means that "there is emotional and value commitment between person and organization; people feel that they 'belong' to a meaningful entity and can realize cherished values by their contributions" (Kanter, 1983, p. 149). With this feeling of pride in belonging to a worthwhile organization having a record of achievement, of being a member rather than merely an employee, the confidence of the individual is bolstered: confidence that the organization will be supportive of creative new practices and will continue to perform well, and confidence also that the individual will be effective and successful in his or her own realm of work in the organization.

Kanter's research revealed that the culture of pride is widely found in organizations that are *integrative*, which means emphasizing the wholeness of the enterprise, actively considering the wider implications of things that they do, and thriving on diversity and stimulating challenges to traditional practices. These organizations tend to be successful to a large extent because their cultures foster a climate of success.

In contrast, Kanter described less-successful organizations as being *segmented*. In segmented organizations, members find it difficult even to discover what is going on beyond their own little sphere of operations, much less to deal with problems that affect the whole organization. People are kept isolated, stratified, away from the larger decisions in the organization, focused on the narrow piece of action in which they are directly involved. In these organizations, people find it difficult to take pride in the organization because they really know little about it and what it is doing. Thus, such organizations are characterized by climates of something other than success.

How Organizational Climate is Created

Figure 7.7 shows that the organizational climate of a school is produced by the dynamic interaction of four variables: ecology, milieu, organization, and culture. People who work in the school, as well as the students there, experience this interaction. Their perceptions of the organization are inevitably molded by that experience. Thus, they come to understand what the place stands for, what is valued and what is not, what is true even if unvoiced, and what is true or untrue of what *is* voiced. As we have said, although all of these subsystems have an impact on the formation of organizational climate, it is generally thought that they do not all have equal impact. However, these four variables—ecology, milieu, organization, and culture—are the levers for change available to the school leader who seeks to shift the organizational climate of a school. Given the dynamic ways in which these subsystems interact, changes in one will result in changes in the others.

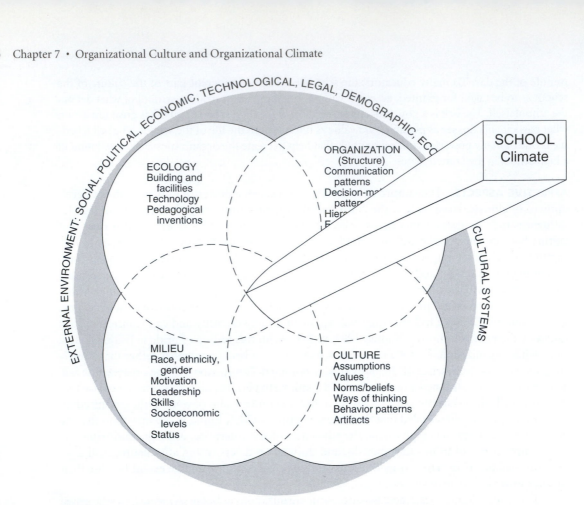

Organizational climate arises from overlapping and interaction of four key organizational factors.

FIGURE 7.7 The organizational climate of the school is the product of the interaction of the four internal dimensions, or subsystems: ecology, milieu, organization, and culture.

For many years, scholars as well as practitioners have tended to concentrate their efforts to change organizations by restructuring the organization, retraining the employees or hiring new people, building new buildings, or using new technology. The expectation usually is that changing one of these factors will result in commensurate changes in other of the organization's subsystems and thus involve the entire organization. However, by the beginning of the twenty-first century, organization theorists as well as practicing leaders were overwhelmingly in agreement that organizational culture is powerful in determining the course of change in an organization. More than a few believe that it is often the most powerful determinant.

GROUP NORMS An important way in which organizational culture influences behavior is through the norms or standards that the social system institutionalizes and enforces. These are encountered by the individual as group norms, which are "an idea that can be put in the form of a statement specifying what members...should do" (Homans, 1950, p. 123). They are, in other words, "rules of behavior which have been accepted as legitimate by members of a group" (Haire, 1962, p. 24). Groups typically exert pressures on an individual to conform to group norms that are more pervasive than the individual is likely to comprehend. These pressures are often felt as an obligation to behave in certain ways, which is often manifested in positive forms, such as support from the group for opinions and behavior that the group approves of and wishes to reinforce.

Especially if an individual highly values the esteem and acceptance of members of the group and, more especially, if the group is highly cohesive, the pressure to conform to group standards and expectations can even influence one's perceptions of reality. One tends to see things in terms of the expectations of the group. Thus, the interaction of the individual with groups reaches far deeper than merely observable behavior: It strongly influences the development of perceptions, values, and attitudes.

PERSON–ENVIRONMENT INTERACTION   Any discussion of organizational culture has its roots in the work of Kurt Lewin, who demonstrated that understanding human behavior requires us to consider the whole situation in which behavior occurs (Lewin, 1936). The term *whole situation* is defined as meaning both the person and the environment. Essentially, then, behavior is a function of the interaction of person and environment. Thus, as we know, B = f (p • e). Consequently, in conceptualizing organizational culture, it is necessary to think of the person and the organizational environment as complementary parts of one situation. They are inseparable.

The perspective of organizational culture helps us to understand that the environment with which people interact is constituted of more than the immediate circumstances in which they find themselves. A crucial aspect of understanding the culture of an organization is to understand the organization's history and its traditions because individuals in an organization are socialized to accept them. Thus, unseen but present in every human encounter with the organization is the understanding and acceptance by participants of values and expectations that are inherent in the tradition of the organization. Organizations normally expend considerable effort, both formally and informally, to transmit and reinforce these values and expectations through socialization processes.

In many U.S. high schools, it is difficult for teachers and administrators alike to conceptualize organizing their work in any other way than by using a bell schedule built on Carnegie units of instruction. Indeed, the tradition of using units as the building blocks of the U.S. high school's daily class schedule is so time honored and so taken for granted that few teachers today even know what a Carnegie unit of instruction is, even though it is one of the most dominant influences on their professional practice.

Carnegie units were invented in 1905 by the Carnegie Foundation for the Advancement of Teaching as a way of standardizing high school instruction so that colleges would have an easier time comparing the transcripts of applicants. It was, and is, a measure of time: 120 hours of classroom instruction. Thus, one unit of a subject requires the student to be present in the classroom for 120 hours. The implications for scheduling are apparent. For example, if one decides to build a schedule around class periods that are 48 minutes long, to allow passing time between classes, then a one-unit class should meet 150 times during the year. This structure lays the basis for the traditional bell schedule that not only wields such power over the behavior of teachers and students but also shapes their perceptions of what school is and ought to be, defines what is possible and not possible, and dictates what is right and what is wrong. This design is a strong tradition in secondary education in the United States. It is often associated with school quality and sound professional practice, and it has continually been reinforced by the teachers' own experience as students in high schools, by their university training, and by their experience as professionals. This system is an illustration of the forces that are always present in organizational culture as part of the unseen, intangible environment that shapes and molds the behavior of participants. The

Carnegie unit illustrates the stubborn persistence that cultural artifacts typically display, surviving to influence thinking and behavior in the organization long after they have outlived their intended purpose.

For many years, educators have doubted that time spent in class is the most useful indicator for gauging what kind and quality of learning a student was achieving. Yet it is reinforced in law and regulation, a venerable hallmark that many people associate with the "quality" of school's instructional program. The Carnegie unit has remained unchallenged for 88 years as one of the key national quality standards in secondary schooling. In 1993, the Pennsylvania State Board of Education, the first state to do so, voted to abolish the use of the Carnegie unit by the end of the century and to establish a set of required academic goals for students to achieve instead. The move—even though applauded by the Carnegie Foundation itself as desirable—has met fiercely entrenched opposition. Today, of course, many U.S. high schools are following block schedules intended to tailor instructional time to the pedagogical requirements of various subjects and also to facilitate changing the ways in which teachers and students work together in class. As used today, block scheduling generally provides more class time for discussion, group work, individual critiques, and other pedagogical techniques in addition to presentations by the teacher.

The term *tradition* used in this sense does not necessarily mean repeating old solutions to newly emerging problems. Some organizations try to create what might be called new cultural traditions in an effort to break the habits of the past and emphasize the value of originality and creativity in finding fresh solutions to problems encountered in the life of the organization. Contemporary examples are readily found in the relatively young entrepreneurial computer firms in the Silicon Valley and other locations that place high value on bold thinking and inventiveness. Apple Computer and Google are among many inventive firms frequently cited as illustrating organizations built on this concept.

Seymour Sarason (1971), whose book, *The Culture of the School and the Problem of Change,* spoke lucidly and persuasively of the necessity of finding ways of altering the patterns of activities, group norms, and the temporal qualities that are characteristic of U.S. public schools before we can hope to change the impact that they have on the people in them. This milieu, which Sarason called the "culture of the school," is not necessarily planned or deliberately created; it tends, instead, to be a phenomenon that is generated from (a) the activities of people in the school (for example, lecturing, listening, moving about according to schedule), (b) the physical objects in the environment (for example, walls, furniture, chalkboard, playground), and (c) the temporal regularities observed (for example, the length of classes, the pattern of the daily schedule, the pattern of the school calendar).

The influence of this interaction among activities, physical environment, and temporal regularities is seen not only as pervasive and relatively stable but also as having great power to mold the behavior of the people in the organization. Sarason (1972) has extended this insight to attempts to plan and create settings in new organizations that presumably would elicit the kinds of behaviors thought to be functional and productive in terms of the organization's mission.

THE INTERACTION–INFLUENCE SYSTEM A central concept in organizational behavior is that of the interaction-influence system of an organization. We should keep in mind that the basic function of organizational structure is to establish patterns of human interaction to get the tasks accomplished (who deals with whom, in what ways, and about what). Thus, departments, teams, schools, and divisions are typical formal structures, whereas friendship groups, people who work in close proximity to one another, and coffee-break groups are typical informal structures. The interactions between and among people thus put into contact with each other in conducting the day-to-day business of the organization establish the norms that are powerful in shaping organizational behavior.

The interaction-influence system of the organization deals simultaneously with structure and the processes of interaction. The two are mutually interdependent in such a dynamic way that they cannot be considered independently. In this sense, the interaction-influence patterns in shaping the organizational behavior of work groups are roughly analogous to the person and environment in eliciting and shaping the behavior of individuals.

The interaction processes in the interaction-influence system include communication, motivation, leadership, goal setting, decision making, coordination, control, and evaluation. The ways in which these interactions are effected in the organization (their characteristics and quality) exercise an important influence on eliciting and shaping human behavior. Efforts to describe the organizational culture of educative organizations are efforts therefore to describe the characteristics of the organization's interaction-influence system.

DESCRIBING AND ASSESSING ORGANIZATIONAL CULTURE IN SCHOOLS

The study of organizational culture presents nettlesome problems to the traditional researcher primarily because important elements of culture are subtle, unseen, and so familiar to persons inside the organization as to be considered self-evident and, in effect, invisible. Collecting, sorting, and summarizing data such as the significant historical events in the organization and their implications for present-day behavior, the impact of organizational heroes on contemporary thinking, and the influence of traditions and organizational myths is a task that does not lend itself to the tidiness of a printed questionnaire and statistical analysis of the responses to it. Over time, as many researchers working independently have demonstrated, it is necessary to get inside the organization: to talk at length with people; to find out what they think is important to talk about; to hear the language they use; and to discover the symbols that reveal their assumptions, their beliefs, and the values to which they subscribe. For that reason, students of organizational culture tend to use qualitative research methods rather than traditional questionnaire-type studies. This approach has raised vigorous debate in many schools of education as to the epistemological value of qualitative research methods as contrasted with the more traditional statistical studies (of the experimental or, more often, survey research types) that have long been the stock-in-trade of educational researchers.

Organizational climate, then, is the study of *perceptions* that individuals have of various aspects of the environment in the organization. For example, in their pioneer study of organizational climate in schools, Andrew Halpin and Don Croft (1963) examined the attributes of leadership and group behavior found to exist in elementary schools. To do this research, they asked teachers to describe their perceptions of certain human interactions in a sample of elementary schools that seemed to result from factors such as the principal's behavior in his or her official role in the hierarchy, the personality characteristics of individual teachers, the social needs of individual teachers as members of a work group, and group characteristics of the teachers in the school such as morale. A major outcome of the Halpin and Croft research was the demonstration that, by using the set of perceptions that the Halpin-Croft questionnaire probed, the organizational climate of schools may be systematically described.

The notion of satisfaction is usually closely associated with the concept of organizational climate. That is, to what extent are the participants' perceptions of the environment of the organization satisfying to them? This association of satisfaction with the perceptions of participants is implicit in some techniques for studying climate, whereas many studies have inquired directly into possible discrepancies between the participants' perceptions of the existing state of affairs and whatever desired state the respondents think ought to prevail.

Studies of organizational climate depend heavily on eliciting the perceptions of participants, which has led to the use of questionnaires in which respondents are asked directly about their perceptions. Although interviews are an effective means of gathering such information, interviewing is time consuming and therefore not as frequently used.

Earlier studies of organizational climate in schools tended to gather data from adults, almost always teachers, with occasional inquiries of principals. In more recent years, the trend in school climate studies has been in the direction of examining the perceptions of students rather than of adults in the school.

Relationship Between Organizational Culture and Organizational Effectiveness

Do various organizational cultures produce different outcomes, in terms of effectiveness, in achieving organizational goals? The issue is far from simple. Measuring organizational effectiveness is, in itself, a complex undertaking, and the traditional need felt by many people in management to control and direct subordinates in the *command* sense of the term tends to tinge discussion of the issue with emotion.

To a large extent, accepted conventions of research and rules of evidence, discussed previously, form the heart of this controversy. It has long been accepted in the logic of science that cause-and-effect relationships are best established by rationalistic research designs such as the controlled experiment. Experimental research, of course, requires one to control the relevant variables under study. A substantial body of carefully controlled experimental research conducted in laboratory settings strongly undergirds the psychological concepts on which students of organizations draw in conceptualizing organizational behavior. However, studies of actual organizations in the real world often must be conducted under conditions where such control is not possible. One of the few large-scale experimental studies on class size research was discussed earlier in this book (Finn & Achilles, 1999); however, most studies of organizational culture and climate rely on causal-comparative and correlational research.

CAUSE AND EFFECT Rensis Likert (1961) sought to link organizational performance to the internal characteristics of the organization. His analysis is that the performance of an organization is determined by a three-link chain of causes and effects.

The first link in the chain is composed of the *causal variables,* which are under the control of the administration. Thus, administration (management) can choose the design of the organization's structure (mechanistic or organic, bureaucratic or flexible). Similarly, administration can choose the leadership style (for example, authoritarian or participative); it can choose a philosophy of operation (for example, teamwork or directive, problem solving or rule following). The choices that administration makes in selecting the options available are critical to and powerful in determining the nature of the management system in the organization (namely, Systems 1, 2, 3, or 4). These choices are seen as causing the interaction-influence system of the organization—in other words, its culture—to have the characteristics that it does have.

Intervening variables flow directly from these causal variables (that is, the choices that administration makes). Thus, the nature of motivation, communication, and other critical aspects of organizational functioning is determined.

End-result variables, the measures of an organization's success, depend heavily, of course, on the nature and quality of the internal functioning of the organization.

This analysis fits nicely with research reports of qualitative research in U.S. public schools—such as Theodore Sizer's *Horace's Compromise* (1984), Ernest Boyer's *High School* (1983), and John Goodlad's *A Place Called School* (1983)—and their counterparts from the corporate world—such as *In Search of Excellence, Theory Z, Corporate Cultures,* and *The Change Masters.* As Rosabeth Moss Kanter (1983) pointed out in the last book, and as we discussed earlier, innovative companies are marked by a culture of pride and a climate of success in which the organizational norms support success-oriented effort—and that depends on the values that the leaders enact in the daily life of the organization.

A now-classic research study lends support for a close relationship between the culture of the school and outcomes. A study of 12 inner-city London schools (Rutter, Maughan, Mortimore, Ouston, & Smith, 1979) posed the following research questions:

1. Do a child's experiences at school have any effect?
2. Does it matter which school a child attends?
3. If so, which are the features of the school that matter?

To measure school outcomes, the researchers used the following dependent variables: (a) student behavior, (b) student attendance, and (c) regularly scheduled public school examinations. The study showed, first, that there was a marked difference in the behavior, attendance, and achievement of the students in various secondary schools. Second, these differences among schools were not accounted for by the socioeconomic or ethnic differences of their students: Clearly, students were likely to behave better and achieve more in some schools than in others. Third, these differences in student behavior were associated with the achievement performance (outcomes) of the school as a whole. These differences in student behavior and performance

> were *not* due to such physical factors as the size of the school, the age of the buildings or the space available; nor were they due to broad differences in administrative status or organization [for example, structure]. It was entirely possible for schools to obtain good outcomes in spite of initially rather unpromising and unprepossessing school premises, and within the context of somewhat differing administrative arrangements...the differences between schools in outcome *were systematically related to their characteristics as social institutions.* (Rutter et al., p. 178)

These latter characteristics (that is, the independent variables) were (a) the behavior of teachers at work, (b) the emphasis placed on academic performance, (c) the provision for students to be rewarded for succeeding, and (d) the extent to which students were able to take responsibility. All these factors, the researchers pointed out, were open to modification by the staff rather than fixed by external constraints. In short, this research strongly suggests that organizational culture (which they call ethos) is a critical factor in student behavior and achievement. Much as Likert did, they pointed out that organizational culture is largely in the control of the people who manage the organization.

Joyce Epstein (1984) reported studies in schools that describe the perceptions of students' satisfaction with school in general, their commitment to school work, and their attitudes toward teachers. Taken together, these are thought by Epstein to describe the quality of school life as the students perceive it. This perception is described as being related, of course, to the behaviors of the students as participants in the organization. To conduct such studies, Epstein developed and validated a 27-item questionnaire designed to be used across school levels (that is, elementary, middle, and high school).

Rudolf Moos (1979) reported large-scale research in the United States, in both secondary school and college settings, that supported the mounting evidence in the literature that the learning and development of students are significantly influenced by characteristics of organizational culture. After studying about 10,000 secondary school students in more than 500 classrooms, he was able to identify characteristics of classroom organizational culture that facilitate academic achievement, on the one hand, and those that induce stress, alienate students, and thereby inhibit learning, on the other. From classroom to classroom, he measured the variances in contextual influences such as (a) stress on competition, (b) emphasis on rules, (c) supportive behavior by the teacher, and (d) extent of innovative activities. They were the independent variables. Moos then correlated these measures with measures of *dependent* variables such as (a) student rate of absence, (b) grades earned, (c) student satisfaction with learning, and (d) student satisfaction with the teacher.

In college settings, Moos studied 225 residence groups (for example, coed and single-sex residence halls, fraternities and sororities), involving about 10,000 students. Using questionnaires, he measured distinctive characteristics of these various groups such as (a) emphasis on intellectuality, (b) social activities, and (c) group unity. He then sought to assess the effects of these variables on dependent variables such as (a) students' concepts of themselves, (b) personal interests and values, (c) aspirations, and (d) achievement.

Essentially, Moos found that students' learning and development are strongly influenced by the nature and qualities of the person-environment interaction in educational settings such as secondary school classrooms and college residence arrangements. An interesting aspect of his research was his attempt to demonstrate how organizational culture and human behavior are influenced not only by the interaction-influence system of the group but also by other factors in the environment such as room design, schedule of activities, and layout of the building. In his view, our knowledge of the causes and effects of organizational culture enables us to create and manage specified learning environments by controlling critical variables (such as competition, intellectuality, and formal structure). This control, in turn, improves our ability to place students in the settings best suited to their needs—settings in which they will feel most comfortable and be most successful. Moos contended that this is highly practical knowledge that can be used to develop administrative policies and pedagogical practices that are effective in dealing with student apathy, alienation, absenteeism, and dropouts.

More recently, there is a substantial body of work supporting a connection between school climate and organizational effectiveness with findings supporting the implementation of *effective school characteristics* introduced in the previous chapter. Here, we report a few of the key studies that have findings representative of most similar studies. In 1999, the U.S. Department of Education sponsored an analysis of over 300 effective school studies to determine if there were any similarities in finding. This study by Vishner, Emanuel, and Teitelbaum (1999) found the following to be school climate predictors of effective high schools: (a) high expectations by staff of student performance, (b) staff development focused on what is important, (c) caring learning environments, (d) parent involvement, and (e) connecting student interest to careers. In another study, Marzano (2003) found the following school-level factors to be associated with effective schools: (a) guaranteed and viable curriculum, (b) challenging goals and effective feedback, (c) safe and orderly environment, (d) parent and community involvement, and (e) collegiality and professionalism. Dependent variables in both studies included both high levels of satisfaction of participants in the school and higher scores on various state and national tests.

In 2013, a large-scale study of middle and high schools in California also supported the above findings. Voight, Austin, and Hanson (2013) compared similar schools in terms of demographics, such as the number of students receiving free and reduced lunch (which is a measure of poverty) and the number of English language learners (ELL students). Schools that did better than expected, which they called "Beating the Odds" Schools (BTO), were measured on standardized tests of math and English language arts and compared to similar schools. The BTO schools had the following school climate characteristics that distinguished them from similar schools not performing as well:

1. High expectation of student performance (student perceptions of staff expectations of their performance)
2. Caring relationships (student perceptions of whether staff cared about them)
3. Meaningful participation (degree to which school provides opportunities for students to participate in activities and decision making)
4. Perceived school safety (degree to which students feel safe)
5. School connectedness (degree to which students feel connected to and respected in the school)

These are all school climate characteristics under the control of the school staff and administration, and all of them can be provided for little to no additional cost. To show how a school can be administered and organized to provide these effective school climate characteristics, we present a "Voices From the Field" example and then we return to a concept introduced in Chapter 1, Rensis Likert's four management systems.

VOICES FROM THE FIELD

Changing the Culture, Making the Grade: Going From an F to Almost a B

Kevin Gordon, former Principal, Gibbs High School, St. Petersburg, Florida

An alumnus of Gibbs High School, I was honored to be asked to take over as principal. However, after several years of leadership changes, disorder, and chaos, Gibbs High School plummeted to a school grade of an F. Never before in the history of Gibbs High or Pinellas County Schools had a high school received such a low grade.

I already had a vision for how I would go about changing the culture and transforming the school. It would have to happen in short order though, as neither the state nor the superintendent were going to give me much time, and early indications were that the local newspaper would chronicle everything that happened.

I could not do the job alone, so I requested who I thought were some of the most talented school-based administrators in the school district to be a part of the administrative team that would assist me in leading the school turnaround and changing the culture. They were both male and female and hailed from local middle and high schools. I was also able to hire a brand new administrator.

Our administrative team met with faculty and staff during the summer to solicit their input and perceptions of the most pressing issues for the administration to address. Unanimously, they agreed the most important issue to address was student discipline. A draft of a new *Master Discipline Plan* was developed based on a review of the previous year's discipline data, with an eye on putting some fortitude behind the hot button offenses and looking for ways to reduce the number of suspensions and referrals. The faculty and staff reviewed, suggested improvements, and ultimately approved the final document.

Administrators visited the homes of students who had 20 or more referrals the year before. The purpose of the visits was to build relationships with parents, inform students that we had new administration, as well as new expectations. We also did a series of automated call-outs to inform students about changes in the Master Discipline Plan that would impact them immediately. We wanted students to have a clear understanding that the new focus at Gibbs High School was on education, that disruptive behavior would not be tolerated, and that violations of the Master Discipline Plan would be strictly enforced: "Welcome to the new, stricter Gibbs High School!"

Aside from discipline, there were tremendous academic issues that needed to be addressed. Out of the nearly 2,000 students, 1,200 of them scored the lowest two levels out of five on the state achievement test. To tackle such a herculean task, I challenged the entire school and student body to improve the achievement test score by 200 points in one year. It was coined the 200-point Challenge. This was the amount of points the school needed to move from an F to a C.

To champion this challenge the staff was trained by Spence Rogers, a training expert in instructional methods and strategies. He did a week-long inservice training and several follow-ups during the year addressing methods, materials, and academic strategies to help us meet the goal we had set. A 200-point Challenge logo was created to place on shirts and door placards. They were used to promote the challenge.

In addition to the 200-point Challenge, a mantra was created that symbolized that success would only occur if the school was totally committed as one body, carrying the same message, sharing the same vision, and on the same mission. We used the phrase from the movie *Drumline*: "One Band, One Sound!" This meant that we, as a group of educational professionals, were on the same page and in complete unison with the mission and vision that was established to accomplish the 200-point Challenge.

Now that the discipline plan was developed and the mission and vision of the school were clearly communicated, it was time to put them into action. As the first day of school approached, posters of the *Master Discipline Plan* were put up in every classroom and grade-level student orientations were organized. The administration had planned on flooding the hallways armed with whistles and loud voices to ensure that students got to class on time. Students would be challenged to memorize the new mission statement and mantra.

The first day was characterized by whistles blowing, loud voices, students scurrying quickly to class—welcome to the new Gibbs High School! The administration and staff worked all summer to prepare for opening day: moving classrooms, hiring teachers, strategically prepping the facility for improved security and management of student flow, visiting challenging students and their parents at home as well as calling on the community to do its part. The time had come for the rubber to meet the road.

After the morning bell, emails began to fly:

"It's amazing how quickly the halls are clearing."
"Know that your hard work is appreciated."
"Mission Accomplished!... Quite the impressive show today whistles and all."
"The kids can feel the change in the air.... I saw it and felt it today"
"One Band, One Sound! Mr. Gordon, thank you for your vision and leadership."
"Things really seem much more under control than they were last year."

In the days and weeks to follow, student orientations were held to ensure that all students understood the new expectations. We also made certain that students, teachers, and staff knew that the changes were all about helping students become successful. All teachers were asked to spend the first 10 days of school focused on building relationships with students, and a specialized team-building curriculum was provided to all teachers who wanted it. The school mission statement was changed and students were challenged to know it. During the orientations each student would recite: "The mission of Gibbs high school is to provide students with the opportunity to get a good education and a high school diploma." The mission was simple, to the point, and easily understood.

It only took a week to have complete order throughout the school. The assistant principals and I walked the halls every period to ensure that students stayed in their classes. Classrooms were visited to determine the nature and level of instruction that was being carried out in the classrooms. We quickly discovered that although students were getting to class on time, the level and frequency of quality instruction needed improvement.

With the help of the Florida Department of Education, we developed a year-long plan focused specifically on lesson plan development. The gradual release template was used as the base for all lesson plans, and teachers were expected to have their lesson plans posted in a prominent place for the administrators to find them as administrators walked through classrooms. Nearly every Wednesday and all professional development days were devoted to training. There were even some Saturdays that staff came in for training, and as often as we could we compensated them for their extra time and effort.

The entire year was spent studying processes and procedure in order to improve them. There were a number of initiatives and special events we undertook to help transform the school. They included a full-day summit that involved students, staff, and the community in discussion groups and idea exchanges. In addition, a week-long freshman transition program called Summer Stomp was developed. It became the model for other high schools in the district. Our first summer attracted more than 225 incoming freshman. Other areas that were developed were a positive behavior support system that rewarded students for good behavior. Students earned G-bucks that they could redeem at the school store for various types of school paraphernalia. This program really helped to build school spirit.

We received tremendous support from the state, the office of the superintendent, and the community. The school turnaround was truly a team effort: teachers giving their all, students doing their best, and the district and state supplying the resources to get the job done. We also had huge support from St. Petersburg College, which provided additional teacher training, college placement testing, and dual enrollment classes.

As a result of these efforts, the school grade improved from an F to a C, missing a B by only six points the first year. Our graduation rate also improved, jumping more than nine percentage points from 72.4% to 81.8%. These improvements were a great accomplishment for the school, its students, staff, and the community. Earning a C was a testament to the fact that hard work really does pay off. No longer would the school have to live under the scarlet letter F. A couple of days after the announcement of the school grade, a big celebration occurred at the football field. There was plenty to be happy about.

FOUR MANAGEMENT SYSTEMS

Having studied organizational climates extensively, Rensis Likert (1961) identified four management systems. We first described Likert's four systems in Chapter 1, and we return to them here as each of the styles is describable in terms of organizational climate and leadership behavior.

- System 1 is called *exploitive-authoritative* (or punitive-authoritarian) and is based on classical management concepts, a Theory X view of motivation, and a directive leadership style.
- System 2 is *benevolent-authoritative* (or paternalistic-authoritarian). It emphasizes a one-to-one relationship between subordinate and leader in an environment in which the subordinate is relatively isolated from others in work-related matters.
- System 3, called *consultative*, employs more of a participative leadership style in which the leader tends to consult with people *individually* in the process of making decisions.
- System 4, the *participative* (or group interactive) model of an organizational system, uses Theory Y concepts of human functioning and emphasizes team interaction in all of the critical organizational processes.

The organization is conceptualized as a roughly pyramidal structure whose basic unit is the face-to-face work group: people who regularly interact (communicate, influence, motivate) at work, together with their supervisor (see Figure 7.8). Examples are department chairpersons and

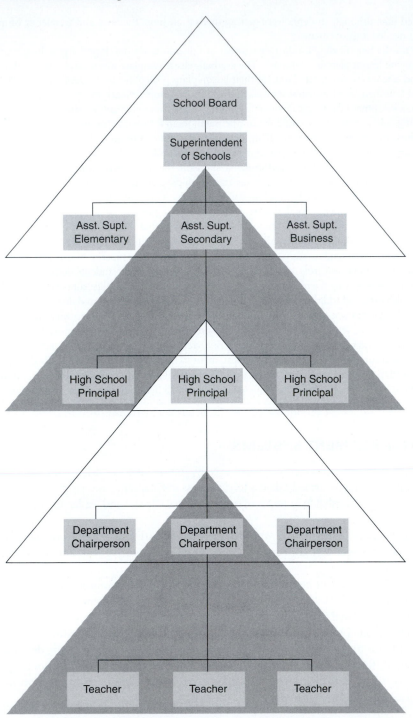

FIGURE 7.8 The linking-pin concept as applied to the decision-making structure of a medium-sized school district.

teachers in the departments, head librarians plus librarians and library aides, grade chairpersons and classroom teachers, and so on. Such groups are (a) small enough to permit the development of an effective group process that facilitates individual participation and (b) close enough to the task to be performed to make effective, creative decisions. To keep such groups coordinated requires effective communication between and among them: The primary work groups must be effectively linked together. Likert pointed out that it is especially essential that groups be linked *upward* in the organization so that the groups lower in the organizational pyramid have the capability of interacting with and influencing higher levels of the organization.

Essentially, then, every supervisor or every administrator is a member of two face-to-face work groups: the group for which he or she is responsible and the group to which he or she is responsible. The total organization is composed of a planned system of such work groups that overlap and are linked together by individuals who have roles in both of the overlapping groups. These individuals serve as "linking pins" between the groups—a role that requires them to facilitate communication, decision making, and other influence processes between levels of the organization and also across the organization.

Such a structure is not totally new in U.S. schooling, of course. The traditional high school principal's cabinet or leadership team, for instance, generally includes chairpersons who link the departments to the cabinet. In turn, the principal is usually a member of a district-wide group comprising other principals, central office people, and the superintendent. The superintendent, in turn, links the superintendent's cabinet to the school board. However, Likert (1961) suggested that, first, such an organizational system can be extended and elaborated to include all facets of the school district organization; and second—and more important—Likert described how such an arrangement can facilitate the development of a more functional interaction-influence system: one that is not characterized by the traditional, directive, downward-oriented concepts of line-and-staff organization but instead is characterized by free communication and influence, up, down, and across the organization, featuring a teamwork approach to problems at all levels.

In sum, "the effectiveness of the interaction–influence system of an organization and the capacity of this system to deal with difficult problems depend on the effectiveness of the work groups of which the structure consists and on the extent to which multiple linkage is provided" (Likert, 1961, p. 181). Considering, therefore, the dynamic interdependence between structure (for example, linked, overlapping groups) and the influence system (for example, directive or collaborative) brings us to the issue of participation in making decisions. One seeking to develop a collaborative interaction-influence system must attend to developing a leadership or administrative style that will develop the skills and motivation of others that support such an approach. In other words, one would seek to move from System 1 to System 4, which conforms to the major approaches to motivation that were discussed in Chapters 5 and 6.

Final Thoughts

The concept of organizational culture has emerged as central not only in the analysis of organizational behavior and organizational effectiveness but also in the day-in and day-out leadership of schools. Organizational culture is the body of solutions to problems that has worked consistently for a group and is therefore taught to new members as the correct way to perceive, think about, and feel in relation to those problems. Over time, organizational culture takes on meaning so deep that it defines the assumptions, values, beliefs, norms, and even the perceptions of participants in the organization. Though culture tends to drop from the conscious thoughts of participants over time, it continues to create powerful meaning for them in their work and becomes "the rules of the game."

Studies of schools have strongly supported the belief that organizational culture is a fundamental factor in determining the quality of educational organizations. Culture cannot be studied directly but is inferred from observed behavior such as language, use of artifacts, rituals, and symbolism commonly encountered in the workplace.

Organizational climate, which is the study of the *perceptions* of participants of certain intangible aspects of the environment, reflects the culture. Studies of organizational climate ordinarily use questionnaires to elicit perceptions from participants. The trend in the study of organizational climate in schools has been away from the study of the perceptions of only adults toward including study of those of students, too.

As the study of organizational culture moved to a central position in organizational behavior in education, it was accompanied by increasing use of qualitative research methods such as participant observation and open-ended unstructured interviews to replace traditional statistical survey-research methods. The use of qualitative research methods makes it possible to produce richly detailed ("thick") descriptions of the organizational culture of schools, which are necessary in order to explain what is happening in them. Qualitative research methods, such as observational research in the school, are based on very clear concepts of the nature of inquiry that are quite different from rationalistic concepts, and they observe rules of procedure and rigor that are equally clear and clearly different from those of conventional quantitative methods.

Much of the research on organizational culture, in both corporate and educational organizations, is related to the effectiveness of the organizations. Many studies describe relationships between performance of the company (in terms such as market share, sales, and profitability) and the organizational culture within the company. Comparable support exists for a similar thesis in education. Since the advent of No Child Left Behind (NCLB), of course, achievement test results have emerged as the only politically acceptable measure of the performance of the school.

A substantial and growing body of empirical evidence, derived from rigorous research in schools and other educative organizations, indicates that the effectiveness of these organizations, in terms of student learning and development, is significantly influenced by the quality and characteristics of the organizational culture. Not surprisingly, the research clearly suggests schools that emphasize supportiveness, open communication, collaboration, and intellectuality, and that reward achievement and success, outperform (in terms of achievement, attendance, dropout rate, frustration, and alienation) those that emphasize competition, constraint and restrictiveness, rules and standard operating procedures, and conformity. By delineating the critical factors involved, the concepts arising from this body of research make it possible and practical to plan and manage organizational culture purposefully. It would be difficult to overemphasize the implications arising from this research for administrative practice in an era marked by declining confidence in schools and school systems and by increasing demands for accountability for performance.

Reflective Activities

1. Using the figures and the discussion in this chapter on school climate, analyze how your organization's interaction-influence system establishes the organizational behavior that affects the climate. In other words, how do people go about their everyday business of interactions that is connected to and influenced by the elements that comprise climate?

2. How would you characterize the system in your organization using Likert's four management systems? That is, which system is most like your organization? How does this management system affect school climate? Give one or two specific examples that support your choices.

3. *Working on Your Game Plan.* This chapter described the overlapping symbolic elements that shape and define the organizational culture of a school. Among them are the myths and stories that people tell about the school, the heroes and heroines who are often recalled, the history and traditions of the school, and the rituals that are

ordinary events in the school. Consider a school that you know well and choose three of the following symbolic elements:

A. Heroes/heroines

B. Stories

C. Myths

D. Rituals

E. Traditions

F. History

G. Values

H. Beliefs

In a paragraph on each of the three elements you have chosen, describe how they are ordinarily manifested in that school. After writing your three descriptive paragraphs, compare notes with others who have done this exercise by reading what you and they have written and discussing the different observations that have been made about the organizational culture of schools.

4. Begin this exercise by reading the following report: Oakland Community Schools Organizations, *Building a District-Wide Small Schools Movement* (Annenberg Institute for School Reform at Brown University, April 2009). It can be downloaded from the Internet. At this writing, the website address was annenberginstitute.org/pdf/Mott_Oakland_high.pdf

This report tells the story of a partnership between the Oakland, California, School District and a community-based agency called Oakland Community Organizations and how the partnership created 10 small schools in a section of the city. It describes how the task was achieved in a city with a population of 43,000 and how the process and its results were systematically studied.

This latter part alone, which describes research methods used in a large and complex organizational change intervention, will be of great interest to our readers. We draw your attention also to page 13 of the report, which lists a series of other case studies of community-organizing initiatives in Austin, Chicago, Los Angeles, Philadelphia, New York City, and Miami. While these do not directly focus on changing schools, they tell a lot about how community organizing is done.

A. Do you think that the size of a school alone has an impact on school culture and climate?
1. If you do, please explain why you think so.
2. How big is too big? What makes you think so?

B. Is community organizing the only way to create small schools? What alternatives do we have?

C. What are some disadvantages to creating small schools to replace big ones?

D. Should high schools and elementary schools have the same size limits? Why?

CRITICAL INCIDENT   Two Schools—Two Different Cultures

Kennedy Elementary School

The principal at Kennedy Elementary, Linda Shoenfeld, is a very organized person. She believes that success in fulfilling her job responsibilities depends on making sure the day-to-day operations of the school and staff function well. Standards are very clear, and tasks are carefully divided among the leadership, office staff, teachers, and nonprofessional staff. Linda is famous for her motto that adorns her office wall: "A school cannot be successful unless it is well managed."

Linda also believes that principals must make logical decisions. She likes order and predictability, and she believes that change should be slow and orderly. She has stated that people need to be able to depend on the principal to analyze problems correctly, use data effectively, and make the correct choice. She talks to other principals, goes to professional meetings, and reads the professional journals for principals, so she is knowledgeable about how to manage schools effectively. She uses her knowledge to make decisions such as the school bell schedule, teacher schedules, budget allocations, and new programs. When teachers are affected by decisions, she relies on her skills to convince them that her decisions are in the best interest of the children.

Linda treats everyone with a degree of respect, and for the most part the staff like her as a person. They believe that she is responsible for making the school what it is today, and although they would like more input into decisions, they appreciate having a stable leader they can depend on to be consistent and fair.

Johnson Elementary School

Principal Margarita Lopez is known for her willingness to try new ideas and experiment to see if they work. She doesn't focus on management aspects of the school, such as book orders and other business chores, which she leaves to others to do. Margarita's leadership philosophy is that she is there to assist others in getting their jobs done. She believes that anyone can be a leader and that his or her ideas are to be respected. This belief often leads to conflict among teachers and with her, but she thinks some conflict and disagreement among professionals is good for an organization. She realizes that some view her leadership style as leading to chaotic situations, but she believes that the organization learns from chaos and that without it the school would stagnate. She sees her job as bringing order to the chaos by making sense of it for everyone, by connecting ideas to theory and research, and by encouraging continual change and improvement.

The staff members view Margarita as a good leader. They appreciate that she allows them a voice in the decisions that are made in the school. They see the school in a constant state of flux that moves the school forward. On the other hand, they also would like some occasional relief from the constant changes that are going on around them.

1. What are the positive and negative attributes of each principal?
2. How are these schools different organizations within which to work? What type of climate and culture would you say characterize each?
3. With which principal would you rather work? Why?

Suggested Reading

Branden, N. (1998). *Self-esteem at work: How confident people make powerful companies.* San Francisco, CA: Jossey-Bass.

One would be hard pressed to name a personal characteristic that is more essential to being effective as a leader than a healthy sense of self-esteem. Your self-esteem has profound effects on your thinking processes, emotions, desires, values, goals, and ways of interpreting events. Self-respect and self-confidence are important aspects of self-esteem, and they are closely tied to your ability to learn, make appropriate decisions, and respond effectively to change. Indeed, Branden believes that self-esteem is the single most illuminating key to your behavior. This book helps readers understand the concept of self-esteem and offers useful advice on how to develop it. This development is important for anyone who wants to be an educational leader, who wants to take responsibility for schools in today's era of great change, and who seeks to develop organizational cultures to make them better.

Combs, A. W., & Avila, D. L. (1985). *Helping relationships: Basic concepts for the helping professions* (3rd ed.). Boston, MA: Allyn & Bacon.

Usually, educational leaders think of themselves as administrators: officers, more or less, in the hierarchical line of authority in the organization. However, if you accept the idea that a powerful way of strengthening schools is to develop their organizational cultures so that they will encourage and support creativity, change, and psychosocial growth, you are taking on the role of a helping professional. Changes in organizational culture cannot be brought about by command; they must be developed from within—from within people individually and from within the social group collectively. Combs and Avila offer valuable understanding about the role of facilitating as a helper, and they give solid advice that you will rarely find in courses on educational administration.

Deal, T. E., & Peterson, K. D. (1990). *The principal's role in shaping school culture.* Washington, DC: U.S. Department of Education, Office of Educational Research and Improvement.

Although some academics still debate whether one can or should deliberately change the culture of schools, the pragmatic practitioner, in view of the mounting evidence of the importance of culture in evoking organizational behavior, tends to conclude that the issue is not whether one can or should, but how to do it. This little publication addresses the process in simple terms and provides the reader with a 10-point program on "how to build an effective culture."

Fullan, M., & Hargreaves, A. (1996). *What's worth fighting for in your school?* New York, NY: Teachers College Press.

This book encourages principals and teachers to think more deeply about school reform, especially about school cultures that have long encouraged teachers to work individually in near isolation in the classroom. The authors make a strong yet quiet case for developing school cultures that facilitate greater collaboration, with teachers working together for improving the work of the school, and explore how principals can support and abet the process.

Levine, S. L. (1989). *Promoting adult growth in schools: The promise of professional development.* Boston, MA: Allyn & Bacon.

This book starts with an examination of the professional lives of teachers and finds what many have found before: that teaching is isolating and inhibiting of personal growth and development. For these reasons, it is unsatisfying and rewarding, and this fact is inevitably reflected in the effectiveness of the schools. Levine goes on, however, to discuss what can be done by school principals and others to change this situation to develop schools as growth-enhancing environments for the adults who work in them. Contains a great deal of useful, practical advice.

McLaren, P. (2007). *Life in schools* (5th ed.). Boston, MA: Pearson.

Life in Schools presents Peter McLaren's philosophy of *critical pedagogy*, which prepares children for life in a society in which there are dominant and subordinate cultures. He discusses class, gender, race, and social issues and their impact on schooling. This book is an excellent example of the implementation of critical theory and critical race theory in schools.

Rubin, H. (1998). *Collaboration skills for educators and non-profit leaders.* Chicago, IL: Lyceum Books.

In working for organizational renewal from the inside out—that is, working with organizational culture and climate—much is said about the need for increased collaboration, teambuilding, and reaching out to engage people in the community. But where do leaders learn the specific skills and techniques for doing this kind of facilitative work? Rubin points out that there is no degree

program in collaborative leadership. The answer, at the moment, is to learn these methods on the job. And this book can help. It is a practical and insightful guidebook by someone who knows and understands schools and nonprofit organizations.

Tieger, P. D., Barron-Tieger, B., & Swick, M. A. (1999). *The art of speedreading people: How to size people up and speak their language.* New York, NY: Little, Brown.

There is little question that the ability to understand others and to address them in their "native" language is a great asset to a leader. This book approaches that problem from the psychological concept of personality typing: Are you an extrovert or an introvert? Sensory or intuitive? Thinking or feeling? Judging or perceiving? The authors help you to understand yourself a little better using these dimensions and then show you how to apply this skill to understanding and interpreting others with whom you communicate. It is a powerful tool for those leaders who choose to work with and through other people in collaborative, collegial, mutually respectful ways.

References

Anderson, C. S. (1982, Fall). The search for school climate: A review of the research. *Review of Educational Research, 52,* 368–420.

Barnard, C. I. (1938). *Functions of the executive.* Boston, MA: Harvard University Press.

Boyer, E. L. (1983). *High school: A report on secondary education in America.* New York, NY: Harper & Row.

Cohen, A. R., Fink, S. L., & Gadon, H. (1984). *Effective behavior in organizations* (3rd ed.). Homewood, IL: Richard D. Irwin.

Deal, T. E. (1985). Cultural change: Opportunity, silent killer, or metamorphosis? In R. H. Kilmann, M. J. Saxton, & R. Serpa (Eds.), *Gaining control of the corporate culture* (pp. 292– 331). San Francisco, CA: Jossey-Bass.

Epstein, J. L. (Ed.). (1984). *The quality of school life.* Lexington, MA: D. C. Heath.

Finn, J., & Achilles, C. M. (1999). Tennessee's class size study: Findings, implications, misconceptions. *Educational Evaluation and Policy Analysis, 21,* 97–109.

Fullan, M. (2001). *Leading in a culture of change.* San Francisco, CA: Jossey-Bass.

Goodlad, J. I. (1983). *A place called school: Prospects for the future.* St. Louis, MO: McGraw-Hill.

Haire, A. P. (1962). *Handbook of small group research.* New York, NY: Free Press.

Halpin, A. W., & Croft, D. B. (1963). *The organizational climate of schools.* Chicago, IL: Midwest Administration Center, University of Chicago.

Heifetz, R. A. (1994). *Leadership without easy answers.* Cambridge, MA: Belknap Press of Harvard University Press.

Homans, G. C. (1950). *The human group.* New York, NY: Harcourt, Brace & World.

Kanter, R. M. (1983). *The change masters: Innovation and entrepreneurship in the American corporation.* New York, NY: Simon & Schuster.

Kilmann, R. H. (1985). Five steps for closing culture-gaps. In R. H. Kilmann, M. J. Saxton, & R. Serpa (Eds.), *Gaining control of the corporate culture* (pp. 351–369). San Francisco, CA: Jossey-Bass.

Kilmann, R. H., Saxton, M. J., & Serpa, R. (1985). Five key issues in understanding and changing culture. In R. H. Kilmann, M. J. Saxton, & R. Serpa (Eds.), *Gaining control of the corporate culture* (pp. 1–16). San Francisco, CA: Jossey-Bass.

Lewin, K. (1936). *Principles of topological psychology.* New York, NY: McGraw-Hill.

Likert, R. (1961). *New patterns of management.* New York, NY: McGraw-Hill.

Marzano, R. J. (2003). *What works in schools: Translating research into action.* Alexandria, VA: Association for Supervision and Curriculum Development.

Marzano, R. J., Waters, T., & McNulty, B. A. (2005). *School leadership that works: From research to results.* Alexandria, VA: Association for Supervision and Curriculum Development; Aurora, CO; Mid-continent Research for Education and Learning.

McLaren, P. (2007). *Life in schools* (5th ed.). Boston, MA: Pearson.

Miskel, C., & Ogawa, R. (1988). Work motivation, job satisfaction, and climate. In N. J. Boyan (Ed.), *Handbook of research on educational administration* (pp. 279–304). New York, NY: Longman.

Moos, R. H. (1979). *Evaluating educational environments.* Palo Alto, CA: Consulting Psychologists Press.

Ouchi, W. (1981). *Theory Z: How American business can meet the Japanese challenge.* Reading, MA: Addison-Wesley.

Peters, T. J., & Waterman, R. H., Jr. (1982). *In search of excellence: Lessons from America's best-run companies.* New York, NY: Harper & Row.

Rutter, M., Maughan, B., Mortimore, P., & Ouston, J. (with Smith, A.). (1979). *Fifteen thousand hours: Secondary schools and their effects on children.* Cambridge, MA: Harvard University Press.

Sarason, S. B. (1971). *The culture of the school and the problem of change.* Boston, MA: Allyn & Bacon.

Sarason, S. B. (1972). *The creation of settings and future societies.* San Francisco, CA: Jossey-Bass.

Schein, E. H. (1985). How culture forms, develops, and changes. In R. H. Kilmann, M. J. Saxton, R. Serpa (Eds.). *Gaining control of the corporate culture* (pp. 17–43) San Francisco, CA: Jossey-Bass.

Selznick, P. (1949). *TVA and the grass roots.* Berkeley, CA: University of California Press.

Sizer, T. R. (1984). *Horace's compromise: The dilemma of the American high school.* Boston, MA: Houghton Mifflin.

Tagiuri, R. (1968). The concept of organizational climate. In R. Tagiuri & G. H. Litwin (Eds.), *Organizational climate: Exploration of a concept.* Boston, MA: Harvard University, Division of Research, Graduate School of Business Administration.

Vishner, M. G., Emanuel, D., & Teitelbaum, P. (1999). *Key high school reform strategies: An overview of research findings.* Washington, DC: U.S. Department of Education.

Voight, A., Austin, G., & Hanson, T. (2013). *A climate for academic success: How school climate distinguishes schools that are beating the achievement odds.* San Francisco, CA: WestEd.

Wilkins, A. L., & Patterson, K. J. (1985). You can't get there from here: What will make culture projects fail. In R. H. Kilmann, M. J. Saxton, & R. Serpa (Eds.), *Gaining control of the corporate culture* (pp. 262–291). San Francisco, CA: Jossey-Bass.

CHAPTER 8

Organizational Change

All that we know about schools as organizations and the behavior of people in them is brought into play when we confront the need to plan and manage reform in them. In fact, the fundamental issue in planning and managing change in a school is the need to bring about the important innovation in the organizational culture of the school, in which the leader finds powerful leverage points for triggering planned and managed organizational change.

Critics of U.S. schooling have a propensity to depict schools as static bureaucracies, stodgy, lumbering about, and unable to adapt to emerging demands for high performance. Although there is some justification for this view, of course, schools are also the product of a long history of change. Transmitted from generation to generation as part of the cultural heritage of the school, this history has been powerful in developing some of the basic assumptions about change that are now well enmeshed in the culture of schools. The patterns of these basic cultural assumptions in the organization—which are normally unchallenged and rarely discussed—have great power to form the beliefs and values of people who work in them and are therefore central in thinking about ways to change things. We are talking about a central element of the foundation of the culture of the school that shapes and molds the abilities of people in the school to conceptualize bold, fresh, creative ways that significantly break with the past and hold out the promise of transforming the school into a high-performance organization. As a point of departure, we turn now to a very brief review of some of the major themes that have shaped the tradition of change in the recent history of schooling.

HISTORICAL CONTEXT FOR CHANGE

Because the Constitution makes no mention of education, each state, at its founding, assumed responsibility for providing public school education in its state constitution. As the nation developed and expanded westward in the nineteenth century, public school education was developed almost entirely as a matter of concern of the various states, and the federal government generally remained uninvolved. Each state created local school districts, which designated local school boards or committees in them to administer and control the state's constitutionally mandated responsibilities for schooling. This arrangement was remarkably suitable for the generations in which the nation was largely agrarian, communities were small, distances between them were great, and the technologically simple systems for transportation and communication were important limiting constraints. Local school districts levied and collected taxes (either directly or indirectly) on property (such as land, buildings, and livestock) within their districts to fund their operations and functioned under the relatively limited and largely benign supervision that the states had chosen as their role. However, powerful winds of social and economic change were freshening by the mid-nineteenth century and would ultimately sweep up the schools: the westward expansion of the nation; the development of science, technology, and industry; a swelling tide of immigration; and a trend toward urbanization. These and other major social-political changes of the time sparked new interest in redefining education's role in the scheme of things. In retrospect, we can see that, as early as 1857, a tectonic shift began in U.S. public schooling, and ever since it has been picking up power for change that continues even now.

In 1857, shortly before the Civil War, congressional representative Justin Smith Morrill of Vermont introduced a bill into the House of Representatives (called the Morrill Act) that would provide 30,000 acres of land for each member of Congress that the state had according to the 1860 census. The land could be used or sold and the proceeds put into endowments to establish educational institutions, called land-grant colleges, to teach not only classical studies but agriculture and mechanical education (hence the formation of colleges that used A&M in their titles, such as Florida A&M University), the sciences, and military tactics. The uniqueness of the land-grant colleges lay in two key concepts underlying them: One concept was to combine the study of traditional academic subjects with the study of more practical subjects such as the sciences and technologies that were emerging at the time, and the other was that these colleges would be owned and operated as public enterprises of the state at taxpayer expense. This bold innovative move was not well received by then-existing institutions of higher education in the United States, which were private preserves dedicated to meeting the needs of students from affluent families who were seeking education in the European tradition to enhance their positions of social privilege. By contrast, the newer land-grant institutions would meet the needs of working-class people who wanted to combine more practical technical studies with studies in the traditional liberal arts. At the outset, the Morrill Act, as it became known, did not have an easy time of it politically: The first time that the bill was passed by both houses of Congress, it was vetoed by a conservative president, James Buchanan, in 1861. It would not be until a second try in 1862, when the Southern members of Congress were absent during the Civil War, that it was passed again by Congress and signed into law by President Abraham Lincoln. This was a landmark intervention by the federal government that not only led directly to the transformation of higher education in the United States but also heralded a new expansion of federal involvement in education that would eventually lead to the inclusion of elementary and secondary education as we see it today. After passage of the first Morrill Act, the states had acquired a powerful partner in education that was not going to go away.

Behind this event, however, an overarching theme hovers almost unseen in the background, a theme that has been at the core of educational debate in the United States since at least the early eighteenth century and that continues today. The immediate questions that we might ask are these: Why did Justin Morrill, the Congress, and Abraham Lincoln all agree in thinking that it was necessary for the government to establish the land-grant colleges? What important public interest was to be served by them? The answers to these questions are too complex for a full discussion here, but one central issue is clear: Concern persisted about the purposes of education. For example, who benefits from education? Is education a private good that benefits only those who have the money and leisure to afford it? Or is it a public good that benefits not only those who receive it but also the body politic? If the latter, what kind of education does the public interest require?

These were the kinds of questions that Benjamin Franklin had raised and for which he proffered answers, as far back as 1749, when he proposed the establishment of an academy in Philadelphia. Franklin's brainchild, the academy, was a bold, new idea: He thought that the academy should focus on teaching the English language, including speaking, spelling, composition, and grammar; and subjects such as arithmetic, mathematics, astronomy, and accounting; history, including English translations of classical Greek and Roman texts; handwriting; the decorative arts; and more. He thought that classrooms in the academy should be equipped with maps and globes; mathematical instruments; apparatus for science and physics experiments; and collections of pictures of machines, celestial mechanics, specimens, architecture, art, and so on. Such an approach to schooling was radically different from the traditional classical schooling at that time, which had been the hallmark of the prestigious Boston Latin School founded in 1635. That school, along with other Latin schools that followed it, emphasized study of the classics and humanities in their original ancient Greek and Latin texts and considered the English language as inferior and unworthy of study. For over a century, such schools in the United States had produced a stream of students who could fluently read and translate the ancient texts and who could discuss their contents in their original languages. Boston Latin School, and others like it, had been established expressly to offer this kind of classical curriculum in order to prepare boys to study for the ministry and the learned professions, and many at the time thought that it did so very well.

A hundred years later, however, things were different, and schools were pressed to meet the challenge of new needs. Franklin's new idea for schooling was announced at the height of the Age of Enlightenment, and it embodied all the new ideas of that great middle-class movement. Franklin was then one of the world's leading Enlightenment scholars, and he saw a need for schools to educate boys who would be prepared to take their places in the practical affairs of business, industry, and commerce that were then burgeoning not only in prosperous Philadelphia but also throughout the Western world. The new need, he saw, was not for more church ministers but for people who had the skills to work in the counting houses; to design, build, and navigate ships that would roam the world; to develop industrial processes and techniques; to fill the emerging needs of government service; and to continue in advanced studies in the arts and sciences. Others saw this need, too, and the academy movement in American schooling flourished and spread as people throughout the growing nation embraced its educational concepts.

Historical Impact on Today's Change Efforts

The history of these themes and these questions illustrates the process of growth and development in education and schooling that have unfolded unceasingly since that time, throughout the centuries and right up until our own time. Educational goals continue to change and develop as social, cultural, and economic realities develop. It is no different in our time and will continue to be so into the future. We are speaking here of change in the organization that has certain basic characteristics, namely, change that

- is *planned and directed* toward the achievement of specific new, higher organizational outcomes. This is in sharp contrast with the unplanned organizational drift that traditionally passes for change in many organizations and that normally occurs over time in any organization. Planned and directed change, on the other hand, seeks to transform an ordinary organization, or even a low-performing one, into a high-performing organization.
- *involves the whole organization*—an entire school or school district—rather than merely pieces of the organization.
- *increases the capacity of the organization* to confront more effectively the continuing need for change now and in the future, leaving the organization stronger, healthier, more resilient, and more adaptable than it was before. This makes planned and directed organizational change very different from the ever-present temptation for a quick fix.

- is *sustainable over time* and thus has a permanence that differentiates it from the constant ebb and flow of fads and fashions that historically has been so characteristic of schools.

In the United States, the terms *school reform, comprehensive school reform,* and *whole school reform* are used interchangeably and embody the four concepts just described. A core defining concept shared by all of these terms is that the reform is intended to change, or re-form, the entire school organization or the entire school system in important ways. This concept arises from systems thinking, which recognizes the dynamic interactive nature of the interrelated parts of the whole organization: We cannot significantly change one part of the school without having an impact on other parts of the interdependent whole. Small-scale changes that have little or no effect on the rest of the organization are viewed as being little more than tinkering.

School reform, which involves *increasing the capacity* of the entire organization to be highly effective in achieving high-performance goals, stands in direct contrast with the long historical tradition in U.S. schooling of repeated, small-scale, piecemeal changes that generally resulted in little significant improvement of the overall learning outcomes of all students. Whereas schools have demonstrated remarkable ability to remain essentially stable and seemingly unchanged, despite a history of numerous small-scale changes over the years, contemporary school reform seeks to lift the organizational performance of schools as a whole. In the larger field of organizational studies, which includes business and industrial organizations as well as nonprofit organizations, such change is generally called simply organizational change. Both terms—*school reform* and *organizational change*—are believed by many to have a moral implication, such as the need to correct existing errors or abolishing malpractice, which requires transforming the organization.

With the advent of the No Child Left Behind (NCLB) Act, with its promises of draconian punishment of schools that fail to demonstrate adequate yearly progress (AYP) in student achievement, it is safe to say that schools in the United States have never before been so focused on the need for *planned*, *controlled*, and *directed* organizational change. This, of course, underscores the need for understanding the processes of organizational change in order for leaders to create effective strategies by which to plan, direct, and control them to achieve the outcomes desired. Clearly, this new era calls for leaders to approach organizational change in ways that are very different from the past.

Educational organizations are expected not only to be vehicles for social change, they are also expected to preserve and transmit traditional values to younger members of society. At the same time, they are expected to prepare them to deal with an ever-changing world, including the rapidly transforming world of work. Thus, schools and other educational organizations must confront not merely change, but also the integration of stability *and* change. And many observers, impatient to bring about change in schools, have pointed out again and again that the more things change in schools, the more they remain the same. As Matthew Miles reminded us:

> Many aspects of schools as organizations, and the value orientations of their inhabitants, are founded on history and constitute … genotypical properties. These are important to the schools; they help maintain continuity and balance in the face of the school's ambiguous mission and its vulnerability to external pressures from parents and others. Therefore, it is likely that, while rapid shifts in specific school practices are relatively more possible, changes touching on the central core of assumptions and structures will be far more difficult to achieve. (Miles, 1967, p. 20)

This is a useful concept for leaders to use in strategic planning for changing schools. It is drawn from biology, which describes how the genetic constitution of the individual produces persistent identifying characteristics, while interaction of the genotype with the environment results in distinctive visible adaptive properties. The notion is that schools as organizations are characterized by a genotypical core of traditions, values, and beliefs that identify them as schools and that differentiate them from other kinds of organizations. It is almost, as the description suggests, as though schools have a genetic predisposition to maintain their identity and core characteristics over time. Yet schools do interact with and are shaped by their ever-changing environments, resulting in the emergence of visible phenotypical properties, which helps explain why exasperated would-be school reformers often feel that the more things change, the more they stay the same.

SCHOOL REFORM AND CHANGE

Clearly, the school reform movement that was kicked off with publication of *A Nation at Risk* in 1983 (National Commission on Excellence in Education, 1983) has been the greatest, most sustained, and most concerted national effort to change the central core of assumptions and structures of the public schools in the history of the Republic. Since its inception, "the country has been searching for some magical way to reform and restructure public schools. We have tried—and are still trying—all sorts of alchemical nostrums we hope will turn our educationally leaden schools into schools of educational gold" (Clinchy, 1993, p. 28). Over the years, the discourses on school reform have been well leavened with bold calls for sweeping changes, such as restructuring education, reinventing schools, turning schools around, and re-creating our educational goals. Yet with so little actual change in U.S. schooling, Seymour Sarason (1990) pondered the seeming intractability of the schools in the face of years of reform effort and predicted the failure of educational reform unless the strategies of change were themselves changed.

The essence of Sarason's analysis was that schools seemed to be intractable only because the strategies selected to carry out reform efforts had largely been ineffective in significantly altering the central core of assumptions and structures—that is to say, the organizational culture—of schools. He explained that the nucleus of that core of organizational behavior is power, particularly the power of assumptions about power: especially whether power is assumed to be authority conferred or denied by one's position in the hierarchy or is assumed to arise from mutual collaboration among people of all levels and at every position in the organization. Thus, Sarason came to understand that *if we want to bring about significant change in the schools, we must come to terms with the power of culture to shape the assumptions and beliefs of people in the school, the power that motivates, the power used in attempts to lead, the power to participate in making important decisions, the power that gives rise to organizational behavior in schools.*

What is there about the strategies and tactics of the reform movement that have generally failed to make much progress in achieving reform? Sarason suggested the problem is that school reform generally avoids dealing with power relationships in the school, which he sees as central to bringing about educational change.

Power Relationships and School Restructuring

School reform literally means to give new form to the school, that is, to change the school in fundamental ways (Sarason, 1990). This concept is popularly called *restructuring*. But the question is as follows: How can schools be restructured? *The key lies in changing power relationships in the school.* How do we bring about such change? Because the public schools are ultimately controlled by the body politic acting through representative political agencies—such as school boards, state legislatures, and the U.S. Congress—political strategies to bring about change in schools can be very powerful. Ordinarily, political change strategies try to change power relationships in the schools by mandate. This is plainly exemplified by the NCLB Act, which mandated a broad array of goals, tests, and changes in the schools along with prescribed rewards and punishments to enforce the mandates that Congress and the Bush administration believed would bring about fundamental change in the functioning of the K–12 schools in the United States and, consequently, would improve their instructional effectiveness. The Obama administration has continued the push for mandates as evidenced in Race to the Top (RTTT), expanding toward mandates of the Common Core Standards, assessments on those standards, and use of assessments in teacher and school evaluation. Clearly, then, those who wield legal hierarchical power can force change on schools by altering the power relationships in them by fiat.

Other outside pressures to reform education has come from business, conservative political organizations, and powerful foundations, such as the Gates Foundation, the Walton Foundation, the Broad Foundation, and the Koch Family Foundations. Ravitch (2010) refers to the latter group of foundations as the "Billionaire-Boys' Club." By using money and social pressures these groups are pushing market-oriented reforms, online education, teacher education reform, and high stakes accountability in the form of teacher and school evaluation systems. With the help of the American Legislative Exchange Council (ALEC), model legislation for these types of state-level reforms is being spread throughout the United States (Ravitch, 2010, 2013). ALEC will be discussed in more detail later in this book.

On the other hand, schools—like other organizations—can be changed from within. Sarason (1990), for example, spoke approvingly about ways of altering power relationships by involving everyone in the organization in the process of change. Sarason pointed out that such a strategy makes two major contributions to our thinking about organizational change in educational organizations. Such a change strategy must

- *conceptualize the organization as a whole*, not as a collection of unrelated parts. This concept would apply to the school district as a whole: The strategy must embrace the idea that the school district is a *system* comprised of interrelated parts such as the elementary schools, the middle schools, and the high schools. And a key to this concept is the systemic relationship of the organization's parts.
- be an explicit educational rationale that seeks to promote the personal and vocational development of everyone. "I use the word *educational*," Sarason explained, "because it aims to expand people's knowledge of and commitment to their [own] individual. . . [personal] growth" (p. 72).

In short, Sarason pointed out that two distinctly different strategy alternatives are possible for changing educational organizations, and few students of organization would disagree:

- A strategy for changing the educational organization from the outside in and from the top down
- A strategy seeking to bring about change from the inside out and from the bottom up

Our choices are the following:

- Change the inner core of cultural assumptions and structures of the school.
- Change the formal, structural aspects of the organization.

The question becomes as follows: Which of the two approaches is more effective?

Aims of Educational Reform

For example, what kinds of changes does educational reform seek to bring about in the schools? What inner assumptions do we seek to change? From his analysis of the rhetoric commonly found in the literature on school change, Sarason (1990) listed five aims that most agree would constitute major changes in the inner core of assumptions that are so difficult to bring about:

- To reduce the wide gulf between the educational accomplishments of children of different social classes and racial backgrounds
- To get students to experience schooling as a process to which they are personally attracted and find motivating, and distinctly not a compulsory obligation they see as confining and boring or even irrelevant to them
- To enable students to acquire knowledge and skills that are not merely rote learning or memorized abstractions, but rather are acquired in ways that interrelate the learning and give personal purpose, now and in the future, to each student
- To engender interest in and curiosity about human accomplishments, past and present. To get students to want to know how the present contains the past—that is, to want to know this as a way of enlarging their own identities: personal, social, and as citizens
- To acquaint students with the domain of career options and how schooling relates to these options in the fast-changing world of work

If these encompass at least a substantial part of the aims of educational reform, why is there so little agreement in the U.S. school reform movement about the strategies and tactics for achieving them? Why is it that, as we described in earlier chapters, there are two major approaches to school reform currently competing with each other? Once again, the answer lies in the different ways in which people conceptualize the problem. It depends, to no small extent, on one's theory of action. We deal with the school reform movements themselves in more detail in Chapter 12 of this book. But in preparation for that, let us now identify and briefly discuss the array of major strategies and tactics of organizational change that are available to organizations generally—schools, corporations, military, or any other kind of organization.

THE TRADITION OF CHANGE IN AMERICAN EDUCATION

Historically, change in schools in the United States was viewed largely as a process of natural diffusion. That is, new ideas and practices arose in some fashion and spread in some unplanned way from school to school and from district to district. The result was that schools generally changed very slowly. In the late 1950s, Paul Mort and Donald Ross observed that it then took about 50 years for a newly invented educational practice to be generally diffused and accepted in schools throughout the country and that the average school lagged some 25 years behind the best practice of the time (Mort & Ross, 1957). Obviously, this is not the best way for new ideas to be disseminated and adopted.

Natural Diffusion Processes

Mort (as cited in Ross, 1958) described this unplanned process of diffusion in U.S. schools as follows:

> Educational change proceeds very slowly . . .
> After an invention which is destined to spread throughout the schools appears, fifteen years typically elapse before it is found in three percent of the school systems . . .

> After practices reach the 3 percent point of diffusion their rate of spread accelerates. An additional twenty years usually suffices for an almost complete diffusion in an area the size of an average state. There are indications that the rate of spread throughout the nation is not much slower. (p. 32)

This point is well illustrated by the introduction and spread of kindergartens. In 1873—nearly 20 years after the introduction of private kindergartens to the United States from Germany—the city of St. Louis established the first public school kindergartens. By the mid-1950s, kindergarten education had been firmly established in the profession as a desirable educational practice, and indeed federally funded projects such as Head Start provided strong stimuli for spurring its development. However, even as late as the 1998-99 school year (125 years after the introduction of kindergartens in St. Louis), only 61% of the nation's schools provided kindergarten education for their children (Institute of Education Sciences, 2013).

For many years, Mort was considered the leading student of educational change in the United States. The main finding of his work was that the primary factor in determining how much lag a school system exhibits in adopting innovative practices was the level, or adequacy, of financial support. Vigorously active in his many years as a teacher and researcher at Teachers College, Columbia University, Mort left a storehouse of knowledge and a large number of devoted students who heavily influenced the thinking of school administrators with regard to the factors that enhance change and innovation in schools. Largely because of this influence, per pupil expenditure has long been considered the most reliable predictor of a school's pattern of adopting educational innovations. For many years, this was known as the cost-quality relationship, and it powerfully affected decisions by state legislatures in matters of state financial aid in support of public schools.

The systematic underpinnings of the cost-quality relationship in education were established in a study of Pennsylvania schools in the 1940s (Mort & Cornell, 1941). Numerous studies dealing with the relationship between expenditure and measures of school output followed, which generally supported the not-too-surprising belief that high expenditure is generally associated with various indicators of superior school output. A troublesome fact was noted rather early in this research, however: It is possible for school districts to have high per student costs and still have inferior schools (Grace & Moe, 1938). Considerable research has been undertaken since 1938 to explore this fact. Most people tended to think that this relationship between cost and quality was linear: That is, more money would tend to ensure higher educational quality, and there was no point of diminishing returns. Since 1965, however, increasing attention has been paid to the possibility that cost-quality relationships in education are actually curvilinear and have an optimum point beyond which additional expenditure fails to yield increased school output (Swanson, 1967). Where additional expenditures have lead to higher student outcomes, the expenditures have been targeted to specific objectives, particularly for disadvantaged children (Grissmer, 2002). In a review of the literature on education productivity studies, Plecki and Catañeda (2009) wrote:

> The upshot of these lines of thinking and research to date are that we know less about the productive impact of policy makers' investments in education than we might wish. To be sure, some analyses highlight certain variables that appear to bear some relationships to student learning. Other studies establish no clear or discernible relationships. The lack of connections and the mixed nature of results across studies may be due to the weaknesses in underlying theory or specification of measures. (pp. 456–457)

They conclude: "Through the use of improved data and more finely tuned methods, . . . a greater focus is now on understanding the ways in which money makes a difference, rather than simply debating the importance of resources" (p. 460). It is beyond the scope of this text to delve into this research, but the areas of primary interest are in teacher quality, class size, early intervention, improving high school, decentralizing authority, and providing incentives to improve performance (Plecki & Catañeda, 2009).

Planned, Managed Diffusion

The *strategy* by which money is spent may have a greater impact on change in schools than conventional indices such as per student expenditure may indicate. One of the more spectacular and better-known attempts to alter significantly the pattern of change in the public schools in the post-*Sputnik* era was undertaken by the Physical Science Study Committee (PSSC) under the leadership of Professor J. R. Zacharias of the Massachusetts Institute of Technology (March, 1963). Briefly, the PSSC group wanted to improve the teaching of physical science in U.S. high schools. Retraining thousands of teachers, developing new curricula for all sizes of school districts, and persuading the local school boards to buy the needed materials and equipment might have taken half a century to accomplish using traditional methods. Instead, within 10 years after the project was inaugurated, high schools were considered to be behind the times if they did not offer a PSSC course.

This incredibly swift mass adoption was achieved by a strategy that involved three phases: (a) inventing the new curriculum, (b) diffusing knowledge of the new curriculum widely and rapidly among high school science teachers, and (c) getting the new curriculum adopted in local schools. This strategy involved the use of a number of new ideas. In addition to bypassing local school districts wherever possible, the PSSC group invested its money in novel and powerful ways. First, by spending $4.5 million in 2 and a half years to hire a full-time professional team, a portable, self-contained curriculum package was developed and tested in practice. This package included filmed lessons, textbooks, teachers' guides, tests, and laboratory guides and apparatus— a completely unified, integrated unit that could be moved *in toto* into almost any high school. Second, physics teachers were introduced to the new techniques by attending institutes, for which they received financial grants and stipends. Some 40 institutes were made available each year throughout the country for this purpose. Third, by providing funds to be matched by the federal government (largely through the National Defense Education Act), the PSSC group persuaded local school boards to buy the package for their schools. The PSSC intervention long served as a model of an outside-in, top-down change strategy led by the federal government.

THREE STRATEGIES OF PLANNED CHANGE

Three major strategic orientations identified in the classic book on change by Bennis, Benne, and Chin (1985) are useful in planning and managing organizational change:

1. Empirical-rational strategies
2. Power-coercive strategies
3. Normative-reeducative strategies

Empirical–Rational Strategies of Change

The traditional processes of unplanned dissemination of new ideas to schools have given way to strategies of planned, managed dissemination intended to spread new ideas and practices swiftly.

Much research and study have been devoted to these strategies, which focus primarily on more closely linking the findings of research to the practices of education. This link requires improving communication between researchers and practitioners (the consumers of research) so that the traditional, scornful distance between them will be replaced by a more productive, collaborative relationship.

This approach sees the scientific production of new knowledge and its use in daily activities as the key to planned change in education. It is referred to broadly as knowledge production and utilization (KPU). Numerous models for implementing the strategy have been proposed and tried over the years; all of these attempt to develop an orderly process with a clear sequence of related steps leading from the original invention or discovery of new knowledge to its ultimate application in practice. The aim is to bridge the gap between theory and practice to shorten the time it takes to change practice in the schools.

RESEARCH, DEVELOPMENT, AND DIFFUSION (R, D, AND D)   Various models for implementing KPU concepts of change appear under different appellations, depending on the number of steps that are seen as important. An R and D model, for example, suggests that someone ought to be conducting research and that someone else ought to be developing some useful products from that research. As in all KPU models, *research* is meant here to be the invention or discovery of new knowledge, regardless of its applicability to immediate problems. In R and D work, the quality and validity of the research are of paramount importance. The model recognizes, however, that the research scientist is not always the person best equipped to translate research findings into useful products.

The *development* phase of R and D includes factors such as solving design problems, considering feasibility in real-world conditions, and cost. Development essentially means translating research into products that are practical for use; these can range from school buildings to student seating, from textbooks to comprehensive packaged curricula, or from instructional techniques to new types of football helmets. In free enterprise societies, this stage has largely been the province of profit-seeking firms that have the necessary financial resources and entrepreneurial skills.

The *diffusion* phase of R, D, and D is seen as a third and distinctive phase; it is, essentially, the marketing activities of R, D, and D. The aim is to make the new products readily available in an attractive, easy-to-use form at a reasonable cost to the adopter.

Of course, the ultimate goal is to get the new ideas into use. Therefore, some treat *adoption* as a separate aspect of the process and may even call it research, development, dissemination, and adoption (RDDA) to emphasize this point. As David Clark and Egon Guba (1967) made clear, the processes of adoption are not simple. They described a three-stage process: (a) *a trial,* during which the new product is tested in some limited way; (b) *installation,* a process of refinement and adaptation to local conditions if the trial appears promising; and finally—if all goes well—(c) *institutionalization,* which means that the innovation becomes an integral part of the system. A test of institutionalization is whether or not the invention continues in use if external support and encouragement are withdrawn (see Figure 8.1).

THE AGRICULTURAL MODEL   It would be difficult to overemphasize the impact that the U.S. experience with planned, controlled change in agriculture has had on the thinking of those who advocate KPU strategies for education. Rural sociologists discovered early the processes and links that facilitated the rapid spread of new and better farming practices through the social system. The development of a network of land-grant universities, agricultural experiment stations, and the ubiquitous county agent are a few of the readily visible key parts of the extensive system that helps farmers

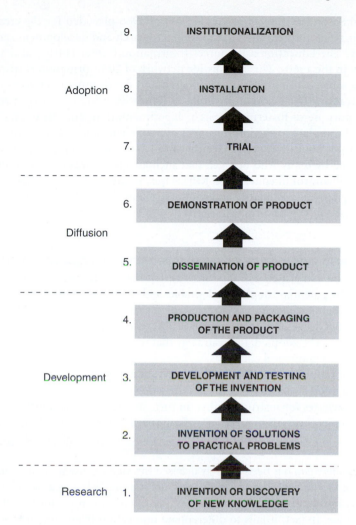

FIGURE 8.1 Concept of the research, development, diffusion, and adoption (RDDA) model of change.

use new, yet proved, knowledge in the practical business of boosting production and lowering costs. When agriculture is compared to the public schools in terms of the speed with which new knowledge and techniques are put into widespread use, it is quickly apparent that agriculture has adopted innovations with far less lag than schools have. Thus, much of the model building and formalistic process development usually found in KPU approaches to change in education is based on efforts to replicate the agricultural model in terms appropriate to education.

Beginning in the late 1950s, federal activity was considerably increased in this direction. For example, the National Defense Education Act (NDEA) of 1958 triggered the production of the spate of innovative curriculum packages that appeared in the 1960s.[1] Title IV of the

---

[1]Such as the Biological Sciences Curriculum Study (BSCS), the Physical Sciences Study Committee (PSSC), the Chemical Bond Approach Project (Chem Bond or CBA), and the School Mathematics Study Group (SMSG).

Elementary and Secondary Education Act (ESEA) of 1965 provided for the creation of 20 regional educational laboratories and 10 educational research and development centers throughout the country. The Educational Resources Information Center (ERIC) also appeared, with federal support, in the 1960s. This nationwide network of 20 information clearinghouses seeks to facilitate the rapid communication of research and development activities in ways useful to those in education. The National Institute of Education (NIE) was organized in 1972 expressly for the purpose of fostering research, experimentation, and dissemination of knowledge that could be applied to the improvement of public education. The creation of a cabinet-level Department of Education in the executive branch of the federal government in 1979 was strongly supported by many who believed that such an agency was needed to exercise greater order, system, and control in educational KPU. Thus, in the span of a quarter-century, the nation moved vigorously to systematize and stimulate planned KPU in education through federal leadership, in place of the traditional, relatively unplanned, scattered, local, and small-scale efforts of the past.

ASSUMPTIONS AND IMPLICATIONS OF KPU APPROACHES TO CHANGE KPU approaches to change are based on two critical assumptions: (a) that the new knowledge (product, technique) will be perceived by potential adopters as desirable, and (b) it is in their own self-interest. It typifies what Bennis, Benne, and Chin (1985) described as an *empirical-rational strategy of change*: That is, the new knowledge or practice is empirically demonstrated to be good, and therefore one rationally expects it to be adopted. It is a strategy that fits neatly into the traditions and values of Western scientific-technological culture.

To facilitate adoption, new ideas have to reach the adopters in practical form. Increasingly, schools are being offered relatively complete instructional delivery systems that seek to provide comprehensive packages for instruction that, in turn, are based on demonstrably effective concepts and are complete enough to meet a significant need of the school. These are often referred to as innovations, and much attention is given to the difficulties of installing innovations in schools.

The term *innovation* has been severely debased through misuse in the literature on organizational change and stability. Some people simply use it more or less as a synonym for "change." But such a broad generalization fails to convey the essence of innovation as it is used in organizational change. In fact, it fails to differentiate innovation from "organizational drift": the inevitable, unplanned, incremental changes that pervade all organizations that exist in a culture whose dominant characteristic is change. Innovation has acquired a pejorative sense in educational circles because of the frequency with which innovations have been introduced, tried, used, and abandoned.

In this book, the term *innovation* is used in referring to planned, novel, deliberate, specific change that is intended to help the organization (a) achieve existing goals more effectively or (b) achieve new goals. One usually speaks of *an* innovation as something that can be specified in terms of

1. concepts,
2. a set of operating procedures, and
3. a relevant technology to which we attach a name (for example, magnet schools, alternative education, Response to Intervention (RTI), the Direct Instructional System for Teaching and Remediation (DISTAR) reading program, individually prescribed instruction, and minimal competency testing).

Thus, not all organizational change can be described as innovation; indeed, as we shall describe shortly, much desirable organizational change is not necessarily innovative in the sense that the term is used here.

The point to be emphasized, however, is that such empirical-rational strategies of change as KPU and R, D, and D tend to focus on innovation. The concept is that good ideas are developed outside the school and are ultimately *installed* in the school. Thus, there is much concern about problems of disseminating the innovation and of installing the innovation in adopting schools. At the installation level, those who favor the innovation see it as empirically proven and view adoption as rational; conversely, they tend to view barriers to installation at the school level as nonrational (if not irrational). At this point, the empirical rationalist becomes concerned not with *educational* change in a broad sense but with *organizational* change to facilitate the adoption process.

OTHER EMPIRICAL–RATIONAL STRATEGIES   To simplify this discussion, we have focused on one empirical-rational strategy, namely, linking basic research to practice by building diffusion networks and stimulating applied research. This process typically involves creating research and development centers, linking state education departments to regional educational laboratories, and developing consortia of universities and school districts. Other empirical-rational strategies for change include the following:

- *Personnel Selection and Replacement*   This strategy includes "clearing out the deadwood" (through dismissal, early retirement, reorganization, transfers), as well as changing the criteria for the certification and employment of new people. Though many proponents of school reform advocate use of this strategy, many administrators confronted with a chronic shortage of teachers consider it problematic. NCLB applied this strategy when it mandated that a Title I school not making adequate yearly progress (AYP) for two years receive a classification as a School in Need of Improvement (SINI); and if in year four continued to miss AYP, corrective action must be taken which could include replacement of leadership and staff.
- *Utopian Thinking*   Futurists seek to develop scientific techniques for improving forecasting of the future. Their efforts are, of course, based on the highly rational premise that skill in predicting the future can be helpful in making decisions in the present. Their empirical-rational attempts to project what *might* exist in the future, what the alternatives *may* be, and what *ought* to be can lead to planned efforts to direct the course of events toward some desired goal, rather than to accept whatever may occur. A focus on the use of technology is a prime example. We see futurists such as Bill Gates and the Gates Foundation supporting efforts to use technology in new ways and to make technology more available.

Power–Coercive Strategies of Change

A power-coercive approach to change differs significantly from an empirical-rational one in its willingness to use *sanctions* in order to obtain compliance from adopters. Sanctions are usually political, financial, or moral. In the power-coercive point of view, rationality, reason, and human relations are all secondary to the ability to effect changes directly through the exercise of power.

One way of exercising political power is to gain control over the political institutions that pass legislation, issue executive orders, and hand down court decisions. This action is commonly accompanied by financial sanctions to heighten their coercive effect. The popularity of this strategy in the United States is visible in the welter of legislation, judicial decisions, and governmental regulations—each with sanctions for noncompliance—that draw so much time and attention from educational policy makers and administrators. The NCLB Act and Race to the Top (RTTT) are exemplars of power-coercive change. NCLB, through Title I funds, and RTTT, through large financial grants to states from economic stimulus money from the American Recovery and Reinvestment Act, require states to implement specific reforms such as the controversial value-added model (VAM) of teacher evaluation in which test scores must be used in the evaluation process. There is no clear research, such as might be the case in empirical-rational change processes, that any value-added models can accurately measure teacher effectiveness. As Doran and Fleischman (2005) asked the following:

> Can any statistical model really sift through all the other factors that may have influenced the student's score (for example, socio-economic status or early learning environment) and isolate the learning that we can specifically attribute to the teacher's methods? (p. 86)

Robert Chin and Kenneth Benne (1969) described the restructuring of power elites as another power-coercive strategy to bring about change. It is well recognized that our society has a power structure in which relatively limited groups have extraordinary power to effect change, either to make things happen or to keep them from happening. Instead of accepting the existing power structure as fixed and inevitable, it is possible to change the power structure. If this is done—either by shifting power to new hands or by spreading power more equitably among more people—it is possible to achieve new goals.

As presented earlier in Chapter 1, critical theory and critical race theory are important to this discussion. This fact has been well illustrated, of course, by the efforts of minority groups and women to gain representation in the key decision-making groups concerning schools, such as school boards, administrative positions, and boards that control finances. It is illustrated, too, by teachers—long maintained in a powerless and dependent state—who have unionized in an effort to shift their power relationships with administrators and school boards to bring about change. A third illustration is the development of political coalitions concerned about the educational welfare of people with challenges—such as physical, educational, and emotional—that has resulted in a series of laws and judicial decisions that have sharply rearranged the power structure in some key areas of educational decision making.

We know that power-coercive strategies of change do not work alone. For example, the University Council on Education Administration (UCEA) conducted a series of three "Voices from the Field" projects between 1999 and 2012 (Acker-Hocevar, Ballenger, Place, & Ivory, 2012). In the third study that included 81 superintendents and 85 principals across the U.S., Kew, Ivory, Muñiz, and Quiz (2012) found that NCLB provided administrators with the power of legislative mandates to hold school staffs accountable for results and the ability to legitimately "pressure teachers to move beyond the status quo to examine the quality of instruction for all students in their classrooms" (p. 18). Nonetheless, NCLB led to

> a number of negative consequences that work against the very objectives intended by the framers of the policy. These include undue pressure to achieve results quickly, a sense of being set up for failure, lack of responsiveness to local issues, narrowing of the purposes of education, and internal inconsistencies. (pp. 18–19)

Normative–Reeducative or Organizational Self-Renewal Strategies

Normative-reeducative strategies for change are different from the first two types of change described above in that both empirical-rational and power-coercive strategies share two assumptions:

1. that good ideas are best developed outside the organization, and
2. that the organization is the target of external forces for change.

Implicit in these strategies is the notion that organizations, when left to their own devices, generally emphasize stability over change and generally are resistant to change; therefore, they must be *made* to change. There is little question that such strategic change orientations are effective under certain conditions. But there is also little question that educational organizations have generally developed strong and flexible cultures that demonstrate remarkable resilience in dealing with these external forces for change by maintaining considerable stability over time and often frustrating even vigorous empirical-rational and power-coercive efforts.

Notice the significant differences between NCLB as a strategy of organizational change in schools and that of the Zacharias-PSSC undertaking that we described earlier. PSSC is an example of the empirical-rational approach of planned, managed change. It sought to improve instructional outcomes by creating and disseminating a carefully planned, coordinated package of curriculum, teacher training, and teaching materials for use in classrooms throughout the nation. It provided schools, and the teachers in them, with practical concepts, skills, and techniques for improving instruction. Teachers involved in a PSSC program generally felt professionally and personally rewarded by the experience of participating. The change strategy of NCLB, on the other hand, was starkly different: to directly exert the invincible political and financial power of the federal government to coerce schools to achieve, in some unstated fashion, ever-higher scores on mandated standardized tests of student achievement. Schools, and teachers in them, have been left scrambling to find acceptable ways of responding to the coercion. Teachers involved tend to feel threatened and diminished by the experience.

These two federal programs of intervention in education clearly demonstrate the theoretical and practical differences between empirical-rational and power-coercive strategies of organizational change in schools. They also clearly demonstrate that the decision to select one strategy over the other is a matter of deliberate choice between competing alternative theories, or understandings, of organization and behavior.

THE RAND STUDY OF FEDERAL PROGRAMS SUPPORTING EDUCATIONAL CHANGE The nature and extent of this frustration are illustrated by research conducted by the RAND Corporation for the U.S. Office of Education. The concerns that led to this research were well expressed in a publication of the National Institute of Education, which reflected the then-prevailing mood of the Congress:

> Over the past decade and a half, the federal government has spent over a billion dollars on research and development on the country's educational problems, and billions more on categorical [financial] aid to schools and districts. Yet, the problems remain intractable, and the repeated research finding that innovations produce "no significant differences" has engendered such frustration that some have begun to despair of the schools' potential for improvement. A disturbingly familiar national

> behavior pattern is beginning to manifest itself in education. We are a "can-do," "quick-fix" society. The answer to a problem is a program. If the program fails, we try another one, and if a whole series of programs fails, we tire of that problem and go on to fresher ones. (Group on School Capacity for Problem Solving, 1975, p. 1)

That was the situation in 1975, and after the first nationwide appraisal of the effectiveness of NCLB by the federal government's venerable National Assessment of Educational Progress (NAEP), it appeared to hold true in 2005. The NAEP study, which compared test results in math and reading since 1990 and also compared the nationwide results from NCLB tests given in 2003 and 2005, revealed that NCLB had produced what could be most enthusiastically described as mixed results. One of the primary goals of NCLB was to reduce the achievement gap between white and minority students, but in 2005 NAEP found at best only modest, if any, gains in that area. Although the appraisal found that math scores in fourth and eighth grades were up in 2005 compared with 1990, the rate of improvement had been slowed after implementation of NCLB compared to the rate of improvement that had occurred in the early 1990s, prior to NCLB. Indeed, one cause for concern from the NAEP study in 2005 was that the data showed greater educational progress in learning outcomes had been made in the years prior to NCLB than in the years after its implementation.

In an effort to understand this situation, RAND undertook a study of federally funded programs that had been designed to introduce and spread innovative practices in public schools. "These change agent programs," Berman and McLaughlin (1978) wrote, "normally offer temporary federal funding to school districts as 'seed money.' If an innovation is successful, it is assumed that the district will incorporate and spread part or all of the project using other sources of funds" (p. iii). (Recall the discussion earlier in this chapter concerning the adoption and institutionalization of innovations, and refer again to Figure 8.1).

The study consisted of a series of related investigations of 293 projects in 18 states sponsored under the following federal programs:

1. ESEA, Title III—Innovative Projects
2. ESEA, Title VII—Bilingual Projects
3. Vocational Education Act, 1968 amendments, Part D—Exemplary Programs
4. Right to Read Program

The research focused on two main issues: (a) the kinds of strategies and conditions that tend to promote change in the school and the kinds that do not and (b) the factors that promote or deter the institutionalization of innovation (which has been tried and adopted) after the federal "seed money" runs out.

Although we make no pretense of summarizing this large and complex research here, the salient finding is clear: The differences among school districts in the extent to which they successfully adopted and implemented innovations are explained not so much by either (a) the nature of the innovation itself or (b) the amount of federal funding but, rather, by the *characteristics of the organization and the management of the local school districts and schools themselves.* For example:

> In cases of successful implementation, the districts were generally characterized by . . . a "problem-solving" orientation. That is, they had identified and frequently had already begun to attack the problem before federal money became available. By contrast, failures in implementation were associated with an "opportunistic"

orientation. These districts simply supplemented their budgets with money that happened to be available [from the new federal program]. (Group on School Capacity for Problem Solving, 1975, p. 1)

School districts that were successful in implementing innovative programs also tended to exhibit other characteristics:

- They tended to reject rigidly packaged innovations that did not permit adaptation to local conditions.
- They were strongly involved in developing their own local materials rather than simply adopting materials that had been developed elsewhere.
- They engaged in continuous planning and replanning rather than in one-shot planning at the beginning of a project.
- They engaged in ongoing training of people as needs arose in the projects and as defined by the participants (rather than in one-shot training at the outset or in having training needs identified by outside "experts").
- Consistent technical assistance was available locally for projects, rather than one- or two-day visits from outside "experts."
- Innovative projects received strong support from key administrators at both the district and the school level (for example, the superintendent of schools and the principal).

In sum, this research gave strong support to the view, long held by applied behavioral scientists, that the organizational characteristics of the target school systems and schools at which empirical-rational and power-coercive strategies of change are aimed are crucial in determining the effectiveness of those schools *and* their capacity to change. In the words of the NIE report, increasing productivity is not primarily a problem that can be solved by installing new accountability systems, teaching administrators improved purchasing techniques, or utilizing superior technology, but is a problem of improving the organizational culture (problem-solving and decision-making structures, incentives to change, skills in managing collaborative planning and implementation, mutual support and communication, opportunities for relevant training, etc.) in which people work.

This development at the local school district and school level is viewed as a necessary precondition to effective utilization of knowledge, no matter how it is produced, packaged, and disseminated:

No matter how good the channels which transmit knowledge and products to practitioners, it appears that such products will spread slowly and see little effective use until schools and districts develop the capacity to engage in an active search for solutions to their own problems, to adapt solutions to the particulars of their own situation, and equally important, to adapt themselves as organizations to the requirements of the selected solutions. (Group on School Capacity for Problem Solving, 1975, p. 5)

Since as early as 1975, federally funded research initiatives indicated that normative-reeducative strategies were necessary to change schools successfully, we wonder why power-coercive strategies continue.

A NORMATIVE-REEDUCATIVE STRATEGY   This orientation, widely known as organizational self-renewal, is based on an understanding of organizations and people in them that is quite different from the orientation usually held by the empirical-rational or power-coercive views, which are essentially classical or bureaucratic and tend to see the organization as a creation apart from people. Organization theory, in this view, "deals with human *response* to organization rather than with human activity in *creating* organizations" (Greenfield, 1973, p. 551).

Normative-reeducative strategies of change, on the other hand, posit that the norms of the organization's interaction-influence system (attitudes, beliefs, and values—in other words, culture) can be deliberately shifted to more productive norms by collaborative action of the people who populate the organization. Andrew Halpin would describe this as shifting from a closed climate to a more open climate. In George Stern's terminology, it would be enhancing the development press of the organizational climate. Rensis Likert would speak of moving away from a System 1 management style toward System 4 (see Chapter 7). Michael Fullan (2001) would describe this as the ability of the organization "to mobilize the *collective capacity* to challenge difficult circumstances" (p. 136).

ORGANIZATIONAL HEALTH To be effective, an organization must consistently perform three essential core activities *over time* (Argyris, 1964):

1. Achieve its goals
2. Maintain itself internally
3. Adapt to its environment

These are the defining characteristics of healthy organizations.

Thus, the organization must be effective and stable, yet capable of changing appropriately. Organizations differ in their ability to accomplish these things; in other words, they exhibit different degrees of *organizational health*. A healthy organization "not only survives in its environment, but continues to cope adequately over the long haul, and continuously develops and extends its surviving and coping activities. Short-run operations on any particular day may be effective or ineffective, but continued survival, adequate coping, and growth are taking place" (Miles, 1965, p. 17). DeGues (1997) suggested, "A healthy living company will have members, both humans and other institutions, who subscribe to a set of common values and who believe that the goals of the company allow them and help them to achieve their own individual goals" (p. 200).

The unhealthy organization, on the other hand, is steadily ineffective. It may cope with its environment effectively on a short-term basis with a crash program, a concentrated drive to meet a particularly threatening situation, or other administration-by-crisis techniques. In the long run, however, the unhealthy organization becomes less and less able to cope with its environment. Rather than gaining in its ability to cope with a situation, it declines in this capacity over time and tends to become dysfunctional.

No single output measure or time slice of organizational performance can provide a reliable, accurate measure of organizational health: A central concern is the organization's continuing ability to cope with change and to adapt to the future. This ability is best viewed in the perspective of time. There are some specific indicators of organizational health; important among them are the following:

1. *Goal focus.* This is the extent to which people in the organization understand and enthusiastically participate in supporting the achievable, appropriate goals of the organization.

2. *Communication adequacy.*   This is vertical and horizontal internal communication and external communication with the environment. It also includes the ease and facility of communication (as opposed to the amount of noise and distortion that can inhibit and confuse communication).

3. *Optimal power equalization.*   An important element of this dimension is the issue of collaboration versus coercion. Are the organization's members coerced or required to work toward the organization's goals, or do they embrace and accept the goals as their own?

4. *Human resources utilization.*   This is the effective use of personnel so that the organization's people feel they are growing and developing in their jobs.

5. *Cohesiveness.*   This is the extent to which participants like the organization and want to remain involved in it in order to influence the collaborative style.

6. *Morale.*   This is exhibited as feelings of well-being and satisfaction.

7. *Innovativeness.*   This is the tendency to devise new procedures and goals, to grow, to develop, and to become more differentiated over time.

8. *Autonomy.*   Rather than being merely a "tool of the environment" that responds passively to outside stimuli, the autonomous organization tends to determine its own behavior in harmony with external demands.

9. *Adaptation.*   Healthy organizations should be able to change, correct, and adapt faster than the environment.

10. *Problem-solving adequacy.*   This includes mechanisms for sensing and perceiving problems, as well as those for solving problems permanently.

VOICES FROM THE FIELD

Changing the Mission and Culture to Become a School of Choice

Brian Mangan, former Principal, Mariner High School, Cape Coral, Florida

After being named Principal of Mariner High School in late May, I was fortunate to have the summer to get to know the school. The school was in the beginning of a transformation both facility-wise and academically. The building just had its 23-year-old air conditioning system replaced, and one of my first facility tasks was the installation of new flooring, followed by renovations throughout a majority of the interior space of the campus as well as some exterior projects. Academically, Mariner was the sole high school in the west zone of the school district of Lee County that did not have a major theme or attractor for students and parents to consider when rising from eighth grade or as a new high school enrollee. This lack of an attractor combined with competition from two brand new high schools and two established high schools with popular programs (International Baccalaureate and Performing Arts) were contributing factors to Mariner being the least selected school in the zone. There was one charter high school in our zone, but we did not feel like we were competing with it. It was small and didn't seem to be attracting those students and families who are interested in traditional public schools. Our main competitors were the other four district high schools.

There was a nascent Math, Science, and Technology (MST) program that had just completed its first year with 40 students enrolled out of a total student population of 1450. In the middle of the summer, I was afforded the opportunity to bring an experienced Assistant Principal for Curriculum (APC) on the administrative staff as well as an Assistant Principal for Administration (APA) who was previously at this school, but released by my predecessor due to budgetary constraints. Hiring these two key administrators would be essential to the twin developments of academics and facility renewal. As the beginning of school approached, it became apparent that there was a need to align the two major projects as well as to integrate a third major resource: teacher capacity.

The first task was to have the Leadership Team define the mission and vision for the school based on staff input. The Leadership Team consisted of the Department Chairs and was led by the Assistant Principal of Curriculum. The foundation for our restructuring was the MST program. We enhanced it to Science, Technology, Engineering, and Math (STEM) and began planning a schoolwide STEM initiative that would be available to all of the students through the development of academies centered on STEM. Next we researched the capacity of the teachers and began to work with key teachers to bring their certifications and professional development in line with STEM concepts. The Assistant Principal for Administration worked with the site foreman, district construction personnel, and maintenance workers to modify the renovations of the interior spaces to create learning spaces that would enable us to implement the STEM academies. Although the original MST students felt as if the rug were pulled from underneath them, as time allowed for the expanded STEM options for students to chart curriculum that appealed to them, students became the biggest proponents and advocates for continued changes to the STEM program.

Over the course of my first year as principal, we synchronized our efforts as a school staff. By meeting with administrators, teachers, and staff members individually, in small groups and large groups, we were able to make decisions and keep the staff informed about what we were trying to accomplish and how it would benefit our students in the future. By recognizing our teachers' "hidden" skills and their desires to be a part of a unique teaching experience, we acquired valuable faculty commitment to the change. By seizing upon STEM, we had clearly separated ourselves from the other high schools in our choice zone and gave students and parents a viable option for their educational experience. By remodeling the campus to support specialized instruction, we were able to offer permanent long-term support to the students and teachers, so the STEM academies would endure over time.

As a staff, we worked on three broad areas continued throughout my principalship at Mariner. First, the renovations were completed by the middle of my second year. Second, the academics were developed into seven major STEM academies by the end of my second year, and course offerings would be broadened in my third year as principal. Third, the teacher capacity was a continuing effort. Professional development never truly ends. Teacher attrition occurred for a variety of reasons, new teachers were hired, and the expansion of academies that occurred because of student interest necessitated continued professional development opportunities. Because of our efforts, Mariner High School moved from the last place (five out of five) to the third spot in the school selection process of incoming freshman. In fact, we have a waiting list, highlighting the success of our efforts.

I was given a new assignment just before the start of what would have been my fourth year as principal. During the summer, the Assistant Principal for Curriculum was promoted to principal of another school. But I keep tabs on my former school, and it is encouraging to know that the program we developed has sustainability despite the leadership change.

ORGANIZATIONAL SELF-RENEWAL   It is a commonplace observation, of course, that many organizations have a tendency to atrophy over time, becoming obsessed with maintaining themselves, increasing their bureaucratic rigidity, and seeking to shore up traditional practices. In a world characterized by rapid change, such organizations tend to be viewed as *un*-healthy; they emphasize maintenance of the organization at the expense of the need for constant adaptability to keep pace with the change in the demands and expectations of its external environment.

The concept of organization self-renewal was first comprehensively described by Rensis Likert (1961). He described managing the interaction-influence system of the organization in ways that would stimulate creativity, promote growth of people in the organization, and facilitate solution of the organization's problems. Matthew Miles and Dale Lake (1967) described an application of the concept to school systems in the Cooperative Project for Educational Development. Later, Gordon Lippitt (1969) elaborated a well-developed approach to the processes of renewal based on the view that every organization has a life cycle (birth-youth-maturity) with different renewal needs at each stage of its existence.

Organization self-renewal postulates that effective change cannot be imposed on a school; rather, it seeks to develop an internal capacity for continuous problem solving. The processes of renewal include the increased capacity to

1. sense and identify emerging problems;
2. establish goals, objectives, and priorities;
3. generate valid alternative solutions; and
4. implement the selected alternative.

An outcome of renewal processes is to shift the culture of the school from emphasis on traditional routines and bureaucracy toward a culture that actively supports the view that much of the knowledge needed to plan and carry out change in schools is possessed by people in the schools themselves. It recognizes that "the optimal unit for educational change is the single school with its pupils, teachers, principal—those who live there every day—as primary participants" (Goodlad, 1975, p. 175).

The self-renewing school possesses three essential characteristics. *First,* its culture supports adaptability and responsiveness to change. Such a culture is supportive of open communication, especially from the bottom up, and places a high priority on problem solving. *Second,* it has a set of clear-cut, explicit, and well-known procedures through which participants can engage in the orderly processes of systematic, collaborative problem solving. *Third,* the school is not an institution relying solely on internal energy, ideas, and resources for solving problems. Rather, it is a school that knows when and how to reach out to seek appropriate ideas and resources for use in solving its problems (Zaltman, Florio, & Sikorski, 1977). More recently, Fullan (2010a) defined the elements for successful reform in self-renewing schools. These schools utilize a leadership coalition that relentlessly focuses on a small number of goals; has high expectations; develops collective and individual capacity focusing on improving instruction; and uses data to determine non-punitive intervention strategies.

THE LEARNING ORGANIZATION   Some organizations, notably low-performing ones, are characterized by a remarkable inability to sense that they have problems—to detect a disconnect with their external environment—and, thus, have little ability to anticipate and adapt to changes in their external environment. In the case of schools, this is commonly observed when the demographics of the community change rapidly, which is common in the United States, as well as when technological changes shift rapidly, which is endemic worldwide. In fast-changing environments, such as those we confront today, school organizations must become increasingly nimble and agile as a matter of survival. That requires developing increased ability to sense, even predict, the problems posed by their environments and invent solutions to them. This is part of the concept of the learning organization: an organization, whether it is corporate or educational, that learns to nimbly adapt to unfolding changes in the environment. This process of increasing the capacity of the organization to learn, to adapt, is often called *organization development.*

Organization development is an approach to increasing the self-renewal capability of school districts and schools. It has been defined in this way:

> Organization development in school districts is a coherent, systematically-planned, sustained effort at system self-study and improvement, focusing explicitly on change in formal and informal procedures, processes, norms or structures, using behavioral science concepts. The goals of organization development include *both* the quality of life of individuals as well as improving organizational functioning and performance. (Fullan, Miles, & Taylor, 1978, p. 14)

The primary goal of organization development is to improve the functioning of the organization itself. Improving the productivity and effectiveness of the organization is seen as largely dependent on developing the organization's capability to make better-quality decisions about its affairs—decisions affecting its structure, its tasks, its use of technology, its use of human resources, and its goals. The primary approach to this process is to develop a work-oriented culture in the organization that maximizes the involvement of the organization's people in more effective decision making regarding matters of importance to them as well as to the goals of the organization. While organization development may very well lead to the adoption of a new program or curriculum, to a restructuring of the organization, or to a commitment to new goals, decisions to adopt new programs are not considered to be first steps in improving the effectiveness of schools and school systems.

Organization development rejects the belief that atrophy is inevitable in organizations. Stated positively, the view is that an organization can—indeed, it must—develop self-renewing characteristics, enabling it to increase its capability, to adapt to change, and to improve its record of goal achievement over time. This concept of system self-renewal sees the organization not as being helplessly buffeted about by exigencies and changes thrust on it, but as growing in its ability to initiate change, as having an increasing impact on its environment, and as developing an increasing capability to adapt to new conditions and solve new problems over time. Perhaps more important is its ability to develop a growing sense of purpose and direction over time. The view is of an energized system marked by increasing vitality and imaginative creativity.

The self-renewal concept is at the center of the difference between organization *development*, on the one hand, and organization *improvement*, on the other. In organization development, the goal is not merely to overcome an immediate problem and arrive at a new "frozen" state of organizational functioning. The concept is one of building into the organizational system the conditions, the skills, the processes, and the culture that foster continual development of the organization over a sustained period of time. This is the bedrock concept on which sustainable change is erected.

Organization development is based on the concept of the organization as a complex sociotechnical system. Such a view of the organization, of course, emphasizes the wholeness of the organizational system and the dynamic interrelatedness of its component subsystems: human, structural, technological, and task. The school, for example, is a sociotechnical system. It comprises subsystems, of course—departments, grade levels, informal groups, teams, and work groups—that are in a constant state of dynamic interrelationship. The school is also a subsystem of larger systems: the school district, for example, and the community in which it functions.

Such a view has fundamental implications for those concerned with administering organizational change; they are translated into certain basic assumptions:

1. To effect change that has long-term staying power, one must change the whole system and not merely certain of its parts or subsystems.

2. Because of the dynamic interrelatedness and interdependence of the component sub-systems, any significant change in one subsystem produces compensatory or retaliatory changes in other subsystems, as we described in Chapter 4.
3. Events very rarely occur in isolation or from single causes. Systems concepts of the organization emphasize the importance of dealing with events as manifestations of interrelated forces, issues, problems, causes, phenomena, and needs. An organization is understood to be the complex system that it is, and ascribing single causation to phenomena or treating events as isolated incidents can mask our full understanding of them.
4. The organizational system is defined not by walls or membranes but by existing patterns of human behavior. These patterns are not static but are in constant dynamic equilibrium—as the concept of force-field analysis illustrates. Therefore, the crucial information that the administrator requires comes from analyzing the specific field of forces at a particular time, rather than from analyzing generalized historical data from the past or from other organizations. Force-field analysis is described later in this chapter.

The main concern for organizational development is the human social system of the organization rather than task, technology, or structure dimensions. Specifically, the focus is on the organizational culture that characterizes the climate of beliefs influencing behavior—such as the ways in which superordinates and subordinates deal with one another, the ways in which work groups relate to each other, and the extent to which people in the organization are involved in identifying organizational problems and seeking solutions to them. Attitudes, values, feelings, and openness of communication are typical concerns in organization development. It matters what people think, how open their communication is, how they deal with conflict, and to what extent they feel involved in their jobs because these kinds of human concerns help determine how much work gets done and how well. People who have learned to keep their thoughts to themselves, to be discreet in proffering a new idea or in voicing doubt or criticism, contribute little to the organization's ability to diagnose its problems and find solutions. The culture of many schools encourages this kind of behavior—leaving decisions to the upper echelons and frowning upon lower-level participants who raise questions.

Commonly, the school's culture carefully structures organizational behavior to minimize open, free, and vigorous participation in central decisions—witness the typical faculty meeting with its crowded agenda of minutiae or the superintendent's pro forma appearances before the staff, which are filled with routine platitudes. Organizations with such characteristics tend to be relatively inflexible, slow to change, and defensive in a fast-changing environment.

One of the great resources available to an organization trying to improve its effectiveness is its own people. By encouraging people to become involved, concerned participants, rather than making them feel powerless and manipulated by unseen and inscrutable forces, the organization can draw ever-increasing strength, vitality, and creativity from its people.

The social systems orientation of organizations means that one cannot change part of the system without affecting other parts of the system. For example, management cannot presume to change the organization without being part of the process. Organizational change is not a matter of "us" (the administration) changing "them" (the teachers and other subordinates) or even of changing "it" (the organization as some sort of entity detached from "us"). The leader must be an active partner involved in the development process to ensure that all subsystems of the organizational system stay appropriately linked together in a dynamic, interactive way. This is one of the identifying characteristics of the increasingly effective organization.

Organization development recognizes that organizations are hierarchical and will continue to be so. When subordinates see that the administration is doing something to the organization in the name of improving its effectiveness—something in which administrators are not involved except as observers—the subordinates are very likely to be wary and less than fully committed. On the other hand, if the administration is already interested in the undertaking, committed to it, and involved in visible ways, subordinates are much more inclined to view the effort as valid and will be more highly motivated to involve themselves. In any organization, subordinates tend to develop highly sensitive antennae that pick up reliable indications of what is really important at higher levels and ignoring all the static and noise that may surround the issuance of official statements.

Peter Senge, one of the early leaders who helped us understand how to create and lead a learning organization, wrote in the forward to Fullan's *All Systems Go: The Change Imperative for Whole System Reform* that change is not possible unless all parts of the system work together and agree on strategies to achieve common goals (Fullan, 2010a). Fullan uses the term "collective capacity" for this process.

A SOCIOTECHNICAL VIEW   Those who are inexperienced in participative approaches to management often think of them as being soft; permissive; and incompatible with the structure, discipline, and power that characterize organizations. In fact, however, what is needed is a new, more effective, approach to management: an approach that stresses more functional administrative structures and seeks more effective organizational behavior. Although the new structures may well be more flexible and adaptable than those of the past, they will not be fuzzy or ill-defined, nor will the more effective work-related behaviors be lacking in clear, exact description and definition.

When the leader recognizes the need for more involvement of faculty and staff in decision making or seeks to move the organization in a more organic or self-renewing direction, does it mean that system, orderly procedures, and control must be abandoned? The answer is, of course, no. The opposite is true: The need is to provide organizational structures that will enhance and facilitate the development of more adaptive decision-making styles to replace the rigid hierarchical structures characteristic of the mechanistic organization.

The shift in organizational system development, then, is not away from the clarity, order, and control associated with traditional views of organizational structure toward an ill-defined, disorderly, laissez-faire administration. What is sought, administratively, is a new and more functional basis for *task* analysis, *structural* arrangements, selection and use of *technology,* and selection and professional development of individual *people* and groups of people on the staff.

FORCE-FIELD ANALYSIS   How can one analyze an organizational learning situation to better understand how to deal with it? Force-field analysis has proven to be a useful analytic approach for both the researcher and the administrator.

Basically, this approach sees a social or organizational *status quo* as a state of equilibrium resulting from the balance between two opposing sets of forces. There are forces for change, sometimes called *driving forces,* and these are opposed by forces for remaining unchanged, sometimes called *restraining forces.* When these force fields are in balance, as in Figure 8.2, we have equilibrium—no change.

Obviously, when one or another of these forces is removed or weakened, the equilibrium is upset and change occurs, as shown in Figure 8.3. On a very simple level, such an imbalance can be the result of the introduction of a new work technique or the acquisition of new skills by participants. But an organization is essentially a stable entity generally characterized by equilibrium;

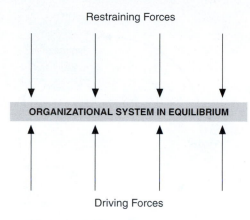

Restraining Forces

ORGANIZATIONAL SYSTEM IN EQUILIBRIUM

Driving Forces

FIGURE 8.2 Force field in equilibrium.

an imbalance brings readjustments that will again lead to a new organizational equilibrium. This simple concept can become very complex when applied to a large-scale organization. But it can also be a practical aid to the administrator who seeks to understand his or her organization better to facilitate either change or stability in the organization. The analytic process of identifying restraining forces and driving forces ranges from a very simple approach at the rudimentary level to rather sophisticated techniques.

Force-field analysis eventually led its creator, Kurt Lewin (1947), to a fundamental three-step change strategy that has come into increasingly popular use. It is predicated on the notion that in order to effect organizational change, it is first necessary to break the equilibrium of the force field: That is, the organization must be *unfrozen*. Once that is done, it is possible to

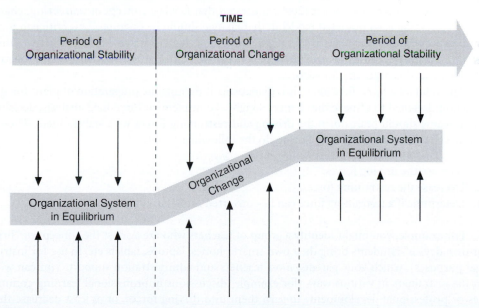

TIME

Period of Organizational Stability

Period of Organizational Change

Period of Organizational Stability

Organizational System in Equilibrium

Organizational Change

Organizational System in Equilibrium

FIGURE 8.3 Imbalance of force field causes organizational change until a new equilibrium is reached.

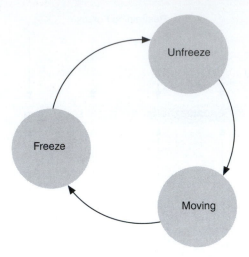

FIGURE 8.4   A three-step change process as an ongoing life cycle of an organization.

introduce *change*—to move the organization to a new level. But no one knows better than educational administrators how fragile change can be and how easily the organization can slip back into its old ways. Therefore, the third step in the three-step change process is *refreezing*. This is an institutionalizing process that serves to protect and ensure the long-range retention of the change. Of course, refreezing smacks of a new *status quo*; in Lewin's view, the desired amount of flexibility could be built in by establishing "an organizational setup which is equivalent to a stable circular causal process" (Lewin, 1951, p. 35). Unfreezing can be a highly traumatic experience to a very rigid and resisting organization, but it can also be built in as a normal part of its life cycle, as suggested in Figure 8.4, in order to achieve greater organizational flexibility over time.

Spillane, Gomez, and Mesler (2009) suggested that Lewin's concept of unfreezing, changing, and refreezing is an outdated model in that change should be ongoing. This criticism is not clear, however, in that no alternative model for "ongoing change" is provided. Surely, there must be some constants necessary to provide stable processes (Cuban, 1993; March, 1981). Proactive, planned changed is necessary for success.

The value of a force-field analysis is diagnostic: it permits the preparation of plans for specific action designed to achieve the changes sought. To implement force-field analysis, decision-making teams should brainstorm the driving and restraining forces with stakeholders. Then to develop a change strategy, identify how to do the following:

1. Increase the driving forces.
2. Decrease the restraining forces.
3. Determine if a restraining force can be converted into a driving force.

For example, you might identify a group of teachers who are against the concept of "bring your own device" (students bring their own smart phones, laptops, tablets etc. to use for instructional purposes), which your parents, most teachers and administration support. You can work with the restrainers in various ways (for example, discussions in professional learning communities or professional development) to turn them into driving forces, or at least decrease their resistance. The success of such a plan depends in large measure on the clarity with which the likely consequences of proposed action are perceived. Of the four major organizational subsystems—task, technological, structure, and human—only the human subsystem has the capacity to react differentially to differing conditions. By decreasing the restraining forces and converting restrainers into drivers, you are using learning organization concepts, improving organizational climate, and therefore improving organizational health. By only focusing on the driving forces, you risk the potential of alienating a significant portion of the human subsystem.

Great art and literature teem with depictions of the heroic achievements of people moved by feelings such as love, faith, courage, and duty. Much of the literature on organizations is concerned with apathy, anger, frustration, and apprehensions of people and their great power to inhibit the organization's goal achievement. Although administrators must be deeply concerned with the work to be performed in the school, the structure of the organization, and the technology that is used, none of these has the capability of resisting plans for action. Only the human subsystem has that capability.

But it is not productive for the administrator to view opposition to change in any form—whether as outright resistance, apathy, skepticism, or whatever—as obdurate behavior. If "increasing the driving forces" is interpreted by the administrator as meaning the stepped-up use of authority and power to get people behind the change effort, it is highly predictable that the result will be strong reactions against the change. Pressure generates counterpressure, and in the school setting, where the administrator's coercive power is sharply limited, it is not likely that the equilibrium of the force field can be broken by such an approach. At the very least, it is predictable that, as the pressure is eventually relaxed—as it must be sooner or later—there will be a tendency for the organization to retreat to its old ways under the pressure of the restraining forces.

In school situations, it is likely to be more effective to help bring the restraining forces into the open as legitimate in the process of change. By creating a culture in which feelings can be expressed instead of secretly harbored, by opening communication and valuing the right to question and challenge, and by helping those who would oppose the forces of change to examine and deal with the concerns that cause their resistance, it is likely that (a) unforeseen probable consequences of proposed actions will be brought into the planning process and, perhaps more important, (b) the level of resistance will be diminished.

As the opposition helps to shape and mold decisions, its views are also shaped, molded, and modified in the process. *To obtain this kind of participation requires the existence of a developmental, or growth-enhancing, organizational culture that characteristically*

1. is intellectually, politically, and esthetically stimulating.
2. emphasizes individual and group achievement.
3. places high value on the personal dignity of individuals.
4. accepts divergent feelings and views in a nonjudgmental way.
5. is oriented to problem solving rather than to winning or losing in intraorganizational skirmishes.

The establishment of orderly problem-solving processes that provide maximum participation for those who will be affected by the change is necessary to develop the collaborative approach suggested here. Although people's perspectives are important, they must be accompanied by effective specific procedures for making them work, thus creating the climate needed and ensuring that the way in which decisions are reached is understood and workable. Development of a new organizational culture and building the group skills needed for open, collaborative decision making require definite training and practice. These goals are not achieved through cognitive understanding and determination alone: They require the development of new insights, new values and commitments, and new group process skills that are best taught and learned in problem-solving situations.

Remember that the creation of a new organizational culture—a new environment for working and solving problems—requires participants to develop new and more effective responses to events, to act differently than they have done in the past. As every educator is keenly aware, such changes in human functioning do not often occur as a result of learning *about* the new, more effective ways of doing things. Opportunities must be provided wherein the new behaviors may be developed in practice: In short, *learning by doing* is required. The goal is to develop new and more productive norms of work-oriented behavior through reeducation.

Change is likely to be stabilized and maintained in the organization over time, when the new, more effective level of performance can be maintained without coercion and without continuous expenditures of administrative energy and vigilance to keep it going. Indeed, this is one practical criterion by which the administrator may judge whether change has been accomplished.

An appropriate plan for organizational change must be cognizant of these realities. It must also recognize that the goal of changing an organization in significant ways presents a challenge in terms of difficulty and in terms of the time required. There are no quick and easy solutions, though there will probably never be a shortage of those who claim to possess such solutions. Hersey and Blanchard's (1977) admonition on this point is highly appropriate:

> Changes in knowledge are the easiest to make, followed by changes in attitudes. Attitude structures differ from knowledge structures in that they are emotionally charged in a positive or a negative way. Changes in behavior are significantly more difficult and time consuming than either of the two previous levels. But the implementation of group or organizational performance change is perhaps the most difficult and time consuming. (p. 2)

THE EFFECTIVENESS OF ORGANIZATIONAL DEVELOPMENT

In reporting on an early major study of organization development in schools, Fullan et al. (1978) pointed out that a problem of assessing efforts to develop the self-renewal, problem-solving capacity of school systems and schools lies in the fact that many change projects are partial, incomplete, short-term activities lacking the planning, scope, and sustained effort required for success. In many cases, for example, a few days of "human relations training" for teachers, or the use of an outside consultant for a few sessions, is incorrectly labeled an organization development project. Often the effort is limited to attempts to reduce conflict or otherwise to ameliorate unpleasant aspects of organizational culture, with little or no intention to alter significantly the organizational structure or processes of decision making.

Researchers at the Center for Educational Policy and Management (CEPM) at the University of Oregon conducted one of the first and most comprehensive research and development efforts in this field. In assessing whether organization development has been successful in a district or school, they caution against accepting superficial claims about *any* effort at change:

> Our experience in looking for outcomes has taught us that they are not simple. . . . Editors of scientific journals and providers of funds should demand detailed documentation when a researcher claims that one or more schools have "installed" or "adopted" some particular new way of doing things. The depth and variety in the

ways that a new structure such as team teaching can be installed or adopted in a school are stupefying, and so are the ways a principal can cover up with verbiage the fact that the innovation really has not taken hold in his [*sic*] school at all. Statements that go no farther than, "In a school that had adopted team teaching the previous year, . . ." or "We shall install team teaching in X schools next year, . . ." should never be accepted without skepticism. (Runkel & Schmuck, 1974, p. 34)

Superficial claims of success only lead to poor school climate. Teachers have a nose for fads, and they become skeptical when the next fad comes around. Individual and collective commitment becomes more and more difficult in a culture of change-for-change sake. To assure teachers that a change is not a fad, Fullan (2010a) identified "resolute leadership" as the key; that is, core leadership of the system (school, district, and/or state) that agrees with the change and provides continuing, long-term support.

Building on the change models he presented in his earlier work in 2001 with *Leading a Culture of Change* and in 2003 with *Change Forces with a Vengeance*, Fullan in 2010 with *All Systems Go: The Change Imperative for Whole System Reform* demonstrates how school systems in the United States, the United Kingdom, and Canada successfully intitiated and sustained reform initiatives. The successful schools and systems began with core beliefs Fullan called a "moral purpose" that includes high expectations, closing the achievement gap, and a focus on limited number of specific, achievable standards of literacy and numeracy. All of this is combined with a belief that all children can learn. The moral purpose is supported with resolute leadership from all educational and political leaders who agree with the purpose and who, although requiring an "intelligent accountability" system, provide more incentives, and few, if any, punishments. Finally, although individual development of teacher capacity is strongly supported, comprised of quality preparation programs, and sustained professional development, the key to success is in collective capacity.

TWO EMERGING QUESTIONS

At this writing, the nation's schools were in the second decade of prodigious effort to implement the many unstated theoretical propositions of standards-based school reform embodied in the NCLB Act. The general theory underlying NCLB has never been explicitly set forth, but two of its principle hypotheses seem to be simple and straightforward: If schools set high standards for learning and specify measurable goals to determine the extent to which individual students achieve those goals, then

1. the learning outcomes of individual students will improve, and
2. the achievement gap that has historically separated students of color and low income from their peers will be eliminated.

It is a novel theory in the history of school change and, as readers of this book well know, NCLB set off a scramble to discover and solve numerous technical problems to implement it in practice—a scramble of discovery still under way. Formative assessments of results were, by mid-2010, disappointing to mixed at best, and this result gave rise to two new questions:

1. Can schools alone achieve the goals of NCLB?
2. Is school reform enough, or is it necessary to reinvent schools as some entirely new and different kind of organization?

Can the Schools Do It Alone?

Because the achievement gap has been so persistent and long-lived (indeed it was a basic reason for NCLB itself being invented) and because historically schools have not been able to close that gap, many people believe that they simply cannot achieve the goal by themselves. Andy Hargreaves (2009) observed the following:

> The turn of the 21st century was marked by a shift from a shared social responsibility to support and create better opportunities for the poor to an expectation that schools and teachers should raise all students' achievement and narrow the gaps between them entirely by themselves. The discourse of equality has degenerated into a demand to close numerical achievement gaps. Responsibility has been lifted from the wider community and placed exclusively on the schools. Too often we hear the mantras, "There are no excuses! Failure is not an option!" (p. 25)

In fact, decades of research on school effectiveness have assembled a body of evidence to support the contention that the differences in the achievement of students are largely due to factors outside the school: differences in family and home life, the communities in which the students live, and society itself (Nichols & Berliner, 2007). And, Hargreaves (2009) added, "Schools can and do make a significant difference, but not all or even most of it. They cannot excel alone; they need communities and society to work with them" (p. 25).

Given this body of research evidence and with the unspectacular results from over a decade of experience with NCLB, there is cause to wonder if a course-correction is in order for the future of the federally mandated enterprise. Hargreaves (2009), asserting that "greater professional accountability must be matched by increased parental responsibility" (p. 26) seconds President Barack Obama's insistence that parents must turn off the TV and the DVD and talk to their children and play with them. Teachers, Hargreaves said, cannot do everything. Parents must do their part, too.

In saying this, Hargreaves was not trying to dump all responsibility on parents, either. Having spent years as a community organizer, surely President Obama well understood the concept of the school being only one important part of educating children. Americans have long understood the need for community support of, and involvement in, the public schools. Community does not mean only the family: it includes health services, social services, and belief-centered organizations; indeed, everything in the community that can support and enrich the learning experiences of children. It has long been a central part of the U.S. tradition of public schools that they are part and parcel of and enmeshed in the community.

In fact, there has been a movement that has been growing, albeit slowly, for over 20 years to encourage the development of "full-service schools" or "community schools." These are schools that embrace the concept of teaching the whole child in a practical way. By partnering with resources in the community, they try to meet not only the intellectual needs of children, but also their mental health and physical health needs, too. At this point in their history, there is no set blueprint for a full-service school (often called a community school); they take different forms in different communities. But they rely on their community partners to provide support services in some or all of such areas as health and dental screening and services, substance abuse, mental health, and counseling (both individual and family). In various organizational patterns, these kinds of services are brought into the school through the presence of professionals from community resource agencies where they have ready access to the children who have need for their services.

An example of such a full-service school exists in affluent Westchester County, NY. Many are surprised to learn that the city of Port Chester has been a pocket of poverty in that county for many years. The Thomas Edison Elementary School in Port Chester, where at times up to 77% of the children were without health insurance, has developed a health center over the years. In the center, healthcare professionals from a community medical agency provide primary healthcare, dentistry, and nutrition counseling to the children. Through other partnerships that Edison Elementary has developed, students and their families are also provided with the services of a mental health counselor and a bilingual family caseworker, too. Edison Elementary has reported not only that its test scores have climbed but also that more immigrant families are now involved in the parent-teacher association (PTA), too.

The focus of the full-service school movement has generally been, in the early years, on healthcare. The National Assembly on School-Based Health Care (NASBHC) reported 1,700 active sites in the United States, and now many schools in the growing movement seek to provide a broader range of community-based services. In 2013, along with 75 state and district school administrators NASBHC supported a letter to the U.S. Congress asking for Congressional support of school-based health centers, and specifically requesting $50 million in fiscal year 2014 to support such efforts.

Is School Reform Enough?

Others, looking at the same history and outcomes of NCLB, come to a very different conclusion: that reforming schools simply doesn't work and is not enough to achieve the goals of NCLB. The contention is that schools, as they presently exist, are basically flawed and are beyond mere incremental improvements, changes, and modifications: we must *reinvent* schools as organizations so that they are transformed into schools that are very different from the schools we know today. Wagner & Kegan (2006) noted: "Our education system was never designed to deliver the kind of results we now need to equip students for today's world—and tomorrow's. The system was originally created for a very different world. To respond appropriately we need to rethink and redesign" (p. 1) to transform the schools.

What does it mean to transform the school? Well, here's one analogy: In the 1960s, IBM's Selectric typewriter was a dramatic technical improvement over the existing manual keystroke typewriter. But merely improving on the Selectric typewriter would never have created the IBM personal computer (PC). The PC is much more than a "reformed typewriter." It is a reinvention of what composing in print is all about (Wagner & Kegan, 2006).

The process of reinventing begins within the leader who creates, within him- or herself, a new vision of what the school should become in the near future and beyond. It could start by reconsidering a core set of values and beliefs that redefine the culture of the school. We are talking about the ways in which the professional practice of teaching is defined and described in schools—moving from one that is centered on teachers engaged in solo practice cloistered in their individual classrooms to teaching practice that is a collegial, collaborative professional enterprise.

> Education as a profession has historically promised a relative degree of autonomy, compared with other professions. Indeed, education organizations have been structured to preserve domains of autonomy and individual craft expertise. Many of our best teachers take great pride in the units of study they create and refine by themselves over time—be it a fourth-grade Native American unit, an advanced placement

biology class, or an innovative laptop computer program. These successes become personal—even, perhaps a source of identity—and it is understandably difficult for educators to open up their practice to scrutiny, share the fruits of their labors with colleagues, or seek constructive criticism from others. For this and other reasons, teachers rarely subscribe to a public, collective knowledge base of professional practice and norms, or engage in collaborative examination of teaching and learning practices. (Wagner & Kegan, 2006, p. 13)

This shift in organizational culture, alone, would be a major change in the right direction in any school.

Final Thoughts

One may choose from three basic strategies in planning and managing organizational change in schools:

1. *Empirical-rational strategies* are based on the concept that change can be fostered by systematically inventing or discovering better ideas and making them readily available in useful form to schools. Adherents of this strategy are often confounded by the difficulties usually encountered in the processes of installing new practices in the target schools. Typical difficulties are (1) ignoring the new ideas, (2) resisting or rejecting the new ideas, or (3) modifying the ideas or practices so that they have been significantly changed by the time they are put in practice.
2. *Power-coercive strategies* are based on the use (or potential use) of sanctions to compel the organization to change. The NCLB Act of 2001 is a compendium of power-coercive strategies complete with required timetables for action, requirements for reporting compliance, and various sanctions and rewards intended to coerce the schools to comply with the demands for prescribed improvement in performance on standardized tests.
3. *Normative-reeducative strategies* are based on the idea of bringing about change in schools by school organizations improving their problem-solving capabilities. This requires shifting the normative values of the school's culture (interaction-influence system) from those usually associated with hierarchical (bureaucratic, mechanistic, classical) organization to more creative, problem-solving norms. Techniques and processes for bringing about organizational self-renewal focus on developing and increasing the skills of the staff members of individual schools in studying and diagnosing their own organizational problems systematically and in working out solutions to them. The term *organization development* is widely applied to these techniques for increasing the self-renewal capacity of schools.

The critical importance of helping schools to develop their own capacity for self-renewal was not widely understood outside the field of organizational behavior until the failure of extensive applications of both empirical-rational and power-coercive strategies to achieve desired levels of success had produced widespread frustration and concern. By improving the organizational health of schools, it is possible to make schools more proactive than defensive and induce them to reach out responsively to adopt new ideas and implement the changing goals of society.

Schools are organizationally different from many other kinds of organizations, such as those in business, the military, and the nonprofit field. They possess special properties (not all necessarily unique) that may well affect the ways in which they should deal with issues of stability and change. For example, as far back as 1978, Fullan et al. told us about the special properties of schools, and these properties have not changed since.

1. *Their goals are diffuse,* usually stated in general, even abstract terms, with effectiveness measurement being difficult and uncertain.
2. *Their technical capability is low*, with a weak specific scientific base underlying educational practice.
3. *They are loosely coupled systems,* which gives rise to coordination problems: Activities are not always clearly connected to goals, and control (for example, accountability) is difficult to establish.
4. *Boundary management is difficult* inasmuch as "the skin of the organization seems overly thin, over-permeable to dissatisfied stakeholders" (Fullan et al., 1978, p. 2).
5. *Schools are "domesticated" organizations,* non-competitive, surviving in a relatively protected environment, and with little incentive for significant change.
6. *Schools are part of a constrained, decentralized system:* 15,000 school districts in the United States with well over 100,000 buildings, each nominally autonomous, yet with many national constraints (for example, standards for test achievement, national textbook market, accreditation and certification requirements, statutes and case law).
7. *Students are compelled to attend.*

In this organizational context, a legacy of study and practical experience that stretches back to the Western Electric Studies in the 1920s underscores the pragmatic necessity of developing and improving people-oriented change strategies in schools.

Reflective Activities

1. Reflect on a major change that has occurred in a school or organization with which you are familiar. Using Kurt Lewin's concept of force-field analysis, identify the driving forces and the restraining forces that were in play prior to and during the change process that helped unfreeze and drive the organization toward change.
2. In the example you chose for Reflective Activity 1, determine which of the three strategic orientations (empirical-rational, power-coercive, or normative-reeducative) was used to plan and manage the change process. Using the content in this chapter, provide specific examples of how the change process followed the particular orientation you identify. Was the process successful in bringing about change that resulted in a positive organizational climate? Why or why not?
3. Find a research article that investigates organizational characteristics and their effects on organizations. Write a short summary that identifies the purpose of the study, the variables being studied, the research methods used, and the findings of the study. Share this information with fellow students. As a class, list those organizational characteristics that have a positive impact.
4. With some fellow classmates, develop an action plan to implement the ideas of Michael Fullan to change your school district into one that focuses on resolute leadership, intelligent accountability, and individual and collective responsibility to achieve its moral purpose.

CRITICAL INCIDENT   The Man for the Job!

Superintendent Aaron Coleman could always count on Ricardo "Rick" Vazquez to fix troubled schools where student behaviors, including gang tensions, were a problem. Rick had saved Aaron from the ire of the school board three different times by going into difficult schools and taking a tough stance with student misbehavior. He took a no-nonsense approach that involved "laying down the law" with students and staff alike. Students were expected to follow the rules, and staff members were expected to uniformly enforce them so that the kids toed the line. Aaron knew very well that part of Rick's "secret" was that, until a few years ago, he had been a very popular and successful middleweight club fighter in the state's boxing circuit. While there had never been even a hint that Rick had, or would, ever lay hands on a kid, all the kids had learned his story from the older guys in the neighborhood, who looked up to him as a role model. And the kids admired the fact that Rick worked out every day and kept in great shape. He was something of a role model for them, too.

Rick strode briskly as usual into the superintendent's office, sure that Aaron was going to ask him to take over as principal of Madison High School. Lately, the grapevine had been rife with the news about how gang behavior, having been seen for the first time last school year, was getting out of hand at Madison. The clerk in the outer office waved him through with a friendly, smiling greeting.

As he approached the desk of Carley, the superintendent's *major domo*, she rose and extended her hand in a warm welcome and said, "Oh, Mr. Vazquez, go right in. He's ready for you. I'm sure he'll be off the phone in just a minute." Rick liked that: to be recognized, to be somebody, to be seen as a winner.

Rick entered the spacious corner office and dropped into a comfortable leather chair in front of the desk, and admired—as he always did—the expansive scene of the front lawn with the flag on the flagpole set against the backdrop of leafy green trees. Putting down the phone, Aaron greeted Rick warmly, "Hi, Rick, you're getting to be my turnaround specialist, y'know that? You have always been able to help me out of trouble spots and I need you this time at Madison High. The school board is down my throat about student achievement, SAT [Scholastic Aptitude Test] scores, attendance, and a lack of parental involvement. And, you know, the Board members are hearing too much about what they call 'gang trouble' there. In general, the place is a mess and I need it cleaned up."

Rick felt good about once again being picked to head a major change effort, this time to lead once-prestigious Madison High to a new and higher vision of excellence. He said, "I'm the man for the job, Aaron. You know you can count on me. This won't be easy. It will take time and extra resources to do the job right, but I'll turn that school around in a few years."

"That's the problem Rick. We don't have years. I need to be able to show the school board major progress at the end of this coming school year, and hopefully we can show them some progress toward our goals by the end of the first semester. As far as extra resources, I'll do what I can, but I can't be seen to show favoritism to you or Madison High, so don't count on much, if any at all. You need to get in there and make the changes necessary to solve these problems. Do what you have to with teacher assignments, but, for Pete's sake, be careful with the union issues. I don't want them all over me like the school board is."

Although a little hesitant about the timeframe and the lack of additional resources, Rick was honored by the superintendent's confidence in selecting him for this critical and tough assignment. Rick was a competitive guy, and he welcomed one more chance to be a winner. He agreed to take the principalship at Madison High.

1. Based on what you know about Rick Vazquez, how do you expect him to approach changes at Madison High School? Do you think his approach will produce sustainable change? Why?
2. What new and higher vision for the future do you think Rick has for Madison High? Do you personally embrace and share that vision?
3. What do you suggest Rick do to make effective changes at Madison and how do you suggest he work with the staff? In your response, cite specific concepts presented in this chapter.
4. How should Rick work with the superintendent?

Suggested Reading

Argyris, C. (1993). *Knowledge for action: A guide to overcoming barriers to organizational change.* San Francisco, CA: Jossey-Bass.

One of the most respected scholars of organizational change offers practical guidance for improving the abilities of organizational members to solve the human problems of working together. Invaluable for the educational leader who wants to improve collegial behavior and implement empowerment on the job.

Darling-Hammond, L. (1997). *A blueprint for creating schools that work.* San Francisco, CA: Jossey-Bass.

A distinguished scholar and observer of U.S. schooling, Darling-Hammond thinks that excessive bureaucratization and administrative red tape in the end leaves teachers little time for teaching. She rails against the "factory model" of the school that processes students instead of teaching them. This problem, she believes, accounts for the relatively poor showing of U.S. students against their contemporaries in other parts of the world. She advocates re-creating schools so that good teachers flourish, and change from the inside out is encouraged. Her data include numerous interviews with people on the firing line, and her emphasis is on learner-centered schools.

Dryfoos, J. G. (1994). *Full service schools: A revolution in health and social services for children, youth, and families.* San Francisco, CA: Jossey-Bass.

Recognizing that schools have become places where all children can learn, Dryfoos believes that community services must become responsive in working with schools in an organized way to help youngsters to learn and develop into responsible, productive adults. Traditional institutions that are primarily responsible for raising and educating children—families and schools—cannot go it alone any more: In many communities, they need help, and the first line of help is from community agencies. If you want to know where the cutting edge of schooling is, read this book.

Fullan, M. (2010). *All systems go: The change imperative for whole system reform*. Thousand Oaks, CA: Corwin.

Fullan presents his change model for whole-system reform based on successful efforts in the United States, Canada, and the United Kingdom. He shows how these states (none in the U.S.) and districts were able to develop *collective capacity*, a concept Fullan suggests is key to whole-system reform.

Hargreaves, A., & Fullan, M. (Eds.). (2009). *Change wars*. Bloomington, IN: The Solution Tree.

This book is a compendium of differing insights from 13 authorities active in the "change wars," as they refer to the current, ongoing international debate on change in schools. It starts out this way: "Anyone who tries to change something in this world, their colleagues, or themselves has a theory of how to bring about that change. This theory may be implicit or explicit, reflectively aware or blindly willful, but it is a theory of change-in-action that is driven by knowledge, experience, beliefs, and assumptions concerning how and why people change, and what can motivate or support them to do so" (p. 1). It then explains a number of practical aspects of change-in-action theory.

Kohn, A. (1999). *The schools our children deserve: Moving beyond traditional classrooms and "tougher standards."* Boston, MA: Houghton Mifflin.

Amazon.com puts it this way: "Teacher-turned-writer Alfie Kohn takes on traditional education giants like E. D. Hirsch, along with practically every state government raising the bar and toughening standards, in this attack on the back-to-basics movement. An established critic of America's fixation on grades and scores, Kohn has written a detailed, methodical treatise that accuses politicians and educators of replacing John Dewey, the father of public education, with test-tutoring king Stanley Kaplan." This book is a must for prospective educational leaders.

Senge, P. (1990). *The fifth discipline: The art and practice of the learning organization*. New York, NY: Doubleday & Company.

Senge observes that the industrial-age assembly line model for education has shaped our schools more than we can imagine—producing generations of "knowers," not lifelong learners, people beautifully prepared for a world that no longer exists. He describes the Comer School Development Program as a genuine pioneer in creating the learner-centered education that will be vital for our future. Drawing on fields from science to spirituality, Senge shows why it matters to have a learning organization. This book has been enormously popular and deserves the attention of all education leaders.

References

Acker-Hocevar, M. A., Ballenger, J., Place, A. W., & Ivory, G. (2012). *Snapshots of school leadership in the 21st century: Perils and promises of leading for social justice, school improvement, and democratic community (The UCEA Voices from the Field Project)*. Charlotte, NC: Information Age.

Argyris, C. (1964). *Integrating the individual and the organization*. New York, NY: John Wiley & Sons.

Bennis, W., Benne, K., & Chin, R. (1985). *The planning of change* (4th ed.). New York, NY: Holt, Rinehart and Winston.

Berman, P., & McLaughlin, M. W. (1978). *Federal programs supporting educational change, Vol. VIII: Implementing and sustaining innovations*. Santa Monica, CA: RAND Corporation.

Chin, R., & Benne, K. D. (1969). General strategies for effecting changes in human systems. In W. G. Bennis, K. D. Benne, & R. Chin (Eds.), *The Planning of Change* (2nd ed., pp. 13-59). New York, NY: Holt, Rinehart & Winston.

Clark, D. L., & Guba, E. G. (1967). An examination of potential change roles in education. In O. Sand (Ed.), *Rational planning in curriculum and instruction* (pp. 111–134). Washington, DC: National Education Association.

Clinchy, E. (1993, December). Magnet schools matter. *Education Week, 8*, 28.

Cuban, L. (1993). *How teachers taught: Constancy and change in American classrooms, 1980–1990*. New York, NY: Teachers College Press.

DeGues, A. (1997). *The living company.* Boston, MA: Harvard Business School Press.

Doran, H. C., & Fleischman, S. (2005). Challenges of value-added assessment. *Educational Leadership, 63*(3), 85–87.

Fullan, M. (2001). *Leading in a culture of change.* San Francisco, CA: Jossey-Bass.

Fullan, M. (2003). *Change forces with a vengeance.* New York, NY: RoutledgeFalmer.

Fullan, M. (2010a). *All systems go: The change imperative for whole system reform.* Thousand Oaks, CA: Corwin.

Fullan, M. (2010b). *Motion leadership: The skinny on becoming change savvy.* Thousand Oaks, CA: Corwin.

Fullan, M., Miles, M. B., & Taylor, G. (1978) *OD in schools: The state of the art* (4 vols.). Toronto, Ontario: Ontario Institute for Educational Studies.

Goodlad, J. I. (1975). *The dynamics of educational change: Toward responsive schools.* New York, NY: McGraw-Hill.

Grace, A. G., & Moe, G. A. (1938). *State aid and school costs.* New York, NY: McGraw-Hill.

Greenfield, T. B. (1973). Organizations as social inventions: Rethinking assumptions about change. *Journal of Applied Behavioral Science, 9*(5), 551–574.

Grissmer, D. (2002). Cost-effectiveness and cost-benefit analysis: The effect of targeting interventions. In H. M. Levin & P. J. McEwan (Eds.), *Cost effectiveness and educational policy.* American Education Finance Association.

Group on School Capacity for Problem Solving. (1975, June). *Program plan.* Washington, DC: National Institute of Education.

Hargreaves, A. (2009). The fourth way of change: Towards an age of inspiration and sustainability. In A. Hargreaves & M. Fullan (Eds.), *Change wars* (pp. 11–43). Bloomington, IN: Solution Tree.

Hersey, P., & Blanchard, K. H. (1977). *Management of organizational behavior: Utilizing human resources* (3rd ed.). Englewood Cliffs, NJ: Prentice Hall.

Institute of Education Sciences. (2013). *Full-day and half-day kindergarten in the United States: Findings from the early childhood longitudinal study, Kindergarten class of 1998–99.* National Center for Education Statistics. Retrieved from http://nces.ed.gov/pubsearch/pubsinfo .asp?pubid=2004078

Kew, K., Ivory, G., Muñiz, M., & Quiz, F. (2012). No child left behind as school reform. In M. A. Acker-Hocevar, J. Ballenger, A. W. Place, & G. Ivory (Eds.), *Snapshots of school leadership in the 21st century: Perils and promises of leading for social justice, school improvement, and democratic community (The UCEA Voices from the Field Project)* (pp. 13-30). Charlotte, NC: Information Age.

Lewin, K. (1947). Frontiers in group dynamics. *Human Relations, 1,* 5–41.

Lewin, K. (1951). *Field theory in social science.* New York, NY: Harper & Row.

Likert, R. (1961). *New patterns of management.* New York, NY: McGraw-Hill.

Lippitt, G. L. (1969). *Organizational renewal: Achieving viability in a changing world.* New York, NY: Appleton-Century-Crofts.

March, J. G. (1981). Footnotes to organizational change. *Administrative Science Quarterly, 26,* 563–577.

March, P. E. (1963). *The physical science study committee: A case history of nationwide curriculum development.* Unpublished doctoral dissertation, Harvard University, Cambridge, Massachusetts.

Miles, M. B. (1965). Planned change and organizational health: Figure and ground. In R. O. Carlson, A. Gallaher Jr., M. B. Miles, R. J. Pellegrin, & E. M. Rogers (Eds.), *Change processes in the public schools* (pp. 11-36). Eugene, OR: Center for the Advanced Study of Educational Administration, University of Oregon.

Miles, M. B. (1967). Some properties of schools as social institutions. In G. Watson (Ed.), *Change in school systems* (pp. 1-29). Washington, DC: National Training Laboratories, National Education Association.

Miles, M. B., & Lake, D. G. (1967). Self-renewal in school systems: A strategy for planned change. In G. Watson (Ed.), *Concepts for social change* (pp. 81–88). Washington, DC: National Training Laboratories, National Education Association.

Mort, P. R., & Cornell, F. G. (1941). *American schools in transition.* New York, NY: Teachers College, Columbia University.

Mort, P. R., & Ross, D. H. (1957). *Principles of school administration.* New York, NY: McGraw-Hill.

National Commission on Excellence in Education. (1983). *A nation at risk.* Washington, DC: Government Printing Office.

Nichols, S. L., & Berliner, D. C. (2007). *Collateral damage: How high-stakes testing corrupts America's schools.* Cambridge, MA: Harvard Education Press.

Plecki, M. L., & Catañeda, T. A. (2009). Whether and how money matters in K-12 education. In G. Sykes, B. Schneider, & D. N. Plank (Eds.), *Handbook of education policy research* (pp. 453–463). New York, NY: American Educational Research Association and Routledge.

Ravitch, D. (2010). *The death and life of the great American school system: How testing and choice are undermining education.* New York, NY: Basic Books.

Ravitch, D. (2013). *Reign of error: The hoax of the privatization movement and the danger to America's public schools.* New York, NY: Alfred A. Knopf.

Ross, D. H. (1958). *Administration for adaptability.* New York, NY: Metropolitan School Study Council.

Runkel, P. J., & Schmuck, R. A. (1974). *Findings from the research and development program on strategies of organizational change at CEPM-CASEA.* Eugene, OR: Center for the Advanced Study of Educational Administration, Center for Educational Policy and Management, University of Oregon.

Sarason, S. B. (1990). *The predictable failure of educational reform: Can we change before it's too late?* San Francisco, CA: Jossey-Bass.

Spillane, J. P., Gomez, L. M., & Mesler, L. (2009). Notes on reframing the role of organizations in policy implementation. In G. Sykes, B. Schneider, & D. N. Plank (Eds.), *Handbook of education policy research* (pp. 409–

425). New York, NY: American Educational Research Association and Routledge.

Swanson, A. D. (1967). The cost-quality relationship. In *The challenge of change in school finance,* Proceedings of the Tenth Annual Conference on School Finance (pp. 151–165). Washington, DC: Committee on Educational Finance, National Education Association.

Wagner, T., & Kegan, R. (Eds.). (2006). *Change leadership: A practical guide to transforming our schools.* San Francisco, CA: Jossey-Bass.

Zaltman, G., Florio, D. H., & Sikorski, L. A. (1977). *Dynamic educational change: Models, strategies, tactics, and management.* New York, NY: Free Press.

Leadership

Like two sides of the same coin, leadership and decision making are inseparable. Leadership cannot be a solo performance. By definition, as we shall see, the only way that leaders can exercise leadership is by working with and through other people, the followers. Thus, leadership is always an ensemble performance. The subject of this chapter, leadership theory, focuses on conceptualizing the range from which one may choose in deciding on a way to engage with others in exercising leadership. Contemporary leadership theory is not neutral in making this behavioral choice: It contends that some ways of working with followers are predictably more effective than others.

On the other side of the coin, decision-making theory focuses on the array of options from which one may choose to implement the leadership theory that has been selected. Decision-making theory is the subject of the next chapter; thus, these two chapters are closely interrelated.

ADAPTIVE LEADERSHIP

In today's fast-paced world dominated by change, the school, and particularly the school leader, must be sensitive to emerging changes in the external environment that call for nimble, deft, rapid responses by the organization. One of the key concepts of organizational theory is the role of change and stability in the environment of the organization in selecting a strategy for leadership.

Certainly, as the pressure to improve the performance of schools has gained momentum and ever-widening support, the need for effective leadership in school administration has been increasingly emphasized. But there are many different and often conflicting ways of thinking about and understanding the nature of leadership. One popular concept or theory of leadership is the time-honored top-down style, which is based on the belief that the best ideas are, or ought to be, found at the higher levels of the organization and are passed down to those at the lower levels, where they are implemented. This traditional understanding of leadership comes to us from the military traditions of ancient Rome, and it is currently exemplified in the No Child Left Behind (NCLB) Act.

Those who supported the enactment of this approach to school reform into federal law in 2001 confidently believed that they knew what had to be done in the schools and classrooms to improve the learning of students. Their beliefs are clearly spelled out in the law itself, which includes the required use of phonics in teaching reading, the regular use of standardized tests to monitor learning, the punishing sanctions to be levied against schools that fail to demonstrate improvement in student learning, and the insistence on using instructional methods that are supported by evidence of their effectiveness derived from "scientific research." Those who advocate this exercise of top-down power from Washington, unparalleled in the history of schooling in the United States, tend to describe it as an exercise in educational or political leadership.

Contemporary scholarly thought about leadership, however, is dominated by the recognition that change, complexity, and uncertainty are dominant characteristics of the environment to which organizations today must nimbly adapt. Margaret Wheatley (1999) popularized the term *chaos theory* in the study of educational organizations and leadership after she studied quantum physics and the science of living systems. Her ideas have introduced the need to find new and better ways to lead under the unstable and unpredictable conditions that confront organizations. Essentially, the leader in these circumstances is confronted with the need to deal with two very different kinds of problems:

- *Some problems are technical (discrete).* They are relatively clear-cut, if not simple, and can be solved by applying technical expertise; the outcome can be predicted with some confidence. Such problems normally can be solved by technically competent individuals and that fact might well favor the use of top-down methods of leadership.
- *Other problems are adaptive (emergent).* These problems, by definition, are so complex and involve so many poorly understood factors that the outcomes of any course of action are unpredictable (Heifetz, 1994). Common examples of adaptive problems include the reduction of crime, the reduction of poverty, and the implementation of educational reform. Solving these kinds of problems requires leadership methods that make the knowledge of many people at various levels in the organization accessible and that facilitate the involvement and cooperation of these people in leadership processes. Therefore, leadership in dealing with adaptive problems, as we shall explain more fully in this chapter, requires collaboration between and among many individuals over time in an iterative process. Heifetz and Linsky (2002) added that adaptive problems

  require experiments, new discoveries, and adjustments from numerous places in the organization or community. Without learning new ways—changing attitudes, value, and behaviors—people cannot make the adaptive leap necessary to thrive in the new environment. The sustainability of change depends on having the people with the problem internalizing the change itself. (p. 13)

In the next chapter, we discuss decision-making processes involving discrete (technical) and emergent (adaptive) problems. Many problems confronting schools today, particularly problems of school reform, are clearly adaptive problems and require adaptive leadership concepts and techniques that are discussed in this chapter. But first we need to review some fundamentals of leadership. The literature is replete with discussions about the dichotomy between leadership and management, so this is where we will begin.

LEADERSHIP AND MANAGEMENT

The rhetoric of reform contends that U.S. schools require leadership, not "mere management." This point suggests that there is a difference between management and leadership *and* that they are mutually exclusive. This view correctly derives from the fact that one manages things, not people, and one leads people, not things. We manage finances, inventories, and programs, for example, but we lead people. There is a qualitative difference between managing and leading and, some contend, they are mutually exclusive. Warren Bennis and Burt Nanus (1985), for example, have told us that "managers are people who do things right and leaders are people who do the right thing" (p. 15). Some blame much of our present dearth of educational leadership on the existence of a managerial mystique, long promoted by schools of business as well as schools of education, that taught managers to pay attention to structures, roles, and indirect forms of communications; to ignore the ideas and emotions of people; and to avoid direct involvement of others in leadership. The result has been a professionalization of management that deflected attention from the real business of schools, which is teaching, and conceptualized leadership as an emphasis on rules, plans, management controls, and operating procedures.

This mistake often manifests itself in the language of those who confuse schooling and teaching with "the delivery of educational services," and who do so with the cool detachment that a merchant might use to speak of the distribution of goods or the manager of a fast-food restaurant might use to describe the essence of serving food. Thus, in schools, we too often see

> an emphasis on doing things right, at the expense of doing the right things. In schools, improvement plans become substitutes for improvement outcomes. Scores on teacher-appraisal systems become substitutes for good teaching. Accumulation of credits in courses and inservice workshops become a substitute for changes in practice. Discipline plans become substitutes for student control. Leadership styles become substitutes for purpose and substance. Congeniality becomes a substitute for collegiality. Cooperation becomes a substitute for commitment. Compliance becomes a substitute for results. (Sergiovanni, 1992, p. 4)

There is little question that as the U.S. public school enterprise became markedly more bureaucratized in the decades from 1945 to 1985, emphasis was placed on the bureaucratic concept of leadership, which we now call management. There is also little question that this myopic focus needs to be corrected, that leadership is badly needed in educational institutions at all levels. But we must be cautious about substituting management-bashing for leadership.

Educational leaders must—as must all leaders—be able to manage. John Gardner (1989) rightly pointed out that leaders often must allocate resources, deal with budgets, and organize the enterprise to enable people to do the work necessary to move the organization toward its vision. He concluded, therefore, that leaders need to be skilled managers, able to deal with the mundane inner workings of organizational life that must be attended to if the vision is to be realized.

Schools are still largely organized and administered as bureaucracies or, as the contemporary pejorative expression has it, using the factory as a model. There is little question that most educational administrators conceptualize their work largely in terms of management of operational routines. Clearly, this emphasis has tended to thwart the development of instructional leadership in schools while emphasizing management. Therefore, U.S. schools are generally in need of more and better leadership. But it is false to argue that principals should be leaders, not managers, because they need to be both.

One of the most common criticisms of educational administrators in the literature on school reform is the charge that they tend to manipulate followers, often by using a veneer of seemingly participative involvement. By indirection, these administrators get followers to pursue ends that the administrators seek while seeming to act on the followers' intentions. Through this manipulation, those who are in power maintain their power, whereas followers are induced to believe that the arrangement is appropriate and legitimate, if not inevitable. Teachers, deeply socialized into the traditional ways of schools—having participated in them since they were

5 years old—generally accept the hierarchical power of principals and superintendents as a reality of life that is both inevitable and legitimate. It is commonplace for teachers who have had their views brushed aside to say to the principal, "Well, just tell me what you want me to do and I'll try my best to do it." This hierarchical power of organizational leaders is an important concept for administrators to understand, and we now turn our attention to the use of power in leadership.

POWER AND LEADERSHIP

There is a vast amount of research on leadership; the literature contains hundreds of definitions of leadership. However, there is general agreement on two factors:

1. Leadership is a group function: It occurs only when two or more people interact.
2. Leaders intentionally seek to influence the behavior of other people.

Thus, any concept of leadership deals with exercising influence on others through social interaction. To understand leadership, we must examine the nature and quality of the social interactions involved. The heart of the matter is power: What kind of power is involved, and how is it exercised?

One must understand that those who lead are necessarily powerful people because power is the basic energy for initiating and sustaining action that translates intention into reality when people try to work collaboratively (Bennis & Nanus, 1985). One cannot lead and be powerless. But the exercise of power is not necessarily oppression—indeed, it cannot be oppressive—in the exercise of leadership as it is being discussed here. Let us explain.

There are different kinds of power through which one may attempt to influence others, and they come from different sources. Understanding leadership requires one to understand the difference between the power of those who lead and the power of those who command. The two are frequently confused with one another. The difference between leadership and command lies in the sources from which power is derived.

Leadership Different from Command

Those who occupy official positions in the hierarchy of an organization exercise vested authority, which is the legitimate right to command. Vested authority rests on legal power that is customarily granted to official positions in the hierarchy such as dean, superintendent, or principal. Because the legal power of office is granted by those higher in the hierarchy, subordinates have no control over it and must yield to it, at least in theory. In practice, of course, such absolute power is rarely found in U.S. educational organizations. When absolute command is exercised, it is often viewed as oppression. Teachers' unions, for example, were created expressly to mediate and limit the arbitrary exercise of power of school boards and school district administrators over teachers; there is no doubt that they have generally been highly effective.

The power of leaders, on the other hand, is voluntarily granted by followers who accept the leader's influence and direction by shared agreement, no matter how informally the agreement is reached. Leaders do not wield legal power vested in an official office; rather, they exercise power that followers have willingly entrusted to them. Why do followers entrust power to leaders? Often, and perhaps at the highest level, because the followers are drawn to the ideas of the leader, because they share the values and beliefs of the leader, and because they are convinced that the leader can represent the followers well in the inevitable conflict with others for control of resources to achieve what the leader and the followers are bound in mutual commitment to achieve.

The key to understanding the difference between the power of officeholders and the power of leaders lies in who controls the power. Followers can, and often do, withdraw the support that they have voluntarily entrusted to the leader. They can also voluntarily increase their grant of support, which increases the power of the leader. The Rev. Dr. Martin Luther King, Jr., for example, is generally acknowledged as one of the great and powerful leaders of the twentieth century, yet he had little legal authority to make his followers do anything. Nevertheless, Dr. King had extraordinary power to influence the behavior of followers and ultimately the course of the nation.

What Dr. King did have was ideas, a set of values and beliefs, and a clear vision of a better, more just, more morally perfect future that embodied all of these ideas and values. It was the intense wish of his followers to share in achieving these goals that motivated them to empower him with their strong, active support. Thus, Dr. King was a very powerful man who could mobilize vast numbers of people for a common purpose and set in motion momentous events, yet he was no oppressor. He had learned much about leadership from studying Mohandas Gandhi, who was a master of the art. Gandhi's work stands as a monument to the effectiveness of leadership: He emerged victorious in 1947 from head-to-head confrontation with the determined oppression of seemingly invincible forces of entrenched colonialism.

Position power, such as that of a superintendent of schools or a school principal, provides the officeholder in the hierarchy with legal authority for at least the potential for forcible domination and coercion. This is not leadership; it is superordination. We must distinguish between the two:

> The source of superordination is *vested authority* [while] the source of leadership is *entrusted authority.* Authority is vested in a superordinate when power resides in the institution, and obedience is owed the superordinate by the subordinate in virtue of the role each occupies, roles the subordinate cannot alter.
>
> Authority is entrusted to a leader when power resides in the followers themselves, and cooperation is *granted* the leader by the follower . . . a judgment . . . the follower can alter. The superordinate may legitimately *compel* subordination; the leader can legitimately only *elicit* followership. The relationship between subordinate and superordinate is *compulsory,* between follower and leader *voluntary.* (Getzels, 1973, pp. 16–17)

Although they do exercise various kinds of power, *leaders engage with followers* in seeking to achieve not only the goals of the leader but also significant goals of the followers. Thus, "[l]eadership over human beings . . . is exercised when persons with certain purposes mobilize, in competition or in conflict with others, institutional, political, psychological and other resources so as to arouse and satisfy the motives of followers" (Burns, 1978, p. 18). This definition of leadership by James MacGregor Burns is as good a definition as we have at this time.

Power Defined

Power is commonly considered to be the capacity to influence others (Louis, 1986), and different kinds of power can be used to exercise that influence. The classic, generally accepted definition of power identifies five kinds, or sources, of power, as described by John French and Bertram Raven (1959):

- **Reward power.**   Controlling rewards that will induce others to comply with the power wielder's wishes
- **Coercive power.**   Having control of potentially punishing resources that will induce others to avoid them
- **Expert power.**   Having knowledge that others want for themselves so much that they will be induced to comply with the power wielder and thus acquire the knowledge or benefit from it
- **Legitimate power.**   Having authority conferred by holding a position in an organization that is recognized by others as having a legitimate right to obedience
- **Referent power.**   Personal charisma of the power holder, or ideas and beliefs so admired by others that they are induced by the opportunity to associate with the power holder *and*, as far as possible, to become more like him or her

The strength of the leader's power depends on the range of the sources of power drawn on. Leaders who draw on one source of power are inherently weaker than those who draw on multiple sources of power. Especially since the advent of teachers' unions and the broadening judicial interpretations of the constitutional rights of teachers, many school principals perceive that their power to lead has been undercut. The official power inherent in the office to coerce teachers into compliance has waned markedly. Although the power to control their compensation also waned in the 1980s and 1990s, with NCLB and Race to the Top (RTTT) mandates to use test scores in teacher evaluation, we are again seeing the power to control compensation increase. In general, however, the degradation of the coercive power of principals has *increased* the need for leadership. Strong school leaders still have access to significant sources of power:

- Many teachers find helping behavior from principals to be highly rewarding if it is nonjudgmental, supportive, collaborative, and caring in the tradition of self-development (McClelland, 1975). When they find such behavior by the principal rewarding enough, their support for the principal increases, and the principal's power to lead increases as a result.
- Teachers continue to recognize the authority of official positions in the organization because they value the organization. They largely defer to the legitimate power of those occupying official positions in the hierarchy of the organization.
- Teachers generally resent and reject principals who pose as pedagogical experts by demanding that lesson plans be submitted for prior approval and principals who conduct critiques of observed teaching in the paternalistic, judgmental manner that they may think appropriate for technical experts. However, teachers view favorably support from principals for fresh ideas. Teachers tend to recognize and see as powerful those principals who are expert in using collaborative, collegial methods of working together to identify and solve mutual problems. Such methods are personally rewarding to teachers at the higher levels of Maslow's concept of motivation (see Chapter 5) and facilitate continuing personal self-growth.
- Principals who have fresh, exciting ideas—who have a vision of the future—that others embrace and want to share are building referent power. Teachers tend to admire principals who express their vision coherently and vividly; who inspire enthusiasm; who involve others in dialogue intended to mold and develop the ideas; and who cause them to see a connection between the vision and their own desire to achieve something meaningful, to be part of a new and better future that is unfolding. This is an important source of power for principals who would be leaders.

These two kinds of power—position power and the authority voluntarily granted to leaders by followers—are not necessarily mutually exclusive. A university dean may have considerable legal clout in decisions regarding reappointment and tenure yet at the same time have power that comes from strong support of a leader by the faculty. The litmus test is who controls the grant of power: A dean who loses the support of the faculty will also have lost considerable power to influence followers and get things done even though his or her official position remains undiminished. Presidents of the United States combine the official power of office with the power from supporters who willingly accord them great power. For example, the collapse of Richard Nixon's presidency after Watergate had little to do with the official legal power of the office of the president; without the support of followers, his position in office was untenable.

TWO-FACTOR LEADERSHIP THEORY ABANDONED

Most of the formalistic theorizing that dominated the study of educational leadership in the 1960s to the 1990s has been largely abandoned. Instead, the seminal insights of Burns, which we have been discussing, gave rise to a new understanding of leadership and have gained ascendancy. The approach prior to Burns's work, which was studied by many present-day educational administrators, generally defined the behavior of leaders in two dimensions:

- One dimension was the emphasis that the leader gives to getting the job done. This was often called *initiating structure* because it often involves structuring the work: delineating the relationship between the leader and the members of the work group; specifying the tasks to be performed; and endeavoring to establish well-defined patterns of organization, channels of communication, methods of procedure, scheduling, and designating responsibilities. It was also often called *production emphasis* or *task emphasis,* for obvious reasons.
- The other dimension was the emphasis that the leader gives to developing friendship, mutual trust, respect, and warmth in relationships between the leader and followers. These behaviors were usually labeled *consideration* or *concern for people* (Halpin, 1966).

Bernard Bass spoke of leaders as tending to be either "follower focused" (i.e., emphasizing concern for people) or "task focused" (i.e., emphasizing rules and procedures for getting the task done):

> A task-focused leader initiates structure, provides the information, determines what is to be done, issues the rules, promises rewards for compliance, and threatens punishments for disobedience. The follower-focused leader solicits advice, opinions, and information from followers and checks decisions or shares decision making with followers. The . . . task-focused leader uses his or her power to obtain compliance with what the leader has decided. The follower-focused leader uses his or her power to set the constraints within which followers are encouraged to join in deciding what is to be done. (Bass, 1981)

This two-dimensional theory held that leadership consists of a mix of these two kinds of behavior and that effectiveness as a leader depends on choosing the right blend in various kinds of situations. The general tendency is for individuals to favor one of these behavioral orientations while placing less emphasis on the other. It would be almost impossible, in U.S. schools at least, for a leader to lack completely both of the two behavioral dimensions of leadership. Students of leadership who wish to denigrate this concept of leader behavior, which has fallen into disrepute in academic circles, often achieve their purposes by reporting that they do not find leaders who are *always* task-oriented or *always* people-oriented.

In the two-dimensional approach to understanding leadership, great emphasis was given to leadership style. For example, one commonly hears complaints that educational leaders in the past emphasized the task, or managerial, dimension of leader behavior—which is often called the *autocratic leadership style*—and few emphasized the consideration dimension—which defines the democratic style of leadership. Thus, individual styles of various leaders were described as tending to be autocratic or democratic, task-oriented or people-oriented, directive or collegial, and one could adopt a leadership style thought to be appropriate to the leader's personality, on the one hand, or the situation in which the leader works, on the other. All of this emanated from efforts to reduce the study of leadership to a science, and therein lay its weakness. In education today, recognition is rapidly growing that leadership cannot be reduced to formulas and prescriptions but must be attuned to the human variables and confusions that normally abound in busy, complex, and contradictory—that is, messy—human organizations.

For readers who want to learn more about some of the most popular two-factor theories of leadership, we suggest the following theories and the primary authors associated with each theory:

- The Ohio State Leadership Studies and the Leader Behavior Description Questionnaire (LBDQ) (Hemphill & Coons, 1957; Stogdill, 1974)
- The Managerial Grid (Blake & Mouton, 1978)
- Situational leadership theory (Hersey, Blanchard, & Johnson, 1996)
- Contingency leadership theory (Fiedler, 1967)

For a thorough description of these and other leadership theories, we recommend Peter Northouse (2010). Northouse's book is about as complete a listing of leadership theories as you can find, and it includes cases and questionnaires for each major theory.

LEADERSHIP AS A RELATIONSHIP WITH FOLLOWERS

Whenever we try to lead people, we become part of their environment and therefore part of their equation for organizational behavior, $B = f(p \cdot e)$. Thus, leaders are not merely concerned with the leadership style and techniques that they intend to use but also with the quality and kinds of relationships that they have with followers. Leadership is not something that one does to people, nor is it a manner of behaving toward people; it is working with and through other people to achieve organizational goals.

What distinguishes leaders from other authority figures is the unique relationship between leaders and followers. Leaders relate to followers in ways that

- Motivate them to unite with others in sharing a vision of where the organization should be going and how to get it there.
- Arouse their personal commitment to the effort to envision a better future and then create it.
- Organize the working environment so that the envisioned goals become central values in the organization.
- Facilitate the work that followers need to do to transform the vision into reality.

How do leaders accomplish these tasks? That depends, first, on what they think leadership is, which is defined in terms of the character and quality of the relationship between leader and follower. This rapport arises from the bedrock assumptions that the would-be leader holds about people and the world in which they work, the world from which all our cultural beliefs and values arise.

Using Douglas McGregor's concepts, one who accepts Theory X assumptions about followers tends to think about leadership pretty much as the stereotype of the traditional boss overseeing a gang in the field or on the shop floor: issuing orders, checking up, and prodding to keep things moving. One who accepts Theory Y assumptions about people at work tends to think about leadership more in terms of collaborating with others to reach organizational goals and achieve the organization's mission, sharing enthusiasm for the work to be done, providing help in solving problems, and supporting and encouraging. In the United States today, people working in education who subscribe to Theory X assumptions commonly mask them behind the kind of Theory X soft behavior, which was discussed in Chapter 1, so they can avoid appearing insensitive and undemocratic. Theory X soft behavior by the leader poses some serious moral and ethical problems, which we will discuss later in this chapter.

The key to understanding leadership, then, lies in understanding your own concept of the human nature of followers and how leaders relate to them. For example, Niccolo Machiavelli's assumptions about human nature were set forth in his advice to a young man of the ruling class in the fifteenth century. Machiavelli's treatise, *The Prince,* once was required reading for students in educational administration and is still widely admired today. It taught that the exercise of leadership by those who inherit positions of power as a privilege of membership in a dominant elite social class required the ruthless exercise of position power, the use of guile and deception when expedient to achieve the leader's personal agenda, and indifference to the concerns of others.

This Machiavellian view of leadership is still very prevalent although it usually is expressed obliquely in cautious terms and is usually disguised in Theory X soft behavior to appear reasonably adapted to the democratic demands of our time. The central idea is that leadership consists largely of commanding and controlling other people. Consider, for example, this observation intended for a mass audience of readers from the management ranks of corporations:

> A leader is a leader only insofar as he [*sic*] has followers. If we want our subordinates to do something and they do not do it, then, plainly, they have not followed our lead. Likewise, if we want our charges to accomplish something, quite apart from how they go about it, and they do not accomplish it, then, again they have not followed our lead. Now these are the only two ways that we can be leaders: we can want certain *actions* and we can want certain *results. The degree in which we get what we want is the measure of our leadership.*
>
> A follower is a follower only insofar as he [*sic*] does what a leader wants in order to please the leader . . . we are all social creatures, and so we want to please the boss . . . Work is done for the boss. We grow for our parents, learn for our teacher, win for our coach. Even the most independent of us presents his [*sic*] work as a gift for the boss. (Keirsey & Bates, 1984, p. 129)

This statement says a great deal about the writers' assumptions about the human nature of followers and how leaders relate to them. On the other hand, consider this statement of assumptions about leadership from a modern military perspective by General H. Norman Schwarzkopf (as cited in Galloway, 1991):

When you lead in battle you are leading people, human beings. I have seen competent leaders who stood in front of a platoon and all they saw was a platoon. But great leaders stand in front of a platoon and see it as 44 individuals, each of whom has hopes, each of whom has aspirations, each of whom wants to live, each of whom wants to do good. (p. 36)

This quote expresses a very different view of human nature than was embodied in Max Weber's now classic work on bureaucracy. Weber's work first appeared in the early years of the twentieth century and became known in the United States only after World War II when translations from the German were published in English. We discuss Weber's views in the following section.

Your Understanding of Human Nature Is Critical

At the turn of the twentieth century, the emergence of giant industrial corporations was transforming society in Europe. Max Weber saw that the old aristocracies could not provide the new kinds of leadership required in the expanding government, business, and industrial organizations of the day. To replace the absolute power inherited by privileged social classes, which was enjoyed by members of the German Junkers of Weber's day and *The Prince* of Machiavelli's day, and to reject the exercise of traditional autocratic rule in modern industrial, commercial, and government organizations that were then emerging around the world, Weber supported the rise of a disciplined and orderly organization composed of offices arranged hierarchically, with legally assigned power and authority descending from the top to the bottom. As discussed in Chapter 3, Weber approvingly gave this kind of organization a name: bureaucracy.

In contrast to autocratic rule, the "law" of the bureaucratic organization lies in its written rules and regulations, official standard operating procedures, written memos, chain of command, and acceptance of the concepts of hierarchical superordination and subordination. It is a vision of organization that is rational, logical, impersonal, formal, predictable, and systematic, and it reflects beliefs about the nature and needs of the human beings who populate the organization. Bureaucratic theory generally holds that people tend to be motivated by the lower levels of Maslow's hierarchy of needs (Chapter 5) with emphasis on pay and benefits, job security, and advancement in rank.

Weber's work has had enormous influence in establishing and maintaining bureaucracy as the most pervasive and credible organizational concept in the world. Yet few who are taught the virtues of bureaucratic organization in their universities understand or even know that it was the same Max Weber, sociologist and theologian, who also wrote powerfully on the Protestant work ethic as a defining characteristic of human nature. Weber was convinced, and convinced many other people at the time, that Protestantism was undergirded by certain fundamental moral and ethical imperatives that were played out in the world of work, the so-called Protestant work ethic, in ways that were superior to those of non-Protestant cultures. Thus, in reality, Weber viewed bureaucracy as embodying and codifying in the world of work certain views of human nature that he believed were inherent in Protestant theology. The two were, in his mind, closely linked.

Let us return to the concept of organizational behavior in which $B = f(p \cdot e)$. In exercising leadership, the leader has an array of options from which to choose in influencing the nature and quality of the organizational environment with which members interact in the course of their daily work. How one chooses depends on one's understanding of what kinds of behaviors are desirable and sought, on the one hand, and how they are likely to be elicited in the organization's environment, on the other. If, for example, you think that Machiavelli understood the realities of modern educational organizations, then his advice on leadership will be appealing and appear practical. If, on the other hand, you think that schools are best understood as bureaucracies, then you will do your best to create a bureaucratic environment for people to work in.

However, if you think of people in Theory Y terms, then you will try to create the organizational environment likely to elicit and support the high motivation and high levels of effort that they will find satisfying in their work. Such an environment is growth-enhancing and engages the members of the organization in personal growth and development as well as in organizational growth and development—that is, a healthy state of increasing ability to identify and solve its own problems in an ever-changing world. An important part of such an organizational environment is the type of leadership that James MacGregor Burns described as transforming (Burns's original term, later called *transformational* or *transformative*).

TRANSFORMATIONAL LEADERSHIP

The idea of transforming, or transformational, leadership was conceptualized by James MacGregor Burns (1978) and has directly influenced the thinking of scholars ever since. Burns's insights were later developed and elaborated by Bernard Bass (1985). They have subsequently been used as the basis of research, such as that of Warren Bennis and Burt Nanus (1985), Rosabeth Moss Kanter (1983), and Judy B. Rosener (1990), each of whom studied corporate leaders, while Thomas Sergiovanni (1992) used the ideas of transformational leadership to organize a critique of school reform.

Transformational Leadership Compared and Contrasted with Transactional Leadership

The heart of Burns's analysis was to compare and contrast traditional transactional leadership with the newer idea of transforming leadership. Having explained that leadership is different from simply wielding power over people, Burns went on to explain that there are two basic types of leadership. In the most commonly used type of leadership, the relationship between leader and followers is based on quid pro quo transactions between them. Transactional educational leaders can and do offer jobs, security, tenure, favorable ratings, and more in exchange for the support, cooperation, and compliance of followers.

In contrast, "the transformational leader looks for potential motives in followers, seeks to satisfy higher needs, and engages the full person of the follower. The result of transforming leadership is a relationship of mutual stimulation and elevation that converts followers into leaders and may convert leaders into moral agents" (Burns, 1978, p. 4). This evokes a third, and higher level of leadership—the concept of moral leadership that began to receive so much attention in education in the 1990s.

Moral Leadership

The concept of moral leadership comprises three related ideas:

- First, the relationship between the leader and those who are led is not one merely of power but is a genuine sharing of mutual needs, aspirations, and values. The genuineness of this sharing is tested by whether the participation of followers is a matter of choice that is controlled by the followers.

- Second, the followers have latitude in responding to the initiatives of leaders: They have the ability to make informed choices about who they will follow and why. As we shall explain more fully, the concept of transforming leadership means that followers voluntarily involve themselves in the leadership process. Among other things, followers voluntarily grant power and authority to leaders and are free to withdraw that grant. Therefore, in the highest level of transforming leadership, which is moral leadership, the followers must have access to alternative leaders from whom to choose, and they must have knowledge of alternative plans and programs they can embrace.
- Third, leaders take responsibility for delivering on the commitments and representations made to followers in negotiating the compact between leader and followers: "Thus, moral leadership is not mere preaching, or the uttering of pieties, or the insistence on social conformity. Moral leadership emerges from, and always returns to, the fundamental wants and needs, aspirations, and values of followers" (Burns, 1978, p. 4). In this sense, moral leadership is very different from the thin veneer of participation that administrators frequently use to give their relationships with followers some patina of genuine involvement while control remains firmly in the administrators' hands.

A Progression

A progression is clearly inherent in the concept of transforming leadership:

- At the lowest level of functioning is the exercise of power to exact the compliance of followers, which is not leadership at all.
- At the entry level of leadership is transactional leadership, wherein the leader and followers bargain with each other to establish a "contract" for working together.
- At a higher level of functioning is transforming leadership, in which the leaders and followers mutually engage in common cause, joined by their shared aspirations and values.
- At the highest level is moral leadership, which demands motivating emotional stimuli, such as a shared mission, a sense of mutual purpose, and a covenant of shared values interwoven with the daily life and practices of ordinary people to inspire new and higher levels of commitment and involvement.

A Process of Growth and Development Through Instructional Leadership

The levels in this progression in transforming leadership increasingly draw on the higher levels of the motivations of followers and, in return, offer increasing opportunities for followers and leaders to grow and develop increasing capacities for effective organizational behavior. Thus, transforming leaders engage the aspirations of followers, tap their motivations, energize their mental and emotional resources, and involve them enthusiastically in the work to be done. This kind of leadership does not merely obtain the compliance of followers; it evokes their personal commitment as they embrace the goals to be achieved as their own, seeing them as an opportunity for a willing investment of their effort. It transforms the roles of both followers and leaders, so they become nearly interdependent; their aspirations, motives, and values merged in mutual commitment to achieve the shared goals. Burns's focus was political leadership, not educational leadership, and he used Gandhi as one well-known exemplar of both transforming and moral leadership. One also thinks of the leadership of Martin Luther King, Jr. But such leadership is not limited to those who appear larger than life on the world stage. Many coaches, in various sports ranging from football to tennis, illustrate effective leadership in their work. Indeed, the metaphor of the coach is popular in speaking of leadership in many kinds of organizations. Many who have followed Burns's scholarly lead have described how readily his concepts of transforming leadership apply to realms other than politics, such as education and business. Increasingly, one finds literature that describes the behavior of people in high-performing schools as being consistent with transformational leadership.

We know that members of educational organizations thrive on the experience of being part of an organization that is constantly growing in its capacity to detect and solve its own problems. A school having such characteristics is seen by teachers as a successful and effective place in which to work. For example, a substantial body of research, such as Dan Lortie's classic *Schoolteacher* (Lortie, 1975), tells us that teachers are highly motivated by feeling successful and effective in their teaching. The more recent body of work by Linda Darling-Hammond (2006; Darling-Hammond & Bransford, 2007; Darling-Hammond & Richardson, 2009) tells us that teachers are successful when they are provided with the necessary resources, such as extensive professional development; and school structures, such as professional learning communities and common planning times. Darling-Hammond also supports National Board Certification by the National Board for Professional Teaching Standards (NBPTS) (Sato, Chung Wei, & Darling-Hammond, 2008), a process that emphasizes a commitment to students and their learning, knowledge in the use of assessment practices, teachers being active members of learning communities in their school, and teachers participating in sustained professional development.

From such studies of teaching and learning, one can conclude that an educational leader in a school might seek to foster a culture that facilitates teaching and enhances the likelihood that one will be successful at it, that energizes and applauds the efforts of teachers, that rewards and supports success in teaching, and that celebrates teaching as a central value in the life of the school. This is the result of instructional leadership at its finest. Such a school is likely to have a history that stresses the importance of teaching, heroes who epitomize achievement in teaching, and rituals and ceremonies that celebrate teaching and the successes of teachers. These are likely to be prominent characteristics of the school that are emphasized daily at all levels of the organization. Thus, one can exercise leadership by working with and through teachers to transform the culture of the school and, in the process, transform the very ways in which the leader and the teachers relate to one another. It is widely believed that the vehicle for bringing about such a transformation is a vision of the future that is better, more desirable, more compelling, and more personally fulfilling than the reality of the present.

IMPLEMENTING TRANFORMATIONAL AND MORAL LEADERSHIP

Educational leaders need to be aware of several important concepts when implementing their theory of practice in educational organizations. These concepts should be helpful in providing practical applications of transformational and moral leadership. These concepts are distributed leadership, professional learning communities, parent involvement, and sustainable leadership. We then end this chapter with a discussion of the study of leadership by Marzano, Waters, and McNulty (2005) that has received wide acceptance in providing direction to educational leaders.

Distributed Leadership

Most organizations to some degree empower members to make decisions. For example, they may have committees that function for a particular purpose, and they are given some level of decision-making authority. In a traditional hierarchical organization, this authority level is minimal. They may have "recommending" authority only, and the official leaders make the decision. The term *distributed leadership* is used to describe the type of leadership that is used in organizations that purposefully empower teams and individuals to make important decisions. Distributed leadership is defined or used in various ways by researchers, but we like the following definition by Spillane and Diamond (2007) to describe the distributed leadership perspective:

> Leadership refers to activities tied to the core work of the organization that are designed by organizational members to influence the motivation, knowledge, affect, or practices of other organizational members. (p. 4)

This definition does not tie leadership to specific individuals in formal leadership positions, such as a school principal. The distributed leadership perspective is a framework for studying leadership and management behaviors and interactions that are "tied to the core work," which in schools is teaching and learning, and the activities are understood from the context of the leaders, the followers, and the situation in which they occur. A key component of this definition is that leadership is "designed by organizational members:" That is, these activities are purposeful and developed by many, not only by the designated leader, and there is broad-based participation of teams and individuals that is not just simple delegation.

Professional Learning Communities

From a practical standpoint, we believe it is best to implement distributive leadership by using the concept of a professional learning community (PLC). Peter Senge (1990) popularized the notion of a learning organization in his book *The Fifth Discipline: The Art and Practice of the Learning Organization*. Senge focused on organizations as systems in which leaders seek to bring people together to collaborate on ways to achieve the organization's goals. Implementation of his five disciplines—personal mastery, mental models, shared vision, team learning, and systems thinking—is the bedrock of a learning community. These concepts have been described for applications in schools most notably by Richard DuFour and Robert Eaker (1998). Professional learning communities are a means to distribute leadership throughout the school and they have the following characteristics

1. Shared mission, vision, and values
2. Collective inquiry
3. Collaborative teams
4. Action orientation and experimentation
5. Continuous improvement
6. Results orientation

Using these characteristics as a guide, all organizational members together develop or revise the mission, vision, and values of the school that results in a collective commitment to its principles and future direction. Then, individual PLCs are formed around common interests to promote the vision and mission. In schools, these common interests may be grade-level teams, cross-departmental teams to work on interdisciplinary curriculum, subject area teams, and so forth. The PLCs work collaboratively to ask questions about what they are doing, where they are going, and how they will get there. Members of PLCs learn together and build the capacity of the school. They question, experiment, collect data, and use results to continually improve the teaching and learning processes that will implement their mission and lead them toward their vision.

So how are schools transformed into PLCs? DuFour and Eaker (1998) tell us that transformation can be achieved through a focus on "the three Cs of sustaining an improvement initiative—communication, collaboration, and culture" (p. 106).

Communication involves the use of many different forms of media and behaviors that inform constituents about the following:

- *What do we plan for?* Focuses attention on current goals and activities.
- *What do we monitor?* Identifies what will be monitored and how data will be collected, and shares data with everyone.
- *What questions do we ask?* These are the tough questions that focus on the mission and vision, such as the following: Are we working on the important learning processes that help students achieve?
- *What do we model?* Everyone models what is important, e.g., the principal actively engages in collaborative teamwork.
- *How do we allocate our time?* Time is set aside for the important aspects of a PLC, such as time to collaborate.
- *What do we celebrate?* Celebrations broadcast what is valued.
- *What are we willing to confront?* Everyone must be willing to confront those who behave in ways that undermine the mission and vision of the school.

Collaboration, the second C, is deliberative. The school's formal leaders must provide opportunities for groups to work together by building time into the school day. Providing collaborative opportunities is perhaps not the most difficult aspect of developing PLCs, but it is the most important. Without collaboration, teachers are isolated in their classrooms, and interaction opportunities occur only in the teachers' lounge or workroom. Collaborative teams, as indicated above, can be formed according to grade levels or subject areas, on the basis of students who are taught by a group of teachers, by areas of schoolwide emphases, or by areas of professional development.

The third C, *culture*, is a focus on the values, beliefs, traditions, and norms of the school. Four strategies for affecting and shaping school culture include the following:

1. Articulating, modeling, promoting, and protecting the shared values that have been identified
2. Systematically engaging staff in reflective dialogue that asks them to search for discrepancies between the values they have endorsed and the day-to-day operation of the school
3. Inundating staff with stories that reflect the culture at work
4. Celebrating examples of shared values and progress in the improvement process with ceremonies and rituals (DuFour & Eaker, 1998, p. 148)

Parent Involvement

One of the values that should be part of any school is the importance of parents or guardians in the involvement of their children's education. Parents should be partners with the school and with their children in the educational experience. Researchers have shown that parent involvement is important in improving their children's achievement. Parents can help motivate their children and help reinforce at home what is important in school. No matter what educational level parents have attained, they can be an important part of the process. Two meta-analyses of 104 research studies on parent involvement confirm the importance of parent involvement. One study of parent involvement at the secondary school level found that family involvement related with higher student achievement across both the general population and minority students (Jeynes, 2007). In another meta-analysis, elementary and middle schools students whose parents were involved in their education

> earn higher grades and test scores and enroll in higher level programs, are more likely to be promoted, pass, earn credits, . . . attend school, have better social skills, demonstrate improved behaviors, graduate and pursue post secondary education. (Henderson & Mapp, 2002, p. 7)

These positive results were consistent across all demographic subgroups.

It is clear that parent involvement in schools, including PLCs, is critical, so how should parents be involved? That is, what is meant by parent involvement? One of the national leaders in the movement to involve parents in schools is Joyce Epstein. Her model for parent involvement has six components; we have provided one implementation example for each area:

1. Parents as providers of the child's basic needs. Provide parent education classes or encourage parents to complete their general education diploma (GED).
2. Communication between the school and the home. Conference with parents when report cards are distributed.
3. Parents as volunteers at the school. Establish school and classroom volunteer programs.
4. Parents as instructors in the home. Inform parents of homework policies and encourage parents to ask children about their homework.
5. Parents involved in school governance. Actively recruit a cross section of parents to serve on the Parent-Teachers' Association (PTA) and to PLC decision-making school teams.
6. Parents working in collaboration with the entire community. Provide parents with information on community resources and services that are available to them, such as health services, social services, recreation, and others. (Epstein, Sanders, Simon, Salinas, Jansorn, & Van Voorhis, 2002)

DuFour and Eaker (1998), in their work on PLCs, emphasized promoting and supporting parenting skills and ensuring that parents are involved in decisions that affect their children. The process of involving parents is not an easy task. Michael Fullan (2005) found in his work with schools that developing ways to involve parents was one of the most difficult problems to solve. But it is worth the effort because once parents are involved in their children's education in meaningful ways, the PLC process is complete. The question then becomes the following: After schools have developed successful PLCs that distribute leadership, involve parents, and begin the improvement process, how do they sustain this process over time?

Utilizing Effective School Research Through Professional Learning Communities

Jim Gasparino, Principal,
Pelican Marsh Elementary School, Naples Florida

Changing demographics in schools, such as a wider variation in socioeconomic status of students or increases in the level of ethnic diversity, are often associated with declining school performance. Pelican Marsh Elementary School faced such changes when we became a Title I choice school allowing students from Title I schools, deemed to be "failing" by the state accountability system, to attend our school. With the arrival of this new group of students, as well as changes of attendance zones, our school faced significant increases in the number of free and reduced lunch students and minority students within the span of a couple of years. We were worried about our student achievement test scores.

In our situation, standardized test scores actually improved as our free and reduced lunch population and diversity rose significantly from about 8% to 33%. Our school had been an A school every year and had consistently scored among the top performing elementary schools in the district and state. So, being faced with this challenge, I had to find a way to bring about changes within the school to meet these new external challenges successfully. It was equally important to recognize that some values and beliefs must never change, such as establishing and maintaining high expectations and believing that all children are capable of meeting those expectations. What did need to change was how we helped our students meet those expectations.

Principals cannot mandate change from their offices, and if they do, they potentially face reluctant teachers. School leaders must be able to develop and communicate their vision of the school so that others may grow to share that vision. With our new student population, we could only work collaboratively—teachers and community—to recognize that our reality had changed and to examine new ways to meet the new reality. There were no new mandates, directives, or programs at our school. What did occur was discussion, examination, and shared professional learning. We did come to recognize that we had to meet our challenges on two fronts—examining both our school culture and instructional strategies, which could only be accomplished successfully through promoting a sense of collective responsibility.

In a culture that seeks to promote collective responsibility, it must follow that if one teacher has a problem, all do. School leaders can only promote collaboration through modeling it and enabling teachers to experience it. We recognized that teaching can be an isolated profession with limited opportunities for consultation among peers. We also recognized our collective knowledge was greater than any one educator's abilities. However, there was no structure, and little time, to work together.

Professional learning communities or PLCs, based on the work of Richard DuFour, presented an opportunity for teachers to support one another and work together to improve student learning. After an initial introduction, a cadre of teachers, our informal leaders, attended training on PLCs with the principal. It was considered critical that as many teachers as possible receive the same training. We also shared the responsibility of training our colleagues. In addition to the train-the-trainer approach, grade-level teams modeled PLC meetings for other teams as well.

PLCs have provided our teachers with the means to promote and implement focused grade-level planning based on the analysis of student performance data and to develop a better understanding of the state standards and benchmarks. The PLCs at Pelican Marsh Elementary represent an interdependent team effort to maintain high expectations for all learners and ensure academic achievement and growth. This team concept is met through collaboration and shared responsibilities, and each team has a learning community facilitator, a team leader, and assigned roles for each team member based on teacher strengths. Each team develops protocols and norms (see example below) to guide their work. Additionally, a member of the administration/leadership team is assigned to each PLC.

The school leadership must recognize their responsibility to provide the learning community with the necessary resources to be effective. To this end, each grade level has a shared, common planning time. Classroom teachers are given a duty-free schedule. Administrators and non-instructional support staff also provide coverage for teachers during assemblies, giving them additional planning time.

We view PLCs as a means to provide the structure necessary for collaborative planning, analysis of student performance, unpacking standards and benchmarks, and promoting conversations about teaching and learning among teachers. This process is accomplished in a cyclical process of assessment, data analysis, examining the standards, changing instruction as needed, and then back to assessment. Teams use the information they gain to help compare strengths and weaknesses across the grade level and discuss instructional strategies, drawing on their collective expertise rather than sitting alone in a classroom.

It is also critical for the school leader to celebrate the work and success of the students and teachers. Recognizing the efforts of all members of the school family serves to sustain a positive, collaborative school culture. PLCs helped us achieve continued success.

Example Norms: 5th Grade PLC Team—Norms

Be on time (9:15 am) and try not to schedule any other meetings during PLC time. If you are going to miss a meeting please let PLC facilitator (Segal) & assigned administrator (Laurie) know

- Stay engaged and be an involved member
- Stay on topic
- Come prepared: bring binder every week, if there is a spreadsheet due please have it filled out in advance
- Don't take the data personally
- Let the team know if you would like to be put on the agenda
- Last Thursday of every month is MTSS (math or writing)
- Roles: Kristin-secretary, Marlana-task master, Julie-co-facilitator, Sharon-production, and Laurie-public relations

Example Protocol

Standards Focused Planning

TEAM MEMBERS PRESENT (X or √ after name)

Guests:_____

School: <u>Pelican Marsh Elementary</u>   Date:_____   PLC Facilitator: ____   Team/Grade: <u>Grade</u>

Leadership Member Present: _____

A. Getting To Know Your Standards
  Strand/Body of Knowledge:
  Standard/Big Idea:
  Benchmark:

What do students need to do to demonstrate mastery of the standard?
Prerequisite Skills/General Knowledge:
Critical Thinking Skills/Real World Application:

B. **Show Your Knowledge of the Standards** (*Cut and paste work product here once created.*)
Diagnostic Rubric for Assignment:
Blue/Exemplary:
Green/Meeting:
Yellow/Review:
Red/Major Intervention:

C. **Analyze Student Achievement** (*Use ASA forms as needed.*)
Date and Agreed Upon Actions for Next Meeting:
Leadership Member: _____ Learning Team Facilitator: _____

Sustainable Leadership

Sustainable leadership has its origins in the sustainable environment movement that was brought to world attention by the report of the Brundtland Commission (formerly the World Commission on Environment and Development and renamed for its chair Gro Harlem Brundtland). Established by the United Nations in 1983, the commission was charged with developing long-term strategies for sustainable development and recommending ways for countries to cooperate in economic and social development. The Brundtland Commission released its report in 1987 and in the foreword, Gro Harlem Brundtland stated the following:

> The Commission has completed its work. We call for a common endeavour and for new norms of behaviour at all levels and in the interests of all. The changes in attitudes, in social values, and in aspirations that the report urges will depend on vast campaigns of education, debate and public participation.
>
> To this end, we appeal to "citizens" groups, to nongovernmental organizations, to educational institutions, and to the scientific community. They have all played indispensable roles in the creation of public awareness and political change in the past. They will play a crucial part in putting the world onto sustainable development paths, in laying the groundwork for Our Common Future. (UN Documents, 1987, Foreword)

The focus of this report was on the importance of working together, worldwide, to create a sustainable future with a focus on development, international economies, population, energy, industrial growth, urban challenges, peace, and the environment. Running throughout the report was a focus on education and sustainable leadership.

The authors and researchers who are most closely associated with the concept of sustainability in the field of education are Michael Fullan, Andy Hargreaves, and Dean Fink, and we will use their work in our discussion of sustainable leadership in education. Based on a longitudinal study entitled "Change Over Time?" by Hargreaves and Goodson (2003), Hargreaves and Fink (2006) outlined the concept of sustainable leadership in schools in their 2006 publication *Sustainable Leadership*. "Change Over Time?" was also the subject of a special issue of *Educational Administration Quarterly* (2006, volume 42, issue 1), which contained five articles outlining the findings of their studies of eight high schools.

Sustainability, as defined by Michael Fullan (2005, p. ix), is "the capacity of a system to engage in the complexities of continuous improvement consistent with deep values of human purpose" (p. ix). Hargreaves and Fink (2006) define sustainable leadership as follows:

> Sustainable educational leadership and improvement preserves and develops deep learning for all that spreads and lasts, in ways that do no harm to and indeed create positive benefit for others around us, now and in the future. (p. 42)

They further describe sustainable leadership by developing each of the seven principles they found contributed to success. Each of the principles of sustainable leadership is described below.

Principle 1: Depth. Learning and Integrity.

Leadership must focus on what is most important to the learning process and that learning must be deep and broad, which is a slow process and does not lend itself to immediate results. Hence, Hargreaves and Fink do not believe in short-term results that should be measured by yearly standardized tests for everyone. They do favor a sample of students that is tested as one data set among many. The area of short-term results is one in which Hargreaves and Fink disagree with Fullan, who supports the commitment to short-term results. For Fullan (2005) short-term results are required by the public to show progress is being made toward long-term goals.

Principle 2: Length. Endurance and Succession.

To preserve leadership over time, it cannot depend on individual leadership. Leadership capacity should be developed in others and distributed throughout the organization. With distributed leadership in place and plans made for leadership succession, the organization can continue to implement its mission with minimal disruption. Fullan expands on this concept by borrowing from Jim Collins and his popular publication *Good to Great.* Collins (2001) found that charismatic leaders do not lead to sustainability unless Principle 2 is implemented.

Principle 3: Breadth. Distribution Not Delegation.

Distributed leadership with true decision-making power is broadly disseminated. The organization needs to monitor how well the distributed leadership is working to ensure that, in the end, an authentic professional learning community is working toward improvement in the teaching and learning process.

Principle 4: Justice. Others and Ourselves.

This principle speaks to the issue of social justice. Individuals and teams must not work to improve their own school at the expense of others. They should not raid other schools for students, teachers, or other resources. At the district level, no school should be treated as though it is special. For example, magnet schools or choice schools should not be treated differently in terms of resources (or they should not exist at all because choice causes competition for students, teachers, and other resources). Schools should cooperate and work together for the greater good of all students.

Principle 5: Diversity. Complexity and Cohesion.

Embracing diversity helps to avoid negative standardization practices such as those fostered by NCLB. Diversity helps bring people with different ideas together to learn from one another. Strong networks from within and among schools and districts, such as the Comer Schools, the Coalition of Essential Schools, and the National Writing Project, increase their sustainability. Certainly, modern technology such as program websites, blogs, and wikis provide easy access to networks among people from all over the world. Networks are also important to Fullan, who believes that networks, both lateral and vertical, build school and district capacity.

Principle 6: Resourcefulness. Restraint and Renewal.

We need to use our resources wisely to ensure that we do not exploit or deplete them, and we must renew those resources to sustain high levels of commitment to the mission and vision. Hargreaves and Fink identify three sources of renewal:

1. *Trust.*   A climate of trust enhances the commitment of members to organizational goals. When there is a lack of trust, the organization cannot move forward and PLCs are impossible to form.
2. *Confidence.*   The organization must have expectations of success. Members must be confident they can achieve their goals.
3. *Emotion.*   Positive emotions are necessary to keep the organization moving toward its mission and vision.

Fullan calls this principle "cyclical energizing." Fullan would agree with Kurt Lewin's concept of the three-step change process as described in Chapter 8: unfreeze, moving, refreeze. People need productive downtime that reenergizes them for continual improvement.

Principle 7: Conservation: History and Legacy.

We need to learn from our past successes and failures. We should not forget the past by simply building something new; we should use organizational memory to build on positive cultural norms. However, we should be purposeful about what past practices we want to abandon and what past practices we want to continue or adapt. At the same time, we should not romanticize the past, which can interfere with our judgment of what was good.

Distributed leadership and sustainable leadership concepts are not without their critics. Henry Levin (2006), professor of economics and education at Teachers College of Columbia University, has been critical of the research base for each and doesn't believe the researchers provide sufficient guidance for practice. But even Levin admits that the work of Spillane on distributed leadership and that of Hargreaves and Fink on sustainable leadership are "useful to generating discussions and further study for students, researchers, and practitioners" (Levin, p. 43). We believe that distributed leadership and sustainable leadership are the right concepts for today's transformational leaders to implement in schools, and for today's researchers in school leadership to study. In the final section of this chapter, we present the work of Marzano, Waters, and McNulty (2005) which lends research evidence to these concepts.

Research on Sustainable Leader Behavior

We focus on one major research study by Marzano, Waters, and McNulty (2005) for two reasons: (a) it is a meta-analysis that analyzes 69 studies of leadership behaviors correlated to student achievement, and (b) this research has had wide impact on school districts around the United States since it was published. The studies in the meta-analysis include a total of 2,802 schools, representing all school levels, with approximately 1,400,000 students and 14,000 teachers. For each study, "a correlation between general leadership and student achievement was either computed or extracted directly from the study" (p. 30). The typical study used in this meta-analysis had questionnaires asking teachers their perceptions of principal behaviors, rather than asking the principals themselves. The average effect size, which they call a correlation, between leadership and achievement for all studies combined was .25. By school type, the correlations were as follows: .29 for elementary schools, .24 for middle or junior high schools, and .26 for high schools. In a hypothetical example, the authors interpret this result to mean that principals in the top half of a normal distribution when compared to principals in the bottom half would have 25% higher pass rates. This improvement is significant. So what do principals who are top performers do that improves student achievement? Marzano, Waters, and McNulty identified 21 specific behaviors which we list here in Table 9.1 in order of highest to lowest correlation to student achievement.

To help our readers interpret these findings, we took liberties with the Marzano, Waters, and McNulty data and categorized the specific behaviors listed in Table 9.1 into general areas of focus in Table 9.2. Listed next to each area of focus are the item numbers from Table 9.1. There is some overlap as some specific behaviors appear in multiple areas of focus, such as item 14, which focuses on communications, school culture, and change leadership.

From our analysis of the specific behaviors, there are five associated with instructional leadership. This result is not surprising, considering much of the literature on school leadership in the last 20 years has focused on the importance of instructional leadership in helping teachers and parents improve student learning.

Marzano, Waters, and McNulty (2005) also performed a factor analysis that resulted in the 21 behaviors being categorized into two lists of behaviors most associated with two types of change strategies. They found that all 21 behaviors were associated with first-order change, that is, change that is incremental and not very disruptive to school routine or culture. All 21 behaviors, they reported, are necessary for the day-to-day, regular management of the school. They found that seven of the behaviors, however, must be the focus of leaders when attempting second-order change, termed "deep change" that "alters the system in fundamental ways, offering a dramatic shift in direction and requiring new ways of thinking and acting" (p. 66). For second-order change to occur, leaders must emphasize the seven behaviors which are listed below (the item number from Table 9.1 appears in parentheses):

1. Is knowledgeable about current curriculum, instruction and assessment practices (item 6)
2. Inspires and leads new and challenging innovations (item 18)
3. Ensures everyone is aware of current theories and practices and makes discussion of these a regular aspect of the school culture (item 14)

TABLE 9.1	Specific Principal Behaviors and Average Correlations	
Specific Principal Behavior		**Average Correlation to Student Achievement**
1. Is aware of details and undercurrents in the running of the school and uses the information to address current and potential problems		.33
2. Adapts leadership behavior to the needs of the situation and is comfortable with dissent		.28
3. Monitors effectiveness of school practices and their impact on learning		.27
4. Is an advocate for the school to all stakeholders		
5. Protects teachers from issues and influences that detract from their teaching time or focus		
6. Is knowledgeable about current curriculum, instruction and assessment practices		.25
7. Establishes a set of standard operating procedures and routines		
8. Provides teachers with materials and professional development necessary for success		
9. Is willing to challenge the status quo		
10. Fosters shared beliefs and a sense of community and cooperation		
11. Involves teachers in the design and implementation of important decisions and policies		
12. Recognizes and rewards individual accomplishments		.24
13. Establishes clear goals and keeps those goals in the forefront of the school's attention		
14. Ensures everyone is aware of current theories and practices and makes discussion of these a regular aspect of the school culture		
15. Establishes strong lines of communication with teachers and students		.23
16. Communicates and operates from strong ideals and beliefs about schooling		.22
17. Is directly involved in the design and implementation of curriculum, instruction, and assessment practices		.20
18. Inspires and leads new and challenging innovations		
19. Has quality contact and interactions with teachers and students		
20. Recognizes and celebrates accomplishments and acknowledges failures		.19
21. Demonstrates an awareness of the personal aspects of teachers and staff		.18

Source: Adapted from Marzano, Waters, and McNulty (2005).

TABLE 9.2   Areas of Focus for Specific Principal Behaviors

Areas of Focus	Item Numbers from Table 9.1
Instructional leadership (includes professional development)	3, 6, 8, 14, 17
Communications	4, 14, 15, 16
Change leadership	9, 13, 18
Decision making and problem solving	1, 2, 11
School culture	10, 14, 16
Relationship building	19, 21
Recognition	12, 20
Order and discipline	5, 7

4. Is willing to challenge the status quo (item 9)
5. Monitors effectiveness of school practices and their impact on learning (item 3)
6. Adapts leadership behavior to the needs of the situation and is comfortable with dissent (item 2)
7. Communicates and operates from strong ideals and beliefs about schooling (item 16)

They warn us, however, that four other behaviors are negatively associated with second-order change:

1. Fosters shared beliefs and a sense of community and cooperation (item 10)
2. Establishes strong lines of communication with teachers and students (item 15)
3. Establishes a set of standard operating procedures and routines (item 7)
4. Involves teachers in the design and implementation of important decisions and policies (item 11)

Deep change can result in certain faculty and staff becoming alienated and principals "pay a certain price for the implementation of a second-order change innovation" (p. 74).

Principals who use the 21 specific behaviors in the Marzano, Waters, and McNulty study are clearly demonstrating transformational and moral leadership. Leadership is distributed and it will sustain over time.

Final Thoughts

This chapter began with a discussion of the difference between leadership and command, with particular attention to the differences in the role of power in both leadership and command. Clearly, organizational leaders have a range of theories of leadership from which to choose in selecting a leadership style.

• For example, one may choose to use a traditional, top-down, directive approach, often thought of as bureaucratic. Such an approach assumes that the best information and the best ideas for solving problems are found in the upper echelon of the organization and should be passed down the line to be implemented by those in the lower echelons. This approach predictably creates a transactional relationship with followers in which motivation and effort are circumscribed by the expectations inherent in the agreed-upon transactional relationship.

• An alternative is to choose a more collaborative, or transformative, leadership style in working with others, in the belief that useful information and good ideas may well be found anywhere in the organization and should be shared in the leadership process. At its best, collaborative leadership creates a transformational relationship with followers in which they are motivated by uniting with others in a mutual commitment to share in solving problems and creating solutions, as well as by the sense of mutual effort, or team membership, involved.

But the major factor in deciding which approach to use in exercising leadership lies in the belief that one approach is more effective in producing better outcomes than the other. Educational organizations today are confronted by demands for near-constant change in dealing with problems that are highly complex, often poorly understood, and ambiguous—and with outcomes that are uncertain. Organizations must be nimble, adaptable, and responsive. The contemporary scientific paradigm of leadership under these conditions is to use a collaborative style that emphasizes teamwork. The goal is to transform the relationship between leader and followers so that participants are energized and motivated by unity of purpose and mutually shared values.

Adult learners, such as teachers, are motivated to learn new ways when they are active participants in their own learning, forging new ideas about the future of their lives at work and participating actively as team members in making the central decisions regarding their work. To move an organization from traditional transactional leadership to transformative leadership requires the development of a new process that is pursued steadfastly over time through which teachers can learn new roles and new skills required for active participation in teamwork and collaboration. This transformative team-building process must include constant attention to the building of greater levels of trust not only between the leader and the followers but among the collaborating followers, too. Thus, transformative leaders understand that leadership is a never-ending process of growth and development—a process of building human capital in the organization. This progress can be achieved by using distributed leadership, which in turn can be achieved by utilizing professional learning communities, and through the 21 specific behaviors of leaders that Marzano, Waters, and McNulty found associated with student achievement. In this way, sustainable leadership can be attained.

Reflective Activities

1. Review the types of power in the French and Raven typology. Describe two leaders in your experience who displayed one or more types of power. Then indicate how effective you believe these leaders were based on the types of power they used.

2. *Working on Your Game Plan.* What leadership theory will you follow: transactional, transformational, or moral leadership? Describe what specific behaviors you will use to implement your theory. Feel free to borrow ideas from this chapter, such as distributed leadership, parent involvement, sustainable leadership, and specific behaviors from the Marzano, Waters, and McNulty study. Then, using your Game Plan ideas, consider the following advertisement and write a letter as directed in application for the position.

"Each Child Is an Individual of Great Worth and Is Entitled to Develop to His or Her Fullest Potential"

Sunny Isles Elementary School District (K–6 ADA 21,350) South Florida's Gulf Coast

Sunny Isles, a culturally and ethnically diverse school district, is seeking outstanding candidates with the following attributes:

Student Advocate • High Integrity • Vision • Energetic • Empathetic • Compassionate • Accountable • Collaborative • Change Agent • Instructional Leader • Effective Communicator

ELEMENTARY PRINCIPAL

Salary: $84,000 to $87,500
Plus excellent fringe benefits
(207 days)

IMMEDIATE OPENINGS
Open Until Filled

Those interested in being considered for this position should submit a letter of interest that describes how their experience, background, aspirations, and goals can serve as a positive influence in the lives of children.

Please Contact
Ronald H. Kirby
Assistant Superintendent, Human Resources
(741) 327-2100 • FAX (741) 327-9601

Please visit our website at:
http://www.siesd.k12.fl.us
(To see the Job Postings' Web page, scroll down to the "Human Resources" banner and click on Employment Opportunities.)

EQUAL OPPORTUNITY EMPLOYER
Culturally Diverse and Bilingual Candidates
Are Encouraged to Apply

CRITICAL INCIDENT   Leadership at North River Middle School

Cliff Jameson, principal of North River Middle School, sat in the superintendent's waiting room to be called in for a special meeting to discuss his school's state test scores—a discussion he dreaded. The scores were down from the previous year, as they had been the year before. In addition, his school did not make adequate yearly progress (AYP), as required by No Child Left Behind (NCLB), and he feared that he was about to be fired as principal.

The superintendent, Linda Thompson, opened her door and welcomed Cliff into the office. She began, saying "Thanks for coming in, Cliff. I know that the teachers in your school get along with you, and they seem to like you. So as a leader, you must be doing something right, but you know that I have been concerned about the standardized test scores and AYP data from your school for the past two years. After we talked last year, the reports you provided about your plans for improvement seemed promising. Tell me how things went from your perspective. Why didn't the scores improve?"

"Linda, thanks for the opportunity to explain things," Cliff began. "To start the year off last year, I met with the different grade levels, and I went over their data pointing out where the problems were. I indicated that each of them had to improve their test scores over last year or their jobs would be in jeopardy based on our new district evaluation system. It was clear to me, looking at the reading test scores, that we had to hold some in-service workshops for all teachers to show them how to teach reading in the content areas. It was also clear to me that, as I visited classrooms, many students were not on task. So I scheduled some classroom management in-service to help improve in this area. The other big area that we focused on was getting the kids prepared for the state test. I helped by providing some test prep software and other materials for all classrooms that focused directly on those areas that would be taught on the test."

"Did you get any input from the teachers about what they thought went wrong and what would help?" asked Linda.

"Of course," Cliff responded. "I asked each of them to send me their ideas and told them that we would discuss them at later meetings, but I got very few comments, and none of them were on target. We did all of the in-service training early in the school year. And I visited everyone's class along with the assistant principals to ensure that teachers were focusing on the basics, that students were on task, and that they were prepared to take the test. We did everything we could based on our analysis of the situation."

"So what went wrong in your opinion, Cliff?" asked Linda.

"Well, as I said, we visited the classes, and we don't think that the teachers followed through with the training well enough and also didn't use the materials to prepare the kids for the test. But things will be much different this coming year."

"Cliff, I have to be honest with you. If your scores go down again, I will have to recommend your removal as principal." Linda asked. "What are your plans to improve the situation at North River?"

"First, we are going to have the same in-service programs as last year, but I plan to bring in expert presenters, who will have more hands-on activities to get the teachers more involved in the training. People learn better by doing, not by just sitting and observing. Second, I have been far too lenient in my evaluations in the past. I am going to recommend probation for all of the teachers whose scores went down by more than five percentile points. This will put a little fire under them and get them motivated. And finally, I am going to work with the administrative team to do more classroom visitations to ensure that things are going as planned. Linda, I know that I can turn this school around, and I appreciate another year at the helm to prove to you that I am a good leader."

1. How would you characterize Cliff Jameson's leadership behaviors? Is he a good leader?
2. Cliff asked the teachers for feedback about what went wrong, but he got very little from them; none of which he thought was appropriate. Why do you think this happened? What techniques could he have used to get more—and more helpful—feedback from the teachers?
3. Cliff said that none of the meager feedback from teachers was on target. How do you interpret what the teachers might really have been saying to him?
4. Place yourself in the superintendent's position. Develop a coaching plan using ideas from this chapter to help the principal meet the goals for this school.

Suggested Reading

Burns, J. M. (1978). *Leadership*. New York, NY: Harper & Row.

This highly readable, Pulitzer Prize-winning volume vividly interprets the contemporary understanding of leadership. The aim of the book is to illuminate the dilemmas of political leadership; hence, it draws many of its examples from great political leaders. However, the lessons for educators are clear and readily understandable. Highly recommended not only for its impeccable scholarship but also for the intellectual quality that is revealed by the open, straightforward writing, which makes its ideas easily accessible.

Drath, W. (2001). *The deep blue sea: Rethinking the source of leadership*. San Francisco, CA: Jossey-Bass.

"Too often," Drath observes, "in thinking about leadership we are like persons standing on the shore, captivated by the dancing, sparkling whitecaps on the ocean and entirely missing the deep blue sea. The whitecaps are real enough, but their source lies within the action of the ocean itself." And it is so with organizations as well, he contends: The deep blue sea to which he refers is our own educational organization, and understanding it lies well below its surface. Thus, he introduces us to a new way of thinking about organizations and exercising leadership in them. He emphasizes, as the contemporary leadership paradigm does, facilitating relationships and meaning between and among people and organizations. Strongly recommended.

DuFour, R., Eaker, R., & DuFour, R. (Eds.). (2005). *On common ground: The power of professional learning communities*. Bloomington, IN: Solution Tree.

The editors and authors of this book have had years of experience as public school teachers and leaders, and have solid academic credentials, too. Now, as consultants, they are in the forefront of the movement to help teachers and principals rebuild the cultures of their schools to meet the new educational goals that the United States has embraced. At the heart of their approach is to help faculty members shift their working environment from that of traditional isolation of teachers in classrooms to developing it into a collaborative, professional learning community.

Fullan, M. (2005). *Leadership & sustainability: System thinkers in action*. Thousand Oaks, CA: Corwin Press.

This short book is important because it is one of the first books to proffer a theory of sustainability for schools. Fullan outlines eight elements that leaders need to implement in order to ensure that the school and the district sustain leadership and change efforts: public service with a moral purpose; commitment to changing context at all levels; lateral capacity building through networks; intelligent accountability and vertical relationships; deep learning; dual commitment to short- and long-term results; cyclical energizing; and the long lever of leadership, which emphasizes the importance of sustainable leaders and the critical mass of leaders who implement the elements of sustainability.

Hargreaves, A., & Fink. D. (2006). *Sustainable leadership*. San Francisco, CA: Jossey-Bass.

The importance of this book is its research base: a series of longitudinal studies of eight high schools in various settings both in the United States and Canada. From this research, the authors developed seven principles of sustainable leadership that are discussed in this chapter of our book. The strength of Hargreaves and Fink's book lies in its research connection and in its practical examples of each of the seven principles.

Heifetz, R. A. (1998). *Leadership without easy answers*. Cambridge, MA: Belknap Press of Harvard University Press.

Heifetz brings an extraordinarily broad background to this discussion of the key concepts of adaptive leadership. He clearly illuminates issues such as distinguishing between adaptive problems and technical problems, and the differences between authority and leadership. His approach is both theoretical and practical, and it is leavened with his own experiences as a medical doctor, a psychiatrist, and a musician. Fullan's work (described above) draws heavily from this book by Heifetz.

Helgesen, S. (1990). *The female advantage: Women's ways of leadership*. New York, NY: Doubleday Currency.

This widely read book argues that men tend to think in linear fashion, lean toward hierarchical organization, emphasize logic, seek power for themselves, are uncomfortable with ambiguity, and are goal-oriented, whereas women tend to think in terms of more global connections rather than in straight lines, emphasize human interaction processes rather than hierarchy, have no great interest in personal power, are easily able to tolerate ambiguity, and are process-oriented. The result, Helgesen argues, is a marked difference in thinking and organizational behavior between men and women—a difference that Helgesen firmly believes gives women a decided advantage as organizational leaders.

Marzano, R. J., Waters, T., & McNulty, B. A. (2005). *School leadership that works: From research to results*. Alexandria, VA: Association for Supervision and Curriculum Development; Aurora, CO; Mid-continent Research for Education and Learning.

This book presents the results of a meta-analysis of 69 leadership studies that found a .25 average effect size for leadership behaviors and student achievement. The 21 top-ranked principal behaviors are presented along with the results of a factor analysis in which the 21 behaviors are categorized into two lists most associated with two types of change strategies. Every student of Educational Leadership should read this book as it has been highly influential across the U.S. in influencing leadership strategies and evaluation of leaders.

Rosener, J. B. (1990). The ways women lead. *Harvard Business Review, 68*(6), 119–25.

Having studied 456 female business executives, Rosener reports that they behave very differently from male leaders in similar positions. She found that men emphasized a command-and-control style (rational decision making, giving orders, appealing to the self-interest of followers), whereas women tended to work more "interactively" (sharing information and power, promoting empowerment, motivating people by appeals to organizational ideals and a shared vision of the future). Many women have found this article appealing, yet it remains highly controversial because the quality of the research design and methods have repeatedly been criticized.

Wheatley, M. J. (1999). *Leadership and the new science: Discovering order in a chaotic world* (2nd ed.). San Francisco CA: Berrett-Koehler.

This is an erudite, witty exploration of new ways of thinking about and exploring science. Not a book focused on education, it draws upon a wide range of sources and people to illustrate the new problems of dealing with uncertainty, emerging new ideas, and rapid change across a broad spectrum of science today. It is highly recommended to educational leaders because it shows us brilliantly that the world of schools is not unique and that leadership problems in the schools are part of a much larger mosaic.

References

Bass, B. H. (1985). *Leadership and performance beyond expectations.* New York, NY: Free Press.

Bass, B. M. (Ed.). (1981). *Stogdill's handbook of leadership: A survey of theory and research* (Rev. ed.). New York, NY: Free Press.

Bennis, W., & Nanus, B. (1985). *Leaders: The strategy for taking charge.* New York, NY: Harper & Row.

Blake, R. R., & Mouton, J. S. (1978). *The new managerial grid.* Houston, TX: Gulf Publishing Company.

Burns, J. M. (1978). *Leadership.* New York, NY: Harper & Row.

Collins, J. (2001). *Good to great.* New York, NY: Harper Collins.

Darling-Hammond, L. (2006). Securing the right to learn: Policy and practice for powerful teaching and learning. *Educational Researcher, 35*(7), 13–24.

Darling-Hammond, L., & Bransford, J. (2007). *Preparing teachers for a changing world: What teachers should learn and be able to do.* San Francisco, CA: Jossey-Bass.

Darling-Hammond, L., & Richardson, N. (2009). Teacher learning: What matters? *Educational Leadership, 66*(5), 46–53.

DuFour, R., & Eaker, R. (1998). *Professional learning communities at work: Best practices for enhancing student achievement.* Reston, VA: Association for Supervision and Curriculum Development.

Epstein, J. L., Sanders, M. G., Simon, B. S., Salinas, K. C., Jansorn, N. R., & Van Voorhis, F. L. (2002). *School, family, and community partnerships: Your handbook for action* (2nd ed.). Thousand Oaks, CA: Corwin Press.

Fiedler, F. (1967). *A theory of leadership effectiveness.* New York, NY: McGraw-Hill.

French, J. R. P., & Raven, B. (1959). The bases of social power. In D. Cartwright (Ed.), *Studies in social power* (pp. 150–167). Ann Arbor, MI: Institute for Social Research, University of Michigan.

Fullan, M. (2005). *Leadership & sustainability: System thinkers in action.* Thousand Oaks, CA: Corwin Press.

Galloway, J. L. (1991). Competence and character. *U.S. News and World Report, 110*(20), p. 36.

Gardner, J. W. (1989). *On leadership.* New York, NY: Free Press.

Getzels, J. W. (1973). Theory and research on leadership: Some comments and some alternatives. In L. L. Cunningham & W. J. Gephart (Eds.), *Leadership: The science and the art today* (pp. 16–25). Itasca, IL: F. E. Peacock.

Halpin, A. W. (1966). *Theory and research in administration.* New York, NY: Macmillan.

Hargreaves, A., & Fink, D. (2006). *Sustainable leadership.* San Francisco, CA: Jossey-Bass.

Hargreaves, A., & Goodson, I. (2003). *Change over time? A study of culture, structure, time and change in secondary schooling.* Chicago, IL: Spencer Foundation.

Heifetz, R. A. (1994). *Leadership without easy answers.* Cambridge, MA: Belknap Press of Harvard University Press.

Heifetz, R. A., & Linsky, M. (2002). *Leadership on the line: Staying alive through the dangers of leading.* Boston, MA: Harvard Business School Press.

Hemphill, J. K., & Coons, A. E. (1957). Development of the leader behavior description questionnaire. In R. M. Stogdill & A. E. Coons (Eds.), *Leader behavior: Its description and measurement* (pp. 6–38). Columbus, OH: Bureau of Business Research of Ohio State University.

Henderson, A. T., & Mapp, K. L. (2007). *A new wave of evidence: The impact of school, family and community connections on student achievement.* Austin: TX, Southeast Educational Development Laboratory. Retrieved from http://www.sedl.org/connections/resources/evidence.pdf

Hersey, P., Blanchard, K. H., & Johnson, D. (1996). *Management of organizational behavior.* Upper Saddle River, NJ: Prentice Hall.

Jeynes, W. H. (2007). The relationship between parental involvement and urban secondary school student academic achievement: A meta-analysis. *Urban Education, 42*(1), 82–110.

Kanter, R. M. (1983). *The change masters: Innovation and entrepreneurship in the American corporation.* New York, NY: Simon & Schuster.

Keirsey, D., & Bates, M. (1984). *Please understand me: Character and temperament types.* Del Mar, CA: Prometheus Nemesis.

Levin, H. M. (2006). Can research improve educational leadership? *Educational Researcher, 35*(8), 38–43.

Lortie, D. C. (1975). *Schoolteacher: A sociological study.* Chicago, IL: University of Chicago Press.

Louis, M. R. (1986). Putting executive action in context: An alternative view of power. In S. Srivastva (Ed.), *Executive power* (pp. 111–131). San Francisco, CA: Jossey-Bass.

Marzano, R. J., Waters, T., & McNulty, B. A. (2005). *School leadership that works: From research to results.* Alexandria, VA: Association for Supervision and Curriculum Development; Aurora, CO: Mid-continent Research for Education and Learning.

McClelland, D. C. (1975). *Power: The inner experience.* New York, NY: Irvington.

Northouse, P. (2013). *Leadership: Theory and practice* (6th ed). Los Angeles, CA: Sage.

Rosener, J. B. (1990). Ways women lead. *Harvard Business Review, 68*(6), 119–125.

Sato, M., Chung Wei, R. C., & Darling-Hammond, L. (2008). Improving teachers' assessment practices through professional development: The case of National Board Certification. *American Education Research Journal, 45,* 669–700.

Senge, P. (1990). *The fifth discipline: The art and practice of the learning organization.* New York, NY: Doubleday.

Sergiovanni, T. J. (1992). *Moral leadership: Getting to the heart of school reform.* San Francisco, CA: Jossey-Bass.

Spillane, J. P., & Diamond, J. B. (2007). Taking a distributed perspective. In J. P. Spillane & J. B. Diamond (Eds.), *Distributed leadership in practice* (pp. 1–15). New York, NY: Teachers College Press.

Stogdill, R. M. (1974). *Handbook of leadership: A survey of theory and research.* New York, NY: Free Press.

UN Documents. (1987). *Our common future: Chairman's foreword. Report of the World Commission of Environment and Development.* Retrieved from http://www.un-documents.net/ocf-cf.htm

Wheatley, M. J. (1999). *Leadership and the new science: Discovering order in a chaotic world.* San Francisco, CA: Berrett-Koehler.

CHAPTER 10

Decision Making

A s we defined it in Chapter 9, the exercise of leadership involves working with and through others—individually and in groups—to achieve organizational goals. When the goals of the organization emphasize

- *stability*, refinement, and continued application of existing practices, and
- *maintenance* of existing levels of performance

the contemporary paradigm of organizational studies supports the use of bureaucratic top-down methods as likely to be highly effective ways of working with and through others. However, when the organization is required to handle successfully

- demands for quick, adroit, nimble responses to rapid, pervasive change in the environment while dealing, at the same time, with
- emerging problems arising from the need for change that are ambiguous and poorly understood, and the outcomes of possible alternative solutions are not knowable in advance,

the contemporary paradigm of organizational studies supports the use of collaborative methods as likely to be more effective ways of working with and through others, which is why, though educational leaders have a theoretical choice between using traditional bureaucratic methods to work with and through others or using collaborative methods, under contemporary conditions in educational practice, collaborative methods are generally the methods of choice.

The two issues of stability and change are contrapuntal: They are inseparable parts of almost every decision in which the educational leader is involved. The effectiveness and quality of decisions that are made in an organization usually reflect the skill with which the leader has orchestrated these two issues.

The fast-paced world of school administration seems, on the one hand, to demand that the leader make decisions quickly, without needless ado, and move on to other pressing business. This velocity creates the temptation to make the decision unilaterally, for the sake of speed and efficiency, and be done with it. On the other hand, it is becoming increasingly clear that healthy organizations characteristically find strength in opening up participation in decision making and empowering relevant people at all levels of the organization to contribute to the quality of the decisions made. There are two reasons for this: First, empowering people to participate in important decisions is highly motivating to them; second, broad participation infuses the decision-making process with the full spectrum of knowledge and good ideas that people throughout the organization have to contribute. This inclusion is especially and particularly important in organizations peopled by knowledge workers, such as schools.

As it is for all organizations, the environment of educational organizations today is dominated by the dynamics of change—fast-paced, pervasive, insistent change. To keep pace—or, better yet, to set the pace—it is imperative that schools be nimble, responsive, adaptable, and capable of constantly developing themselves from within (or, as the popular phrase has it, reinventing themselves). It is an increasingly competitive environment. The secure monopoly that school districts once had is no longer secure because attention is increasingly focused on results in the form of student achievement and because competitors promise to produce better results than the established public schools have accomplished. In a real sense, the competition is global, not merely local, because clients of educational organizations anxiously compare the results posted by local schools with those in other parts of the world. In this context, the educational leader is constantly making judgments about how to make a decision—more particularly, who should be involved in making it and how these others should be involved in the process.

Therefore, this chapter focuses on participative decision making. It begins, however, with a brief background discussion on decision making in general and a discussion of so-called rational decision making. We then discuss the realities of working in schools, how these realities influence the behavior of leaders in their decision-making efforts, and the need to develop a theory of decision-making practice. The Vroom-Yetton normative leadership model is presented, which offers guidance in determining how to make decisions, in terms of involving other people. This is a very important guide to leadership action and should be studied closely for the implications it has for effective leader behavior. The chapter closes with a suggestion for a simple, practical paradigm for shared decision making and a decision-making flowchart for team decision making.

The significance of decision making at the organizational and administrative level has a long history. For example, in a landmark book, Herbert Simon (1950) observed that "a general theory of administration must include principles of organization that will insure correct decision-making" (p. 1). By 1959, Daniel E. Griffiths had proposed a theory that administration *was* decision making. He maintained that,

- first, the structure of an organization is determined by the nature of its decision-making processes;
- second, that an individual's rank in an organization is directly related to the control exerted over the decision process;
- and third, that the effectiveness of an administrator is inversely proportional to the number of decisions that he or she must personally make. (1959)

Griffiths's theory, which was highly influential in educational circles for many years, highlights two important concepts: (a) The administrator's task is to ensure that an adequate decision-making process is in place in the organization; and (b) because such a process is in place, the effective administrator makes relatively few decisions personally, although those few may be particularly potent in their impact on the organization. In this view, the administrator's influence resides more firmly in creating and monitoring the processes through which decisions are made by the organization than in personally making large numbers of the many decisions that are required in any busy complex organization.

However, Simon, Griffiths, and their colleagues at that time envisioned that decision making could be rationalized, made logical, systematized, and optimized by applying logical-mathematical methods to the solution of educational problems. Many people believed them then, and many still would like to. With the passage of time, however, it has become apparent that many of our most entrenched educational problems are so ambiguous, multifaceted, and complex that they simply cannot be reduced to algorithms into which various quantitative data can be plugged to yield optimum educational decisions. Indeed, since the mid-twentieth century, there has been growing understanding that the human complexities of organizational life in commerce as well as in education sharply limit the usefulness of such decision-making approaches in many kinds of organizations.

INDIVIDUAL VERSUS ORGANIZATIONAL DECISION MAKING

An important issue that enters many discussions of decision making is being raised here: the question of individual versus organizational decision making. On the one hand, there is the widely held expectation that persons in administrative positions will personally "be decisive." What that means is far from clear, but it is often taken to mean making decisions swiftly, without delay or temporizing and, clearly, with minimum ambiguity. It also often implies that the individual tends to make decisions that conform to certain accepted qualitative standards: For example, decisions are well informed and ethically acceptable. Thus, discussions of administrative decision making often focus on the personal behaviors of individuals who are construed to be "decision makers."

On the other hand, because administration is defined as working with and through other people to achieve organizational goals, it is important to consider the mechanisms by which the organization (and not merely the individual) deals with decision making. In this perspective, the issue begins to turn on the ways in which the *organization* "acts" (or "behaves") in the process of making and implementing *organizational* decisions, rather than on the idiosyncratic behavior of the person in administrative office. For many of the clients of organizations (students and parents, for example), the individual roles of administrators in decision-making processes are obscure and perhaps irrelevant, whereas the "behavior" of the organization is most relevant. In this view, the vital decision-making functions are organizational—although administrators may be seen as implicated.

This point was illustrated in one university when the heating system was constantly malfunctioning, classrooms were chronically unkempt, and student seating was typically in disrepair. Students were astounded when, in the spring, an ambitious project was undertaken to beautify the campus by planting flowers and shrubs and setting sculptures among the trees. This action, of course, prompted outcries from students, such as the following: "What is wrong with this university? It obviously doesn't care what happens in the classrooms. All that matters is what visitors see on the outside!" The implication was that, regardless of the persons who might be involved in the process, somehow the decision-making processes of the university, as an organization, had gone awry.

The discussion of decision making in this chapter recognizes that the personal decision-making style of the administrator is important insofar as it gives rise to the ways in which the organization, as an entity, goes about the unending processes of identifying problems, conceptualizing them, and finding ways of dealing with them. The individual decision making of persons in administrative office takes on significance as organizational behavior chiefly because of its inevitable impact on the behavior of others and on the decision-making processes of the organization itself.

This emphasis on the responsibility of the administrator for the nature and quality of the decision-making processes used in an organization is compatible with the contemporary view that the administrator is a key actor in the development of the culture of the organization. That is, decision-making practices are not so much the result of circumstances inherent in a given organization (the kind of place a school is) as they are the choices of those in authority (namely, administrators) about how decisions *ought* to be made. These choices are closely tied to assumptions held by administrators on issues that are now familiar to the reader, such as the following:

- What motivates people at work
- The relative values of collaboration versus direction in the exercise of leadership in the workplace
- The desirability of a full flow of information up, down, and across the organization
- The best ways of maintaining organizational control and discipline
- The value of involving people throughout all levels of the organization in decision making

RATIONALITY IN DECISION MAKING

Even an elementary understanding of contemporary approaches to decision making in organizations requires brief consideration of some of the ways in which we have learned to think about the issue. Those who live in the Western world tend to use and accept logic, rationality, and science when thinking about concepts such as decision making. This propensity reflects generally held assumptions in our culture about the ways in which we ought to go about making decisions. These assumptions have formed the core of our thinking about such matters.

During the three centuries since the Reformation, the history of Western thought and culture has been dominated by the rise of science, technology, and industry. Scientific thought, with its strong emphasis on logical rationality, has become almost ingrained in the institutions of our culture. Thus, in seeking explanations of our experiences, we are accustomed to respect the rationality of logical positivism. In short, we tend to see the solution to all sorts of problems as requiring the application of engineering approaches. This penchant was reflected in Max Weber's analysis of bureaucratic organization. It was epitomized by the work of Frederick Taylor, who adapted the principles and methods of science to a form of "human engineering" in the workplace and sought to create a science of management that could be applied to everyday problems in the organization. Taylor called it *scientific management* and, as Donald Schön pointed out, "Taylor saw the . . . manager as a designer of work, a controller and monitor of performance . . . [seeking through these roles] to yield optimally efficient production" (Schön, 1983, p. 237).

The concept of management as a science grew steadily during the first half of the twentieth century, but World War II stimulated its development enormously. This growth was due to three factors associated with the war:

- The great emphasis on the roles of science and technology in winning the war
- The development of operations research and systems theory (These theories involved the application of the rational logic of mathematics modeling to the solution of complex problems ranging from how to reduce the loss of shipping to submarine attack to how to increase the effectiveness of aerial bombing.)
- The unprecedented scale of organizing that was required to manage the global dimensions of the conflict

The post-World War II era was one of great optimism and energy, when industry and business moved rapidly to exploit the markets that abounded as a result of the years of wartime shortages everywhere. Confidence in science and technology boomed, and the rational, logical methods associated with science soared in acceptance and prestige. It was common to refer to the wartime Manhattan Project as a model for conceptualizing and solving problems: "After all, if we could build an atomic bomb we ought to be able to solve this problem." Government expenditures for research surged to new heights on the "basis of the proposition that the production of new scientific knowledge could be used to create wealth, achieve national goals, improve human life, and solve social problems" (Schön, 1983, p. 39).

In 1957, the Soviet Union launched *Sputnik I*. The United States reacted with another spasm of emphasis on the logic of applying mathematics and science to the solution of problems. Under the leadership of President John F. Kennedy, the United States began a large-scale effort to develop new space technology. Before long, the U.S. educational infrastructure found itself involved in meeting the demands of the space program for scientists and mathematicians, as well as managers trained to apply the concepts of those disciplines to complex organizational challenges. The new rallying cry became, "If we can put a man on the moon, why can't we solve this problem?" The implication was that the National Aeronautics and Space Administration (NASA) had—since its inception under the presidency of Dwight Eisenhower—developed and demonstrated the effectiveness of a model for complex decision making that was applicable to all sorts of problems, social as well as technological.

During the post-World War II era, another similar model—widely admired and emulated—was proffered by medicine. It emphasized clinical-experimental research as the basis of knowledge:

> The medical research center, with its medical school and its teaching hospital, became the institutional model to which other professions aspired. Here was a solid base of fundamental science, and a profession which had geared itself to implement the ever-changing products of research. Other professions, hoping to achieve some of medicine's effectiveness and prestige, sought to emulate its linkage of research and teaching institutions, its hierarchy of research and clinical roles, and its system for connecting basic and applied research to practice. The prestige and apparent success of the medical and engineering models exerted great attraction for the social sciences. In such fields as education . . . the very language . . . rich in references to measurement, controlled experiment, applied science, laboratories and clinics, was striking in its reverence for those models. (Schön, 1983, p. 39)

This is precisely the view and the hope that is so very much in evidence among the supporters of the No Child Left Behind (NCLB) Act as it was created and as it began to unfold in practice.

Rational Decision-Making Models

It is not surprising that students of decision making tried to develop and assist administrators to master, a *science* of making better-quality decisions through the analysis of decision-making processes. An early and major contributor in this effort was Herbert Simon. Simon's analysis identified three major phases in the process of making decisions (Simon, 1960):

- First, there is *intelligence activity*. In view of the influence of World War II on postwar thought, Simon used the term *intelligence* much as military people do: the search of the environment that reveals circumstances that call for a decision.

- The second phase is *design activity*: the processes by which alternative courses of action are envisioned, developed, and analyzed.
- The third phase in Simon's analysis is *choice activity*—the process of actually selecting a course of action from among the options under consideration.

Simon's great stature as a scholar and his popularity as a consultant to numerous prestigious corporations ensured wide acceptance of his pioneering approach to decision making, which now stands as classic work. Many who were to follow would create a substantial body of literature devoted to efforts to improve his conceptualization, usually by elaborating the number of steps to be found in the process. Thus, one finds numerous models proffered in the extensive literature on decision making. Two basic assumptions incorporated in almost all of them are based on Simon's work: the assumption that decision making is an orderly, rational process that possesses an inherent logic; and the assumption that the steps in the process follow one another in an orderly, logical, sequential flow (which some refer to as linear logic). Such models, and the assumptions on which they are based, became important in the training of administrators and have been widely applied in planned, systematic ways to real-world organizations in the hope of improving their performance.

Peter F. Drucker, a leading organizational scholar whose thinking was very influential in corporate circles from the 1960s to the 1980s, listed the following steps in a rational decision making process (Drucker, 1974):

1. Define the problem.
2. Analyze the problem.
3. Develop alternative solutions.
4. Decide on the best solution.
5. Convert decisions into effective actions.

Such a formulation was seen as helping the administrator to organize decision making and make it more systematic, an alternative to intuitive, perhaps haphazard, knee-jerk responses to the flow of events in the busy environment of organizational life. Drucker's model, much elaborated and detailed, was widely applied in corporate and governmental organizations throughout the United States, and it was accepted by many as the essential logic of administrative thought.

Nevertheless, even as the number of models proliferated and efforts to install them in organizations intensified, a widespread disparity between the theoretic notions of the scholars and actual practices of administrators was also apparent. It was noted, for example, that decision making usually does not terminate with either a decision or the action to implement a decision. In the real world, decision making is usually an iterative, ongoing process whereby the results of one decision provide new information on which to base yet other decisions. Thus, feedback loops were added to some process models to ensure that the outcomes of decisions would be considered when future decisions were pondered.

Eventually, recognition of this cyclic nature of decision-making processes caused some students of the subject to abandon conventional lists of steps and linear flowcharts in favor of circular depictions. Both the feedback loop concept and the circular concept of decision-making processes illustrate two additional assumptions commonly found in the literature on decision making:

1. Decision making is an iterative, cyclical process that proceeds over time to provide successive approximations of optimal action;
2. Reaching optimal decisions is the central goal of decision making.

It has long been obvious, however, that people in an organization do not tend to search end-lessly and relentlessly for the best way of achieving goals. They engage in decision-making proce-dures to seek alternative ways of doing things only when the organization's performance seems to be falling below some acceptable level. This "acceptable level" of performance is usually not the highest level of performance possible; rather, it is one that is good enough to fit the organization's percep-tion of reality and values. Once those in the organization sense the need to seek some alternative way of doing things, they tend to seek a course of action that is perceived as sufficient to alleviate the need for action. That is, they tend to make a decision that will relieve the proximate problem but are unlikely to seize the moment as an occasion for moving to some optimal level of performance. This widespread tendency in organizations is called *satisficing* (March & Simon, 1958).

LIMITS ON RATIONALITY IN DECISION MAKING

As we have explained, much of the scholarly literature on decision making—both organizational and individual—represents the efforts of academicians to uncover and describe the logic as-sumed by them to be inherent in decision-making processes. Based on these efforts, a number of models of decision-making processes have been developed. These models, it has often been assumed, can be useful in facilitating the learning of this logic by administrators so that logic may be applied in their work. Many people—including practicing educational administrators, legislators, and school board members trained at a time when these assumptions were essentially unchallenged—persist in the belief that more rigorous application of these efforts to practice is essential to improving organizational performance. Recall our discussion in the previous chapter about *discrete* and *emergent* problems. Although a simple, rational decision-making model may be applied to a discrete problem by one individual having all the needed information, emergent problems are the domain of more complex decision-making processes.

Emergent problems, with their ambiguity and uncertainty are the dominant issues of the real world of the educational administrator. Organizations, their goals, their technologies, and their environments have become so complex that it is difficult to connect causes with effects, ac-tions with outcomes. For example, the volatile nature of the economic, social, and political envi-ronments of the educational organization makes it difficult to predict the course of future events with any certitude. This condition is not limited to educational organizations by any means; it is of pressing importance in all forms of organizational life. This volatility has caused researchers to reexamine organizational life more carefully in recent years and, in the process, to question old assumptions concerning the logic and rationality of decision making.

The Gap Between Theory and Practice

Scholars commonly seek to improve the performance of administrators by instructing them in the application of rational, logical models of decision making to their work. Still one of the most practi-cal decision-making theories, Victor Vroom and Philip Yetton's (1973) contingency model points out with remarkable clarity that the central issue in contemporary leadership is participation in the process of making decisions. The issue is often confused by value-laden arguments over the relative merits of a hard-nosed, directive administrative style as contrasted with a more consultative style. Even the eminent Peter Drucker (1974) lapsed occasionally into contrasting "democratic manage-ment," "participatory democracy," and "permissiveness" with the supposed successes of autocratic, tyrannical management that makes decisions by fiat. Clearly, the complexities of modern organiza-tions require decision-making processes that are carefully selected with an eye to the probability of effectiveness in view of the contingencies in the situation. There may be situations in which an autocratic style is most effective and other situations that call for highly participatory methods for greatest effectiveness. As Vroom and Yetton see it, the problem for the leader is to analyze the contingencies in each situation and then behave in the most effective manner.

Vroom and Yetton (1973) specified how leaders ought to behave in order to be effective in view of specific contingencies. The Vroom-Yetton model is not prescriptive, but it can be described as a normative model because it tries to tie appropriate leader behavior to specific contingencies.

VROOM AND YETTON'S FIVE LEADERSHIP STYLES

Vroom and Yetton have developed a taxonomy of five leadership styles, as follows:

Autocratic Process (Types AI and AII)

Style I: AI. Leader (manager, administrator) makes the decision using whatever information is available.

Style II: AII. Leader secures necessary information from members of the group, then makes the decision. In obtaining the information, the leader may or may not tell followers what the problem is.

Consultative Process (Types CI and CII)

Style III: CI. Leader shares the problem with relevant members of the group on a one-to-one basis, getting their ideas and suggestions individually without bringing them together as a group; then the leader makes the decision.

Style IV: CII. Leader shares the problem with members as a group at a meeting, then decides.

Group Process (Type GI)

Style V: GI. Leader, acting as chairperson at a meeting of the group, shares the problem with the group and facilitates efforts of the group to reach consensus on a group decision. Leader may give information and express opinion but does not try to "sell" a particular decision or manipulate the group through covert means.

Notice that Vroom and Yetton have described these leadership styles in behavioral terms (for example, "leader decides" or "leader shares the problem with the group") rather than in general terms (for example, "directive style" or "participative style"). They do not imply that one style is more highly valued than others or that an issue must be addressed in terms of which behavior works in the specific situation.

Seven Situation Issues

In the Vroom and Yetton model, analysis of the situation begins with yes or no answers to the following questions:

   A. *Does the problem possess a quality requirement?* One quality might be time: Is this a decision that must be made now, with no time to consult others? Other quality factors might be the

desirability of stimulating team development or keeping people informed through participation.

B. *Does the leader have sufficient information to make a good decision?*
C. *Is the problem structured?*
D. *Is it necessary for others to accept the decision in order for it to be implemented?*
E. *If the leader makes the decision alone, how certain is it that others will accept it?*
F. *Do others share the organizational goals that will be attained by solving this problem?*
G. *Are the preferred solutions to the problem likely to create conflict among others in the group?*

Decision-Process Flowchart

The leader can quickly diagnose the situation's contingencies by answering yes or no to each of the seven questions listed above, as they are arrayed on the decision-process flowchart (see Figure 10.1). As the flowchart shows, it is possible to identify 14 types of problems in this way, and the preferred way of dealing with each becomes evident as one follows the chart from left to right.

For example, given a problem, the first question is the following: Does the problem possess a quality requirement? In effect the question is as follows: Is one decision preferable to or more rational than another? If not, then questions B and C are irrelevant, and one follows the flowchart to question D: Is acceptance of the decision by others important to implementing it? If the answer to this question is no, then the leader may utilize type AI (solution style "I" in the chart) which is to make the decision alone, using information available. If acceptance by others is important, however, then question E must be asked: If I make the decision, am I certain others will accept it? If yes, the leader makes it alone (type AI), but if not, then the group makes the decision together (type GI or solution style "V" in the chart). The flowchart clearly suggests there is a logical basis for utilizing various leadership styles for maximum effectiveness under specific describable circumstances.

Early research conducted in a variety of organizations made it clear that practicing managers and administrators rarely used such models in their work. Henry Mintzberg, Duru Raisinghani, and Andre Theoret reported that normative decision-making models have no influence on the behavior of middle- and upper-level corporate managers (Mintzberg, Raisinghani, & Theoret, 1976). James G. March (1981) found that decision makers, in fact, tended to make sense of problems not by applying logical models to them but by assessing what kinds of options are actually available to be used in solving them. Paul C. Nutt (1984), after examining 78 different organizations, concluded the following:

> Nothing remotely resembling the normative methods described in the literature was carried out. Not even hybrid variations were observed. … The sequence of problem definition, alternative generation, refinement, and selection, called for by nearly every theorist seems rooted in rational arguments, not behavior. Executives do not use this process. (p. 446)

A national survey of senior high school principals indicated a similar situation among that group of administrators (National Association of Secondary School Principals, 1978).

Thus, we have an obvious gap between theory and practice. What does this gap mean? It could suggest that the administrators and managers whose behavior was studied by the researchers were ill-trained and, therefore, unable to use the decision-making models available to them. An

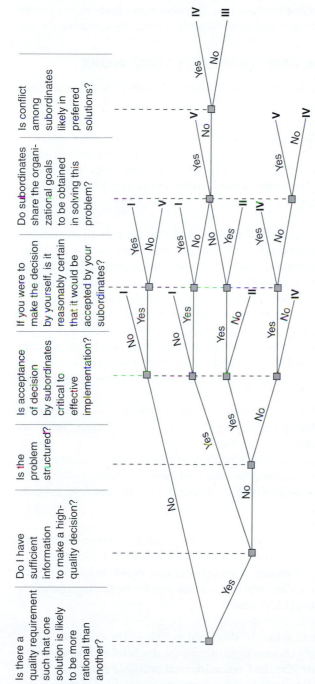

I. You solve the problem or make the decision yourself, using information available to you at the time. II. You obtain the necessary information from your subordinate(s), then decide on the solution to the problem yourself. You may or may not tell your subordinates what the problem is when you are getting the information from them. The role played by your subordinates in making the decision is clearly one of providing the necessary information to you, rather than generating or evaluating alternative solutions. III. You share the problem with relevant subordinates individually, getting their ideas and suggestions without bringing them together as a group. Then *you* make the decision that may or may not reflect your subordinates' influence. IV. You share the problem with your subordinates as a group, collectively obtaining their ideas and suggestions. Then *you* make the decision that may or may not reflect your subordinates' influence. V. You share a problem with your subordinates as a group. Together, you generate and evaluate alternatives and attempt to reach agreement (consensus) on a solution. Your role is much like that of a chairperson. You do not try to influence the group to adopt "your" solution, and you are willing to accept and implement any solution that has the support of the entire group.

FIGURE 10.1   Vroom-Yetton normative leadership model.

Source: From Luthans, F. (1977). *Organizational behavior* (2nd ed.). New York, NY: McGraw-Hill, p. 458. Reproduced with permission of McGraw-Hill.

equally plausible explanation is that the decision-making models espoused in the scholarly literature arise from assumptions about the nature of administrative work that do not reflect the conditions that the administrator on the job actually encounters. This disconnect leads us to consider
research that describes the behavior of managers and administrators as it actually occurs on the job.

THE NATURE OF MANAGERIAL AND ADMINISTRATIVE WORK

Henry Mintzberg (1973) reported research that presented detailed descriptions of the activities
of the chief executives of five organizations as they were observed in their daily work. The executives whose behaviors were thus recorded were (a) the manager of a consulting firm, (b) the
president of an industrial company, (c) the manager of a hospital, (d) a manager of a consumer
goods concern, and (e) the superintendent of a suburban school district. This research strikingly
reveals, first, that the executive's work is very diverse and requires a broad range of skills and,
second, the pressure that appears to be inherent in the work. More specifically, Mintzberg developed five propositions from his observations:

1. Administrators and managers do a great deal of work, and they do it at an unrelenting
   pace. Each day, they attend a number of previously arranged meetings as well as a number
   of unplanned conferences and interactions, deal with a substantial volume of mail and paperwork, and handle numerous phone calls. There are seldom any real breaks in the work.
2. In doing their work, administrators characteristically devote a brief period to each of a
   large number of decisions, and these tend to center on specific, well-defined issues and
   problems. Important and trivial activities arise in juxtaposition to one another in an unplanned, random way, requiring quick mental shifts from topic to topic. There are many
   brief contacts with people interspersed with planned meetings of prolonged duration and
   other activities (such as desk work, telephone calls, unscheduled meetings, and tours)
   worked into the daily schedule.
3. Administrators prefer to deal with active problems that are well-defined and nonroutine.
   Routine information (such as recurring reports) is given low priority, whereas "fresh" information (even if of uncertain quality) is given high priority.
4. Verbal communication is much preferred. (In Mintzberg's original study, it accounted for
   over three-fourths of the executives' time and two-thirds of their activities.)
5. Managers maintain working relationships with three principal groups: superiors, subordinates, and outsiders.

This research suggests a great deal about the ways in which administrators make decisions, particularly about why few seem to use formal decision-making models in their work. The
rhythm of the administrator's workday constitutes a driving force that evokes behavior in ways
that are not likely to enter the mind of the contemplative scholar pondering the logic he or she
seeks to find in the situation. As Mintzberg (1973) noted:

> The work of managing an organization may be described as taxing. The quantity of
> work to be done, or that the manager chooses to do, during the day is substantial and
> the pace is unrelenting. After hours, the chief executive (and probably many other
> managers as well) appears to be able to escape neither from an environment that rec-
> ognizes the power and status of his position nor from his [sic] own mind, which has
> been well trained to search continually for new information. (p. 30)

In conducting his observations of the administrators he studied, Mintzberg developed a technique that required the frequent recording of code symbols that described behaviors being observed during numerous short timeframes during the day. Eventually, these coded entries were reduced and arrayed statistically to produce a detailed, quantified description of the observable behaviors that occurred over the total period of time during which observations were carried out.

A number of studies using the Mintzberg technique have examined the on-the-job behavior of educational administrators such as superintendents of schools and school principals (Morris, Crowson, Hurwitz, & Porter-Gehrie, 1981, 1984; Pitner, 1978). This research has confirmed that Mintzberg's propositions apply to the work of school administrators who work long hours at an unrelenting pace. Their work is characterized by many brief interactions, mostly verbal. Meetings, phone calls, and paperwork account for almost every minute from the moment they enter the office in the morning until they leave in the afternoon or evening.

Mintzberg's use of the term *unrelenting pace* needs a little clarification here. One could conjure up the image of an assembly line worker being driven at his or her task by the inexorable rush of work coming down the line, never stopping, never varying, which is not what Mintzberg appeared to mean in describing the work of managers. In the manager's work situation, time becomes an important resource. Unlike the situation of the teacher, however, time for the administrator is a fluid resource rather than a constraining one.

For the teacher, critical time constraints (such as the school year, the school day, the bell schedule, and fixed constraints such as bus schedules and lunch schedules) sharply limit what he or she can do. Administrators, on the other hand, can—and often do—have considerable latitude to vary the pace of their work as it seems appropriate to them. They can take extra time to carefully consider some unimportant issues at length, if they wish, and seek to save time by making a series of rapid decisions on other matters. Or the administrator who wishes to do so can vary the use of time resources by stretching the workday into the evening, or the workweek into the weekend, and the work year into the summer and holidays, which is, of course, what many educational administrators commonly do. Thus, the "unrelenting pace" is not necessarily an unvarying pace; it is one in which characteristically the work to be done is never completed, and there is always more to be done. One never knows when the task is finished.

These characteristics of administrative work combine with the ambiguity inherent in the educational system—an ambiguity arising from the unclear goals and priorities of schools and school systems, uncertain methods of evaluating administrative performance, and problematic preferences exercised by various constituency groups—to put considerable pressure on educational administrators. One result, and an additional source of pressure, is that they—like administrators in other fields—seldom stop thinking about their work.

How Administrators Think

Research suggests that a source of confusion in the minds of scholars who study organizations and the behavior of administrators in them may be the fact that academic people and administrators tend to think about administrative work in different ways. The models for decision making described in the beginning of this chapter are the products of persons conditioned in the belief that highly logical, linear thinking, sometimes called *scientific thinking*, is the single most appropriate way of exploring problems and seeking alternatives in the decision-making process. Such observers, largely academics, tend to expect to see administrators behave in much the same ways that they themselves do. They maintain "that thinking is visible in the form of long reflective episodes during which managers sit alone, away from the action, trying to make logical inferences from facts. Since observers do not see many episodes that look like this, they conclude that managers do not do much thinking" (Weick, 1983, p. 222). Indeed, much of the in-service training for administrators that emphasizes the so-called models for decision making is little more than an effort to train administrators in formal methods of reflective thought. The assumption underlying such training is that one can improve the decision-making behavior of administrators by improving their skills in logical, reflective thought.

But why do researchers report so few occasions in which administrators are observed, as scientists frequently are, thinking reflectively—cogitating, mulling over a problem, considering alternatives in the dispassionate calm of a quiet retreat? Karl Weick proposes three possible explanations. First, they do think but not while they are on the job: "[T]hey think at home, on airplanes, in the john, on weekends. . . . Thus, the reason researchers do not see managers think is that managers do not think when the observers are around" (Weick, 1983, pp. 222–223). The second possibility is that, essentially, managers do not think because they have reduced uncertainty to such an extent and anticipate the future so well that they are confronted by few situations in which they are perplexed or bewildered. The third possibility proposed by Weick (and the one he considers most likely) is that managers think all the time, but researchers have missed that fact because, while researchers look for episodes evidencing reflective thinking, managers go at the thinking process quite differently. That is, thinking is inseparably woven into, and occurs simultaneously with, managerial and administrative action.

Thus, when administrators tour, read, talk, supervise, and meet with others, all of those actions contain thought, and, indeed, they *are* the ways in which administrators do their thinking. "Connected ideas, which are the essence of thought," Weick (1983) explained, "can be formed and managed *outside* the mind, with relatively little assistance from the mind. This is how managers work, and this is why we are misled when we use reflection as an index of how much their work involves thinking" (p. 222). Thus, most of the thinking that administrators do is woven into their actions when their actions are taken with attention, intention, and control; that is, they pay attention to what is happening, impose order on their actions, and correct their performance when it strays from accepted standards.

In considering the ways in which administrators think about their work, it is important to bear in mind that the organizational environment in which the work is done is characterized by ambiguity, uncertainty, and disorder: It is, in a word, messy. Situations that require decisions are often fluid and are therefore difficult to analyze, even after the fact; they are subject to a number of interpretations, often conflicting; and (as will be explained more fully later) they are often not clearly bound and labeled. In the daily flow of action, administrators typically engage in brief, spontaneous, face-to-face, verbal interaction with others. They are, in other words, constantly "fighting fires." But, as Weick (1983) wrote,

> fighting fires, which managers do all the time, is not necessarily thick-headed or slow witted. Firefighting has seemed like mindless activity because we have used scientific activity as the ideal case for comparison, because we have thought of thinking as a separate activity that stops when people put out fires, because we have presumed that the only time people think is when they make distinct decisions or solve clearcut problems ... and because we keep examining things as if they occurred in sequences rather than simultaneously. (p. 236)

A crucial issue is implied in this view: whether administration is, or can be, a science in the traditional sense or whether it is, instead, an art or a craft. Many continue to pursue the notion of administration as the application of management science to organizational problems (much as engineering is the application of physics and mathematics to other sorts of real-world problems), as envisioned earlier in the twentieth century. Those holding this view tend, of course, to emphasize the development of technical rationality in organizational decision making. Others—cognizant of the great complexities of human organizations and the uncertainty, instability, and uniqueness that are commonly found in them—recognize the importance of intuitive judgment and skill, the sense of proportion and appropriateness in the context of the traditions and values of the organization's culture. Schön, like Weick, found the thinking of managers closely entwined with the action demanded in their work. Schön (1983) observed:

> Managers do reflect in action. Sometimes, when reflection is triggered by uncertainty, the manager says, in effect, "This is puzzling; how can I understand it?" Sometimes, when a sense of opportunity provokes reflection, the manager asks, "What can I make of this?" And sometimes, when a manager is surprised by the success of his own intuitive knowing, he asks himself, "What have I really been doing?" (pp. 240–241)

Thus, Schön makes clear that the term *art* has a two-fold meaning in describing administration: intuitive approaches to understanding situations and also one's reflection, in a context of action, when one encounters events that are incongruent with his or her intuitive understandings.

The reader should note that, in this discussion, we are talking about *trained* intuition (Blackburn, 1971). The point is that we can learn—through both formal education and socialization into the organization's culture—to see a complex system as an organic whole as well as being trained (as we commonly are) to see individual parts of the whole. This crucial point is difficult for some observers to accept, perhaps for two main reasons. One is that, in the strong tradition of technical rationality that has long been emphasized in Western culture, the logic of breaking complex phenomena down into relatively simple, quantifiable parts has been thoroughly ingrained in many of us. It seems so sensible, so right, that holistic approaches to complex problems are suspect. It is also probable that recent research on right- and left-hemisphere brain functioning is important to our understanding here. One mode of consciousness, associated with the left hemisphere, is generally described as analytic, rational, sequential, convergent, logical, objective, and linear. The other, associated with the right hemisphere, is characterized as intuitive, holistic, pattern-recognizing, artistic, subjective, and nonlinear. Unquestionably, emphasis has been placed on training left-brain functions in education that stresses logical-positivistic approaches to decision making. If we are to improve the way we apply right-hemisphere functioning to our decision making, it is likely that we will also have to improve our training strategies (Pondy, 1983).

Thus, it is argued that administrators are thinking all the time, that their thinking is closely intertwined with the actions (decisions) they take, and that everyday thinking almost never represents a sequence of steps. These facts suggests that formal models for decision making have little relevance to everyday administrative thinking and that to try to implement them would run counter to the real world as administrators experience it. In the real world, problem situations are experienced holistically and the steps found in the usual decision-making models are considered simultaneously rather than serially. This view suggests that emphasis on holistic thought—which seeks understanding of the complexities, interconnections, ambiguities, and uncertainties of educational organizations—might be more fruitful in decision making than the linear and step models proffered in the past.

The Influence of Organizational Culture on Decision Making

Earlier in this book, the concept of organizational culture was discussed as being at the core of understanding organizational behavior such as decision making. Organizational culture involves the norms that develop in a work group, the dominant values advocated by the organization, the philosophy that guides the organization's policies concerning employees and client groups, and the feeling that is evident in the ways in which people interact with one another. Thus, it clearly deals with basic assumptions and beliefs that are shared by members of the organization. Taken together, these define the organization itself in crucial ways: why it exists, how it has survived, what it is about. In the process of developing and becoming part of the way of life in the organization, these values and basic beliefs tend to become solidly—almost unquestioningly—established as "the way we do things here." In this way, they shape the view of the world that members bring to problems and decision making. We speak of intuition in the processes of thinking; organizational culture plays a large role in shaping that intuition because the assumptions and beliefs that compose the essence of organizational culture are largely taken for granted by participants. This fact is especially so in educational organizations because those who work in them are generally highly socialized to the values and central beliefs of the organization through long years of commitment to them.

Consider the educational and work history of professionals in schools and institutions of higher education. Most of these people entered school at the age of five or (at most) six and have remained in educational organizations, with only brief absences (such as for military service or child rearing), almost continuously throughout their formative years and the later years in which they established themselves as full adult members of society. As a result, they have strong tendencies to accept the values of education and educational organizations and, as professionals in these organizations, are highly committed to their core values, central beliefs, and goals. In the long process of being so thoroughly socialized into the organization—first as student, and, ultimately, as professional—those who work in educational organizations tend to accept the "rules of the game" for getting along and "the ropes" that must be learned in order to become accepted as a member.

In other words, these individuals become members of a set of persons who have a long history of sharing common experiences. These shared experiences have, over time, led to the creation of a shared view of the world and their place in it. This shared view enables people in the organization to make sense of commonplace as well as unusual events, ascribe meaning to symbols and rituals, and share in a common understanding of how to deal with unfolding action in appropriate ways. Such sense making was described by Karl Weick (1983) as being central to understanding how people in organizations attribute credibility to interpretations they have made of their experience. Such a shared view is developed over a period of time during which the participants engage in a great deal of communicating, testing, and refinement of the shared view until it is eventually perceived to have been so effective for so long it is rarely thought about or talked about anymore: It is taken for granted. This process constitutes the development of an *organizational culture*. And, as Deal (1985) informed us, it is culture that largely determines how one perceives and understands the world; culture is the concept that captures the subtle, elusive, intangible, largely unconscious forces that shape thought in a workplace.

Mintzberg's analysis, which is supported by a number of studies in educational organizations, makes it clear that administrators spend little time in reflective thought. They are active; they spend much of their time communicating, interruptions are frequent, and they have little opportunity to be alone in peace and quiet. But as Schön and Weick have pointed out, that does not necessarily mean that administrators do not think; it means that their thinking is closely intertwined with their action on the job.

But is their thinking merely random, perhaps geared to the last person with whom they talked or the latest crisis that has emerged? Probably not. Organizational culture is a powerful environment that reflects past experiences, summarizes them, and distills them into simplifications that help to explain the enormously complex world of the organization. In this sense, Weick (1979) indicated the organization—the school, the university—may be understood as a body of thought that has evolved over time and that guides the administrator in understanding what is going on and how to deal with it. This body of thought embodies a highly complex array of subtleties, inconsistencies, and competing truths: It reflects the complexities and delicate balances of the administrator's world. Efforts to reduce this complexity through simplification processes such as imposing decision-making models on it are not likely to be very workable. In this view, therefore, the culture of the organization represents significant thinking prior to action and is implicit in the decision-making behavior of administrators.

The role and power of organizational culture to shape and mold the thinking and, therefore, the decision making of people in organizations is not a new concept by any means. Only recently, however, has it received widespread serious attention from organizational analysts and administrative practitioners alike as an approach to improving the decision making of organizations.

Closing the Gap Between Theory and Practice

What guidance does the theoretic and research literature offer for practicing administrators attempting to implement these newer concepts in decision making? One answer is that, in selecting an administrative style to use in practice, one needs to examine one's assumptions about what is the most effective approach to administrative practice. Let us consider briefly how some of the important points of this text come together at this juncture to see where they lead us in administrative decision making.

Administration has been defined as *working with and through people to achieve organizational goals*. It has long been accepted that the functions of administration are planning, organizing, leading, coordinating, and controlling. But the persistent puzzling question throughout the twentieth century was the following: What are the most effective ways of performing these functions? As we have described, there are conflicting ways to approach administrative practice: Classical approaches and human resources approaches are the leading contenders among the currently competing systems of analysis through which administrative practice is interpreted. Except for those administrators who choose to pursue a mindless eclectic course in their professional work, the administrator must choose among these competing systems of analysis in deciding how to go about his or her professional work. The choice that the administrator makes rests largely on assumptions about the nature of organizations and the people in them.

THEORY OF PRACTICE

How will you make decisions as a leader? What theories about the decision-making process will you follow? The assumptions that form the foundations of one's professional practice constitute, in the language of Chris Argyris (1971) and Donald Schön (1983, 1987), a theory of practice. But we do not always practice what we preach; the actual theory of practice that one uses in deciding what to do is not always explicit, clear, and well-reasoned. Indeed, given human frailty, we often espouse one theory but act on the basis of another, perhaps conflicting, theory. We commonly witness administrators verbalizing their commitment to values that support improving the quality of work life in educational organizations while engaging in actions that are perceived by role referents to be antithetical to such improvement. Thus, as individuals—often enlightened and well-intended—we act out the conflict between opposing ideas about organizations and people that has characterized organizational theory for decades.

Human Resources Development—A Theory of Decision Making

There is a pattern in the history of the competition between the two major conflicting systems of analysis. Over the course of the twentieth century, the classical (or bureaucratic) approach gradually lost credibility, in the analysis of *educational* organizations at least, because the organizational problems of schools and universities deepened even as the application of bureaucratic attempts at solution grew and multiplied. Simultaneously, as more sophisticated research was pushed forward, the credibility and usefulness of human resources approaches grew steadily, and that pattern seems likely to continue into the foreseeable future. This pattern is clearly evident in the body of research literature that is being discussed in this text, and it is called *human resources development* (HRD). HRD is based on the overlapping theories and concepts of scholars such as Chris Argyris (1971), Abraham Maslow (1970), Frederick Herzberg (1966), Rensis Likert (1961), James March and Herbert Simon (1958), Douglas McGregor (1960), William Ouchi (1981), and Karl Weick (1979, 1983).

Recall that McGregor (1960) described two sets of conflicting assumptions that administrators tend to hold about people and their attitudes toward work: Theory X, the belief that people are lazy and will avoid work if they can, and Theory Y, the belief that people seek responsibility and want to perform satisfying work. These concepts are now well understood by many administrators. Maslow's concept of motivation is based on a hierarchy of needs in which satisfied needs are seen as not motivating people but in which unsatisfied needs can be motivators. Herzberg's work identified what he called maintenance factors (such as compensation and working conditions) as not being motivators but as being essential in order for motivating factors (such as satisfaction arising from achievement in the work itself and a sense of autonomy on the job) to be effective. Maslow and Herzberg's theories of motivation are detailed in Chapter 5.

Likert (1961) conceptualized four management styles (System 1 through System 4), each using different styles of leadership, motivation, and conflict management that have predictable outcomes in terms of organizational culture as well as end results in terms of organizational effectiveness. Further, and perhaps more important, Likert pointed out that it is the administrator—who has options from which to choose in deciding what the philosophy of management is to be, how communication is to be carried out, and how decisions shall be made in the organization—who bears major responsibility for the culture that develops in an organization. Vroom and Yetton lent strong support to Likert's views by demonstrating that administrators are key actors in controlling decision making in the organization, and that this control is exercised by the decision-making style that administrators choose to use.

Argyris (1971) emphasized the need to develop greater harmony and consistency between the goals of organizations and the human needs of people who work in them, which requires replacing directive administrative styles with more participative styles.

James March and Herbert Simon (1958) pointed out that ambiguity and uncertainty characterize the natural state of affairs in organizations, rather than the patterns of predictability and order that administrators have traditionally sought to find in them. Thus, streams of problems, solutions, participants, and opportunities for making choices swirl around, occasionally resulting in decisions, though rarely arrived at in the sequential fashion usually envisioned by formal, rational decision-making models.

Karl Weick (1979, 1983) made it clear that, instead of the close hierarchical cause-and-effect linkages that classical theory assumes to be present in organizations, the instructional activities of schools are characteristically loosely coupled. This loose coupling not only calls traditional assumptions about management methods into question but also creates new visions of how schools can be managed to reduce the rigidity and ineffectiveness so frequently observed in them.

William Ouchi (1981) and others—including Terrence Deal (1985), Michael Fullan (2005), Rosabeth Moss Kanter (1983), Edgar Schein (1968, 1985), and Marshall W. Meyer (1977)— have explained that there are various ways of exercising administrative control in organizations. Although traditional bureaucratic hierarchy is one way, and is often thought to be the only way, in fact, the norms of the culture of an organization evolving throughout its history are an exceedingly powerful means through which administrators exercise influence over others. The cultures of some organizations are more effective than others in implementing HRD concepts of motivation, leadership, conflict management, decision making, and change.

These HRD perspectives on organization provide a set of assumptions on which to base the practice of administration that are clear alternatives to classical perspectives. Those who choose to use classical bureaucratic perspectives on organization continue to push hard for reducing ambiguity through increasing the use of rules and close surveillance, striving for greater logic and predictability through more planning, increased specification of objectives, and tighter hierarchical control. Whereas contemporary best thinking in management emphasizes tapping the motivations and abilities of participants while recognizing that disorder and illogic are often ordinary characteristics of effective organizations, taken together, the assumptions of HRD constitute a theory of decision making, the centerpiece of which is participative methods, resulting in the *empowerment* of others.

PARTICIPATIVE DECISION MAKING

Much of decision making revolves around issues of participation in solving problems and making decisions. *Participation* is defined as the mental and emotional involvement of a person in a group situation that encourages the individual to contribute to group goals and to share responsibility for them (Davis, 1972). Participation as "mental and emotional involvement" is the notion of ownership of (or buying into) decisions, genuine ego involvement, not merely being present and "going through the motions." Such involvement is motivating to the participant and thus releases his or her own energy, creativity, and initiative. One of the pioneers in human relations theory, Mary Parker Follett (1941), distinguished participation from *consent,* which is the major feature of voting on issues or approving proposals. This ego involvement, this sense of ownership, also encourages people to accept greater responsibility for the organization's effectiveness. Having bought into the goals and the decisions of the group, the individual sees him- or herself as having a stake in seeing them work out well, which, in turn, stimulates the development of teamwork so characteristic of effective organizations.

The use of participative decision making has two major potential benefits: (a) arriving at better decisions and (b) enhancing the growth and development of the organization's participants (for example, greater sharing of goals, improved motivation, improved communication, better-developed group-process skills). As a practical guide for implementing participative processes in educative organizations, three factors in particular should be kept in mind: (a) the need for an explicit decision-making process, (b) the nature of the problem to be solved or the issue to be decided, and (c) criteria for including people in the process.

Participative Decision Making and Empowerment

Participative decision making requires the interaction of power and influence from two sources: the power and influence of the administrator and the power and influence of others in the organization. In educational organizations, these others are generally faculty members, students, and/or community members. When the organization is conceptualized as a traditional bureaucracy, which emphasizes the top-down exercise of hierarchical power, the power of administrators is ordinarily viewed as being in conflict with that of others. Indeed, in such a view, the administrator tends to consider it important to garner power, expand it if possible, and limit the power and influence of others. Unionized teachers, on the other hand, consider it important to resist the expansion of the administrator's power and seek to enlarge their own power. These are important elements in establishing and maintaining control of decision making in the organization when the participants are responding to traditional values and beliefs.

Administrators who embrace these traditional views of organization and administration may view the management of participative decision making in the organization as requiring a conflict management approach. In the traditional organization, characterized by employer-worker relationships that we now tend to associate with the stereotypical factory model, the power and influence of the administrator dominates the decision-making process, and the followers have little ability to influence the course of events.

In traditional organizations, which are markedly hierarchical, the process of deciding how to make decisions is largely controlled by the administrator, not the followers. In such an organization, the process from autocratic decision making toward collaborative decision making resides largely in the extent to which the administrator sees power sharing as a win-win proposition, a desirable state of affairs, rather than a threat to administrative hegemony. Many present-day educational organizations, though still hierarchical, have developed collaborative cultures to such an extent that reverting to the autocratic model would be difficult; the administrator is not so much confronted with the issue of whether others will be involved in decision making but, rather, how and to what extent they will be involved.

Participative or Democratic?

One of the most common, and most serious, errors that leaders can make in organizational decision making is to confuse participative decision making with democratic decision making. It is common to hear a principal exclaim, "Democratic decision making doesn't work! I can't hold a meeting and call for a vote every time we need to make a decision! There just isn't time for that," which is quite right. And the teachers do not want to be involved in making every decision; they do not have time for *that*, either. Let's look at some of the issues involved.

In the first place, the concept of democracy is a political one; it refers to government by the people, either directly or through representatives. It generally implies majority rule as determined by voting. It also rests on a specific concept about the relationship between the government and the governed: The governed, the body politic, exercise ultimate power over the government in the voting booth. We commonly think of the government as being at the top of a hierarchical organization with the people at the bottom, but this structure is a little misleading because, in the end, the Constitution really has created a government of the people, by the people, and for the people. This concept does not translate to educational organizations.

Educational organizations are inherently hierarchical. The school board is created by the body politic; it simply is not the province of teachers, for example, to control the organization by vote. The board can, and usually does, appoint a superintendent of schools and create an organization through which it manages the schools in the district. We say "usually does" because about 1% of school districts in the United States elect superintendents—only in Alabama, Florida, and Mississippi. Traditionally, school boards have managed the school system directly by creating a central office bureaucracy that reports to the board. A common complaint about school boards is that the boards tend to micromanage to a fault. One of the current approaches to school reform challenges that time-honored arrangement and proposes that school boards stop managing schools directly. School boards can do this by using school site management organization (called school-based management or school-based decision making), in which individual schools have more freedom to make their own decisions but are responsible to the school board for educational results. Alternatively, school boards can enter into contracts with other entities, such as charter school boards or for-profit school management corporations, to operate the schools and be responsible to the school board for educational results. However, the bottom line is that, at the school district level, the organization is hierarchical, and power is exercised asymmetrically from the top down.

At the school level, there surely may be certain issues that, from time to time, the principal might wish to have decided by a ballot of the teachers. But there is scant support in scholarly and research literature for turning the affairs of the school over to the ballot box. School principals and other administrators are educational leaders, and we have discussed the relationship between followers and leaders by which leaders are granted power to act as leaders. The Vroom and Yetton model presented in this chapter provides the leader guidance in organizing and managing *participative* decision making and that should not be confused with *democratic* decision making.

Sometimes, on some issues, teachers do want to be involved and expect the principal to make decisions and tell them what the decision is. Clearly, this process is time-efficient for everyone and is a normal way of operating on relatively simple and routine matters. At other times and on other issues, however, teachers want to be more involved—and the greater their involvement, the more time is required of them. But teachers are busy people. For that simple and practical reason, therefore, teachers usually participate in making joint decisions with the principal on a relatively limited number of issues that are considered to be very important. The principal can,

BOX 10.1

Will School Boards Disappear?

It is beyond the scope of this text to go into detail about school board decision making, except to say school boards continue to be a source of controversy. Underwood (2013) reported on the American Legislative Exchange Council's (ALEC) attempt to reduce or eliminate the decision-making authority of democratically elected school boards in Wisconsin. The many bills ALEC sponsored in Wisconsin for 2013 promote the privatization of education such as vouchers for all students to attend any school of their choosing. "What happens," Underwood wrote, "to our democracy when we return to an educational system where access is defined by corporate interest and divided by class, language, ability, race, and religion?" (p. 19). Who will make decisions about local educational policy? (ALEC is discussed in more detail in Chapter 12).

however, find many kinds of appropriate ways to involve others in decision making, so participation is optimized yet the process is time-efficient.

But too often the gap between theory and practice is evident. Research conducted by members of the University Council on Education Administration (UCEA) provided an example between what types of decision-making structures *should* occur and what often happens in the field. UCEA conducted a series of three "Voices from the Field" projects between 1999 and 2012 (Acker-Hocevar, Ballenger, Place, & Ivory, 2012). In using the voices of 81 superintendents and 85 principals across the United States, Touchton, Taylor, and Acker-Hocevar (2012) found that although superintendents and principals understood and believed they should include stakeholders in important decisions, they often failed to do so at sufficient levels.

> Superintendents and principals agreed that giving voice, listening, and involving stakeholders were important and necessary to making decisions that were in the best interest of students, both at the school district and school levels . . . however, both groups believed it was complex and time consuming. These two factors, complexity and time, along with the lack of stakeholder understanding of accountability for decisions, made consistent and appropriate implementation of participative decision making problematic. (p. 138)

The main recommendation from this study was that superintendents and principals should establish a decision-making system to include "processes, structures, and procedures... and an ethical framework for decision making that school leaders, teachers, students, and community constituents agree to as part of the decision-making system" (p. 140). Most importantly, in following critical theory (as discussed in Chapter 1) Touchton, Taylor, and Acker-Hocevar emphasized that role responsibilities should deliberately include historically under-represented populations who have not been given a voice in the decision-making system.

In participative decision making, all organizational members have the right to be heard, express their views, express feelings, and offer knowledge and information. Thus, they have a right to be part of the process. As the organization becomes experienced in participative methods, it may very well shift, over time, from the traditional top-down model across a range of optional ways of working together to the level of true collaboration. However, nowhere in this process is it inherent that the leader is bound by the vote of subordinates. In that sense, a school is not a democracy; at its best, it is a participative organization.

An Explicit Decision-Making Process

Participation can mean many things. All too often, the process, when not properly attended to, can be seen by participants as vague and ill-defined. Under such conditions, people are not sure when to participate or what their proper role is in the process.

The most important decision that a group makes is *to decide how it will make decisions.* This is often one of the most obscure facts of organizational life: People often do not know who makes decisions or how they are made, let alone how they individually may participate in the process. It is important, therefore, for the organization to develop an *explicit, publicly known set of processes for making decisions that is acceptable to its participants.* Later in this chapter, we present two models of how teams can make collaborative decisions.

The best time to grapple with this problem is before it is necessary to make a decision. One way of initiating this process is to convene a meeting of a school faculty (or other work group) for the purpose of reviewing the recent performance of the group. After selecting a few *specific, recent,* decision-making episodes, the group can assess its experience by asking a few questions, such as the following: Were we the right group to make this decision? What were the processes by which this decision was reached? Do we all agree that we know how the decision was reached? How do we feel about that way of solving this problem? Should we use similar procedures next time or should we make some changes? What suggestions do we have for (a) identifying and defining problems, (b) deciding how to deal with them (and who should be involved), and (c) keeping everyone informed about what is going on?

Simple steps such as the ones listed above can begin to focus on the importance attached to the *way* that problems are defined and dealt with—a focus on group process. To be successful, it must be accompanied by an emphasis on developing a climate in the group that supports open communication and stresses the skills required for revealing and working through differences among members of the group.

Who Identifies the Problem?

Many would contend that, as one contemplates involving others in creating an explicit group decision-making process, an even more fundamental question must be confronted: Who decides what problem requires a collaborative solution or decision? As has been said many times, the most important step in making a decision is to define the problem. Whoever defines the problem literally controls the decision-making process.

At the lowest levels of group involvement, it is the administrator who decides not only what the problem is but also what the solution is. However, as one increases the freedom of others to participate in the decision-making process—that is, as one increases the empowerment of the group—a central question becomes the following: Who defines the problem? The trend toward greater empowerment of others is marked by the administrator tending to identify the problem, but leaving the options for solving the problem somewhat open to others. At the highest levels of participation, the administrator and the other participants become involved in a more genuine collaborative process of, first, mutually agreeing on the definition of the problem itself and, second, jointly deciding how to deal with it.

Emergent and Discrete Problems

We introduced in the previous chapter different types of problems organizations face. These are emergent (adaptive) and discrete (technical). Participative decision making has salience primarily because it tends to produce decisions of better quality than those reached by even highly capable individuals. But some kinds of problems are best solved by experts, whereas other kinds of problems are best solved by groups. To achieve decisions of the highest possible quality, therefore, it is necessary to analyze the situation. Indeed, one of the indicators of a highly skilled group is that its members are able to make such analyses, thereby knowing what problems the group should try to work through and what problems it should refer to appropriate experts.

Some problems have the following characteristics: (a) The elements of the problem are relatively unambiguous, clear-cut, and often quantifiable; (b) the elements of the problem are readily separable; (c) the solution to the problem requires a logical sequence of acts that may be readily performed by one person; and (d) the boundaries of the whole problem are relatively easy to discern. Problems of this kind may be called *discrete,* and they may well be solved best by an expert or the organization's leadership. Heifetz (1994) called these Type I problems.

Some problems are quite different: (a) The elements of the problem are ambiguous, uncertain, and not readily quantifiable; (b) the elements of the problem are so dynamically intertwined that it is difficult to separate them on the basis of objective criteria (in fact, obtaining measurements may be difficult); (c) the solution to the problem requires the continued coordination and interaction of a number of people; and (d) the dimensions and nature of the problem cannot be fully known at the time of decision but will come into better view as iterative processes of dealing with the problem cause it to unfold over time. These types of problems may be called *emergent*. The highest-quality solutions to problems of this kind are likely to come from a group of people who (a) are in the best position to possess among them the knowledge necessary to solve the problem and (b) will be involved in implementing the decision after it is made. Heifetz (1994) used the terms Type II and Type III problems to describe emergent issues. He stated that

we can separate these adaptive situations into Types II and III. In Type II situations, the problem is identifiable but no clear-cut solution is available. The doctor may have a solution in mind but she cannot implement it. And a solution that cannot be implemented is not really a solution; it is simply an idea, a proposal.

. . . Type III situations are even more difficult. The problem definition is not clear-cut, and technical fixes are not available. (pp. 74–75)

A typical discrete problem in a school district is handling school supplies. The myriad problems involved in consolidated purchasing, warehousing, and distributing supplies to schools are relatively clear-cut and can be ordered into a logical sequence by an expert. Indeed, compared with the skilled business manager—with his or her intimate knowledge of the budget, contract law, purchasing procedures, and the vagaries of the school supply market—a group of school district administrators trying to deal with the problem of getting the right supplies, at the right price, to the right places, on time could well be a matter of the blind leading the blind. Similarly, laying out school bus routes for maximum economy and efficiency is normally a discrete problem. The use of mathematical models and computer simulations, now relatively common in larger districts, requires the use of experts who have the requisite technical skills and the techniques for grasping the full dimensions of the problem.

Policy issues in public education, on the other hand, are very often emergent problems. In the example provided above by Heifetz, a Type II emergent problem might be clear-cut: The principal knows that professional development on the Common Core Standards implementation is required, but without the cooperation or buy-in by the teachers, it cannot be implemented, or at least it cannot be not implemented successfully. The matter of implementing competency-based education, for example, clearly qualifies as an emergent problem. Often the issue confronts school district administrators on the level of "How shall we implement the decision that has been handed down to us?" rather than the level of "Should we do it?" Type III problems are not clear-cut. For example: How do we close the achievement gap? How should we assess students? A decision to take on a Type III issue requires commitment from many people, continuous close collaboration and free flow of communication, and recognition that success depends on an iterative process of decision making as the extent and implications of the problem become apparent.

Many of the problems encountered in the course of day-to-day administrative practice are emergent. Indeed, as education grows more complex, there appears to be less and less certitude that many important issues can be resolved by experts who pass their solutions on to others to implement. Appropriate solutions require free and open communication among a number of individuals who pool and share information. Close collaboration is necessary to weigh and evaluate information in the process of developing an informed judgment about which of several alternatives might be best. Commitment to the implementation of the solution is essential in order to maintain the collaboration that is the basis of the iterative processes of decision making.

Who Should Participate?

An erroneous assumption that is often made about participative decision making is that its intent is to involve everyone in every decision. Clearly, this technique is neither practical nor desirable. Edwin Bridges (1967) has suggested two rules for identifying decisions in which it is appropriate for teachers to participate:

1. *The Test of Relevance.* "[W]hen the teacher's personal stakes in the decision are high," Bridges has stated, "their interest in participation should also be high." Problems that clearly meet this test concern teaching methods and materials, discipline, curriculum, and organizing for instruction.
2. *The Test of Expertise.* It is not enough for the teacher to have a stake in the decision; if his or her participation is to be significant, the teacher must be competent to contribute effectively. In dealing with the physical education department's program schedule, for example, English teachers may be able to contribute little or nothing. (p. 52)

We would add a significant third test to use when deciding which problems to consult teachers about the following:

3. *The Test of Jurisdiction.* Schools are organized on a hierarchical basis; the individual school and staff have jurisdiction only over those decision-making areas that are assigned to them, either by design or by omission. Problems may be *relevant* to teachers, and the teachers may have the requisite *expertise,* but—right or wrong—they may not have *jurisdiction,* that is, it might not be in their decision-making *domain.* Participation in making decisions that the group cannot implement can lead to frustration at least as great as that caused by simple nonparticipation.

Desire of Individuals to Participate

Another practical consideration is whether individuals themselves wish to be involved in making a decision. The demands of time and personal interest inevitably require each person in the organization to establish (albeit imprecisely, perhaps) some priorities for his or her time and energies. In his classic work, *The Functions of the Executive,* Chester Barnard (1938) pointed out that there are some things in which some individuals simply are not interested; he spoke of such matters as falling within the individual's *zone of indifference.* To seek active involvement of teachers in matters to which they are essentially indifferent is, of course, a way to court resistance in various forms. It is common, for example, for school principals to seek the involvement of teachers, either on a limited basis (for example, limiting participation to expressing views and opinions) or on low-level problems (reserving important decisions for themselves). There is little wonder that teachers are often indifferent to such participation.

There are areas of decision making in which teachers take great personal interest over a sustained period of time; in effect, these areas may be described as *zones of sensitivity* (Owens & Lewis, 1976), which represent "personal stakes," as it were, and could include areas such as teaching assignments and evaluation of professional performance. When dealing with problems that

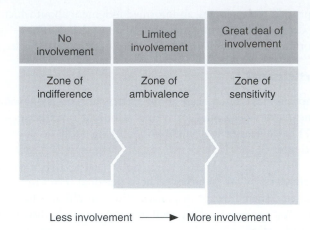

FIGURE 10.2   Zones of involvement in decision making.

fall within a staff's zone of sensitivity, a high degree of participation in a group-process mode of decision making would, of course, be indicated. The principal would enhance his or her authority with such involvement.

A third category of problems are those in which teachers have something at stake, but not enough to make them especially concerned as individuals. These fall in the *zone of ambivalence.* For example, it may be difficult for everyone on the staff to become concerned about preparing the agenda for a professional conference day or scheduling an assembly program. Thus, to avoid needless negative feelings from teachers who feel that they are already overburdened by the bureaucratic demands of administrators, involvement of teachers in problems of this sort has to be selective. To be effective, such involvement should be restricted. For example, have a small representative group deal with the problem or simply be sure to keep everyone informed as the problem is resolved. Figure 10.2 graphically depicts the three *zones* of involvement.

Undoubtedly, there will be clusters of issues to which teachers may be sensitive, ambivalent, or indifferent, but it is not possible simply to assume these generalizations; some assessment should be part of the diagnosis in each situation.

Participation Requires High Level of Skills

One persistently under-recognized problem in implementing participative decision-making methods is the need to provide participants with training in the group process skills that are needed to make collaboration work well. The intention to collaborate in making decisions is simply not sufficient in itself. And it is not sufficient that only the administrator be skilled in participative methods; It is essential that all participants understand and know how to play their roles effectively.

All too often, it is assumed that every educated adult knows how to take part in a meeting and do it well. That assumption can be a mistake, especially if one seeks to develop collaborative, collegial participation in making decisions in the organization. The mistake becomes more serious as the importance of the decision increases and the consequences of the decision loom larger in the lives of the people involved. At its best, participative decision making in educational organizations uses collaborative group methods, whereas our larger society outside the school generally emphasizes competitive group methods. For example, whenever we have a meeting, we often assume that the best way to make decisions is by voting when in fact voting is a highly competitive process because some people become winners and others become losers. That may be highly appropriate in our democratic political system, but it is generally not appropriate in organizational decision making where the goal is neither victory nor compromise but consensus and empowerment, not win-lose but win-win.

To date, the teaching and practice of collaborative group skills have been nearly absent from university programs of preparation for both teachers and administrators. Therefore, to engage in and develop participative decision making in education, it is important for decision-making groups to have adequate support in the form of access to on-the-job training and technical consultation to help members refine their skills as effective group members. Trust building, conflict management, problem solving, and open communication are among the important skill areas in which members of collaborative groups need ongoing support. Some training and skill development can be done through lectures and workshops, but third-party consultation, in which groups can get impartial feedback on the functioning of their group at work and reflect on their own experiences with the process, is essential.

VOICES FROM THE FIELD

Collaborative Decision Making

Jorge Nelson, former Head of School in Vienna, Austria;
Currently Head of School at Myanmar International School,
Burma

As the new Head of School of a top regional private independent school, I found out only after arriving on campus the first week on the job how deeply divided the faculty was over my new appointment. One faction had clearly wanted the secondary school principal, a 25-year veteran employee of the school—and the only other candidate in the final pool—to be the new Head of School. The new gymnasium was even named after him! The other faction was quite happy to embrace the newly appointed head.

It was not a healthy situation moving forward, and I was determined to meet the challenge during the first all-day orientation meeting of the school year scheduled for the next week when faculty and staff arrived to begin work. I planned to use a shared decision-making process I learned about during my doctoral studies in educational leadership, and which I successfully applied in other schools in the past. I knew I needed to bring the faculty together or else!

In preparation of the meeting, I invited everyone in the entire school, all 77 employees including non-certified staff and maintenance department members, to the all-day workshop. We arranged the session for groups of seven to sit at tables in the library. The table groups were arranged heterogeneously, not by department, to break up any cliques that had been maintained, some of which had been in existence for almost the entire 40-year history of the school.

At the orientation everyone wore a name tag, so the new and veteran faculty would be comfortable with learning everyone's names. I had them sit in a large circle, away from the table, and I led them in a simple icebreaker whereby each employee would state his or her name and then tell how they felt about their name. Their novel, personal, and sometimes humorous comments about their own lives broke the ice successfully and helped level the playing field amongst the certified and non-certified staff. The whole exercise took about two and a half hours for everyone to speak, but it was worth the time as everyone got to know more about their co-workers, and the ice was melted.

After the coffee break, I distributed a written assignment for each group to work on. The title of the assignment read: "Top Ten of the Top Ten: Small group identification of the Top Ten issues needing to be addressed by the entire school community and then individual voting for your own individual Top Ten of the Top Ten." In this assignment, I used a variation of the nominal group technique.

The directions of the assignment read: "a) Each group will create a team name for themselves based on a local fruit or vegetable; b) The team will then have one hour for an open, frank, positive discussion amongst themselves about issues facing the school community based on the mission and vision of the school; c) After the discussion, the team scribe will list the Top Ten issues agreed upon in consensus; d) The teams will post the Top Ten around the library walls so everyone can see each team's 'Top Ten List.'" This exercise took the rest of the morning. We then had lunch together at our tables.

After lunch, I began by asking each team's spokesperson to present their team's "Top Ten List" to the entire group. Each spokesperson had approximately 10 minutes to describe the list—about one minute per line item. After every team had their say in front of the entire group, I handed out ballots for each employee to list his or her individual Top Ten issues from the 11 Top Ten lists posted around the library. I collected the ballots from everyone and thanked them for a successful day. I immediately collated the data and sent out the results to all employees. The results of this data-based survey became my to-do list for running the school my first year on the job.

It is important to note that I only facilitated the process. I did not include my opinion in any of the discussions. I observed and listened the entire day. The exercise took only one day, yet the entire group of school employees came together, debated, and arrived at a consensus on important issues. At the end of the day, everyone had their personal say by voting on the "Top Ten of the Top Ten." I trusted the team of professionals, both certified and non-certified, to do a good job in identifying what challenges needed to be addressed, and they did. I now knew what to do to make this school more successful and a happier place in which to work. With my to-do list developed by the faculty and staff, there was ownership and buy-in from the entire school community already—day one!

PARADIGMS FOR COLLABORATIVE DECISION MAKING

Confusion can be a very real hazard in organizational decision making. Unless participants know just what procedures the organization is using to arrive at decisions and what their own role and function will be in the procedures, the advantages ascribed to democratic or participatory decision making may well be nullified. It would be difficult to find research support for describing ambiguity in the decision-making processes in a school as a virtue. In addition to knowing *how* people are to participate in decision making—that is, what their role and functions will be—they must know *when* they will participate.

It is also important that participants understand the orderly steps of the decision-making process as the organization moves toward a decision. These steps can be charted, which can make some of the critical choices to be made more apparent. A skeleton of a proposed decision-making paradigm using the rational decision making process presented earlier in this chapter might resemble the one in Figure 10.3 which shows the four steps typically involved in reaching a decision: (a) defining the problem, (b) identifying possible alternatives, (c) predicting the consequences of each reasonable alternative, and (d) choosing the alternative to be followed. In Figure 10.3, these four steps are identified by the numbers along the *time* dimension. In practice, individual administrators and their staffs might employ other series of steps, perhaps labeled differently; the suggested paradigm is readily adaptable to any sequence of decision-making behavior. Along the *behavior* dimension, a choice must be made about who is going to perform each necessary decision-making function. Here, broken lines indicate choices of action open to

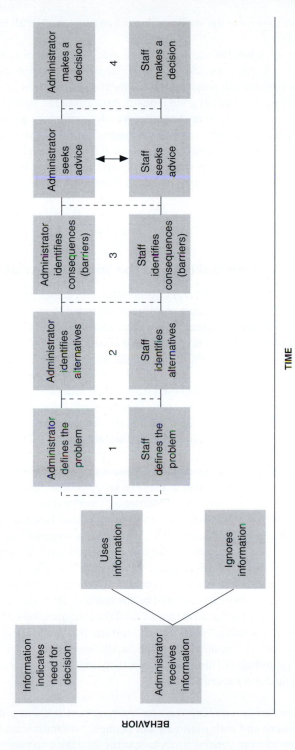

FIGURE 10.3 A paradigm for shared decision making in the school.

the administrator: to involve the staff members at any one step, at all of them, or indeed not to involve them at all.

In other words, when the administrator receives (or becomes aware of) information indicating the need for a decision, the choice is clear: He or she can either use or ignore the information. If the decision maker elects to act on the information, he or she can logically proceed either by (a) defining the problem or (b) giving the information to the staff members and asking them to define the problem. From then on, the process of decision making can comprise any combination of participation that the decision makers desire. The administrator can handle every phase of the process alone or can utilize any combination of participation by the staff. But we must bear in mind that the administrator has no monopoly on the initiation of participation. The concept of participative decision making requires that all members have access to the means of initiating decision-making processes.

But what specific processes can a group follow in their decision making? We introduce a team decision-making model, the Total Teamwork System (TTS), next.

School-Based Decision Making and the Total Teamwork System

School-based decision making (SBDM), sometimes called site- or school-based management, involves "an organizational and political initiative intended to give parents, teachers, and others a greater voice in school governance" (Kowalski, Lasley, & Mahoney, 2008). Some suggest the definition of this process should be placed on a continuum from simply giving the principals more power in the schools they administer—typically called site-based management—to allowing an elected group of stakeholders among teachers, staff, and parents set policy and make implementation decisions for the school—typically called school-based decision making (Valesky, Horgan, Caughey, & Smith, 2003). As teams of individuals, generally called the *site council*, meet to administer a school, they need to be trained in the decision-making process, as noted above. In using a model of team decision making, they can systematize and streamline the decision-making process.

An empirically-based, decision-making model and training program for teams was developed by one of the authors of this text as part of a group of researchers at the Center for Research in Educational Policy at the University of Memphis (Valesky et al., 2003). Based on a 4-year study of how decisions were made by teams in schools using school-based decision making, the model, named the Total Teamwork System (TTS), comprises a series of four primary questions that decision-making teams ask themselves. The initial research used the work of Vroom and Yetton, which was described earlier in this chapter. Vroom and Yetton's model of seven questions was reduced to just four in the TTS. Some of Vroom and Yetton's questions were unnecessary in this model, and others were adapted as dictated by the research findings.

The researchers found that when teams used the four questions in the TTS model, their decisions were judged as positive. When they did not use this model, decisions led to poor results, such as a win-lose feeling among team members, disagreements, poor implementation of decisions, and a general feeling of failure among participants. The researchers explained why a team decision-making model is needed:

> Participative decision making requires learning new skills in order to be effective. Good intentions and enthusiasm are not enough. You must learn to work effectively as a team, to go from general issues to specific strategies, to negotiate, to communicate both within and outside your decision-making group, and a host of other skills.

We've all been on committees that don't accomplish their goals. Sometimes this is because people disagree, sometimes it's because people don't understand exactly what they are to do, sometimes it is because people don't know how to reach decisions, or sometimes it's because meetings get bogged down. In almost all cases, these problems could be avoided if participants knew more about group decision making. Effective group decision making requires certain skills and most importantly an agreed-upon process for decision making—it doesn't come naturally. (Horgan & Valesky, 1993, pp. 4–5)

The four questions the TTS model uses to guide teams to effective decisions are as follows:

1. Is this an issue or question that falls within the legitimate domain of our group?
2. As stated, is the issue appropriate for a meaningful discussion or should the question be rephrased?
3. To deal effectively with this issue, should we seek further information?
4. Is acceptance by those outside the committee necessary for successful implementation?

Below is a description of what a team should consider as they answer each of these questions. In addition, Figure 10.4 is a flowchart of this process, which includes each of these questions.

Is this an issue or question that falls within the legitimate domain of our group? Teams may receive an issue or problem from any number of sources. One of the organization's leaders may give it to the group to handle, one of the team members may bring up an issue at a meeting, or maybe a parent or a student brings an issue to the team. These issues may be very important, but sometimes they are not really in the team's domain. That is, the team doesn't have the authority or should not accept the authority to decide on a particular issue. Perhaps it is a policy decision that should be made by someone or some group at a higher level in the organization. Perhaps the issue comes under the authority of another individual or group, and you would be usurping that authority. In these cases, the group should delegate to a different decision-making authority. On the other hand, if your team believes an issue is in the team's domain, then you need to ask yourselves the next question.

As stated, is the issue appropriate for a meaningful discussion or should the question be rephrased? Concerns, issues, or problems that are brought before a decision-making team come in two basic forms that may need rephrasing before the team deliberates further. The first form that may need rephrasing is when a concern is stated in a very general way. In this case, general issues may need to be made specific. For example, a parent group may tell your team that discipline needs to be improved. Before your team can deal with this issue, you need to identify why they believe this, which behaviors they are concerned about, where and when these behaviors occur, and so forth. Perhaps after getting answers to your questions, you find that the specific concern is actually bullying that is occurring in the ninth grade, particularly in physical education classes.

The second form of a concern that may need rephrasing is when it is too specific. In this case, the team may want to rephrase the issue as a policy concern. For example, suppose a teacher complains to a team that she always gets assigned remedial classes. Because this specific concern is about one teacher, perhaps a general policy issue related to teacher assignment is really the problem that your team should tackle. The decision-making team can then determine if the newly rephrased concern is really in their domain or not. If not, they can pass it on to the appropriate group. If it is in their domain, they go to the next question.

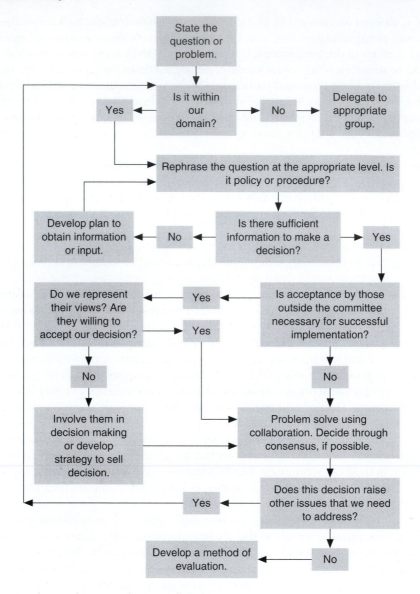

FIGURE 10.4 The Total Teamwork System flowchart.

Source: Reprinted from Valesky, T. C., Horgan, D. D., Caughey, C. E., & Smith, D. L. (2003). *Training for quality school-based decision making: The Total Teamwork System.* Lanham, MD: Scarecrow Press, p. 8. Reprinted with permission from Scarecrow Press, a member of Rowman & Littlefield Publishing Group.

To deal effectively with this issue, should we seek further information? There is no need to spend a team's time discussing an issue if there isn't sufficient information to make a decision. Good decisions are based on data, and often the data gathering and analysis take longer than making the decision itself. The team needs to determine its data needs, delegate information-gathering responsibilities, and table the decision until all the facts are gathered.

Once the necessary information is ready, your team should revisit question two above to be sure it is still phrased correctly, and then move on to the last question when ready.

Is acceptance by those outside the committee necessary for successful implementation? If people outside the committee must carry out the decision, and the team is not sure those people are willing to accept the decision, then those people need to be brought into the decision-making process. On the other hand, if your team believes it can fairly represent the view of others who will implement the decision, then it can go ahead and make the decision. If the final decision brings up new issues that need to be addressed (e.g., implementation guidelines for policy), then those issues will recycle through this TTS model.

Any decision that a team makes needs to be evaluated for its effectiveness; therefore, an evaluation plan needs to be designed and follow-up responsibilities must be assigned. This evaluation process requires the team to reflect later on its decision and revise it if necessary—again, based on data.

Data-Based Decision Making and Total Quality Management

Using data to explore whether or not an educational program is effective is certainly not a new concept. Program evaluation, according to Rossi, Lipsey, and Freeman (2004) has deep roots in education—becoming commonplace by the end of the 1950s. Before the system of accountability required by NCLB, education research was typically the domain of school district administration, university researchers, and governmental entities. Indeed, principals reported that after NCLB, they began using data more often in the decision-making process, and specifically disaggregating the data (Touchton, Taylor, & Acker-Hocevar, 2012). In addition, NCLB started a major national focus on having teachers, principals, and other school-based staff involved in conducting research, often called *action research*, which was defined by Gall, Gall, and Borg (2007) as

> a form of applied research whose primary purpose is to increase the quality, impact, and justice of education professionals' practice. We use the term *action research* to include what is sometimes called *practitioner research, teacher research, insider research,* and (usually when carried out by teacher educators on their own practice) *self-study research.* (pp. 597–598)

Kurt Lewin—the same person who gave us B = f (p • e)—also coined the term *action research* (Lewin, 1948), and he provided the same basic model we still use when describing how to carry out action research. This model was popularized by the Total Quality Management (TQM) movement based on the work of W. Edwards Deming (1986): PDCA (Plan-Do-Check-Act) or PDSA (Plan-Do-Study-Act). Deming called this the Shewhart Cycle, named for Walter A. Shewhart, who is known as the *Father of Statistical Quality Control.* The PDSA cycle can be depicted as shown in Figure 10.5. Deming preferred to use the PDSA rather than PDCA, as the term *check* reminded him of an administrator's role of *inspecting* results, which he said comes after the fact, is too late, and is costly. One of Deming's 14 *Principles of Transformation* (i.e., transforming management to improve the organization) was to "improve constantly and forever the system of production and service" (p. 49). Hence, organizational structures should be in place to continually monitor and improve. Two additional Deming principles are connected to this discussion: "[E]liminate numerical quotas" (p. 70) and "take action to accomplish the transformation" (p. 86). In other words, it is management's job to quit inspecting for quotas (such as year-end testing only) and to implement the Shewhart Cycle by taking action to accomplish the transformation.

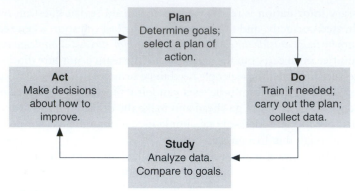

FIGURE 10.5 The Shewhart and Deming Cycle: Plan-Do-Study-Act (PDSA).

In current education parlance, we use the terms *data-based decision making* and *data-driven decision making* in implementing action research. Picciano (2006) noted that data-driven decision making uses data analysis (the *study* part of PDSA) as part of the process, but "it does not replace the experience, expertise, intuition, judgment, and acumen of competent educators" (p. 6). Piccciano's comments on action research were as follows:

> Action research projects can vary significantly and frequently do not follow the standard format (purpose, hypothesis, methodology, findings) that usually characterize other research studies. Action research methodology (qualitative or quantitative) can be adopted, statistical procedures may be used or not, and methodologies may be mixed and matched to meet goals. (p. 49)

The sophistication of the action research in which schools engage depends on the purpose and goals (or *plan* in the PDSA), the time staff members have to devote to the PDSA process, and the research and statistical analysis skills of the staff. Advanced skills are not typically needed in most action research projects, but when they are needed, schools should look to their central office staff for assistance or to local universities where faculty and advanced graduate students may be found who may be eager to collaborate. For the most part, however, school staff members do not need advanced research or statistical skill levels to participate in effective data-based decision making. It does not have to be overly complicated to analyze and use data in decision making. As Kowalski et al. (2008) defined data-based decision making, it is "the process of compiling, reviewing, sharing, and using data to assist in improving schools, particularly, enhancing student achievement" (p. 103). Their model for implementing data-based decision making includes four phases: collecting, connecting, creating, and confirming. Let's look at each of these areas:

COLLECTING During the *Do* phase of the PDSA cycle, data are collected while program implementation occurs. As Deming warned, we should not wait until the end of a program to inspect the results. Collecting and analyzing data during the implementation process allow us to adjust implementation to achieve better results. So, we determine what data are needed (both qualitative and quantitative data), what data are available to us, and then we plan on collecting the data we do not have readily available. There are many ways to collect data, and decision-making teams need to decide how to collect the data needed. Box 10.1 lists some TQM tools that can be used to collect and analyze data at the school site. In addition, many school districts have *data warehouses* in which more than just standardized test scores and grades may be maintained. With a good technology interface, and staff trained in how to retrieve the data, school-based teams can download some of the data needed.

CONNECTING Kowalski et al. (2008) defined connecting as "analyzing the data from different perspectives or combining it with other data" (p. 112). In the *study* phase of PDSA decision-making teams do *data mining*, i.e., combing through and digging deep into the data, and *data disaggregation*, which is separating data by various student characteristics, to connect the data and find relationships to better understand the phenomenon under investigation.

CREATING This is the *act* phase of PDSA in which decision-making teams take action on what they find in the data, using their best judgment as professionals to make decisions to improve the process. Kowalski et al. stated:

> Creating is planning and taking action on the data. If a gap exists between where your students are and where you want to them to be, creating means developing goals and strategies to address that gap and then closing it in ways to foster student success. (p. 113)

CONFIRMING Also part of *act* in PDSA, is determining if what you have been doing accomplished your original goals.

> In this stage, you are evaluating your efforts, learning from feedback, and starting the cycle again. You compiled data. You analyzed it and communicated it to others, developed goals, and identified strategies to make a difference. In the confirming state, you are reflecting on whether your efforts made the difference you hoped for. (Kowalski et al., 2008, p. 114)

Examples of using the TQM philosophy, tools, and processes in education are schools that follow the Malcolm Baldrige National Quality Award criteria, more simply known as the Baldrige Criteria. In 1987, the U.S. Congress passed the Malcolm Baldrige National Quality Improvement Act, Public Law 100-107, which was passed to improve business and industry, and later adapted for schools. Today, a public-private partnership exists to award the stamp of "quality" to those organizations meeting the award criteria. This partnership exists under the direction of the National Institute of Standards and Technology (NIST), which is an agency of the U.S. Department of Commerce. In education, the Baldrige Criteria include the following areas (National Institute of Standards and Technology, 2013):

1. Leadership
2. Strategic planning
3. Customer and market focus
4. Measurement, analysis, and knowledge management
5. Human resources focus
6. Process management
7. Organizational performance results

BOX 10.2

Examples of Basic Total Quality Management Tools used to collect and analyze data.

1. Qualitative Tools:
   a. Brainstorming: Team generates ideas collaboratively.
   b. Cause and effect charts (also called Fishbone charts because the chart looks like a fishbone): Problems are identified with lines off the main horizontal line representing causes, and lines off main causes representing sub-causes.
   c. Flowcharts: A visual depiction of a process from start to finish is presented.
   d. Multi-voting: Typically used after brainstorming generates multiple possibilities, this technique uses individual voting and team discussions; individuals rank their top three to five choices; votes are tallied; team discusses; voting then occurs; and the process is repeated as needed.
   e. Affinity diagrams: While brainstorming, ideas are organized and grouped according to their "affinity" to other ideas.
   f. Force field diagrams: A visual description of driving forces and restraining forces in the change process are portrayed.

2. Quantitative Tools:
   a. Pareto charts: Graphic diagrams of most frequent causes of a problem are listed.
   b. Histograms: Bar charts that describe distributions of variables are created.
   c. Control charts & graphs: These techniques use of a number of simple charting tools to visually depict data (e.g., pie charts and line charts); spreadsheet programs typically have numerous graphs available.
   d. Run charts: Line charts are created depicting a variable's value over a time line; these charts typically show the average, and upper and lower control limits.
   e. Scatterplots: These charts show the relationships of two variables in an X and Y axis chart; they can be created in a spreadsheet using a scatter chart.

   For more detail and visuals of these tools and other TQM tools there are many helpful websites. One of the better websites is skymark.com/resources/tools/management_tools.asp

For additional information about the Baldrige Criteria see the website of the National Institute of Standards and Technology at nist.gov/baldrige/publications/business_nonprofit_criteria.cfm where you will find education award criteria and application information. By the way, Malcolm Baldrige was the Secretary of Commerce at the time the law was enacted.

Final Thoughts

The wish to simplify organizational decision making and render it more rational has spawned a large number of decision-making models, each of which seeks to reveal the order and logic of organizational life. A common puzzle, however, is that administrators are infrequently observed—even after training—using such models in their work or spending prolonged periods of time in episodes of reflective thinking. Recent research is giving rise to the understanding that (a) educational organizations and administrative work are far more complex than had formerly been believed and (b) administrators go about the thinking that precedes decision making in ways that differ significantly from that of scholars and researchers. Events in the organizational world rarely occur in a neat sequence; more rarely still does one thing occur at a time. Rather, the administrator is typically confronted with ambiguous circumstances in which a number of events are unfolding simultaneously, various goals and values of the school may be in conflict, and truth may take several forms, yet the need for decisions presses inexorably on at a relentless pace.

Many organizational problems are not well understood at the time that decisions must be made. They may be described as being emergent problems—that is, they tend to be ambiguous and difficult to define, and the information needed to solve them is scattered among a number of people. Dealing with emergent problems leads to an iteration of diagnosis and solution by a process of successive approximation over time.

Under these conditions of ambiguity and uncertainty, which are characteristic of educational organizations, the trend in organizational decision making in education has been in the direction of empowering teachers and others to participate more fully in making important decisions. This trend is not merely an organizational response intended to placate individuals who have long felt alienated and even oppressed by the traditional top-down decision-making processes of hierarchical organizations. It is primarily intended to improve the quality of decisions by drawing on the knowledge and experience of key people who are closest to the action in the core enterprise of the school:

teaching. At the same time, empowerment through participation in decision making tends to meet intrinsic motivational needs of individuals more adequately and to strengthen the growth-enhancing qualities of the organization's culture in ways and to a degree that traditional decision-making methods simply cannot match.

Shifting from traditional methods to participative methods requires administrators to develop a new understanding of power, a new sense of administrative wisdom. Traditionally, it was believed that only limited power was available in the organization and that the wise administrator would garner all of it. Thus, empowering teachers and others to participate in decision making would be viewed by the administrator as losing power by giving it away to others. Modern empowering administrators, on the other hand, understand that one gains power by sharing it with others because, in collaborative effort, the power available to the group multiplies.

The intention to share power with others and increase participation in decision making is, in itself, insufficient to ensure success. Such efforts must be accompanied by the support of ongoing technical training and consultation to help all participants, administrators and others alike, to master the group process skills that are essential to making empowerment succeed. They must also be accompanied by the development of defined and publicly known processes through which one participates in the collaborative process.

Reflective Activities

1. Make a list of three to five discrete problems you believe typically should be handled by principals. Why do you believe the principal should categorize each of these areas as discrete?
2. With what type of emergent problems have you been involved when deciding on solutions in the past? Choose one memorable problem and describe the process that was used in the decision-making process. How was the leader involved in organizing the decision-making process? Was the solution acceptable to those in the organization? Did the decision-making

process follow steps similar to the Total Teamwork System (TTS)?
3. *Working on Your Game Plan.* In this chapter, several models of decision making were presented. As a future leader, explain what model of decision making you will use to lead your organization. State the type of organization, the decision-making structures you envision for it, and your philosophy about how decision making should unfold. Include in your Game Plan about decision making, how you will approach the issue of data-based decision making.

CRITICAL INCIDENT   Deciding How to Decide

Dr. Alex Mahdi began his first principalship at Lincoln Middle School after receiving his doctoral degree from the nearby state university. While taking his university classes, he became committed to the idea of collaborative decision making, which he believed empowers staff. Alex understood from the superintendent that the previous principal was very authoritarian, and he rarely got input on decisions. Partly because of this, the school climate was very poor, and many teachers requested transfers over the years. The superintendent stated that she was looking for someone who could change the decision-making culture at Lincoln and turn around the school climate problems. So when he took over Lincoln Middle, Alex wanted to empower the staff to make decisions.

At the first faculty meeting of the year, Alex told the staff that his vision for Lincoln Middle School included collaborative decision making. He informed the staff that they would be heavily involved in decision-making processes. Alex set up many committees, such as the discipline committee, reading across the curriculum committee, professional development committee, parent-teacher association committee, and many more. In addition, he chaired the Lincoln Middle School leadership committee, which was composed of the assistant principals and the department

chairs. All teachers served on at least one committee in addition to their department-level committees. Staff members were involved in decision-making activities at the monthly staff meetings.

At the end of the first year, Alex sent out a climate survey to the staff. To his surprise, there were low marks related to decision making in the school. On the survey, teacher comments focused on two themes: (1) They found that committee work was too time consuming, and (2) they didn't feel like there was a process to make decisions on the committees, which contributed to the time required for committees to make decisions.

Alex was not sure what to do with this new information. He still believed that collaborative decision making was the key to staff empowerment.

1. What do you suggest that Alex do in reaction to the survey data? What might he do to analyze and resolve the problem?
2. What process described in this chapter would you recommend the committees follow when making decisions?
3. If you were the principal, would you reorganize the committee structure and, if so, what process would you use to do so?

Suggested Reading

Bolman, L. G., & Deal, T. E. (1984). *Modern approaches to understanding and managing organizations.* San Francisco, CA: Jossey-Bass.

The chapter titled "Applying the Human Resource Approach" describes the basis for the human resources management approach to decision making and considerations in applying it in practice. Includes discussions of participative methods, organizational democracy, and organization development.

Cunningham, W. G. (1982). *Systematic planning for educational change.* Palo Alto, CA: Mayfield Publishing Company.

One of the better discussions of formal decision-making procedures based on conventional, logical linear models. Features a description of decision tree analysis that can be very effective in dealing with discrete problems. See the chapter titled "Decision Making."

Kanter, R. M. (1983). *The change masters: Innovation and entrepreneurship in the American corporation.* New York, NY: Simon & Schuster.

This is a classic book on change and using data. The chapter titled "Dilemmas of Participation" explores problems and apparent dilemmas confronting administrators seeking to implement participative decision-making methods and suggests ways of dealing with them.

Kowalski, T. J., Lasley, T. J., II, & Mahoney, J. W. (2008). *Data-driven decisions and school leadership: Best practices for school improvement.* Boston, MA: Pearson.

This is a complete book on everything school leaders need to know about data-based decision making. It contains chapters on school reform, group decision making, research on data decision making, collecting and analyzing data, technology and information management, and several chapters related to applying data-based decisions. This book does an outstanding job of connecting theory and practice in data-driven decision making.

Valesky, T. C., Horgan, D. D., Caughey, C. E., & Smith, D. L. (2003). *Training for quality school-based decision making: The total teamwork system.* Lanham, MD: Scarecrow Press.

This book is designed to train decision-making teams in an empirically based group decision-making process. This decision-making model, based on Vroom and Yetton's normative model, uses four questions empirically determined to lead to effective decisions. Each chapter of the book describes in detail how to answer the questions, and there are activities for teams to practice team decision making.

Wynn, R., & Guditus, C. W. (1984). *Team management: Leadership by consensus.* Columbus, OH: Charles E. Merrill Publishing Company.

An excellent resource for readers who want a detailed, practical guide for implementing participative management in educational organizations.

References

Acker-Hocevar, M. A., Ballenger, J., Place, A. W., & Ivory, G. (Eds.). (2012). *Snapshots of school leadership in the 21st century: Perils and promises of leading for social justice, school improvement, and democratic community (The UCEA Voices from the Field Project).* Charlotte, NC: Information Age.

Argyris, C. (1971). *Management and organizational development.* New York, NY: McGraw-Hill.

Barnard, C. I. (1938). *The functions of the executive.* Cambridge, MA: Harvard University Press.

Blackburn, T. R. (1971). Sensuous-intellectual complementarity in science. *Science, 172,* 1003–1007.

Bridges, E. M. (1967). A model for shared decision making in the school principalship. *Educational Administration Quarterly, 3*(1), 52–59.

Davis, K. (1972). *Human behavior at work: Human relations and organizational behavior* (4th ed.). New York, NY: McGraw-Hill.

Deal, T. E. (1985). Cultural change: Opportunity, silent killer, or metamorphosis? In R. H. Kilmann, M. J. Saxton, & R. Serpa (Eds.), *Gaining control of the corporate culture.* San Francisco, CA: Jossey-Bass.

Deming, W. E. (1986). *Out of crisis.* Cambridge, MA: Massachusetts Institute of Technology, Center for Advanced Engineering Study.

Drucker, P. F. (1974). *Management: Tasks, responsibilities, and practices.* New York, NY: Harper & Row.

Follett, M. P. (1941). The psychology of consent and participation. In H. C. Metcalf & L. Urwick (Eds.), *Dynamic administration: The collected papers of Mary Parker Follett* (pp. 210–212). New York, NY: Harper & Row.

Fullan, M. (2005). *Leadership & sustainability: System thinkers in action.* Thousand Oaks, CA: Corwin Press.

Gall, M. D., Gall, J. P., & Borg, W. R. (2007). *Educational research: An introduction.* Boston, MA: Pearson Education Inc.

Griffiths, D. E. (1959). *Administrative theory.* New York, NY: Appleton-Century-Crofts.

Heifetz, R. A. (1994). *Leadership without easy answers.* Cambridge, MA: Harvard University Press.

Herzberg, F. (1966). *Work and the nature of man.* Cleveland, OH: World.

Horgan, D. D., & Valesky, T. C. (1993). Empirically based training for school-based decision making. *National Forum of Educational Administration and Supervision Journal, 10*(3), 3–15.

Kanter, R. M. (1983). *The change masters: Innovation and entrepreneurship in the American corporation.* New York, NY: Simon & Schuster.

Kowalski, T. J., Lasley, T. J., II, & Mahoney, J. W. (2008). *Data-driven decisions and school leadership: Best practices for school improvement.* Boston, MA: Pearson.

Lewin, K. (1948). *Resolving social conflicts: Selected papers on group dynamics.* New York, NY: Harper & Row.

Likert, R. (1961). *New patterns of management.* New York, NY: McGraw-Hill.

Luthans, F. (1977). *Organizational behavior* (2nd ed.). New York, NY: McGraw-Hill.

March, J. G. (1981, December). Footnotes to organizational change. *Administrative Science Quarterly, 26,* 563–577.

March, J. G., & Simon, H. A. (1958). *Organizations.* New York, NY: John Wiley & Sons.

Maslow, A. (1970). *Motivation and personality* (2nd ed.). New York, NY: Harper & Row.

McGregor, D. M. (1960). *The human side of enterprise.* New York, NY: McGraw-Hill.

Meyer, M. W. (1977). *Theory of organizational structure.* Indianapolis, IN: Bobbs-Merrill Educational Publishing.

Mintzberg, H. (1973). *The nature of managerial work.* New York, NY: Harper & Row.

Mintzberg, H., Raisinghani, D., & Theoret, A. (1976). The structure of "unstructured" decision processes. *Administrative Science Quarterly, 21*(2), 246–275.

Morris, V. C., Crowson, R. L., Hurwitz, E., Jr., & Porter-Gehrie, C. (1981). *The urban principal: discretionary decision-making in a large educational organization.* Unpublished manuscript, University of Illinois at Chicago.

Morris, V. C., Crowson, R. L., Hurwitz, E., Jr., & Porter-Gehrie, C. (1984). *Principals in action: The reality of managing schools.* Columbus, OH: Charles E. Merrill.

National Association of Secondary School Principals. (1978). *The senior high school principalship.* Reston, VA: National Association of Secondary School Principals.

National Institute of Standards and Technology. (2013). Baldrige Performance Excellent Program. U.S. Department of Commerce. Retrieved from http://www.nist.gov/baldrige/publications/education_criteria.cfm

Nutt, P. C. (1984). Types of organizational decision processes. *Administrative Science Quarterly, 29*(3), 414-450.

Ouchi, W. (1981). *Theory Z: How American business can meet the Japanese challenge.* Reading, MA: Addison-Wesley.

Owens, R. G., & Lewis, E. (1976). Managing participation in organizational decisions. *Group and organization studies, 1*(1), 56–66.

Picciano, A. G. (2006). *Data-driven decision making for effective school leadership.* Upper Saddle River, NJ: Pearson.

Pitner, N. J. (1978). *Descriptive study of the everyday activities of suburban school superintendents: The management of information.* Unpublished doctoral dissertation, Ohio State University, Columbus.

Pondy, L. R. (1983). Union of rationality and intuition in management action. In S. Srivasta (Ed.), *The executive mind.* San Francisco, CA: Jossey-Bass.

Rossi, P. H., Lipsey, M. W., & Freeman, H. E. (2004). *Evaluation: A systematic approach.* Thousand Oaks, CA: Sage.

Schein, E. H. (1968). Organizational socialization and the profession of management. *Industrial Management Review, 9*(2), 1–16.

Schein, E. H. (1985.) *Organizational culture and leadership.* San Francisco, CA: Jossey-Bass.

Schön, D. A. (1983). *The reflective practitioner: How professionals think in action.* New York, NY: Basic Books.

Schön, D. A. (1987). *Educating the reflective practitioner.* San Francisco, CA: Jossey-Bass.

Simon, H. A. (1950). *Administrative behavior.* New York, NY: Macmillan.

Simon, H. A. (1960). *The new science of management decision.* New York, NY: Harper & Row.

Touchton, D., Taylor, R., & Acker-Hocevar, M. (2012). Decision-making processes, giving voice, listening, and involvement. In M. A. Acker-Hocevar, J. Ballenger, A. W. Place, & G. Ivory (Eds.), *Snapshots of school leadership in the 21st century: Perils and promises of leading for social justice, school improvement, and democratic community (The UCEA Voices from the Field Project)* (pp. 121–145). Charlotte, NC: Information Age.

Underwood, J. D. (2013, May). School boards beware: Influential national network calls for elimination of school boards. *Wisconsin School News.* Wisconsin Association of School Boards. Retrieved from http://www.wasb.org/websites/wisconsin_school_news/File/2013May/Underwood%20Commentary.pdf

Valesky, T., Horgan, D. D., Caughey, C. E., & Smith, D. L. (2003). *Training for quality school-based decision making: The total teamwork system.* Lanham, MD: Scarecrow Press.

Vroom, V. H., & Yetton, P. W. (1973). *Leadership and decision making.* Pittsburgh, PA: University of Pittsburgh Press.

Weick, K. E. (1979). Cognitive processes in organizations. In B. M. Staw (Ed.), *Research in organizational behavior* (Vol. 1, pp. 41–74). Greenwich, CT: JAI Press.

Weick, K. E. (1983). Managerial thought in the context of action. In S. Srivastva (Ed.), *The executive mind.* San Francisco, CA: Jossey-Bass.

CHAPTER 11

Conflict and Communications in Organizations

Because educational organizations exist only to foster cooperative human endeavors and to achieve goals that cannot be achieved by individuals acting alone, their organizational ideals normatively emphasize cooperation, harmony, and collaboration. Contemporary literature on schools ordinarily stresses virtues such as empowerment, participation, and collaboration, with little mention of competition and conflict. Yet, as James MacGregor Burns (1978), who gave us transformational leadership theory, wrote, "the potential for conflict permeates the relations of humankind, and that potential is a force for health and growth as well as destruction. . . . No group can be wholly harmonious . . . for such a group would be empty of process and structure" (p. 37). Thus, because conflict is pervasive in all human experience, it is an important aspect of organizational behavior in education.

Conflict can occur even within a single individual (so-called *intrapersonal conflict*), typified by approach-avoidance conflict, the common situation in which the person feels torn between the desire to achieve two goals that are incompatible. This tension leads to feelings of stress and—not infrequently—behavior manifestations (for example, indecisiveness) and even physiological symptoms (for example, hypertension, ulcers). Howard Gardner's concept of *intrapersonal intelligence*, introduced in an earlier chapter, becomes important in this discussion. Conflict runs the gamut of social experience—between individuals, between groups, and between whole societies and cultures.

Conflict can occur *within* persons or social units; it is *intra*personal or *intra*group (or, of course, *intra*national). Conflict can also be experienced *between* two or more people or social units: so-called *inter*personal, *inter*group, or *inter*national conflict. In this chapter, we are not attempting to deal with the broad, general phenomenon of conflict; we will confine the discussion to conflict in organizational life—*organizational conflict* (that is, *intra*organizational conflict), which most commonly involves interpersonal conflict and intergroup conflict. (See the discussion in a previous chapter on Gardner's concept of *interpersonal intelligence*.)

THE NATURE OF CONFLICT IN ORGANIZATIONS

In bureaucratic theory, the existence of conflict is viewed as evidence of breakdown in the organization: failure on the part of management to plan adequately or to exercise sufficient control. In human relations theory, conflict is seen as evidence of failure to develop appropriate norms in the group. Traditional administrative theory has therefore been strongly biased in favor of the ideal of a smooth-running organization characterized by harmony, unity, coordination, efficiency, and order. Human relations adherents might seek to achieve this through happy, congenial work groups, whereas classical adherents would seek to achieve it through control and strong organizational structure. Both, however, tend to agree that conflict is disruptive: something to be avoided. One of the more dramatic developments in the literature on organizations has been a reexamination of these positions, resulting in some more useful views.

In the vast body of scientific literature, there is no consensus on a specific definition of conflict. There is general concurrence, however, that two prerequisites are essential to any conflict: (1) divergent (or apparently divergent) views and (2) incompatibility of those views (Thomas, 1976).

Thus, Morton Deutsch (1973) said simply that "a conflict exists whenever incompatible activities occur." But this incompatibility produces a dilemma—conflict becomes "the pursuit of incompatible, or at least seemingly incompatible, goals, such that gains to one side come out at the expense of the other" (p. 10). When incompatibility results in one side coming out ahead, we are confronted with the classic, zero-sum, win-lose situation that is potentially so dysfunctional to organizational life; everyone strives to avoid losing and losers seek to become winners. The focus of contemporary application of behavioral science to organizations is precisely as follows: to manage conflict in the organization so that hostility can be either avoided or minimized. This process is *not* the management of hostility; it is the management of conflict that reduces or eliminates the hostility emanating from it.

Conflict Different From Attacks

A distinct difference exists between organizational conflict and its attendant hostility, on the one hand, and destructive attacks, on the other; to treat them as being alike can be a serious mistake. Kenneth Boulding (1962) suggested that we distinguish between malevolent hostility and nonmalevolent hostility. Malevolent hostility is aimed at hurting or worsening the position of another individual or group, with scant regard for anything else, including the consequences for the attacker. Nonmalevolent hostility, on the other hand, may well worsen the position of others but is acted out for the purpose of improving the position of the attacker. Malevolent hostility is often characterized by the use of issues as the basis for attack, which are, in reality, not important to the attacker except as a vehicle for damaging the opposition.

Malevolent hostility can, in turn, give rise to "nefarious attacks" (Wynn, 1972, p. 7). These are characterized by the following:

1. the focus on persons rather than on issues;
2. the use of hateful language;
3. the use of dogmatic statements rather than questions;
4. the maintenance of fixed views regardless of new information or argument; and
5. the use of emotional terms.

The key difference between such attacks (whether malevolent, nefarious, or otherwise) and legitimate expressions of conflict lies in the motivation behind them, which is often not easily discernible. Although considerable (and often vigorous) conflict may erupt over issues such as improving school performance, ways of desegregating a school system, or how to group children for instruction, the parties to the conflict may well be motivated by essentially constructive goals. The key is whether the parties involved want to work with the system or are motivated by a wish to destroy it.

Warren Bennis (2010) described, for example, how—in a period of student disruption at the State University of New York at Buffalo—he labored hard and long to deal with a student takeover of the campus, using his not inconsiderable skills as a third-party facilitator. But it was all to no avail. Looking back, Bennis came to realize that he really had not been in a two-party conflict management situation at all. The students—to the extent that they were organized— were committed to a set of political goals that had little to do with the educational goals that the university administrators embraced. In this case, the conflict was largely a device being used to achieve carefully masked goals. The student confrontations and rhetoric were often, in fact, malevolent with little intention of coming to agreement. Any public education administrator needs to be sensitive to this problem and to be aware of the significant difference between attacks for the sake of destruction and vigorous expression of essentially constructive—though sharply divergent and perhaps unwelcome—views.

Contemporary Views of Conflict

Conflict in organizations is now seen as inevitable, endemic, and often legitimate because the individuals and groups within the human social system are interdependent and constantly engaged in the dynamic processes of defining and redefining the nature and extent of their interdependence. Important to the dynamics of this social process is the fact that the environment in which it occurs is itself constantly changing. Thus, as Chester Barnard (1938) pointed out, "inherent in the conception of free will in a changing environment" (p. 36) are social patterns characterized by negotiating, stress, and conflict.

There is conflict in any well-led organization because, as we saw in the chapter on organizational change, leaders marshal and organize resources sometimes *in conflict with others*. By definition, leaders marshal resources (people, money, time, facilities, materials) to achieve new goals. Given the finite resources available in an educational organization, there will invariably be competing ideas of what to do with those resources: how to use the time, how to involve people, where to spend the money, how to schedule facilities, and so on. Thus, when leadership is present, people in the organization must experience conflict as a normal part of organizational life. The central issue, then, is neither whether organizational conflict is present nor the degree to which it is present. The central issue is how well conflict is managed in the organization.

Effects of Organizational Conflict

This is an important issue because frequent and powerful hostility arising from conflict can have a devastating impact on the behavior of people in organizations. Psychological withdrawal from the hostility—such as alienation, apathy, and indifference—is a common symptom that keenly affects the functioning of the organization. Physical withdrawal—such as absence, tardiness, and turnover—is a widely occurring response to conflict in schools. Physical withdrawal is often written off as laziness on the part of teachers who have been spoiled by soft administrative practices. Outright hostile or aggressive behaviors—including job actions, property damage, and minor theft of property—are teacher responses to conflict situations that appear to be too difficult to handle or totally frustrating.

Indeed, the behavioral consequences of conflict in educational organizations can be, to put it mildly, undesirable. Ineffective management of conflict (for example, a hard-nosed policy of punishment for offenses, get-tough practices in the name of administering the negotiated contract, emphasizing the adversarial relationship between teachers and administrators) can— and frequently does—create a climate that exacerbates the situation and is likely to develop a

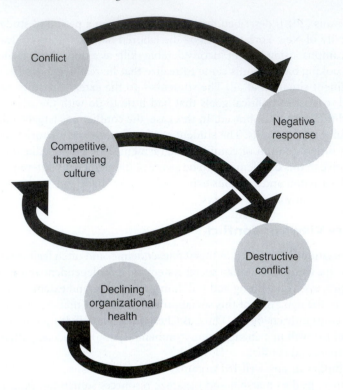

FIGURE 11.1 An ineffective conflict-response-climate syndrome leads to a lower state of organizational health.

downward spiral of mounting frustration, deteriorating organizational climate, and increasing destructiveness, as shown in Figure 11.1.

Obviously, the health of an organization caught in this syndrome tends to decline. Effective management of conflict, on the other hand, can lead to outcomes that are productive and enhance the health of the organization over time, as shown in Figure 11.2. The point to be emphasized is that conflict in itself is neither good nor bad; it is (in value terms) neutral. Its impact on the organization and the behavior of people largely depends on the way conflict is treated.

The Criterion: Organizational Performance

To speak of organizational conflict as good or bad, or as functional or dysfunctional, requires one to specify the criteria used in judging. Some people—many with a humanistic bias—simply find conflict repugnant and seek to abolish it wherever it may be found. Others are concerned about the internal stress that conflict often imposes on individuals. These problems, in themselves, are not of central concern in *organizational* terms. After all, there are also people who relish conflict, find it zestful, and seek it out. The issue, then, is the impact of conflict on the performance capability of the organization as a system.

Again, the problems of measuring the productivity of educational organizations and the discussion of the relevance of the school's system or school's internal conditions (that

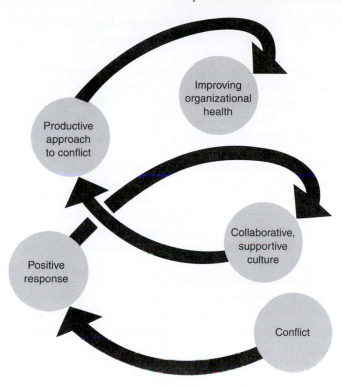

FIGURE 11.2   An effective conflict-response-climate syndrome leads to an improved state of organizational health.

is, organizational culture, interaction-influence system) come to the fore. The functional or dysfunctional consequences of conflict on educational organizations are understood best in terms of organizational health, adaptability, and stability.

Modern motivation theory makes it clear that challenge, significance, and the need to solve problems are important attributes of work that people find interesting, enjoyable, and motivating. Also, as has been seen, concepts of participative leadership rest on the conviction that many people in the organization have good ideas and high-quality information to contribute to making better decisions in the organization. In this view, Kenneth Thomas (1976) observed that

> [t]he confrontation of divergent views often produces ideas of superior quality. Divergent views are apt to be based upon different evidence, different considerations, different insights, different frames of reference. Disagreements may thus confront an individual with factors which he had previously ignored, and help him to arrive at a more comprehensive view which synthesizes elements of his own and others' positions. (p. 891)

Finally, there is growing reason to believe (based on both research and expert opinion) that conflict causes people to seek effective ways of dealing with it, resulting in improved organizational functioning (for example, cohesiveness, clarified relationships, clearer problem-solving proce-dures). Speaking of society in general, Deutsch (1973) observed that

> conflict within a group frequently helps to revitalize existent norms; or it contributes to the emergence of new norms. In this sense, social conflict is a mechanism for adjustment of norms adequate to new conditions. A flexible society benefits from conflict because such behavior, by helping to create and modify norms, assures its continuance under changed conditions. (p. 9)

He went on to caution that rigid systems that suppress conflict smother a useful warning signal, thereby maximizing the danger of catastrophic breakdown.

We all have witnessed repeatedly the wisdom of these observations in national and inter-national events of great and small magnitude. Educators in the United States also have seen it closer to home, where fearful explosions of pent-up hostility have, not infrequently, followed long periods of frustration brought on by organizations that thought they had either crushed or nimbly avoided impending conflict.

Although few who really understand conflict would advocate its deliberate use in organi-zational life, fewer still would advocate seeking its elimination or avoidance. Rather, by apply-ing concepts of conflict management, organizations can minimize the destructive potential of conflict, on the one hand, and make conflict as productive, creative, and useful as possible, on the other.

THE DYNAMICS OF ORGANIZATIONAL CONFLICT

Hostility

Many people say that they do not like conflict, avoid it whenever they can, and may even fear it. This point is important to recognize because it leads to one of the least productive and most common approaches to conflict management: denial and avoidance. Therefore, it is not splitting hairs to point out that the aftermath to an episode of conflict is ordinarily more troubling than the conflict itself. Badly managed organizational conflict can generate hostility among the par-ties, and this factor can lead to hate, retribution, and antagonism.

A key goal of any approach to conflict management is to eliminate or reduce—to manage—the hostility arising from the conflict. But the time to intervene is before conflict arises, rather than afterward. It is important for members of the organization to learn to talk openly about conflict and to discuss what conflict is and the strategies and tactics that may be used to encourage it (yes, encourage it) in ways that will be productive for everyone.

Although numerous writers have compiled a long list of the causes of organizational con-flict, Louis Pondy's classifications are considered by most to have considerable merit in today's schools. He classified three basic types of *latent* conflict:

1. When the organization's resources are insufficient to meet the requirements of the subu-nits to do their work, there is *competition for scarce resources* (for example, budget alloca-tions, assigned teaching positions, reduced space or facilities).
2. When one party seeks to control the activities "belonging" to another unit (and the second unit seeks to fend off such "interference"), the issue is *autonomy* (for example, protecting one's "turf").

3. When two parties in the organization must work together but cannot agree on how to do so, the source of conflict is *goal divergence* (for example, the school principal and the director of special education have differing views about how mainstreaming issues are to be settled). (Pondy, 1967)

A Contingency View

These latent sources of conflict are unlikely to disappear from organizational life. Therefore, it is important to develop a culture that supports productive approaches to conflict management. Because there are a number of causes of conflict—even when classified or grouped, as above—it is obvious that there is no one best way of managing conflict. As John Thomas and Warren Bennis (1972) put it:

> An effective paradigm incorporates what might be termed a "situational" or "contingency" framework, a point of view reflected in much of the current theoretical and empirical work in organizational theory. There is a primary emphasis upon diagnosis and the assumption that it is self-defeating to adopt a "universally" applicable set of principles and guidelines for effecting change or managing conflict. (p. 20)

As a basis for the necessary organizational diagnosis, two concepts concerning conflict are often used: One seeks to understand the internal dynamics of the events that occur in the process of conflict; the other seeks to analyze the external influences that tend to structure the conflict.

A Process View of Conflict

Conflict between two parties appears to unfold in a relatively orderly sequence of events, and, unless something intervenes, the sequence tends to be repeated in episodes. Each episode is highly dynamic, with each party's behavior serving as a stimulus to evoke a response from the other. Each new episode is shaped in part by previous episodes.

One model of such a process is suggested by Kenneth Thomas in which an episode is triggered by the *frustration* of one party in reaction to the act of another (for example, denial of a request, diminishment of status, disagreement, or an insult). This friction causes the participants to *conceptualize* the nature of the conflict—often a highly subjective process that suggests ways of defining and dealing with perceived issues in the conflict, which is followed by *behavior* intended to deal with the conflict. As Kenneth Thomas explained, understanding the bases for this behavior is a complex matter, but key elements surely include a mix of (a) a participant's desire to satisfy the other's concern (cooperative-uncooperative) and (b) the participant's desire to satisfy his or her own concern (assertive-unassertive). *Interaction* of the parties follows, of course; this is a highly dynamic phase of the process. It can involve escalation or deescalation of the conflict, depending on factors such as the trust level that is established, biases and self-fulfilling prophecies that get in the way, the level of competition between the participants, and the openness and sensitivity each has to the other. The *outcome* of all this—the last stage in an episode of conflict—is not merely some agreement on substantive issues but also includes residual emotions (for example, frustration, hostility, trust—either increased or decreased). These outcomes have potentially long-term effects on the aftermath of a conflict episode, particularly as they set the stage for ensuing episodes.

In commenting on the aftermath as part of a sequence of episodes, Louis Pondy (1967) pointed out that

> if the conflict is genuinely resolved to the satisfaction of all participants, the basis for a more cooperative relationship may be laid; or the participants, in their drive for a more ordered relationship, may focus on latent conflicts not previously perceived and dealt with. On the other hand, if conflict is merely suppressed but not resolved, the latent conditions of conflict may be aggravated and explode in more serious form. . . . This legacy of a conflict episode is . . . called "conflict aftermath." (p. 320)

A Structural View of Conflict

Although a process approach to conflict describes it as a *sequence of events,* a structural view tends to describe conflict in terms of the *conditions that influence behavior.* For example, every organization has rules and procedures (written and unwritten, formal and informal) that regulate behavior (for example, who talks with whom about what). Rules and procedures often serve to avoid or manage conflict by clarifying issues such as how and when to proceed, and who has what responsibility. Of course, they can also cause or exacerbate conflict by becoming dysfunctional, such as when they lead to rigid, repetitious behavior that does not readily allow for exceptions (the typical bureaucratic "hardening of the categories").

Not infrequently, rules and procedures so complicate the processes of working out a relatively simple conflict through direct negotiation that they, in fact, create conflict. For example, in one school district, an elementary school principal discovered that an order for a certain kind of paper had been cut sharply by an administrative assistant in the office of the assistant superintendent for business. When the principal contacted the administrative assistant to straighten out the matter, she was reminded that her complaint should be routed through the assistant superintendent for elementary education, who could take it up with the assistant superintendent of business, and so on. Needless to say, considerable conflict ensued, much time was lost, and the needed paper finally arrived at the school—in time for the *following* year. The point is that simple rearrangements in the way that even minor decisions are made and differences are negotiated can influence the course of conflict in organizations.

Another structural factor lies in the kinds of people found in the organization, with particular reference to their personality predispositions, such as their attitudes toward authority and the extent and flexibility of their responses to others. In selecting new personnel, for example, many school districts and schools are attracted to candidates who seem to fit in over candidates who might add diversity to the staff.

Another structural factor influencing the incidence and nature of conflict in an organization is the social norms of the organization: the social pressures, for example, to "stand up and fight" or "not rock the boat." The creation of organizational cultures that smooth over friction and frown on open challenge and questioning can make it very difficult to identify and confront conflict at all. Similarly, when secretiveness and restricted communication represent the organizational norm, it is difficult to know if a latent conflict exists, let alone to plan ways of dealing with it. Many administrators of educational organizations instinctively understand this fact and make it a rule to put as little communication in writing as possible, to assemble people for meetings as infrequently as possible, and—when meetings *must* be held—to be sure to control the proceedings tightly to minimize the risk of opening up issues that might cause trouble.

Todd Whitaker (2002), who wrote a very popular book to assist principals in dealing with individuals who create conflict, suggested using frequent communications and meetings to minimize hostile, harmful conflict. He suggested principals use opportunities to bring conflict to the forefront; it will only fester if ignored. In meetings and written communications, principals can positively reinforce those individuals who are working to support the organization's goals, thereby sending a message to those less positive individuals about behavioral expectations.

Thus, the structural factors that shape conflict in organizations are strongly influenced by structural factors in the organization itself (Likert & Likert, 1976). Likert and Likert advocated developing a more responsive interaction-influence system through System 4 leadership, developing a supportive climate, deemphasizing hierarchical status, and using consensus for productive (win-win) problem solving.

An Open-Systems View of Conflict

Thus far, we have been discussing organizational conflict entirely in terms of the internal functioning of educational organizations, and this topic will continue to be the focus of the chapter as a whole. It is vital, however, not to lose sight of the fact that these organizations are open systems: They are interactive with their environments, and much that goes on within them reflects changes in the external environment.

The University Council on Education Administration (UCEA) conducted a series of three "Voices from the Field" projects between 1999 and 2012. Using the third study (Acker-Hocevar, Ballenger, Place, & Ivory, 2012) that included 81 superintendents and 85 principals across the United States and representative of both genders as well as various ethnic/racial backgrounds, Alsbury and Whitaker (2012) analyzed superintendent and principal responses to outside forces and stress levels. They reported as follows:

> Although superintendents agreed with the intent of NCLB, they were dissatisfied and frustrated with the implementation of the law. Components of the law such as AYP, particularly related to special education, and highly qualified teachers posed difficulties for superintendents. Lack of funding to implement NCLB was another stressor for superintendents. (p. 173)

Alsbury and Whitaker also reported superintendents felt a great deal of pressure dealing with many community groups with divergent interests, as well as "power issues with members of their boards of education. Terminating employees seemed to cause a lot of angst for small-district superintendents in terms of their relationships with boards and communities" (p. 174). Another source of conflict for superintendents was dealing with the "teachers' unions and in the context of making decisions in the best interests of students" (p. 175).

Similar to superintendents, principals reported pressures of dealing with the implementation of No Child Left Behind (NCLB). Prominent complaints were dealing with the issue of recruiting and maintaining highly qualified teachers, and meeting Adequate Yearly Progress (AYP) requirements for subgroups. In addition, and similar to superintendents, principals reported problems with parent and other stakeholders:

> Principals often struggled with their desire to solicit input and the simultaneous political pressures of community members or board members wanting decisions to go their way. Coupled with pressures from boards and community members was working with the teachers' unions within the decision-making process. (Alsbury & Whitaker, 2012, p. 179)

Another good case in point is P.L. 94-142 (currently known as Individuals with Disabilities Education Act [IDEA]), which was passed by Congress and signed into law on November 29, 1975. It is a classic example of power-coercive change strategy and probably set the stage for more widespread conflict in U.S. public schooling—at all levels—than anything since the *Brown* school desegregation decision about two decades earlier. At the highest levels, it raised conflicting constitutional issues: the interpretation of the Tenth Amendment that education is a state responsibility and a matter of local control versus the view that P.L. 94-142 is an exercise of federal responsibility to ensure full civil rights and equal opportunity for the unserved (and inadequately served) population of children with disabilities.

However, the law also raised conflicts all along the line, from Washington, DC, to the most remote school classroom in the nation. For example, it sought to redefine the prerogatives of teachers to control instruction and related decision making by mandating the inclusion of parents in a participatory role in planning individualized instruction and in a formalized appeal process. The parent—formerly an outsider confined to an advisory role—suddenly became one of the insiders with new authority in relation to the teacher.

The ability of schools to deal productively with this conflict thrust on them from the larger environment was unclear even as late as 1990 because external initiatives to mandate increasing control of the classroom decisions of teachers were still increasing in number and scope. However, it is a clear and unambiguous illustration of how conflict—very much involving the internal functioning of schools and school systems—can be imposed on them by rapid change in the external system.

Gerald Griffin and David Rostetter (1978) speculated about whether Randall Collins's (Collins, 1975) five hypotheses on coercive efforts to deal with coercion and conflict might apply. As Griffin and Rosetter pointed out:

1. Coercion leads to strong efforts to avoid being coerced.
2. If resources for fighting back are available, the greater the coercion applied the more counter-aggression is called forth.
3. If resources are not available but opportunities to escape are, the greater the tendency to leave the situation.
4. If resources for fighting back and opportunities to escape are not available, or if there are other strong incentives for staying in the situation (material rewards or potential power), the greater coercion that is applied, the greater the tendency to comply with exactly those demands that are necessary to avoid being coerced.
5. If resources for fighting back and opportunities for escape are not available, the . . . tendency to dull compliance and passive resistance increases. (p. 4)

In this view, coercion leads to a conflict-hostility-resistance syndrome *within* the organization, nothing like the synergistic, creative, problem-solving culture that characterizes effective organizations. Only time will tell what effect federal initiatives, based on traditional concepts of schools as organizations, will ultimately have.

APPROACHES TO ORGANIZATIONAL CONFLICT

When conflict arises, the almost instinctive response of the parties involved is to adopt a strategy—backed by determination—to *win*. To most people, winning means, ipso facto, that the other party will *lose*.

The focal point of conflict management is the win-lose orientation and how to deal with it. It is important, first, to understand the dynamics and consequences of win-lose approaches to conflict and, second, to see what alternatives are available.

The Win-Lose Orientation to Conflict

The dynamics of win-lose conflict and their consequences for organizational behavior are well known. In the 1950s and 1960s, students of group dynamics conducted extensive research on the phenomena of group conflict—including both experimental work and field observation studies (see the discussion of group dynamics and human relations in Chapter 3) (Deutsch, 1949; Sherif & Sherif, 1953; Sherif, Harvey, White, Hood, & Sherif, 1961).

Early in the study of organizational conflict, and still current thinking, Blake, Shepard, and Mouton (1964) observed "a win-lose orientation to conflict is characterized by one basic element. The contesting parties see their interests to be mutually exclusive. No compromise is possible. One must fail at the price of the other's success" (p. 18). The parties to the conflict come to believe that the issues can be settled in one of three ways: (a) a power struggle, (b) intervention by a third party who possesses some sort of power greater than either of them (and this can include public opinion or moral suasion), or (c) fate. This approach has two consequences according to Likert and Likert (1976). Conflict *between parties* causes deep negative feelings and typically results in hostility and failure to arrive at acceptable solutions for both parties. In addition, *within groups* conflict typically results in expectations that members will tow the party line and diversity of opinion is not acceptable. Leaders close ranks around their most ardent supporters which sets the stage for in-group dissension.

Experimental studies of conflict made it clear that the perception of individuals and groups is very much involved in conflict—often becoming distorted as the episode unfolds (Blake, Shepard, & Mouton, 1964; Deutsch, 1973; Sherif & Sherif, 1953). And, of course, "perception is the key to behavior. The way people see things determines the way they will act. If their perceptions are distorted, the distortions are reflected in their behavior" (Likert & Likert, 1976, p. 61). We may believe we are communicating one message, but the receiver may be interpreting the message in a different way. Thus, judgment is adversely affected by the conflict experience: One tends to become blindly loyal, to become hostile to members of the other group, and to denigrate not only their ideas but also their worth as people. Leaders of the opposition—formerly seen as mature, able people—are now seen as irresponsible and incapable. Indeed, even cognition is affected: In studying proposed solutions to the conflict, it becomes difficult or impossible to see merit in proposals put forth by the other side even though they may be in substantial agreement with one's own ideas. Thus, agreement becomes elusive. *Any* sign of questioning about the position of one's group or any approval of proposals put forth from the other side is viewed by associates as backing down. Winning becomes everything. The ability to identify alternatives, to be objective, and to suspend judgment while seeking to understand are all badly distorted as one increasingly shares the gung-ho drive of the group for victory.

In terms of the process model of conflict (described earlier), win-lose is a way of conceptualizing the conflict and gives rise to predictable patterns of behavior in the interaction between parties to the conflict as the episode unfolds. But the consequences, it should be clear, are not limited to the shape and character of the conflict itself. Each of the groups involved in the conflict is powerfully affected in the aftermath. Usually, hostility between the winning group and the losing group is intensified, and subsequent episodes may be expected.

Commonly, the losing group rejects its leaders; very likely it will, in time, begin reappraising what went wrong and start preparing to do better next time. Powerful emotional reactions (resentment—even hatred—and anxiety) are likely to continue to distort the group's functioning, reducing the likelihood that it will develop a climate supportive of self-renewal and creative problem solving. Thus, win-lose solutions to conflict tend to build long-term dysfunctional behaviors that result in a downward spiral of organizational climate, performance, and overall organizational health. A central concern of conflict management, then, is to seek more effective ways of conceptualizing conflict as a basis for more effective behavior.

A Contingency Approach to Conflict

Contingency approaches to management are predicated on the concept that diagnosis of the situation is necessary as a basis for action. In dealing with conflict, the contingency view holds that there is no one best way of managing it under all conditions, but that there are optimal ways of managing conflict under certain conditions. An important aspect of conflict management, then, is to consider (a) alternative ways of managing conflict and (b) the kinds of situations in which each of these various alternatives might be expected to be the most effective, not only in dealing with the critical issues but also in doing so in a way that strengthens the organization.

Diagnosing Conflict

In the first place, it is helpful to ascertain whether conflict *does* exist between the parties or whether a conflict only *appears* (to the parties) to exist. The criterion is whether the two parties seek goals that are actually incompatible.

Frequently, what appears to be a brewing conflict between two parties is, in fact, a misunderstanding. When the problem is recognized as one of distorted perception, as discussed earlier, it is probable that the misunderstanding can be dealt with through explicit goal setting and improved communication. This process often requires training individuals and groups in skills such as group goal setting and prioritizing, as well as in communication skills (for example, active listening, seeking feedback to check the receiver's perceptions, using multiple channels).

If a conflict *does* exist (that is, the parties do have goals that are mutually incompatible), then it is necessary to select a method of dealing with it as productively as possible from among the many options available. The general principle is that a win-lose approach tends to be the least productive, while a win-win approach—in which both parties win something (though not necessarily equally)—tends to be the most productive.

Collaboration is a process in which the parties work together to define their problems and then engage in mutual problem solving. As a mode of dealing with conflict, this process requires, first, that the parties involved must want to try to use it (and will give time and effort to participating). The process also requires that the people involved possess (a) the necessary skills for communicating and working in groups, effectively coupled with (b) attitudes that support a climate of openness, trust, and frankness in which to identify and work through problems.

In situations in which the *will* to do this exists but the skills are not well developed, a facilitator can be brought in to help the groups learn the necessary skills and engage in the collaborative processes (the facilitator does not get involved in the substance of decisions, merely the processes for making them). This is the highest level of win-win conflict management because it leaves the groups with new skills and new understandings that they can use in dealing with future problems. It is, of course, a form of organization development (organizational self-renewal). The best part of collaborative approaches to problem solving is the healthy sense of ownership or commitment to the solution arrived at that is unmatched by other approaches. In Likert and Likert's terms, it is System 4 management.

Bargaining, compromise, and other forms of splitting the difference have some elements in common with collaborative problem solving: (a) The parties must be willing to engage in the process (though sometimes they are legally required to do so); (b) there is some move toward collaboration (though usually this is restricted to the negotiators); and (c) the process is basically conciliatory and not in flagrant conflict with the organization's well-being. If the bargaining goes to mediation or arbitration, the outside third party plays a role quite different from that of the group-process facilitator in a collaborative process: The outside third party in mediation or arbitration *does* have the power to make judgments and impose decisions on the parties in conflict. The goal of bargaining is to develop a long-term relationship between the parties and provide them with a mechanism for dealing with future problems. But bargaining is not a collaborative approach: It recognizes that the two parties are essentially adversaries and may use information as a form of power for strategic purposes.

Neither party wins in the typical bargaining/compromise situation, but then neither party loses. Although the term *bargaining* is readily associated with labor-management relations, negotiation processes are, in fact, widely employed within organizational settings to resolve conflicts. For example, when two administrators confer to work out some problems between their divisions, it is not uncommon for them to use negotiating and compromise techniques systematically. If the negotiations do bog down, the administrators may take the problem to their immediate superordinate for mediation (a common feature of the so-called bureaucratic mode of conflict management).

Avoidance (withdrawal, peaceful coexistence, indifference) is often employed when dealing with conflict. Avoidance is useful when (a) it is not likely that the latent conflict really can be resolved ("live with it") or (b) the issues are not important enough to the parties that they are willing to devote the time and resources to work them out. As Blake et al. (1964) pointed out, avoidance can be in the form of a ceasefire, wherein two groups engaged in a long-term struggle decide to keep in contact, still entrenched in their positions, but not to get locked into combat with each other. An interesting outcome of various avoidance responses to latent conflict is that, although conflict is not inevitable, agreement is impossible. Thus, a hostile aftermath is avoided, but the underlying problems are not dealt with; the latent conflict—with all its hazardous potential—remains, ready to become manifest at any time.

Power struggle is, of course, the effort by each party to win, regardless of the consequences for the other party. Although conflict, in itself, may be seen as having some potential benefit for organizations (or, at least, as being nondestructive), this mode of dealing with it is viewed almost universally as being destructive. It is the classic win-lose situation.

Dealing with Conflict

As Heifetz and Linsky (2002) pointed out:

> When you tackle a tough issue in any group, rest assured there will be conflict, either palpable or latent . . . most people have a natural aversion to conflict . . . but your default mindset . . . is probably to limit conflict as much as possible. Indeed, many organizations are downright allergic to conflict, seeing it primarily as a source of danger, which it certainly can be. Conflicts can generate casualties.
> . . . Thus, the challenge of leadership when trying to generate adaptive change is to work with differences, passions, and conflicts in a way that diminishes their destructive potential and constructively harnesses their energy. (pp. 101–102)

An important aspect of diagnosis for the conflict manager is to ascertain the way each party to the conflict has conceptualized the situation. In his classic work on conflict management, Kenneth

TABLE 11.1 Levels of Cooperativeness and Assertiveness for Five Orientations of Dealing with Conflict

Orientation	Dimensions of Conflict (Levels)	
	Cooperativeness	Assertiveness
Competitive (Domination)	Low	High
Avoidant (Neglect)	Low	Low
Accommodation (Appeasement)	High	Low
Sharing (Compromise)	Medium	Medium
Collaborative (Integration)	High	High

Thomas (1976) contended that it is common, in a conflict situation, to emphasize the extent to which a party is willing to cooperate with another party but to overlook a second critical factor: the party's desire to satisfy his or her own concerns. Thus, in his view, two critical behavioral dimensions shape the way one conceptualizes conflict:

1. *Cooperativeness:* the extent to which one wishes to satisfy the concerns of the other
2. *Assertiveness:* the extent to which one wishes to satisfy her or his own concerns

Thus, in diagnosing conflict as conceptualized by the parties involved, the issue becomes more than merely a matter of cooperating or acting professionally: Cooperation can be viewed as literally a sacrifice of one's own needs.

From this analysis, Thomas identified five principal perspectives that may be used in conceptualizing conflict and behaviors commonly associated with those perspectives:

1. *Competitive* behavior is the search to satisfy one's own concerns at the expense of others, if need be. As shown in Table 11.1, it is a high assertive-high uncooperative orientation. The effect is domination of the situation (as, for example, in hard-nosed contract negotiations in which nothing is yielded and every advantage is exploited). It is the classic win-lose view of conflict.
2. *Avoidant* (unassertive-uncooperative) behavior is usually expressed by apathy, withdrawal, and indifference. This position does *not* mean that there is an absence of conflict but that it has been conceptualized as something not to deal with. Hence, the latent conflict remains and may be viewed differently at another time.
3. *Accommodation* (high cooperativeness-low assertiveness) is typified by appeasement: One attends to the other's concerns while neglecting his or her own. This orientation may be associated with a desire to maintain a working relationship even at some sacrifice of one's interests.
4. *Sharing* orientation (moderate assertiveness-moderate cooperation) often leads to compromise (trade-offs, splitting the difference, horse trading).
5. *Collaborative* orientation to conflict (high assertiveness-high cooperativeness) leads to efforts to satisfy fully the concerns of both parties through mutual problem solving. The solution to the conflict is a genuine integration of the desires of both sides. The concept is win-win.

This approach to the analysis of conflict helps one to assess the kinds of strategies (for example, bargaining, power, or collaboration) that might be most useful in managing conflict. The goal, of course, is to manage the conflict so that it will be as productive as possible for the organization while minimizing destructive consequences. It is important, therefore, to consider the potential long-run consequences resulting from the aftermath of conflict.

For example, avoidance or appeasement can be appealing responses because—in the short run—they are likely to head off the difficulties of seeking genuine solutions. They have the added advantage of requiring the least in terms of organizational energy, time, and resources. But they do not solve the problem that triggered the conflict, nor do they develop the organization's capacity to deal productively with conflict.

Bargaining (compromising) does help to develop the internal capacity of the organization to deal with conflict. But bargaining is not designed to produce optimal solutions: In the process of horse trading, neither side emerges completely satisfied, and quite likely the more skilled, hard-nosed negotiator will walk away with more than his or her opponent does. Bargaining is essentially an adversarial—if not downright underhanded—procedure using "dirty tricks" and wily ploys to gain advantage. These tactics often engender resentment and mistrust, both dysfunctional attitudes in organizational life.

Competitive win-lose power plays and collaborative problem solving require the most energy, time, and resources. The essentially different consequences of each mode have already been described. Because the aftermath and long-term consequences of win-lose power struggles are well known to be dysfunctional and those of collaboration are known to be functional, few who are concerned about enhancing the organization's performance would fail to choose collaboration—whenever practical—as the most desirable conceptualization of conflict and competition as the least desirable.

Dealing with Difficult Individuals

Every organization is likely to have some individuals who are difficult. Todd Whitaker's book (2002), *Dealing with Difficult Teachers*, provides real-world advice for handling problems with individual teachers who may be burned-out, ineffective, or just plain difficult and uncooperative. Too often principals avoid dealing with these individuals because of the work and stress involved in doing so. But to ignore the problem is to avoid performing the principal's most important role—providing a positive learning environment for every child. Teachers who are rude, negative, or hostile help create a negative organizational climate, and they potentially do untold harm to children. It is the principal's responsibility to either change the behavior of these individuals from negative to positive (or at least neutral) or remove them from the school. Removing them is one of the most difficult and stressful roles of the principal's job and careful documentation of all violations of district and school policy and procedures makes removal a bit easier. Prior to any attempts to remove an individual, with exception of willful or dangerous neglect of duty, Whitaker provided some helpful suggestions in dealing with difficult people:

1. Look for opportunities to reinforce positive behaviors, though Whitaker humorously commented that "sometimes you have to squint" (p. 31) because positive behaviors may be seldom exhibited. When observed, take the opportunity to praise them in front of others if appropriate, that is, the praise must be authentic.
2. Give them responsibilities appropriate to the situation. This advice may go against one's instincts, but as Herzberg informed us, giving someone responsibility is a powerful motivator. When appropriate, involving peers can potentially have several positive outcomes,

including building positive relationships with others; and when paired with positive people, the difficult teachers have good role models to emulate.

3. Raise difficult teachers' discomfort levels in terms of their negative behaviors. This process includes approaching them about their negative behaviors, which in turn will help them accept responsibility for their situation.

4. Help difficult teachers improve their *interpersonal intelligence*. "Principals must share with them how they are coming across" to others (Whitaker, 2002, p. 57).

5. Establish expectations that negative behaviors are not acceptable in the school and that they help create poor school climates. Two critical times or locations for high expectations of positive behaviors are during all meetings and in the teachers' lounge.

How one communicates or approaches difficult teachers (or anyone for that matter) is critical to one's effectiveness. Whitaker wrote:

> Make sure that you do not treat them in the manner that they treat others. Never raise your voice, use sarcasm, or treat them rudely. It is also critical that we do not take a confrontational or argumentative approach. . . . Realize that your positive and productive teachers want these negative staff members dealt with, but they want it done in a professional manner. (p. 27)

When having difficult discussions or in any way being critical of an individual's behavior, never do so in front of others. In other words, don't embarrass them in front of their peer or superiors. It will only make them more defensive and does nothing to correct their negative behaviors.

Finally, the principal should be sure all leaders in the organization understand and apply the above principles of dealing with difficult people. Assistant principals, team leaders, PLC facilitators, and other leaders should be trained in dealing with difficult individuals as they are even more likely to encounter negative behaviors. Difficult staff members can be intimidating and stressful for any leader.

Dealing with Stress From Conflict

With conflict comes stress, and leaders generally feel the most stress as they are expected to manage the conflict, as Heifetz and Linsky (2002) pointed out. Drawing attention to tough questions and bringing conflicts to the surface to deal with them will increase stress on all individuals involved, which, in turn, increases stress levels. Heifetz and Linsky suggested that leaders can create a "holding environment" (safe place) within which to deal with the tough issues (e.g., hiring an outside facilitator, going on a retreat to a different location, establishing a culture that disagreement is fine, but not hostility). As group and individual tensions increase due to normal conflict, leaders can "lower the temperature" by doing the following:

1. Address the technical aspects of the problem.
2. Establish a structure for the problem-solving process.
3. Temporarily reclaim responsibility for the tough decision.
4. Employ work avoidance mechanisms.
5. Slow down the process of challenging norms and expectations. (p. 111)

Item number 4 in the above list needs some explanation. Heifetz and Linsky simply mean that leaders give individuals and groups temporary breaks from the conflicting situations as needed. Item number 5, slowing down the process of challenging norms and expectations, is difficult in education because of expectations of stakeholders and pressures brought by the outside environment (e.g., NCLB) to make significant and continual improvements.

In the UCEA "Voices from the Field" project, Alsbury and Whitaker (2012) reported that superintendents and principals coped with stress at a personal level with "stress-reduction activities, like meditation, relaxation training, physical exercise, health and wellness programs, and time-management training. Indeed, school leaders reported that the most effective coping mechanisms included physical exercise, talking with friends, and venting to their spouse" (p. 184). Alsbury and Whitaker recommended school districts develop programs to help administrators deal with stress, including setting up effective mentoring and networking relationships, as well as professional development programs to help administrators develop coping mechanisms for job-related stress. They suggested this process would also assist the district in meeting its goal of providing higher quality, sustainable leadership in schools as these programs will reduce burnout caused by physical and mental exhaustion.

Final Thoughts

Organizational conflict has been discussed in this chapter chiefly in terms of two-party clashes within the organization. Whereas conflict was once thought to signal a failure of the organization, it is increasingly recognized as a normal and legitimate aspect of human social systems. Thus, conflict is not only inevitable, but, contrary to earlier views, it can serve a useful function by stimulating creative solutions to problems.

Whether organizational conflict is destructive or constructive depends to a large extent on how it is managed. Healthy organizations—characterized by well-developed problem-solving mechanisms and a collaborative climate—are able to identify conflict and deal with it in a collaborative way that leaves the organization stronger and better developed rather than weakened and wracked with hostility.

Ways of handling conflict in school districts and schools have been heavily influenced by the people who have been consulted for advice or by third-party intervention. Especially with the spread of collective bargaining, school districts have turned increasingly for advice to people trained and conditioned to view conflict in adversarial, combative terms (lawyers and, not infrequently, professional negotiators and mediators), rather than people trained and conditioned to view it as a phenomenon of organizational behavior (applied social scientists, organizational psychologists). Too often this decision has produced essentially destructive, win-lose strategies and tactics.

This chapter has proposed a way of diagnosing conflict in a given situation as a basis for choosing an appropriate management strategy. Clearly, there is no one best way of managing conflict in organizations. There are a number of ways, each suited to circumstances in a particular situation. The basic principle in choosing a way of managing conflict, however, is to use the approach most likely to minimize the destructive aspects (for example, hostility) and to maximize the opportunities for organizational growth and development.

Finally, no phase of conflict management is more critical than diagnosing the situation. Frequently, the processes of conceptualizing, or analyzing, conflict confuses effects with causes. For example, a superintendent of schools asked a consultant, "What are some of the ways that I can deal with conflict in this school district?" When asked what kind of conflict he was talking about, the superintendent replied, "Well, you know, we had that teachers' strike and it was pretty bad here. Now the teachers are back at work, but we have a lot of bad feeling everywhere. You know—hostility. We have to do something about it. What can we do?" Although, as we have explained, hostility is an important aspect of conflict, it is important to bear in mind that hostility does not describe a conflict itself. Hostility is an emotional reaction that is all too often part of the outcome or aftermath of an episode of conflict. But trying to ameliorate hostile feelings is, perhaps, dealing with a symptom rather than a cause. If we fail to diagnose the conflict correctly and deal with the causes, the conflict will continue under the surface, ready to manifest itself at a later time.

Reflective Activities

1. *Handling Conflict:* Complete the following four cases that make up the conflict management activity by author Allan Dornseif (1996). *Please place the number 5 for your most likely response, the number 4 (next most likely), to 1 (least likely) next to the courses of action you would take under each of the four cases that follow. Answer based on what you would most likely do if you were the person described in the situation.*

CASE ONE

Pete is the lead teacher of a five-teacher middle school teaching team. Recently, he has noticed that Sarah, a teacher from across the hall, has been dropping in on Linda, the reading teacher in Pete's team, almost every fifth period to borrow something and chat a few minutes. It's only for a short time, but class noise and attention appear to be worsening. Others on the team seem to have some resentment of the minor intrusion. If you were Pete, you would:

_____ **a.** Talk to Linda and tell her to limit conversations to break periods.

_____ **b.** Ask the principal to tell the other team members to keep their teachers in their own classrooms.

_____ **c.** Talk to both teachers the next time you see them together, find out what they are up to, and inform them of the problem as you see it.

_____ **d.** Say nothing now; it would be silly to make a big deal out of a few minutes.

_____ **e.** Try to keep the rest of the team at ease; it is important that they all work well together.

CASE TWO

Ralph is head of the new computerized management system. His department consists of a state-of-the-art computer system and a staff of five. The work is exacting. Inattention or improper procedures could create costly damage to the system, bad output, or a serious breach of confidential information. Ralph suspects that Jim is drinking too much, maybe even on the job; at the least, he appears to be a bit "high." Ralph feels that he has some strong indications, but he knows he does not have evidence. If you were Ralph, you would:

_____ **a.** Talk to Jim outright, tell him what you suspect and why, and that you are concerned for him and for the operation of the department.

_____ **b.** Ask Jim to keep his habit off the job; what he does *on* the job is part of your business.

_____ **c.** Not confront Jim right now; it might either turn him off the job or drive his drinking further underground.

_____ **d.** Tell Jim that drinking on the job is illegal and that if he gets caught you will do everything you can to see that he is fired.

_____ **e.** Keep a close eye on Jim to see that he is not making serious mistakes.

CASE THREE

Sally is the district curriculum specialist and has been appointed by the superintendent to gather data for teaching improvement. On separate occasions, two teachers on the committee have come to her with different suggestions for reporting test results. Because the superintendent will see the progress the teams are making, Paul wants to send the test results directly to the superintendent and then to the teaching teams. Jim thinks the results should go directly to the teaching teams, so they can take corrective action right away. Both ideas seem good; the superintendent has been extremely busy completing this project, and there is no specific procedure for routing the reports. If you were Sally, you would:

_____ **a.** Decide who is right and ask the other person to go along with the decision.

_____ **b.** Wait and see; the best solution will become apparent.

_____ **c.** Tell both Paul and Jim not to get uptight about their disagreement. It is not that important.

_____ **d.** Get Paul and Jim together and examine both of their ideas closely for the best approach.

_____ **e.** Send the data to the superintendent with a copy to the lead teachers (although this approach is a lot more work for staff and will be more expensive).

CASE FOUR

Jean is president of the Parent-Teacher Association (PTA). From time to time in the past, the school council and the staff have "tapped" the PTA for volunteers to augment several projects, which has not been a problem because parents have been very willing to cooperate. Lately, however, there is an almost constant demand for volunteers to help on various new projects. Many parents are no longer available and the rest of the "real workers" must now make up for the shortage. Parents are beginning to complain that they are being used. If you were Jean, you would:

_____ **a.** Let it go for now; the extra projects will be over soon.

_____ **b.** Try to smooth things over with the volunteers, the council, and the principal. Everyone is doing this for the kids, after all. We cannot afford a conflict.

_____ **c.** Tell the council and the staff they can each have only two volunteers.

_____ **d.** Go to the principal and council chair and talk about how these demands for additional help could best be met without overloading the volunteers.

_____ **e.** Go to the council chair and get him to call off or postpone the council's projects.

Activity Score Sheet Directions   For each case, write the number you placed next to each letter. The column with the highest number shows your preferred method of resolving conflict in these types of situations.

Insert Ranking for Each Letter

Case					
One	d.	e.	a.	b.	c.
Two	c.	e.	b.	d.	a.
Three	b.	c.	e.	a.	d.
Four	a.	b.	c.	e.	d.
Totals					
Style					
	Retreat	Reconciliation	Harmony	Muscle	Collaboration

Now that you have your scores, let's relate them to the style for dealing with conflict. When faced with a controversy, we often rely on an instinctive approach that reflects our attitudes and behavior. From our background and experiences, most of us have developed an approach that we prefer and with which we are most comfortable as we face potential conflict situations. Two issues are at stake, however, in group conflict situations. The values we assign to these two issues determine our preferred strategy of dealing with conflict. We can approach a potential conflict situation with five possible methods, each of which is described below.

Reflect on your scores based on the styles of dealing with conflict below. Are your scores what you would expect?

Muscle

When using this method, the need for confrontation is high to accomplish goals and establish or maintain one's status, but it is low in its need to maintain harmonious feelings and smooth working relationships. This style is assertive, aggressive, and competitive, which creates a win-lose situation. People using this approach often feel they have moral certitude in their position. "I am the boss. Just do it!"

Most people view this approach as one that other people use, not themselves. Because more people rely on a muscle approach, however, it may be an unconscious personal choice.

Reconciliation

Reconciliation is the opposite of using muscle. Here the concern for people, feelings, and smooth working relationships is high, while the need to accomplish goals and maintain status is low. This style is one of accommodating, giving in, and acquiescing to preserve relationships while resolving the conflict, at least temporarily. Sometimes we say "agreeing to disagree" or "peaceful coexistence." Usually, it means that we quietly sweep the issue under the rug and hope it stays there (it rarely does).

Harmony

Bargaining or negotiation is about equal in its need to maintain harmony in relationships and to accomplish goals. It is a "middle ground," aimed at achieving compromise in order to resolve conflict. This approach is used when the pressure to win is not too great, and the parties find it possible to work out an equitable bargain or to "split the difference." In this situation, there is no loser, but there is no winner either.

Retreat

Avoiding or withdrawal is the other end of the muscle approach. It is low on both the need to maintain relationships and the need to accomplish goals. This approach is aimed at not becoming involved with conflict and the strong feelings it may generate. Retreat is usually a temporary solution.

Collaboration

Solving problems through the collaboration of people and groups attempting to reach consensus on issues is high both on the need to maintain relationships and the need to accomplish goals. It is aimed at finding a new set of goals that incorporate the ideas and concerns of both parties, which leads to growth in the working relationship. This style stresses working together for a mutual solution to conflicts.

Facing the issues together, all parties need a strong commitment to finding a solution to which all can agree. This approach requires a high investment of energy with no guarantee that the problem can be solved effectively. It is the most positive approach, however, which engenders trust. Its success makes it more likely to be used in future conflict situations.

Each of these approaches has its own advantages and disadvantages, its strengths and weaknesses. In itself, no one style is "better" than another. However, each approach has a different thrust and different consequences. Constructive conflict management calls for the ability to read the situation and apply the best strategy.

Different stages of conflict may call for different approaches. In the initial stages of bargaining, for example, both parties are likely to use muscle to establish the issues in which they are most interested. Later, as bargaining continues, each party must assume a negotiating style if a compromise is to be reached. If the parties can develop a mutual trust, the problem-solving approach of collaboration is best for the long term.

2. Review Louis Pondy's three basic types of latent conflict. For each type of conflict (competition for scarce resources, autonomy, and goal divergence), provide an example from your experience. Using Kenneth Thomas's model of conceptualizing conflict, identify the type of orientations that were involved in each scenario. Who were the players in the conflict, and what strategies did they and the organizational leaders use to respond to the conflict? Did the outcomes have positive or negative effects on organizational health?

3. Review the critical incident at the beginning of the chapter, and apply the knowledge you learned from this chapter to add to your responses to the questions.

4. *Working on Your Game Plan.* Meetings with staff members present prime opportunities for educational leaders to engage in conflict management. In school meetings, however, conflict is often latent: unrecognized, "papered over," ignored and thus denied, or simply not acknowledged. Latent conflict is almost impossible to manage productively. Therefore, a first step in managing conflict is to make the conflict manifest: Acknowledge it; get it on the table so that it can be described, discussed, and managed. A common problem in school staff meetings, however, is that people behave in tacitly agreed-on ways to prevent conflict from being acknowledged and managed. As described in this chapter, this response is ordinarily attributable to the fear of hostility.

Reflect on your own experience with staff meetings at school now that you have read this chapter. Prepare three key coaching tips that you might offer a school principal for improving the planning and conducting of staff meetings and thus incorporating conflict management strategies and tactics. Start each of your coaching tips with a specific recommended action or procedure. Then describe your rationale for recommending the action.

For example, one might recommend that the principal form an advisory group made up of staff members who will work collaboratively to develop the agendas for staff meetings. The model for doing this might very well be the Tannenbaum-Schmidt model. The rationale for this recommendation is twofold: First, empowering teachers to exercise greater influence over the meetings that they must attend will have a salutary effect in improving the climate of the meetings and thus increase consensus; second, this process will, in turn, make it easier, and more likely, that issues of conflict can be acknowledged and discussed.

CRITICAL INCIDENT   Conflict in the First-Grade Team

At James Madison Elementary School, there is conflict among the five teachers in the first-grade team, and the principal, Miriam Jackson, is not sure how to handle the situation. Miriam is uneasy because the conflict is affecting instruction in the first grade, and it is causing concern among teachers in other grade levels.

The problems started two years ago when the district required all schools to align their instructional strategies, assessments, and curriculum to the state standards. While attempting to do this on a team level, Miriam saw that there was a split on the first-grade team about basic reading philosophy. Two team members were in the phonics camp, and three were firmly in the whole-language camp. Although everyone understood that any reading program must be a blend of both philosophies, they disagreed about what should be taught first, and therefore what approach should be the main focus of the curriculum. This dissension led to many arguments, some of which were very hostile, about the instructional strategies that would be used in the first grade.

Last year, Miriam basically told them that they needed to work this out among themselves, but she observed little progress in their ability to work together in the last 2 years. Team meetings were very stressful for the team leader, who was in the whole-language camp. Teachers in the phonics camp told Miriam that they were being shunned and threatened with their jobs by the team leader and the other teachers. At faculty meetings, the conflict on the first-grade team led to school-wide arguments on the subject of reading, and Miriam was very concerned that the overall school climate has declined because of this conflict. She wondered how she can turn this challenge into an opportunity.

1. How should Miriam handle this conflict so that the issues related to the hostility among teachers and issues related to the curriculum are resolved?
2. Can she do it in a way that might benefit the whole school?

Suggested Reading

Beckhard, R. (1967). The confrontation meeting. *Harvard Business Review, 45*, 149–155.

This journal article describes "an activity that allows a total management group, drawn from all levels of the organization, to take a quick reading on its own health, and—*within a matter of hours*—to set action plans for improving it" (p. 149). It provides a specific design for a one-day meeting that can be used to deal with the stress of a crisis that helps the group (1) diagnose the situation, (2) set goals and priorities collaboratively, (3) develop a plan of action, and (4) implement the plan on both a short- and long-range basis.

Derr, C. B. (1975). *Managing organizational conflict: When to use collaboration, bargaining and power approaches.* Monterey, CA: Naval Postgraduate School.

This book proposes a contingency approach, pointing out that collaboration, bargaining, and power approaches are all appropriate in the management of organizational conflict under certain conditions. The author explains how to diagnose the contingencies in different situations and discusses the benefits and drawbacks for each strategy under varying conditions.

Likert, R., & Likert, J. G. (1976). *New ways of managing conflict.* New York, NY: McGraw-Hill.

After analyzing the causes of increasing organizational conflict, this book describes procedures for substituting System 4 (win-win) problem-solving strategies for the win-lose approach that usually leaves one party in a conflict frustrated and embittered. This is a highly specific, practical how-to book with some explicit applications to schools that should be helpful to practitioners.

Whitaker, T. (2002). *Dealing with difficult teachers* (2nd ed.). Larchmont, NY: Eye on Education.

Todd Whittaker is a popular author among students of educational leadership. In this book, he identifies key methods to assist future leaders in working effectively with teachers who behave in ways that create negative school climates. He shows that a direct, assertive approach is critical to address problem behaviors, and he clearly describes how to assist a teacher to become a positive force in the school or, if necessary, to use disciplinary measures to remove the teacher.

Yankelovich, D. (1999). *The magic of dialogue: Transforming conflict into cooperation.* New York, NY: Simon & Schuster.

Leaders in the ongoing struggle to forge a broad consensus on the goals, purposes, and methods of schooling must continually strive to improve communication among the parties to the debate. In this book, the author, a social scientist and scholar in communication, offers methods to help leaders master communication skills that they need to be more effective in resolving problems and achieving shared goals. The term *dialogue*, as Yankelovich uses it, has a specific meaning and is not merely a synonym for "conversation." He shows how to use dialogue to strengthen relationships, dissolve stereotypes, overcome mistrust, achieve mutual understanding, and shape visions grounded in shared purposes. Some have objected that this book is merely a systematic presentation of common sense. The problem, however, is that common sense is often one of the first things out the window when opposing forces face conflict over schooling. This valuable book takes the leader back to fundamentals—always a good idea, as any athlete will testify, when things are not going well.

References

Acker-Hocevar, M. A., Ballenger, J., Place, A. W., & Ivory, G. (Eds.). (2012). *Snapshots of school leadership in the 21st century: Perils and promises of leading for social justice, school improvement, and democratic community (The UCEA Voices from the Field Project)*. Charlotte, NC: Information Age.

Alsbury, T. L., & Whitaker, K. S. (2012). Pressure of outside forces, stress, and finding balance. In M. A. Acker-Hocevar, J. Ballenger, A. W. Place, & G. Ivory (Eds.). *Snapshots of school leadership in the 21st century: Perils and promises of leading for social justice, school improvement, and democratic community (The UCEA Voices from the Field Project)* (pp. 169–187). Charlotte, NC: Information Age.

Barnard, C. I. (1938). *The functions of the executive*. Cambridge, MA: Harvard University Press.

Bennis, W. (2010). *Still surprised: A memoir of a life in leadership*. San Francisco, CA: Jossey-Bass.

Blake, R. R., Shepard, H. A., & Mouton, J. S. (1964). *Managing intergroup conflict in industry*. Houston, TX: Gulf Publishing Company.

Boulding, K. E. (1962). *Conflict and defense: A general theory*. New York, NY: Harper & Brothers.

Burns, J. M. (1978). *Leadership*. New York, NY: Harper & Row.

Collins, R. (1975). *Conflict sociology: Toward an explanatory science*. New York, NY: Academic Press.

Deutsch, M. (1949). The effects of cooperation and competition upon group process: An experimental study. *American Psychologist, 4*, 263–64.

Deutsch, M. (1973). *The resolution of conflict: Constructive and destructive processes*. New Haven, CT: Yale University Press.

Dornseif, A. (1996). *Pocket guide to school-based decision making* (No. 5). Arlington, VA: Association for Supervision and Curriculum Development.

Griffin, G., & Rostetter, D. (1978, March). *A conflict theory perspective for viewing certain problems associated with Public Law 94–142*. Paper presented at the meeting of the American Educational Research Association, Atlanta, GA.

Heifetz, R. A., & Linsky, M. (2002). *Leadership on the line: Staying alive through the dangers of leading*. Boston, MA: Harvard Business School Press.

Likert, R., & Likert, J. G. (1976). *New ways of managing conflict*. New York, NY: McGraw-Hill.

Pondy, L. R. (1967, September). Organizational conflict: Concepts and models. *Administrative Science Quarterly, 12*, 296–320.

Sherif, M., Harvey, O. J., White, B. J., Hood, W. R., & Sherif, C. W. (1961). *Intergroup conflict and cooperation: The robbers cave experiment*. Norman, OK: Institute of Group Relations, University of Oklahoma Book Exchange.

Sherif, M., & Sherif, C. W. (1953). *Groups in harmony and tension*. New York, NY: Harper & Brothers.

Thomas, J. M., & Bennis, W. G. (1972). *Management of change and conflict*. Baltimore, MD: Penguin Books.

Thomas, K. (1976). Conflict and conflict management. In M. D. Dunnette (Ed.), *Handbook of industrial and organizational psychology*. Chicago, IL: Rand McNally.

Whitaker, T. (2002). *Dealing with difficult teachers* (2nd ed.). Larchmont, NY: Eye on Education.

Wynn, R. (1972). *Administrative response to conflict*. Pittsburgh, PA: Tri-State Area School Study Council.

CHAPTER 12

School Reform

The last two decades of the twentieth century and the beginning of the twenty-first century witnessed a remarkable quickening and expansion of efforts to reform U.S. schools. It is almost certain that these efforts will continue and that they will dominate the environment of educational leadership well into the twenty-first century. As explained briefly in Chapter 4, the term *school reform* often means very different things to different people because they use various theories in trying to understand and explain issues such as education, schools as organizations, and human behavior.

The term generally connotes planned efforts by those external to the school to cause changes, or restructuring, to occur within the school. Chapter 7 described in some detail three major theoretical strategies that dominate the field:

- Empirical-rational strategies
- Power-coercive strategies
- Organizational self-renewal strategies

To be effective, power-coercive strategies require the exercise of power so overwhelming that the organization is compelled to change in response. Adherents of power-coercive strategies for school reform normally start out with little concern for, or interest in, organizational behavior issues in the schools. The third category of school reform seeks to change schools from the inside out through processes of organizational self-renewal. As described in Chapter 8, when the leader's theory of practice is based on the strategy of organizational self-renewal, organizational behavior issues are central in the leader's practice.

Many of the reforms faced by schools are a direct result of initiatives of the U.S. Department of Education, and typically these reforms follow a power-coercive strategy. Although some reforms required of state education systems are based on empirical-rational thinking, they are implemented through coercive policies, so district or school-based reforms are not generated through organizational self-renewal methods. Prime examples were the requirements in No Child Left Behind (NCLB) such as annual testing that became high stakes assessments for children, teachers, schools, and school districts.

The U.S. Department of Education is a driver of reform in education. In 2010, the Obama administration released *A Blueprint for Reform: The Reauthorization of the Elementary and Secondary Education Act* in which it presented its priorities and strategies for improving education in elementary, secondary, and post-secondary education (U.S. Department of Education, 2010). This strategic plan became the basis for the administration's reform policy from 2011 to 2014 and listed the following goals:

> *Goal 1:* Postsecondary education, career and technical education, and adult education. Increase college access, quality, and completion by improving higher education and life-long learning opportunities for youth and adults.

> *Goal 2:* Elementary and secondary. Prepare all elementary and secondary students for college and career by improving the education system's ability to consistently deliver excellent class-room instruction with rigorous academic standards while providing effective support services.

> *Goal 3:* Early learning. Improve the health, social-emotional, and cognitive outcomes for all children from birth through third grade so that all children, particularly those with high needs, are on track for graduating from high school college-ready and career-ready.

> *Goal 4:* Equity. Ensure and promote effective educational opportunities as well as safe, healthy learning environments for all students regardless of race, ethnicity, national origin, age, sex, sexual orientation, gender identity, disability, language, and socioeconomic status.

> *Goal 5:* Continuous improvement of the U.S. education system. Enhance the education system's ability to continuously improve through better and more widespread use of data, research and evaluation, transparency, innovation, and technology.

> *Goal 6:* U.S. Department of Education capacity. Improve the organizational capacities of the department to implement this strategic plan.

In his introduction to the strategic plan, Secretary of Education Arne Duncan writes that reaching President Obama's goal of regaining the lead in the highest proportion of college graduates in the world

> will require comprehensive education reforms from cradle to career, beginning with children at birth, supporting them through postsecondary education, and helping them succeed as lifelong learners who can adapt to the constant changes in the diverse and technology-driven workplaces of the global economy. (U.S. Department of Education, n.d., p. 1)

To support these reform efforts, over $4 billion was included in the original Race to the Top (RTTT) program as part of the American Recovery and Reinvestment Act of 2009 (AARA). You may know AARA by the term "stimulus," which was money pumped into a failing economy. It worked to a large degree, although the pundits are still arguing whether it was too much or not enough money. Nonetheless, RTTT dangled the money carrot before the states, and those who applied and "won" the money (22 states by the summer of 2013) had to fulfill the requirements of RTTT, which to most seemed to be a kinder, gentler NCLB. To help achieve the Department of Education goals, RTTT attempted to advance four areas of reform in K-12 schools:

1. adopting rigorous standards and assessments that prepare students for success in college and the workplace;
2. recruiting, developing, retaining, and rewarding effective teachers and principals;
3. building data systems that measure student success and inform teachers and principals how they can improve their practices;
4. turning around the lowest-performing schools. (U.S. Department of Education, 2013).

To receive an award, a state had to provide evidence or plans to meet these four areas of reform. The competitive grant application indicated several priorities, the first and most important of which was for the state to identify a comprehensive approach to education reform. The state had to show commitment from sufficient school districts to use funds "to increase student achievement, decrease the achievement gaps across student subgroups, and increase the rates at which students graduate from high school prepared for college and career" (U.S. Department of Education, 2009, p. 4). The highest priority goals included in this comprehensive approach to reform were a requirement for developing common standards, improving teacher and principal effectiveness based on performance, improving teacher and principal preparation programs, and turning around low performing schools. The second highest priority was to present a plan to promote STEM education (Science, Technology, Engineering, and Mathematics) in elementary, secondary, and post-secondary education. Other priorities of less importance in the award decisions were for innovations in improving pre-K through third grade learning outcomes including school readiness; expansion of statewide data systems to merge data on all educational programs and human resources information; coordination and alignment, vertical and horizontal, of educational programs from early childhood through workforce development and community agencies (such as child welfare and juvenile justice); and school-level conditions for reform, innovation, and learning, including school climates to promote such activities (U.S. Department of Education, 2009).

In her critical commentary, Diane Ravitch (2013) concludes that NCLB and RTTT have actually led to federal control of education unlike any time in the past. Washington dictates education reform by giving or withholding funding, and by doing so effectively negates the promise of "federalism—a calibrated balance among federal, state, and local governments" (p. 314). We provide this information above as a context for the subsequent discussions in this chapter on the landscape of reform in education.

MARKET-BASED SCHOOL REFORM

Some who would reform public schooling in the United States believe that the notion of public schools being democratically controlled by the body politic should be abandoned in favor of indirect control through the marketplace. This view of school reform tends to be shared by two main groups: market-oriented theorists who see government organizations as inferior to market-oriented organizations, and business investors who see private control of education as a potential source of vast profits.

There are three primary vehicles for the delivery of market-oriented education reforms that are beginning to flourish in some states.

- *Charter Schools* These schools are autonomous nonsectarian schools that are formed by nonprofit or for-profit companies. They are given a charter (contract) by the school district, a public university, or the state board of education to operate and receive state funding per each child enrolled. Some states also include startup costs by providing some capital money for buildings. In the charter, the charter school indicates how it will be organized, what type of curriculum and services it will offer to the students and parents/guardians, how it will be funded, and how it defines its autonomy from the public schools. The original rationale for allowing such schools is twofold: one, charter schools will operate under a philosophy distinct from the local public schools, giving parents and guardians added choices of how to educate their children; and two, through competition with charter schools, public schools will improve. In the 2012-2013 school year, 42 states and the District of Columbia had legislation authorizing some type of charter schools (Center for Education Reform, 2013). The states that did not authorize charter schools were Alabama, Kentucky, Montana, Nebraska, North Dakota, South Dakota, Vermont, and West Virginia.

• *Vouchers* Vouchers are also called tuition vouchers or scholarships. In some states, parents and guardians are provided a state tuition voucher, usually about the same amount of money as the average per-pupil cost per child, which they may use in the school of their choice. Eligibility for vouchers differs by state, but they are usually reserved for students who have disabilities or students who attend failing schools as defined by the state. As of August 2012, 10 states and the District of Columbia permitted vouchers (Arizona, Florida, Georgia, Indiana, Louisiana, Mississippi, Ohio, Oklahoma, Utah, and Wisconsin). Two additional states, Maine and Vermont allow vouchers for students in small towns and rural areas where public schools are not easily available (Alliance for School Choice, 2012; U.S. Department of Education, 2009).

• *Tax Credits or Tax Deductions* Tax credits or deductions are allowed to either individuals or corporations who provide money to scholarship organizations. The scholarships are then given to individuals who use them to attend the school of their choice, public or private. These scholarships work much like vouchers, except that individual or corporate money, not public funding, is used. In some states, like Florida, public money in the form of vouchers cannot be used in private schools (*Bush v. Holmes*, 2006), whereas there is no such limitation on scholarship money. At the end of 2012, 13 states participated in this market-based reform (Arizona, Florida, Georgia, Illinois, Indiana, Iowa, Louisiana, Minnesota, New Hampshire, Oklahoma, Pennsylvania, Rhode Island, Virginia) (Alliance for School Choice, 2012; U.S. Department of Education, Office of Innovation and Improvement, Office of Non-Public Education, 2009).

Origin of Market-Based Reforms

One of the early and widely popular expositions of this iconoclasm was the book *Politics, Markets, and America's Schools,* by John Chubb and Terry Moe, which was published in 1990 by the Brookings Institution. In this scholarly polemic, all educational reforms ever tried were totally dismissed and the authors' own theoretical concept—sometimes called the voucher system—was argued as being flawless, though, at that time, it had never been tried. Markets, the authors insisted, by their very nature, foster the autonomy that is required for schools to be effective. In the marketplace, they theorized, the ineffective schools simply disappear for want of customers to purchase their products. With this simple, strongly argued proposal, Chubb and Moe (1990) stirred a national debate on parent-student choice in the marketplace as an alternative to direct democratic control of public schooling that had prevailed in the United States for well over a century.

To work, free-market school reform requires the existence of schools to make up a market in which parents and students can actually shop for the school of their choice willing to accept their vouchers. By 1998, pilot state-approved voucher programs were functioning in Milwaukee and Cleveland, cities that permit vouchers to be used in either religious or nonreligious private schools. In 1999, the Florida legislature passed the first statewide voucher program, titled the Opportunity Scholarship Program, but in 2006, in *Bush v. Holmes,* the Florida Supreme Court struck down this law, citing that it violated the Florida constitution provision that the legislature shall provide for a uniform system of public schools. In a similar setback to voucher programs,

TABLE 12.1   State Voucher Programs That Were Enacted

State	Description	Year Enacted
Arizona	Vouchers for students with disabilities	2006
	Vouchers for foster-care children	2006
	Vouchers for students in low-performing schools (may attend private schools)	2011
Florida	Vouchers for students in failing schools (Note: This program was terminated by the Florida Supreme Court at the end of the 2005–2006 school year.)	1999
	Vouchers for students with disabilities	1999
Georgia	Vouchers for students with disabilities	2007
Indiana	Vouchers to assist students from low- and middle-income families	2011
Louisiana	Vouchers for students in low-performing schools (may attend private schools)	2008
	Vouchers for students with disabilities	2010
Maine	Voucher-like tuition assistance for students in small towns and rural areas	1873
Mississippi	Vouchers for students with dyslexia	2011
Ohio	Vouchers for students in Cleveland	1995
	Vouchers for autistic students	2003
	Vouchers for students in underperforming schools	2006
Oklahoma	Vouchers for students with disabilities	2010
Utah	Vouchers for students with disabilities	2005
	Vouchers for all students (Note: The implementation of this program was not supported by the required statewide referendum of November 2007.)	2007
Vermont	Voucher-like tuition assistance for students in small towns and rural areas	1869
Wisconsin	Vouchers for students from low-income families in Milwaukee	1990
	Vouchers for students from low-income families in Racine	2011
District of Columbia	Vouchers for students from low-income families (Note: This program is federally funded.)	2004

Sources: Data compiled from U.S. Department of Education, Office of Innovation and Improvement, *Education Options in the States* (2009), retrieved from http://www.ed.gov/parents/schools/choice/educationoptions/index.html; Alliance for School Choice (2012), *School Choice Yearbook 2011-2012*, retrieved from http://www.allianceforschoolchoice.org/school-choice-facts

Louisiana's State Supreme Court ruled in May 2013 that state funds designated for schools, called the Minimum Foundation Program, could not be used for nonpublic schools. Proponents of these vouchers, including Governor Jindal, vowed to continue the voucher programs by finding new money not included in the Minimum Foundation Program. Tables 12.1 and 12.2 display the types of voucher and tax credit programs for each state.

Despite what may seem to educators to be a great deal of news coverage and public discussion, the public is somewhat confused about or unaware of school vouchers, charter schools, and tuition tax credits. In November 1999, nine years after the appearance of the Chubb and Moe book, Public Agenda conducted a study that revealed that 63% of people interviewed across the country reported knowing "very little" or "nothing" about vouchers. By 2008, this number

TABLE 12.2   State Tax Credit Programs That Were Enacted as of August 2007

State	Description	Year Enacted
Arizona	Tax credits for individuals for contributions to scholarship organizations	1997
	Tax credits for corporations for contributions to scholarship organizations	2006
Florida	Tax credits for corporations for contributions to scholarship organizations	2001
Georgia	Tax credits for individuals and corporations for contributions to scholarship organizations	2008
Illinois	Tax credits for parents for education expenses	1999
Indiana	Tax credits for individuals and corporations for contributions to scholarship organizations	2009
Iowa	Tax credits for parents for education expenses	1987
	Tax credits for individuals for contributions to school tuition organizations	2006
Louisiana	Tax credits for individuals and corporations for contributions to scholarship organizations	2012
Minnesota	Tax credits and tax deductions for parents for education expenses	1955/1997
New Hampshire	Tax credits for corporations for contributions to scholarship organizations	2012
Oklahoma	Tax credits for individuals and corporations for contributions to scholarship organizations	2011
Pennsylvania	Tax credits for corporations for contributions to scholarship organizations	2001
Rhode Island	Tax credits for corporations for contributions to scholarship organizations	2006
Virginia	Tax credits for individuals and corporations for contributions to scholarship organizations	2012

Sources: Data compiled from U.S. Department of Education, Office of Innovation and Improvement (2009); *Education Options in the States,* retrieved from http://www.ed.gov/parents/schools/choice/educationoptions/index.html; and Alliance for School Choice (2012), *School Choice Yearbook 2011-2012,* retrieved from http://www.allianceforschoolchoice.org/school-choice-facts

improved somewhat, with 40% indicating they did not know enough about school vouchers to have an opinion, while 37% favored vouchers and 24% opposed. Yet when asked specifically if they favored or opposed allowing students and parents to choose a private school to attend at public expense, which is a definition for vouchers, 50% opposed the idea and 44% favored it. It is clear that, when given the definition of vouchers, the public mostly oppose the idea. Yet the Phi Delta Kappan/Gallup Poll published yearly indicates a trend that favors vouchers. In 2006, only 36% favored vouchers (Bushaw & Gallup, 2008). But in 2012, this percentage increased to 44% (Bushaw & Lopez, 2012).

Concerning charter schools, the 2008 Phi Delta Kappan/Gallup Poll, revealed that 51% favored charters, 35% opposed them, and 14% did not have an opinion. By 2011, those in favor of charter schools peaked at 70%, but then dropped to 66% in 2012 (Bushaw & Lopez, 2012). These percentages were similar in 2008 among Democrats and Republicans, with an equal percentage opposing charters, and only 4% more Republicans favoring them. However, charter schools are becoming a politically-charged concept with 80% of the republicans favoring them but only 54% of the democrats in 2012. Overall however, the trend in favor of charter schools is declining, which could suggest that, as the public learns more about the actual success of charter schools to improve the achievement levels of students versus that of public schools, they see charter schools as a less desirable choice. This opinion is certainly the case among democrats. Traditionally, the public has rated the public schools where their own children go to school very highly, with 77% giving them an A or B rating (up 13% in the last 20 years), and only 6% giving them a D or F rating. Whereas when asked to rate the public schools nationally, 48% rated them an A or B, and 17% rated them a D or F. This dichotomy between ratings of one's own public schools and those nationally is perplexing, but one explanation is that the politicians and pundits often speak of the failures of public schools, which leaves a lasting impression on the public about the public schools in general.

Economic Theory and School Reform

The origin of the concept of school vouchers is generally credited to Milton Friedman, a staunchly conservative economist and winner of the Nobel Prize for economics in 1976. Friedman developed economic views that were strongly opposed to those of John Maynard Keynes, which dominated economic and political thought for most of the twentieth century. Keynes advocated public works programs and other government spending programs in free markets to stimulate employment and the economy, and to provide social programs such as healthcare and education. After World War I, until well after World War II, Keynesian economics underlay the economic and political policies of many Western nations, including the New Deal of the United States.

Friedman was a pioneer of the now-fashionable idea of open markets free of government interference or control. In that context, Friedman developed the notion that schooling should not be a service provided by the government but should be part of the free-market system (Friedman, 1955, 1995). Although Friedman did very little to put the idea into practice, many of his followers have done so. Thus, the theory that drives market-based school reform, including voucher plans, arises from economic thought. We will not try to delve deeply into economic theory here, but some points are highly relevant to the idea of tuition vouchers and market-based school reform and should be considered by school leaders.

Economics is the science of how a society chooses to allocate scarce resources to best meet competing needs (Friedman, 1976). Education Professor Herbert J. Walberg has been a leader in trying to adapt market theory to the organization and control of public schooling in the United States. Walberg and Bast (2001) explain that economic activity takes place in four sectors: governments, households, civic or nonprofit institutions, and the marketplace. Each sector has its own rules and ends. Activity in government and civic institutions, for example, generally takes the form of voting, giving, or receiving commands. Within households, rules commonly resemble a kind of primitive communism. In the marketplace, the primary activities are purchase, sale, savings, and investment. In this context, one can look at schooling as an economic issue because the necessary resources—money for requirements such as buildings, facilities, equipment and materials, teachers, and administrators—are scarce and must be bid for in competition with other demands. Whereas people in the United States have traditionally chosen to make decisions about schooling within the framework of democratic political control, it is plausible to the free-market advocate that we can choose to shift from that public policy value to the marketplace if we wish. Naturally, in a booming economic era that characteristically celebrates free-market entrepreneurship and denigrates government, the free-market protagonists tend to view this as highly desirable.

A large problem looms before the free-market advocate and everyone else who entertains this seemingly simple idea: the enormous size and complexity of the public schooling enterprise in the United States, which are rendered incalculably greater when one considers the scope of the human variables involved in this vast and complex human social system. In the United States, for 2010 and 2011, we are talking about 14,166 school districts with 98,817 public schools (an increase of about 12,000 since 2005), of which 5,274 were charter schools (National Center for Education Statistics, 2013). Because the notion of rational choice lies close to the heart of economic theory, how can one be confident that—in an enterprise of this enormous human and social scale as well as obvious diversity—rational choice can and will prevail in the arena of the free marketplace? Fortunately, Walberg believes, there is a disarmingly simple answer. It should be well understood by school leaders because it has immense implications for leadership and organizational behavior in an era of market competition and school vouchers. Whereas education leaders are intensely interested in the complexities of human issues such as motivation, collaboration, and conflict management, we are told that the economist chooses to ignore such things:

> The economist solves the problem of complexity by assuming as little as possible about the motivation of the actors he is studying ... [and] asserts only that human agents will tend to choose rationally among the choices they face.... Rational choice theory is silent on whether or not the agents' ends are rational or desirable in any way except that they are voluntarily chosen by the agent over other ends. (Walberg & Bast, 2001, p. 8)

In other words, the incentives and the rules of the marketplace give rise to behavior, and the economist is not particularly involved in the values or attitudes that may or may not contribute to the decision-making processes of either individuals or societies. Economists most often emphasize the notion of *rational* choice—that is, making decisions in the marketplace that are perceived to be in one's economic self-interest. This is, of course, very troublesome from the organizational behavior perspective—which assumes that nothing is more important in understanding organizations than the psychosocial factors in the human dimension of the organization.

Much of the work of those who favor free-market strategies in educational reform is financially supported by conservative think tanks and often cited by conservative news columnists such as William Raspberry, whose column appeared in the *Washington Post* and was widely syndicated until his death in 2012. Both the think tanks and those who elect to represent them tend to advocate, as a transcendent truism, the ideology that free-market solutions to public policy issues are intrinsically superior to all other solutions. This ideology applies in particular to those solutions that they like to call "government" solutions (as in *government schools,* a term that appears frequently in discussions of market-driven school reform). Walberg, for example, has written numerous tracts—closely reasoned and carefully documented—to forcefully argue this thesis. But the sources on which Walberg depends for evidence to support his strident advocacy of abandoning public schooling and embracing for-profit corporate schools in the marketplace are very thin on research and long on opinions that express ideological chutzpah from the economic realm of academe. In Walberg's copious and finely detailed ad hominem arguments, one is hard-pressed to find a scintilla of support for even the possibility that government schools and their administrators have a shred of value. Economist Thomas Sowell, whose work was described in Chapter 2, similarly assails public education as a partisan advocate instead of revealing the balanced temperament and perspective that one normally associates with scholarly analyses. For example, Sowell is so anxious to destroy the roots of professional preparation for teaching—that is, the preparation programs in teacher education in U.S. colleges and universities—that he argues the contracts of all the professors of education should be bought out and the faculty members dismissed so that the programs in which they teach may be eradicated. As you will see a little later in this chapter, the American Association for Higher Education vigorously differs with that suggestion.

In addition to a survey of present-day evidence of the superiority of private enterprise and free competition in education compared to all other approaches, Andrew Coulson (1999a) has sought to develop a historical rationale to advance the claims of marketplace approaches to schooling. His discourse in *Market Education: The Unknown History* ranges from the ancient civilizations of Athens and Rome, through the Islamic world and the Middle Ages, to nineteenth-century Great Britain and the United States. His intent is to demonstrate that what he calls market education has consistently been shown to be superior to all other approaches since the time of Aristotle. Coulson (1999b) sums up the findings of his study this way:

> [A] recurrent theme emerged from the hum of the centuries: Competitive educational markets have consistently done a better job of serving the public than state-run educational systems. The reason lies in the fact that state school systems lack four key factors that history tells us are essential to educational excellence: choice and financial responsibility for parents, and freedom and market incentives for educators. School systems that have enjoyed these characteristics have consistently done the best job of meeting both our private educational demands and our shared educational goals.

Perhaps. Some readers, however, see in this scholarly discourse merely evidence that the dynamic tension inherent in the controversy of marketplace versus democratic control of schooling has waxed and waned for millennia, that it has often been as contentious as it is today, and that its long run on the stage of history testifies to the fact that it has, despite Coulson's claim, never been resolved. His claim should be taken lightly because he is director of the Cato Institute's Center for Educational Freedom, a conservative think tank whose mission, in part, is "to increase the understanding of public policies based on principles of limited government, free markets, individual liberty, and peace." In a policy brief for the Cato Institute, Neal McCluskey and Andrew Coulson (2007) argue that NCLB has failed to improve public schools, a claim with which we would not disagree, and they advocate for the abolition of the U.S. Department of Education, NCLB, and all federal spending on education, designating all education policy to the states. Without evidence of the effectiveness of the free markets, McCluskey and Coulson recommend dismantling the "government schools" in favor of only a free-market education system based on charter schools, tuition tax credits, and the like. Their only rationale is that this is the only way to obtain a free-market system.

Advocates of marketplace concepts of schooling have been very influential in suggesting new alternatives to traditional ways of providing public schooling, such as the idea of school choice and vouchers, which merit thoughtful consideration. They have raised serious doubt about the viability of public schooling as it has been known in the United States for well over a century. It seems highly probable that their proposals will have a deep effect on the organization and administration of public schooling in the United States for years to come. One group that has listened attentively to the widespread discontent of U.S. citizens about the state of public schooling, as well as the proposals from the free-market advocates, is that small but growing group of investors who see public schooling as a rare opportunity for potentially high—possibly huge—profits on their business investments in education at all levels.

School Reform as Investment Opportunity

Perhaps you remember Michael Milken, the former junk bond king. Well, he is an education entrepreneur now. He heads a corporate conglomerate known as the Knowledge Universe that owns a number of companies that span preschool education to corporate training. In 1998, he met with Arthur Levine, president from 1994 to 2006 of Teachers College, Columbia University, to discuss issues of corporate involvement in public education reform. "The message was," President Levine later recalled, "you guys are in trouble and we're going to eat your lunch." This point of view was understood by Levine not as a direct challenge but as a predatory threat.

Many investors, not a few with very deep pockets, have heard the unhappiness over public schooling in the United States—especially the notion of searching for marketplace alternatives to the existing system—and have been attracted to it as a potential high-profit investment. Many investors plunged into the business beginning in the late 1990s, often riding the stock market boom of the time by raising hundreds of millions of dollars in venture capital to finance yet-to-be-developed enterprises (Wyatt, 1999). These efforts were commonly represented by well-known individuals from public life who would be easily recognized and trusted by investors. Former governor of Tennessee Lamar Alexander, once hailed as an "education governor" and a presidential hopeful, provided leadership for such an investment group. William F. Weld, a former governor of Massachusetts, who had faced stiff political resistance to his advocacy of for-profit schooling, sought to help Leeds Equity Partners III raise a huge venture capital fund investment in for-profit schooling beginning with $150 million in startup money. By 2003, William F. Bennett, well-known perennial critic of public education, was heading a business called K12, which relied heavily on the Internet to provide curriculum and instruction to partner schools in California, Colorado, Idaho, Ohio, and Pennsylvania, as well to individuals throughout the nation who desired support and guidance in providing homeschooling for their children. A number of relatively small companies have tested the waters in for-profit educational management with varying degrees of success.

By 2003, the largest and best known of the for-profit, education-management corporations was Edison Schools, Incorporated. It was founded as The Edison Project in 1992, after obtaining an initial contract to manage four schools with about 2,000 pupils. The corporation grew during the next decade, with a number of reverses and recoveries along the way. In the 2002–2003 school year, Edison claimed that it managed 150 public schools with some 84,000 pupils enrolled in 23 states and the District of Columbia. Based on these statistics, Edison liked to advertise that it was the third largest school system in the United States, which is a bit of a stretch, of course, because few would describe its schools as comprising a school system. Nevertheless, Edison Schools had clearly established itself as the pacesetter in the business of managing public schools for profit. Edison was a publicly traded equity corporation that has consistently lost money throughout its history, even as its number of clients has grown. Consequently, the price of its stock declined markedly as this process unfolded.

On December 21, 2001, a few hours after the classrooms of the Philadelphia public schools had been emptied for the annual holidays, Governor Mark Schweiker of Pennsylvania and the mayor of Philadelphia, John Street, announced a takeover by the state of the city's floundering school system. This decision was to have been a major coup for Edison Schools, which had arranged, as part of the deal, to take over the management of 45 of the city's failing schools and thus hoped to make a major breakthrough in the development of its business. Philadelphia was the seventh largest school district in the United States, and the takeover was the largest in history, involving some 210,000 students and 27,000 employees. However, when the secretly negotiated deal became public, a firestorm of controversy resulted. An advertising blitz costing over $400,000 may have boomeranged on Edison in a community that was deeply concerned about the future of its educational enterprise. In the end, Edison was awarded 20 schools to manage, while six other community agencies, including universities and charter school operators, were awarded the rest. The 45 schools, including Edison's 20, were the lowest achieving schools in the district. The school district also selected 21 schools that were also low achieving, but not quite as low as the 45, to be restructured but administered by the district, with intensive staff support and extra funding per pupil for the first year. In addition, 16 schools, called the Sweet 16, which were administered by the district, were given additional funding but no additional support. With the exception of eight schools administered by Temple University and the University of Pennsylvania, the remaining 45 schools received from $100 to $300 more per pupil in 2002–2003 than the 21 district schools under restructuring, and in 2005–2006, all 45 schools received from $450 to $780 more than the district schools. The Sweet 16 had $550 more per pupil in 2002–2003 and $450 in 2005–2006. This administrative structure allowed for a research study that could compare the charter school success in improving student achievement to the other district schools.

Two studies by the RAND Corporation and Research for Action were completed in 2007 and 2008. The 2007 study collected data on the first four years of the state takeover, through spring 2006. The researchers in this study found that, after four years, none of the privately managed schools or the district schools exceeded gains made by schools elsewhere in Pennsylvania, that no positive effects were found among the 45 schools by provider (for-profit, nonprofit, and universities), and no effects were found for the Sweet 16. The 21 restructured schools, however, had significantly positive effects in math for all years, and reading the first year, when compared to the rest of the schools in the district. The authors of the study concluded that there was no evidence to support spending additional taxpayer money on private management companies (Gill, Zimmer, Christman, & Blanc, 2007). The second study in 2008 tracked longitudinal data from 2000 through 2007, allowing the authors to track student movement from traditional public schools to charter schools, and vice versa. Using student-level data, not school-level, and controlling for student demographics, the researchers found the charter schools and traditional public schools in Philadelphia were indistinguishable, that charter schools in operation for four years were no different in student achievement than those in operation three years or less, and that there was no competitive effect of charters on nearby traditional public schools (Zimmer, Blanc, Gill, & Christman, 2008).

Philadelphia turned out to be a test case for Edison Schools, and it seemed to be a failure. Edison's director was Benno C. Schmidt, Jr., former president of Yale University. The most interesting person to join Edison was John Chubb (yes, the same Chubb discussed earlier in this chapter), who was one of the original seven members of the organization and who later became its Senior Executive Vice President for Development. Its chief executive officer was Christopher C. Whittle, who created and formerly headed Whittle Communications, the firm that offered the highly controversial Channel One to the nation's junior and senior high schools. Edison's chief operating officer was Christopher Cerf, a noted Washington litigator who practiced before the Supreme Court and was associate counsel to former president Bill Clinton. With the failure in Philadelphia, there has been a shakeup at Edison Schools. The name has changed to EdisonLearning and Christopher Whittle, Benno Schmidt, and Christopher Cerf are no longer listed anywhere on their website (edisonlearning.com/), and the CEO was Jeff Wahl. In 2008, Chris Whittle engineered Edison Schools to be bought out by Terry Stecz, who took the company private. Although EdisonLearning still manages charter schools, it has changed the focus from managing charter schools to providing various learning services to districts, such as online courses, evaluation systems, intervention programs in math and reading among other Supplemental Educational Services.

One of the more lucrative markets for entrepreneurs has been in the area of Supplemental Educational Services (SES, not to be confused with Socio Economic Status in this section). Under NCLB, SES services are to be provided to low-income families whose children attend Title I schools designated as "in need of improvement" for more than a year or those not meeting the Adequate Yearly Progress (AYP) for disadvantaged students. These services, provided outside regular school hours, include tutoring and other remedial assistance in reading, language arts, and math. SES providers can be nonprofit entities, for-profits businesses, private schools, or the local public schools themselves. Research is not clear on the effectiveness of SES, with some studies showing positive results (Harding, Harrison-Jones, & Rebach, 2012; Zimmer, Gill, Razquin, Booker, & Lockwood) and some indicating no gains to minimal gains (Allen, 2008; Burch, 2007; Burch, Steinberg, & Donovan, 2007; Heinrich, Meyer, & Whitten, 2010; Heistad, 2006; Rickles & Barnhart, 2007). Some studies have shown the neediest students may not be taking advantage of SES (Heinrich, Meyer, & Whitten, 2010).

In 2011, the U.S. Department of Education established "ESEA Flexibility," to permit State Education Agencies (and hence local school districts) to waive the SES requirements among other specific requirements of NCLB. As of 2013, 34 states had been approved for ESEA flexibility. For up-to-date information on SES requirement and changes to implementation policies of the ESEA, see the following website of the U.S. Department of Education: 2.ed.gov/nclb/choice/help/ses/index.html

Before we leave this section on market-based reforms, we want to mention online PK-12 education, which is becoming one of the entrepreneurial magnets as it has massive potential for expansion. Most states now offer free online options for K-12 students; many states developed their own courses and virtual schools, and they will pay for online charter school education or online education courses and "virtual schools" from for-profit companies. A major scandal broke in Maine in 2012 related to two companies, who along with the director of Jeb Bush's Foundation for Excellence in Education, suggested legislation, state education policies, and gubernatorial decrees for the commissioner of education in Maine. An article in the *Portland Press Herald* from May 20, 2013, included the following about the companies involved:

> K12 Inc. of Herndon, Va., and Connections Education, the Baltimore-based subsidiary of education publishing giant Pearson, are both seeking to expand online offerings and to open full-time virtual charter schools in Maine, with taxpayers paying the tuition for the students who use the services.
>
> . . . More often they have worked through intermediaries. K12 Inc. donated $19,000 to a political action committee that supported LePage's candidacy [Maine's Governor] in 2010. K12 and Connections Education provided support to Jeb Bush's foundation and to a controversial corporate-funded organization for state legislators, the American Legislative Exchange Council, or ALEC. Both K12 and Connections Education built relationships with Maine lawmakers and officials who introduced laws and policies beneficial to the companies' bottom lines. (Woodard, 2013)

Louisiana also experienced a similar scandal in 2013, in which students were unknowingly enrolled in courses from a private for-profit company from Texas. At the time of this writing, the commissioner of education from Louisiana expressed regret about the incident and started an investigation to determine how this mistake occurred and how to prevent it in the future. Similar stories will undoubtedly unfold as online education continues to expand.

Current Status of Charter Schools

Although charter schools at the end of 2013 represented approximately 5% of all public schools (about 3% of all students) in the U.S., this number has increased from about 2% (less than 1% of all students) in 2000–2001. The charter school movement is growing in the United States, and it continues to be touted as a viable alternative by some politicians, including President Obama's administration, and by the private entrepreneurs. According to Miron and Gulosino (2013), in 2011–2012 there were 97 for-profit EMOs (educational management organizations) representing 36% of all charter schools in the United States serving 44% of all students enrolled in charter schools, and 201 nonprofit EMOs at the end of 2010–2011. (Table 12.3 identifies the largest for-profit EMOs that had 10 or more schools each in 2012–2013. To the best of our knowledge, the EMOs listed are all for-profit organizations.

Miron and Gulosino (2013) listed 31 nonprofit EMOs with 10 or more schools, The largest nonprofits in 2011–2012 were the KIPP (Knowledge Is Power Programs) Foundation (approximately 98 schools and 35,000 students); Cosmos Foundation (approximately 47 schools and 23,500 students); Responsive Education Solutions (approximately 36 schools and 11,000 students); Aspire Public Schools (approximately 30 schools and 11,000 students; and Concept Schools (approximately 26 schools and 8,000 students).

With the advent of SES money made available through NCLB, and SES services required by NCLB, many of the charter school EMOs have moved into the business of providing tutoring services through a variety of delivery modalities. One extreme example is the Richard Milburn Academies that once administered 13 charter schools, but now has no schools, moving to tutoring services and distance education courses for school districts.

Two of the major national associations for charter schools are the National Alliance for Public Charter Schools and the NACSA, the latter of which claims membership of charter schools that represent over half of the approximately 5,714 charter schools in the country. NACSA provides resources and services to charter schools, and, in their guide of principles and standards for authorizers, they focus on three areas to promote quality charter schools: maintain high standards for schools, uphold school autonomy, and protect student and public interests (National Association of Charter School Authorizers, 2012). NACSA describes six different types of charter school authorizers permitted by legislation in the 42 states and Washington, DC, that allow charter schools. All but six allow Local Education Agencies (LEAs) to authorize charters, and LEAs authorize the most charters—approximately 53% of all charters in the country. Other authorizes include the following: State Education Agencies (SEAs; 20% of all charters), independent chartering boards established by SEAs (14%), higher education institutions (8%), not-for-profit organizations (4%), and noneducational government entities such as municipalities (1%). Overseeing 26% of all charter schools are five authorizers: Texas Education Agency, Arizona State Board for Charter Schools, Los Angeles Unified School District, Chicago Public Schools, and North Carolina Department of Education (National Association of Charter School Authorizers, 2010). NACSA represents a promising trend in a move toward organizing charter schools and providing information to organizers about developing and maintaining quality charter schools. NACSA even has a guide on how to close failing charter schools. While NACSA represents a positive step nationally for charter school quality, it also indicates the permanency of charters in U.S. education.

So, let's understand how we got to this point and where we are now. Under the George W. Bush administration, the U.S. Department of Education (commonly referred to as ED for Education Department) heavily promoted market-based reforms. In fact, ED supported market-based reforms through efforts to promote state legislation expanding parental school choice opportunities and through funding efforts. For example, between 2000 and 2008, ED provided approximately $1.8 billion in startup money for charter schools and over $320 million to fund facilities acquisition. ED recommends that states provide 100% funding to charters equivalent to what public schools receive, including comparable facilities (U.S. Department of Education, 2008). In its 2008 report on charter schools, ED cites only positive research findings

TABLE 12.3 Largest For-Profit Educational Management Organizations (EMOs) at the End of Academic Year 2013

Name of EMO	Approximate Number of Schools	Approximate Number of Students	Website and Notes
Academica	100*	30,000	academica.org/
Accelerated Learning Solutions	10	1,300	als-education.com/index.php (FL only)
Charter School Associates	15	3,000	edline.net/pages/CSA (FL only)
Charter Schools USA	58	50,000	charterschoolsusa.com (mostly FL; also GA, IL, IN, LA, MI, NC)
Chicago International Charter Schools	15	5,500	chicagointl.org/
Connections Academy, Inc.**	26	30,000	connectionsacademy.com/home.aspx (online schools and services only)
Constellation Schools	22	4,500	constellationschools.com/default.aspx (only in OH)
CS Partners	19	6,000	charterschoolpartners.com/about/
Edison Learning	11 schools, and 391 partnerships	450,000 served in 25 states	edisonlearning.com/
Educational Services of America	250 partnerships	13,000	esa-education.com/AboutUs.aspx
Global Educational Excellence	11	4,000	gee-edu.com (MI, OH)
Imagine Schools	71	44,000	imagineschools.com/ Operate in 12 states and DC
K-12	57	87,000	K-12.com (online only)
Leona Group	68	19,000	leonagroup.com/index.htm (AZ, FL, MI, OH, IN)
Mater Academy, Inc.	17	12,200	materacademy.com/index.jsp (all in Miami, Florida)
Mosaica Education	90 (12 in U.S.)	16,000	mosaicaeducation.com/
National Heritage Academies	75	48,000	heritageacademies.com (nine states, most in MI and OH)
Nobel Learning Communities	180	N/A[†]	nobellearning.com/
Somerset Academy	38	8,500	somersetacademyschools.com (most in FL)
Victory Schools	15	7,500	victoryschools.com (8 schools in NY; others in PA and NJ)
White Hat Management	45	14,000	whitehatmgmt.com (mainly in OH and CO)

[†]N/A = not available.

*Academica lists over 100 schools, but many of those are listed in collaboration with Mater Schools and Somerset Academy. Most are in Florida and Utah.

**Connections Academy is owned by Pearson Inc. There were tentative agreements in seven additional states to open schools.

about the success of charters, although some of its own research refutes positive findings (see the Braun, Jenkins, and Grigg study below). In 2010, with his RTTT funding initiative, President Barack Obama's administration continued to promote charter schools. Arne Duncan, Obama's choice for Secretary of Education, continued to be a strong proponent of charter schools as he had been when he was superintendent of the Chicago school system. Indeed, a quick glance at the ed.gov website on school choice shows it promotes school choice options for parents and provides guidance to school districts on how to create "strong district public school choice programs" (see 2.ed.gov/admins/comm/choice/edpicks.jhtml?src=ln). Ed.gov also provides funding for charter school programs and in fiscal year 2011 awarded large grants to New York ($28.2 million) and Florida ($21.4 million). Strong support for charter schools and other market-based reforms also comes from state politicians, and support appears on state education department websites. For example, the Florida Department of Education website includes the following statement: "Charter schools are largely free to innovate, and often provide more effective programs and choice to diverse groups of students" (Florida Department of Education, 2013). Why are the Washington and state policy makers promoting charter schools? Is there evidence that charter schools are more educationally effective than other forms of schooling?

Some studies support charter school effectiveness in increasing student achievement (Gronberg & Jansen, 2001; Hanushek, Kain, & Rivkin, 2002; Sass, 2006), but these studies have not been conclusive because similar methodological studies found contrasting results, showing that charter schools produce lower achievement than traditional public schools (Bifulco & Ladd, 2006a; Eberts & Hollenbeck, 2001). One of the studies that received a lot of national attention and that supported a positive impact of charter schools on student achievement was written in 2004 by Caroline Hoxby, a professor at Harvard University (Hoxby, 2004). The data included a national sample of charter schools from 37 states. The Hoxby study, however, was reanalyzed by Joydeep Roy and Lawrence Michel, who noted that Hoxby's analysis

> suffers from the fact that *her method of comparing charter schools to their neighboring regular public schools (and to those neighboring public schools with a similar racial composition) inadequately controls for student backgrounds.* In her sample of matched schools there are often significant differences in the demographic and socioeconomic characteristics of the students. (Roy & Michel, 2005, p. 2).

In their analysis of Hoxby's data, Roy and Michel found that her conclusions were not correct. When controlling for ethnicity and socioeconomic status, the advantages of charter schools disappeared.

In another large-scale, national study, researchers sampled 150 charter schools and 6,764 noncharter public schools and found that charter schools performed significantly lower in both math and reading on the 2003 National Assessment of Educational Progress (NAEP) (Braun, Jenkins, & Grigg, 2006). This study was published on the National Center for Education Statistics website, which is an arm of the U.S. Department of Education. When adjusting student test scores for student characteristics, they found that charter schools scored .11 standard deviations lower in reading and .17 standard deviations lower in math. The authors caution that these results do not take into account potential differences in prior student achievement or parental and student motivation to move to a charter. Similar findings were confirmed in 2006 by Ron Zimmer and Richard Buddin in a study of urban charter school performance in Los Angeles and San Diego. They found that charter schools performed no better than public schools and in some cases were outperformed by public schools. In addition, this study found that charter schools did not have a positive achievement effect for Black, Hispanic, or limited English proficiency students (Zimmer & Buddin, 2006).

Supporting the above findings was a well-designed study using 2003 NAEP math scores from fourth- and eighth-grade students that went beyond comparisons of public schools with charter schools, and also compared Catholic, Lutheran, and Christian private schools. When looking only at raw achievement scores, public schools appear to underperform when compared to other types of schools. After controlling for student demographics and location, however, public schools significantly outperformed or were equal to all other school types. Public schools outperformed all other school types at the fourth-grade level, and outperformed Catholic schools and Christian schools at the eighth-grade level; Christian schools scored significantly lower than all other school types in both grades (Lubienski & Lubienski, 2006). Later, these same authors used a longitudinal dataset of mathematics achievement that followed children from kindergarten in 1998 through fifth grade in 2004. While public school students' initial mathematics achievement was slightly lower in kindergarten, they significantly surpassed Catholic schools and were equal to all other private schools by the fifth grade (Lubienski, Crane, & Lubienski, 2008). Both of these studies help dispel the belief that private schools outperform public schools and that parents will choose the best-performing schools for their children.

A major longitudinal study of charter schools was released in 2013 by the Center for Research on Education Outcomes (CREDO) at Stanford University, following schools from opening through their fifth year. This study included 1,372 schools from 25 charter management organizations (CMOs), which are public entities, and 410 schools from 38 EMOs. They defined EMOs as an "organization that provides school operations to independent charter schools and CMOs under contract" (Peltason, 2013, p. 3). The major findings have some good news for charters in general and EMOs in particular:

> CMOs on average are not dramatically better than non-CMO schools in terms of their contributions to student learning. The difference in learning compared to the traditional public school alternatives for CMOs is -.005 standard deviations in Math and .005 in reading; both these values are statistically significant, but obviously not materially different from the comparison.
>
> . . . CMOs post superior results with historically disadvantaged student subgroups. They produce stronger academic gains for students of color and students in poverty than those students would have realized either in traditional public schools (TPS) or in many categories what would have learned in independent charter schools.
>
> . . . The average student in an Educational Management Organizations (EMOs) posted significantly more positive learning gains than either CMOs, independent charter schools or the traditional public schools comparisons. Their results were also relatively more positive for black and Hispanic students and English Language Learners (ELLs).
>
> . . . Poor first year performance simply cannot be overlooked or excused. For the majority of schools, poor first year performance will give way to poor second year performance. Once this has happened, the future is predictable and extremely bleak. For the students enrolled in these schools, this is a tragedy that must not be dismissed. (Peltason, 2013, pp. 5–8)

The last finding is important for authorizers of charter schools to recognize and use to carefully monitor initial success. In terms of achievement comparisons to traditional public schools, results for charters showed better scores for math than reading achievement. Traditional public schools did outperform multistate CMOs and both reading and math, but non-multistate CMOs outperformed traditional public schools. In addition, although the results show significant positive performance for charters in most comparisons, the winners were only marginally better, with small effect sizes. The U.S. Department of Education uses an effect size of .25 in the *What Works Clearinghouse* (discussed later in this chapter), to identify education practices meeting "rigorous scientific evidence." The CREDO data does not meet this standard. Although these results are promising for charter schools, there has been no independent analysis of the CREDO study, so we advise some caution in accepting these findings as conclusive of charter school success. We have no doubt, however, proponents of charter schools will use this study to support their cause. In a similarly designed study released in 2009 (Center for Research on Education Outcomes, 2009), CREDO found that charter schools performed worse than traditional public schools in both math and reading. They also found those of lower socio-economic status, Blacks, Hispanics, and ELLs performed significantly worse than those in traditional public schools, but again the effect sizes were relatively small. CREDO findings in both of their studies support the notion that charter schools improve over time, unless the schools start out as very low performers.

Is there a difference in the effectiveness of for-profit charter schools and nonprofit charter schools? In a well-designed study on charter schools in Michigan, authors Hill and Welsch (2006) found, after controlling for a variety of school and district characteristics, for-profit charter school students scored significantly lower on academic achievement tests than did students in nonprofit schools. One might suspect that this is due to for-profit charters spending less per pupil than nonprofits, but this is not the case. When controlling for spending, there was no difference in the results, indicating that policies other than spending in for-profit charter school policies are responsible for their poor performance (Hill & Welsch, 2006).

What about the contention by charter school advocates that charter schools will fuel competition and motivate noncharter public schools to perform better? When defining competition as the percentage of students (6% or more) in charter schools in a district, Hoxby (2002) found that in Michigan there is a large competitive effect. Certainly, the percentage of schools in a district may be an indicator of competition resulting from parental dissatisfaction with traditional public schools, but it may also be a result of state policy and charter school marketing campaigns. The key question about the effectiveness of charter school competition is whether traditional public schools feel the pressure and respond to the pressure by increasing their test scores. As noted earlier in this chapter, this was one of the major reasons why states justified approving charter schools. In one study, a competitive effect was found based on the distance that charters were located from noncharters (Holmes, DeSimone, & Rupp, 2003). In contrast, Richard Buddin and Ron Zimmer (2006) found no competitive effects in a study of California charter schools compared to public schools.

In another study of competitive effects of charters, Scott Imberman (2009) measured student achievement gains by comparing charter schools in Los Angeles that were within 1.5 miles of a traditional public school. He found that charter schools actually have a deleterious impact. Math and language scores fell in traditional public schools, while reading scores were unaffected. Imberman projects several possible explanations:

- The district loses funding for each student who leaves for a charter.
- The charters draw higher socioeconomic students away from the traditional public schools.
- The charters attract high-quality teachers from the traditional public schools.

One of the disturbing findings about enrollment in charter schools is that there is a high level of segregation in most states (Frankenberg & Lee, 2003). In 2003, the number of black students enrolled in intensely segregated minority charters (90% or more minority) was almost twice as much as in traditional public schools. Frankenberg and Lee concluded the following:

> There is little evidence from this analysis that the existence of charter schools helps to foster more integrative environments, especially for minority students. At a time when the public schools are more segregated for minority students than thirty years ago, any reform that is publicly funded and intensifying the increasing public school segregation deserves very careful evaluation. (p. 36)

Several recommendations to increase diversity in charter schools were suggested:

- Locating charters at the boundaries of segregated neighborhoods
- Providing transportation
- Providing full information to families about the charter schools (including racial segregation data)
- Accepting students on a first come-first serve basis with no screening
- Providing a welcoming environment for diverse populations

In many states, implementing these suggestions would mean redesigning charter school legislation and policy to conform to these recommendations.

These findings have been confirmed by several studies (Bifulco & Ladd, 2006b; Institute on Race and Poverty, 2008; Ni, 2007; Renzulli, 2006). For example, in Minnesota, the first state to pass charter school legislation (1991), the number of nonwhite students in charter schools in 1995 was three times higher than traditional public schools, and this statistic remained about the same through 2008. This fact is disconcerting because the proponents of charter schools have argued that charter schools would improve racial segregation by promoting additional choices for parents.

Yet, there are some promising data identified in a study by Lee and Lubienski (2011) in which they examined trends in racial composition over time as the number of charter schools have increased. They compared data available from the National Center of Educational Statistics from 34 states and Washington, DC, during 2001–2002 as well as 2007–2008. They use an exposure index, which measures the degree to which majority students are exposed to minority students in schools. Findings include the following:

1. In 23 of 35 states, charter schools are less integrated than public schools.
2. There has been a modest increase over time of integration in both public and charter schools when analyzing all data.
3. However, 17 of the 35 states showed worse integration over time (AK, AR, CO, DC, ID, IN, KA, MN, MO, NV, NM, OK, OR, RI, SC, VA, WY).

Lee and Lubienski explain that in some states, statute and policy make it easier for authorizers to approve charters in urban areas, which typically have higher minority populations. Furthermore, parents are more likely to look for schools having populations of similar racial/ethnic background.

Vouchers

Vouchers are another controversial, market-based reform that has been the focus of researchers. Research studies that have been sponsored and published by conservative think tanks such as the Manhattan Institute, the Heritage Institute, or the Hoover Institute have consistently resulted in positive effects for school choice programs. One such study, by Jay Greene and Marcus Winters (2008), concludes that the Florida McKay scholarship program, which provides vouchers to any student with a disability to attend the school of her or his choice, results in competition that helps improve the public school achievement of students with disabilities. Because the quality of think tank publications varies so widely, The Think Tank Review Project, established by the Education and the Public Interest Center (EPIC) at the University of Colorado at Boulder and the Education Policy Research Unit (EPRU) at Arizona State University, reviews the quality of these publications that may have potential for influencing education policy. In reviewing the Greene and Winters' study, Jon Yun (2008) found several weaknesses in the study's design, most important of which was the conclusions were based on the unsubstantiated assumption that the selection bias that occurred due to nonrandomization underestimated the competitive effect. Yun argued that this presumption was incorrect and that other potential sources of selection bias actually lead to underestimating the effect of the voucher program. Yun concludes: "Any attempt to use this report for decision-making or policy evaluation, prior to validation using different methods and more robust approaches, should be viewed with extreme skepticism" (p. 7).

In reviewing eleven studies completed between 1999 and 2008 on the effect of vouchers on students and on public schools, Cecilia Rouse and Lisa Barrow (2008) conclude the following:

> [T]he best research to date finds relatively small achievement gains for students offered education vouchers, most of which are not statistically different from zero. Further, what little evidence exists about the likely impact of a large-scale voucher program on the students who remain in the public schools is at best mixed, and the research designs of these studies do not necessarily allow the researchers to attribute any observed positive gains solely to school vouchers and competitive forces. The evidence to date from other forms of school choice is not much more promising. As such, while there may be other reasons to implement school voucher programs, one should not anticipate large academic gains from this seemingly inexpensive reform. (p. 17)

In their analysis of the research, Rouse and Barrow (2008) noted that a few studies showing African American students benefitting from voucher program were not designed well enough to preclude alternative analyses. Although the studies showing benefits of vouchers to African American students have received wide publicity, those studies have not found benefits to these students. One such example is a study by Clive Belfield (2006), who found that the Cleveland voucher program did not benefit African American students. The Cleveland Scholarship and Tutoring Program received a great deal of national attention when the U.S. Supreme Court in its 2002 decision in *Zelman v. Simmons-Harris* (2002) reversed a federal district court ruling that granted summary judgment to the plaintiffs, who sought to enjoin the voucher program on grounds that it violated the establishment clause. The net effect of this Supreme Court ruling was to permit public funds to be funneled to private schools, including religious schools.

In a review of a report about the Milwaukee Parental Choice Program (MPCP), Cobb (2012) found methodological and data analysis problems with the findings of the School Choice Demonstration Project (Cowen, Fleming, Witte, Wolf, & Kisida, 2012), which received a great deal of national attention by politicians. Cowen et al. reported students who used a voucher to attend private school in eighth or ninth grades, when compared to a sample of Milwaukee Public School (MPS) students: a) were more likely to graduate high school; b) were less likely to enroll in a two-year or technical post-secondary institution; c) were more likely to enroll in a four-year post-secondary institution; and d) dropped out of high school for similar reasons, most notably a poor academic experience. They admit there are no findings in their study, or in previous School Choice Demonstration Project reports, supporting differences in academic achievement for voucher students compared to traditional education students, and "they *do not* support a comprehensive conclusion that the MPCP necessarily provides a better learning environment than MPS" (Cowen et al., 2012, p. 17). Cobb's review of the Cowen et al. study criticized the findings on its methodological approach of keeping 56% of the voucher students in the sample even though they were no longer in a choice program by twelfth grade. Cowen et al. based their findings on "exposure" to the voucher program, rather the long-term persistence in the program. Cobb concludes, "The problem is that we do not know exactly where they graduated high school or for how long they were enrolled in a voucher program school. This one caveat alone calls into question the usefulness of nearly the entire study" (p. 5).

Finally, in another study that has received a lot of attention, Chingos and Peterson (2012) studied the use of school vouchers on college enrollment in New York City. They did not find any impact on college enrollment overall, but they did report a significant impact for African American students whose enrollment rate increased 24%. This study traced the use of vouchers on students from elementary school through college. In reviewing this study for the National Education Policy Center, however, Goldrick-Rab (2012) found methodological errors: "Contrary to how it was presented, the main finding of this new report *should* be that, using a rigorous experimental design in which vouchers were randomly assigned to students, the estimated college enrollment rates of students with and without vouchers *were not different* from one another" (p. 6).

Successes of Market-Based Reforms

Market-based reform legislation has grown rapidly in the U.S. over the last 20 years, and one of the organizations that helps write and encourage this market-based education legislation is ALEC, the American Legislative Exchange Council. ALEC recommends specific legislation to its members who then sponsor that legislation in their states. ALEC also sponsors research to support its views, which can be considered conservative. It is a highly political, republican organization, although it has a few democratic members as well. Private corporations can also join, and among some its corporate sponsors are Reynolds American, ExxonMobil, National Rifle Association, and Corrections Corporation of America. ALEC holds conferences during which representatives from these companies write draft legislation with legislators in attendance who receive "scholarships" to attend (Dannin, 2012).

ALEC defines its formula for success as follows:

For more than 35 years, ALEC has been the ideal means of creating and delivering public policy ideas aimed at protecting and expanding our free society. Thanks to ALEC's membership, the duly elected leaders of their state legislatures, Jeffersonian principles advise and inform legislative action across the country. Literally hundreds of dedicated ALEC members have worked together to create, develop, introduce and guide to enactment many of the cutting-edge, conservative policies that have now become the law in the states. The strategic knowledge and training ALEC members have received over the years has been integral to these victories. Since its founding, ALEC has amassed an unmatched record of achieving ground-breaking changes in public policy. Policies such as teacher competency testing, pension reform, and Enterprise Zones represent just a handful of ALEC's victories in the states. (American Legislative Exchange Council, 2013, "About-ALEC")

ALEC drafts legislation on many issues related to its conservative mission, many of which are about PK-12 education. In fact, ALEC has a special task force on education, which focuses on teacher tenure, privatization of education, and collective bargaining. We have seen the results of ALEC legislation in these areas, most notably in Arizona, Georgia, Louisiana, Ohio, Tennessee, Oklahoma, and Wisconsin (Underwood & Mead, 2012). In an analysis of model bills, Dannin (2012) states:

> The ALEC bills examined here demonstrate strong opposition to public-sector work and workers and take the view government illegitimately usurps private enterprise. In other words, ALEC contends that the natural and best operation of the education and financial ordering is through private companies in a system in which unions do not exist. ALEC acts on that view through many strategies to move public work to the private sector and to bar union representation and negotiation. (p. 530)

In a 2013 ALEC *Report Card on American Education: Ranking State K-12 Performance, Progress, and Reform* (Ladner & Myslinski, 2013), the authors graded every state on how its market-based initiatives are enacted into state policies including the following: academic standards, charter school laws, private school choice, teacher quality policies, and online learning options. Highest grades went to Arizona (B+), Washington, DC, (B−), Florida (B), Georgia (B−), Idaho (B−), Indiana (B+), Louisiana (B), Michigan (B), Ohio (B), Oklahoma (B+), Pennsylvania (B−), Utah (B−), and Wisconsin (B−). Interestingly, although they reported the National Assessment of Education Progress (NAEP) state results, they did not use these results in their grading systems, and hence, there was no correlation between NAEP scores and the assigned state grades.

An independent review of this ALEC report

> indicates that it is based more on an explicit ideological agenda than on compelling evidence on the effectiveness of these policies. The report draws selectively from research literature to make claims about these policies, which are not supported by a reading of the wider literature. Moreover, much of the research they highlight is quite inferior and unsuitable for supporting the claims made. In fact, some of the evidence in the report actually contradicts the authors' assertions that their preferred policies are more effective. (Lubienski & Brewer, 2013, p. 1)

Our conclusions, based on reading the research literature on market-based reforms, are simple. Market-based reforms have not been shown to be more effective than traditional public schools in improving student achievement either in schools that receive vouchers or in charter schools, nor have market-based reforms increased traditional public school achievement by challenging the public schools in a competitive market. The assumption from market-based proponents that the private sector is inherently better than traditional public schools is flawed. This fact gives reason to question the claims that public schools are failing, and reason to question the current efforts of school reform that focus on privatization through charter schools and choice through vouchers. If, however, the rationale for market-based reforms were simply to give parents more choices in where to send their children to school, then alternative forms of schooling such as the use of vouchers and charter schools may be justified. Indeed, Belfield and Levin (2009) agreed that one of the major benefits of market reforms is increased choice, yet they did not find revolutionary improvements in education the advocates of choice have predicted, and they even suggested if choice were applied universally, it could lead to inequalities of opportunity unless specific opportunities were made available to students of lower SES.

An early supporter of market-based reforms, Frederick Hess (2009) blamed the lack of success (and future success) of market-based reforms on a number of factors: choice programs are not well funded; there are restrictions on the financial support for facilities construction; and states have specific policies on admission, staffing, and curriculum that hinder success. He further chastised both the proponents and opponents of market-based reforms for not allowing "creative destruction" of the education system which is the hallmark of market-driven strategies—allowing for "ongoing opening, closing, and franchising that open competition implies" (p. 510). Hess was pessimistic that current efforts of market-based reforms would succeed, and he concluded that

> given the hesitance of both the public and reformers toward market-based school reform, political efforts to promote specific deregulatory measures—such as relaxing the licensure of teachers and administrators, allowing money to follow students more readily from school to school, or instituting more flexible compensation— might ultimately prove to have a more dramatic effect on educational provision than proposals for choice-based reforms. (p. 510)

Perhaps Hess is right. Yet, the number of charter schools has been increasing in the last decade as evidenced earlier in this chapter. Notwithstanding Hess's disappointment about the speed of reforms, to many it seems that "creative destruction" is occurring with many charters opening and closing—some closed by the authorizing agencies and other closing on their own due to financial constraints, low enrollment, and other reasons. Scandals have also taken their toll on some charters such as financial mismanagement and sudden closings by owners with little warning to families and staff. There is even a website devoted solely to charter school scandals (see charterschoolscandals.blogspot.com/).

All of these corporate incursions into schooling for profit are of recent vintage, few if any predating 1990, so their track record is thin at best. Naturally, those who are invested in them and who work in them are busily trying to put the best foot forward and are making claims that are often more hopes than evidence of success. Nevertheless, it is clear that there is at least a market niche for their products, and they are working hard to reach their ambitious goals. Entrepreneurs work in ways that are very different from those of the bureaucrats in the world of public schools. One great difference lies in the fact that entrepreneurs bring startup money to the project, sometimes substantial amounts of it. Thus, they are able to undertake a project with strong resources and a long-term perspective because they can depend on substantial financing from their investment capital, which allows them to ride out the inevitable surprises and difficulties that arise in a startup project. Unlike the restrictive mind-set of public school bureaucracies, in which new programs must demonstrate their effectiveness almost at once, entrepreneurs are willing to spend money in order to make money and are determined to have the time that is necessary to develop the project and make it work. While at this point there is little evidence that the students attending for-profit schooling achieve at higher levels than those attending government schools, it appears certain that their growing financial backing will make them increasingly serious competitors as time goes on. But their strength comes from more than money: They have ideas that seriously challenge the traditional orthodoxy of both the pedagogical and the organizational ideas of public schooling.

Privatization and Virtual Education in Higher Education

Higher education has also attracted serious attention from investors. Leeds Equity Partners III, mentioned earlier, is focusing on providing professional training and certification in fields such as business, law, psychology, and medicine. The organization believes that training in these fields can be offered profitably if it can harness the Internet as a vehicle for instruction. Many students, it reasons, would be attracted to programs that permit them to pursue studies without taking much time off from work to commute to even local campuses. Productivity Point International, one of Michael Milken's groups, offers an extensive array of online courses geared to the needs of businesspeople for software technical training. The University of Phoenix, the largest private university (publically traded) in the nation, has established nearly 200 campuses in 43 states and offers an extensive list of degree-granting programs that range from undergraduate through doctoral degrees in specialties that have great appeal to working professionals. With heavy reliance on online instruction and other distance-learning techniques, plus campuses placed to be handy to a large population of prospective students, the University of Phoenix does not try to emulate traditional universities but instead offers programs that are a clear alternative for busy working people.

Many established public universities have already felt this competition and have plunged into the development of distance learning, making it more convenient for students to attend campuses in their own communities, with less need for commuting. For example, the Florida legislature in 2013, debated opening a new virtual university, but instead funded the University of Florida to expand its online offerings. Other states, such as California, Kentucky, and Michigan, have virtual websites serving as clearinghouses for its state institutions' online programs. Canada also has an extensive virtual university offering online classes from all accredited Canadian universities. Other major virtual institutions include the British Open University, Open University of Australia, and in the United States National Universities Degree Consortium. The latter is a venture offering degree programs though eight state universities around the country. No doubt, as private school education continues to intrude on state university market share, more public universities will band together to compete, while providing quality at a lower price.

An annual survey of online education in the United States is conducted by the Sloan Consortium. The report released in 2013 (Allen & Seaman, 2013) was based on the responses of 2,800 chief academic officers, also called Provost or Vice-President for Academic Affairs. The number of post-secondary students enrolled in 2002 in at least one online course was 1,602,970 (9.6% of total enrollment), which increased to 6,714,792 (32% of total enrollment). The percentage of students taking courses increased every year since 2002, and the number of all post-secondary institutions offering online courses also increased from 71.7% in 2002 to 86.5% in 2012.

Can we assume that online courses are more efficient than traditional face-to-face courses? In terms of the effort it takes faculty to teach courses, this is not the case. Allen and Seaman (2013) report that 46% of the respondents believe faculty effort is greater for online courses, while only 9.7% disagree. And what about the quality of the coursework? Is it better or inferior to traditional instruction? Although still high, there was a drop in the percentage of respondents who indicated online courses were inferior or somewhat inferior between 2011 and 2012 (32.4% to 23%). The respondents also indicated that online courses had lower retention rates than traditional classes.

These findings are certainly troubling, and it behooves institutions, both K-12 and higher education, to insure the infrastructure to provide online education is of high quality, that instructors are highly trained in the technology and pedagogy, and that instructors receive adequate time to provide high-quality instruction and feedback to the online students.

By now you have probably heard of a MOOC. A MOOC, or a Massive Open Online Course, can enroll thousands of students at the same time. In 2013, there were three main MOOC developers: Coursera, edX, and Udacity (Kolowich, 2013). Allen and Seaman (2013) found 2.6% of higher education institutions in 2013 had at least one MOOC, with another 9.4% in the planning stage, and that most MOOCs are currently offered by large public, doctoral degree granting institutions. They found the majority of academic leaders did not believe MOOCs were sustainable, though no reasons were provided. Some of the problems reported by Meisenhelder (2013) are that only 10% of all students successfully complete a MOOC, and students do not interact with faculty or receive feedback except from one another. In 2013, these courses were all free, but plans were underway to find ways to charge tuition. According to Kolowich (2013), Udacity was working with Georgia Institute of Technology to offer a master's degree in computer science for only $7,000, but the Georgia Institute of Technology website noted this degree was a pilot program funded by AT&T. There is no doubt that MOOCs will continue to impact university programs in the near future.

STANDARDS-BASED SCHOOL REFORM

Chapter 1 described and discussed standards-based school reform, which has been growing steadily and gathering strength since the first educational summit meeting was convened by President George Herbert Walker Bush in 1989. Educational leaders should recognize that this is very different from market-driven strategies: It operates from different assumptions and different theories of action. At the core, standards-based school reform is a political strategy; it accepts and seeks to work within the direct democratic political system under which public schooling has been controlled in the United States for some two centuries. At the operational level, it is an organizational strategy; more exactly, it seeks to greatly strengthen the hierarchical command-and-control power of the states over public schooling. Let us explain.

After being ratified by New Hampshire in 1788, the Constitution went into effect. Within a year, elections were held, and on April 30, 1789, George Washington was inaugurated as president, John Adams was inaugurated as vice president, the elected members of the two houses of Congress took office, and the federal government was organized and started operating from its headquarters on Wall Street in New York City. It was a busy year in New York: Courts had to be organized, judges appointed, emissaries commissioned to foreign nations, a financial crisis arising from the debts incurred by the states during the American Revolution had to be straightened out, and national defense had to be provided for—but no one in New York had to think about education. It was not in the federal Constitution.

At the same time that so much was going on in New York, however, each of the 13 states was engaged in writing and adopting its own constitution. The framers of the constitutions in each of the states quickly noted that nothing had been said about education in the federal Constitution. Therefore, each state included in its constitution a commitment to provide for schooling.

In time, after the adoption of a state constitution, the legislature of each state—as representatives of the body politic—wrote and adopted statutes that spelled out how the mandate for public schooling in the state constitution would be carried out. There were differences in the constitutional language from state to state and differences in the statutory arrangements, too. But from the beginning, there was also a remarkable consistency among the states about how public schooling would be organized and governed under state authority. From this process of representative democracy, a pattern and structure developed—ultimately in all 50 states—that was original and unique in the world. It was, and still is, a source of admiration and bafflement for people around the world: Like jazz, it is distinctly American.

For each state to provide public schooling, the state legislators had many options for arrangements from which to choose. They could have easily created a centralized bureaucratic organization, like the department of motor vehicles, or the state police, or the state court system. They all chose not to do this, however, and all adopted one pattern, with variations: to decentralize the organization and administration of public education.

The pattern was to create school districts within the state. In some states (notably those in New England), the boundaries of the school district usually are identical to the boundaries of the town. In many states, the boundaries of the school district are coterminous with the boundaries of the county or parish. Some state legislatures created school districts whose boundaries did not coincide with the boundaries of towns, the cities, or counties, which makes it possible to have several school districts in a single county or even within a single city.

Despite these political and organizational variations, school districts have in common a unique characteristic: They are created by the state for the purpose of conducting *state* business at the local level, in this case, education. Thus, school districts have a local school board, usually elected but sometimes appointed, to carry out the state responsibility to provide for education in the district. In carrying out their mandate, school boards are under the general supervision of the state education department and, through them, the state legislature. Thus, while education is a responsibility of the state and there is a state education bureaucracy that oversees the local school districts, we in the United States speak often about the importance of local control.

Perhaps the clearest and simplest example of this political concept in practice was seen in New England. For nearly 200 years, it was common practice in New England towns to have an annual school meeting, separate from the annual town meeting, to discuss educational matters, adopt the school budget, and elect members to the school board or school committee, which is still the practice in some small New England towns today.

This arrangement for the organization and administration of public schooling emerged at the beginning of the second millennium as a critical issue in education reform. We shall come back to this issue when we examine the significant new proposals that were put forward by the Education Commission of the States (1999) to reform public schooling through changes in school governance. But for the moment, let us return to the strategy of reform through education standards and the relationship that it has with the basic concepts that underlie the traditional governance arrangement just described.

Instead of seeking to bypass or extirpate the public control of schooling through political processes, as advocates of market-driven approaches would, the advocates of standards-based school reform have sought to work within and strengthen the existing system. Beginning with the first summit meeting on education in 1989, forces were set in motion to reenergize the existing political arrangements and make them work powerfully for school reform. The forty-first president of the United States, George Herbert Walker Bush, convened and participated in that first summit meeting, and principal invitees included the governors of the states—many of whom came—which not only lent weight to the proceedings but also attracted the press and their cameras: It became an important and widely publicized media event. Other important actors were invited and attended, including state governors (including young governor William Jefferson Clinton who played a prominent role), legislators, movers and shakers from the corporate world, and key state-level bureaucrats, whose participation and support were critical to making high-level decisions become reality "back home" in the states. Instead of being marginalized or bypassed, these key actors were involved as important participants in action plans for school reform. In a sense, they were owners of the ideas and thus were committed to seeing that they worked. The federal government was becoming more involved in education. The six Bush era "America 2000" goals were built upon by the Clinton administration, which became "Goals 2000" in 1994 under the Goals 2000: Educate American Act. However, the new republican controlled Congress became suspicious of too much federal control of education, and national standards were downplayed. The second National Education Summit took place in 1996, but this time it was sponsored by the National Governors Association who joined with business executives. President Clinton played a minor role in this summit. The result of this conference was the support for tough state standards, and the businesses pledged to look for the existence of state standards before setting up shop in a state. The final summit in 1999 sustained the focus on state standards and in addition emphasized the accountability of education to these standards through rigorous testing.

For good or ill, the standards-based school reform movement is a classic example of command-and-control organization and management. The concept is that educational standards are determined at the state level and turned into mandates that are passed down the hierarchy to the school district to be implemented. Compliance is generally monitored by the state by administering mandatory statewide standardized tests. It is a strategy that follows the long-established, political-legal arrangements that the states themselves created when they wrote their constitutions—except for one point: It marginalizes participation at the level of the local school district. Whereas the tradition for organizing and administering schooling in the states has tended to give considerable weight, if not primacy, to local control, the current standards-based movement of school reform strongly reasserts the authority of the state. Conceptually, the standards-based school reform movement reasserts the primacy and authority of the state in educational policy and practice and redefines the authority relationship between the school district and the state that had developed over a period of many years.

As described in Chapter 2, the standards-based school reform movement has been vigorous and powerful. The three National Education Summits were attended by politically powerful people: the president, many governors, legislators, and corporate executives. Predictably, these initiatives have produced dramatic widespread changes in schooling, which became evident when standardized tests mandated by the states increased in frequency. It was soon underscored when the test results began to be used by states to develop "report cards" to grade individual schools with sometimes dire consequences for the schools that were deemed to be failing. Soon, school districts began to use the tests in deciding who was qualified to be promoted from grade to grade and who was qualified to graduate from high school. This development has become known as high-stakes testing. All of these initiatives were proposed and advocated at the three educational summit meetings held between 1989 and 1999.

The history of this top-down movement is striking in how little attention has been paid to critical issues at the school level and at the level of individual students that result from the energetic top-down exercise of coercive power, such as the following:

• The impact that new standards and high-stakes testing has on the daily experience of pupils and students in school.
• The curricular, instructional, and organizational transformations that they demand of schools.
• The long-term effects of this new concept of school experience on the pupils and students themselves—for example, on their educational and career planning.

The presidents of the National Education Association and the American Federation of Teachers were invited to attend the 1999 summit meeting as a first step in reaching out to the teaching profession. The reformers were planning steps to tie test results to the compensation of teachers as well as to the promotion of students through the grades and, ultimately, graduation from high school. At the same time, there was a rising tide of alarm expressed by parents who were dismayed as they began to understand the possible consequences to their children of high-stakes testing in the new era of tougher educational standards. Perhaps reacting to that alarm, Secretary of Education Richard W. Riley issued a call in his seventh annual State of American Education speech in 2000 for a "midcourse review" of the standards movement. This was not a call to halt the movement but to "make sure everybody understands what the standards movement is all about." State leaders and educators, he said, "need to listen hard to legitimate concerns." He went on to point out that standards should be challenging but realistic, adding that "[s]etting high expectations does not mean setting them so high that they are unreachable except for a very few."

Common Core State Standards

We must turn our attention to the CCSS. In a major switch in states-rights philosophy, state legislatures are rapidly replacing the states' standards with what can be called "national standards"; although some states are having second thoughts and considering repealing their support. At the time of this writing, 46 states, four territories, and the Department of Defense have adopted the CCSS as their own. Only the following had not yet adopted them fully: Nebraska, Minnesota, Virginia, Texas, and Puerto Rico. Minnesota has adopted the English language arts standards only, but they have not joined one of the consortia as of yet.

What was (is) wrong with the individual state standards? One reason for the change has been the push from critics of the many different state standards for common standards, so children could move around the country, or even the same state, and essentially learn similar standards in similar grade levels. Another criticism regarding assessments, particularly international assessments, was the difficulty in comparing across states or nations since what one learned in fifth grade in Tokyo was not the same as in Alabama, or Finland, or Wisconsin, and so on. But perhaps the biggest criticism of state standards was they were (are) an "inch deep and a mile wide." Are the CCSS a solution to these criticisms? The authors of the new standards believe they are. But the critics of CCSS believe they will lead to a national curriculum.

The CCSS were developed through the Council of Chief State School Officers (CCSSO) and the National Governors Association (NGA)—two of the most prominent organizations in education reform in the last several decades. Recall, the CCSSO was instrumental in supporting the development of the Educational Leadership Policy Standards (formerly ISLLC Standards). The authors of the CCSS state the following:

The criteria that we used to develop the college- and career-readiness standards, as well as these K-12 standards

- Are aligned with college and work expectations;
- Include rigorous content and application of knowledge through high-order skills;
- Build upon strengths and lessons of current state standards;
- Are informed by top-performing countries so that all students are prepared to succeed in our global economy and society; and,
- Are evidence and/or research-based. (National Governors Association Center for Best Practices, 2010a, p. 1)

The standards were developed with the goal of readiness to enter college or the workforce, and they include College and Career Readiness (CCR) standards, which are more general than the specific K-12 standards. In the standards for ELA (English Language Arts) and literacy in content areas, each set of standards begins with CCR standards that are the same for all grades and content areas, and subsequent grade-specific standards translate corresponding CCR standards into assessment-like expectations. The expectations for student mastery are as follows:

> Students advancing through the grades are expected to meet each year's grade-specific standards, retain or further develop skills and understandings mastered in preceding grades, and work steadily toward meeting the more general expectations described by the CCR standards. (National Governors Association Center for Best Practices, 2010b, p. 4)

In a move to placate critics who complain about the loss of state control of education, the authors suggest the standards allow states and teachers to determine how standards are achieved; for example, specific writing standards are provided but not "a particular writing process or the full range of metacognitive strategies that students may need to monitor and direct their thinking and learning" (p. 4). In the mathematics standards document, it specifically states "these standards themselves do not dictate curriculum, pedagogy, or delivery of content" (National Governors Association Center for Best Practices, 2010c, p. 84).

One of the key elements of the English language arts and literacy in history, social studies, science, and technical subjects is that literacy is taught at an early age using informational passages from content areas to reinforce the learning of core subjects and to align with similar goals of the National Assessment of Educational Progress (NAEP). In grades K through five, there is a balance of reading literature and informational passages, but changes to 30% literature (fiction and nonfiction) by 12th grade and 70% informational text. Table 12.4 illustrates the connection between the 10 CCR writing standards in the English language arts and literacy in the content area and grade specific standards for grades K through two. Table 12.5 illustrates the connection between the 10 CCR writing standards in the English language arts and literacy in the content area and grade specific standards for high school.

TABLE 12.4   Example of College and Career Readiness (CCR) Standard and Grade Specific Standards.

CCR Standard: Write arguments to support claims in an analysis of substantive topics or texts, using valid reasoning and relevant and sufficient evidence for Grades K to 2.

Kindergartners	Grade 1 Students	Grade 2 Students
Use a combination of drawing, dictating, and writing to compose opinion pieces in which they tell a reader the topic or the name of the book they are writing about and state an opinion or preference about the topic or book (e.g., *My favorite book is* …).	Write opinion pieces in which they introduce the topic or name the book they are writing about, state an opinion, supply a reason for the opinion, and provide some sense of closure.	Write opinion pieces in which they introduce the topic or book they are writing about, state an opinion, supply reasons that support the opinion, use linking words (e.g., *because*, *and*, *also*) to connect opinion and reasons, and provide a concluding statement or section.

Source: Table adapted from National Governors Association Center for Best Practices, 2010b.

TABLE 12.5   Example of College and Career Readiness (CCR) Standard and Grade Specific Standards for High School.

CCR Standard: Write arguments to support claims in an analysis of substantive topics or texts, using valid reasoning and relevant and sufficient evidence.

Grades 9–10 Students	Grades 11–12 Students
Write arguments to support claims in an analysis of substantive topics or texts, using valid reasoning and relevant and sufficient evidence.	Write arguments to support claims in an analysis of substantive topics or texts, using valid reasoning and relevant and sufficient evidence.
a. Introduce precise claim(s), distinguish the claim(s) from alternate or opposing claims, and create an organization that establishes clear relationships among claim(s), counterclaims, reasons, and evidence.	a. Introduce precise, knowledgeable claim(s), establish the significance of the claim(s), distinguish the claim(s) from alternate or opposing claims, and create an organization that logically sequences claim(s), counterclaims, reasons, and evidence.
b. Develop claim(s) and counterclaims fairly, supplying evidence for each while pointing out the strengths and limitations of both in a manner that anticipates the audience's knowledge level and concerns.	b. Develop claim(s) and counterclaims fairly and thoroughly, supplying the most relevant evidence for each while pointing out the strengths and limitations of both in a manner that anticipates the audience's knowledge level, concerns, values, and possible biases.
c. Use words, phrases, and clauses to link the major sections of the text, create cohesion, and clarify the relationships between claim(s) and reasons, between reasons and evidence, and between claim(s) and counterclaims.	c. Use words, phrases, and clauses as well as varied syntax to link the major sections of the text, create cohesion, and clarify the relationships between claim(s) and reasons, between reasons and evidence, and between claim(s) and counterclaims.
d. Establish and maintain a formal style and objective tone while attending to the norms and conventions of the discipline in which they are writing.	d. Establish and maintain a formal style and objective tone while attending to the norms and conventions of the discipline in which they are writing.
e. Provide a concluding statement or section that follows from and supports the argument presented.	e. Provide a concluding statement or section that follows from and supports the argument presented.

Source: Table adapted from National Governors Association Center for Best Practices, 2010b

What you will notice from the Tables 12.4 and 12.5 is the progression of the same CCR standard from grade-to-grade, and at the high school level specific grade-level standards are combined for grades nine and 10 and for grades 11 and 12. The authors of the standards indicate this provides greater flexibility to schools to accommodate schedules and offerings.

Although this discussion and examples presented have been for the English language arts and literacy content areas, the similar contexts apply for the math standards. The difference is CCR standards for math are not exactly the same across all grade levels. Though similar, they build in complexity with additional CCR standards added in the middle grades and high school grades. Not all math standards are CCR standards, so the math standards document identifies CCR standards with a plus sign (+). Geometry is the only domain, or groups of similar standards, contained in all grades (National Governors Association Center for Best Practices, 2010c). Table 12.6 shows how the standard domains are laid out by grade level.

So what do the professional experts and the research literature report about the new standards? Are they effective? Can they be effective?

TABLE 12.6 Common Core State Standards Domains in Math

Standard Domains*	Grade Levels					
	K	1–2	3–5	6–7	8	9–12
Counting and Cardinality	✓					
Operations and Algebraic Thinking	✓	✓	✓			
Number and Operations in Base Ten	✓	✓	✓			
Number and Operations in Base—Fractions			✓			
Measurement and Data	✓	✓	✓			
Geometry	✓	✓	✓	✓	✓	✓
Ratios and Proportional Relationships				✓		
The Number System				✓	✓	✓
Expressions and Equations				✓	✓	
Statistics and Probability				✓	✓	✓
Functions					✓	✓
Modeling						✓
Algebra						✓
Number and Quantity						✓

*Domains are clusters of similar standards.

Source: Table adapted from National Governors Association Center for Best Practices, 2010c

We agree with McTighe and Wiggins (2012) that educators need to take the time to become familiar with the background materials about the standards before diving into standards for individual grade levels. Together, teachers need to understand the entire context, or gestalt, of the CCSS by reading the introductory material as well as specific information about "what is not covered," and they should become familiar with the appendices, which are very helpful to understanding how the standards can be implemented. For example, the appendices in the ELA standards provide examples of graded work to illustrate various levels of student mastery. McTighe and Wiggins admonish the user of the new standards to not simply use them within grade level in a sequence as presented, but to backward-map the curriculum by determining what it is you want the student to be able to do. McTighe and Wiggins state the following:

> If a curriculum simply marches through lists of content knowledge and skills without attending to the concomitant goal of cultivating independent performance, high-schoolers will remain as dependent on teacher directions and step-by-step guidance as 4th graders currently are. The resulting graduates will be unprepared for the demands of college and the workplace. (p. 9)

For ELL and students with disabilities (SWD), the authors of the standards indicate these students should be expected to master the standards. The caveats are that for ELLs they may not have "native-like control of conventions and vocabulary" (p. 6), and for SWDs accommodations should be employed to provide for the widest range of student participation. We doubt this is sufficient direction for school districts and teachers in working with ELL and SWD populations for mastering the standards and accompanying assessments.

At the time of this writing, there is major pushback from both liberals and conservatives about using the CCSS. Although it seems like an odd mix of critics, both sides are worried about the erosion of local or state rights in terms of who controls the curriculum. But for states to get a good chunk of the RTTT money, they must show they are using standards that will result in students who are college ready. So states adopting the Common Core can gain approval easily since college readiness is supposedly built into the standards. Notwithstanding the carrot of using money to gain acceptance of the Common Core, there is strong pressure in some states to roll back their decision to adopt the Common Core and return to their state standards—most notably in Michigan, Ohio, and Tennessee. Support from the National Education Association also waned after seeing how the standards were causing implementation problems and understanding how assessments of the standards would be used for teacher evaluation—and in some states for pay increase decisions. Perhaps the most telling decision of how the fight over CCSS will play out is the Republican National Committee's decision in April 2013 to oppose the standards. In the summer of 2013, proponents of Common Core were beginning to fight the opposition's criticisms and to market the standards (Ujifusa, 2013).

Assessing the Common Core State Standards (CCSS)

One of the criticisms of the CCSS is the way in which the U.S. Department of Education handled the assessment process. Unfortunately, instead of choosing one group, or allowing individual states, to develop an assessment, they chose to allow consortiums of states to bid for assessment development grants. In 2010, the U.S. Department of Education (ED) through RTTT awarded $330 million to two groups of states to develop assessments aligned to the CCSS: The Partnership for Assessment of Readiness for College and Careers (PARCC), which in summer 2013 included 22 states plus the U.S. Virgin Islands, and Smarter Balanced Assessment Consortium, which included 24 states. Common assessments by these consortiums will be in English language arts and math only. States are responsible for additional subject area tests. The assessments are planned to be in place for the 2014–2015 school year, and at the time of this writing pilot testing was being completed and some problems were being reported with test delivery via computer. Smarter Balanced will use computer adaptive testing, in which the computer adjusts the level of difficulty based on student responses. A correct response will increase the difficulty of the next question, and an incorrect response will be followed with an easier question. PARCC will use computers to deliver the assessment, but the format will not be "adaptive" to student responses. The cost of the infrastructure to use computer technology for test administration will be borne by the states. Additional costs for states will be approximately $27 per student, which Smarter Balanced claims is currently less than states spend on existing assessments (Smarter Balanced Assessment Consortium, 2013). Smarter Balanced also indicates on its website that it is working with PARCC to ensure comparability across the two assessments. Both consortia claim their tests will be an improvement over traditional state tests by doing a better job of assessing critical thinking skills.

Critics of this assessment process see little change in high stakes testing from the experience with NCLB. Since RTTT states must have teacher and principal evaluations based on performance, the stakes are indeed high. In addition, since the stakes are high, these assessments are viewed as the force that will drive the curriculum.

Another alarming result of high-stakes testing has been seen in cheating scandals across the United States, including some high-profile scandals in New York, Washington, Atlanta, and El

Paso. The pressure to improve test scores and close the achievement gap has caused superintendents, principals, and teachers to change test scores to inflate their results. The U.S. Government Accountability Office (GAO) reported in a national survey of testing between 2010 and 2012 that "40 states detected potential cheating during the past two school years and 33 states confirmed at least one instance of cheating" (Government Accountability Office, 2013, p. 8).

The Condition of Education

Most of the indicators in the 2012 *Condition of Education* compiled by the National Center for Education Statistics are good news for educators. These data are presented below. Based on our own government data, it is not clear to us why education is still highly criticized as failing by many politicians, the media, and yes, some educators. Let's look at some of the most recent data available. Here are some of the positive trends from the 2012 *Condition of Education*:

1. The percentage of 3- to 5-year-olds enrolled in full-day preprimary programs increased from 32% in 1980 to 58% in 2010.
2. Although the average NAEP (National Assessment of Educational Progress) reading score was not measurably different for fourth graders between 2009 and 2011, eighth graders improved by one point. However, there has been notable improvement since 1992 for both grade levels as the percentage at or above the proficient level has increased.
3. For math, in grades four and eight, the average scores in 2011 were higher on NAEP than the average scores for those grades in all previous assessment years: in fourth grade from a scale score of 213 in 1992 to 241 in 2011; in eighth grade from 263 in 1992 to 284 in 2011.
4. Twelfth-grade math NAEP scores also improved for the two years reported: a scale score of 150 in 2005 to 153 in 2009.
5. The percentages of high school graduates who took mathematics courses in geometry, algebra II/trigonometry, analysis/precalculus, statistics/probability, and calculus while in high school were higher in 2009 than in 1990.
6. Dropout rates in public schools for all subgroups have decreased over a 15-year period: from 12.1% in 1990 to 7.4% in 2010.
7. Graduation rates have improved somewhat from 73.7% in 1991 to 75.5% in 2009.
8. Over the 35-year period between 1975 and 2010, the rate of immediate college enrollment after high school ranged from a low of 49% in 1979 to a high of 70% in 2009.
9. A larger percentage of full-time teachers held a post-baccalaureate degree in 2007–2008 than in 2003–2004. Forty-nine percent of elementary school teachers and 54% of secondary school teachers held a post-baccalaureate degree in 2007–2008, compared with 45% and 50%, respectively, in 2003–2004.
10. In higher education, the number of associate's degrees increased between 2000 and 2010 by 50%; the number of bachelor's degrees increased by 33% between 2000 and 2010; the number of master's degrees increased by 50%; and the number of doctoral degrees increased by 34%.
11. Post-baccalaureate enrollment has increased every year since 1983, reaching 2.9 million students in 2010. In each year since 1988, women have comprised more than half of post-baccalaureate enrollment. In 2010, post-baccalaureate enrollment was 59% female.

Now, here are the challenges we are facing:

1. The percentage of public school students in the United States who were ELLs was higher in 2009–2010 at 10% (or an estimated 4.7 million students) than in 2000–2001 at 8% (or an estimated 3.7 million students).

2. The number of children and families living below the poverty line has increased for all subgroups, though higher for Native American, Black, and Hispanic families.
3. The percentage of public school students in the United States who were ELLs was higher in 2009–2010 at 10% (or an estimated 4.7 million students) than in 2000–2001 at 8% (or an estimated 3.7 million students).
4. The number of children and youth ages three through 21 receiving special education services was 6.5 million in 2009–2010, or about 13% of all public school students. Some 38% of the students receiving special education services had specific learning disabilities
5. Twelfth-grade reading scores have been erratic—bouncing from a high scale score of 292 on the NAEP in 1992 to a low of 286 in 2005—only to increase to 288 in 2009, the last date of 12th-grade reporting.
6. The achievement gap between White students compared to either Black or Hispanic student using NAEP scores is still a problem although there is some good news. See below.

The Achievement Gap

The achievement gap is the difference in performance between different racial subgroups. Although the *Condition of Education 2012* (2012) did not analyze achievement score gaps between subgroups, *The Condition of Education 2011* (2011) did. Here is what was reported in 2011:

Mathematics:

- In fourth grade, the achievement gap was improved six scale score points for Black students compared to White students between 1990 and 2009; in 1990, the gap was 32 points, and in 2009, the gap was 26 scale score points.
- In fourth grade, the gap for Hispanics compared to Whites in 2009 was 21 points, not measurably different from 1990.
- In eighth grade, the gaps were 32 points for Black students and 26 points for Hispanic students compared to White students; neither was measurably different from 1990.
- In 12th grade, the gaps were 30 points for Black students and 23 points for Hispanic students compared to White students; neither was measurably different from 1990.

Some progress was made in fourth grade in reducing the achievement gap between Black students compared to White students since 1990, but no other narrowing in the gaps had occurred in other grade levels.

Reading:

- In 2009, for grades four, eight, and 12, Whites students scored higher than both Black and Hispanic students, but none of the gaps were measurably different from 1992 or 2007.
- In 2009, the gaps in NAEP scale score points between White and Black students for grades four, eight, and 12 were 26 points, 26 points, and 27 points respectively.
- The gaps between White and Hispanic students for grades four, eight, and 12 in 2009 were 25 points, 24 points, and 22 points respectively.

You can see from these scores that Hispanic students scored higher than Black students, but only by a few scale score points. Overall, since 1992, there has been no significant narrowing of the reading achievement gaps. Certainly, there is much room for improvement.

A 2006 report by Jaekyung Lee and published by The Civil Rights Project at Harvard University did not find achievement gains or a narrowing of the achievement gap between racial/ethnic groups or between socioeconomic groups. This report indicated that, although many states and the U.S. Department of Education boasted achievement gains and positive gap trends using state tests, these gains were not confirmed by NAEP in grades four and eight—and that because NAEP existed well before the state tests that were created as a result of NCLB, NAEP is a better indicator of national trends both before (from 1991–2001) and after (2002–2005) with NCLB. Lee reported that modest gains in achievement and in reducing the gap were made in math immediately after NCLB, but the scores returned to the same levels of gains as before NCLB. Although gains have been reported in NAEP for math in both grades four and eight, the same growth patterns were in place before NCLB, which means that NCLB is not the reason for the gains. Reading gains remained flat both before and after NCLB was enacted. There were no significant changes in the gaps either before or after NCLB. The findings were the same for the early state adopters of accountability reform, or the so-called first-generation accountability states, namely, California, Florida, Kentucky, Maryland, New York, North Carolina, and Texas (all of which had more experience with accountability reform efforts), when compared to the second-generation states. In the forward to this report, Gary Orfield wrote that the achievement gaps for NAEP were showing positive narrowing in the 1970s and 1980s "when more of the civil rights and anti-poverty efforts of earlier reforms were still in operation" (Lee, 2006), but after 1983, reforms that responded to *A Nation at Risk* did not show similar positive reductions in the achievement gap. This legacy continues with NCLB. No reports have been issued at the time of this writing for RTTT.

High-stakes testing has resulted in additional, unanticipated outcomes. In a metasynthesis of 49 qualitative studies on high-stakes testing, Au (2007) makes the following conclusions: "[T]he tests have the predominant effect of narrowing curricular content to those subjects included in the tests.... [I]n a minority of cases, high stakes tests have led to increases in student-centered pedagogy and increases in content knowledge integration" (p. 264). So while it is possible to have positive curricular outcomes in some schools, this is not the case in most schools. The tests have the effect of top-down mandates to change the curriculum based on what the policy makers believe the tests should measure. Another unintended consequence of high-stakes graduation tests is that significantly more students drop out of school prior to graduation, and these students are more likely to be poor and minority group members (Marchant & Paulson, 2005). In addition, Marchant and Paulson indicate the states that have graduation exams have lower SAT scores. The reason for this phenomenon is most likely that a narrowing of the curriculum and a focus on traditional teaching methods to help students prepare for the tests does not prepare them for the type of questions encountered in the SAT that require reasoning. This fact is particularly alarming because "the SAT has even been equated to an intelligence test, measuring students' ability to learn, not mastery of what was learned" (p. 4). In arriving at similar findings regarding higher dropout rates, Nichols, Glass, and Berliner (2005) conclude, "there is no convincing evidence that the pressure associated with high-stakes testing leads to any important benefits for students' achievement" (p. iii). More recently Hargreaves and Braun (2013) concluded the following:

> We find that over more than two decades, through accumulating statewide initiative
> in DDIA [data driven improvement and accountability] and then in the successive
> Federal initiatives of the No Child Left Behind Act and Race to the Top, DDIA…has
> come to exert increasingly adverse effects on public education, because high-stakes
> and high-threat accountability, rather than improvement alone, or improvement

and accountability together, have become the prime drivers of educational change. This, in turn, has exerted adverse and perverse effects on attempts to secure improvement in educational quality and equity. (p. ii)

The implications from these findings are critical to policy makers who continued their focus on high-stakes testing at the national and state levels. Reforms at the state level focused on the use of high-stakes testing as the primary measure of accountability. This pressure promoted teaching to the test, a narrowing of the curriculum to focus on math, reading, and (to some extent) science, and a focus on traditional teaching methods over cooperative learning and integrated thematic projects that foster creative thinking. It is not surprising then that the state tests showed improvement, but not surprising that SAT scores decline. In addition, states have manipulated their state test score proficiency levels. When kept low, these levels falsely show that more individuals are "proficient" but at the same time show a larger achievement gap; and when proficiency levels are set at a high level, they show a narrowing of the achievement gap because fewer students in all racial/ethnic categories will reach the higher levels.

PISA and TIMSS

We know there are criticisms of where the United States stands in comparison to other countries based on the PISA test (Programme for International Student Assessment) and TIMSS (Trends in International Mathematics and Science Study). For a number of reasons, we do not value these comparisons, nor do many other researchers. In response to reviews critical of U.S. performance in international tests, Carnoy and Rothstein (2013) concluded that "conclusions like these, ... are oversimplified, frequently exaggerated, and misleading. They ignore the complexity of test results and may lead policymakers to pursue inappropriate and even harmful reforms" (p. 2). We concur with this analysis, which is prescient of problems associated with future international comparisons.

Summary Findings of EPI Study

We end this section with the results from a report by the Economic Policy Institute's Broader, Bolder Approach to Education (Weiss & Long, 2013), which was an in-depth study of Chicago, New York City, and Washington, DC, school districts, chosen

because all enjoyed the benefit of mayoral control, produce reliable district-level test score data from the National Assessment of Educational Progress (NAEP), and were led by vocal proponents who implemented versions of this reform agenda. Indeed, former reform leaders in all three cities have become high-profile national proponents who disseminate the agenda across multiple districts and states. (p. 3)

These high-profile reform leaders were Arne Duncan, Michael Bloomberg, and Michelle Rhee, respectively, in Chicago, New York City, and Washington, DC. The conclusion from this report summarized much of the research literature about market-based reforms and high-stakes testing. Here is a summary of the findings from this report:

- Test scores increased less, and achievement gaps grew more, in "reform" cities than in other urban districts.
- Reported successes for targeted students evaporated upon closer examination.

- Test-based accountability prompted churn that thinned the ranks of experienced teachers, but not necessarily bad teachers.
- School closures did not send students to better schools or save school districts money.
- Charter schools further disrupted the districts while providing mixed benefits, particularly for the highest-needs students.
- Emphasis on the widely touted market-oriented reforms drew attention and resources from initiatives with greater promise.
- The reforms missed a critical factor driving achievement gaps: the influence of poverty on academic performance.
- Real, sustained change requires strategies that are more realistic, patient, and multipronged.

In the next section, we discuss possible solutions to failed power-coercive strategies, and we share some research on what does work to improve schools.

WHOLE-SCHOOL REFORM

Whole-school reform (also called comprehensive school reform [CSR]) is predicated on two basic elements that have been learned about school reform since the mid-1980s and that are now widely incorporated into the theory of practice of many education leaders:

- First, we have not been very successful at learning how to improve the effectiveness of schools by using top-down, command-and-control methods from the federal level, the state level, or even the school district level.
- Second, there has been a great deal of demonstrated success in improving the effectiveness of schools by working to renew individual schools from the inside out. This approach means that every school is expected to meet the same standards, but every school writes its own script.

Increasing School Autonomy

Effective CSR depends on giving schools more power to determine what best meets the needs of a school. The terms used to describe this type of power structure are site-based management or school-based decision making, which is an effort to decentralize decision making in the system by shifting some important decisions from the central office of the state or the district to the school. In some cases in which the concept was enthusiastically embraced by the central office, important instructional, personnel, and financial decisions were delegated to the schools. These decisions were then made by principals and teachers. In management jargon, this process creates a flatter organization. Layers of bureaucracy are stripped away, decisions are made close to where the work is done, and less time is devoted to bureaucratic paperwork and delays; the happy result should be that the school is more responsive, more nimble, more quickly adaptable, and more effective. This management strategy has become nearly standard procedure in revitalizing for-profit organizations in the corporate world, while it remains highly unusual in the world of public schools, with some exceptions. In 1990, the Kentucky Education Reform Act actually mandated the use of site-based management in all public schools, requiring that each school establishes a school council including the principal, three elected teachers, and two elected parents. The school council participates in decisions about the school budget and curriculum, hires teachers, and hires the next principal when the position is vacated. In a similar mandate, Florida schools are required by statute to have a school advisory council (SAC) to include elected teachers, parents, staff, students, and community members, and with the majority of the members being nondistrict employees. Although the Florida legislature had at times funded SACs up to $10 per student to spend on school improvement projects ($5 beginning in 2008–2009 and no money beginning in 2009-2010), they have little other authority except as in an advisory capacity to the school administration. They "approve" the School Improvement Plan (SIP) each year, but the SIP is typically developed by the school staff with little input from the SAC. This procedure is not true school-based decision making, though better than having no SAC.

Sadly, however, experience with site-based management in public schooling has been mixed. Some school districts, mostly moderate-size suburban districts, have implemented on-site management to good effect. However, in many instances, especially in city school districts, where schooling problems often seem intractable, school boards and their central office bureaucracies are reluctant to cede their power to schools. School site-based management frequently results in limited authority being transferred to the schools, and decision making at the school level ranges from marginal to illusory.

The question remains: What undermines the effectiveness of principals and teachers? The answer of a longtime student of New York City education, Diane Ravitch, strikes a chord with those who are experienced at working in schools:

> [W]hat undermines the effectiveness of principals and teachers is a school system that seeks to restrict initiative by imposing an elaborate command-and-control mechanism, that attempts to manage all of its employees through uniform and burdensome mandates and regulation, that stamps out efforts to find a different (perhaps better) way of educating children, and that lacks meaningful standards for what children should learn but has elaborate standards for the delivery of mediocre services. (Ravitch & Viteritti, 1997, p. 4)

Although a one-time supporter of NCLB including market-based reforms, Diane Ravitch (2010) studied the results of NCLB carefully and decided it supported a testing industry that "hijacked" (p. 15) the standards movement and took decisions about how to teach away from the school level. She supports a national curriculum that is balanced and, by including the arts, does not narrow the curriculum to only math and reading. Yet, she supports allowing teachers to determine how to implement the curriculum.

> Congress and state legislatures should not tell teachers how to teach, any more than they should tell surgeons how to perform operations. Nor should the curriculum of the schools be the subject of a political negotiation among people who are neither knowledgeable about teaching nor well educated. Pedagogy—that is, how to teach— is rightly the professional domain of individual teachers. Curriculum—that is, what to teach—should be determined by professional educators and scholars, after due public deliberations, acting with the authority vested in them by schools, districts, or states. (pp. 225–226)

Thus, school reform is recognized as an issue in organization and behavior: The crux is recreating the school organization—the operational level of the school district—to energize teachers and principals, motivate them, encourage them to collaborate in mutual problem solving, and engage their personal commitment to achieving their own deeply held goals and aspirations. It involves organizing to encourage the development in the school of a culture of leadership, energized motivation, shared decision making, and—above all—a growth-enhancing climate of success for both children and adults. Fullan (2011) concurs. He outlined four criteria for evaluating the effectiveness of the "drivers" (i.e., policies and strategies, for successful whole system reform). Do the drivers:

1. foster intrinsic motivation of teachers and students;
2. engage educators and students in continuous improvement of instruction and learning;
3. inspire collective or team work; and
4. affect all teachers and students—100 per cent?

> The right drivers—capacity building, group work, instruction, and systems solutions—are effective because they work directly on changing the culture of the school system (values, norms, skills, practices, relationships).
>   . . . The glue that binds the effective drivers together is the underlying attitude, philosophy, and theory of action. (pp. 3–5)

Support for School Leaders

The concept is one of shifting authority and responsibility from the central office bureaucracy of the school district to the individual school so that the school can become more nimble, more adaptable, and increasingly effective. The autonomy that comes with site-based management brings greater opportunity for the school leader to be more effective in making a difference. It also greatly increases responsibility for results. As the central office bureaucracy is diminished, the school leader can look there less and less for guidance or to pass responsibility up the line. Whole-school educational reform is transforming the school principalship into a very different, very demanding opportunity for those who want to be leaders.

Under these changed circumstances, school leaders must not allow themselves to be isolated. More than ever, school leaders need support; they need to reach out and connect with people who have something pertinent and useful to offer: ideas, collegiality, support, feedback, helpful experience, people skills, or knowledge needed for this new era. One can no longer assume that senior people in the bureaucracy know the answers to contemporary leadership problems: Very often the most effective help must come from peers who are facing similar problems.

Many schools have turned to comprehensive school reform (CSR) models that can be adopted or adapted for their schools. Because CSR models essentially reorganize the school through packaged programs, they are to some extent a top-down driven reform process, and because NCLB authorizes the use of federal funding, including Title I, only for programs that are supported by "scientifically-based research," the choices for school reform efforts are not always those of the local school alone. Nonetheless, CSR models are being implemented widely in schools across the United States and internationally. To make good decisions about which CSR models will be most effective for a particular school, decision makers need to turn to the research for support.

Research Support for CSR Models

In one of the most comprehensive studies on CSR models, Geoffrey Borman and his colleagues completed a meta-analysis of studies on the 29 most popular CSR models (Borman, Hewes,

Overman, & Brown, 2003). Published in 2003, this study continues to be cited by current researchers. Borman et al. used the following criteria to categorize the CSR models:

- **Strongest Evidence of Effectiveness**   Ten or more studies with statistically significant and positive achievement results using comparison groups; at least five third-party studies were included.
- **Highly Promising Evidence of Effectiveness**   Five or more studies with statistically significant and positive achievement results using comparison groups; at least three or more third-party studies were included.
- **Promising Evidence of Effectiveness**   Two or more studies with statistically significant and positive achievement results using comparison groups; at least one third-party study was included.
- **Greatest Need for Additional Research**   There was only one study that lacked positive statistical significance.

The results for each of the above categories, including the effect size that indicates the overall percentage of a standard deviation increase over comparison groups, are displayed in Table 12.7.

In 2006, using a research design model similar to Borman and his associates, the Comprehensive School Reform Quality Center (CSRQ Center), which is operated by the American Institutes for Research, has sponsored research to evaluate various CSR models. This research is particularly helpful for all school levels. The CSR models are rated on rubrics that evaluate programs in the following categories:

- Evidence of positive effects on student achievement
- Evidence of positive effects on additional outcomes
- Evidence of positive effects on parent, family, and community involvement
- Evidence of a link between research and model design
- Evidence of services and support to schools to enable successful implementation

The researchers completed a review of the literature, in which they screened over 1,500 studies to arrive at 41 studies that met rigorous research design criteria. Studies that met rigorous designs were considered conclusive studies. CSR programs were rated by categories of effectiveness based on the following criteria:

- **Very Strong Evidence of Effectiveness**   Ten studies with at least five rated as conclusive and 75% of outcomes significantly positive with an effect size of .25 or higher.
- **Moderately Strong Evidence of Effectiveness**   Five to nine studies with at least three rated conclusive, and 51% to 75% significantly positive outcomes with an effect size of .15.
- **Moderate Evidence of Effectiveness**   Two to four studies with at least one rated conclusive, and with 26% to 50% significantly positive outcomes with an effect size of at least .15.
- **Limited Evidence of Effectiveness**   One study with 1% to 25% of outcomes significantly positive.
- **Zero Evidence of Effectiveness**   No study outcomes were significantly positive.

In arriving at a summary report on each of 18 CSR models for middle school and high schools, none met the criteria for "very strong," and none met the criteria for "moderately strong." They did find five CSR programs that met "moderate" evidence of effectiveness; these

TABLE 12.7 The CSR Models and Effect Size, Ranked by Category	
Strongest Evidence of Effectiveness	**Effect Sizes**
Direct Instruction	.21
School Development Program (James Comer)	.15
Success for All	.18
Highly Promising Evidence of Effectiveness	
Expeditionary Learning Outward Bound	.19
Modern Red School House	.26
Roots and Wings	.38
Promising Evidence of Effectiveness	
Accelerated Schools	.09
America's Choice	.22
ATLAS Communities	.27
Montessori	.27
Paideia	.30
The Learning Network	.22
Greatest Need for Additional Research	
Audrey Cohen College System	N/A*
Center for Effective Schools	N/A
Child Development Project	N/A
Coalition of Essential Schools	N/A
Community for Learning	N/A
Community Learning Centers	N/A
Co-nect	N/A
Core Knowledge	N/A
Different Ways of Knowing	N/A
Edison Schools	N/A
High Schools That Work	N/A
High/Scope	N/A
Integrated Thematic Instruction	N/A
MicroSociety	N/A
Onward to Excellent II	N/A
Talent Development	N/A
High School	N/A
Urban Learning Centers	N/A

*N/A = not applicable.

Source: This table was created from data from Borman, G. D., Hewes, G. M., Overman, L. T., and Brown, S. (2003). Comprehensive school reform and achievement: A meta-analysis. *Review of Educational Research*, *73*(2), pp. 155–156.

were America's Choice, First Things First, School Development Program, Success for All Middle Schools, and Talent Development High School. Several studies met the criteria for "limited" evidence of success; these were Expeditionary Learning, Knowledge Is Power Program (KIPP), Middle Start, More Effective Schools, and Project GRAD. Programs that had no evidence of effectiveness were Accelerated School Plus, ATLAS Communities, Coalition of Essential Schools, High Schools That Work, Making Middle Grades Work, Modern Red Schoolhouse, Onward to Excellence II, and Turning Points (Comprehensive School Reform Quality Center, 2006a).

The CRSQ center evaluated 20 CSR models for elementary schools with more showing stronger evidence of effectiveness than for middle or high schools (Comprehensive School Reform Quality Center, 2006b). No model was rated as "very strong"; however, two were rated as "moderately strong": Direct Instruction (full-immersion model) and Success for All. Seven were rated as "moderate": Accelerated School Plus, America's Choice, Core Knowledge, Literacy Collaborative, National Writing Project, School Development Program, and School Renaissance. Six were rated as having "limited" evidence of effectiveness: ATLAS Communities, Different Ways of Knowing, Integrated Thematic Instruction, Modern Red Schoolhouse, Pearson Achievement Solutions (formerly Co-nect), Ventures Initiative, and Focus Systems. Programs that had no evidence of effectiveness were Breakthrough to Literacy, Coalition of Essential Schools, Community for Learning, Comprehensive Early Literacy Learning, First Steps, and Onward to Excellence II.

Another source of information for CSR programs is a website entitled *What Works Clearinghouse* established by the Institute for Education Sciences (IES) of the U.S. Department of Education (Institute for Education Sciences, 2013). This website provides publications and reviews to assist practitioners in deciding "what works." They provide intervention reports that summarize research findings on specific interventions such as those presented in Table 12.7 above: practice guides from experts who study the literature and provide recommendations on instructional techniques, single study reviews on interventions, and quick reviews on recent research. In addition, the user can search for what works, and the site provides guides to show the extent of evidence and how much improvement to expect from various interventions. Users can search multiple domains such as dropout prevention, ELLs, literacy, math, and student behavior, among others. Searches can be delimited to individual or multiple grade levels, to levels of intervention effectiveness, the extent of evidence (meaning how much research support the findings), and the delivery method (individual, small group, whole class, and whole school). The website provides a wealth of information for administrators and teachers to use in their decision making about what works best for their schools. The *What Works Clearinghouse* has received some criticism for providing no information about the difficulty of implementing interventions and "not enough information to understand the characteristics, or causal influences, that separate effective curricula from those that are not" (Smith & Smith, 2009, p. 383).

Schools need to be very deliberate when deciding to adopt CSR models for their schools. Principals and staff should collaboratively decide that a particular model is best for their students, and part of the decision-making process should include reading the research studies about models of interest. Also, they need to be aware of startup expenses and yearly maintenance costs. The Borman study reported a range in yearly costs from $47,000 for James Comer's School Development Program to $282,000 for Roots and Wings and Success for All. According to Datnow (2005), higher costs tend to create problems for the sustainability of CSR reforms, yet the Borman study suggests that these costs can be offset by using Title I funding.

Response to Intervention (RTI)

We cannot leave the area of comprehensive school reform (CSR) without mentioning the response to intervention (RTI) initiative. RTI is a CSR that provides differentiated instruction to students who are struggling academically. Although many people think of RTI as a special education program, it is a general education initiative used in all classrooms. One reason RTI may be linked to special education is that its origins can be traced to changes in the Individuals with Disabilities Education Act (IDEA) of 2004, which stated the following:

> [W]hen determining whether a child has a specific learning disability as defined in section 602, a local educational agency shall not be required to take into consideration whether a child has a severe discrepancy between achievement and intellectual ability in oral expression, listening comprehension, written expression, basic reading skill, reading comprehension, mathematical calculation, or mathematical reasoning. (Individuals with Disabilities Education Act, 2004)

The previous method of determining a specific learning disability (SLD) waited for the child to show this discrepancy, and therefore the child was far behind his or her peers before intensive remediation occurred.

The RTI model typically uses a tiered approach to identify at-risk students and then provide interventions. There can be from two to four tiers in state or district models, but a typical approach might use something like the following three-tiered approach to assist students:

Tier 1

All students in the school are provided with high-quality, researched-based instruction differentiated to meet the needs of all learners. Progress data is maintained on all learners, and data is reviewed periodically to ensure that no student needs additional support.

Tier 2

Those students identified in Tier 1 as needing additional support are provided increasingly intensive instruction. They may be removed from the classroom or provided differentiated instruction in the classroom in small groups or individually. They are returned to the regular classroom instruction when data indicate that the students are successful.

Tier 3

Students who do not respond to support provided in Tier 2 are provided individualized, intensive instruction that is targeted to student academic difficulties.

Only when students in Tier 3 do not respond to interventions are they referred for special education assessment.

The concept of RTI is supported by many leaders and researchers in education, including special education professionals. A synthesis of 18 early reading intervention studies found positive results for students participating in interventions, particularly when the interventions were provided in the early grades and in smaller groups (Wanzek & Vaughn, 2007). Problems with RTI exist, however, in several areas. First, many teachers see RTI as simply another program to implement without sufficient support, including professional development. Second, what interventions should be provided and who decides how (individualized or standardized for groups), when, and where (pull-out, push-in, or classroom) to implement them? It seems clear that RTI works to remediate students, but before one can claim that RTI is effective as a CSR, implementation procedures need to be formalized in states, districts, and schools.

The *What Works Clearinghouse* provides several practice guides providing recommendations for instructional and school practices that show success in improving students' achievement at each RTI tier. For example, the following two recommendations have "strong" research evidence for success in improving math achievement in middle and elementary schools for Tiers 2 and 3:

1. Instruction during the intervention should be explicit and systematic. This process includes providing models of proficient problem solving, verbalization of thought processes, guided practice, corrective feedback, and frequent cumulative review.
2. Interventions should include instruction on solving word problems that is based on common underlying structures. (Gersten, Beckmann, et al., 2009, p. 6)

To assist struggling students with reading, Gersten, Compton, et al. (2009, p. 6) suggest the following recommendation has "strong" evidence to help at the Tier 2 level:

Provide intensive, systematic instruction on up to three foundational reading skills in small groups to students who score below the benchmark score on universal screening. Typically, these groups meet between three and five times a week, for 20 to 40 minutes.

VOICES FROM THE FIELD

RTI Interventions in a Small Rural High School

Steve Ritter, Principal, Lakeland High School, Deepwater, Missouri

Our intervention system is goal-oriented towards all students graduating from high school. We identified problems hindering our students from being successful in our school. We took a collaborative approach by coming together and discussing a variety of ways we could assist students in our school when they were not meeting academic expectations. Prior to my arrival at Lakeland, there were no interventions, alternative programs, or assistance programs for struggling students. Through the assistance of many of our faculty and staff members, we established a system of interventions for our students.

We began at Tier 1 with discussions about what high quality instruction looked like in the classroom. We discussed a variety of instructional methods, ways to engage students in the classroom, examples of differentiated instruction, and interdisciplinary activities where our elective courses were supporting the content and processes of the core content area. The first intervention in this process had to be examining how we were teaching. We had to review if we were meeting the needs of the variety of learners in our classroom. We also looked at data to find areas where we needed to improve and provided additional focus to those areas in each course as well as looking at research-based best practices to improve our instruction.

For our students who were still struggling, we implemented several programs to assist a large number of students in Tier 2. We established an intervention period we call Academy. Academy is a twenty-four minute period where students can work on homework, get assistance from their Academy teacher, or visit another teacher for assistance. We also have added some interventions within Academy based on individual student data. We added a math tutoring lab that is supervised by our high school math teacher. He supervises four to six tutors and six to 12 tutees during this time for four days a week. Our junior high math teacher also put together a math tutoring lab. She supervises several eighth-grade students who conduct tutoring to other seventh- and eighth-grade students. Both teachers assist in tutoring students in the room as well. We have added an after school homework help program and a Saturday school program for students who need assistance with managing and completing their homework.

Some students continue to struggle in their classes, so we have turned to alternative education programming by utilizing an online learning system in Tier 3. This program is used for the After School Credit Recovery (ASCR) program. ASCR provides students who have failed classes an opportunity to recover lost credit. The program also provides an alternative presentation of the content, which can be used in Tiers 1 and 2 with struggling learners as well. The most intense intervention is the use of the Missouri Options program. The Missouri Options program allows schools to prepare students for taking the GED. Students who pass the GED through the Missouri Options program are able to obtain a regular high school diploma from their school at the same time as their kindergarten cohort group. Putting these programs together was no small feat. With a faculty of 16 teachers and 180 students in grades seven through 12, it required a great deal of teamwork to make this happen.

The new intervention system forced us to structure our school day differently than in the past, and the new programs have provided us the opportunity to bring about changes and more student success. However, the biggest key to our success is having the right people in the right place. We have a counselor who has excelled in collaborating with stakeholders. He routinely gathers teachers together to discuss student academic and behavior progress during the school year. When needed, he gathers together the student, the student's parents, teachers, and me, and we work out a plan with all involved to find what programs can lead to greater student success. We even formed a contract between the student, parents, counselor, and principal stating what everyone would do to assist the student towards success and mandating certain intervention programs for the students. While the counselor coordinates these meetings, we have many other team players in the process.

The teachers play a large role in our intervention process. We have teachers doing little things, like checking assignment sheets, meeting with students before and after school to monitor homework progress, and being informal mentors to students. Our librarian coordinates our online learning system for the flexible scheduling during the school day and the After School Credit Recovery (ASCR) program. A teacher and the librarian supervise the ASCR program four days a week. Two other teachers and the Special Education teacher help with the Saturday school homework program. The involvement of more than 75% of our faculty in the intervention system has benefited a large number of our students. It has also made it easier for the faculty as a whole to embrace the new systems. One of the other keys to making a reform or change sustainable is to have the faculty see the results. Last school year, three of our 39 seniors would not have graduated from high school without our Tier 3 interventions. This year, we have two of our 29 students who would not be graduating without the Tier 3 interventions. It is our hope that as more practices are implemented in the Tier 1 and Tier 2 levels we will have fewer students requiring the most extreme interventions.

We also know that we can do better and do more for our students. We are seeing great success and improvement in academic achievement in math. Teachers are willing to invest into the new practices when they see the positive results of the changes. This fact can also hold true for students. We have several students who after a short time in Tier 2 interventions begin to see success. We enjoy the opportunity to celebrate with them and keep them on that path. However, we will also continue to look to improve. We will continue to implement interventions where our data shows gaps. We know our next goal is to focus on reading comprehension. We will continue to look at data, create a plan of action, and implement interventions to meet our goal of graduating all our students.

TEACHER EDUCATION AND SCHOOL REFORM

As school reform unfolded, increased attention inevitably focused on the education of teachers. Not only was there rising dissatisfaction with the achievement of students in schools, and therefore with the quality of instruction that they received, but also there was a rising teacher shortage by 1999. The shortage loomed ominously as enrollments in schools rose while, at the same time, school reform efforts were pushing class sizes down. The problem was compounded by the fact that with increased employment and educational opportunities available to women, the once seemingly endless supply of bright young women filling the need for teachers in school classrooms had dwindled sharply.

At the same time, many colleges and universities took the position that teacher education was unworthy to be included in the august ranks of academe. Yale University's example was not atypical: It simply abolished the small department of education that it once had. In many institutions of higher education, schools or colleges of education struggled with little support and often were isolated from either the leadership of the university or the faculty in the other schools. By 2000, however, universities were being called both to account and to take responsibility for meeting the need to educate and train the 2.5 million new teachers who would be needed in the United States in the first decade of the twenty-first century. The two main drivers for reform in schools or colleges of education are the U.S. Department of Education and the accreditation process by two professional organizations: National Council for Accreditation of Teacher Education (NCATE) and the Teacher Education Accreditation Council (TEAC).

Accreditation of Teacher Education Programs

Although there are two teacher education accreditation organizations, the main player is the National Council for Accreditation of Teacher Education (NCATE) and within NCATE, the Council for the Accreditation of Education Preparation (CAEP), which as of 2014 accredited 670 programs. The other accrediting organization is the Teacher Education Accreditation Council (TEAC), which as of 2014 accredited approximately 173 programs. There are approximately 500 teacher preparation programs in the U.S. not accredited.

NCATE began to reform its standards for accreditation of colleges of education during the 1990s when criticisms of colleges of education began to increase. It is NCATE's policy to revise the standards every seven years, and each successive revision of the standards for accreditation increased pressure on colleges of education to focus on candidate (student) success both in college and after securing a job. One of the indicators even requires surveys of employers on the effectiveness of graduates. In the fall of 2013, CAEP approved new standards. Their five standards are as follows:

Standard 1: Content and Pedagogical Knowledge

Standard 2: Clinical Partnerships and Practice

Standard 3: Candidate Quality, Recruitment, and Selectivity

Standard 4: Program Impact

Standard 5: Provider Quality, Continuous Improvement, and Capacity (Council for the Accreditation of Education Preparation, 2013)

Standard 4 is about the results of preparation programs, including employer satisfaction data, the promotion and retention of candidates, and the satisfaction rates of graduates about their preparation program. Although not required for the accreditation process, NCATE suggests colleges of education provide PK-12 student-learning data as evidence in reporting the success of its graduates.

Federal Focus on Colleges of Education

The U.S. Department of Education (ED) released a document in 2011 titled *Our Future, Our Teachers: The Obama Administration's Plan for Teacher Education Reform and Improvement* (U.S. Department of Education, 2011). In this document, ED singles out the various departments of education in the states for not reporting sufficient numbers of low-performing teacher preparation programs and, therefore, suggests there are many more low-performing teacher education programs needing remediation than are reported. Obviously, the states have different criteria of what constitute low performance than ED does. Much of the ED findings are based on a report by The Education Schools Project (Levine, 2006) that suggested remediation for teacher preparation programs should involve

- better recruiting efforts, increased admissions and graduation standards;
- updated programs that include extensive clinical components;
- improved faculty quality (mostly doctoral-level faculty);
- programs lasting five-years with student majoring in subjects they will teach;
- shifting most preparation programs to doctoral-degree granting institutions;
- improving the accreditation process that will not allow low-performing programs to be accredited;
- requiring all preparation programs to be accredited.

As described in the preceding section, NCATE suggests colleges of education report PK-12 learning results connected to its graduates, but the Obama administration will require this of RTTT states, as has already been done in Louisiana, North Carolina, Tennessee, and New York City. Through Title II funding, the Obama administration in fiscal year 2012 budgeted $185 million for teacher preparation program reforms, of which $110 million went to $10,000 scholarships for the TEACH grant program to attract high-quality individuals to high-quality traditional or alternative teacher education programs. Since 38% of the students were minorities in 2012, but only 14% of the teachers were Hispanic or African American, much of this money is also set aside to attract minorities into the teaching profession. Lastly, the Obama administration's plan to improve teacher education used RTTT funds to support professional development for new and veteran teachers (U.S. Department of Education, 2011).

A BROADER, BOLDER APPROACH TO EDUCATION

The influential Economic Policy Institute took the initiative in 2008 to bring together many leaders in education, civil rights, health, social welfare, and housing to look at the research and develop a policy statement for education and social change. The list of original signers of the resulting document, entitled *A Broader, Bolder Approach to Education,* include President Obama's secretary of education, Arne Duncan; Tom Payzant, former assistant secretary of education; Julian Bond, chair of the NAACP; James Comer; Linda Darling-Hammond; Joyce Elders, former U.S. surgeon general; John Goodlad; James Heckman, recipient of the Nobel Prize in Economics in 2000; Susan Neuman, former assistant secretary of education; William Raspberry, former newspaper columnist; Diane Ravitch, former assistant secretary of education; Janet Reno, former U.S. attorney general; Richard Rothstein; Ted Sizer; and many other leaders. In June 2008, a full-page advertisement was taken out in the *Washington Post* and the *New York Times* to deliver their message to the public. These advertisements included the following recommendations to improve student achievement and narrow the achievement gaps among different racial/ethnic groups and socioeconomic levels (Economic Policy Institute, 2013):

1. Pursue an aggressive school improvement strategy, including ensuring smaller classes in early grades for disadvantaged children, attracting high-quality teachers to hard-to-staff schools, improving teacher and school leadership training, making a college preparatory curriculum accessible to all, and paying special attention to recent immigrants.
2. Provide developmentally appropriate and high-quality early childhood, preschool, and kindergarten care and education that promote not just academic readiness but positive lifetime social, economic, and behavioral outcomes for low-income children.
3. Address children's health, including routine pediatric, dental, hearing, and vision care for all infants, toddlers, and schoolchildren to minimize health problems that impede school success. Full-service school clinics can overcome the absence of primary-care physicians in low-income areas and address poor parents' inability to miss work for children's routine health services.
4. Improve the quality of out-of-school time. Low-income students learn rapidly in school but often lose ground after school and during summers. Successful out-of-school and extended day programs not only focus on remediation but also provide cultural, organizational, athletic, and academic enrichment that middle-class children routinely enjoy.

The message from this statement is that schools alone cannot resolve the complex social and economic problems that children encounter and that a new national approach must be developed, so the economic and social problems that create large disadvantaged populations can be corrected to level the playing field. In this way, children will enter school at similar levels of readiness to learn. The full statement addresses the weaknesses of NCLB and its focus on high-stakes testing as well as its assumption that low student achievement is caused by bad schools.

It is time to change the rhetoric that blames only schools for the lack of major progress in improving student achievement and the increasing concerns about the economic competitiveness of the United States. Although the ideas expressed in *A Broader, Bolder Approach to Education* are not new, with the credibility of the authors of this document and an administration in Washington, DC, that seems to listen a little more to the professionals than the previous one, the time seems ripe for pushing these ideas to the forefront of the education debate and supporting the education policy that will enact such reform.

Final Thoughts

In the early twenty-first century, school reform was the single overarching concern that drove, with great energy, the direction that public education was taking in the United States. Three major strategies for school reform—each based on a different theory of action—jousted with one another for dominance in the highly competitive arena. The advocates of two of these strategies—market-based reform and standards-based reform—started out professing little interest in issues of organizational behavior in schools.

One group reasoned that the power of market competition would somehow coerce schools to do whatever they had to do to become more effective, or they would simply not survive in the marketplace. The standards-based reform group reasoned that the exercise of overwhelming down-the-line political and bureaucratic coercion would produce a similar result. Those that promote the third school reform strategy, comprehensive school reform (CSR), suggested that curriculum delivery models must be standardized throughout the school. Although research does not support the first two strategies, market-based reform and standards-based reform, there is some evidence that a few CSR models show promise.

Higher education is beginning to show a heightened awareness of the connections among the university, teacher education, and the effectiveness of public schooling. There was some hope that reforming teacher education and educational research at the university level might trigger a powerful and far-reaching transformation in the practice of education, much as the reform of medical education had transformed the practice of medicine early in the twentieth century.

More recently, highly placed individuals are calling for reforms to the economic and social structures that create hardships in the form of poverty, among other factors. The schools alone cannot overcome these hardships. Through *A Broader, Bolder Approach to Education*, these individuals hope to influence policy makers to look beyond schools for solutions.

We end this text with a quotation from Diane Ravitch (2010), which happens to be the last comment in her book, *The Death and Life of the Great American School System*:

> At the present time, public education is in peril. Efforts to reform public education are, ironically, diminishing its quality and endangering its very survival. We must turn our attention to improving the schools, infusing them with the substance of genuine learning and reviving the conditions that make learning possible. (p. 242)

Education is not failing as we have seen from the NCES data, but the general public mostly hears that U.S. education is going downhill fast. Education may be in peril, but only because of those who would force change with sometimes dubious results, rather than create conditions to permit schools to improve through organizational self-renewal.

Reflective Activities

1. Research whether your state has any legislation permitting charter schools. If it does, find the total number of charters in the state and the number of charter schools in your district. Discuss your findings with your classmates. Does anyone in your class work in a charter school? If so, discuss with them their experiences of working in charter schools.

2. Select one of the comprehensive school reform (CSR) initiatives identified in this chapter. Go to the research literature, or to the *What Works Clearinghouse,* and find a recent study that evaluates the school reform you chose. Locate at least one primary article research study, either quantitative or qualitative. Do not choose an article that simply talks about the program components or one that is a "war story" that touts the program's effectiveness by stating how well the authors "think" it worked in a school or district. Find an article that describes the program's effectiveness based on dependent variables such as test scores, school climate, and qualitative interviews and observations by researchers. Read it and then summarize its findings in one or two paragraphs. Share your summary with others in your class. Discuss the pros and cons of each of the reform initiatives. Which of these reforms has great promise in helping schools improve?

3. *Working on Your Game Plan.* At this point, you now have parts of your game plan that you have been working on, along with some further ideas about educational organization and leadership. Now the challenge is to review these thoughts, written and not yet written, and pull them together to develop a more complete draft statement about your understanding of organizational behavior in education—a first draft of your personal game plan for educational leadership. A way to get started would be to identify 10 to 20 "this I believe" kinds of statements about educational leadership and educational organizations. After each statement, write a sentence or two that explains briefly why you hold that belief.

   For example, we might start out with this statement: *If highly motivated teachers are important to educational excellence, then a school must have a climate that is open and growth enhancing.* We think this in large part because the literature on motivation, notably Maslow's and Herzberg's theories, suggests that people are highly motivated by opportunities in which they can grow and mature as individuals. The research literature on organizational climate also supports the view that a growth-enhancing climate is highly motivating.

   How would you, at this point, define your game plan as a work in progress?

CRITICAL INCIDENT   District Test Scores Decline Once Again

Superintendent Christa Mason received the state's test scores and was not pleased. Not only did the district as a whole perform worse than last year, a higher percentage of high school students than last year will not graduate this year until they pass the 11th-grade assessment. In fact, 58% of 12th graders who needed to pass the assessment did not. These students will have one more chance in the summer to score higher than the cut-off score, or they will receive only a diploma of attendance. To make matters worse, a larger percentage of third graders than last year will be retained because of their low scores.

Last year, one high school, two middle schools, and five elementary schools were deemed academically deficient by the state's department of education, and each of these schools received intensive technical assistance from the state to assist them in developing plans to increase the test scores. None of these schools improved this year. In addition, all schools that last year performed below the state average in reading and/or math had to develop written plans for improvement that were approved by the school board. Over 75% of them failed to improve their scores.

Superintendent Mason and the district's leadership have worked with the state's superintendent association and the state school board association to change the governor and legislature's primary focus on the state assessment test for graduation and third-grade retention. These efforts have not succeeded, however, in changing the state accountability law. In the meantime, the district leadership must work with the school principals to develop a response to the continuing problem of low test scores. The superintendent would like to continue with the plans that have been in place since last year because she believes these plans will work if they are given sufficient time. But she knows the school board will demand a different response. They have already warned her that if the scores are low this year, they will want the replacement of principals and teachers whose students scored poorly. She also knows that her contract, recently renewed for another year, will be in jeopardy next year.

Superintendent Mason knows that this news will place the district, the schools, and especially the students in a very difficult position. The local newspaper has already asked the superintendent for an interview today to discuss the results prior to their article in tomorrow's edition, which will run a front-page headline about the district's poor test scores.

1. How do you believe the superintendent should respond to the newspaper interview?
2. What is your opinion of this type of state accountability system?
3. Should the district and individual schools adopt specific Comprehensive School Reform models to help the schools improve? If so, which ones would you suggest? If not, what recommendations do you have for helping the schools improve?

Suggested Reading

Chubb, J. E., & Moe, T. M. (1990). *Politics, markets and America's schools.* Washington, DC: Brookings Institution.

Historically, this is an important book because it was so instrumental in popularizing the idea of school vouchers. It is scholarly, carefully written, and analytic. But it is suspect for many readers because it totally dismisses all forms of education reforms except what the publisher, the Brookings Institution, has advocated for years. Their central argument is that the two alternatives discussed—democratic control and market control—have very different consequences for the organization and performance of schools. Markets, the authors contend, foster the autonomy that schools need to make themselves more effective, and democratic control, they contend, fosters bureaucracy that smothers autonomy and hence effec-tiveness. Every school leader should read—no, carefully study—these challenging ideas.

Goodlad, J. I. (1998). *Educational renewal: Better teachers, better schools.* San Francisco, CA: Jossey-Bass.

Goodlad masterfully interweaves the culture of the schools and the processes by which the teachers in those schools are educated to work in them. The question is as follows: What comes first—good schools or good teacher-education programs? The answer, according to Goodlad, is that both must come together.

Kohn, A. (1999). *The schools our children deserve: Moving beyond traditional classrooms and "tougher standards."* New York, NY: Houghton Mifflin Company.

This is a book about tougher standards versus better education: the costs of overemphasizing achievement, the arrogance of top-down coercion, the case against standardized testing, and confusing harder with better. It's a good book, insightful, fact-filled, and provocative, and it deserves a place in every discussion about school reform.

Kozol, J. (2005). *The shame of the nation: The restoration of apartheid schooling in America.* New York, NY: Crown.

Much of this book is a sequel to his previous work in which he examines and exposes the lack of attention and funding to the impoverished schools in the nation, particularly the urban poor. This book presents his findings from visiting about 60 schools in 30 school districts in 11 states. Kozol also examines the impact of high stakes testing and the dramatic effects the accountability movement has had on students, teachers, and principals.

Ravitch, D. (2010). *The death and life of the great American school: How testing and choice are undermining education.* New York, NY: Basic Books.

A previous proponent of charter schools, high-stakes testing and accountability movements, Diane Ravitch changed her beliefs after studying the research over approximately a 10-year period. She now bemoans the results of market-based reforms in taking the most talented students and leaving the lower performing students to the public schools. She also believes that high-stakes testing has resulted in teaching to the test and establishing a *de facto* national curriculum devoted to math, reading, science, and writing—devoid of the humanities.

Ravitch, D. (2013). *Reign of error: The hoax of the privatization movement and the danger to America's public schools.* New York, NY: Alfred A. Knopf.

This book made the *New York Times* nonfiction bestseller list. Diane Ravitch provides insights from research to support her claims that market-driven reforms, high stakes testing, value-added teacher evaluation, and other reforms brought on through NCLB and RTTT are destroying the public school system in the United States. This book is a must read for all educators.

Sarason, S. B. (1998). *Charter schools: Another flawed educational reform?* New York, NY: Teachers College Press.

Sarason has long been one of the most sensitive and supportive observers of the problems of public schooling. In this discussion, he draws on his impressive understanding of the creation of organizational settings to raise tough questions about—not challenges to—the idea of charter schools. It may seem strange to some that he draws on a variety of examples, including the history of the Manhattan Project, to examine the problems of charter schools, but he does, and with a remarkably helpful effect.

Vance, M., & Deacon, D. (1995). *Think out of the box.* Franklin Lakes, NJ: Career Press.

We think that we have done well to have gotten this far without mentioning the notion that one should "think out of the box." However, the idea may have started with this book. If you like your management thought light and easy, this is the book for you. It has been phenomenally successful in corporate management circles.

References

Allen, I. E., & Seaman, J. (2013). *Changing course: Ten years of tracking online education in the United States.* Babson Survey Research Group. Retrieved from http://sloanconsortium.org/publications/survey/changing_course_2012

Allen, M. A. (2008). *Assessing the effectiveness of supplemental educational services in urban Florida school districts.* Unpublished doctoral dissertation, University of Florida, Gainesville.

Alliance for School Choice. (2012). *School choice now: The year of school choice: Choice yearbook 2011–2012.* Retrieved from http://www.allianceforschoolchoice.org/school-choice-programs-in-america-the-facts

American Legislative Exchange Council (2013). *About ALEC.* Retrieved from http://www.alec.org/about-alec/history/

Au, W. (2007). High stakes testing and curricular control: A qualitative metasynthesis. *Educational Researcher, 36,* 264.

Belfield, C. R. (2006). *The evidence on educational vouchers: An application to the Cleveland scholarship and tutoring program* (Publication No. 163). New York, NY: National Center for the Study of Privatization in Education, Teachers College, Columbia University.

Belfield, C. R., & Levin, H. M. (2009). Market reforms in education. In G. Sykes, B. Schneider, & D. N. Plank (Eds.), *Handbook of education policy research* (pp. 513–527). New York, NY: American Educational Research Association and Routledge.

Bifulco, R., & Ladd, H. F. (2006a). The impacts of charter schools on student achievement: Evidence from North Carolina. *Education Finance and Policy, 1,* 50–90.

Bifulco, R., & Ladd, H. F. (2006b). School choice, racial segregation, and test-score gaps: Evidence from North Carolina's charter school program. *Journal of Policy Analysis and Management, 26*(1), 31–56.

Borman, G. D., Hewes, G. M., Overman, L. T., & Brown, S. (2003). Comprehensive school reform and achievement: A meta-analysis. *Review of Educational Research, 73*(2), 125–230.

Braun, H., Jenkins, F., & Grigg, W. (2006, August). *A closer look at charter schools using hierarchical linear modeling.* Washington, DC: U.S. Department of Education, National Center for Educational Statistics. Retrieved from http://nces.ed.gov/nationsreportcard/pubs/studies/2006460.asp

Buddin, R., & Zimmer, R. (2006, September). Charter school outcomes in California. Paper presented at the meeting of the National Conference on Charter School Research, Vanderbilt University, Nashville, TN.

Burch, P. (2007, May). *Supplemental education service under NCLB: Emerging evidence and policy issues.* Denver, CO: University of Colorado, Educational Policy Research Unit.

Burch, P., Steinberg, M., & Donovan, J. (2007). Supplemental Educational Services and NCLB: Policy assumptions, market practices, emerging issues. *Educational Evaluation and Policy Analysis, 29,* 115–133.

Bush v. Holmes, 919 So. 2d 392 (Fla S.C. 2006).

Bushaw, W. J., & Gallup, A. M. (2008, September). Americans speak out—Are educators and policy makers listening? The 40th annual Phi Delta Kappa/Gallup poll of the public's attitudes toward the public schools. *Phi Delta Kappan, 90,* 9–20.

Bushaw, W. J., & Lopez, S. J. (2012). Public education in the United States: A nation divided. *Phi Delta Kappan, 95*(1), 9–25.

Carnoy, M., & Rothstein, R. (2013). *What do international tests really show about U.S. student performance?* Washington, DC: Economic Policy Institute. Retrieved from http://s2.epi.org/files/2013/EPI-What-do-international-tests-really-show-about-US-student-performance.pdf

Center for Education Reform. (2013). K-12 Facts. Retrieved from http://www.edreform.com/2012/04/k-12-facts/

Center for Research on Education Outcomes. (2009). *Multiple choice: Charter school performance in 16 states.* Stanford, CA: CREDO.

Chingos, M. M., & Peterson, P. E. (2012). *The effects of school vouchers on college enrollment: Experimental evidence from New York City.* The Brown Center on Education Policy at Brookings and Harvard's Program on Education Policy and Governance. Retrieved from http://www.brookings.edu/research/papers/2012/08/23-school-vouchers-harvard-chingos

Chubb, J. E., & Moe, T. M. (1990). *Politics, markets, and American's schools.* Washington, DC: Brookings Institution.

Cobb, C. D. (2012). *Review of Report 30 of the SCDP Milwaukee evaluation.* Boulder, CO: National Education Policy Center. Retrieved from http://nepc.colorado.edu/thinktank/review-Milwaukee-Choice-Year-5.

Comprehensive School Reform Quality Center. (2006a, October). *CSRQ Center report on middle and high school comprehensive school reform models.* Washington, DC: Comprehensive School Reform Quality Center. Retrieved from http://www.csrq.org/MSHSreport.asp

Comprehensive School Reform Quality Center. (2006b, November). *CSRQ Center report on elementary school comprehensive school reform models.* Washington, DC: Comprehensive School Reform Quality Center. Retrieved from http://www.csrq.org/CSRQreportselementaryschoolreport.asp

Coulson, A. J. (1999a). *Market education: The unknown history.* New Brunswick, NJ: Transaction Publishers.

Coulson, A. J. (1999b, May 14). Are public schools hazardous to public education? *Education Week.* Retrieved from http://www.edweek.org/ew/articles/1999/04/07/30coul.h18.html?qs=andrew+coulson

Council for the Accreditation of Education Preparation. (2013). *CAEP accreditation standards.* Washington, DC: NCATE. Retrieved from http://caepnet.files.wordpress.com/2013/09/final_board_approved1.pdf

Cowen, J. M., Fleming, D. J., Witte, J. F., Wolf, P. J., & Kisida, B. (2012). *Student attainment and Milwaukee parental choice program: Final follow-up analysis.* SCDP Milwaukee Evaluation Report No. 30. School Choice Demonstration Project, University of Arkansas. Retrieved from http://www.uark.edu/ua/der/SCDP/Milwaukee_Eval/Report_30.pdf

Dannin, E. (2012). Privatizing government services in the era of ALEC and the great recession. *University of Toledo Law Review, 43*(3), 503–531.

Datnow, A. (2005). The sustainability of comprehensive school reform models in changing district and state contexts. *Educational Administration Quarterly, 41*(1), 121–153.

Eberts, R. W., & Hollenbeck, K. M. (2001). *An examination of student achievement in Michigan charter schools* (Working Paper 01–68). W. E. Upjohn Institute for Employment Research Staff. Retrieved from http://research.upjohn.org/up_workingpapers/68/

Economic Policy Institute. (2013). *Broader, bolder approach to education.* Retrieved from http://www.boldapproach.org/

Education Commission of the States. (1999). *Governing America's schools: Changing the rules.* Report of the National Commission on Governing America's Schools, executive summary. Denver, CO: Education Commission of the States.

Florida Department of Education. (2013). Charter schools. Retrieved from http://www.floridaschoolchoice.org/information/charter_schools/

Frankenberg, E., & Lee, C. (2003). Charter schools and race: A lost opportunity for integrated education. *Education Policy Analysis Archives, 11*(32), Retrieved from http://epaa.asu.edu/epaa/v11n32/

Friedman, M. (1955). The role of government in education. In R. A. Solow (Ed.), *Economics and the public interest* (pp. 123–144). New Brunswick, NJ: Rutgers University Press.

Friedman, M. (1976). *Price Theory.* Chicago, IL: Aldine.

Friedman, M. (1995). Public schools: Make them private (Briefing paper No. 23). Washington DC: Cato Institute. Retrieved from http://www.cato.org/pubs/briefs/bp-023.html

Fullan, M. (2011). *Choosing the wrong drivers for whole system reform.* Seminar Series Paper 204. East Melbourne, Victoria, Canada: Centre for Strategic Education. Retrieved from http://www.edsource.org/today/wp-content/uploads/Fullan-Wrong-Drivers1.pdf

Gersten, R., Beckmann, S., Clarke, B., Foegen, A., Marsh, L., Star, J. R., & Witzel, B. (2009). *Assisting students struggling with mathematics: Response to Intervention (RtI) for elementary and middle schools* (NCEE 2009-4060). Washington, DC: National Center for Education Evaluation and Regional Assistance, Institute of Education Sciences, U.S. Department of Education. Retrieved from http://ies.ed.gov/ncee/wwc/pdf/practice_guides/rti_math_pg_042109.pdf

Gersten, R., Compton, D., Connor, C. M., Dimino, J., Santoro, L., Linan-Thompson, S., & Tilly, W. D. (2009). *Assisting students struggling with reading: Response to Intervention and multi-tier intervention for reading in the primary grades. A practice guide.* (NCEE 2009–4045). Washington, DC: National Center for Education Evaluation and Regional Assistance, Institute of Education Sciences, U.S. Department of Education. Retrieved from http://ies.ed.gov/ncee/wwc/pdf/practice_guides/rti_reading_pg_021809.pdf

Gill, B., Zimmer, R., Christman, J., & Blanc, S. (2007). *School restructuring, private management, and student achievement in Philadelphia.* Santa Monica, CA: RAND Corporation.

Goldrick-Rab, S. (2012). Review of "The effects of school vouchers on college enrollment: Experimental evidence from New York City." Boulder, CO: National Education Policy Center. Retrieved from http://nepc.colorado.edu/files/ttr-voucherscollege.pdf

Government Accountability Office. (2013). K-12 education: States' test security policies and procedures varied. Briefing for the Secretary of Education. Retrieved from http://www.gao.gov/assets/660/654721.pdf

Greene, J. P., & Winters, M. A. (2008, April). *The effect of special education vouchers on public school achievement: Evidence from Florida's McKay scholarship program.* (Civic Report No. 52). New York, NY: Manhattan Institute for Policy Research. Retrieved from http://www.manhattaninstitute.org/html/cr_52.htm

Gronberg, T. J., & Jansen, D. W. (2001). *Navigating newly chartered waters: An analysis of Texas charter school performance.* Austin, TX: Texas Public Policy Foundation.

Hanushek, E. A., Kain, J. F., & Rivkin, S. G. (2002). The impact of charter schools on academic achievement (Unpublished paper). Stanford University.

Harding, H. R., Harrison-Jones, L., & Rebach, H. M. (2012). A study of the effectiveness of Supplemental Educational Services for Title I students in Baltimore City Public Schools. *Journal of Negro Education, 81*(1), 52–66.

Hargreaves, A., & Braun, H. (2013). *Data-driven improvement and accountability.* Boulder, CO: National Education Policy Center. Retrieved from http://nepc.colorado.edu/files/pb-lb-ddia-policy.pdf

Heinrich, C. J., Meyer, R. H., & Whitten, G. (2010). Supplemental Education Services under No Child Left Behind: Who signs up, and what do they gain? *Educational Evaluation and Policy Analysis, 32*(2), 273–298.

Heistad, D. (2006). Evaluation of supplemental education services in Minneapolis Public Schools: An application of matched sample statistical design. Minneapolis, MN: Minneapolis Public Schools.

Hess, F. M. (2009). A market for knowledge? In G. Sykes, B. Schneider, & D. N. Plank (Eds.), *Handbook of education policy research* (pp. 501–512). New York, NY: American Educational Research Association and Routledge.

Hill, C. D., & Welsch, D. M. (2006). *Is there a difference between for-profit versus not-for-profit charter schools?* (Paper No. 166). New York, NY: National Center for the Study of Privatization in Education, Teachers College, Columbia University.

Holmes, G. M., DeSimone, J., & Rupp, N. G. (2003, May). *Does school choice increase school quality?* (Paper No. 9683). Cambridge, MA: National Bureau of Economic Research.

Hoxby, C. (2002). How school choice affects the achievement of public school students. In P. T. Hill (Ed.), *Choice equity.* Stanford, CA: Hoover Institute. Retrieved from http://media.hoover.org/documents/0817938923_141.pdf

Hoxby, C. (2004). *Achievement in charter schools and regular public schools in the United States: Understanding the differences.* Cambridge MA: Department of Economics, Harvard University.

Imberman, S. A. (2009, January 1). *The effect of charter schools on achievement and behavior of public school students: An instrumental variables approach.* University of Houston. Retrieved from http://www.class.uh.edu/faculty/simberman/charter_compet_12-08.pdf

Individuals with Disabilities Education Act 20 U.S.C. § 1400 (2004), Sec. 614(b) (6) (A).

Institute of Education Sciences. (2013). *What works clearinghouse.* Retrieved from http://ies.ed.gov/ncee/wwc/default.aspx

Institute on Race and Poverty. (2008, November). *Failed promises: Assessing charter schools in the twin cities.* University of Minnesota Law School. Retrieved from http://www.irpumn.org/website/projects/

Kolowich, S. (2013, August 8). MOOCs may not be so disruptive after all. *The Chronicle of Higher Education, 59,* 45.

Ladner, M., & Myslinski, D. J. (2013). *Report Card on American education: Ranking state K-12 performance, progress, and reform.* Washington DC: American Legislative Exchange Council. Retrieved from http://www.alec.org/publications/report-card-on-american-education/

Lee, J. (2006). *Tracking achievement gaps and assessing the impact of NCLB on the gaps: An indepth look into national and state reading and math outcome trends.* Cambridge, MA: The Civil Rights Project at Harvard University. Retrieved from http://www.civilrightsproject.ucla.edu/ (This project moved to UCLA in 2007.)

Lee, J., & Lubienski, C. (2011). Is racial segregation changing in charter schools? *International Journal of Education Reform, 20*(3), 192–209.

Levine, A. (2006). *Educating school teachers.* Washington, DC: The Education Schools Project. Retrieved from http://www.edschools.org/teacher_report.htm

Lubienski, C., & Brewer, T. J. (2013). *Review of "Report Card on American Education: Ranking State K-12 Performance, Progress, and Reform."* Boulder, CO: National Education Policy Center. Retrieved from http://nepc.colorado.edu/thinktank/review-report-card-ALEC-2013/

Lubienski, C., Crane, C., & Lubienski, S. T. (2008). What do we know about school effectiveness? Academic gains in public and private schools. *Phi Delta Kappan, 5,* 689–695.

Lubienski, C., & Lubienski, S. T. (2006). *Charter, private, public schools and academic achievement: New evidence from NAEP mathematics data.* New York, NY: National Center for the Study of Privatization in Education, Teachers College, Columbia University.

Marchant, G. J., & Paulson, S. E. (2005). The relationship of high school graduation rates and SAT score. *Education Policy Analysis Archives, 13*(6). Retrieved from http://epaa.asu.edu/epaa/v13n6/

McCluskey, N., & Coulson, A. J. (2007, September 5). End it, don't mend it: What to do with No Child Left Behind. *Policy Analysis* (No. 599). Washington, DC: Cato Institute, Individual Liberty, Free Markets, and Peace. Retrieved from http://www.cato.org/pub_display.php?pub_id=8680

McTighe, J., & Wiggins, G. (2012). *From Common Core standards to curriculum: Five big ideas.* Retrieved from http://jaymctighe.com/resources/articles/

Meisenhelder, S. (2013, fall). Mooc mania. *Thought and Action,* pp. 7–26.

Miron, G., & Gulosino, C. (2013). *Profiles of for-profit and nonprofit education management organizations: Fourteenth Edition—2011–2012.* Boulder, CO: National Education Policy Center. Retrieved from http://nepc.colorado.edu/publication/EMO-profiles-11–12

National Association of Charter School Authorizers. (2010). *The state of charter school authorizing.* Retrieved form http://www.qualitycharters.org/images/stories/publications/2010_facts_report.pdf

National Association of Charter School Authorizers. (2012). *Principles & standards for quality charter school authorizing.* Retrieved from http://www.qualitycharters.org/images/stories/publications/Principles.Standards.2012_pub.pdf

National Center for Education Statistics. (2011). *The condition of education 2011.* Retrieved from http://nces.ed.gov/programs/coe/indicator_mgp.asp

National Center for Education Statistics. (2012). *The condition of education 2012.* Retrieved from http://nces.ed.gov/pubsearch/pubsinfo.asp?pubid=2012045

National Center for Education Statistics. (2013). *Number and types of public elementary and secondary schools from the common core data: School year 2010–11* (data file). Available from http://nces.ed.gov/quicktables/

National Governors Association Center for Best Practices, Council of Chief State School Officers. (2010a). *Common core state standards (Introduction).* Washington, DC: National Governors Association Center for Best Practices, Council of Chief State School Officers. Retrieved from http://www.corestandards.org/assets/ccssi-introduction.pdf

National Governors Association Center for Best Practices, Council of Chief State School Officers. (2010b). *Common core state standards for English language arts and literacy in history/social studies, science, and technical subjects.* Washington, DC: National Governors Association

Center for Best Practices, Council of Chief State School Officers. Retrieved from http://www.corestandards.org/assets/CCSSI_ELA%20Standards.pdf

National Governors Association Center for Best Practices, Council of Chief State School Officers. (2010c). *Common core state standards for mathematics.* Washington, DC: National Governors Association Center for Best Practices, Council of Chief State School Officers. Retrieved from http://www.corestandards.org/assets/CCSSI_Math%20Standards.pdf

Ni, Y. (2007, March). *Are charter schools more racially segregated than traditional public schools?* (Policy Report No. 30). East Lansing, MI: Michigan State University, Education Policy Center.

Nichols, S. L., Glass, G. V., & Berliner, D. C. (2005, September). *High stakes testing and student achievement: Problems for the No Child Left Behind act.* Tempe, AZ: Education Policy Research Unit at Arizona State University.

Peltason, E. H. (2013). *Charter school growth and replication* (Vol. I.). Retrieved from http://credo.stanford.edu/pdfs/CGAR%20Growth%20Volume%20I.pdf

Ravitch, D. (2010). *The death and life of the great American school system: How testing and choice are undermining education.* New York, NY: Perseus Books.

Ravitch, D. (2013). *Reign of error: The hoax of the privatization movement and the danger to America's public schools.* New York, NY: Alfred A. Knopf.

Ravitch, D., & Viteritti, J. P. (Eds.). (1997). *New schools for a new century: The redesign of urban education.* New Haven, CT: Yale University Press.

Renzulli, L. A. (2006). District segregation, race legislation, and black enrollment in charter schools. *Social Science Quarterly, 87,* 618–637.

Rickles, J. H., & Barnhart, M. K. (2007). *The impact of supplemental educational services on student achievement: 2005-06.* Los Angeles, CA: Los Angeles Unified School District Planning, Assessment, and Research Division Publication No. 295.

Rouse, C. E., & Barrow, L. (2008). *School vouchers and student achievement: Recent evidence, remaining questions* (Publication No. 163). New York, NY: National Center for the Study of Privatization in Education, Teachers College, Columbia University.

Roy, J., & Michel, L. (2005). *Advantage none: Re-examining Hoxby's finding of charter school benefits* (Briefing Paper No. 158). Washington, DC: Economic Policy Institute.

Sass, T. R. (2006). Charter schools and student achievement in Florida. *Education Finance and Policy, 1*(1), 91–122.

Smarter Balanced Assessment Consortium. (2013). *Frequently asked questions.* Retrieved from http://www.smarterbalanced.org/resources-events/faqs/#2450

Smith, M. S., & Smith, M. L. (2009). Research in the policy process. In G. Sykes, B. Schneider, & D. N. Plank (Eds.), *Handbook of education policy research* (pp. 372–397). New York, NY: American Educational Research Association and Routledge.

Ujifusa, A. (2013). Common core supporters firing back. *Education Week, 32*(31), section 1, 18–19. Retrieved from http://www.edweek.org/ew/articles/2013/05/15/31standards_ep.h32.html?tkn=ONYFxpOiJZHkT5Yqw1UVLep2x1q5YIlyWQba&cmp=clp-edweek

Underwood, J., & Mead, J. F. (2012). A smart ALEC threatens public education. *Phi Delta Kappan, 93*(6), 51–55.

U.S. Department of Education. (2009). *Race to the Top executive summary.* Retrieved from http://www2.ed.gov/programs/racetothetop/executive-summary.pdf

U.S. Department of Education. (2010). *A blueprint for reform: The reauthorization of the elementary and secondary education act.* Retrieved from http://www2.ed.gov/policy/elsec/leg/blueprint/blueprint.pdf

U.S. Department of Education. (2011). *Our future, our teachers: The Obama administration's plan for teacher education reform and improvement.* Retrieved from https://www.ed.gov/teaching/our-future-our-teachers

U.S. Department of Education. (2013). *Race to the Top fund.* Retrieved from http://www2.ed.gov/programs/racetothetop/index.html

U.S. Department of Education. (n.d.). *Strategic plan for Fiscal Years 2011-2014.* Retrieved from http://www2.ed.gov/about/reports/strat/plan2011-14/plan-2011.pdf

U.S. Department of Education, Office of Innovation and Improvement. (2008). *A commitment to quality: National charter school policy forum report.* http://www2.ed.gov/admins/comm/choice/csforum/report.html

U.S. Department of Education, Office of Innovation and Improvement. (2009). *Education options in the states.* Washington, DC: U.S. Department of Education. Retrieved from http://www.ed.gov/parents/schools/choice/educationoptions/index.html

U.S. Department of Education, Office of Innovation and Improvement, Office of Non-Public Education. (2009). *Education options in the states: State programs that provide financial assistance for attendance at private elementary and secondary schools.* Retrieved from http://www2.ed.gov/parents/schools/choice/educationoptions/educationoptions.pdf

Walberg, H. J., & Bast, J. L. (2001). Understanding market-based school reform. In M. C. Wang & H. J. Walberg (Eds.), *School choice or best systems: What improves education?* Mahwah, NJ: Lawrence Erlbaum.

Wanzek, J., & Vaughn, S. (2007). Research-based implications from extensive early reading interventions. *School Psychology Review, 36,* 541–561.

Weiss, E., & Long, D. (2013). *Market-oriented education reforms' rhetoric trumps reality: The impacts of test-based teacher evaluations, school closures, and increased charter school access on student outcomes in Chicago, New York City, and Washington, D.C.* Washington, DC: Broader, Bolder Approach to Education. Retrieved from http://www.epi.org/files/2013/bba-rhetoric-trumps-reality.pdf

Woodard, C. (2013, May 20). Special report: The profit motive behind virtual schools in Maine. *Portland Press Herald*. Retrieved from http://www.pressherald.com/news/virtual-schools-in-maine_2012-09-02.html?pagenum=full

Wyatt, E. (1999, November 4). Investors see room for profit in the demand for education. *The New York Times*, p. 1.

Yun, J. T. (2008, May 22). Review of "The effect of special education vouchers on public school achievement: Evidence from Florida's McKay scholarship program." Boulder, CO, and Tempe, AZ: Education and the Public Interest Center & Education Policy Research Unit. Retrieved from http://epicpolicy.org/files/TTR-Yun-Manhattan-MCKAY_FINAL_.pdf (No Child Left Behind section).

Zelman v. Simmons-Harris, 536 U.S. 639 (2002).

Zimmer, R., Blanc, S., Gill, B., & Christman, J. (2008). *Evaluating the performance of Philadelphia's charter schools.* Santa Monica, CA: RAND Corporation.

Zimmer, R., & Buddin, R. (2006). Charter school performance in two large urban districts. *Journal of Urban Economics, 60*(2), 307–326.

Zimmer, R., Gill, B., Razquin, P., Booker, K., & Lockwood, J. R., III. (2007). *State and local implementation of the No Child Left Behind act: Title I school choice, supplemental educational services, and student achievement* (Vol. I). Washington, DC: U.S. Department of Education, Office of Planning, Evaluation and Policy Development.

GLOSSARY

Administration   Working with and through other people to achieve organizational goals.

Bargaining   The process of negotiating the terms of an agreement that involves give-and-take and, often, compromise.

Behaviorist psychology (behaviorism)   The branch of human psychology that deals with the study of directly observable objective evidence of behavior, such as measurable and quantifiable responses to stimuli, and specifically eschews introspective evidence, such as emotions, perceptions, motives, thoughts, and attitudes. (*See also* cognitive psychology; social psychology; and humanistic psychology.)

Bureaucracy   Literally, from the French (after Max Weber), rule or authority of offices. Thus an organization characterized by a pyramidal hierarchy of authority in the form of official offices, top-down centralized decision making, emphasis on rules and regulations, and impersonality in human interactions. Contrast with human resources development.

Change process   The life-cycle theory of organizational change, which views change as an endless process in the life of an organization, is the most widely acclaimed theoretical model. It is a three-stage model that starts with (1) unfreezing existing practices and behaviors, followed by (2) the development of new practices and behaviors, then (3) institutionalizing and standardizing the newly developed practices and behaviors.

Charter schools   Public schools that operate under special charter from the state, or under contract from a school board, that frees them from certain restraints and requirements so that they can pursue innovative teaching methods that are expected to improve the achievement of students.

Classical organizational theory   A theory of organization that embodies basic ideas from bureaucracy and scientific management such as the scalar principle, unity of command, and span of control.

Cognitive psychology   The branch of human psychology that studies the mental processes that mediate between stimulus and response, especially such processes as creativity, perception, thinking, and problem solving. (*See also* behaviorist psychology; social psychology; and humanistic psychology.)

Collaborate   To work jointly with others, especially in intellectual efforts such as solving problems and setting goals.

Common Core State Standards (CCSS)   Academic standards in mathematics and English language arts that in 2014 were adopted by 46 states. Developed through a joint venture of the Council of Chief State School Officers (CCSSO) and the National Governors Association (NGA)

in an attempt to develop standards to prepare high school graduates to enter college or careers.

Conflict, organizational   A situation in which two or more parties hold divergent, or apparently divergent, views that are incompatible.

Contingency theory   The concept that no single approach to organization and administration is superior to all others in all cases; that the best approach is contingent upon variable factors in the context of the situation.

Critical race theory (CRT)   As defined by Solórzano (1997)—see chapter 1—CRT is scholarship and discourse on race and racism in an attempt to eliminate racism and racial stereotypes from society, including laws, social policy, and organizational cultures. When applied to education, CRT seeks to provide equity in educational opportunity for students of color and to eliminate racism from schools.

Critical theory (CT)   CT is a type of social criticism sensitive to shortcomings in social institutions for allowing only a limited voice in governance to marginalized groups.

Espoused theory   Theory to which one publicly subscribes. Superintendents of schools, for example, often espouse a culture of collegiality, trust, and teamwork as essential to the school district's plan for achieving educational excellence.

Exception principle   The classical principle of organization that recurring decisions should be codified in standardized written form such as rules, standard operating procedures, regulations, and operations manuals, thus freeing administrators to deal only with exceptions to the rules.

Expectancy theory   A theory of motivation—a person is motivated if he or she believes in his or her capacity to successfully performing a task and whether or not it is of importance to them; the latter is called the *valence*, or value, of performing the task.

Feedback   The flow of information that an organization or an individual receives that provides information about the impact that the behavior of the organization or the individual is having on others.

Homeostasis   The tendency of an open social system to regulate itself so as to stay constantly in balance with its environment, which permits it to adapt to changes in the environment.

Hostility   Behavior intended to hurt or worsen the position of another individual or group.

Human capital   The concept that the knowledge that people have—their skills, attitudes, and social skills—are valuable assets to the organization and, because they are assets, can increase or decrease in value over time, depending on how they are managed.

Human relations   Broadly refers to the interactions among people in all kinds of social situations in which they seek through mutual action to achieve some purpose. Applicable to two people seeking to develop a happy and productive life together, organizations such as a business firm or school, or entire societies.

Human resources development   A set of assumptions about organization that emphasizes the primacy of the conscious thinking of persons in the organization, their abilities, and their socialization to the values and purposes of the organization as a basis for coordination and motivation. Contrast with bureaucracy.

Humanistic psychology   An approach to the study of human psychology that focuses on human interests, values, dignity, and worth and recognizes the capacity of human beings to increase self-realization through reason. (*See also* social psychology.)

Leadership   After James MacGregor Burns, the processes of mobilizing, in conflict or in competition with others, institutional, political, psychological, and other resources so as to arouse and satisfy the motives of followers. Thus, a dynamic interactive relationship between members of a group and an individual collectively acknowledged by the group as a leader.

Motivation   The forces that cause people to behave as they do. Thought by behaviorists to be extrinsic (the carrot and the stick) and by others to be intrinsic (cognitive and emotional, e.g., feelings, aspirations, attitudes, thoughts, perceptions).

Naturalistic research   Research conducted in the natural setting using observational methods that are designed to avoid distorting or disturbing the natural setting.

Neoclassical organization theory   Classical organizational concepts that are manifested in contemporary form. For example, the educational standards movement, high-stakes testing, and accountability programs are based on classical concepts of organization and hence are neoclassical ideas.

Organization   An orderly, functional social structure (such as a business, political party, or school) characterized by identifiable people who are members of the organization and an administrative system.

Organization development   Any of a variety of processes by which an organization improves its ability to make better-quality decisions about its affairs.

Organization self-renewal   The concept that effective change cannot be successfully imposed on an organization from the outside but is a process of developing an increasing internal capacity for continuous problem solving and goal setting.

Organizational behavior   Both a field of scientific inquiry that seeks to understand the behavior of people in organizational contexts and a field of professional practice that seeks to apply that knowledge from the social sciences to practical problems of organizational leadership and administration.

Organizational climate   After Renato Tagiuri, the characteristics of the total environment in a school building. Often called the "atmosphere," the "tone," the "personality," or the "ethos" of the school.

Organizational culture   Those enduring traditions, values, and basic assumptions shared by people in an organization over time that give meaning to the work of the organization and establish the behavioral norms for people in the organization.

Organizational health   The extent to which the organization, over time, achieves its goals, maintains itself internally, and adapts to changes in its environment. The healthy organization shows a pattern of increasing its ability to do these things over the course of time.

Performance-based assessment   An alternative to machine-scored multiple-choice tests in assessing student achievement. Normally requires the student to perform tasks such as writing an essay, demonstrating the method of solving a problem, or conducting a science demonstration.

Power   The ability to exercise control, authority, or influence over others either as an official right of office or by mutual agreement with the others.

Qualitative research   Research that seeks to understand human behavior and human experience from the point of view of those being studied rather than the point of view of the researcher.

Rationalistic research   The concept that controlled experimental research is the epitome of research methods but that nonexperimental methods are acceptable if they are quantitative and observe certain procedural safeguards.

Reflective practice   A process in which one reflects on and thinks through the dissonances that inevitably arise between theory and practice and seeks to bring about greater harmony between espoused theory and theory of action.

Reify   To think of an abstraction, such as organization, as though it were material and concrete. People often reify organizational structure, although it is intangible.

Scalar principle   Commonly, the concept of line and staff, which holds that authority in the organization should flow in as unbroken a line as possible from the top policy-making level down through the organization to the lowest member.

School choice   The concept that parents may choose the schools their children may attend at public expense rather than the schools that the school district may designate. Ordinarily, public, private, or religious schools may be chosen.

School reform   A generic term that includes all kinds of efforts to improve the apparent effectiveness of schools. The three principal competing approaches to school reform are (1) market-based strategies, (2) setting and enforcing content standards, and (3) school improvement and development.

Scientific management   The view of management that formalizes differentiated roles between management and workers; the asymmetrical exercise of power and discipline from the top down, in which management plans and sets goals and workers execute the required tasks. Originated with the work of Frederick W. Taylor.

Self-actualization To achieve or attain one's maximum potential as a human being.

Self efficacy After Bandura, how much one believes he or she is capable of performing a task. It influences the choices we make, how much effort we put into those choices, and how long we persist in our choices if we encounter difficulties. Related to expectancy theory.

Self-esteem To have a sense of confidence, pride in oneself, and self-respect.

Site-based management Attempts to shift decision making from the central administrative offices of the school district to the school.

Social psychology The branch of human psychology that studies group behavior and the influence of social factors (such as group norms) on the personalities, attitudes, motivations, and behaviors of individuals. (*See also* behaviorist psychology; cognitive psychology; and humanistic psychology.)

Social sciences Collectively, the scholarly and scientific disciplines devoted to the study of human society and the relationships between individuals in and to society. Usually includes sociology, psychology, anthropology, economics, political science, and history.

Social system A collectivity of individuals who are bound together by common bonds or purposes. Herds of cattle and flocks of birds are social systems in the animal world. Among humans, street gangs and lunch groups are examples of informal social systems. Church congregations, schools, and business firms—being more clearly structured—are examples of more formal social systems.

Social systems theory The concept that organizations are best understood as dynamically interactive social systems.

Sociometry The study of interpersonal relationships using quantitative methods that reveal the strength and direction of preferences between and among individuals in a social system.

Sociotechnical systems theory The concept that an organization is best understood as the dynamic interaction of four subsystems: technology, structure, task, and people.

Span of control The principle of classical organizational theory that the number of people reporting to a supervisor should be limited to a number thought to be manageable.

Standards, academic content Specification of those things that every student should know and be able to do in the so-called core subjects (usually, but not necessarily

limited to, mathematics, the sciences, geography, and the English language). Advocates of academic content standards normally believe that they should apply equally to all students, regardless of linguistic or cultural heritage, special learning needs, race, or socioeconomic status.

Standards, discipline-based Performance standards established for student learning in various academic disciplines, such as mathematics, music, the English language, economics, reading, sciences, history, geography, foreign languages, and physical education.

Standards, performance Define and specify what minimal information and insights or skills students must acquire in order to meet the specifications framed by academic content standards. Students are usually expected to demonstrate their levels of achievement in the academic content standards either on some form of standardized paper-and-pencil tests or by performing tasks, such as writing an essay.

Systems theory The concept, generally accepted in both the physical and social sciences, that all observations of nature are embedded in complex, dynamically interactive systems.

Theory Systematically organized knowledge that is thought to explain things and events that are observed in nature.

Theory in use Also called *theory of action* is the actual theory that is manifest in the behavior of an individual or group. One's theory in use, or theory of action, may differ from the espoused theory (see above). It is inferred from the behaviors of individuals rather than from their words. Dissonance between espoused theory and theory in use is commonplace in organizational leadership.

Theory of practice The broad theoretical amalgam that guides and gives direction to one's professional practice, as distinguished from a practice in which one responds in *ad hoc* fashion as events unfold.

Total quality management An approach to management, adopted from business and industrial management, that focuses on satisfying the client and, to achieve that end, emphasizes involving workers in continual decision-making processes that seek unending improvement in the way the organization functions.

Unity of command The classical principle of organization that no one in an organization should receive orders from more than one superordinate.

Voucher A chit or written authorization drawn upon the public treasury, usually issued by a state, that can be used by parents to pay tuition for the schooling of their children at a private school, a religious school, or an out-of-district public school.

NAME INDEX

SUBJECT INDEX